Women and the English Renaissance

Women and the English Renaissance

*Literature
and the Nature of Womankind,
1540–1620*

LINDA WOODBRIDGE

University of Illinois Press
Urbana and Chicago

This book is printed on acid-free paper.

Publication of this work was supported in part
by a grant from the University of Alberta.

Published simultaneously in Great Britain by The Harvester Press

Library of Congress Cataloging in Publication Data

Woodbridge, Linda, 1945–
Women and the English Renaissance.

Bibliography: p.
Includes index.
1. English literature—Early modern, 1500–1700—History and criticism.
2. Women in literature. 3. Women—Great Britain—History—Renaissance,
1450–1600. I. Title.
PR429.W64W66 1983   810'.9'352042   82–24792
ISBN 0–252–01027–2

For Roland, Dana, and Rachel

Acknowledgments

Thanks are due

to my Department, for funding research assistance and typing.

to my University, for a grant in aid of publication.

to the staff of the University of Illinois Press, especially Carole Appel and Cynthia Mitchell, for all their help.

to the editors of *Atlantis, Mosaic,* and *English Literary Renaissance* for permission to reprint small portions of my essays originally appearing in their journals.

to Linda Pasmore, a professional typist of genius and a sympathetic friend.

to Herbert Coursen and Arthur Kinney, who generously read and commented on the manuscript.

to Harriett Hawkins, who with the patience of Job read and commented on the manuscript twice, in two different versions.

to the good teachers who have taught me and inspired me, especially Marjorie Schroeter and Mabel Chester, excellent teachers of my childhood, and Paul Jorgensen and Robert Dent, excellent teachers of my youth.

to my parents, Viola and Richard Taylor, for their understanding.

to my little daughters Dana and Rachel, resolutely dainty in pink ballet costumes for all my talk of Amazons, who have demonstrated—by surviving the writing of this book—the toughness of womankind.

to my respected colleague and dear co-vivant, Roland Anderson, who with the patience of Grissill listened to my theories, lightened my discouragements, read all the page proofs, and throughout the entire course of this project did more than his half of the housework.

Contents

Exordium   1

PART ONE: THE FORMAL CONTROVERSY

Chapter One: The Genre	13
Chapter Two: The Early Tudor Controversy	18
Chapter Three: The Elizabethan Controversy	49
Chapter Four: The Jacobean Controversy to 1620	74
Chapter Five: The Influence of the Formal Controversy	114

PART TWO: TOWARD THE HERMAPHRODITE

Chapter Six: *Hic Mulier* and *Haec-Vir*	139
Chapter Seven: Civilian Impotence, Civic Impudence	152
Chapter Eight: Saints of Sonnet and the Fight for the Breeches	184
Chapter Nine: The Gossips' Meeting	224
Chapter Ten: Pistolas in the Playhouse	244

PART THREE: THE WOMAN-HATER

Chapter Eleven: The Stage Misogynist	275
Chapter Twelve: *Swetnam the Woman-hater Arraigned by Women*	300

Peroratio: Hot Ice and Wondrous Strange Snow   323

Bibliography   329
Index   345

Exordium

THE STUDY OF WOMEN and the English Renaissance is a perilous quest, and many who have undertaken it have successfully navigated between the Quicksand of Unthriftihood and the Whirlpool of Decay only to find themselves in very deep waters.

The topic is gargantuan. Scholars who have done battle with this giant in the past have always had to lop off limbs. Francis Utley terminated his analytical index to the argument about women, *The Crooked Rib,* at the year 1568, noting that the topic required "the pruning shears."[1] Louis B. Wright, in "The Popular Controversy over Women" in *Middle-Class Culture in Elizabethan England,* carried the study from the 1540s to 1642 but lopped off the topic's weightiest limb, the drama, which he disposed of in a single footnote: "The drama, of course, is full of commentary on women. Jonson and Middleton are severe on women, while Heywood is usually found defending them." Gamaliel Bradford manfully tackled both dramatic and nondramatic literature in his charmingly ridiculous book *Elizabethan Women.* The result was that he proceeded through Elizabethan literature at a full gallop, striking off such sparks as these: "The taint of allegory clings to some extent about the most fully developed of Spenser's heroines"; "Of pure, modest, and charming women Jonson has few." And even at that, he lopped a fairly substantial limb: "The women of Shakespeare have been written about with a depth and beauty which it would be vain for me to attempt to equal; they have been written about with a richness of inanity which it would be impossible for me to surpass. Perhaps they have been written about enough." Katharine Rogers's ambitious overview, *The Troublesome Helpmate: A History of Misogyny in Literature,* taking as its province literature from Homer to Edward Albee, is necessarily brief in its treatment of the English Renaissance and purposely does not address the positive half of the debate about woman.[2]

Quite apart from its daunting size, the topic is fraught with special perils. Both the negative and the positive sides of the formal Renaissance debate about womankind have presented stumbling blocks; the attack

upon women—based on a vast storehouse of antifeminist jest and satire—has been scrupulously avoided by most Victorian and post-Victorian
scholars. The blazing fires of Jacobean misogyny are seldom accorded
more than a footnote to the discussion of Baroque malaise; the drama's
antifeminism is dismissed as fare for the groundlings. This scholarly
quickstep is occasioned in part by prudery (so much of Renaissance antifeminism is bawdy) and in part by chivalry: where is the scholar so
ungentlemanly as to dwell at length on matters so unflattering to the fair
sex? For the rare scholar, the chivalric impulse has led to fervent denun-
ciations of Renaissance misogyny; the Rev. A. B. Grosart, discussing in
1880 the Swetnam controversy of Jacobean times, pontificated: "It may
be affirmed that the man who has low thoughts of woman *qua* woman
proves himself to be low. . . . It is just what we might expect to find the
books against Woman, whether earlier or later, to be the productions of
(self-evidently) mean, degraded, and impure Writers. . . . It is an outrage and an offence for any man to 'rail' and accuse so splendid a piece
of God Almighty's workmanship as Woman. . . . Woman is to be rev-
erenced, loved, and transfigured with celestial radiance."[3] But for most
lay scholars, the better part of chivalry has been silence. The great variety
of Renaissance misogynist tempers, from sprightly wit to scurrilous
venom, has prompted no more response from most modern commentators than the raising of a critical eyebrow. Readers interested in the
nature of Renaissance literary misogyny get small satisfaction from
scholars: literary historians have spared our sensibility but frustrated our
curiosity. And even the few who have taken up the topic have confused
the issue by portraying literary misogyny, rather than male supremacy,
as public enemy number one for womankind.

The positive side of the Renaissance debate about women has elicited
an odd, but perhaps predictable, response: in the defenses of womankind
against literary detraction, some writers have discerned the infancy of
modern feminism. During each of this century's several periods of feminist activism, social and literary historians, from Violet Wilson in 1924
to Juliet Dusinberre in 1975, have attempted to locate the origins of modern
English and North American feminism in the English Renaissance—
possibly because major writers of the English Renaissance like Shakespeare and Spenser provide so many female characters to work with,
possibly because the word *Renaissance* itself sounds so promising.[4] (Could
the age that gave us the printing press, Protestantism, and gunpowder
prove remiss where women are concerned?) Louis B. Wright saw in the
English Renaissance "new trends of thought . . . which quickened the
processes leading to the so-called freedom of woman in modern society"
and regarded Renaissance defenses of women as "early landmarks in the
literature of woman's rights" (pp. 507, 465). Carroll Camden suggested

in *The Elizabethan Woman* that the Elizabethans were way ahead of us in their theory of women: "Too often we have discovered, with the smug air of the scientific explorer, what the Elizabethans well knew" (p. 9). In *Shakespeare and the Nature of Women,* Juliet Dusinberre found the English Renaissance seething with feminist ferment.

As I said, this response is odd but predictable: predictable because the assumption that feminism is identical with kindness to women is a common befuddlement; odd because modern feminism is the belief in the essential intellectual, emotional, and moral equality of the sexes, an equality which underlies apparent differences which feminists believe are mainly attributable to cultural influences, and the concomitant belief that this equality of essence makes logical and just the demand for equality of rights and opportunity for women.[5] But Renaissance defenses of women constantly emphasize the differences between women and men, make assumptions about female "nature," ignore cultural influences on female behavior.

The writer who tries to assess the implications for real life of the Renaissance formal debate about the nature of women is constantly at risk; and this holds true, too, for the way women are portrayed as characters in literature outside the formal debate. The relationship between literature and life is a very slippery subject. What, for example, does the popularity of the Patient Grissill story tell us about certain periods of literary history? Does this story reflect a world populated by submissive wives? Or is it a male wish-fulfillment fantasy peculiar to a world where hardly any real wives are submissive? When one piece of literature claiming that a majority of women are unchaste is balanced by a contemporary piece claiming that a majority of women are chaste, are we to view the problem as one of conflicting statistics on the behavior of real women and content ourselves with the pious wish that this was the sort of thing a parish register could tell us? Or are we to regard the two pieces as complementary attempts at behavior modification, designed to discourage unchastity by ridiculing it and to encourage chastity by praising it? Or should we simply conclude that literature bears no relation to life? If citizens are often cuckolded in the drama patronized by the aristocracy, do we assume that this is slice-of-life realism, or do we argue that aristocrats would not have demanded so many theatrical cuckoldings if they had been able to cuckold citizens in the flesh? Are there cases where the very prominence of a theme in literature argues *against* its being a representation of real life?

Renaissance literature dealing with women has long been adduced by social historians as evidence of attitudes toward women which prevailed in the real world. In discussing Renaissance belief in the superiority of women, Carroll Camden in *The Elizabethan Woman* cites four works be-

longing to what I shall call the formal controversy—William Bercher's
The Nobility of Women, Jane Anger's *Protection for Women,* Rachel Speght's
A Mouzell for Melastomus, and Anthony Gibson's *A Woman's Worth,*—
alongside a matrimonial handbook, a sermon against wife beating, a tract
against female transvestism, and a devotional work (pp. 17–18, 273). He
assumes that all are accurate reflections of Renaissance attitudes and that
all can be taken with the same degree of seriousness and literalness. Catherine M. Dunn seeks enlightenment on the superiority question in other
works of the formal controversy: from Castiglione's *The Courtier,* Agrippa's *Treatise of the Nobility and Excellency of Womankind,* and Tilney's *Flower
of Friendship* she concludes that "women were considered inferior not
only in power and position, but in nature as well. . . . Morally they were
evil, since they were descendants of Eve, though for the propagation of
the race they were a necessary evil. Some writers did grant women a
limited goodness, while only a very few thought them morally equal or
even superior to men." These pronouncements she gathers together under the title "the traditional social theory" and believes that this theory
eventuated in an "accepted way of life" for women in the real world.[6]
Coryl Crandall seeks in the Swetnam controversy "the prevailing attitude among the majority of the 17th century middle class."[7] Ruth Kelso
writes of literary attacks on women, "We must believe that under the
extravagance of expression there was a real antagonism."[8] Wright repeatedly suggests that individual attacks on, or defenses of, womankind
were direct responses to contemporary events, whether historical (the
murder of Sir Thomas Overbury) or literary ("the attacks on women
reached even the cloisters of Oxford and influenced one learned youth,
Christopher Newstead, to publish *An Apology for Women*"): that such
writings might have been no more than set pieces in an established literary genre, possibly composed in entire ignorance of, or indifference to,
contemporary murders or satires, he seems not to consider. The formal
controversy he includes with ballad and sermon, and characterizes all as
literature for "the Elizabethan shopkeeper," explaining that "writers reflecting the trend of middle-class opinion arose to defend woman against
her traducers" (pp. 497, 465).

Conclusions about popular attitudes, drawn from the Renaissance formal debate about womankind, have been used to divine authors' attitudes toward the female characters they created: Daniel Stempel believes
that "our knowledge of Elizabethan mores can come to our aid" in interpreting Shakespeare's Cleopatra and to this end cites the misogynists'
half of the formal debate to conclude that Elizabethans officially believed
"Woman was a creature of weak reason and strong passions, carnal in
nature and governed by lust."[9] Since this sort of thing goes on, it is

essential to determine whether this formal debate did reflect Renaissance attitudes toward women.

Both the operation of literary convention and the principles underlying the artificial construction of literary *personae* are widely understood; but some genres, more than others, tempt us to forget them. Just as love poetry, no matter how conventional, can bring out the biographical critic lurking in us all, so controversialist literature has its own biographical temptations: we tend to assume that what is argumentative in form must represent the author's serious attempt to persuade.[10] But the Renaissance inherited from the Middle Ages an almost aesthetic view of debate. Peter Ramus held the view that, in the words of Marlowe's Faustus, "to dispute well [is] logic's chiefest end," and the four debates of *The Courtier,* if they end in enlightenment, begin as recreation. Writers like Gosynhyll and Pyrrye wrote formal essays on both sides of the woman question, damning and praising women with equal conviction. R. Warwick Bond cites evidence indicating that the formal debate about womankind was a prescribed exercise in medieval universities, a vehicle for acquiring and demonstrating logical and rhetorical skill,[11] and, indeed, the technique of arguing both sides of the same question as practice in rhetoric goes back to the first of the Greek Sophists, Protagoras of Abdera. All this suggests that we will establish personal motives for the composition of formal attacks on and defenses of women about the same time we are certain of the Dark Lady's identity. And it makes questionable the use of such writings as evidence of Renaissance attitudes toward women.

Another tendency of those who seek reality behind the formal debate about women is to assume that the women writers who engaged in the controversy must have taken it seriously and personally. Helen Andrews Kahin views Jane Anger as sincerely indignant and emotional in her 1589 defense of women, in contrast to John Lyly, who in his writings on women struck poses, Kahin believes, of sophisticated insincerity.[12] The complexity of this particular issue, and the probable biases that cloud it, are evident from the fact that Ruth Kelso, who uses writings about women as documents of social and intellectual history, presents evidence purporting to demonstrate that women took formal misogynistic tracts with deadly seriousness, punishing the offending authors (p. 9), while Francis Utley, who treats controversialist writings about women as literature, argues that women were active and good-humored participants in a controversy about women which was a "very courtly game," maintaining that "the opposition was fictional; the pretense that the eagerly listening women who were a conditioning factor of satire must be elaborately apologized to or deprived of a view of the sinning poem was pretense and nothing more" (p. 30).

The purely literary approach, like the approach of the social or intellectual historian, has its dangers. We must make due allowances for jest, irony, aesthetic distance, dramatic objectivity. But are we to assume that what is literary can have *no* basis in real life, real emotion, real attitude? Utley criticizes commentators like Gray, Pinkerton, and Grosart for misunderstanding medieval jest: "If they had satirized women with the words of the Middle Ages they would have meant them, and how could society exist if women were abolished?" (p. 29). Victorian critics may well deserve lampooning; but a view of literature as bearing no relationship whatsoever to the lives and beliefs of real human beings is no more appealing than its opposite extreme, the too-pat biographical and social conclusions of the utterly literal-minded.

Even more unsatisfying than the assumption that literature has no basis in human lives or attitudes is the assumption that what is intended as literature can have no effect on human lives and attitudes. "Medieval satire accepted the thorn in the side and made a jest of it," Utley assures us, secure in the confidence that jest is both blameless and harmless (p. 30). I cannot share that confidence: I believe that Utley underestimates both the capacity of the average reader to take literally what was intended in jest and the power of jest itself, even when understood as jest, to color, often permanently, our attitudes toward the objects of jest. And I believe that, as life often imitates art, the image of Woman in literature has long influenced the behavior of living women. Feminists in our time have combatted the sex-role stereotyping of textbooks and television; I will try to show that Renaissance women were, for a few years, successful in reshaping the drama's image of women. Then, as now, women recognized literature's power to intimidate or to inspire.

As a compromise between two extreme views, first that all Renaissance writings about women are fair game for social and intellectual history and second that any Renaissance writing that establishes itself as literature by taking the form of dialogue, verse, narrative, or drama is off limits for social and intellectual history, I propose that some kinds of Renaissance writings about women are fairer game for social and intellectual history than others. What I shall describe, in part 1, as the formal controversy about women was, I believe, largely a literary game, with very tenuous roots in real contemporary attitudes. The more complex and generically mixed controversy I shall describe in the opening chapter of part 2, arising from historically documented female transvestism, bore a considerably clearer relationship to contemporary reality. (In the remaining chapters of part 2, I shall widen this discussion to embrace non-controversialist literature of varying degrees of canonicity, from Henry Hutton to Shakespeare.) In part 3, I shall discuss ways in which these two strains converged to produce at the same time new literary conventions and new ways of looking at contemporary reality.

I will focus on the years 1540 to 1620: in the seminal years 1540 to 1542, five documents of the formal controversy were published, while the years 1615 to 1620 saw intense activity in both the formal controversy which is the subject of part 1 of this study and the transvestite controversy which is the subject of part 2. Both controversies had roots in pre-sixteenth-century literature, and both had a life after 1620; but the most interesting and most representative work in the controversies was done between the two poles of the Elyot/Gosynhyll/Vaughan/Agrippa controversy of the early 1540s and the Swetnam/*Hic Mulier* controversies of the years 1615 to 1620.

It is customary to refer to a number of documents in these two controversies as pamphlets and to the Swetnam controversy in particular as a "pamphlet war." *Pamphlet,* however, is an insidious term: it denotes merely a literary work bound in a certain way; but since it connotes hasty composition, ephemerality, a popular and undiscriminating readership, and hack work, it is prejudicial to the serious consideration of these works. (Renaissance authors more often call their opponents' works pamphlets than their own.) The term is misleading, too, in its conjured image of inflammatory rhetoric (usually in prose) and fervor—approaching zealotry—for a cause; I want to argue for considerable aesthetic detachment and a sense of play in the formal controversy, which especially in Tudor times was often conducted in poetry; its authors should not be envisioned as pamphleteers. I have, therefore, dispensed with the term *pamphlet.*

My contribution to the large and complex topic of women and the English Renaissance will be, I hope, to clarify the terms of reference with which we approach the topic in future. By emphasizing the role of literary convention, I hope to retard the wholesale appropriation of literary materials as documents in the history of popular attitude; by showing how certain recurrent literary structures and character types seem to reflect the real world, I hope to remind the strictest aesthetician that there is some connection, however sublimated or oblique, between female literary figures and women of flesh and blood. Before we can explore the point at which life and literature intersect and the ways in which life and literature interact—and such explorations are very much the business of a feminist literary critic—we must be clearer in our own minds than we have been so far that life and literature are not the same. To such a clarification this book addresses itself.

The reader should come to this topic prepared for a dizzying sense of topsy-turviness. With regard to the genre I identify as the formal controversy, I will argue that misogynistic attacks on women were responses to defenses of women and not the other way around, that the purpose of attacks and defenses was (from at least one perspective) the same, that Renaissance attacks on women are more congenial to modern feminism than are Renaissance defenses of women. At other points I will argue that literary misogynists are intended as tools in the defense of women, that hostility toward the opposite sex was recognized as a step toward normal sexual maturity, that Shakespeare's transvestite heroines reveal his essential conservatism about sex roles, that Renaissance literature dramatizes the serious consequences of jest, that in creating a substantial number of its female literary characters the Renaissance ignored its own theory of womanhood, that the Renaissance typically characterized womankind in general as weak and timid while portraying individual women as sturdy and aggressive. It was an age of paradox, an age which appropriately cherished the symbol of the hermaphrodite, and the age thrusts forth its paradoxes to tease anyone who contemplates it.

It is hard to know quite where to begin, when confronting the strange paradoxical dragon that is Women and the English Renaissance; but adopting Sidney's principle that where the hedge is lowest one may soonest leap over, I will begin with Renaissance formal debate on women, it being an easier task to connect that controversy with literary recreation than to connect my second sort of controversy with life. It is hard to know where to leave off, too: I have passed over much fascinating material in proverb, epigram, sermon, epyllion, and ballad which deals with types of women or with individual women to focus on that in literature which has implications for the *nature* of women, partly because the topic of women and the English Renaissance indeed requires the pruning shears, and partly because of my own feminist interest in the history of theory about women. Whether or not the reader is feministically inclined, I think she or he will find that, as Gamaliel Bradford so winsomely put it, "the subject is one of considerable interest and varied charm."

NOTES

1. See the Bibliography for publishing information on works cited by author and title in the text.

2. Katharine Rogers, *The Troublesome Helpmate*. Chapters 3 and 4 deal with the Renaissance.

3. Introduction to A. B. Grosart's edition of *Swetnam the Woman-hater Arraigned by Women*.

4. Violet Wilson, *Society Women of Shakespeare's Time;* Juliet Dusinberre, *Shakespeare and the Nature of Women*.

5. My definition of feminism here, it should be noted, is in sharp contradistinction to the definition offered by Coryl Crandall, who in the introduction to a scholarly edition of *Swetnam the Woman-Hater Arraigned*

by *Women,* defines feminism as belief in the superiority of women—the opposite of antifeminism. Belief in the equality of the sexes Crandall sees as a compromise view. This formulation has a certain semantic symmetry but leads inevitably to confusion, since the word *feminism* is not used this way today. Even in a Renaissance context, the reservation of this important term for a very specialized phenomenon is not useful. In fact, I have never seen in a Renaissance work a thoroughgoing and wholly serious argument for the absolute superiority of women over men.

6. Catherine M. Dunn, "The Changing Image of Woman in Renaissance Society and Literature" in *What Manner of Woman: Essays in English and American Life and Literature,* ed. Marlene Springer, pp. 15–16, 34–35.

7. Coryl Crandall, "The Cultural Implications of the Swetnam Anti-Feminist Controversy in the 17th Century," p. 136.

8. Ruth Kelso, *Doctrine for the Lady of the Renaissance,* p. 10.

9. Daniel Stempel, "The Transmigration of the Crocodile," pp. 63, 65.

10. Even so generally sensible a critic as Katharine Rogers, perfectly aware that "misogyny was a popular theme for rhetorical exercises" (*Helpmate,* p. 76), can sometimes be observed leaping into a biographical quagmire with both feet: " 'Let every one loath his Ladye,' Euphues (and Lyly) concluded, 'and bee ashamed to bee hir servaunt . . . flye women' " (*Helpmate,* p. 111).

11. Introduction to R. Warwick Bond's edition of William Bercher's *The Nobility of Women,* p. 56.

12. Helen Andrews Kahin, "Jane Anger and John Lyly," pp. 31–35.

Part One

❧

THE FORMAL CONTROVERSY

Not one word I ever utter can be taken for granted
as an opinion growing out of my identical nature.

—John Keats

❧

CHAPTER ONE

The Genre

Lᴵᴛᴇʀᴀʀʏ ᴀᴛᴛᴀᴄᴋꜱ upon and defenses of women were widespread in
European literature of the late Middle Ages and Renaissance: Ruth Kelso,
in *Doctrine for the Lady of the Renaissance,* has analyzed continental (and a
few English) controversialist writings on women by topic; Francis Utley,
in *The Crooked Rib,* has analyzed English (and some continental) controversialist writings on women by genre. Utley's careful generic analysis
of the *querelle des femmes* has done us the service of focusing attention on
the literary qualities of such writings; his fine distinctions among *chanson
d'aventure, chanson de mal marié, débat, exemplum* collection, proverb, parody of courtly love, and others have made possible a precision in describing individual pieces as members of small generic subtypes. Utley's generic
categories, however, allow for the inclusion of much material on women
which is nonargumentative and which, while demonstrating the faults
of individual women, often makes no comment on the nature of Woman,
from the sadistic shrew-taming poem *A merry Ieste of a Shrewde and curste
Wyfe lapped in Morrelles skin* to the "rebellious lover" poems of the Petrarchan tradition. I would like to suggest another formulation, still (like
Utley's) literary in focus—that a number of controversialist works about
women can be grouped together as one genre, which I shall call the formal controversy about women. This formulation combines some of
Utley's genres and excludes others.

Works of the formal controversy possess certain features in common.
All foster a sense of genuine debate, positing an opponent whose probable arguments the author anticipates and rebuts. Sometimes the opponent appears in person as a speaker in a dialogue; but even when he is
not present his existence is always acknowledged, at least as a rhetorical
construct. These works do not merely lash out at women in bitterness,
as does the title figure of *The Golden Boke of Marcvs Avrelivs,* but argue a
thesis about Woman, with the help of logic and rhetoric. In Tudor and
early Jacobean times, the opponent was usually hypothetical; not until

after 1615 did authors regularly direct rebuttals to specific, traceable works of other authors in print.

All works of the formal controversy address the nature of Woman in general: they do not limit themselves to wives as does Erasmus's *A mery dialogue, declaringe the propertyes of shrowde shrewes, and honest wyues* or the anonymous *The Batchelars Banquet* (an English version of *Le Quinze Joyes de Mariage*), or to prostitutes, as does the anonymous *Dialogue betwene the comen Secretary and Jelowsy touchynge the vnstablenes of harlottes* or Erasmus's *Of the yong man and the euill disposed woman,* or to individual women, as does Marston's *The Insatiate Countess.*

All formal works deal exclusively with the nature of Woman: although a formal controversy might be incorporated as one book of a larger work, as is Book III of Castiglione's *The Courtier,* or appended to another work, as *A Cooling Card for Euphues and All Fond Lovers* is appended to Lyly's *Euphues,* or function as an epistolary interlude in a novella, as does the formal controversy in Barnabe Rich's *Brusanus, Prince of Hungaria,* scattered misogynistic insults or brief defenses of womankind by dramatic characters do not belong generically to the formal controversy as I define it.

All works of the formal controversy use *exempla*—historical and/or literary examples, usually biblical and classical in origin, of good women or bad. All of these works catalogue women's faults or virtues: works devoted to one fault, like Charles Bansley's *A treatyse, shewing and declaring the pryde and abuse of women now a dayes,* which deals mainly with women's sartorial extravagance, or Skelton's *The Tunning of Elinor Rumming,* which deals mainly with feminine bibulousness, do not meet the genre's requirements.

All formal controversies argue their case theoretically, relying heavily on abstractions, rather than bringing their charges against women or vindications of women to life as object lessons. This genre does not embrace either fictionalized accounts of women, like Greene's *Penelopes Web . . . A Christall Mirror of feminine perfection,* or *Mamillia. A Mirrour or looking-glasse for the Ladies of Englande,* or like John Dickenson's *Fair Valeria;* nor does it embrace drama devoted to female behavior, like Phillip's *Comedy of Patient and Meek Grissill,* Chapman's *The Widow's Tears,* or Heywood's *How A Man May Choose A Good Wife From A Bad.*

The characteristic literary modes of the formal controversy are the classical oration and the dialogue. The former employs a single *persona,* the latter two or more speakers. The formal controversy, thus stylistically diversified, is still one genre, just as comedy can be called one genre through its various permutations, from poetry to prose, from romantic to satiric to musical.

The formal controversy existed in medieval times, as is documented in the works collected by Utley. Humanism, however, gave it its characteristic Renaissance form, most evident in its rhetoric, its humanist arguments, and its addition of classical materials to the characteristic set of *exempla*. The dialogue *Interlocucyon with an argument betwyxt man and woman whiche of them could proue to be most excellēt,* translated from French and published in English about 1525, is still essentially medieval; its *exempla* are biblical—Eve, the Virgin Mary, Hester, Judith, Delilah, Sara, and Mary Magdalene, although Helen of Troy does put in an appearance. In most later Renaissance works, biblical and classical *exempla* are mixed, reflecting the Christian/humanist synthesis.[1] The classical and the Judeo-Christian traditions both contained favorable views of women: the classical tradition offered Plato's remarks on the equality of women; the Judaic had its Deborahs, Sarahs, and Esthers; the medieval Christian tradition contributed Mariolatry, with its probable influence on the adulation of woman in the literature of courtly love. But these traditions bequeathed a heritage of antifeminism as well: patristic misogyny, which entered early into the Christian tradition, was perfectly compatible with Aristotelian notions of women's innate imperfection. Hence the usefulness of both traditions to both defenses and attacks.

The most important single source of classical *exempla* used in the formal controversy between 1540 and 1620 is Boccaccio's *De Claris Mulieribus* (Concerning Famous Women), a mid-fourteenth-century collection of 104 brief biographies of women. Included here are misogynists' favorites like Deianira and Clytemnestra; defenders' favorites from the common trio Ceres-Minerva-Carmenta to regulars like the Sybils, the Amazons, Penelope, Sappho, Lucrece, Portia, Zenobia, Dido, and Veturia; and a few examples employed with equal dexterity by attackers and defenders—Semiramis, Medea, Cleopatra. Boccaccio's ambivalent treatment of the third group facilitated their use by both sides: he emphasizes Semiramis's remarkable administrative and military talents as well as her monstrous sexuality, Medea's great skill in magic as well as her murderous inclinations; the debater could take his pick of which qualities to emphasize. The formal controversy's euhemerist habit of considering classical goddesses as mortal women, foolishly elevated to divinity by the ignorant, is also fully in evidence in *De Claris Mulieribus.* Many of Boccaccio's examples were gleaned from Ovid's *Metamorphoses,* and some Renaissance controversialists may have taken their examples directly from that popular source or from other classical or early Christian sources—Ovid's *Fasti* and *Heroides,* Livy's *Historiaram ab Urbe Condita,* Plutarch's *Mulierum virtutis,* Augustine's *De Civitate dei,* Valerius Maximus's *De Factis Dictisque Memorabilibus.* Many simply relied on the works of other Renaissance controversialists, sometimes, I suspect, picking up names from the works of their contemporaries and fleshing out the *exempla* by reference to lexicons like those of Balbus, Perottus, Calepine, Stephanus, Elyot, Cooper, or Thomas. But Boccaccio is the one place where the majority of the standard examples are gathered together.

This material was widely disseminated during the Renaissance. *De Claris Mulieribus* was followed by a number of compilations of female biographies, including Christine de Pisan's *Le Livre de la Cité des Dames,* 1405 (translated into English as *The Boke of the Cyte of Ladyes,* 1521), Foresti of Bergamo's *De Plurimis claris sceletisque Mulieribus,* 1497, Ravisius Textor's *De Memorabilibus et Claris Mulieribus,* 1521, and Chaucer's *Legend of Good Women,* 1372–1386 (seven of Chaucer's ten "good women" appear also among the biographies of *De Claris Mulieribus*). An anonymous translator rendered twenty-one of Boccaccio's biographies into English in the early fifteenth century. A precise source study on the formal controversy would be difficult and probably inconclusive.

The genre as it developed in England was strongly influenced by the work of two continental humanists, both of whom resided in England in early Tudor times—the German Henry Cornelius Agrippa, who wrote his *De nobilitate et praecellentia Foeminei sexus* in Latin around 1509, and the Italian Baldassare Castiglione, who wrote *Il Cortegiano* in Italian between 1508 and 1516. Sir Thomas Elyot, who inaugurated a flurry of writings in the genre in 1540, may well have known the works of both foreign humanists; but Agrippa's treatise lay unpublished until 1529 and did not become available in English translation until 1545; Castiglione's did not appear in English as *The Courtier* until 1561. I will discuss these works in the order in which they became accessible in English.

While the cross-fertilization of ideas is difficult to trace through the international humanist circle which included Agrippa, Castiglione, Erasmus, More, Colet, Vives, and others, many of whom knew each other personally and most of whom knew each other's work, the nature and status of women was an important concern of the whole group. The feminist tendencies of these early humanists has, I think, been overestimated; but they came closer than most practioners of the formal controversy about women to engaging real issues.

Although Louis B. Wright includes works of the formal controversy under the rubric "The Popular Controversy over Woman,"[2] the formal controversy is not really a "popular" genre, in the sense that ballads about shrews can be called "popular." Antifeminist treatises often sold well, but the controversy is hardly a proletarian genre. Several of its authors had close ties with the Christian-humanist intellectual community: Elyot, Agrippa, and Castiglione stand out, but even the literary ingenue Edward More, who defended women in the 1560s, had some connection with the Christian humanists, in being the grandson of Sir Thomas More. The genre, with its learned lists of exemplary women and its appeals to ancient authority, demanded at least the trappings of erudition; as an exercise in bestowing originality on a rhetorical set piece, it required both technical virtuosity and familiarity with a wide sample of work in the genre, much of which was available only in foreign languages. Individual works of the genre have been characterized in the past in terms of emotional outburst, chivalric fervor, patristic neurosis. I prefer to regard most of them as a kind of intellectual calisthenics, a few of them as acrobatics of a high order, fit for international competition.

As for the connection of these productions to their authors' own relationships with and attitudes toward the living women who were their contemporaries: despite the controversialists' own conventional allegations that their opponents had been soured by marriage to shrews or mistreatment by whores, there is not a scrap of external evidence to suggest any connection with real life at all.

NOTES

1. There was a precedent for the biblical/classical amalgam: as Utley points out, patristic misogynists too had drawn examples from both sources (p. 5). Whether the Renaissance controversy was influenced by patristic practice or reinvented the mode in accordance with the constant habit of Christian humanism, this mixture of source material was congenial to the Christian humanist temperament, whatever its origins.

2. *Middle-Class Culture in Elizabethan England,* chap. 13.

CHAPTER TWO

The Early Tudor Controversy

THAT THE BRIEF, intensive formal controversy which flourished during the early 1540s was inaugurated by an author of no less distinguished reputation than Sir Thomas Elyot is an important fact. Francis Utley has argued that the Renaissance *querelle des femmes* was carried on mainly by "hacks like Gosynhill and Pyrrye" (p. 90). But although popularizers were involved in the controversy, it is significant that with Sir Thomas Elyot's *The Defence of Good Women,* 1540, the Renaissance formal controversy gained at its inception the prestige of humanist credentials.[1]

Elyot's prose dialogue was influenced by the thinking of the Spanish humanist Vives, who resided in England while tutor to Katharine of Aragon. If Elyot's ideas about women, like his mentor's, favor maidenly modesty and womanly piety too much to be called "feminist" in the modern sense, that is the case with a majority of Renaissance defenses of women: defenders and detractors alike trafficked in stereotypes which are remote from, and even antithetical to, modern feminism. Elyot's stereotype of a "good" woman suggests that modesty, piety, and home-keeping are the essence of decent womanhood, while in fact these were only the ideals of his own culture, ideals which treatises like his were designed to promote; and he insists on the subservience of wives.

According to Foster Watson, *The Defense* is "probably the first imitation in English of the Platonic dialogue,"[2] and it is easy to see why this form suggested itself: it provides a literary forum for debate and offers a method for discrediting erroneous opinion by embodying it in a speaker of questionable integrity. Elyot's antifeminist detractor, Caninius, speaks "like a cur." The literary habit of likening the misogynist to a canine, visible throughout the controversy, probably stems from the fact that the classical misogynist Diogenes was always called a dog; his followers were Cynics, a word derived from the Greek κύων—dog. Elyot's defender of women, Candidus, is "benigne" and "gentill." The respective temperaments of these two are a paradigm for the genre: defenders typically adopt a posture of sweet reasonableness in contrast to the vitriolic abuse of the "snarling" and "barking" detractor.

Candidus employs a strategy conventional to the formal defense: he impugns the motives of the detractor, accusing him of harboring a sour-grapes attitude. Because Caninius's advances have been repulsed by one woman, Candidus suggests, he has taken emotional refuge in the opinion that all women are worthless: he is of "the company, whiche disappointed somtime of your purpose, ar fallen in a frenesy [i.e., frenzy], and for the displesure of one, do spring on all women the poyson of infamie" (Sig. Bv). He also accuses Caninius of having got his notions of feminine inconstancy from poetry; informed as it is by bawdry (the loves of the gods, and so forth), poetry gives the reader a distorted notion of what women are like. The contemporary poetry that dealt most prominently with women was Petrarchan poetry, newly imported into England at the time Elyot's *Defense* was written, but since the dialogue is set in classical times, direct allusion to Petrarchan poetry would have been inappropriate. One reference to a poetry of weeping and sighing, however, indicates that it was partly the Petrarchans Elyot had in mind (Sig. [A6]–[A6]ᵛ).

Candidus notes that while historians and philosophers have written of some bad women like Helen of Troy, many more are good: he adduces a number of historical-literary examples from Penelope to Portia and reminds his opponent that Plato and others argued the equality of women. Caninius, not to be outdone in knowledge of Greek philosophers, brings up Aristotle's contention that women are imperfect, delight in rebuking and complaining, and are never content. Candidus discredits Aristotle by reference to his dissolute life. Caninius urges women's physical weakness, lack of courage, inconstancy, and dearth of judgment. Women are "weaker than men, . . . they lacke hardinesse, and in perilles are timerous, more delicate then men" (Sig. [B7]). Candidus, delighted to be able to turn Caninius's Greek philosopher against him, cites Aristotle's belief that men and women were designed as complements and that women are perfect at least for the task they were designed for: looking after the house takes neither strength nor courage. He adds, in a more palatable argument, that men are not honored for brawn, but for reason; he forces Caninius to agree that women possess reason, on the grounds that homemaking requires more reason than does bread-winning. (It would seem that Caninius gives up this point too easily.) Candidus buttresses his argument for feminine reason by adducing wise and learned women of classical literature and legend—Carmenta (alias Nicostrata), who invented the Latin alphabet, Minerva or Athena, honored as a goddess for inventing armor and introducing horticulture, the

Muses as bestowers of the liberal arts, Diotima, Cassandra, and the Sybils.

Candidus now discomfits his guest by announcing he has invited a woman to dinner. "I pray you of this matter say to her nothynge," begs the embarrassed Caninius; Candidus replies, "Thus do they all that be of your facion, In wise womens absence speke reprochefullye, and whan they be present, flatter them plesauntly" (Sig. [C8]ᵛ). The dinner guest is the martial queen Zenobia, who establishes herself as an insufferable prig by declaring that she is seldom away from home so late in the evening and expressing pious hopes that she will not be slandered or propositioned during dinner. If this means of certifying her as a "good" woman does not endear Elyot much to the modern reader, things begin to look up when she informs the company that as a young woman she held off getting married until she had studied moral philosophy. The reader is lulled into the expectation of a serious discursus on education for women— until she recounts what she learned from philosophy, the sum of which was "to honour our husbandes nexte after god: which honour resteth in due obedience" (Sig. Diiᵛ). Zenobia claims that education helps a woman please her husband, which (it would appear) is the main goal of education for women. Things do not, however, remain at this feministically bleak pass forever; Zenobia tells how, after being widowed, she ruled her country, rebuilt fortifications against the besieging enemy, made good laws, and enforced them justly. Candidus holds Zenobia up as a shining example of womanhood. Caninius recants.

The closing segment of the *Defense* is noteworthy as one of the few Renaissance texts to view with approval the independence, assertiveness, and erudition of a widow—widows being perhaps the most heavily satirized class of women in Renaissance literature. Zenobia's capability in politics and warfare demonstrates the relative freedom to act, in a man's world, that was inherent in a widow's position, as in a reigning queen's. Elyot did, however, make the portrait less threatening by softening Zenobia's aggressiveness. He has her emphasize that her learning, pursued during a protracted maidenhood, lay quiescent while she was a wife, conducing during marriage only to chastity and the defense of her sexual reputation. Only after she was widowed did her education come to the aid of more active administrative, diplomatic, and military talents. Elyot renders Zenobia acceptably "feminine," too, by altering history. The historical Zenobia had played the aggressor: after her troops conquered Egypt in A.D. 270, she claimed imperial stature, although in her husband's day her realm of Palmyra had been part of the Roman Empire. Historically, the Romans attacked Zenobia only in response to her initial acts of aggressive rebellion; Elyot creates the impression that as queen of a sovereign state Zenobia merely took the defensive against Roman incursions on the territory she held in trust for her male children. Renaissance defenders of women often take this tack when faced with military-minded females; they praise martial women only when they act in defense of their country or their children, particularly under siege. This habit was perhaps conditioned by the figurative language of Petrarchan poetry, where the lady's heart was so often a fortress under siege. But it is also a natural expression of the entrenched Western conception of woman as passive, man as active.

Elyot's treatise differs from most succeeding defenses (and attacks) in introducing no biblical examples: in the dialogue's classical setting, Christian reference would be out of place.

Foster Watson suggests that the *Defense* was written out of sympathy with Katharine of Aragon: "her death in 1536 may, indeed, have been the occasion for the production of this booklet" (pp. 212–13). Posthumous sympathy, however, seems an odd motivation for defending women. Watson here displays the usual tendency of scholars to assume that works of the formal controversy were direct responses to personal emotions and contemporary events and then to look (almost always in high places) for a woman to whose actions or character the literary document can in some way be attached. But Elyot's motivation may have been purely literary. He had before him an example of the medieval formal controversy cast in dialogue, the *Interlocucyon with an argument betwyxt man and woman whiche of them could proue to be most excellēt,* published a decade or so before he began the *Defense,* which might easily have inspired a humanist to recast the old biblically-oriented argument in classical terms. Elyot might have wished to experiment with the dialogue as he had encountered it either in Plato or in the colloquies of Erasmus, then being translated into English. Certainly Elyot's argument has a bookish quality throughout: both the *exempla* and the character of Zenobia are probably from Boccaccio's *De Claris Mulieribus;* the character of Caninius is dependent partly on the classical model of Diogenes as shaped by anecdotal traditions; references are made to classical and Petrarchan poetry. Elyot takes obvious delight in the dramatic opportunities dialogue provides: he allows Candidus to exhibit his cleverness in turning the tables on Caninius in the Aristotle argument and enjoys staging the discomfiture of Caninius when Zenobia enters. When Candidus accuses Caninius of having got his ideas of women by reading rather than experience, Caninius argues that reading is a quite natural source of such ideas: "By the consent of al autours my wordes be confirmed, and your experience in comparison thereof is to be littel estemed" (Sig. Aiiiiᵛ). Both disputants take a recreational view of the debate: Caninius makes little jests, and Candidus replies good-humoredly: "Now in good faith that is merily spoken" (Sig. Aiiii^v), "In good faith Caninius ye ar a mery companion" (Sig. Biiii^v).

Pastorals have been written by people one suspects of having hardly any interest in sheep; and Elyot's *Defense of Good Women* is a piece of literature, written out of a long literary tradition which it modifies but whose conventions it nonetheless observes. One need not look beyond that tradition, toward dead queens or living queans, to account for Elyot's choosing to write theoretically about women.

Another dialogue, indebted to Elyot's, was published in 1542. Robert Vaughan's *A Dyalogue defensyue for women, agaynst malycyous detractours* uses seven *exempla* identical to seven in Elyot's list—Carmenta, the Muses, Minerva, Diotima, Leontium, Cassandra, the Sybils: he cites them in Elyot's order and describes them in similar terms.[3] The *Dialogue,* however, owes less generically to the Platonic/Erasmian dialogue than to the medieval bird debate.[4] A chattering pye (magpie), rejoicing in his own malicious ingenuity, is the detractor of women; a virtuous falcon defends. The contrast between the two speakers' personalities is similar to the contrast between Caninius and Candidus, but more extreme: the pye is ebulliently raucous; the falcon maintains a tone of sober dignity ("the fawcon moste gentyll, with sober behauour"). In the Renaissance, even male defenders of women were expected to be ladylike.

Vaughan speculates on detractors' motives. First, he suspects (as had Elyot) that misogynists have turned against all women after betrayal by one; he counsels readers to keep an open mind about women despite unpleasant personal experiences: "Euer consyder, it is a made [i.e., mad] affection / To iudge all unparfyte, thoughe one lacke parfection" (Sig. Aii^v). Second, detractors may be motivated by pure malice, directed at women because they are relatively defenseless. Third, he hints obscurely that misogynistic tracts are written to gain great men's favor.

The falcon maintains that to slander Woman is to slander her creator, to call God "a bongler or a botcher" (Sig. Aiiii). The pye cheerfully replies that the Devil is God's creation too. (The falcon, having no ready answer to this, wisely lets the pye take the offensive for the duration of the argument.) The pye argues that women are inferior because physically weak. The falcon responds humanistically: human dignity does not depend on size or physical strength; if it did, one would grant superiority to animals, many of which surpass man in physical strength. The pye reasons that if "humayne perfection" consists of reason and knowledge, women are still inferior: reason and knowledge are exactly what women lack; the falcon replies with a brief catalogue of learned women from Carmenta to Diotima to the Sybils. At the mention of women in history, the pye adduces Eve; the falcon counters with the Virgin Mary. The pye maintains that women are fickle, their affections mutable; the falcon, anticipating a fine passage in *Haec-Vir,* a 1620 defense of female transvestism (see part 2), answers that mutability is the order of the whole world. He points out that men can play false too, break promises too; he adduces historical and biblical examples.

The pye alleges that women have caused wars, citing Helen of Troy; the falcon maintains that Helen was abducted. The pye calls women cruel and shrewish; the falcon responds that women's cruelty in matters of love is nothing to the cruelty and violence of men at war; women are tender-hearted by nature, learning cruelty only by men's example. The pye holds women lazy and extravagant, bringing their husbands into debt; the falcon counters that most homemakers are models of thrift and industry, and nourishers of mankind. The pye insists on women's vanity, adding that women dress finely to entice men, the falcon that women do not entice, men seduce. (This question runs through the Renaissance controversy; it is the question debated in the trial scene in the play *Swetnam the Woman-hater Arraigned by Women.*) The pye contends that women's seducibility proves them witless, the falcon that it is more blameworthy to importune than to be importuned. He returns to clothing, demurring again at the misogynist's habit of generalizing—even conceding that some women dress for vanity or provocation, indiscriminate condemnation of the whole sex is unreasonable. The pye remains an indiscriminate condemner: "If one be nought, so be all the rest"; the falcon rejoins, "Some men be murderers, shulde I therefore call / All mankynde murderers?" (Sig. Dii^v). The undaunted pye states categorically that men are morally superior to women; the falcon replies that ever since Cain, the first murderer, men have committed all sorts of violent crimes. The pye argues that while man may historically have been guilty of more violent sins, women have been guilty of more sensual sins. The falcon denies this. When the pye complains that the falcon is making women out to be perfect, the falcon concedes that no human being is perfect but insists that women are "more godly than men" (Sig. Ei^v). After the pye recants, the piece closes with sober religious reflections in the author's own voice: Vaughan sees detraction of women as an affront to God. The humanist arguments (including an account of the aptness in Greek and Latin of contemporary Englishwomen) and the devoutness of the closing remarks lend an aura of high seriousness. Still, the author's personal commitment to the status of women does not declare itself. This is another work of primarily literary motivation. If sincere concern about Woman is present, it is effectively muffled: aesthetic distance is created by the venerable bird-debate genre, arguments ossify into ritual, and the witty misogynist is a conventional character.

The mention of "malicious detractors" in Vaughan's title is likely no more than a curtsey to the genre's formal expectations. A pre-1542 edition of Gosynhyll's *School House of Women* has long been posited, partly to locate the malicious detractor to whom Vaughan refers.[5] But the book Vaughan vaguely alludes to in his opening lines is not necessarily a satire on women, at Utley assumes;[6] in fact, as Vaughan describes it, it sounds like a defense: "I red an oracyon / Most pleasauntly set forth, with flowers rethoricall / Descrybynge the monstruous vyce of detraction." Despite Vaughan's indebtedness to Elyot, Elyot's *Defense* is not a "oracyon." Vaughan's allusion here is more probably to a defense which *is* an oration, Gosynhyll's *Mulierum Pean,* the opening stanza of which is very close to Vaughan's opening stanza, with its calendric-zodiacal imagery and its winter setting.[7] *Mulierum Pean,* however, is undated, although usually assigned to about 1542, the year Vaughan's *Dialogue* was published: it is difficult to say who is echoing whom. In either case, though, we have a succession of three defenses of women—Elyot's, Vaughan's, and Gosynhyll's—all of which represent themselves as "defenses" against misogyny but whose traceable literary antecedents are not misogynistic attacks but other defenses. The clear implication is that these pieces were not composed as sincere and pious vindications of a maligned sex but as exercises in a literary genre.

Edward Gosynhyll's attack on women, *The Scole house of women,* and his defense of women, *Mulierum Pean,* exemplify the formal controversy's second main literary form, the classical oration. At the risk of becoming enmired in Renaissance pedantry, I will examine their oratorical structure, for this reason: it has long been assumed that Gosynhyll's work has no form whatsoever. Utley claims that Gosynhyll "has little plan other than to salt his rambling series of charges against the sex with proverb, jest, and example" (p. 256), and he goes so far as to aver that "if there is one thing the Scholehouse lacks, it is rhetoric in the renaissance sense of inner form and outward polish" (p. 276). Such pronouncements encourage readers to ignore the possibility of literary motivations on Gosynhyll's part, to view his works as extempore effusions, literature for shopkeepers, candid expressions of the common man's beliefs about women. The conclusion of several scholars that these two works, connected by explicit mutual cross-reference and alike in virtually all stylistic features, must be by different authors reflects the assumption that both the *School House*'s satire on women and *Mulierum Pean*'s praise of women are disingenuous outpourings of an author's personal feelings, and as such could not have been composed by the same author.[8] As a counter to such biographical fallacies, I want to argue that whatever Gosynhyll's works may lack in "outward polish," if there is one thing they possess, it is "rhetoric in the Renaissance sense of inner form."

Renaissance formal instruction in the skills of argument was based on classical rhetoric, stemming from Aristotle's *Rhetoric* and channeled through Latin rhetoricians. Two common rhetoric texts were Quintilian's *Institutio Oratoria* and the anonymous *Rhetorica ad Herennium,* ascribed to Cicero. Outside the pieces cast in dialogue form, most essays of the formal controversy follow the structure laid down for what Quintilian called judicial oratory, the two uses of which, according to Quintilian, are attack and defense.[9] The judicial oration was usually divided into five parts— the *exordium* or introduction, *narratio* or statement of facts, *confirmatio* or proof, *refutatio* or refutation of opposing arguments, and *peroratio* or conclusion. Some rhetoricians combined *confirmatio* with *refutatio.* Some added further parts, such as the *partitio,* a forecast of structure, the *propositio,* a statement of theses to be demonstrated, and the *digressio,* a digression. While a certain amount of latitude was allowed the Renaissance "orator," the basic method and structure were clear and easy to follow. Anyone who had a case to argue, offensive or defensive, would likely adopt this form, as did Sir Philip Sidney in *The Defense of Poesy.* Formal Renaissance debaters of the woman question were no exception. That even such a disorganized essay as Joseph Swetnam's *Arraignment of Lewd, Idle, Froward and Unconstant Women* was considered a classical oration is indicated by one of its critic's reference to its introduction as the *exordium.*

Gosynhyll's formal attack, *The School House of Women,* is slightly unusual in being cast in rhyme royal. But the Renaissance freely adapted classical forms to its own literary traditions. Shakespeare provides two orations in *Julius Caesar,* Brutus's in prose, Antony's in blank verse. Gosynhyll's structure establishes the work as a judicial oration, despite its verse form inherited from the Middle Ages.

The *exordium* occupies the first four stanzas. Here Gosynhyll characterizes the treatise as a response to another work: "A fole [i.e., fool] of late, contryued a boke / And all in prayse of the femynye." This book, a pun reveals, is *Mulierum Pean,* which in its turn claims to be a response to *The School House.* The publishing history of these two works is the essence of confusion.[10] It is probable that Gosynhyll intended this double self-rebuttal to humorous effect. But it may also have arisen from the demands of the form: the judicial orator, in an adversary situation, would naturally allude to his opponent. Gosynhyll maintains the illusion of genuine opposition through the fact that *The School House* is unsigned, while *Mulierum Pean* appears under his own name. The *exordium* includes a standard disclaimer: only wicked women merit his criticism; the good should not take offense. His attempt to disarm opposition, by characterizing as wicked any woman who registers an objection, is also a standard ploy: "Perchaũce the women, take displeasure / Bycause I rubbe them,

on the gall / To them that good be, paraduenture / It shall not be mater-
yall / The other sorte, no force at all / Say what they wyll, or bendeth
the brewe [i.e., brow] / Them selfe shall proue, my saynge trewe."

The *propositio* is marked with a pointing hand in the 1560 edition: "Eche
other man, in generall / And name[ly] those that maryed be / Gyue
euident, testimonyall / Affermynge the same, yf I wolde lye / And thus
reporte, that femynye / Ben euyll to please, and worse to truste / Crabbed
& comberous, when them selfe luste" (Sig. [A]ᵛ–Aii). Gosynhyll delivers
considerably more than he promises—a discussion of deceit, ill temper,
and wilfulness—but he delivers what he promises.

The School House, like most formal attacks, uses the *narratio* to list
women's faults: the catalogue is long and enthusiastic. Women "haue
tonge at large, voyce loude & shryl." Their raucousness grows out of
their "frowarde wyll" (Sig. Aii). Women harbor grudges, having an in-
fallible memory for slights. Women are deceitful, given to evasions and
duplicity. They are creatures of sense, not reason; rather than listening to
the voice of male reason in any argument, they will "tell theyr owne tale
to the ende." Though women's reason is "not worth a torde [i.e., turd] /
Yet wyll the woman, haue the last worde" (Sig. Aiiᵛ). They are malicious: "Malyce is so rooted, in theyr harte / That seldome a man, maye
of them here / One good worde in a whole longe yere" (Sig. Aiiᵛ).

Gosynhyll confesses that, for all women's unpleasantness, men cannot
do without them because of the "many sondry commodytyes" women
provide. The only "commodity" he mentions is sex, into which women
lure men by certain tricks, such as kissing "with open mouthe / . . .tongue
to tongue" (Sig. Aiiᵛ-Aiii). Wooing a woman is perilous. A man must
take infinite pains to please her, and if he once displeases her she will
weep. A man can gain the sexual favors of almost any woman, since
women are frail. However, this is dangerous; once she gives in to a man,
a woman will claim he promised to marry her. Women are promiscuous;
no matter how kind a man is to his mistress, when he turns his back
another man will "come aloft" with her (Spenser used "come aloft" to
mean "experience orgasm" [cf. *Faerie Queene,* III.x.48.5]; that is probably the meaning here). If a woman becomes pregnant, she will pressure
one of her lovers to marry her, claiming the child is his: the paternity
being greatly in doubt, she will swear he resembles whoever she has
chosen to bully into marriage. If the man escapes marriage, he will have
to subsidize the woman's removal to a different locale, where she can
begin her old tricks all over again. If he makes the mistake of marrying,
he will suffer through the usual trials of pregnancy for husbands. The
wife will lie in bed all day, feigning illness, while the husband is kept
busy fetching such things as the whims of pregnancy demand. She will

spend every day tippling with gossips who visit her during her confinement. This section of the *School House* is likely indebted to that lively French satire on matrimony, *Le Quinze Joyes de Mariage,* which Gosynhyll knew either in its French original or in an English translation published in 1507 (STC 15258; second edition 1509).

In the 1560 edition, a pointing hand signals the beginning of a *digressio* about gossips (see chapter nine). Gosynhyll sets this off from the rest of the *narratio* by making it a dialogue between an old gossip and a young one. It is still, however, part of the discussion of married women's faults; the gossips complain about their husbands and discuss husband management. Here Gosynhyll explains his title. Women school each other in vicious behavior; this is the "schoolhouse of women": "Thus lerne the yonger, of the elders guiding / Day by day, kepynge suche scoles / The symple men, [they] make as foles" (Sig. [A4]). (A secondary meaning of the title is that Gosynhyll proposes to school women in proper behavior.) The *digressio* ends after the penultimate stanza of Sig. Bi[v]; in the following stanza Gosynhyll returns to where he left off three pages earlier, with wives' faults and husbands' miseries. He marks this return with a stanza devoted to the proverb "hanging and wiving go by destiny," concluding, "I am well sure / Hangynge is better, of the twayne / Sooner done, and shorter payne" (Sig. Bi[v]).

Wives have various deceitful shifts to gain freedom to commit adultery, from feigned pilgrimages to midwife duties. The result of cuckoldry—and this is important to understanding Renaissance fanaticism on the subject—is uncertain paternity: "The blynde, eateth many a flye / So doth the husbande, often ywys [i.e., indeed] / Father the chylde, that is not his" (Sig. Bii). Other faults are related to women's incorrigible lechery. Looking-glass vanity and extravagant adornment are adjuncts to sexual appetite: physical attractiveness is intended mainly to allure. Dainty diets and expensive liquor serve as aphrodisiacs. Gosynhyll's opinion that women are "farre more lecherous" than men (Sig. Bii[v]) was a common refrain and is noteworthy for being almost the only item in the Renaissance misogynist catalogue that has not been widely reiterated in the twentieth century. Denigration of woman appears to be the constant. In the Renaissance, when lust was an abomination, women were condemned as lustful; now, when sexual fulfillment is salvation, men (despite the findings of Kinsey and others) are very often said to possess the stronger sexual urge.[11]

After feminine wiles ("Wepe they or loughe they, all is one thynge / They deale most craftly" [Sig. Biii]), Gosynhyll turns to wives who seek political power through their husbands. Here is a hint of his social class: he envisions political ambition in terms of desire not to be queen, but to be the mayor's wife: "Who so wyll thryue / and office bere, in towne and citye / Muste nedes be ruled, by his wyue / . . Bycause her selfe, wolde honoured be" (Sig. Biii). Like a bourgeois Lady Macbeth, such a wife spurs her husband by suggesting that only fear stands in his way, wondering aloud whether he is "a man or a mowse." These three stanzas on ambition are a small *digressio,* set off in the 1560 edition by a leaf device; then Gosynhyll returns to marital misery: "Of all the dyseases, that euer wore / Weddynge is nexte, vnto the gowte" (Sig. Biii).

Gosynhyll relates an old anecdote: the two shrewish wives of Socrates were once enraged with the philosopher for laughing at them when they were arguing with each other. Joining forces, they broke a full piss pot over his head. Socrates's response brings the *narratio* to a close:

> He helde hym pleased, and well content
> The pysse ran downe, by hys chekes twayne
> Wel wyst [i.e., knew] I (sayde he) what it ment
> And trewe it is that all men sayne
> That after thondre, commeth rayne
> Who hath a wyfe, is sure to fynde
> At home in hys house, many a fow[l] wynde
>   (Sig. Biii^v).

Gosynhyll now sets about refuting opposing arguments. For some reason, rather than using *Mulierum Pean* in his *refutatio* he introduces a conversation he alleges to have had with an unspecified woman. This woman brings up some stock arguments in favor of feminine worthiness:

> A certayne wyfe, sayde to me ones [i.e., once]
> I wolde thou knewe it, god made vs
> Neyther of earth, stocke, ne stoens [i.e., stones]
> But of a thynge, muche precyous.
> Of a ribbe of a man, scripture sayth thus
> Because the woman, in euery nede
> Shulde be helpe to the man, in worde & dede.
>
> Man made of earth, and woman of man
> Is of a thynge, moste principall
> Whiche argueth well, sayth she then
> By iudgemente iuste, and reason naturall
> That we be euer, substanciall
> And yet ye men, of vs bable
> That women alwayes, are varyable
>   (Sig. Biii^v–[B4]).

Gosynhyll refutes this argument by pointing out that all Eve helped Adam to was the apple and original sin, and it is appropriate that woman was made of a bone. First, the rib was crooked, and so is woman's nature. Second, bones are stiff and unyielding, as is woman's wilfuless. Third, two bones together will rattle, and two women together make a terrible "clytter clatter" (Sig. [B4]). His description of feminine talkativeness is graphic: "Where many gese be, be many tordes / And where be women, are many wordes" (Sig. [B4]^v). He also offers an alternate version of woman's creation: a dog ran off with Adam's rib before God could fashion a woman. Since the dog ate the bone, God had to make woman from one of the dog's ribs, which accounts for women's barking at their husbands.

Another popular anecdote follows—that of the man whose wish that his dumb wife could speak was granted by the Devil. Since "frō that day forwarde, she neuer ceased / Her boyster bable," the man entreated the Devil to take away the wife's tongue again. "Not so sayd the deuyll, I well medle nomore / A deuyll a woman to speke may constrayne / But all that in hell be, can not let [i.e., stop] it agayne" (Sig. Ci).

Taking up the claim that woman is a helper to man, he acknowledges that "all men saye / That woman to man, is most comforte"; however, they mean this "a nother way": whether by irony or semantic confusion, what men really mean by "most comforte" is "vtter extorte" (absolute torture). The reason men accuse women of being "varyable" or inconstant, as the "certain wife" has complained, is that it is true: he tells an anecdote about the devil and a false wife.

Gosynhyll now advances to the *confirmatio,* the proof. Here he reiterates the major charges of his *propositio*—women are "crabbed" (Sig. Cii^v), "comberous" (Sig. Ciii^v), untrustworthy (Sig. Di^v), wilful (Sig. Cii^v)—and reminds the reader of subsidiary charges like lewdness, talkativeness, inability to keep a secret. In choosing his methods of proof, he follows the advice of classical rhetoricians. Among various modes of proof, Quintilian gives most attention to evidence to witnesses, historical and literary example, and appeal to authority. For evidence of witnesses, Gosynhyll appeals to the experience of male readers: "We se, by experyence / Euery daye, before our iye / And by reporte, of men of credence" (Sig. Cii). Throughout this section, he appeals to the male reader as "thou" or "you." One such passage seems to indicate that Macbeth's was a common case:

> In case thou take, the matter lyght
> As a man of peace, loue and concorde
> Then wyll she wepe, anone forth ryght
> And gyue [thee] many, and euyll worde

and byd [thee] gyrd, to [thee] thy sworde
and saye yf I, had maryed a mon
This thynge shulde not, be longe vndon
                                    (Sig. Ciii).

Gosynhyll appeals to the authority of Solomon (Sig. Dii^v, Diii), but his most important proof is historical and literary example. This was true of most controversialists and has the sanction of Quintilian: "Of all descriptions of proof the most efficacious is that which we properly term *example:* that is, the adducing of some historical fact, or supposed fact, intended to convince the hearer of that which we desire to impress upon him. . . . The same is the case with regard to examples taken from fictions of the poets, except that less weight will be attributed to them" (I, pp. 363, 366). That Gosynhyll intends his examples as "proof" is clear from his calling one of them "the profe" (Sig. Cii^v) and from his statement, "Examples here of, diuers there be / To a proue [i.e., prove] my sayeng" (Sig. [C4]). Gosynhyll draws historical examples from biblical sources (Eve, Jezebel, Herodias, Lot's wife, Delilah, Athaliah, Job's wife, Pharaoh's wife) and classical sources (Messalina, Cicero's wife). He of course considers the biblical to be "historical." His literary examples are classical (Pyrrha, Myrrha, Byblis, Pasiphaë, Helen of Troy) and modern (women in Boccaccio).

In the *peroratio,* or conclusion, Gosynhyll negates his initial assurance that he criticizes only bad women: "In the woman / Is lytell thynge, of prayse worthye" (Sig. Diii^v). He grants that his adversaries' claim that of all creatures, women are the best, would be true were it not for two small sins of womankind, summed up in the proverb "[they] can neyther do, nor saye well" (Sig. Diii^v). An afterword ("Go forth lytell booke") includes another attempt to forestall rejoinder: the very act of objecting to his criticisms will prove the criticisms justified: "Rub a scalde horse, vpon the gall / And he wyll byte, wynse and went" (Sig. [D4]). Here Gosynhyll makes a belated appeal to authority, summoning Solomon, David, Jerome, Juvenal, Cato, and Ovid as witnesses to the truth of his accusations.

The closing lines of *The School House* indicate that its main intent was comic: he wrote it "that the masculyne, might hereby / Haue somme what to [i]este, with the femyny" (Sig. [D4]^v). The essay's jesting intent is underlined by its sprightly and puckish tone: this writer so offends as to make offense a skill, and it would be a ham-fisted interpreter indeed who traced this sort of antifeminism to the sober misogyny of a St. Jerome. One is reminded more of Chaucer's Jankyn, reading antifeminist literature to the Wife of Bath with all the effrontery of the clown daring jests with Cleopatra, all for the joy of sending into a rage someone of whom he is quite tolerably fond. It is a teasing tone, a tone that was to be echoed by many ensuing detractors. The stance is not unattractive: Gosynhyll posits a world where men jest *with* the "femyny," where women are secure enough in their sense of equality to laugh along with men even when the joke is at their own expense or at most to counterattack in the same spirit of fun.

Some of Gosynhyll's antifeminist lore comes from jest books. The story of the dumb wife and the devil can be found in *A Hundred Merry Tales,* ca. 1525; the story of Socrates and the piss pot is a widespread jest to which Chaucer alludes in the Wife of Bath's prologue (ll. 727–732): a version appears in *Tales and Quick Answers,* 1535. Many feminine faults which Gosynhyll enumerates had long been the subject of jest.

What are we to make of the classical structure and the trappings of Christian humanism conjoined with material whose proper literary environment was the jest book? This is probably part of the joke. It is a pedantic version of the mock-heroic mode, where the essential silliness of the subject matter is exposed by the loftiness of the style. Gosynhyll's technique is double-edged: women's piss-pot antics are shown unworthy of Christian-humanist treatment; but at the same time, the earthiness of the examples exposes the stuffiness of the pedantic superstructure, and the controversy itself becomes the object of laughter. The effect is not unlike that achieved by the Nun's Priest's Tale in treating the predestination controversy. One might view Gosynhyll as a middle-class arbiter between the lofty theorizing of intellectuals and the earthy jokes of the people: the Socrates anecdote, where the rarefied heights of Greek philosophy yield to the common man's sufferings from shrewishness, was an inspired choice among available jests.

But Gosynhyll's intimation that jest is harmless underestimates jest's power. Almost all formal misogynistic attacks of the Renaissance represent themselves as jest; wit and humor loom very large in Western misogyny. Literary jest has not been without its effect on real women. If women are not taken seriously, it is partly because they have been viewed for so many centuries through the eyes of jesters. Husbands can evade serious discussion of marital difficulties because jesters have taught them to dismiss even legitimate wifely complaints as shrewishness or female hysteria. Employers are reluctant to hire women to do physical labor because of the jokes about women's weakness and timidity. The spirit of Gosynhyll and his fellows, embodying generations of genial misogyny, hovers over everything a woman says and does: a woman cannot debate an issue without fearing criticism for female illogicality, cannot take a moral stand without suspecting that her auditors consider her a scold, cannot hold a simple conversation without wondering whether she is talking too much. Women have internalized all the old jokes: was that the jokes' purpose all along? Beginning by paying her the insidious compliment that she is magnanimous enough to laugh at herself, the jester ends by inducing in a woman through his jokes the same contempt for herself that he feels for her. A bitter fool.

Many theorists of jest have recognized in laughter a tool for asserting and maintaining superiority. Hobbes attributes laughter to "the apprehension of some deformed thing in another, by comparison whereof [the laughers] suddenly applaud themselves"; he remarks gratifyingly that "it is incident most to them that are conscious of the fewest abilities in themselves, who are forced to keep themselves in their own favor by observing the imperfections of other[s]."[12] Freud, noting that "by making our enemy small, inferior, despicable or comic, we achieve . . . the enjoyment of overcoming him," suggests that many jokes are directed at women out of male sexual frustration (Freud's belief that a man makes smutty jokes when he "finds his libidinal impulse inhibited by [a] woman" is not very different from Elyot's opinion that the misogynist is one who, repulsed by a woman, is "fallen in a frenesy").[13] Bergson concludes that "in laughter we always find an unavowed intention to humiliate, and consequently to correct our neighbour."[14]

Quintilian recognized the power of jest and advised orators on its uses. "Though laughter may appear," he wrote, "a light thing, as it is often excited by buffoons, mimics, and even fools, yet it has power perhaps more despotic than any thing else, such as can by no means be resisted" (I, p. 432). Humor is difficult to combat because he who protests even against a cruel jest can always be accused of not being able to take a joke. The charge that feminists have no sense of humor has arisen from feminist protests against misogynistic jokes. Such protests may be futile: the misogynist always comes off as the genial and urbane man, the protestor as a scowling and joyless prig. Nevertheless, feminists are quite right to see the joke as a major enemy. Many of the damaging stereotypes which hamper us all in our daily lives have been built up gradually, piece by piece like great mosaics. And the pieces are jokes.

When Gosynhyll turned his hand to a formal defense, he used no jests. He might well have done so, since his defense includes a counterattack upon men. But there was simply no body of antimasculist jests on which he could draw. Indeed, *antimasculist* is not even a word, as no male counterpart of the word *misogynist* exists. An anthology of antimasculist humor would be among the world's shortest books.

In *The prayse of all women, called Mulierū pean,* Gosynhyll says one January night he dreamed an assembly of women accused him of having written *The School House of Women,* a book which, to their "grefe," reviles all women (Sig. Aii). They urge him to publish *Mulierū pean,* which he has already written. One of the women, the goddess Venus, commands him to sharpen his pen and write as she bids. The first few stanzas are clearly dictated by Venus, but where her dictation leaves off and the "original" *Mulierum Pean* is meant to begin is not clear. The *exordium,* at any rate, consists of an attack on male detractors of womankind: the first was Adam, who after the apple incident "made excuse / The faute [i.e., fault] allegynge to the femynye" (Sig. Aii^v), and men have been blaming the world's evils on women ever since. Fish, fowls, and even worms manage to get along with the females of their species, but human males have "maners so rude" that with no cause they "rayle and iest" at womankind (Sig. Aii^v). Eve was created "to helpe and assyst" Adam, and men are unable to get along without women, whatever they say in jest.

The *narratio* varied markedly from one formal defense to the next. Rhetoricians were undecided as to its proper use in a defense. In an attack, the *narratio* consisted of the facts surrounding the accusation, but in a defense, simply denying the accusation did not really qualify as a *narratio.* Quintilian had suggested that a defense's *narratio* might be the place to query the accusation and the facts adduced in its support. Gosynhyll chooses this course. He accuses his "opponent" of having been overzealous in prying into feminine faults, "nothynge lefte out" (Sig. Aiii). He also questions the validity of his opponent's adducing literary examples without acknowledging that "poetes do fayne [i.e., feign]" (Sig. Aiii). He charges his opponent with distorting the evidence by glossing over what does not suit his argument: "What that makes nat, for your purpose / Shall be interpretate, with a lewde glose" (Sig. Aiii). He calls his opponent's examples "Faynt and feble" (Sig. Aiii). Here, as if realizing that he is drifting into the *refutatio,* Gosynhyll has Venus direct him to postpone the specific refutation "tyll thou may espye / A place therefore more necessary" (Sig. Aiii). Gosynhyll devotes the balance of the *narratio* to the virtues of women, which counters the list of feminine faults in *The School House.*

Gosynhyll here incorporates another kind of oration, that which Quintilian calls the "panegyric or laudatory" and Cicero the "epideictic" oration, the uses of which were described as "praise and blame." Cicero advocated the use of the epideictic oration as part of other types of oration: "If epideictic is only seldom employed by itself independently, still in judicial and deliberative causes extensive sections are often devoted to praise or censure."[15] This is how Gosynhyll uses it.

Gosynhyll opens his praise of womankind by noting that women are necessary to the continuance of the human race. Women are nurturers, looking after men when they are sick or injured. Women give men certain pleasures that men cannot offer each other. Women were involved in the founding of civilization: Ceres invented agriculture, Carmenta the alphabet; Pallas Athena (Minerva) was the artificer of wool and oil (for which her name was given to Athens). Though he probably mined these *exempla* from Boccaccio's *De Claris Mulieribus,* or perhaps from the rather fancier sources he actually cites, Gosynhyll may have been acting in this passage on a hint from Quintilian, who had recommended the panegyric oration for praise of the gods: "In praising the gods, we shall . . . eulogize the peculiar power of each, and such of their inventions as have conferred benefit on mankind. . . . In respect to inventions, we extol, in praising Minerva, that of the arts . . . in praising Ceres, that of corn" (I, pp. 219–20). (All early Tudor defenses praise Carmenta and Minerva for benefits conferred on mankind; Gosynhyll's addition of Ceres, however, is unusual.[16]) Gosynhyll rounds off this discussion with Sappho's skill in poetry and the Sybils' in prophesy.

One common theme in defenses, that men ought to show respect for womanhood out of gratitude to their mothers, Gosynhyll expands into a panegyric to motherhood. Pregnancy's exotic cravings, for antifeminist writers a trial of husbands, Gosynhyll views as one of the tribulations of expectant motherhood: "The stomake seldome satysfyde / For many sondry meates prouyde / Longe for more than she may gete, / And many a sory morsell ete" (Sig. Bi).[17] Childbirth endangers a woman's life; the agony of labor pains is an "urgent grefe" (Sig. Bi). Convalescence after childbirth is difficult: the husband, seldom sensitive to the wife's weakened condition, leaves her to manage housework alone. Child care is so exhausting that if men were to undertake it their arms and shoulders would ache and they would go lame. The mother of an infant gets little or no sleep; she is awakened at all hours to breast-feed the child and comfort him when he cries. "the man may lye and snowre [i.e., snore] full fast" while the wife walks the baby around the bed chamber or rocks its cradle until her arms ache. A mother must habituate herself to unappetizing smells, as she must clean up a baby who is "vnclene beneth" (Sig. Bi^v); her life is one continual round of changing and washing diapers. "Thus hathe the mother all the care / All the labour and dyssease / Where as the father dothe what hym please" (Sig. Bi^v). When the child is a year old, the mother must hold him constantly lest he get into mischief, and breast-feeding becomes a problem: the child has teeth and will bite. Men would be much less patient if they were responsible for child care, Gosynhyll suggests, much likelier to strike an offending child. If men remember all the trouble their mothers took, "Howe be it ye haue no better sporte / Than of the woman euyll to report?" (Sig. Bii).

This is a fine passage, possessed of a homely charm and a sure grasp of domestic detail. A discussion of dirty diapers brings us closer to the universal female condition than do pronouncements on Ceres and Minerva or debates about the relative culpability of Adam and Eve. But the potential for feminism in this passage is not realized. The stereotype of women's innate nurturing qualities is promoted; the assumption care is women's work is not seriously challenged. The moral is not men should share child rearing and housework on a regular basis, but simply that men should demonstrate their gratitude to women for performing these demeaning tasks (which "the man wolde sure dysdayne" [Sig. Bii]) by not writing antifeminist treatises.

Gosynhyll's *refutatio* is directed at the arguments of *The School House* and at erroneous popular opinion. He first takes up the tale of the Devil and the dumb wife, varying it considerably. In *The School House*, the anecdote deals with one man who cured his wife's dumbness by applying aspen leaves to her tongue on the Devil's instructions. In *Mulierum Pean*, Gosynhyll turns this into a creation myth:

> Some saye the woman had no tonge
> After that god had her create
> Untyll the man toke leues longe
> And put them vnder her palate
> An aspyn leffe of the dyuel he gatte
> And for it moueth with euery wynde
> They saye womens tongues be of lyke kynde
>   (Sig. Bii).

This he refutes by an appeal to authority: "All the clerkes [i.e., writers on theology] that euer were / Do wryte the same and testefye / That god made all thynge parfetlye [i.e., perfectly] / Howe shulde the woman then tonge haue none / And be of goddes creacyon?" (Sig. Bii^v).

The topic of creation leads into the problem of Eve: "Because that Eue our prime parent / The wyll of god dyd ons [i.e., once] transgresse / They blame all women in lyke consent" (Sig. Bii^v). The refutation of the misogynist's argument from Eve is lengthy. Gosynhyll objects to sweeping generalities about women, implying that Eve is no more than one example: "Nat euery man of one compleccyon / Nor euery Woman of one condycyon" (Sig. Bii^v). He questions the logic of blaming Eve more than Adam: both partook of the apple. He maintains that the Virgin Mary atoned for Eve's sin. In the cult of the Virgin Mary elaborated during the Middle Ages, Mary had become almost the female equivalent of Christ: as Christ redeemed mankind from the sins of Adam, so Mary redeemed womankind from the sins of Eve. Although the formulation is essentially medieval, formal defenders use this argument all through the Renaissance. Gosynhyll advances the notion, mentioned in *The School House*, that Eve was made of better material than was Adam. Man, he argues, is only the adjective, woman the noun of created beings. He further defends Eve with the *felix culpa* argument: the Fall of Man was fortunate in that it eventuated in the Savior's incarnation. The woman was chosen to initiate this fortunate offense—a mark in favor of womankind.

To demonstrate that God favors womankind, a small *digressio* discusses biblical women assisted by God to bear children in old age. If this seems to the modern reader like a sign of divine favor that women could well do without, that is doubtless a modern prejudice.

Returning to Adam as the first detractor, Gosynhyll argues that God was unimpressed by Adam's logic in blaming sin on the woman; He put a curse of hard work on Adam. Eve was punished by sorrow in childbearing, true; but labor pains, he argues, are only a penance, not a curse.

Gosynhyll's *propositio* is delayed for rhetorical effect, a tactic approved by rhetoricians: "Thus all thynge pondred in balance playne / God fauoureth alwayes the femynitye / We then to haue them in dysdayne / Standeth nat well with equytye / And who so sayde the good rare be / I durst auenture my heed to lose / To proue he lyeth" (Sig. Ci). The word *prove* in the last line introduces the *confirmatio*, the proof.

Gosynhyll possesses extensive documentation: "Thousandes or two I dare well say / Of them that yet here lyuyng be / In ful recorde forth bryng I may" (Sig. Ci); he could provide anyone interested with the names and addresses of such women (Sig. Ci). For the time being, however, he contents himself with historical example. He introduces anecdotes about good women of the Bible—Sarah, Rebecca, Judith, Deborah, Jael, Hester (Esther), Ruth, Anna, the Virgin Mary, Mary Magdalene, Martha, the woman of Canaan. He intermingles with these tales a running counterattack on men, adducing examples of bad men in the Bible and commenting, "Stubberne and styffe is the masculyne" (Sig. Cii^v), "Men can fyght and braule / And kyll eche other comenly / Whiche is nat sene in the femynyne" (Sig. Ciii^v). He appeals to authority: "God them marked gracyously" (Sig. [C4]); "God preferred the woman" (Sig. [C4]). Having proved his case by holy writ, he turns to the classics. He still speaks judicially, in terms of witnesses: "For more wytnes I shal reporte / Of later tyme" (Sig. Ei). Gosynhyll's classical examples are predictable—Lucrece, Penelope, Portia. He gives some prominence to Coriolanus's mother, perhaps because her son was one man who repaid his debt of gratitude to his mother. A sensible debater, he omits the fact that Coriolanus paid his debt with his life.[18]

Suddenly Gosynhyll backtracks to take up a biblical example he has "forgotten." This apparent evidence of hasty composition or failure to revise is in fact a deliberate device sanctioned by Quintilian: "Sometimes we may pretend that something has escaped our memory, with a view to introduce it into a place better suited to our purpose" (I, p. 290). The placing of this final historical example, near the end of the *confirmatio*, better suits Gosynhyll's purpose because it is his best example—the biblical Susanna story, appropriate because Susanna was assailed by detractors, who slandered her to cover up their own attempt at seducing her. This example obliquely impugns the motives of the detractor of women, implying that those who slander women are those who have themselves been frustrated in lewd attempts on feminine honor—exactly the accusation Elyot's Candidus raises against the detractor Caninius. Gosynhyll's emphasis on Daniel, the child raised up by God to confound Susanna's detractors, suggests a parallel between Daniel and Gosynhyll: both, Gosynhyll implies, were chosen by God to defend the honor of women.

Gosynhyll comments on modern women that in estates he has visited the lady of the manor oversees baker, brewer, butler, and cook. Sketching out the demanding and complicated nature of running a great household, he notes that the realm's great ladies perform these tasks well: "My lady must receyue and paye / And euery man in his offyce controll / And to eche cause gyue ye and nay / Bargayne and bye . . . " (Sig. Eiii). Historians have lately devoted attention to the responsibilities of Renaissance noblewomen; such considerations did not entirely escape the notice of Renaissance theorists of women.

Gosynhyll's last "proof" is a remark on language: even common idioms pay tribute to women: "A further profe . . . / By comune reporte we here eche day / The chylde is praysed for his mother wytte" (Sig. Eiii).

The *peroratio* of *Mulierum Pean* states that this defense will cause misogynists to recant. The afterword (again, "Go forthe lytell boke") reveals authorship: in case the reader misses "Gosynhyll" three times in acrostic, the author declares his name, "Edwarde Gosynhyll."

How seriously did Gosynhyll offer his reflections on women in these two essays? The debater who rebuts himself can be suspected of holding the Ramist view that to dispute well is logic's chiefest end. The facility with which one writer can argue opposing propositions must caution the reader against too blithely accepting any Renaissance pronouncement on women as reflecting the attitudes of his contemporaries. The emphasis on jest is telling—the incorporation of jest-book anecdotes, Gosynhyll's own description of *The School House* as a "iest," the jest implicit in the act of self-refutation. Gosynhyll excuses his misogyny on the grounds that his work is jest, apparently regarding formal jest as safely "literary," by definition insulated from real life. And the formal elements of his work mark it as a self-conscious literary exercise, to which personal feelings about women are irrelevant.

The structure of the oration is impeccable in both essays; in the absence of other evidence we must assume Gosynhyll worked this out for himself. His careful, often subtle positioning of examples, his imaginative blend of classical structure with native verse form, his fairly disciplined control of tone combine to make these essays works of some literary sophistication: all the indications are that Gosynhyll saw himself as a stylist. It is an injustice to characterize him as a catchpenny poet. Imitating classical orations is a hard way to catch a penny.

The fact that it was the *judicial* oration that served as the model for the formal controversy has implications for the later development of the controversy. By the early seventeenth century, controversialists were frequently using judicial imagery. Joseph Swetnam entitled his diatribe *The Arraignment of Lewd, Idle, Froward, and Unconstant Women*. One of his opponents featured in her rejoinder the arraignment of Swetnam, before a tribunal of women, on charges of public misogyny. This controversy culminated in the play *Swetnam the Woman-hater Arraigned by Women,* which staged a trial scene: lawyers for prosecution and defense argued the sexes' relative culpability. The persistently legal atmosphere of the later controversy has roots in the rhetoric of the early controversy; the accusation/defense format adapted from classical rhetoricians carried the seeds of dramatic situation. Nearly all of Quintilian's illustrative examples are drawn from hypothetical courtroom proceedings. The image of a trial, with Woman as defendant, hovers over the whole controversy. And the position of Woman as "the accused" placed severe limitations on constructive discussion of women and their role in society. The formal controversy was prevented by its own rhetoric from becoming more than a literary pastime. How could the sincerest advocate discuss the economic deprivations or social disadvantages of a client who stands accused of high crimes and misdemeanors? Little wonder that defenders defined their task primarily as clearing the client of charges against her.

The defenses by Elyot, Vaughan, and Gosynhyll, whatever their literary merits, accomplish little more for women's cause than to create a stereotype of the "good" woman to counter the misogynist's stereotype of the "bad." The portrait of Woman as by nature a tender-hearted, homekeeping, obedient, motherly, uncomplaining washer of befouled diapers does little to advance the argument for the equality of women. The next defense, however, while no less firmly grounded in literary tradition, evidences considerable potential for genuine feminism.

When the great Heinrich Cornelius Agrippa von Nettesheim, scholar of international reputation, theorist of magic, at once humanist and critic of humanist pursuits, undertook a defense of women, something out of the ordinary was to be expected. It is true that his defense, *De nobilitate et praecellentia Foemenei sexus,* called in Clapham's 1542 translation *A Treatise of the Nobilitie and excellencye of woman kynde,* is more generously endowed than any other early Renaissance defense with tedious lists of great women in biblical and classical history: women who inspired the love of Greek gods, beautiful women in the Bible, good wives of the

Bible and the classics, great female names in religion, philosophy (Diotima *et al*), prophecy (the Sybils *et al*), oratory and poetry (Sappho *et al*), government (Semiramis, Dido, the Amazons), warfare, invention, and even—an Agrippan touch—magic. (Circe and Medea are, eccentrically, praised as better magicians than the male Zoroaster.) The Virgin puts in her statutory appearance, along with the women to whom Christ first showed himself after the resurrection, who serve as a contrast to the all-male cast of malefactors involved in his trial and crucifixion. And Agrippa promotes a view of parents that cannot help striking the modern reader as painfully unfair to both sexes: the "chiefest offyce and duetye of woman," he declares (now ignoring Sappho, the Amazons, and the rest) "is to conceyue" (Sig. C); in the course of defending childrearing as a worthy occupation, Agrippa avers that fathers have little influence on children, that mothers love children more than fathers do because they correctly perceive that children have "more of theyr mothers substance, than of theyr fathers" (Sig. Cᵛ), and that children love their mothers more than their fathers.[19] He furthers stereotype by noting that women are more pitying and merciful than men: women, to whom milk is given, are nourishers by nature. (Woman's milk as a symbol of her gentle, nurturing qualities was a commonplace; Shakespeare twice employs it in ironic reversal: two of his least nurturing female characters, Goneril and Lady Macbeth, accuse their husbands of "milky gentleness" and of being "too full o' the milk of human kindness.")

But if Agrippa's treatise is predictable in these particulars, it is predictable in no others. His initial flat statement of the complete spiritual and intellectual equality of the sexes sparkles in an age when other defenders contented themselves mainly with shaming the unchivalrousness of detractors. Dismissing physical differences between the sexes as negligible, Agrippa announces a credo: "The woman hathe that same mynd that a man hath, that same reason and speche, she gothe to the same ende of blysfulnes. . . . Betwene man and woman by substance of the soule, one hath no higher preemynence of nobylytye aboue the other, but both of them naturally haue equall libertie of dignitie and worthynesse" (Sig. Aiiᵛ). This, however unorthodox, is nothing to what follows: the rest of the essay argues the superiority of women in every area except equality of divine substance. The arguments Agrippa marshalls in support of this amazing thesis are ingenious if not outrageous: many have that bright casuistical flair that characterizes the work of Neoplatonists; a few are almost certainly tongue-in-cheek.

On the sticky problem of our first mother, Agrippa expends a good deal of ingenuity. Eve was God's last and hence highest creation (since God was clearly working his way up the Great Chain of Being); she was made of nobler material, formed, unlike Adam, of animate substance. In explaining away Eve's part in the unpleasantness of the apple, Agrippa with a lawyer's mind locates a loophole: God forbade eating the fruit *before* Eve's creation; the stricture therefore did not apply to her. God deliberately declined to deny the fruit to Eve; he wished her, as a superior being, to be free of the rules governing the inferior Adam: "For god wolde [i.e., willed] her to be fre[e] from the begynning. Therfore the manne sinned in eatynge, not the woman. And all we synned in Adam, not in Eva" (Sig. Cv^v). This astonishing, thoroughly heretical, and perfectly delightful theory is not persuasive, and Agrippa must have known it was not. Although it is true that Adam is warned away from the fruit before Eve's creation, Eve demonstrates in her conversation with the serpent that she has been informed of the rules: "But of the fruit of the tree which is in the midst of the garden, God hath said, Ye shall not eat of it, neither shall ye touch it, lest ye die" (Gen. 3:3, KJV). Eve clearly believes that "ye" includes herself, and since she does die, there is no doubt that God intended her to be included. Although Agrippa tries to buttress his argument by maintaining that "the man knew well he dyd amisse; but the woman being deceyued, erred ignorãtly" (Sig. [C6]), he accomplishes no more than to render gullible his supposed superior creature. The argument remains the purest sophistry. Considering that Agrippa's argument has no smaller effect than to recreate Woman as a separate species, exempt from original sin, it is difficult to believe that his intention was other than to amuse his readers with the joy of outrageous ingenuity exercised for its own sake. Among all the defenses of Eve, it remains my personal favorite; but I cannot believe it was meant to be taken seriously.

No more can one take seriously Agrippa's treatment of the ghastly Old Testament episodes where God commands the victorious Israelites to kill all male captives and keep the women as prizes; Agrippa considers this evidence of the excellency of womankind! And then there is hair. Agrippa's contention that women are given long hair for modesty's sake was a commonplace: it went along with the argument that women's privy parts are more privy than men's; women are more modest than men by nature. What smacks of ingenuity for its own sake is the treatment of baldness and beards: first, women are superior because they do not go bald, baldness being an affront to human dignity by spoiling the appearance of that seat of reason, the head; second (diametrically opposed to the baldness argument), men are inferior because they possess beards: excessive hairiness reduces a human being to the animal level (Sig. [B8]). The manifest absurdity of these arguments, particularly when taken together, militates against serious intent.

Human physicality calls forth more logical curiosities: women are cleaner than men (Agrippa claims that men dirty the bathwater more), and women

are finer because it is worthier to void "superfluous humours" by "se-
crete partes" than by the face, "the moste worthy part of a mannes body"
(Sig. [B8]ᵛ). (This somewhat obscure remark seems to mean that menstruation is less disgusting than spitting.)

One of Agrippa's pleasantest moments is his defense of that univer-
sally-rued vice of womankind, talkativeness. "And is not a womā better
spoke, more eloquent, more copious and plentyfull of wordes than a
man?" he unblushingly inquires, no doubt fully cognizant of the chagrined agreement to be expected from most readers. His defense is humanistic: "Is it not right faire and comendable, that women shulde excelle
men in that thing, in whiche men chiefly passe all other beastes?" (Sig.
Ciiiᵛ, Ciiii). The argument is far from unreasonable: it is a logical extension of the humanist glorification of speech as a distinctive attribute of
humankind; but it must have struck contemporaries, accustomed to satiric diatribes on women's irrepressible prattling, as perverse. Again, the
argument is almost certainly facetious.

The real shock is Agrippa's contention that, given women's superiority, Christ as God would surely have descended to earth in female form
had it not been necessary to exhibit humility, since the sin he had come
to expiate was pride: "He toke vpon hym manhode, as the more humble
and lower kynde, and not womankynde, the more hygher and noble"
(Sig. [C6]ᵛ). One can imagine clergymen fainting in their studies upon
reading such a passage. And if one were not already convinced that
Agrippa's tongue is planted firmly in his cheek, one could be left in very
little doubt after encountering those venerable biblical bogey-women,
Delilah, Lot's daughters, and Job's wife, now metamorphosed into examples of the superior power of womankind. When all this is capped
with fantastic natural history (all eagles and the phoenix are female, all
basilisks are male) one feels that here is no more than a rival "iest."

A later translator, Henry Care, who in 1670 refurbished this work as
a rejoinder to a recent work listing women's imperfections alphabetically,
took it as an elaborate jest, placing it in the classical tradition (revived in
the Renaissance) of rhetorical paradox.[20] The translator's preface suggests
that the piece might gain pardon if not applause in an age of extravagant
opinions and wild conceits; it is no worse than the paradoxical praises of
tyranny, injustice, ugliness, and folly (here he names Erasmus's *The Praise
of Folly*) which have gone before. Agrippa wrote it, Care suggests, for
love of perversity: he enjoyed "stemming the impetuous Tide of popular
opinion," as witness *The Vanity of the Arts and Sciences,* Agrippa's attack
on humanist learning.

I see nothing in Agrippa's essay to preclude its being a rhetorical paradox. Agrippa called the work an oration.[21] In form it is close to an
epideictic oration, though an occasional foray into *refutatio* (see Dii, [D8])

brings it closer at times to the more typical judicial oration. But Agrippa's use of this god-praising oration for that which is seldom praised, his outrageous arguments, his main thesis that flies in the face of received opinion, would seem to establish the work as rhetorical paradox. It is similar in kind to Montaigne's *Apology of Raymond Sebonde,* that trenchant argument for the superiority of animals to mankind that George Boas has discussed as part of the paradox tradition.[22] Such a view gains strength, if anything, from the pains Agrippa takes to deny that his arguments are sophistical (Sig. Aiii): this seems a hint to the reader to view the work in a certain light. But Henry Care is unjust in assuming that the paradox's motive is love of perversity, its main purpose wit for its own sake. Paradoxical literature from Montaigne's *Apology* to Erasmus's *The Praise of Folly* exhibits serious intent: the need for such outlandish arguments to maintain an extreme opinion is meant to reflect on the outlandishness of argument that would be necessary to maintain the opposite extreme. Montaigne's argument for animal superiority undermines extravagant humanist claims for the superiority of mankind, while Erasmus's panegyrics to folly call into question the age's complacent reliance on the wisdom of this world. The rhetorical paradox is an overcorrection, pointing up the untenable nature of one extreme position by demonstrating the feasibility of arguing its opposite.[23] Paradox is not like the mock-heroic mode, where the inadequacies of the subject are exposed by the inflated terms in which it is celebrated; Agrippa's hyperbolic praise of women is not an ironic vehicle for laying bare the sex's unworthiness but a graphic demonstration of the absurdities one must resort to if one claims superiority for either sex.

Like the sonnet, paradoxical works contain a *volta,* a point at which the author takes leave of outlandish argument and outrageous example and quietly asserts the mean between extremes that must represent the attitude of the reasonable thinker. Montaigne leaves behind tales of enamored elephants and soberly objects to human presumption; Erasmus's lively and ironic enumeration of human follies yields to devout reflections on the foolishness of mankind and the wisdom of God. And Agrippa, as if his ingenuity had reached its outer limit with the eagles, phoenix, and basilisks, turns sober and begins arguing straightforwardly what was always the real issue—the case for equality.

Agrippa now decries the double standard of sexual morality, argues that women's evil has been overestimated because most writers are male, and reminds the reader (with a near-anthropological modernity) that women's social and political inferiority in contemporary Europe is not based on natural law and has not, at other times and in other cultures, invariably obtained. He recalls marital equality in ancient Rome, Roman legal guarantees for joint ownership and disposal of marital property and for wives' right of inheritance; he notes ancient arguments for women's equality and rights, citing Lycurgus and Plato. Adducing other cultures where women had more rights than they now have—the Cantabrians, Scythians, Thracians—he observes, "That is nowe forbydden by lawes, abolished by custome, extincted by education. For anon as a woman is borne euen from her infancy, she is kept at home in ydelnes, & as thoughe she were vnmete for any hygher busynesse, she is p[er]mitted to know no farther, than her nedle and her threede" (Sig. [F8]–[F8]ᵛ). Women are forbidden to hold office, pleade a case at law, be guardians or tutors, preach God's word (here he notes women preachers in the Bible). In his ringing conclusion, Agrippa stands head and shoulders above his contemporaries as a realist in the study of sexual politics. Controversialists seldom went farther than to judge women good or bad by the degree of their conformity to a code of behavior seen as part of the natural order. Agrippa questioned the existence of "natural" order, viewing women's condition as a product of forces less natural than cultural: "And thus by these lawes, the women being subdewed as it were by force of armes, are constrained to giue place to men, and to obeye theyr subdewers, not by no naturall, no diuyne necessitie or reason, but by custome, education, fortune, and a certayne Tyrannicall occasion" (Sig. G, Gᵛ). In the light of this statement, Agrippa's lists of great women in history take on new meaning: women have done more in the past than they are doing now, because contemporary society denies them the education and the legal rights they must have to perform what they are capable of. Not content with praising or blaming Woman as she now exists, Agrippa suggests reasons for the actual inferiority of so potentially excellent a creature. His initial coy disavowal of sophistry contrasts strikingly with the gravity of his final affirmation: "For neyther Ambition, nor the cause of myne own commendation, but my dutie and the very truthe moued me to wryte" (Sig. [G3]). The serious turn the work has taken, and the accuracy of his social analysis, incline me to believe him.

When Agrippa recognizes the opposition, he does not characterize it as misogynistic insult and jesting detraction: "There be somme men," he tells us, "whyche by relygion, clayme authoritie ouer women, and they proue theyr tyranny by holy scripture" (Sig. Gᵛ). The enemy, Agrippa sees, is not the misogynist but the male supremacist. The distinction is crucial: many men who have loved women have been male supremacists; open misogyny has always been less difficult for women to deal with than has well-intentioned paternalism of the sort in which defenders themselves indulged. The formal controversy's potential usefulness was undermined by the way defenders of women persistently depicted literary misogyny, "malicious detraction," as the major obstacle to women's happiness.[24] Agrippa could play the literary game as well as any—better than most; but in sensing the game's ultimate irrelevance to women's struggles for freedom and dignity, he stood virtually alone. He saw that women suffer less from literary insults than from being "constrained to give place to men, and to obeye theyr subdewers."

The rhetorical paradox is itself a kind of jest—an intricate and exquisite jest, preëminently vulnerable to misinterpretation.[25] Agrippa's feminist use of this mode reminds us that while composition of a defense is no guarantee of true authorial concern about the woman question, neither does literary sophistication evidence lack of such concern. One sometimes senses authorial "sincerity" in controversialist works, as I do with Agrippa; such impressions may frequently be wrong. But whatever the author's personal attitude toward women, it remains clear that the formal controversy, for all its preoccupation with stylistic finesse, could occasionally produce a thinker capable of laying philosophic foundations for modern feminism.

Of the five pieces comprising the early Tudor controversy, defenses of women outnumber attacks by four to one. A similar proportion obtained all through the period under examination: of the thirty-five works of the formal controversy which I shall discuss, only nine are pure formal attacks on women; the others are either defenses or dialogues in which defender triumphs over detractor. This numerical disparity suggests that the defense was the formal controversy's basic format, the attack a variant. Defenses of women were always inclined to be theoretical and philosophical, while formal attacks were slapdash composites of jest and anecdote on which formal structure was superimposed with some strain. The looser hold of intellectual methodology over *The School House of Women* can be seen in comparison with *Mulierum Pean: Mulierum Pean* employs about fifty *exempla*, cites sources in notes, and avoids jest; *The School House* employs just over twenty *exempla*, provides no notes, and covers deficiencies of argument with jokes.

It seems most probable to me that the formal attack on women received what structure and even what logic it had by imitation of formal defenses. Misogyny lurks in many corners of culture, from proverb to myth to jest to stereotype: this potent force does not need formal statements of theory or logical rationales and seldom generates them for any but literary purposes. Renaissance evidence, at least, suggests that far from being responses to misogynistic attacks, defenses of women provided literary models for misogynistic attacks. The paradoxical generation of attack as response to defense is manifest in the startling fact that both Gosynhyll's *School House* and *Mulierum Pean* stem in part from the same unacknowledged source—Agrippa's defense.

Thirty of *Mulierum Pean*'s and eight of *The School House*'s *exempla* also appear among Agrippa's *exempla;* of these, several are very rare else-where in the formal controversy—Messalina, Queen Athaliah, Mary the sister of Moses. In cases where variant names or spellings are possible, Agrippa and Gosynhyll make the same choices—Mary rather than Miriam as Moses's sister; the Queen of Saba, not Sheba; Jahel, not Jael; Loth, not Lot. Both follow Livy (or Boccaccio) in naming Coriolanus's mother Veturia, rather than adopting Plutarch's Volumnia. In one section, we can follow Gosynhyll's deconstruction of Agrippa with the utmost clarity. In *Mulierum Pean,* Pilate's wife is followed immediately by the woman of Canaan. In Agrippa, these two *exempla* are separated by some extremely dubious examples of feminine virtue; Gosynhyll has appropriated three of these—Delilah, Lot's daughters, and Job's wife—for *The School House* and then continued with the indubitably virtuous woman of Canaan for *Mulierum Pean.* Gosynhyll likely noticed that the negative examples, which mark Agrippa's work as rhetorical paradox, were more suitable to formal attack, and he duly sorted positive from negative in making his own division of the topic. Such evidence suggests that Gosynhyll, far from being overcome with remorse after writing *The School House* and repenting with *Mulierum Pean,* probably worked on the two pieces simultaneously.

Whether Gosynhyll read Agrippa in the Latin edition of 1529 or 1531, published at Antwerp and Lyons, which suggests an awareness of the international literary scene one hardly expects of a popular scribbler, or used Clapham's 1542 translation, which would place the Gosynhyll works later than is usually assumed and indicate that *Mulierum Pean* echoes Vaughan's 1542 defense rather than the other way around, Gosynhyll's indebtedness to Agrippa shows attack spawned by defense. Gosynhyll himself describes *The School House* as a response to "a boke . . . in prayse of the femynye." It is difficult to imagine an author transmuting a rhetorical paradox into two complementary judicial orations, tightroping his way through an aggressive defense and a defensive attack, while bursting with misogynistic spleen or mellowing into palinode. In the early Tudor controversy, we are not in the presence of Renaissance Attitudes Toward Women. We are in the presence of art.

NOTES

1. I use the 1545 edition, STC 7658. The only extant copy of the 1540 edition, at the Huntington Library, is not listed in the STC. References to the STC in my notes and Bibliography are to Pollard and Redgrave's *Short-Title Catalogue of Books Printed in England, Scotland, & Ireland and of English Books Printed Abroad, 1475–1640*. References to the Wing *Short-*

Title Catalogue, which goes beyond 1640, will be distinguished as "Wing STC." A number of the documents I discuss in this volume, including *The School House of Women; The Arraignment of Lewd, Idle, Froward, and Unconstant Women; Ester Hath Hanged Haman; The Worming of a Mad Dog; Hic Mulier; Haec-Vir,* and *Monodia,* will be reprinted in *Half Humankind: English Texts and Contexts of the Controversy about Women,* edited by Katherine Usher Henderson and Barbara F. McManus (Urbana: University of Illinois Press, in press).

2. Foster Watson, *Vives and the Renascence Education of Women,* p. 211.

3. Vaughan says that the work was given to him by a friend. Utley outlines the case for and against Robert Burdet as author (pp. 323–24). Catherine Henze ("Author and Source for *A Dyalogue Defensyve for Women*") concurs in the attribution to Burdet and points up parallels between the *Dialogue Defensive* and Elyot's *Defense.* For the sake of convenience, I shall consider Vaughan the author.

4. The medieval bird debate often dealt with women; see Utley, p. 239. Utley suggests that Vaughan's *Dialogue* may have been indebted to Thomas Feylde's *A contrauersye bytwene a louer and a Jaye,* written some time between 1509 and 1535. Feylde's poem is interesting for its humanist classical learning, but it is more a commiseration than a debate, and its influence on Vaughan's dialogue is not easy to see.

5. Cf. Wright, p. 468: "The *Schole house of women* immediately provoked replies and imitations, one of the most vigorous retorts being *A Dyalogue defensyue for women, agaynst malycyous detractoures* (1542), attributed to Robert Vaughan." I do not know, incidentally, of any imitations of the *School House* dating to this period.

6. Utley, p. 273. Vaughan's omission of all punctuation from line endings (except at the ends of speeches) led Utley, I believe, to misread the relevant passage on Sig. Aiii, which he quotes thus:

> I red an oracyon
> Most pleasauntly set forth, with flowers rethorycall
> Descrybynge the monstruous vyce of detraction
> The dowghter of eunye [*sic*], the furye infernall . . .
> Bryngynge Innocentes, in to paynes depe
> And from theyr good names, it doth them cast downe
> By readynge this Aucthour.

Utley's ellipsis after "infernall" is misleading: the omitted lines further describe detraction, which is the antecedent of the pronoun "it" in "from theyr good names, it doth them cast downe"; Utley's ellipsis makes the antecedent of "it" appear to be "readynge this Aucthour." The rest of the sentence beginning "By readynge" (not quoted by Utley) indicates that Vaughan agrees with the author of the "oracyon": "By reading this Aucthour, I was pensyfe in my harte / As one that had proued, his wordes to be trewe." By Utley's reading, the work antecedent to Vaughan's dialogue is a satire on women; by my reading, it is a protest against detraction. It should be noted that Vaughan does not even say that the "oracyon" was about women: those whose good names are cast down by detraction are merely called "Innocentes." Utley's reading has been colored by his assumption that defenses of women are answers to satires on women.

7. Utley (pp. 293–94) cites other parallels between the *Dialogue* and *Mulierum Pean*.

8. Utley (pp. 251–52) cites four scholars who "reject Gosynhill's authorship of the *Scholehouse* with something like finality."

9. Marcus Fabius Quintilianus, *Quintilian's Institutes of Oratory*, I, p. 240.

10. For a lucid account of the confusions obscuring the publishing history of *The School House* and *Mulierum Pean*, see Utley, p. 251 ff.

11. For "the charge that woman is more lustful than man," Katharine Rogers suggests three "underlying motives: a sexual ascetic is likely to project his own lustful feelings upon women; an ambivalent lover will accuse his mistress of unfaithfulness or sexual insatiability which make her unworthy to be the object of a man's love; and a patriarch is apt to worry constantly that the wife he owns may rebel against his sovereignty by giving her body to other men" (*Helpmate*, p. 54).

12. Thomas Hobbes, *Leviathan, Parts I and II*, p. 57.

13. Sigmund Freud, *Jokes and Their Relation to the Unconscious*, pp. 103, 100.

14. Henri Bergson, *Laughter*, p. 477.

15. Marcus Tullius Cicero, *Rhetorica ad Herennium*, pp. 183–85. This work, dubiously Cicero's, I ascribe to Cicero for the sake of convenience.

16. Other sources for the Ceres exemplum might have been Ovid's *Metamorphoses*, Christine de Pisan's *City of Ladies*, or Castiglione's *The Courtier* (not available in English when Gosynhyll wrote). Gosynhyll footnotes the *Metamorphoses*, but his grouping Ceres/Carmenta/Pallas together, with no intervening *exempla*, suggests the influence of Christine, who discusses these three consecutively. The *City of Ladies* appeared in English translation in 1521.

17. Gosynhyll may here have been influenced by Agrippa, who cites women's ability to digest "coles, erth, stones" and other oddments craved during pregnancy as evidence of women's marvelous constitutions (*A Treatise of the Nobilitie and excellencye of woman kynde* [Sig. Ciii-Ciii^v]). For Gosynhyll's debt to Agrippa, see below.

18. In the section devoted to women of classical antiquity appears a stanza on Queen Hester which has apparently been misplaced by the printer. It belongs on Sig. [C4]^v, immediately following the first stanza.

19. This argument would probably have been recognized in Agrippa's day as a deliberate reversal of Thomas Aquinas's extension of Aristotle's physiological theories, which demonstrated that a child loved his father more than his mother, since the father forms the child "in a more excellent manner than the mother, because the father is the active principle; the mother, in contrast, is the passive and material principle" (*Summa*

Theologica, Secunda Secundae, Question 26, Article 10 [my translation]). Agrippa's bland inversion of so familiar a dogma would almost certainly have provoked suspicion that his work was tongue-in-cheek.

20. Care entitled his translation, to which he made some additions of his own, *Female Pre-eminence; or, the Dignity and Excellency of that Sex, above the Male.* Wing STC 784.

21. In the opening sentence of Agrippa's epistle "Clarissimo viro domini Maximiliano . . . ," prefixed to the 1531 version of *De Nobilitate* in the complete works published in Latin at Lyons.

22. George Boas, *The Happy Beast in French Thought of the Seventeenth Century.*

23. Rosalie L. Colie advances a similar theory of the way paradox works: "One element common to all . . . kinds of paradox is their exploitation of the fact of relative, or competing, value systems. . . . The paradox is an oblique criticism of absolute judgment or absolute convention" (*Paradoxia Epidemica: The Renaissance Tradition of Paradox,* p. 10).

24. A similar problem of misdefinition dogs Katharine Rogers's *The Troublesome Helpmate.* Rogers completely abandons her topic, described in her subtitle as *A History of Misogyny in Literature,* while discussing the nineteenth century, a period poor in literary misogyny: here she focuses instead on paternalism. Misogyny and paternalism are, I think, alternate strategies of the male supremacist; I suspect that Rogers's main interest is in the way literature can function as an instrument of male supremacy, but by focusing on literary misogyny she often allows herself to be sidetracked onto the less important question of whether individual authors were woman-haters in their private lives.

25. Even critics who recognize Agrippa's work as a paradox can misunderstand the way the argument works. Warwick Bond, for example, while viewing Agrippa as a "paradox-monger," charges him with lack of "fairness in urging the women's claims. . . . If sometimes he rises to eloquence in declaiming against the wrongs that woman suffers at the hands of tyrant man, at others he resorts to a line of argument which fatally prejudices her cause" (introduction to his edition of William Bercher's *The Nobility of Women,* pp. 83–84).

CHAPTER THREE

The Elizabethan Controversy

AFTER LYING DORMANT through the 1550s,[1] the formal controversy was resurrected in 1560, when the printer John Kynge blitzed the market with a number of works on women. Among miscellaneous pieces on women—*The Proud Wife's Paternoster, Nice Wanton, A dialogue betwene the comen Secretary and Ielowsy touchynge the vnstablenes of harlottes*—Kynge published in that year fresh editions of *Mulierum Pean* and *The School House of Women* and a new rejoinder to *The School House*, Edward More's *A Lytle and Bryefe tretyse, called the defence of women, and especially of Englyshe women, made agaynst the Schole howse of women*.

In his *Defence of Women*, More testifies to having perused a copy of *The School House* on the strength of its subtitle, "wherin man may rede a goodly prayse of the condicyons of women," which he soon found cruelly deceptive. He was then moved, he says, to write a defense of women. In 1560, Kynge bound More's defense with *The School House*, having entered both in 1557–58. One wonders how and when More acquired his copy of *The School House*, which had probably been out of print for some fifteen years. It is possible that Kynge, planning a new edition of *The School House*, commissioned More's rejoinder. But More seems an odd choice: he was only twenty and had never written for publication (*The Defense* is his only recorded work); in any case this seems a great deal of trouble for Kynge to take, especially since he probably already possessed the rights to another defense, *Mulierum Pean*. More's own story may be true—that he wrote his defense after somehow coming across *The School House*, presumably the edition of ca. 1542. Conceivably, it was More's approaching Kynge about publishing his defense that prompted Kynge to put out a new edition of *The School House*. Be this as it may, More's remark helps explain the continuity of the genre: the remarkable similarities among works of the formal controversy published over a number of years are understandable if such books remained easily accessible after they lapsed out of print. *The School House* was in the private library of Captain Cox the mason in 1575.[2] More too may have found it in a private library, probably (given his education and family background) of a more intellectual sort than Cox's. Productions of the formal controversy were apparently not discarded as ephemera.

But is there necessarily any candour in More's story about his shocked perusal of *The School House?* Indignation at literary misogyny was a conventional pose of the formal defender and could appear in a total vacuum of formal misogyny. More could easily have composed his defense in imitation of earlier defenses, mentioning *The School House,* perhaps known to him by title only, as a sop to convention. More's youth may be less pertinent to his idealism than to the state of tutelage which dictated that he compose a formal defense as a literary exercise; certainly the antifeminist epigram on More's title page suggests neither idealism nor indignation. Considering the textbook quality of formal defenses, the youth of a number of practitioners is of interest: one of the three women who wrote defenses in response to Joseph Swetnam emphasized that she was being educated by her mother; another was under twenty. Agrippa wrote *De Nobilitate* in his early twenties.

More relates his incensed disbelief that one born of woman could display such spite against the sex as does the author of *The School House.* The filial ingratitude of misogynists is hardly a new note: Gosynhyll had sounded it in *Mulierum Pean,* and it was to be sounded again and again, up to and beyond Troilus's hesitance, for the sake of mothers everywhere, to turn misogynist because of one bad experience with a woman: "Let it not be believ'd for womanhood! / Think, we had mothers; do not give advantage / To stubborn critics, apt . . . / to square the general sex / By Cressid's rule" (*Troilus and Cressida,* V.ii.129–133).[3] More's modest disclaimer that his inexperienced youth may not be equal to the task, and his wish that a married man would take it on, are succeeded by a fervent declaration of purpose couched in the language of chivalry: he will be women's "Champyan bold" (Sig. Aiv).

More flirts with the idea of women as victims of an unjust social system: "And as the pore & nedy man hanged is sometyme / When the rycher skapeth, for a greater cryme, / So doth the sely [i.e., innocent] woman of eche degree and sorte / Runne in slaunder undeserued, by meanes of mens reporte" (Sig. Aiv.) The observation is fairly sophisticated: women of all social classes ("of eche degree") are in the same position as lower-class men: both lack the social and economic power to defend themselves. But by limiting women's predicament to "slander," More fails to engage the real problem. Detraction was a serious offense in an age which had staked much on earthly immortality, on the preservation of one's fame and good name for posterity (cf. Falstaff's "Will [honor] not live with the living? No. Why? Detraction will not suffer it"

[*1 Henry IV,* V.i.140–142]), but concentrating on slander itself distracted attention from legal inequities, social prejudice, and a host of other problems more serious for women than antifeminist insults.

More's obligatory defense of Eve is hardly feminist. The Devil who tempted her was male; and Adam ate of the apple too, tempted by the Devil, whose words Eve simply repeated verbatim. Besides, More argues, women are weak and frail by nature, as is the will of God.

Like Gosynhyll in *Mulierum Pean,* More focuses on the difficulties of a woman's life: wakeful nights of child nursing, the penalty for Eve's transgression, should be punishment enough; detraction should cease. He adds rather feebly that whatever their faults, English women are at least more chaste than Italian women.

More trudges stolidly through virtuous women of biblical and classical renown (Susanna, Judith, Lucrece), concluding that "women are ryght honest, and men are very lewede [i.e., lewd]" (Sig. Cii^v). When he takes arms against charges of extravagant dress, he may be toying with the idea that opulently attired wives are status symbols to display their husbands' wealth: "A woman hauing nothing but at her husbandes hande / That he thus maynteneth her . . . who ought to beare the blame? / Not she that weareth them, but he that byeth the same" (Sig. Cii^v); but More is probably not that astute; the argument has the aroma of a legal quibble. And although More points out that farthingales and other outlandish fashions were invented and constructed by male tailors and that foreign fashions are brought back by male merchants who want their wives to wear them, he is still only shadowboxing with the economics and social significance of fashion. He misses an opportunity to remark that contemporary men dressed extravagantly too.

More's most important point is in reference to shrewishness. He argues that wives' remonstrances over husbandly vices such as drinking should not be interpreted as scolding: they are, in fact, justified rebukes. The grievances of alleged shrews in Renaissance literature are often genuine, but railers against scolding were seldom willing to admit this fact. I shall later have more to say about "justifiable shrewishness."

More's form is, again, the judicial oration. The *exordium* comprises his description of himself and of the shock of reading *The School House,* and his promise to be women's "champion." In the *narratio* he dismisses the charges against his client, womankind, as undeserved slander, concentrating on the charges against Eve. The *confirmatio* includes remarks on the goodness of women in the face of the difficulties of motherhood and the trials of attempted seduction by men, backed up by biblical and classical example. The *propositio* is probably "women are ryght honest, and men are very lewede." The *refutatio* replies to specific charges, such as extravagant dress, use of cosmetics, and scolding. The possible confusion in More's mind between chivalrous defense and judicial pleading was one that perennially haunted the controversy.

More's poem is not rooted in social or political reality; it exists not in a world where real women demand rights but in a world where books answer books. More's indignation is most likely a calculated posture: he handles the genre too comfortably to be quite as unfamiliar with its conventions as his opening remarks suggest.

That the decision to publish Thomas Hoby's translation of Castiglione's *The Courtier* in 1561 was influenced by recent activity in the formal controversy is a distinct possibility.[4] The translation, complete by 1556, had been in the hands of the printer, William Seres, for some years before publication. The printer's preface makes obscure reference to certain parts of the book "beeing misliked of some, that had the perusing of it," but *The Courtier* is hardly seditious. One suspects that the printer feared that he would not sell enough copies to offset the cost of printing so lengthy a book. But with Kynge's launching three works of formal controversy with such confidence in 1560, Seres might well have been moved by the fact that Book III of *The Courtier* was a specimen of the same genre. The title page, the description of contents, and the translator's preface of the 1561 edition all advertise that the work features prominently a discussion of women; this suggests that Seres printed *The Courtier* with an eye to current controversy. In his dedicatory epistle, Hoby states that he translated Book III first and only later decided to translate the other three books. At the beginning of Book III he notes that he translated this book at the request of the Lady Marquess of Northampton, in 1551. Whatever else it may have accomplished, if the formal controversy was responsible for giving the world *The Courtier* in English, it deserves some honorable mention in literary history for that alone.

Lord Gaspar Pallavicino is Castiglione's antifeminist detractor, abetted at times by Ottaviano Fregoso (Lord Octavian) and one Phrisio. Gaspar has a witty female opponent in the Lady Emilia Pia, and women have a champion in Lord Julian de Medici. The stage is set for the discussion of women towards the end of Book II—significantly, during a discussion of jesting. Although in the collection of impenetrable jokes which comprises much of Book II, Castiglione avoids antifeminist humor, the question of women does arise. First is the question of whether bawdy humor is appropriate when ladies are present: Gaspar believes that bawdy humor is ladies' favorite sort, alleging that he has been "ready to blushe for shame at woordes which women have spoken to me oftener than men" (p. 178); other speakers judge bawdiness before ladies unseemly. The ladies make no comment. Second is the question of whether men's witty seductions or women's witty cuckoldings can be considered "merrie pranks"—what we would call practical jokes. During the debate on this question, Boccaccio's ribaldries are placed within the antifeminist tradition: one speaker informs Gaspar that "John Boccaccio was (as you be) without cause an ennemye to women" (p. 203). Third is the question of antifeminist humor—how far it should be tolerated and what harm (if any) it does. The majority opinion is that such humor does little damage unless a woman's chastity is impugned. The humorist who went this far would be guilty of a gross breach of chivalry, "bicause in this point women are in the number of selie [i.e., innocent] soules and persons in miserye, and therfore deserve not to be nipped in it, for they have not weapon to defende themselves" (p. 190). They belong to an earlier-mentioned category of unfortunates about whom jesting would be "bytter and discourtious"; for example, the maimed. (It would be rude to inquire of one without a nose, "And where doest thou fasten thy spektakles?" [p. 170].) Such jesting can destroy a woman's only source of honor, her sexual "credit."

Julian is uneasy about antifeminist humor of any sort. That such humor can eventuate in indiscriminate contempt is demonstrated during this very debate: Lord Octavian argues that antifeminist humor serves the useful function of reminding women that they are very imperfect creatures, "of litle or no woorthynesse in respect of menne" (p. 199), and Gaspar states categorically that "fewe menne of woorthynesse there be that generally set any store by women" (p. 203). Julian rebukes both. Octavian's remark, although in jest, was inappropriate, he argues, because it provoked Gaspar to make an even more offensive remark in earnest. Gaspar is put rather curtly in his place; he has given too much weight to Octavian's remark because of Octavian's superior social position (the comment is reminiscent of Robert Vaughan's speculation that antifeminist attacks were prompted by a desire to please great men). More important, Octavian's humor opened the door to cruel and false statements, unanswerable because couched in jesting terms. "Bicause manie times credit is geven to men of great authority," Julian says, "although they speake not the full truth, and also whan they speake in boorde [i.e., jest], the L. Gaspar hath suffered himselfe to be lead by the L. Octavians woordes to saye that Men of wisdome sett no store by [women], which is most false" (p. 205). Julian here meets squarely a knotty problem—the elusiveness of detraction, the difficulty of responding appropriately to cruel allegations which dodge serious answers by masquerading as a bit of fun. But Castiglione's emphasis is so far exclusively upon detraction, about what is said about women, not about the status of women in the real world.

The women's responses to these exchanges serve as a paradigm for female responses to Renaissance misogyny. Sometimes the women laugh off the misogyny, refusing to dignify slander by responding to it: "Here the L. Emilia in like maner smilinge, said: Women neede no defendoure againste an accuser of so small authoritie" (p. 179). Sometimes they impute to the detractor the standard sour-grapes motive: "Let the L. Gaspar alone in this his froward opinion, risen more bicause he could never finde woman that was willynge to loke upon him, then for anye want [i.e., lack] that is in women" (p. 179). Sometimes they maintain an ambiguous silence, whether of becoming modesty, rage, resignation, or despair one cannot know: "Syns [i.e., since] I see the Ladyes so quyet and beare these injuries at youre handes so pacyently as they doe, I wyll hensefurth beleave that some parte of that which the L. Octavian hath spoken is true: namely that they passe not to be yll reported of in everye other matter, so theyr honesty be not touched" (p. 204). At one point they launch a concerted physical attack on Gaspar Pallavicino, becoming the harridan horde of misogynists' imaginings; they are precursors of the theatrical Joseph Swetnam's tormentors. But all is in fun: "Then a greate parte of the women there . . . arrose upon their feete, and ran all laughyng toward the L. Gaspar, as they wold have buffeted him and done as the wood women did to Orpheus, saing continually: Now shall we see whether we passe to be yll spoken of or no" (p. 204). (Gaspar shrugs off the attack: "Where thei have not reason on their side, they will prevaile by plaine force" [p. 204].) And finally they look for a male champion. Emilia has doubts about this course: "I pray God it fall not to oure lott to give this enterprice to anye confederate with the L. Gaspar, least [i.e., lest] he facion us for a gentilwoman of the Court, one that can do nought elles but looke to the kitchin and spinn." (Phrisio interjects, "In deede that is an office fitt for herr" [p. 206].) The discussion of the ideal gentleman was led by a man, but despite Emilia's obvious qualifications—wit, good sense, outspokenness—the task of leading the discussion of the ideal gentlewoman falls to Julian.

Book III is wholly devoted to limning the ideal female courtier. Although it has become fashionable in our middle-class age to decry the snobbishness of that ideal, it was the aristocracy in the Renaissance that came to terms with feminism in anything resembling the modern meaning of the word. It was Agrippa, writing to please Margaret of Austria, governor of Franche-Comté and the Netherlands, who voiced the revolutionary opinion that women's status in society is determined by culture rather than by God. It was Castiglione, writing for the court of Urbino (and Sir Thomas Hoby, translating at the behest of the Lady Marquess of Northampton), who proclaimed physiological distinctions irrelevant and understood women's desire for liberty. In England, the upper-class girl shared her brothers' Latin and Greek tutor, while middle-class girls were barred from grammar school; the aristocratic lady fought off the

Roundheads and held the manor together in her husband's absence, while the middle-class wife was debarred from the weavers' guild. The aristocracy gave England a queen who reigned as one of the nation's greatest monarchs; the middle class could boast no lady mayor of London.)

The third night's conversation at Urbino proceeds once the Duchess has overridden Gaspar's and Phrisio's objection that the topic of women is of no importance to anyone. Julian takes up his task with a good will, even though (feministically speaking) he gets off to a shaky start by insisting that as a man should "showe a certein manlinesse full and steadye, so doeth it well in a woman to have a tendernes, soft and milde, with a kinde of womanlie sweetnes in everye gesture . . . , that in goyng, standinge and speakinge . . . , may alwayes make her appeere a woman without anye likenes of man" (p. 216).

Julian accepts some aspects of the double standard: "She ought also to be more circumspect and to take better heed that she give no occasion to be yll reported of, and so to beehave her selfe, that she be not onlye not spotted wyth anye fault, but not so much as with suspicion. Bicause a woman hath not so manye wayes to defende her selfe from sclaunderous reportes, as hath a man" (p. 216). But there are "vertues of the minde that ought to be commune [i.e., common] to her with the Courtier"—wisdom, nobleness of courage, constancy (p. 216). Few writers of the period conceded these particular virtues to women.

When Gaspar remarks that he assumes that any virtue Julian attributes to woman will apply chiefly to her role as housewife and mother, Julian, here a dubious champion, responds, "It is not comlye [i.e., comely] for a woman to practise feates of armes, ridinge, playinge at tenise, wrastling, and manye other thynges that beelonge to men" (pp. 219–20). Aretino (who else?) replies, "Emonge them of olde time the maner was that women wrastled naked with men, but we have lost this good custome" (p. 220). Aretino is an early practitioner of a tactic familiar in our own day—the insinuation that women who interest themselves in masculine pursuits are mainly desirous of gang rape. Cesar Gonzaga asserts a simple fact: "In my time I have seene women playe at tenise, practise feates of armes, ride, hunt, and do (in a maner) all the exercises beeside, that a gentilman can doe" (p. 220). (Ah, were it not for that "in a manner"!) Julian yields, wishing only that women would practice such athletics in a manner not too "boisterous," adding that women, while free to take up almost any activity, should do so with "soft mildenesse"—for example, restricting their musical endeavors to instruments less "unsightly" than trumpets or drums (p. 220).

Julian proceeds to the *Seventeen* magazine school of ideal womanhood: "Where she is somwhat fatter or leaner than reasonable sise, or wanner, or browner, [she should] helpe it with garmentes . . . feiningly" (p. 221)—

advice going back to Ovid. He describes the accomplished young lady: "This woman [will] have a sight in letters, in musike, in drawinge or peincting [i.e., painting], and skilfull in daunsinge" (p. 221). Lady Emilia must by this time be certain that kitchen and spinning wheel are just around the corner in this inauspicious conversation. But matters are to improve.

Julian insists that constancy ("staidenesse"), courage, temperance, strength of mind, and wisdom make a woman not merely an agreeable companion but a decent human being. "I wonder then, quoth the L. Gaspar smilinge, sins you give women both letters, and staidnesse, and noblenesse of courage and temperance, ye will not have them also to beare rule in Cities and to make lawes, and to leade armies, and men to stand spinning in the kitchin" (pp. 221–22). Julian answers (smilingly), "Perhappes [too], this were not amisse" (p. 222). Plato, he notes, approved of women overseeing cities and leading armies; Julian believes many women could handle political and military leadership as competently as men.

Gaspar disavows hatred of women, excusing their imperfections on Aristotelian grounds: they were made imperfect by nature. However, "to esteame them above that they are, me thinketh a plaine errour" (p. 223). Here Julian begins to show his mettle as a social thinker. Women are not imperfect, he declares; moreover, there is no essential difference between men and women. (Physiological differences are unimportant: while men are stronger than women, males of great physical strength are hardly granted greater social status than other males;) the converse is usually true. (Kate Millett was still trying to persuade readers of this point some 450 years later.) What matters in humans, says a humanist Julian, is the mind; and here the sexes are equal: ("What ever thinges men can understande, the self same can women understande also") (p. 224).

Julian adduces great women in history, objecting to the prejudice of male historians. He suggests that God is not necessarily male, adducing great classical myths of hermaphrodism: "Orpheus said that Jupiter was both male and female: and it is read in Scripture that God facioned male and female to his likeness. And the Poetes manie times speaking of the Goddes, meddle the kindes together" (p. 226). This is too much for Gaspar, who takes refuge in a cheap shot: "I woulde not . . . we should entre into these subtill pointes, for these women will not understande us" (p. 226). Heartened by this witticism, he soon essays another, purloined from Aristotle: ("Generallye everye woman wisheth she were a man, by a certein provocation of nature, that teacheth her to wishe for her perfection") (pp. 226–27). Julian does not deny that all women wish they were men; he answers Gaspar "sodeinlye"—the suddenness indicating, I think, both impatience with Gaspar's fatuous jesting and the dawning on Julian of a new, radical insight. (The L. Julian answered sodeinlye: The seelie poore creatures wish not to be a man to make them more perfect, but to have libertye, and to be ridd of the rule that men have of their owne authoritie chalenged over them) (p. 227). Julian has reached the same conclusion Agrippa had reached: "The women being subdewed as it were by force of armes, are constrained to give place to men, and to obey theyr subdewers, not by no naturall, no diuyne necessitie or reason, but by . . . a certayne tyrannical occasion" (Agrippa, Sig. G-G^v).[5] On recognitions like these, a feminist movement can be built. Significantly, Emilia does not realize the importance of what Julian is saying; she treats it as a digression and calls him back to his purpose. Soon the discussion becomes conventional. Eve is adduced by the antifeminist forces; Julian counters with the Virgin Mary. Virtuous and wicked women are catalogued—Carmenta, Ceres, Pallas Athena, the Sybils, Diotima, Sappho, Portia the wife of Brutus, Octavia the wife of Mark Antony, Cleopatra, Semiramis.

Contemporary female rulers are not neglected: Anne of France, Margaret of Austria, Isabella of Spain exemplify women's aptness for rule. (Was this one of the sections that was "misliked of some" during Mary Tudor's reign?) Cheerfully ignoring these examples, Gaspar announces, "The world hath no profit by women, but for gettyng of children. But the like is not of men, whiche governe Cities, armies, and doe so manye other waightye matters, the whiche (sins you will so have it) I will not dispute, how women coulde do, yt sufficeth they do it not" (p. 250). Julian suddenly becomes very tired and cannot go on; the gauntlet is taken up by Cesar Gonzaga.

Gonzaga uses an *ad hominem* argument to discredit Gaspar's charge that women are more lecherous than men: those who make such claims are commonly impotent old roués—a new twist on the sour grapes argument. (A similar allegation was to be used against Swetnam in the play *Swetnam the Woman-hater Arraigned by Women*.) He also rails against guileful male seduction attempts: here as elsewhere in *The Courtier* Petrarchan protestations are viewed as deceitful prologues to open lechery. He grants, however, that some courtly lovers are sincere, noting that courtly love has inspired men to courage in battle and adeptness at dancing; would not the world be poorer had a woman not inspired Petrarch to write love poetry? Another speaker evinces serious concern over the deception of women by false protestations of love; Julian revives to comment, "Bicause men be nowadayes so craftye, that they make infinite false semblantes, and sometime weepe, whan they have in deede a greater lust to laughe . . . I would saye that she should not be light of credence that she is beloved" (p. 267).

The adulation of women in Petrarchan poetry had several unfortunate side effects. Such deification, by making Woman more than human, re-inforced the antifeminist contention that she was other than human. Pe-trarchan etherealization and desensualization of women led (in literature, at least) to intense disillusionment with any woman displaying normal sensuality. And the unrelenting hyperboles provoked a backlash which contributed to the antifeminism of formal satires and plays of the late 1590s and early 1600s. *The Courtier* suggests another problem: Petrar-chanism was open to abuse by cynical male deceivers. Julian's remarks show how far middle-class mores had penetrated the aristocratic code; while any courtly love relationship worthy of the name had, since the twelfth century, been adulterous, Julian primly advises women that the way to distinguish true love from false is that the former involves a firm offer of matrimony. Frederick voices the traditional aristocratic ethic—that adultery is justified because most women are forced by their parents to marry old, disagreeable men; but Julian is firm.

Throughout, the women conduct themselves with what can only be described as ladylike demeanor—in the original, technical sense of the word *lady*. Genuine anger, if its exists, is sublimated in polite amuse-ment. The ideal of ladylike behavior still stood in the way of militant feminism when Christabel Pankhurst found herself incapable of muster-ing the saliva to spit on a policeman; for many it stands in the way now. This ideal can be traced in a line of descent to the Lady Emilia, whose potential feistiness is turned by its dictates into perpetual polite smiles.

Castiglione's form, the multiple-speaker dialogue, resembles the Pla-tonic dialogue: one speaker in each book directs discussion; but these speakers do not triumph so thoroughly as Socrates does in Plato. Gaspar remains unpersuaded by Julian's arguments, and even speakers who sup-port Julian's basic position on women disagree with him about details. *The Courtier* gives less sense of a mentor, leading his followers step by step toward a rational, predetermined conclusion, than does Platonic dia-logue. Castiglione creates more sense of actual controversy, genuine questioning, genuine opposition. *The Courtier* is more sophisticated than Elyot's *Defense* in a number of ways, not least of which is its very incon-clusiveness. There is no easy recantation for Gaspar, as there had been for Elyot's Caninius. As *The Courtier* ends, we know that Gaspar's miso-gyny will continue. This dramatized fact—that logic cannot overcome prejudice—casts doubt on the efficacy of the formal controversy as a mode of improving the status of women.

Agrippa and Castiglione came closer than any other writers of the Renaissance formal controversy to embracing beliefs fundamental to modern feminism; they also forged the genre of the formal controversy, giving it its characteristic Renaissance form. It is interesting, then, to find Agrippa's treatise wedded to Castiglione's dialogue in William Bercher's

The Nobility of Women, dedicated and dated in 1559 but not printed until 1904. R. Warwick Bond, who edited the manuscript for a private printing by the Roxburghe Club, traces the by-paths and indirect crook'd ways by which Bercher met the work of Agrippa and Castiglione: the Italian Lodovico Domenichi, whom Bond dubs "that abominable plagiarist" (p. 75), appropriated Book III of *The Courtier,* larding the arguments of its defenders with weighty chunks of material borrowed without acknowledgment from Galeazzo Flauio Capella and from Agrippa's *De Nobilitate,* the latter borrowed at second or third hand from an Italian translation (which may or may not have been by Domenichi) of a French translation of Agrippa's original Latin. The resultant ponderous work was subsequently translated into English and abridged by about two-thirds by William Bercher, whom Bond believes knew neither Castiglione's *Courtier,* which was being translated at about the same time by Hoby, nor Agrippa's *De Nobilitate,* either in Latin or in Clapham's translation.

This involved process was rather typical of the formal controversy, which was always a cosmopolitan continental traveller, picking up manners and styles in this land or that, for whom plagiarism was no more serious an offense than the aping of foreign fashions.

The formal controversy was a sophisticated game for international literati: the sport came in demonstrating the infinite permutations which a fixed canon of argument and *exempla* might yield. The old arguments were pranked up as poetry, as prose treatise, as dialogue, as judicial oration set to poetry, as treatise grafted onto dialogue, like dressing up a doll in a series of ensembles. Uniformity of topic and example were to the formal controversy what meter is to a poem—a norm against which tiny variations could play, to the reader's delight. Regularity of form, like a literary Olympic Committee, made possible international competition on an equal footing. Which author could most ingeniously exonerate Eve? Who could mint the wittiest libel? Little wonder the formal controversy so seldom engaged questions of importance to living women.

In 1568 appeared a graceful little imitation of *The Courtier,* Edmund Tilney's *A brief and pleasant discourse of duties in Mariage, called the Flower of Friendship.* Tilney alludes to Castiglione in his opening lines and, like Castiglione, creates a courtly discussion of a set topic, with one speaker leading each day's discussion;[6] but instead of delineating the ideal courtier, Tilney's characters define the ideal husband and, on the second day, the ideal wife. Erasmus and Vives are among the speakers; the mantle of Gaspar Pallavicino falls upon Gualter of Cawne, a "merie gentleman" who plays the jesting antifeminist detractor.

As Utley points out, *The Flower of Friendship* is "essentially a skilfully written matrimonial treatise" (p. 117); it is, however, one of the only extant matrimonial treatises to place the husband's "particular duties" before the wife's and to give the husband as much responsibility for marital happiness as the wife. Another novelty is Tilney's Isabella, who indulges in occasional jibes against husbands and dissents from orthodox ideas on wifely subjection. *The Flower of Friendship* is a generic hybrid uniting marriage sermon with formal controversy.

Tilney improves on Castiglione in allowing the second day's discussion to be led by a woman, Lady Julia. Among the ideal wife's attributes Julia predictably lists chastity first, followed closely by modesty and obedience. Isabella disagrees: "As meete is it," she declares, "that the husband obeye the wife, as the wife the husband, or at least that there bee no superioritye betwene them, as the auncient philosophers haue defended" (Sig. [D8]). Erasmus intervenes, arguing absolute male authority. Julia agrees. She advocates extremes of homekeeping: the only way a woman can maintain her reputation for chastity is never to leave the house. Echoing Erasmus's *Coniugium,* she advises the wife of a habitual drunkard to treat him with loving gentleness rather than shrewishness. Her attacks on extravagant attire and cosmetics are conventional. While it is pleasant to see a female speaker defending women, it is sadly true that as a champion of women, Lady Julia is considerably less able than her prototype in *The Courtier,* Lord Julian.

C. Pyrrye, in *The praise and Dispraise of Women, very fruitfull to the well disposed minde, and delectable to the readers thereof,* ca. 1569, imitates Gosynhyll in attacking women in one poem and defending them in the next. Like Edward More, he claims, in his second poem, to have run across a book of unsurpassed misogyny, namely the first poem. (Since he takes credit for writing both, the fiction seems awkward to us but suggests that the Renaissance accepted as natural an author's exercising his wit on both sides of this question.) The first is an admirably thorough compilation of charges against women—pride, cruelty, lack of foresight, intemperance, love of extremes, moodiness, "wandering wit" (women are always changing their minds), inconstancy, talkativeness, vanity, covetousness, impatience, credulity, drunkenness, superstition, lust, deceit, passion for "dainty meat," extravagant dress, use of cosmetics, vengefulness, ingratitude, irreligion, spitefulness, rancorousness, shrewishness, materialism, mincing walk, penchant for slander and character defamation, and habit of walking about with naked breast. Bad women in history, literature, and the Bible make their wonted appearance.

Pyrrye's self-refutation, "the prayse of Women," impugns the motives of misogynists: they may attack women because women are too weak to counterattack or because they have been scorned by some woman. This poem is, with a few changes, a plagiarism of *Mulierum Pean,* often word-for-word. Pyrrye renders Gosynhyll's rhyme royal in paired four-line stanzas, padding out the eighth line as best he can.[7] His changes flatten out the original and rob it of its charm: for example, he removes the dirty diaper passage from the section on women's tribulations.

The formal controversy did not always appear full-blown, in carefully developed treatises; it was sometimes sketched in cameo, with the names of a few exemplary women stamped on it like a generic signature. Such is the case with a pair of poems in *Tottel's Miscellany*. The first, "Against women, either good or bad," introduces the defenders' favorite Penelope and the detractors' favorite Helen of Troy. The world boasts few Penelopes, the poem argues, and many Helens; both cause trouble: "For one good wife Vlisses slew / A worthy knot of gentle blood: / For one yll wife Grece ouerthrew / The towne of Troy." The poet concludes, "[Since] bad and good / Bring mischief: Lord let be thy will, / To kepe me free from either yll." The next poem, "An answere," blames all on the Ulysseses and Parises of the world. Another formal attack appears in George Turberville's *Epitaphes, Epigrams, Songs and Sonets*, 1567: "Disprayse of Women that allure and loue not" (pp. 59–62) asserts that despite ancient paeans to Lucrece and Penelope modern readers should not jump to conclusions about female virtue. Times have changed: no more Grissills, Lucreces, and Cleopatras inhabit the world. Modern women are deceitful; their beauty allures unsuspecting males, whom they murder with disdain. Though they weep crocodile tears, they secretly enjoy their lovers' misery. The reader is advised to shun women, keeping in mind those old bogeywomen Medea, Circe, Cressida, and Helen of Troy.

A cameo defense appears in the last tale of George Pettie's *A petite pallace of Pettie his pleasure*, 1576: one Alexius, after initial resistance to matrimony, falls in love and "vttereth great commendation of woman kinde" (p. 217), which follows the usual pattern. Women were made of the "purified mettall of man, wheras man was made of ye grosse earth" (p. 217). Alexius echoes one of Agrippa's more outrageous arguments: "Wheras men receiue from *Adam* origynall sinne, women are altogether voide of that infection" (p. 217). The *refutatio* tackles Aristotle's theory that women wish to be men because everything seeks for its perfection; Alexius believes that a woman wishes to be a man "that shee might be free from the filthinesse whiche men did force her to . . . like as ye litle chicke being caught by the kyte, would wish with all his heart hee were a kite, and yet the kind of kites is not to be thought better then of the chicken" (pp. 218–19). If women can govern households, they can govern countries; it is only the "malicious spite" of men that prevents them from doing so (p. 220). The *confirmatio* adduces Carmenta, Ceres, Semiramis, Zenobia, Deborah.

The best-known cameo controversy is the one John Lyly appended to *Euphues*. In "A Cooling Carde for Philautus and all Fond Louers," a misogynistic set piece, women are "the gate to perdition" (p. 39); they entice with "wanton glaunces" and allure with "wicked guyles" (p. 39ᵛ); they are cruel, scornful, immoderate, and have tears "at commaunde-ment" (pp. 40, 43, 45); they revel in cosmetics, ointments, periwigs, jewels, fine array (pp. 43ᵛ–44). Euphues enlists the authority of an early misogynist: "Learne of . . . *Diogenes* to detest women bee they neuer so comely" (p. 41), inserting the usual disclaimer: "I meane not . . . to fall out with women as altogether guyltie" (p. 39); only the altogether guilty are intended. The attack's seriousness is undercut by dramatic irony: the reader is aware that Euphues's misogyny is only the unlucky lover's sour-grapes response; an additional irony is that this sententious moralizer comes fresh from having betrayed the friend he now lectures. Further, Euphues appends a defense: in "To the graue Matrones and honest May-dens of Italy," Euphues assures women that he is "not so dogged as *Di-ogenes* to abhorre all Ladyes" (p. 45ᵛ). He opposes to his list of bad women (Helen of Troy, Jezebel) a list of good women (Penelope, Deborah).

In 1589, Thomas Nashe tried his skill at a formal attack, *The Anatomie of Absurditie, Contayning a breefe confutation of the slender imputed prayses to feminine perfection.* To save the opposition the trouble of impugning his motives, Nashe announces he has turned misogynist as a result of dis-appointment in love two summers ago. (This wry twisting of a familiar convention should not send scholars in search of a lost lady.) Confirming the formal controversy's primarily literary orientation, Nashe's main in-terest is the literary misdemeanors of his fellow authors. Having "runne through Authors of the absurder sort, assembled in the Stacioners shop," he rails at their "vnsauery duncerie" (Sig. Ai). He was moved to attack women because so much of the unsavory duncery appears in literature having to do with women—love poetry, romances, works whose dedi-cations flatter the female reader: "Many of them to be more amiable with their friends of the Feminine sexe, blot many sheetes of paper in the blazing of Womens slender praises . . . neuer remembring, that as there was a loyall *Lucretia,* so there was a light a loue *Lais,* that as there was a modest *Medullina,* so there was a mischiuous *Medea,* that as there was a stedfast *Timoclea,* so there was a trayterous *Tarpeya,* that as there was a sober *Sulpitia,* so there was a deceitful *Scylla,* that as there was a chast *Claudia* so there was a wanton *Clodia*" (Sig. Aii). Here is another case of an attack on women being produced in response to defenses of women, rather than the other way around.

Nashe conventionally fears arraignment by angered females ("But per-haps Women assembling their senate, will seeke to stop my mouth by most voices" [Sig. Aii]), lists wicked women, catalogues women's vices. He anthologizes antifeminist quips from Aristotle, Diogenes, Pythagoras, Socrates, Demosthenes, Democritus, Plutarch, Seneca, Marcus Aurelius, Plautus, Valerius, Theophrastus, Cicero, Plato, and Homer.

The same year, Jane Anger, whose name may or may not be allegorical but who insists she is a woman writing for women, produced *Iane Anger her Protection for Women. To defend them against the scandalovs reportes of a late Surfeiting Louer, and all other Venerians that complaine so to bee ouer cloyed with womens kindnesse,* 1589. Juliet Dusinberre, in declaring that Jane Anger's pamphlet protested "against the denigration of women in *Euphues*" (p. 6), follows the conclusion of Helen Andrews Kahin in her odd essay "Jane Anger and John Lyly," in which Kahin states that "the content of *Euphues his Censure to Philautus* had been included in Lyly's *Euphues the Anatomy of Wit* . . . as early as 1578" (pp. 31–35). What she can mean by "content" I cannot say; the fact is that *Euphues his Censure to Philautus,* which Kahin believes provoked Anger's response and which she seems to attribute to Lyly (p. 32), is by Robert Greene and has little more in common with Lyly's work than the borrowed names; it has virtually nothing to do with the controversy about women. It is difficult to believe that the "surfeiting lover" Jane Anger had in mind was Euphues. Anger quotes at least three times from the offending work (Sig. B^v, B4^v, C4); none of these quotations appears in *A Cooling Card.* Anger seems to refer to a specific book, rather than to misogyny in general; Kahin's alternate suggestion that it may have been the lost work listed in the Stationer's Register as *Boke his Surfeyt in love, with a farewel to the folies of his own phantasie,* 1588, is reasonable. We need not, however, assume with Kahin that this essay "must have leaned heavily on Lyly": the material Anger refers to was the formal controversy's stock-in-trade; possible influences on this lost work are almost unlimited. The fact remains, though, that here is another defense with no traceable antecedent attack. Even the author Anger quotes might have served as an excuse for her writing a formal defense, more than as a reason.

The *Protection* has two dedications, one to gentlewomen and one "to all VVomen in generall." The author adjusts her tone to suit class differences, exercising ladylike restraint in the former and growing more vehement in the latter, which opens with a strident "Fie on the falshoode of men." But the style of the essay itself is often aureate; Lyly's influence is not far to seek. Anger views the formal controversy as a literary exercise; male authors, she believes, use it as a vehicle for showing off literary style. But she views the genre as so overworked as to be a last refuge of the unimaginative: "Their mindes are so caried away with the manner, as no care at all is had of the matter: they run so into Rethorick, as often times they overrun the boundes of their own wits, and goe they knowe not whether. If they haue stretched their inuention so hard on a last, as it is at a stand, there remaines but one help, which is, to write of vs womē" (Sig. B).

Anger's essay injects new life into a stagnating genre. Perfectly aware of the genre's conventions—she denounces satirists of women as dogs, "barking" and "snarling" (Sig. C^v)—she plays new tunes upon the old scales: her opponent, she says (at the point at which the opponent's integrity was usually impugned), was at the time of writing old and diseased, if not clinically dead (Sig. D1). In the process of acquitting Helen of Troy, on grounds of justifiable cuckoldry, Anger creates a delightful new mythology of the cuckold's horns: "But that Menalaus was serued with such sauce it is a wonder: yet truely their Sex are so like to Buls, that it is no maruell though the Gods do metamorphoze some of them, to giue warning to the rest . . . for some of them wil follow the smocke as Tom Bull will runne after a towne Cowe. But, least [i.e., lest] they should running slip and breake their pates, the Gods prouident of their welfare, set a paire of tooters on their foreheades, to keepe it from the ground" (Sig. B2).

Women's legendary wilfulness and contrariety Anger blames on men: "Wee are contrary to men, because they are contrarie to that which is good" (Sig. B3). Like Edward More, she argues that men misconstrue justified rebukes as shrewishness: "Our tongues are light, because earnest in reproouing mens filthy vices, and our good counsel is termed nipping iniurie, in that it accordes not with their foolish fancies. Our boldnesse rash, for giuing Noddies nipping answeres, our dispositions naughtie, for not agreeing with their vilde mindes, and our furie dangerous, because it will not beare with their knauish behauiours" (Sig. B3^v).

Anger's *refutatio* argues "if I'm one you're another": bad women in history are balanced by bad men. Of the venerable women / woe-men pun she remarks, "If women breede woe to men, they [men] bring care, pouertie, griefe, and continual feare to women, which if they be not woes they are worser" (Sig. B4). Male writers have neglected male vices: "I would that ancient writers would as well haue busied their heades about disciphering the deceites of their owne Sex, as they haue about setting downe our follies" (Sig. C). Like Castiglione, Anger acknowledges the dangers of the Guileful Petrarchan: "Imagination onely is sufficient to make them assay the scaling of halfe a dozen of vs in one night, when they will not stick to sweare that if they should be denied of their requestes, death must needes follow" (Sig. C3).

The *confirmatio* discusses women's good qualities, including helpfulness, chastity, and constancy: "Our virginitie makes vs vertuous, our cōditions curteous, & our chastitie maketh our truenesse of loue manifest" (Sig. C^v). Eve is praised with an old chestnut: "[Adam] being formed

In principio of drosse and filthy clay . . . GOD making woman of mans fleshe, that she might bee purer then he" (Sig. C).

Anger must circumvent religion: Christian doctrine, as interpreted in the Protestant Renaissance, insisted on woman's subjection.[8] She sophistically and half-seriously argues (judiciously avoiding "God"), "The Gods knowing that the mindes of mankind would be aspiring, and hauing throughly [i.e., thoroughly] viewed the wonderfull vertues wherewith women are inriched, least they should prouoke vs to pride, . . . they bestowed the supremacy ouer vs to mã" (Sig. B2ᵛ).

Anger has noticed the literary association of women with food: men are "rauenous haukes, who doe not onely seize vpon vs, but deuour vs" (Sig. B3); of the lover-turned-misogynist syndrome, she notes, "The Lion rageth when he is hungrie, but man raileth when he is glutted" (Sig. B3ᵛ).

Helen Andrews Kahin seeks reality behind the controversy: "As a participant in the literary quarrel about women, John Lyly belonged with those authors who wrote both for and against the sex as the occasion demanded, whereas Jane Anger was a member of that smaller and usually more sincere group who, steadfast to one point of view, wrote specific and often emotional replies to particular pamphlets. Indeed, the patent sincerity and righteous indignation of Jane's answer are in marked contrast to the sophisticated insincerity of Lyly" (p. 35). But judging the "sincerity" of any author is a tricky business. Some authors appear seriously indignant only because their style is too crude to earn them praise for sophisticated insincerity. And "patent sincerity and righteous indignation" can themselves be a sophisticated pose. Any good controversialist adopts a tone calculated to stir the reader: whether moral indignation will serve better than detached amusement is a decision she must make deliberately; the better polemicist she is, the more deliberately she will make it. Controversial writing is even less amenable than other literature to the spontaneous overflow of powerful feelings. "Patent sincerity" is really a charge of insufficient artistic detachment. Is it because she is a woman that "Jane" is charged with emotionalism and sincerity? To assume that female writers were sincerely indignant, male writers playing gracefully with a convention, is merely sexist. I see no more reason for taking Anger's treatise as an emotional outburst than for taking Gosynhyll's that way, or Lyly's.

Anger's apparent "steadfastness to one point of view" is helped along by the fact that no other work of hers has survived. The *Protection* does not smack of unpremeditated passion; its dry wit and sardonic reversals of familiar conventions bespeak conversance with a tradition. Her defense of women's intelligence combines a tone of tough-minded sexual realism with an academic tone: "It hath bene affirmed by some of their sex, that to shun a shower of rain, & to know the way to our husbands bed is wisedome sufficient for vs womē. . . . Give me leaue like a scoller to proue our wisdome more excellēt then theirs" (Sig. Cᵛ-C2); her sprinkling of Latin tags and classical allusions, less pretentious than Lyly's or Greene's, shows a woman capable of intellectual operations more complex than mastering directions to the bedroom. This circumspect rhetorical strategy cannot be called emotional. Anger's enjoyment of her ingenuity in devising antimasculist insults argues aesthetic detachment that precludes hot tears flowing at the time of composition. If this is emotion, it is emotion recollected in some tranquillity.

The Renaissance espoused rather rigid notions of the appropriateness of certain styles to certain subjects: what terms could a Tamburlaine use but "high astounding terms"? Controversialists' stances varied within a narrow range—from moral indignation to scornful ridicule. These are Anger's stances; we should consider the role of literary tradition before making social assumptions based on the anger of Anger.

Euphues had paved the way for the incorporation of the formal controversy in prose fiction. Placing it in a narrative context opened up new possibilities: it could be used to characterize, to comment on the action, even to advance the plot. The old doll had been given yet another new ensemble. In *The Aduentures of Brusanus Prince of Hungaria,* 1592, Barnabe Rich followed Lyly's lead. When Brusanus's friend Dorestus falls in love with Moderna, he resolves, according to Brusanus (who is "an open enemy to woman-kinde" [p. 60]), "to try what he could do in a bad matter" by writing "in the praise of women, as *Erasmus* wrote a booke in the praise of folly" (p. 68). (Once again, defense precedes attack.) "Like a champion in the defence of women," Dorestus produces a brief defense in which he says Eve was made of superior material, calls male dominance "vsurped prerogatiue," clicks his tongue about misogynists' "slaunderous and false reportes," and lists a few feminine virtues (pp. 59–60). To cure him of this madness, Brusanus writes a formal attack, cataloguing antifeminist sentiments of Marcus Aurelius, Seneca, Diogenes, Socrates, Aristotle, Pythagoras, and Tertullian, listing women's faults, and adducing bad women in history. To this, Dorestus responds with a formal defense. In his *refutatio,* he attacks Brusanus's authorities: these philosophers "were some of them Parasites, some Epicures, some Jesters, some railers, some infected with pride, some with couetousnes, but most lasciuious" (p. 81). (The charge of jesting is interesting.) He impugns classical detractors' motives: their misogyny resulted from an unfortuate experience with one woman. This is most apparent in the case of Marcus Aurelius, whose wife Faustina must indeed have been a trial;

but other ancient misogynists were also notoriously inept with women: Aristotle was bridled and ridden by his mistress; a woman hanged Terence in a basket (this anecdote was more typically told of Virgil); Socrates's wife brained him with a piss pot. Misogyny from such sources, he argues, is suspect. Dorestus discusses women's virtues and men's faults, and his list of good women in history is standard: what is original is that upon receiving this missive, Brusanus recants and, as a sign of his new-found admiration for the female sex, elopes with Dorestus's love Moderna.

The controversy took a slightly different turn with the translation from Italian of an attack/defense pair, *Of Marriage and VViuing. An Excellent, pleasant, and Philosophicall Controuersie, betweene the two famous Tassi now liuing, the one Hercules the Philosopher, the other, Torquato the Poet,* 1599. Ercole attacks; Torquato defends.

The first treatise, *The Declamation of Hercules Tasso, a learned Philosopher, against Marriage or wedding of a Wife,* cites Thales Miletius, who avoided marriage in youth by declaring it was too soon to marry and in maturity by declaring it was too late (other formal attacks ascribe this to Diogenes). Tasso uses what might be called a "balancing formula," adducing various ancient authorities who saw contrary types of women as equally undesirable: "If thou marry one that is faire, she will grow to be common: If one that is fowle, she will waxe loathsome" (Sig. B^v); "If [she] should chaunce to be good . . . must I loose her . . . If shee should be badde, I must beare with her perforce: If poore, I must supply her wants & necessitie: if rich, I must support her pride and insolencie: If foule, I must loathe her: and if shee be faire, I must keep a watch and guard ouer her" (Sig. B2-B2^v). This formula, traced by the Tassos to Bias, Prieneus, Bion of Boristhenes, Antisthenes, Mirthus, and Pitacus Mitalenus, but probably most readily available in Theophrastus's *De Nuptiis,* was to become a stock feature of the later Renaissance formal controversy. It had made previous appearances in English in *The Wife of Bath's Prologue* (ll. 248–255), in an exchange of poems between N. Vincent and G. Blackwood in *Tottel's Miscellany* in 1557, and in two epigrams in George Turberville's *Epitaphes, Epigrams, Songs and Sonets,* 1567 (p. 73^v); its best-known Renaissance manifestation is in Swetnam's *Arraignment* (see below).

In enlisting the support of Demosthenes, Metellus, Cato, Homer, Euripides, Terence, Aristophanes, Cicero, Plautus, Protagoras, Diogenes, Menander, Hesiod, Varro, Plato, Socrates, Petrarch, Philemon, and Alphonsus of Aragon to demonstrate the folly of marrying a woman, Tasso abets the tendency, noticeable in Nashe's *Anatomy of Absurdity* and Rich's *Brusanus,* for the later Tudor controversy to rely more heavily on appeal to authority than had the earlier controversy, which had favored historical and literary example for "proof" of its assertions.

Although Tasso claims he wrote out of "a certaine youthfull Capri-chious Humour"—the usual "all in fun" disclaimer—the work displays such contempt for women's intellect and disgust with the female body as to make the jest unpalatable. Referring to "the base indignitie and corrupt wickednes of womens nature" (Sig. C2ᵛ), Tasso echoes Aristotle in averring that "euery Woman would willingly bee a Man and euerie Idiot and Foole, learned and wise" (Sig. C3ᵛ). He maintains that "an unworthie and contemptible thing is a woman" (Sig. C4); women are no more than receptacles for spent semen: they are "not framed for any other respect or vse, then for a Receptacle of some of our Excrementall humors: standing vs in the same steed, as the Bladder, the Gaull, and such other vncleanly members of our bodie" (Sig. C3). Woman is under the moon's pernicious influence, as evidenced by disgusting physical at-tributes—menstruation, thick phlegm, "driueling spettle," "smoking vapors comming from the stomack," "scuruy scabs," and "rewmaticke Catars" (Sig. [C4]).⁹ Contemporary formal satires in English were re-galing readers with matters scabrous and excremental, but the English formal controversy had never evinced disgust with female physicality. In fact, the formal controversy native to England is a decorous genre, in whose annals one seldom encounters anything more offensive than Go-synhyll's witticisms about goose turds.

Women's characteristics are, according to Tasso, "sleepie & heauie: sluggish & slowe: slothfull & dull: vnmindful & forgetfull: simple & sot-tish: cold & chilly: vnpleasing & unsauory: fearfull & timerous: astonisht & amazed: malitious & enuious: irksom & loathsom: carping & biting: fond & vain: curious & precise: insatiable, and vnsatisfied: iealous & sus-pitious: miserable & couetous: froward & pettish: ignorant & assish: proud & insolent: bold and impudent: a great liar, & a smooth dissembler" (Sig. [C4]). Like much proverbial wisdom, this is blithely inconsistent: "Smooth dissembler" sorts ill with "simple & sottish," "fearful & timerous" with "carping & biting," "insatiable" with "chilly." Women's faults often can-celled each other in formal controversy; this was part of the jest.

Tasso argues that St. Paul commanded women to cover their heads in church because "men are the Images and glorie of God" and women are a lower species "betweene man and vnreasonable creatures" (Sig. D3). To the standard quotation "Man is the Head of the Woman, as our Sa-viour Jesus Christ is chiefe ouer the Churche," Tasso adds the quaint remark that man is the head, woman the "goutie foote" (Sig. D2ᵛ).

Disturbed by modern "equality for women" movements ("these vnworthie women, who too too malepert and insolent, dare with theyr Brazen and bolde faces, venture to call themselues mens Companions" [Sig. D2]), Tasso emphasizes aggression in his list of women's faults—domineering shrewishness, pride, spite, gossiping, impudence, and boldness. Mothers-in-law are a great trial; they teach their daughters shrewishness. If one does not want children, there is no point to marriage; if one does want children, he risks having daughters.

A Defence or Answere vnto the foresaid Declamation, written by that famous Poet and Orator, Torquato Tasso opens with the wry comment that Ercole Tasso has, in spite of all, just got married. (The two works were first published in Italian in 1598.) Torquato feels that under the circumstances, Ercole should recant and publish a defense; "But that which you would not doo, some eloquent Gentlewoman will (perhaps) take in hand" (Sig. [H^v]). Meanwhile, Torquato defends by accepting the argument of Pitacus Mitalenus, a reversal of Thales Miletius: "If . . . thou take a faire woman, it will be a pleasure vnto thee, and if a foule one, why, then she will not be common" (Sig. [H4]), and by praising female beauty in Neoplatonic terms: physical beauty reflects spiritual beauty. Demonstrating that Ercole's authorities praise women at times, he accuses Ercole of taking their remarks out of context. Women are necessary to cities and commonwealths, Tasso points out; the Amazons did without men, but no society can do without women. He adduces exemplary women.

Another import was Anthony Gibson's *A Womans Woorth, defended against all the men in the world. Proouing them to be more perfect, excellent and absolute in all vertuous actions, then any man of what qualitie soeuer.* 1599, a translation from Alexandre de Pont-Aymeri's French original.[10] Solidly in the formal tradition, *A Woman's Worth* begins by noting that Reason (in the person of Athena) is female and proceeds to the usual *exempla;* the inclusion among Penelope, the Sybils, and other defenders' favorites of such questionable worthies as Delilah and Lais, favorites of the opposition, and the appearance of that fabled shrew Xantippe (Socrates's wife) among examples of women who outshone their husbands, lends credence to the suspicion (voiced in Gibson's introduction) that the work is a rhetorical paradox. But the work displays little paradoxical ingenuity, being mainly a praise of the stereotypical "good" woman. Women are more temperate than men, more liberal and charitable, humbler, more beautiful; their graces act as a civilizing force in society, their tearfulness is a virtue indicating tender-heartedness. Women are simple souls, easily seduced. They are made of better stuff; Adam was made "of slime and dung." A small objection against the double standard is entered: "[Men] will approue that good in themselues, which they thinke bad and condemne in women" (p. 30). Appended to *A Woman's Worth* is *An other defence of womens vertues, written by an Honorable personage, of great reckoning in Fraunce,* which employs conventional arguments and *exempla.*

The Praise of vertuous Ladies. An inuectiue against the discourteous discourses, of certain Malicious persons, written against Women, another formal defense, appears in Nicholas Breton's *The Will of Wit,* 1597. The date of composition is a problem: *The Will of Wit* was entered in the Stationer's Register in 1580, although no edition before 1597 survives. But two passages in *The Praise of Virtuous Ladies* are extremely close to passages in Jane Anger's *Protection for Women,* 1589: "Some will say, Women are foolish: hee neuer heard that the wisedome of a Woman, should be no more then to goe out of the raine, when shee is in it, and know her husbands bedde from another mans. But now a dayes men be so phantasticall (I dare not say foolish) that if a Woman bee not so wise as to make a man a foole, shee is no wise Woman" (pp. 67ᵛ–68); "thinke this sufficient commendation for a Woman, if shee bee a Virgin for chastitie, with Virginitie vertuous, of condition courteous" (p. 70ᵛ). Did Anger borrow from a lost edition of *The Will of Wit,* published before 1589, did Breton borrow from Anger after 1589, adding *The Praise of Virtuous Ladies* to the collection of pieces previously printed (or merely entered) as *The Will of Wit,* or did both borrow from a common source? Whatever the answer, we have yet another case of defense imitating defense.

That Breton is burlesquing the genre is clear as early as the Dedicatory Epistle:

> Gentlemen & others to whose viewe shall come this woonderfull peece of worke of the praise cf womẽ (considering how little cause of commendation, is found in a number of them.) I beseeche you, before you begin to read: resolue with your selues, to take in good part, what you thinke I haue written against my conscience. And though I haue perhaps, as great cause to write the contrarie, in respect of the little good that I haue founde in some: Yet the hope of good, that I haue to find by fauour of some one, (none such) hath made me in the behalfe of women generally, (for her sake) say as much as I wish all to approue. (Sig. R)

Like Nashe in *The Anatomy of Absurdity,* Breton is impugning his own motives, but in a neat inversion: authors conventionally turned misogynist after an unpleasant experience with one woman; Breton has turned defender before a pleasant experience with one woman. The fact that the pleasant experience is only anticipated, that the treatise itself is a means to its consummation, makes this work a species of masculine wiles, a seduction by defense. But no one would look for the lady: Breton is playing with a convention; neither biographical fact nor societal attitude can be deduced from this wholly literary exercise.

Breton enjoys himself with the Eve question: since Eve, made of Adam's rib, was a part of Adam, the temptation was pure self-deception by Adam. He also has fun with filial gratitude: "Some men may thinke, that some one Woman hath hired me, to flatter all, or else, by flattering of all, I shuld hope of fauour of some one. [This is what he has just confessed to.] Some will say, perhaps hee hath a Woman to his mother" (Sig. R3ᵛ). Breton gallops through conventional material, flippantly defending and wryly half-defending. Not all women are obstinate and cruel; for husbands, it is the luck of the draw. Women are wanton, but so are men. Women's greed and illiberality he denies without explanation. Some women may be inconstant, but Penelope, Lucretia, and Cleopatra were constant. The charge of female deceit is made by men who have been foolish enough to trust women in the first place. At the end, Breton reverses convention by promising amends to men.

Parody signals the decline of a tradition; it is a delightful, inventive phase of any genre's life history, but it heralds decrepitude. By the end of Elizabeth's reign, the formal controversy was well past the first blush of youth, well past the last blush of middle age. But like the queen, the genre was to attract suitors into old age.

NOTES

1. I deliberately resist the temptation to speculate on why the controversy lay dormant: to link its revival to the death of Queen Mary and accession of Queen Elizabeth would be easy, but hitching the controversy's wagon to Elizabeth's star is the fallacy I have complained of before—the assumption that works of the formal controversy were direct responses to contemporary events, reflecting current attitudes toward certain women in high places. The fact is that we just don't know why the controversy lay dormant in the 1550s; I think we must leave it at that.

2. See *Captain Cox, his Ballads and Books; or, Robert Laneham's Letter* (Hertford: Stephen Austin, 1890); for new light on Laneham, see David Scott, "William Patten and the Authorship of 'Robert Laneham's Letter' (1575)."

3. References to Shakespeare in my text are to *The Complete Works*, ed. G. B. Harrison.

4. I use W. E. Henley's edition of Hoby's translation.

5. It is difficult to believe that Agrippa and Castiglione, working at exactly the same time on the two pieces of literature which shaped the Renaissance formal controversy and which approach true feminism more nearly than any other documents of that controversy, had no contact with each other's work. Some *exempla* do suggest one author's direct familiarity with the other. Castiglione mentions, within six lines, Aspasia, Diotima, Corinna, and Sappho (p. 239), while Agrippa mentions Aspasia/Diotima and Sappho/Corinna on consecutive pages (Sig. Evᵛ, [E6]); these four names are not found in conjunction in any of the formal controversy's standard sourcebooks, and Aspasia, Diotima, and Corinna are otherwise rare in the controversy. Agrippa cites Semiramis, Thomiris, and Artemisia in the space of five paragraphs (Sig. [E8]–Fii), while Castiglione sets these three in the same sentence (p. 248); Thomiris and

Artemisia are otherwise rare in the controversy, and Castiglione's spelling ("Thomiris" in Hoby, "Tomiris" in the Italian) approximates Agrippa's "Thomiris"; compare "Thamyris" in Boccaccio's *De Claris Mulieribus,* "Tamyris" in *De Claris'* source (Justinus's *Epitoma Historiarum Philippicarum Pompei Trogi*), "Tomyris" in Valerius Maximus's *De Factis Dictisque Memorabilibus.* (Interestingly, Spenser was to mention Semiramis and Thomiris in the same breath [*FQ,* II.x.56], with the spelling "Thomiris." Was he familiar with the early Renaissance controversy?) Other rare *exempla* shared by the two works are Amalasunta and Theodelinda.

Agrippa wrote *De Nobilitate* about 1509; Castiglione wrote and revised *Il Cortegiano* between 1508 and 1516, and there was plenty of opportunity before and during these years for the two men's paths to cross. Castiglione spent 1506 in England on a diplomatic mission, where he created a great stir in humanist circles; Agrippa spent 1510 in England on a diplomatic mission and was introduced to humanist circles by John Colet, whose guest he was. Agrippa was in Castiglione's native Italy from 1511 to 1518, where as a theologian he attended the council of Pisa; Castiglione, at work on *Il Cortegiano* during this period, was in public prominence in Italy from 1508 to 1525, commanding the papal troops and moving among artists, writers, and divines. Among examples of illustrious women rulers in *Il Cortegiano,* Castiglione includes Margaret of Austria, daughter of the Emperor Maximilian, the woman to whom Agrippa dedicated *De Nobilitate,* written while he was in the service of Maximilian. The Maximilian connection might well have brought the two together: Maximilian married the niece of Lodovico Sforza in 1493, and Castiglione was in the service of Lodovico Sforza in 1496, only a few years before Agrippa entered Maximilian's service. Castiglione and Agrippa may have met in person; if not, Castiglione's manuscript is known to have circulated widely before publication, and Agrippa's may have done the same. Castiglione finally published his in 1528, Agrippa in 1529. Some influence in one direction or the other is far from unlikely. Unfortunately, Henry Morley does not mention Castiglione in his two-volume *Life of Henry Cornelius Agrippa von Nettesheim,* and Julia Cartwright does not mention Agrippa in her two-volume *Baldassare Castiglione, the Perfect Courtier: His Life and Letters, 1478–1528.*

6. Ernest J. Moncada, while acknowledging the similarities to Castiglione, also presents evidence of Tilney's indebtedness to Pedro de Luján's *Coloquios matrimoniales* ("The Spanish Source of Edward Tilney's *Flower of Friendshippe*").

7. Here, for comparison, are two passages, the first from *Mulierum Pean* and the second from *The Praise and Dispraise of Women:*

> 1. Pallas the doughter of Iupyter
> Through her entere and pured brayne
> The goddesse named of the artyfycer
> Of wolle and oyle, fyrst founde the vayne
> For whiche inuencyon the story is playne

Preferred she was before Neptune
To gyue the name to Athenes towne.
                              (Sig. [A4]ᵛ)

2. And Pallas eke through pured braine,
      So doth the story tell:
    Of oyle and wolle first founde the vaine,
      Which is a great iewell.
  Wherfore they did her then prefer,
      before Lady Neptune:
    To geue the name as pleased her,
      Vnto Athenes towne
                              (Sig. Ciii).

The passages could hardly be closer. While neither can be called accomplished poetry, Gosynhyll at least has some notion of who Neptune is.

8. See my essay "'What Says the Married Woman?': Marriage Theory and Feminism in the English Renaissance," listed in the Bibliography under L. T. Fitz.

9. The physiological theories Tasso draws on here date back to Aristotle and Galen; they were under attack in medical circles by the late sixteenth century. See Ian Maclean, *The Renaissance Notion of Woman: A Study in the Fortunes of Scholasticism and Medical Science in European Intellectual Life,* chapter 3.

10. Gibson says that translation was done by "a friend," who may have been Anthony Munday.

CHAPTER FOUR

The Jacobean Controversy to 1620

As James's reign opened, the formal controversy showed signs of moribundity. No home-grown formal attack on women appeared in England between 1592 and 1615. Two formal defenses straggled onto the early Jacobean scene, unaware that the parade had passed them by.

Lodowick Lloyd's *The Choyce of Iewels,* 1607, follows the formal defense's usual format, with one change: it omits the conventional reference to recent slanders which have moved the author to defend the gentle sex, simply plunging into the statutory catalogues of good women in history without explanation. The omission makes Lloyd's defense the clearest extant example of a defense existing in complete independence of formal misogyny, indicating once again that the defense was the genre's basic format—a thrust masquerading as a parry. Lloyd's biblical and classical exempla are conventional, except for the inclusion of certain dubiously virtuous figures like Helen of Troy and Medusa, which combine with Lloyd's provocative closing remark, "*Socrates* so confest, that *Zantippe* his wife did him as much good at home by chiding, to learne him patience; as he did in Schoole to learne his schollers Phylosophy" (Sig. F3ᵛ), to suggest that the defense was intended as a rhetorical paradox. If so, it is a crude one.

I. G.'s *An Apologie for Women-Kinde,* 1605, comes closer to fulfilling formal conventions; it mentions detraction: "Then fondlings cease the female sexe to blame" (Sig. C). But again, no antifeminist work is named: the *Apology* is another independent defense. It is an undistinguished piece, in pentameter couplets quite unheroic. Women deserve better, the author feels, but he can't manage much more. He would have liked to write an epic in women's praise. He opens with an epic convention, invocation of the Muse: in fact, rather charmingly, he invokes all nine, calling upon them to "infuse high thoughts into my dullard sprite, / And guide my trembling hands, whilst I indite / The sacred honours of your fellowe Sexe, / Which mens vnlawfull tirannye doth vexe" (Sig. [A4]). Perhaps his humble talents require the help of eight extra Muses, or perhaps this

is simply the traditional point that the Muses were women. He owns
that "this subject was more fitte / For peerlesse *Homers* or for *Virgils*
witte, / The *Florence-Petrarkes, Tassoes,* or *Ronsardes,* / *Sidnyes* or *Spen-
cers*" (Sig. [A4]^v). Four of these are writers of epic; but I. G., "whose
fruitlesse braine is like a barren rocke" (Sig. B), soon settles for the old
judicial oration. The way he handles it shows that while he has absorbed
the usual *exempla* from previous defenses, he has not mastered the oration's structure: he hopelessly jumbles *refutatio* with *confirmatio,* and his
argument is hard to follow. But there are some interesting moments.

Eve's prelapsarian beauty he describes in a Petrarchan blazon, complete with "Corrall lippes" (Sig. B2^v). If Eve was the worshipped Petrarchan mistress before the Fall, after the Fall she became the wife: "[God]
tooke the rule out of the womans handes, / Making her thrall vnto su-
biections bandes. / That was before mans pow'rfull gouernesse, / His
mistresse, loue, his wife, his Empresse" (Sig. B3^v).

I. G. comments on women's lack of military prowess:

Tis true they judge the fight of armes is least,
Man by his reason differs from a beast;
Likewise Sage nature hath not wrought so strong,
Their Corpes [i.e., body], nor armes, ne yet their legges so long,
As mens she hath: but framed them moste fit,
To entertaine each combatte with their witte.

(Sig. D2^v)

Introducing a concern central to the Jacobean view of womankind (see
my part 2), I. G. disdains the common notion that peacetime is effeminate and hence unworthy. War, says I. G., is fit for beasts; if women find
intellectual combat more congenial, women are the more fully human:
to humanity's proper pursuits, physical prowess is irrelevant. He calls
war "brutish, rude, and cruell killing armes, / Of bloudy Mars, from
whom comes naught but harmes" (Sig. D3). I. G. is confronted by two
facts, however: first, some very aggressive women are abroad in the
modern world, making an issue of their physical strength (perhaps the
women in masculine attire?—see below); and second, the literature of
defense cites many women renowned for military prowess. The contemporary mannish woman he condemns: "And truth to say, without all
spight or hate, / Those mannish queans are moste degenerate" (Sig. D3).
But he catalogues with approval ancient women "with stout courage,
and vndaunted bouldnesse" (Sig. D3), whom he assumes were *not* "mannish queans."

I. G. makes a revealing comment about order. What he means by "mens
vnlawfull tirannye" in his invocation becomes clear in his remark that
God's making Eve subject to Adam is no sanction for male "tyranny":

Yet did he [i.e., God] not her cast in slauery,
Nor any baser foule seruilitye.
But left her guidance to her husbands will,
Onely for order yeilding to him still.
So Abell was subiected vnto Cain,
Yet Cadets [i.e., younger sons] Iudge th'authoritie is vaine.
And 'tis a point that euery one can tell,
The younger borne most what doe farre excell.

                              (Sig. B3ᵛ–[B4])

"Tyranny"—treating women like slaves, assuming they are moral inferiors—is as illogical as seeing younger brothers as inferior to elder
brothers. By the law of primogeniture, the elder inherits: but this does
not reflect moral worth; it is a social expedient, "onely for order." Wives
are subject to husbands, then, to maintain order in society, but are not
ultimately inferior. The Renaissance found the concept of marital equality incomprehensible because its view of order was hierarchical. The universe was ordered by the Great Chain of Being, society by social classes.
Throughout, degree was observed: lower classes obeyed higher. In this
orderly scheme, wives had to keep their place. Just as in *Coriolanus,* where
the commoners are wrong to overstep their prerogatives but Coriolanus
is equally wrong to evince contempt for the commoners, so a husband
who behaves "tyrannously" is as culpable as a wife who tries to dominate
her husband. I. G. argues that women's subjection does not make them
despicable; they are despicable only if they rebel against subjection.

I. G., for all his praises, is defensive about women; his essay is dotted
with concessions like "tis true they judge the fight of armes is least,"
which imply criticisms to which his essay is a response. But defensiveness was a generic hallmark; women were always defendants in the formal controversy. The existence of these two defenses in a vacuum of
formal attack suggests again that authors adopted the formal defense as
a genre, in a package with all its conventions, just as a poet might pen a
Petrarchan complaint whether or not he had lately been victimized by a
scornful lady's killing frown. We need not assume that a defense of women
is a response to anything; what misleads us into doing so is that the genre
is, by convention, structured and argued like a response.

Within a few years, the formal controversy revived. In 1613 Barnabe
Rich published a putative defense of women which is largely indistin-
guishable from a formal antifeminist treatise. *The Excellencie of good women*
employs some defense conventions, without the formal defense's careful
structure or internal logic. Made of the "purified mettall of man," woman
was "the last and therfore the perfectest handy worke of the Creator"
(Sig. [A4]). Worthies are listed—Carmenta, Zenobia, Sappho. The virtues are of the feminine gender in Latin. Christ's persecutors were men,

but many women helped him. However, there have been bad women—
Delilah, Jezebel. Rich repeats the verdict he had reached in *Faultes faults,
and nothing else but faultes,* a nonformal attack on women and other un-
worthies he had published in 1606: nowadays it is hard to tell good women
from bad because all of them dress like whores. Rich sets up a dichotomy
between wife and harlot, assuming that all women will be one or the
other. The qualities of a good woman are those of a good wife—obedience, sobriety, gravity, chastity, diligence, thrift, home keeping. Faults
were a specialty of Rich's ever since *Faults, Faults, and Nothing Else but
Faults,* and here, defining virtue as the absence of faults, he displays his
old zest on the topic. Contemporary women wear makeup, dress extravagantly, are impudent, audacious, bold. Women's provocations undermine justice in peacetime; women's temerity undermines military discipline
in wartime. Nowadays women must have coaches and other "newfan-
gled vanities" (p. 20); they run up huge bills at the mercers, the tailors,
the goldsmiths.

Suddenly Rich pulls himself up, as if recalling that this is a *defense* of
women. He goes back to women's virtues. A good woman, relishing
housework, keeps at home; she is no "gadder about the streetes" (p. 23).
A good woman is not idle, as are most women nowadays. She does not
"follow delicacies" as do most women nowadays (p. 27). By now Rich
is once again in full cry against women. He launches into another diatribe
against harlots: any woman who does not come up to his standard is to
be considered one. Rich's mode of arguing is unintentionally comic. His
constant habit is to mention briefly a virtue which consists of abstinence
from some vice and then to burst into a diatribe against that vice, leaving
the impression that most women are prone to vice. For example, his
dictum that a good woman keeps silence leads to the biblical reflection
that "a *Harlot* is full of words" (p. 29), and off he goes again. With Rich,
the formal defense has clearly drifted from its moorings.

In William Goddard's *A Satirycall Dialogve Or a Sharplye invectiue conference, betweene Allexander the great, and that truelye woman-hater Diogynes,*
1616, the classical misogynist Diogenes initially adopts the lying traveller
role: he has observed such wonders as a twenty-year-old woman still a
virgin, a widow who wept real tears over her husband. As he enters into
formal dialogue, Goddard stacks the cards in Diogenes's favor: Alexander's part is limited to feeble assertions that things aren't really that bad.
Alexander's defense of marriage consists of a praise of sexual delights:
"Why hee that's mary'd is in heaun all night." Disposing of this is child's
play for the Cynic:

> There lett him bee, for I had rather dwell
> A thousand tymes, a single man in hell.
> I am assurd that ther'es noe Divell cann

> (Like to a wife) torment a mary'd man.
> Il'e none of them, I'me euer worse a yeare
> When once I doe, a womans tongue but heare
> It galls my gutts when I a woman see
> Ile not once come, where such straunge creatures be.
>
> (Sig. B^v–B2)

Diogenes descants on husbands' miseries: "Who would be bound to scrape, pinch, carke, and care / For brattes, (perhaps) that gott by others are?" (Sig. B4). The tub he lives in is too small to accommodate a wife: "It must not be a smale howse that cann hold / A silent man, ioynd with a shrill-tongud schold. / Nowe will hir gossipps come; then praie nowe where / Is roome for them to chatt, and make good cheere?" Nor would there be room for the wife's lovers. If he had to marry, Diogenes would marry a woman with no head, no body, and no limbs; she would have no tongue with which to lash him, no equipment with which to cuckold him, no hands with which to box his ears (Sig. B4^v). Alexander adduces women's modesty. Diogenes scoffs: women feign blushing as they turn on tears; alone together, they will talk bawdy all night. He once eavesdropped on three sisters who were relating sensual dreams; these he retails at great length, with salacious zest. One sister's dreams drove her into such a sexual frenzy that all that kept her chaste was fear of pregnancy (Sig. C4); if she were rich she would buy a different man for every night of the year (Sig. D). Alexander accuses Diogenes of hasty generalization: "Cause one is badd therefore must they be all?" (Sig. D^v). Diogenes denies the haste: he has done exhaustive research. Once, he dressed as a woman to spy into women's abuses; infiltrating a gossips' meeting, he heard the usual talk (see chapter 9).

Diogenes sees women as insatiable in lust, ingenious in deceit: universal cuckoldry results. He echoes (or is echoed by) the opening lines of a contemporary play, S. S.'s *The Honest Lawyer*: "Who hath tenn *Herculesses* strengths in's loines / . . . Shall be assurd the horne, on's browe to fynd" (Sig. E4). Alexander reiterates, "Thou muste not for some fewe condemn em all" (Sig. E4^v), and accuses Diogenes of filial ingratitude: "Thou talkst, as yf thou were noe womans sonn" (Sig. E4^v). But he retires defeated, stung by Diogenes's parting shot (a clever play upon Alexander's famous lament): "Goe seeke thee out an other world to wynn / And putt the women of this world therein" (Sig. F).

The humorous tone of his obligatory apology shows that Goddard does not expect women to be offended: perhaps Diogenes turned woman-hater from unsavory personal motives; anyway, he is dead, and women can take comfort in the hope that he has gone to hell. The poem closes, "Excuse my worke, it paintes the Cynnick forth / And to the Wise it nothinge staines your worth" (Sig. F^v). Goddard employs one of the formal controversy's two main literary forms, the dialogue, but his is the only surviving dialogue of the formal controversy in which attacker clearly gets the better of defender: the dialogue was used mainly by defenders of woman rather than by attackers. And Goddard's dialogue is generically impure in Diogenes's use of contemporary women as *exempla*.

Arthur Newman's *Pleasures Vision . . . A Short Dialogve of a Womans Properties, betweene an old Man and a Young*, 1619, reasserts the tradition in something closer to its original form. Newman's misogynist, an old man, speaks of frailty, adducing Eve. A young man defends Eve and notes that women are necessary to the race's continuance. The old man says women lack true reason, are wily rather than intelligent. The young man says that women are men's "helpes," that they are pretty, that Virtue is feminine in gender, that women would not sin if men did not tempt them. The old man accuses women of wilfulness, flattery, and moral laxity. There are no Penelopes nowadays. Yes, counters the young man, there are. The old man adduces dissembling and feminine wiles: "They sport, and toy . . . / Then frowne, then rage, then hate, and then disdaine" (Sig. D3). Women are constant cuckolders. To the young man, this is just because women are easily seducible, owing to their honest, trusting natures. The old man answers that if that were true, it would show women gullible; but in truth it is women who allure rather than men who seduce. The young man primly reminds him that women are the weaker vessels: it ill becomes men to slander such a loving sex. The old man says women only pretend to love men, in order to get what they want. The young man, a fellow of few ideas, reiterates that men deceive women. The old man alleges that women cannot keep a secret. The young man replies that men deceive women. The old man says that women are inconstant. The young man accuses the old man of harboring a sour-grapes attitude, since he is past it. The old man takes umbrage. The young man argues against blaming all women because "some one of them" was wicked. The old man accuses the young man of being a woman in disguise. The young man reiterates that women are beautiful and necessary to male well-being. In a postscript, he backs down on one item: "Many of them are good, and many ill, / Yet all in this erre, all must haue their will" (Sig. [D8]^v). Except for the sparsity of biblical and classical examples, the dialogue is in line with convention. Its tone indicates the persistence of jest as a prominent element in the controversy.

Christopher Newstead says he wrote *An Apology for Women; or, Womens Defence*, 1620, because of "many Hyperbolizing selfe-conceitists, who deeme it their greatest grace, to be able to disgrace women." He objects to antifeminism that passes itself off as humor and shows some understanding of the pernicious effect jokes can have: "No intentions can make absolute euills good," he believes. Much that has called itself jest has been cruel: "Iests should be . . . pleasing, not piercing." Antifeminist humor creates or buttresses certain habits of mind: "They haue got such an habit in speaking ill of them in iest, that they know not how to speake well of them in earnest."

Newstead argues, after Plato, that woman differs from man "onely in a materiall designation, hauing one and the same specificall essence" (p. 2). Instead of exonerating Eve, he proclaims her irrelevant. Sex roles have changed since creation days: "It is true, at first, when there was but two actors, vpon this Theater of the world, woman was the Syren, that allured man vnto euill: but now each man with *Teresias,* is metamorphosed into a woman: pleasures and delights, are the ingendring Serpents, that haue womanized their affections: Men were the more perfect by nature: but women now then they" (p. 3).

Newstead divides women into three types—the very good, the pretty good, and "the dregges and scumme . . . of woman kinde" (p. 6). He enumerates women's virtues, with conventional supporting *exempla.* He takes male friendship off its pedestal: "There is greater Sympathy of affections in friendships . . . betwixt man & womā, then man and man" (p. 22). He scoffs at the Petrarchan charge of inconstancy, which so often came down to the lady's preferring one suitor to another: "They must . . . first loue, ere they bee inconstant" (p. 23). A pleasant moment is Newstead's contention that all misogynists in history have been gluttons. (Later, he argues that women are more intelligent than men because they eat less, adducing the proverb "Fat panches make leane pates" [p. 32].) Possibly reflecting the aggressive public behavior of women during the period in which this piece was written (see part 2), Newstead devotes considerable attention to female fortitude and magnanimity. He defines fortitude as self-control, a conquest over the passions that is more difficult than a military victory—and more accessible to women. But many women excel at war—the Amazons, Artimesia, who fought among Xerxes's army with "virill audacity" (p. 18), Semiramis, Boudicca, Joan of Arc. Many women are stronger than men, but the greater strength of most men is irrelevant to human worth. Beasts are stronger than men: "Valour consists in the minde, not in the body" (p. 20). Women sometimes show valour in encouraging men to be warlike: Helen of Troy, surprisingly, serves as an example. Even the caveman stereotype is enlisted to prove that women feel at home in the life of action: Venus preferred "bloudy *Mars*" to "timorous and fairefac't *Apollo*"; Katherine of France and others enjoyed being wooed with the sword.

Newstead concludes with the glories and hardships of motherhood. Women are nurturers, perfect teachers of religion, morality, eloquence, manners. Women love children more than men do, Newstead argues with no apparent malicious intent, because they are certain the children are their own. Nothing is worse than ingratitude toward one's mother.

Newstead's assumption that literary misogyny, though intended in a spirit of fun, has the power to wound living women is shared by other Jacobean commentators. William Heale, in an intensely serious denunciation of wife beating, lays much at the door of literary antifeminism: "It is a custome growne so common to vnder valew [women's] worth, as everie rymer hath a libell to impeach their modestie; everie phantastike a poeme to plaine their vnfaithfulnesse; The Courtier though he weare his Mistresse favour, yet stickes not to sing his Mistresse shame; The Cobler though in himselfe most disgracefull, yet wants [i.e., lacks] hee not a ballade for their disgrace" (*An Apologie for Women,* 1609). Such ideas are a distinguishing mark of the Jacobean controversy: the medieval tolerance of antifeminist jest as recreation, still viable in Tudor times, was wearing thin. There are two ways in which one might regard such a shift in attitude toward the relationship between literature and life. First, one might, with Utley, regard the medieval/Tudor attitude toward jest as the more sophisticated, arguing that the medieval mind had a surer grasp of the distinction between literature and game on the one hand, and life on the other (or one might ascribe Jacobean suspicion of jest to the humorlessness of advancing Puritanism or the gloom of impending civil war). Second, one could attribute late Renaissance suspicion of antifeminist jest to an enhanced Jacobean sense of the power of jest, even of the power of literature, to shape the lives, attitudes, and behavior of living people. I incline toward the second view. To mistake for high seriousness what is intended as jest is an error, but to assume that what is intended as jest can have no effect on living people is equally erroneous. To maintain that some two thousand years of insults have had no effect on women's self-respect would be as foolish as to deny that many who have insulted women in jest have contemned them in earnest.

The problem of game versus reality, seriousness versus jest, bedevils the confrontation which comprises the most intense Jacobean activity in the formal controversy. *The Araignment of Lewde, idle, froward, and vnconstant women: Or the vanitie of them, choose you whether,* published under the pseudonym Thomas Tel-troth but written by one Joseph Swetnam, provoked the confrontation. The work went through at least ten editions by 1637, and at least six more by 1880. It was also translated into Dutch.[1] Its success is hard to understand. Everything in it was dismally stale, a good deal of it plagiarized from works like *The Golden Book of Marcus Aurelius* and *Euphues.* It is longer than most misogynistic attacks, but one cannot call it sustained—rambling or long-winded, perhaps. One explanation might lie in Swetnam's revival (or borrowing) of Euphuistic prose style, which might have appealed as a novelty.[2] But the main sales booster must have been its very notoriety: it was answered with three direct rebuttals, one indirect rebuttal, and a play. This disproportionate response must have aroused public curiosity about Swetnam's work.

Swetnam probably had no inkling of the furore the *Arraignment* would create. The title page complacently promises a work "pleasant for married Men, profitable for young Men, and hurtful to none." Like his forebears in the formal controversy, Swetnam counted on women's good humor. In this case he counted wrong.

In the first of two dedicatory epistles, addressed to women, Swetnam is deeply remorseful: "When I first began to write this booke . . . I vowed for euer to be an open enemy vnto women, but when my fury was a little past, I began to consider the blasphemy of this infamous booke against your sectes [i.e., sex]; I then tooke my pen and cut [it] in twenty peeces." Since he published the tract anyway, this is transparently insincere. "I wrote this booke with my hand," he assures women, "but not with my heart." Men, he pretends to believe, will never see this epistle with its Petrarchan affectations like "blasphemy." And women will never see the snarling dedication to men: "Before I doe open this trunke full of torments against women, I thinke it were not amisse . . . to driue all the women out of my hearing, for doubt least [i.e., lest] this little sparke kindle into such a flame, and raise so many stinging Hornets humming about my eares, that all the witt I haue will not quench the one nor quiet the other." But he knew both sexes would read both dedications and expected them to share a good laugh over the essay. The hornet business is one of several references to the expected counterattack. "I know women will barke more at me, then *Cerberus* the two headed Dog did at *Hercules*"; "I knowe women will bite the lippe at me and censure hardly of me." All this was conventional. Utley traces through medieval misogynistic works "the pretense that the eagerly listening women . . . must be elaborately apologized to or deprived of a view of the sinning poem" (p. 30). But in this case, the fiction came true: three of the authors who responded in print to Swetnam were women. Women *did* "censure hardly" of Swetnam; it would seem that they *were* seriously offended. Or were they? The problem of assessing seriousness is in this case complicated by the fact that Swetnam's literary opponents were women (or so they claim). Whether they were more "serious" than Swetnam himself is a matter for debate. But first to Swetnam.

The attack begins where convention demanded it begin: women "were made of the ribbe of a man, and that their froward nature sheweth; for a ribbe is a crooked thing good for nothing else, and women are crooked by nature." Eve, "by her aspiring minde and wanton will . . . quickly procured mans fall, and therefore euer since they are & haue been a woe vnto man" (Sig. B).

A passage borrowed from *The Golden Book of Marcus Aurelius* introduces a section on the faults of women: "The Lyon being bitten with hunger, the Beare being robbed of her young ones, the Viper being trode on, all these are nothing so terrible as the fury of a woman. A Bucke may be inclosed in a Parke, a bridle rules a horse, a Woolfe may be tyed, a Tyger may be tamed, but a froward woman will neuer be tamed, no spur will make hir goe, nor no bridle will holde hir backe" (p. 2). Women are opinionated, unheedful of good advice, jealous, short-tempered, proud, bold, vindictive, ungrateful, dissembling. A woman never forgets an injury. Sirens all, women allure men to their destruction.

After citing Diogenes and Socrates, Swetnam discusses miseries of husbands, who suffer from the extravagance, pride, and cruelty of a wife who will withhold sexual favors until she gets something she wants. She harangues her husband in bed, "saying, I might haue had those which would haue maintained me like a woman, where as nowe I goe like nobody: but I will be maintained if thou were't hanged: with such like words she will vex thee, blubbering forth abundance of dissembling teares (for women doe teach their eies to weepe) for doe but crosse a woman although it be neuer so little, shee will straight way put finger in the eye and cry" (p. 8).

Swetnam complains about feminine wiles: "She will be now merry then againe sad; now laugh then weepe, now sick then presently whole" (p. 11). Women are wilful, perversely yearning for independence: "Except a woman haue what she will, say what she list, and goe where shee please, . . . thy house will be so full of smoke that thou canst not stay in it" (p. 12). Wife beating is sadly ineffectual: "There is no way to make hir good with stripes except thou beate hir to death" (p. 12).

Appealing to authority, Swetnam cites Solomon's misogyny in *Proverbs*. Women are parasites: "Men I say may liue without women, but women cannot liue without men" (p. 14); "Man must be at all the cost and yet liue by the losse, a man must take all the paines and women will spend all the gaines, a man must watch and ward, fight and defẽd, till the ground, labour in the vineyard, and looke what hee getteth in seauen yeares, a woman will spread it abroad with a forke in one yeare" (p. 15). Women's idleness had merited inclusion in Swetnam's title; women's parasitical ingratitude arouses his greatest ire: "Eagles eate not men till they are dead but women deuour them aliue, for a woman will pick thy pocket & empty thy purse, laugh in thy face and cutt thy throat, they are vngratefull" (p. 16).

Swetnam quotes biblical authorities who disapproved of whoredom and lists famous whores of history, which lets him retail a few racy anecdotes. Great men of history have been ruined or at least discomfited by loose and devious women—Samson, David, Aristotle, Hercules, Demosthenes, Plato, Socrates, Hannibal, Julius Caesar, Holofernes, and, of course, Adam. Harlots are not admirable, according to Swetnam. But at least they are classifiable. He frets over a paradoxically unclassifiable class of women—"vnmarried wantons." The never-married woman who indulges her lust without remuneration loses her identity: "You haue . . . made your selues neither maidens, widowes, nor wiues" (p. 27). Nor, of course, whores—quite. Like many of his contemporaries, Swetnam organizes his views of women by a kind of sexual taxonomy: the Renaissance rejoiced in systems of classification. As human beings might be divided into sub-classes along social lines (royalty, aristocracy, commonalty), religious lines (clergy, laity), spiritual lines (the saved, the damned), or into dichotomies like military/civilian, so women had their own sub-classes—usually maid/wife/widow, plus whore. Such categorization defined women solely on grounds of their relationships with men. "Maid" was a special case: it meant both "unmarried" and "virgin." Sexual activity did not declassify the others: a cuckolding wife was a bad wife, but still a wife; a promiscuous widow a bad widow, but still a widow. Even a whore had a fixed category; if she reformed she was an "honest whore," but still classifiable as a whore. But a maid who lost her virginity became nothing. Like the itinerant actor, she was classless and therefore feared. This is one reason Renaissance writers tended to assign the label "whore" to any unmarried non-virgin: it was a way of assimilating the puzzling maid/not maid into a recognizable category: to categorize was to understand. The unchaste never-married woman was a special sort of monster; her crime was heinous because it disrupted the schematic order of the world, on which so much Renaissance doctrine depended.

Swetnam's section on faults closes with the elderly proverb, "Men . . . are touched but with one fault, which is drinking too much, but it is said of women that they haue two faultes, that is, they can neither say well nor yet doe well" (p. 28). He reverses the balancing formula; women, despite their own faults, are hypercritical of their husbands': "Women will account thee a pinch-penny if thou be not prodigall, and a dastard if thou be not ventrous . . . if silent, a sot, if full of words, a foole. . . . If thou be cleanly in thine apparrell they will terme thee proud, if meane in apparrell a slouian" (p. 28).

In chapter 3, on marriage, Swetnam's problems with logic and tone become extreme. He vacillates confusedly among three positions—that no wise man should marry, because all women are bad; that no wise man should marry, because women's unpredictability makes it impossible to distinguish good women from bad; and that no man should marry in haste, because by careful inquiries, he can distinguish a good woman from a bad. Arguing the first position, he may adopt a Gosynhyllian tone of sprightly cynicism; arguing the third, he may echo Erasmian marital doctrine or mimic the marriage sermon. At one moment, he employs anecdote to show a blindfolded choice of a wife from a gaggle of maidens as sensible a proceeding as any; at the next, he soberly exhorts, "If thou espie a fault in thy wife, thou must not rebuke her angerly or reproch-fully, but onely secretly betwixt you two" (p. 53). The essay is a galli-mawfry of proverb, sermon, anecdote, moral maxim, invective, in which sobriety mingles indiscriminately with pure sass. Swetnam repeats him-self endlessly and shamelessly, unblushingly serving up proverbs and verbal formulae two and three times, without so much as a change in wording; the treatise suffers from verbal diarrhea and is irritating to read.

Swetnam's use of the balancing formula is well-known:

> There are six kindes of women which thou shouldest take heede that thou match not thy selfe to any one of them, that is to say, good nor bad, faire nor foule, rich nor poore, for if thou marriest one that is good thou maist quickly spill [i.e., spoil] her with too much mak-ing of her . . . and if bad, then thou must support her in all her bad actions, and that will be so wearisome vnto thee that thou hadst as good drawe water continually to fill a bottomlesse tub: if she be faire then thou must doe nothing else but watch her: and if she be foule and loathsom who can abide her: if she be rich then thou must fore-beare her because of her wealth: and if she be poore then thou must maintaine her. (pp. 36–37)

But soon he embarks on a formal defense, citing the Virgin, Sara, Su-sanna, Lucrece, and sympathizing with the miseries of mothers. Swet-nam has created a tossed salad of woman lore, without having given the matter the least thought. Two consecutive paragraphs cancel each other. The first concerns the immutable nature of the sexes, emphasizing the dichotomy between men's military and women's civilian world; "Is it not strange that men should bee so foolish to doat on women who differ so farre in nature from men? for a man delights in armes & in hearing the ratling drums, but a woman loues to heare sweet musicke on the Lute, Cittern, or Bandora: a man reioyceth to march among the mur-thered carkasses, but a woman to dance on a silken carpet: a man loues to heare the threatnings of his Princes enemies, but a woman weepes when she heares of wars: a man loues to lye on the cold grasse, but a woman must be wrapped in warme mantles: a man tryumphes at warres, but a woman reioyceth more at peace" (pp. 38–39).

Swetnam was apparently unaware that such notions were currently being questioned (see part 2). In the next paragraph he contradicts them: woman has no nature at all: "If a man talke of any kinde of beast or

fowle, presently the nature is knowne: as for example, the Lyons are all
strong and hardy, the Hares are all fearefull & cowardly, the Doues are
all simple, and so of all beasts and fowle the like, I meane few or none
swaruing from his kinde: but women haue more contrary sorts of behauiour then there be women, and therefore impossible for a man to
know all, no nor one part of womens quallities all the daies of thy life"
(p. 39). This is a basic tenet of feminism—that individual women cannot
be understood by stereotypes about women's "nature." Swetnam, however, views failure to live up to stereotype as pure female perversity.

He talks interminably about women's interminable talking. Women's
tongues are sharp, ceaseless, and unable to keep a secret. On the choice
of a wife, he has nothing new to say, but says it anyway: "The best time
for a young man to marry, is at the age of twenty and fiue, and then to
take a wife of the age of seauenteene years or there about, rather a maide
then a widdow, for a widdow she is framed to the conditions of another
man & can hardly be altred, so that thy paines will be double, for thou
must vnlearne a widdow and make her forget and forgoe her former
corrupt and disordered behauiour" (p. 46). A diatribe against widows is
tacked on as a postscript to the disorganized treatise; this topic he tackles
with his usual sparkling originality: "If she be rich she will looke to
gouerne, and if she be poore then art thou plagued both with beggery
and bondage; againe, thy paines will be double in regard of him which
marrieth with a maide, for thou must vnlearne thy widowe, and make
her forget her former corrupt and disordered behauiour, the which if
thou take vpon thee to doe, thou hadst euen as good vndertake to wash
a Blackamore white, for commonly widowes are so froward, so wasp-
ish, and so stubborne, that thou canst not wrest them from their wills,
and if thou thinke to make her good by stripes thou must beate her to
death" (p. 59). Swetnam includes what in his view is the typical widow's
harangue:

> She thundereth out a thousand iniuries that thou dost her, saying,
> my Corne he sendeth to the market, and my Cattell to the fayre,
> and looke what he openly findeth he taketh by force, and what I
> hide secretly he priuily stealeth it away, and playeth away all my
> money at dice. Loe thus he consumeth my substance and yet hateth
> my person, no longer then I feede him with money can I enioy his
> company, now he hath that he sought for he giueth me nothing else
> but froward answeres and foule vsage, and yet God knowes of pure
> loue I married him with nothing, but now his ill husbandry is like
> to bring to ruine both me and my children, but now all this while
> she doth not forget to tell of her owne good huswifery, saying, I sit
> working all day at my needle or at my distaffe, and he like an vnthrift
> and a whoremonger runneth at randome. (pp. 61–62)

A clear case of justifiable shrewishness; but Swetnam does not care if the charges are true. He only sees they are "wearisome as hell."

Swetnam ends his own wearisome harangue with the question, "Why do I make so long a haruest of so little corne?" Why indeed?

Swetnam has plundered the formal controversy, carrying off an unsorted booty of the controversy's conventions, arguments, authorities, jests, and *exempla,* along with miscellaneous shards of misogyny snapped up from nonformal literature; but he neither respects nor understands the genre. Swetnam is a football player who rushes to the fifty yard line with his arms full of shoulder pads, helmets, and shin guards, panting and eager, but who doesn't know a fair catch from a touchdown.

Although Swetnam published the *Arraignment* under a pseudonym, he must have taken few pains to conceal his identity: the first rejoinder, Rachel Speght's *A Movzell for Melastomvs, The cynicall Bayter of, and foule mouthed Barker against Evahs Sex; or, An Apologeticall Answere to that Irreligious and Illiterate Pamphlet made by Io. Sw. and by him Intituled "The Arraignement of Women",* 1617, calls him Io. Sw. on the title page, makes an acrostic on his name (Sig. B), and addresses a dedicatory epistle to Joseph Swetnam. Dedicating a debunking rebuttal to the debunkee was an unusual move, and Speght employs it effectively. Her first dedicatory epistle, to women, uses the chivalric diction traditional to "champions" of women: she will "encounter with a furious enemy" (Sig. A3); she is "armed" and carries a "buckler" (Sig. [A4]); she faces "the persecuting heate of this fierie and furious Dragon" (Sig. [A4]^v); women of all classes will convene as "spectators of this encounter" (Sig. [A4]^v). In the second epistle, to Swetnam, she is already taking on the dragon, boldly accusing him of possessing an "idle corrupt braine" (Sig. B^v), of being illiterate, illogical, and impious. The image is that of a fearless, militant woman who uses her own name, opposing a treacherous coward who fires from behind bushes, hiding behind a pen name until she smokes him out. It is, as I will show in part 2, the cherished image of the day—assertive woman confronting effeminate man.

This dedication repeats two adjectives from the subtitle—"irreligious" and "illiterate." The *Arraignment* is irreligious because Swetnam quotes Scripture out of context, perverting its meaning, because criticism of women libels the Creator, and because biblical examples are interspersed with "heathenish" materials. This last is a new note: the formal controversy had always mingled biblical with classical examples; Swetnam's mixture does not differ in kind from earlier mixtures. The Bible and the classics were twin fountains of Renaissance thought; rare is the Renaissance writer who does not draw upon both. Speght herself quotes the classics. But her early uneasiness over heathen reference anticipates the piety of her essay: she answers a jest with a sermon. Although Speght was apparently a clergyman's daughter, her pious tone is not necessarily any more than a rhetorical ploy, and a shrewd one at that. An excellent way of countering a flippant, jesting opponent is to adopt a tone that makes flippancy and jest inappropriate; the appeal to religion is an excellent strategy for doing just that.

By "illiterate," Speght means poor writing at every level—organization, logic, documentation, grammar. The epistle to Swetnam concentrates on poor logic; she relegates most other compositional errors to an appendix. Coryl Crandall finds Speght "excessively concerned" with Swetnam's grammar.[3] But Speght's heavy emphasis on style is evidence that her objections to his work are primarily literary. Here again, as in the case of Jane Anger, the temptation is to assume that Speght was personally affronted by literary misogyny, simply because she was a woman. But her cool emphasis on style, grammar, and logic, her attention to Swetnam's *literary* misdemeanors, make one wonder about the extent of her injuries.

Speght calls Swetnam on his opening gambit, which had been an attempt to discredit, in advance, any rejoinders: "I know I shall be bitten by many because I touch many, but . . . whatsoeuer you thinke priuately I wish you to conceale it with silence, least in starting vp to finde fault you proue your selues guilty of these monstrous accusations which are heere following against some women: and those which spurne [i.e., kick] if they feele themselues touched, proue themselues starke fooles in bewraying their galled backs to the world, for this booke toucheth no sort of women, but such as when they heare it will goe about to reproue it" (*The Arraignment,* Sig. A2ᵛ). Swetnam argues (using the "galled horse" proverb Gosynhyll had used in the same context) that a woman who objects to his views only demonstrates her own wickedness; Speght feels she must rebut this before objecting to his views. Swetnam's argument, she shows, is invalidated by its undistributed middle term: "As for your . . . aduice vnto Women, that whatsoeuer they doe thinke of your Worke, they should conceale it, lest in finding fault, they bewray their galled backes to the world; in which you allude to that Prouerbe, *Rubbe a galled horse, and he will kicke:* Vnto it I answer . . . that though euerie galled horse, being touched, doth kicke; yet euery one that kickes, is not galled: so that you might as well haue said, that because burnt folks dread the fire, therfore none feare fire but those that are burnt" (Sig. B2ᵛ). Criticizing Swetnam's logic is good strategy: a recurrent misogynist's allegation was that women are incapable of logic. After thus disposing of Swetnam's self-protective clause and setting herself up as a cool, logical analyst, she exposes another inconsistency: "In your Title Leafe, you arraigne none but lewd, idle, froward and unconstant women, but in the Sequele (through defect of memorie as it seemeth) forgetting that you had made a distinction of good from badde, condemning all in generall, you aduise men . . . not to match with any of these six sorts of women, *viz. Good* and *Badde, Faire* and *Foule, Rich* and *Poore"* (Sig. B3). Speght seems unaware that this balancing formula was conventional, or that announcing that one wrote only of bad women and then assuming that all women are bad was one of the oldest conventions of antifeminist literature. It had always been part of the joke: an author implied that he had to insert a disclaimer to prevent assault by multitudes of outraged women; when by degrees he implied that all women are bad, the assumption was that women readers would not be logical enough to notice what he was doing. Speght notices; she again proves women capable of logic but lays herself open to the charge of having missed the joke. One can imagine Swetnam smiling over Speght's dedicatory epistle, reminding his friends that women have no sense of humor. I suspect she did miss the joke and had little knowledge of the controversy's conventions. But her insistence that Swetnam is illogical, rather than inappropriately flippant, may be a deliberate refusal to see anything funny in misogynist insult.

Despite her combat imagery, Speght's tone is more condescending than belligerent. The epistle's title, "Not vnto the veriest Ideot that euer set Pen to Paper, but to the Cynicall Bayter of Women, or, metamorphosed Misogunes, Ioseph Swetnam," avoids a ranting tone by conceding that Swetnam may be only the second or third greatest idiot who ever set pen to paper: denying Swetnam even the dubious grandeur of preëminence among idiots, she also quietly announces that her essay, unlike his, will avoid hyperbole. Speght knows she cannot afford to fulfil stereotype by emotional ourbursts: her stance must be that of the controlled, responsible intellectual. But she is unwilling to be ladylike; her combat images show that her quiet militancy is still militancy. The poems in praise of the author stress Speght's youth: she is not yet twenty. A disciplined writer, for a teenager.

The body of Speght's essay, *A Mouzell for Melastomus* (A Muzzle for Black Mouth), is single-mindedly Christian. Determined to avoid Swetnam's crude disharmonies, Speght separates her dignified defense from her biting criticism of Swetnam's idiocies, relegating the latter to an appended essay with a separate title page. Her organization is in marked contrast to Swetnam's scatter-shot methods: on pages 3 and 4, for example, she lists four common antifeminist views and takes each up in turn. Her structure, however, is not that of the traditional formal defense. She begins where formal defenses began, with Eve, only because that is the obvious opening for a Christian discussion of women. She mentions biblical women but compiles no traditional lists. Many common defense motifs—the miseries of pregnancy and childbirth, women's

nurturing qualities, female contributions to the arts, science, warfare—
are absent. Much traditional material was excluded by Speght's decision
not to mingle pagan lore with Christian, but Speght may have been largely
unaware of the formal controversy. The genesis of her essay differs cru-
cially from the genesis of most earlier defenses: hers really is what earlier
defenses pretended to be—a response to an attack in print.

Speght appeals to the highest authority: "The worke of Creation being
finished, this approbation was giuen by God himselfe, That *All was very
good:* If All, then *woman*" (p. 3). Her first defense of Eve is no defense at
all: "Sathan first assailed the woman, because . . . she being the weaker
vessel was with more facility to be seduced" (p. 4). The second is hardly
more feminist: "Woman sinned . . . but so did the man too: And if *Adam*
had not approoued of that deed which *Eue* had done . . . hee being her
Head would haue reproued her" (p. 4). Third, Eve meant well: she gave
Adam the fruit "to make her husband partaker of that happinesse, which
she thought by their eating they should both haue enioyed" (p. 6). This
is pretty feeble too. Finally Speght falls back on the Virgin Mary. She
acquits herself better when arguing that the rallying cry of medieval ascetic misogyny, St. Paul's "It is good for a man not to touch a woman,"
grew out of historical circumstance: marriage was temporarily inadvis-
able among endangered Corinthian Christians; Paul's words need not be
elevated into principle. She objects, too, to Swetnam's assumption that
Solomon's misogyny reflected his wisdom. To turn against women because one's concubines are vicious is to prove nothing about womankind.

Speght's historical relativism is impressive; it was a rare quality. Most
writers who drew lessons for mankind from history ignored cultural
differences and temporal changes.[4] Speght's view of history, even biblical
history, approaches Agrippa's: neither will accept past views of women
unqualified by historical and cultural context. Speght has the makings of
a thinker and a feminist; the question "because women have been responsible for housework in the past, must they always be so?" would
not have shocked her. (Indeed, she argues that men ought to help with
housework. Male pigeons spell female pigeons in egg sitting; cocks help
hens build nests. Can't human males do likewise? [pp. 12–13].) But Speght
would draw the line at ingenious rereadings of Genesis that get Eve completely off the hook, or at Agrippa's sophistical Scripture-twisting, proving woman man's superior, because she has a scholar's reverence for the
text and too much intellectual honesty to distort the written word's plain
meaning, and because she is a Christian: blasphemous Scripture-twisting
is what she taxes Swetnam with. Speght's feminism is hobbled by her
faith: she believes that although the Bible does not promote misogyny,
it does not allow for feminism either. Man was designated woman's su-

perior by God; a husband should not tyrannize a wife, but he is still her head. Speght mentions equality when using an old proverb: "Man was created of the dust of the earth, but woman was made of a part of man, after that he was a liuing soule: yet was shee not produced from *Adams* foote, to be his too low inferiour; nor from his head to be his superiour, but from his side, neare his heart, to be his equall" (p. 10). But she elsewhere accepts the husband as the wife's "head." Equality was poetic and proverbial; Speght did not demand it of real marriages.

After the epilogue's benedictory "To God onely wise be glorie now and for euer, AMEN" (Sig. E3), Speght begins afresh with *Certaine Qvaeres to the bayter of Women*. Her tone changes; she is now the hard-nosed literary critic cum censorious grammarian. She apologizes for this essay's relative disorganization: "[I am] not altogether ignorant of that Analogie [i.e., proportion, balance] which ought to be vsed in a literate Responsarie: But the Beare-bayting of Women [Swetnam's subtitle], vnto which I haue framed my Apologeticall answere, beeing altogether without methode, irregular, without Grammaticall Concordance, and a promiscuous mingle mangle, it would admit no such order to be obserued in the answering therof, as a regular Responsarie requireth" (Sig. F). Speght believes there is a proper rhetorical form for attacks and defenses, which she criticizes Swetnam for violating and regrets she cannot follow herself. That this form was the classical oration as outlined by Cicero and Quintilian is suggested by Speght's identifying Swetnam's introduction as the *exordium* (Sig. F2). Any educated writer, attacking or defending anything, would think so automatically of the classical oration that Speght, unaware as she seems to be of the formal controversy, expects criticism for choosing another form. This goes far toward explaining the structural similarities among attacks and defenses; it also accounts for the aroma of textbook exercise that clings to works of the formal controversy. A reader eager for a discussion of women that comes to grips with real issues will likely be put off by Speght's analysis of Swetnam's grammatical and stylistic errors. But the formal controversy did not often deal in real issues: it was mainly a game. Speght may have been genuinely concerned about libels upon womankind; but she was equally concerned that Swetnam had violated the rules of the rhetorical game.

Speght's emphasis on formal aspects of argument also demonstrates that she is educated. Like Margaret Tyler, who had defended women's right to learning,[5] Speght believes in women's right to enter the jealously guarded male preserve of intellectual endeavor. Although prefatory verses praise her learning, Speght would like to be more learned; her mention of stealing hours for studying from "feminine" pursuits is part modesty and part resentment: "I am young in yeares, and more defectiue in knowledge, that little smattering in Learning which I haue obtained, being only the fruit of such vacant houres, as I could spare from affaires befitting my Sex" (Sig. F). But *Certain Queries* shows that she is at least more learned than Joseph Swetnam, thus puncturing stereotypes about the relative erudition of the sexes.

But Speght does not take her own erudition too seriously. For misquoting Scripture, Swetnam merits the title of blasphemer; citing Leviticus 24:14–16, which subjects blasphemers to the death penalty, she concludes: "The *Bayter of Women* hath blasphemed God, *Ergo,* he ought to die the death" (p. 34); but this is a playful syllogism; another jest follows. Quoting Swetnam's dismissal of marriage, "If thou marryest a still and a quiet woman, that will seeme to thee that thou ridest but an ambling horse to hell, but if with one that is froward and vnquiet, then thou wert as good ride a trotting horse to the diuell," Speght with mock sobriety counsels Swetnam to marry at once; he is certain to go to hell and "it would be too irkesome for you to trauaile so tedious a iourney on foote" (pp. 34–35). Speght is capable of using humor to ridicule her opponent; but unlike Swetnam, she does not mix humor indiscriminately with serious matter.

Speght picks up on the discrepancy between Swetnam's invective on feminine idleness and his account of the *Arraignment*'s genesis, which opens "musing with my selfe being idle" (p. 36). Authors who write books condemning idleness, which are composed and read during idle hours, are in an odd position. The prosperity which made women idle created markets for authors. Swetnam is here like "a Fencer, which teacheth another how to defend himselfe from enemies blowes, and suffers himselfe to be stricken without resistance" (p. 36); appropriate, since Swetnam was apparently a fencing master; his only other known work is *The Schoole of the noble science of defence,* a treatise on fencing.

Ultimately, Swetnam's illiteracy is at least as irksome as his misogyny: "Whoso makes the fruit of his cogitations extant to the view of all men, should haue his worke to be as a well tuned Instrument, in all places according and agreeing, the which I am sure yours doth not: For how reconcile you those dissonant places aboue cited? or how make you a consonant diapason of those discords wanting harmony?" (p. 36).

Speght's is an able defense. It is not feminist, partly because any sallies she makes into the territory of equality come up against the wall of her own Christian beliefs, and partly, I suspect, because she was not terribly involved in the woman question. Her emphasis on literary style is a reminder that the formal controversy was a literary battle. Neither defenders nor attackers looked in their hearts and wrote. They looked in their Quintilians and wrote.

In 1617 another woman erupted into print. *Ester hath hang'd Haman; or, An Answere To a lewd Pamphlet, entituled, The Arraignment of Women.*

With the arraignment of lewd, idle, froward, and vnconstant men, and Hvsbands was published under the pseudonym Ester Sowernam. "Sowernam" is the converse of Swetnam: this author thought the name was pronounced "Sweetnam" and found this ironic. (The short *e* pronunciation is more appealing, I think.) "Ester" alludes to the biblical heroine who rid her country of the pestiferous Haman. Casting Swetnam as a public enemy, the allusion recalls the formal controversy in which Esther (Hester) was so familiar an example. A riddling description of the author alludes to Swetnam's discussion of the woman neither maid, wife, nor widow: "Written by *Ester Sowernam,* neither Maide, Wife nor Widdowe, yet really all, and therefore experienced to defend all." Sowernam's riddle, if it does not mean that the author is a man imagining feminine responses, is probably a protest against categorizing women by marital status and sexual experience. It may mean that she has been maid, wife, and widow successively and is "therefore experienced to defend all," alluding perhaps to Speght's excusing herself from discussing widows on grounds of inexperience: Sowernam dismisses Speght as "the Maide" (Sig. A2ᵛ). Sowernam's "yet really all," however, suggests that she is maid, wife, and widow simultaneously, a paradox implying that marital status is irrelevant, that a woman possesses an indestructible self, unalterable by sexual or marital experience.

The first dedicatory epistle provides a rare insight: "Vpon my repaire to *London* this last *Michaelmas* Terme; being at supper amongst friends, where the number of each sexe were equall; As nothing is more vsuall for table-talke; there fell out a discourse concerning women, some defending, others obiecting against our Sex: Vpon which occasion, there happened a mention of a Pamphlet entituled *The Arraignment of Women,* which I was desirous to see. The next day a Gentleman brought me the Booke" (Sig. A2). The punctuation, unfortunately, obscures the sense. Does "as nothing is more vsuall for table-talke" refer to the balance of sexes or to the table-talk's consisting of controversy about women? Semicolons separate this clause from both contiguous clauses. If the former was intended, the passage shows that Renaissance hosts took care to achieve a balance of the sexes. If the latter was intended, it is evidence that controversy about women was practiced as conversational as well as literary recreation. The fact that "As" is capitalized, and "there" is not, supports the latter interpretation. Sowernam's reference to the dinnertime debate is casual and matter-of-fact. She displays no indignation and wastes no energy describing the speakers or their arguments. She is on good enough terms with one male guest to borrow a book from him the next day; no spleen against the male sex is exhibited here.

This glimpse into the controversy's social life ratifies a view of formal controversy as game. Its insults are bantering jibes between friends who count on each other's good humor and who, while claiming superiority for one sex, know the game would be impossible without at least conversational equality between the sexes. Gosynhyll, when he spoke of jesting "with the femynye," must have had in mind such a party as Sowernam describes, where the men light heartedly rag the women, who laugh or pretend to be angry. Book III of *The Courtier,* which posits such a party, is replete with references to smiling and laughing.

Sowernam determined to extend the game into print. Whoever she was, like Speght she had some classical education; she may have fancied herself as an author. But after beginning her rejoinder, "Word was brought mee that an Apologie for women was already vndertaken, and ready for the Presse, by a Ministers daughter" (Sig. A2ᵛ; she later identifies Speght's essay by title [p. 6]). This put Sowernam in an awkward position: she could not persist without declaring Speght's efforts inadequate. This unsisterly course she took: "Whereas the Maide doth many times excuse her tenderness of yeares, I found it to be true in the slendernesse of her answer, for she vndertaking to defend women, doth rather charge and condemne women" (Sig. A2ᵛ). She perhaps has in mind Speght's defense of Eve, which rather made things worse. But Sowernam learned quite a lot from Speght's essay. She follows Speght in accusing Swetnam of blasphemy: antifeminist writers had been lambasting women for centuries on biblical authority without incurring the charge of blasphemy; Sowernam was clearly influenced by Speght's original approach. Sowernam also profits from Speght's separation of pious defense from scrappy attack on Swetnam: Sowernam attacks Swetnam under the fresh heading *The Arraignment of Joseph Swetnam* (p. 27) after completing her formal defense. Pagan examples she relegates to a separate section of the defense, with its own dedicatory epistle: "In my first Part I haue . . . strictly obserued a religious regard, not to entermingle anything vnfitting the grauitie of so respectiue an Argument. Now . . . I am determined to solace my selfe with a little libertie" (p. 16). Speght's example has taught Sowernam to be careful with tone; she preëmpts the charge of scolding by adducing the extremity of the provocation: "If in this answere I doe vse more vehement speeches then may seeme to correspond the naturall disposition of a Woman; yet all iudicious Readers shall confesse that I vse more mildnesse then the cause I haue in hand prouoketh me vnto" (Sig. B).

Unlike Speght, Sowernam is perfectly conversant with the controversy. In one dedication, where she calls upon chivalrous London apprentices to resist misogynists, she inverts the misogynist's assurance that he censures only bad women: "Let not the title of this Booke in some poynt distaste you, in that men are arraigned, for you are quit by Nonage": they escape arraignment by not yet being men. "None are here arraigned," she promises, but "old fornicators" (Sig. [A4]ᵛ). Sowernam

recognizes the extent of literary misogyny: "It hath euer beene a common custome amongst Idle, and humerous Poets, Pamphleters, and Ri-
mers, out of passionate discontents, or hauing little otherwise to imploy
themselues about, to write some bitter Satire-Pamphlet, or Rime, against
women" (p. 31). She addresses herself to the tradition, not merely to
Swetnam, whose knowledge of tradition is sadly limited: she will "examine all the obiections which are most materiall, which our adversarie
hath vomited out against woman, and not onely what he hath obiected,
but what other authors of more import then *Ioseph Swetnam* haue charged
vpon women: alas, seely man he obiecteth nothing but what he hath
stolne out of English writers, as *Euphues,* the *Palace of Pleasure,* with the
like" (p. 32). Sowernam knows English literature well enough to catch
Swetnam's plagiarisms from Lyly and Pettie, and she knows her classical
misogynists too. Swetnam has small Latin and less Greek: "He neuer
read the vehement and profest enemies against our sexe, as for *Gracians,
Euripides, Menander, Simonides, Sophocles,* with the like amongst Latine
writers *Iuvenall, Plautus, &c*" (p. 32). Like Speght, Sowernam proves she
is better educated than at least one man.

Her chagrin at Swetnam's impressive sales is part jealousy and part
disgust with public taste. With so many clever, literate misogynists to
choose among, why does the public buy Swetnam's dismal drivel? Women
have superior literary judgement; the illiterate masses buying Swetnam
are male: " 'Tis pittie but that men should reward you for your writing. . . . As for women, they laugh that men haue no more able a champion" (p. 43). Sowernam's reason for borrowing a copy of Swetnam is
clear: she would not bolster his ego by increasing his sales; her remarks
may even be a call for a boycott by other women. Like Speght, Sowernam worries about the advisability of responding to Swetnam; in the
past, women have always remained aloof from the literary doings of
misogynists (she must not have heard of Jane Anger): "Amongst the rable
of scurill writers, [Swetnam] now present hath acted his part, whom
albeit women could more willingly let passe, then bring him to triall and
as euer heretofore, rather contemn such authors thē deigne them any
answere, yet seeing his booke so commonly bought vp, which argueth
a generall applause; we are therfore enforced to make answere in defence
of our selues, who are by such an author so extreamely wronged in publike view" (p. 32).

But protesting against jest is dangerous. When, perhaps emulating
Speght, Sowernam tries to expose Swetnam's illogic, she falls flat:

> Now to shew to what vse woman was made, [Swetnam] begin-
> neth thus. *At the first beginning a Woman was made to bee an helper to
> Man: And so they are indeed, for they helpe to consume and spend, &c. . . .*
> Marke a ridiculous ieast in this: Spending and consuming of that

which Man painfully getteth, is by this Authour the vse for which
Women were made. And yet (saith hee in the Argument) *most of them
degenerate from the vse they were framed vnto.* Woman was made to
spend and consume at the first: But women doe degenerate from
this vse, *Ergo, Midasse* doth contradict himselfe. Beside this egre-
gious folly, he runneth into horrible blasphemy. VVas the end of
Gods creation in VVoman to spend and consume? Is *helper* to be
taken in that sence, to helpe to *spend? &c.* Is spending and consum-
ing, *helping?* (pp. 2–3)

But the joke depends on the equivocation on "helping"; Sowernam takes
as illogic what is a mere pun: she has missed the joke. But her protest
against "ridiculous ieast" is intriguing. Was Sowernam beginning to perceive that many Renaissance attitudes toward women originated in ridiculous jests, that serious consideration of "women's issues" was hampered
by the debate's jest-book quality? Did she sense that dressing up misogyny as a literary genre was deliberately obfuscatory, that concealed within
clouds of comic rhetoric and anecdote was a core of ugly attitudes which
the very tone prevented women from exposing and protesting against?
If she did, Sowernam makes a tactical error in doing battle with the cloud
itself. Again and again, she tries logical analysis on old jokes; for example, "If Woman receaued her crookednesse from the rib, . . . how
doth man excell in crookednesse, who hath more of those crooked ribs?"
(p. 3). She might better have taxed Swetnam with hackneyed writing—
the crooked rib joke was a literary antique—or of substituting jest for
thought. That she played the old game probably demonstrates that she
didn't see through it.

Where Speght's metaphor had been military, Sowernam's is legal: she
does not battle Swetnam but arraigns him. Reflecting the litigiousness of
women in the contemporary drama (see part 2), she turns Swetnam's
arraignment metaphor into a small play, "*Joseph* Swetnam his Endite-
ment." Despite his guilty conscience, Sowernam's Swetnam feebly pleads
"not guilty" before a judge, jury, and accuser, mostly women. He fears
prejudice—"The selfe and the same persons [are] Judges and Accusers"
(p. 31)—but is not certain how the prejudice might work: being women,
they might fall in love with him. To vitiate the charge of prejudice, the
women adjourn and bind him over for later trial.

Sowernam's essay thus contains the germ that developed into the play
Swetnam the Woman-hater Arraigned by Women (see part 3). Her indictment
scene provides hints for the play's characterization of Swetnam—his almost casual reaction to his indictment, his inability to resist an antifeminist joke even before a female judge and jury, his confidence that his
own attractiveness will mitigate his accusers' fury. This looks like a faithful replica of the historical Swetnam as we see him through *The Arraign-*

ment—a vain, conceited fellow with a cheerful confidence in his limited abilities that is so pathetically misplaced as to be almost endearing, a man whose moral stance is so confused that he can enter a plea against his conscience, a man who declines to defend himself, rather to his accusers' discomfiture. A man who, when accused, takes refuge in a joke.

For long stretches of the essay, Sowernam plays the old game. She answers Swetnam in his own terms, slipping back into the now exhausted and unproductive mode of the formal controversy. Eve was the last and therefore the highest creation. The Virgin Mary atoned for Eve's sin. Elizabeth, Anna, the woman of Samaria, Mary Magdalene put in regulation appearances. Good women from the classics are listed, and they are the same old good women—Ceres, inventor of agriculture, Carmenta, inventor of the alphabet, Diana, the Graces, the Muses, and the rest.

Men, Sowernam charges, are inconsistent: at one moment they promulgate proverbial wisdom about the love of a good woman ("if they haue a sonne . . . who is of a wild and riotous disposition, such a father shall presently be counselled, helpe your sonne to a good wife, marry him, marry him" [p. 24]); at the next they write satires on women; then Petrarchan poetry adulating Woman as a goddess. Does she recognize the elements of literary convention in proverb, satire, or Petrarchan poetry? Is her failure to distinguish between the stance of a literary *persona* and the attitudes of living men a rhetorical ploy, or sheer lack of literary sophistication? It is very difficult to know.

Sowernam is more convincing when she sticks plainly to life rather than attempting literature. Men, she notes, set higher standards for women than for men:

> What an hatefull thing is it to see a woman ouercome with drinke, when as in men it is noted for a signe of goodfellowship? and . . . for one woman which doth make a custome of drunkennesse, you shall finde an hundred men: it is abhorred in women, and therefore they auoyd it: it is laughed at and made but as a iest amongst men, and therefore so many doe practise it: Likewise if a man abuse a Maide & get her with child, no matter is made of it, but as a trick of youth, but it is made so hainous an offence in the maide, that she is disparaged and vterly vndone by it. So in all offences those which men commit, are made light and as nothing, slighted ouer; but those which women doe commit, those are made grieuous and shamefull. (p. 24)

Whatever misogynists say, they believe women morally superior: "In no one thing, men doe acknowledge a more excellent perfection in women then in the estimate of the offences which a woman doth commit: the worthinesse of the person doth make the sinne more markeable" (p. 24).

This attempt to unearth subconscious male attitude might have been refined upon; she might have suggested that men set higher standards for women as a sop to their own consciences: with a wife as the repository of family virtue, a husband is released from virtue's tedious necessities. (Capitalists' wives are encouraged, on this principle, to play Lady Bountiful, to relieve by little charities the miseries caused by their husbands' business practices. This phenomenon, prominent in Victorian times, was visible in the Renaissance.) But as an essay into the complexities of male psychology, it is not a bad start. Especially promising is Sowernam's thesis that social conditioning, not Nature, decides which sex will be more given to alcoholism and which more careful of sexual reputation.

Much misogyny, Sowernam thinks, results from men's attempt to shift guilt onto someone else. Male rationalizing began with "the woman whom thou gavest to be with me, she gave me of the tree, and I did eat." To illustrate the scapegoat habit, she examines the Erasmian view of shrewishness and treats it with the contempt I think it deserves:[6]

> Drunkards, Leachers, and prodigall spend-thrifts . . . when they come home drunke, or are called in question for their riotous misdemeanours, they presently shew themselues, the right children of *Adam*. They will excuse themselues by their wiues, and say that their vnquietnesse and frowardnesse at home, is the cause that they runne abroad. An excuse more fitter for a beast then a man. If thou wert a man thou wouldest take away the cause which vrgeth a woman to griefe and discontent, and not by thy frowardnesse encrease her distemperature: forbeare thy drinking, thy luxurious riot, thy gaming, and spending, and thou shalt haue thy wife giue thee as little cause at home, as thou giuest her great cause of disquiet abroad.
> (p. 44)

Sowernam too has the makings of a feminist. Her acquiescence in the genre's conventions, however, hampers the potential. She shakes her finger at Swetnam's evasion of true argument without recognizing its full significance—that the formal controversy only created the illusion of true argument, that only an extraordinary artist—an Agrippa or a Castiglione, not a Swetnam or a Sowernam—can successfully confront real issues within the context of a literary parlor game. Sowernam seems to have wanted it both ways—to take part in a sophisticated literary sport and to engage questions of importance about women. Castiglione managed to do both, with a fair degree of success. Agrippa managed to do both, only at the expense of having his essay dismissed as perverse and self-contradictory for 300 years. Sowernam does not manage to do both. She does not play the game very well: she wields logical exegeses like quarter-staves, to batter the treacherous gossamer of jest; and her mental sinews have too little elasticity to grasp radical ideas about equality for women.

Sowernam's Christian faith is also a barrier to her feminism: the Bible undeniably insists that wives are to be obedient to husbands. Sowernam tries hard to wrest a feminist argument even from that: "She is commanded to obey her husband; the cause is, the more to encrease her glorie. Obedience is better then Sacrifice: for nothing is more acceptable before God then to obey: women are much bound to God, to haue so acceptable a vertue enioyned them" (pp. 9–10). But this line of argument will hardly result in feminism as we know it.

One passage does suggest potential for a feminist movement: "*Ioseph Swetnam* hauing written his rash, idle, furious and shameful discourse against Women, it was at last deliuered into my hands, presently I did acquaint some of our Sexe with the accident, with whom I did aduise what course we should take with him. It was concluded . . . wee would not answere him either with *Achilles* fist, or *Stafford*-law; neither plucke him in pieces as the *Thracian* woman did *Orpheus,* for his intemperate rayling against women: But as he had arraigned women at the barre of fame and report; wee resolued at the same barre where he did vs the wrong, to arraigne him" (p. 27). It would be important, historically, for women to band together against oppressors. Feminism is a corporate venture; mutual support is essential to its survival. But the attack on the misogynist is a literary convention: Castiglione had referred to the attack on Orpheus when describing the merry attack upon Gaspar Pallavicino led by Emilia. We can deduce little from such a passage about sisterhood in the Renaissance.

It is noteworthy that Sowernam's friends advise justice, not revenge. This avoids the charge of vengefulness and is important as a feminine intrusion on the male preserve of justice. But it also reflects the perennial felt necessity to be ladylike.

One woman who acknowledged no such constraint was the pseudonymous Constantia Munda, the third woman to answer Swetnam. In *The Worming of a mad Dogge; or, A Soppe for Cerbervs the Iaylor of Hell,* 1617, Munda is the first female "defender" to indulge the pleasure of a good rant. She describes her essay as "no Confvtation bvt a sharpe Redargution of the *bayter of Women*": "redargution" implies vigorous reproof as well as refutation, and Munda is not niggardly of reproof. There is little "confutation"; Munda's essay is unique among rejoinders to misogyny in offering no defense of women whatsoever. Perhaps she assumed that against such manifest idiocy, women need no defense. Or perhaps she was deliberately repudiating the formal controversy, deliberately refusing to play the old game.

A dedication to Swetnam sets the tone, with the calculatedly disgusting vocabulary of formal satire—all diseases and bad smells:

> Could the straine
> Of that your barren-idle-donghill braine,
> As from a Chymick Limbeck so distill
> Your poyson'd drops of hemlocke, and so fill
> The itching eares of silly swaines, and rude
> Truth-not-discerning rusticke multitude
> With sottish lies, with bald and ribald lines,
> Patcht out of English writers that combines
> Their highest reach of emulation but to please
> The giddy-headed vulgar: whose disease
> Like to a swelling dropsie, thirsts to drinke
> And swill the puddles of this nasty sinke. . .

Swetnam has a "spungie pate" (Sig. B), an "idle addle coxcombe" (p.
12), a "peevish and pettish nature," "dogged frompard frowardnesse,"
"male-contented desperation," a "currish disposition" (p. 14), and a "de-
generous and illiberall disposition" (p. 20). His mind "is troubled and
festered with the impostume of inbred malice, and corrupt hatred" (p.
20), which has resulted in a work of "impudent detraction" (Sig. B), of
"viperous scandals" (p. 6), of "leuitie ioyn'd with degenerate cowardize"
(p. 8). Joseph Swetnam is a "mangie rascall" (p. 33).

Munda's pugnacity leaps from every line. Sowernam had envisioned a
courtroom, Speght a chivalric combat. Munda presents herself as a street
scrapper, her confrontation with Swetnam as an open brawl; a gang of
women will pounce on Swetnam and savage him. This is no debate: it is
a mugging. Munda fears no reprehension for scolding: "Ile take the paines
to worme the tongue of your madnesse, and dash your rankling teeth
downe your throat: tis not houlding vp a wispe, nor threatning a cucking-stoole shall charme vs out of the compasse of your chaine, our pens
shall throttle you, or like *Archilochus* with our tart Iambikes make you
Lopez his godson: we will thrust thee like *Phalaris* into thine owne brazen
bull, and baite thee at thy owne stake, and beate thee at thine owne
weapon" (p. 16). Archilochus was a Greek satirist of fabled bitterness,
iambics that bludgeoning satire Sidney defined as "a bold and open crying
out against naughtiness"—a fair description of Munda's style. She bursts
with spleen:

> But as [Speght] hath beene the first Champion of our sexe that
> would encounter with the barbarous bloudhound, and wisely dammed
> vp your mouth, and sealed vp your iawes lest your venomed teeth
> like madde dogges should damage the credit of many, nay all inno-
> cent damosels; so no doubt, if your scurrilous and deprauing tongue

breake prison, and falls to licking vp your vomited poyson, to the
end you may squirt out the same with more pernicious hurt, assure
your selfe there shall not be wanting store of Helebore to scoure the
sinke of your tumultuous gorge, at least we will cram you with
Antidotes and Catapotions, that if you swell not till you burst, yet
your digested poyson shall not be contagious. (pp. 15–16)

Munda's very syntax suggests breathless rage: unwilling to interrupt the
volcanic flow, she seldom comes to a full stop. Two consecutive sen-
tences on pages 20 and 21 contain 138 and 243 words. The essay is pep-
pered with neologisms: standard English proved inadequate to convey
Munda's wrath.

Occasionally, she relaxes into condescension and ridicule. She characterizes Swetnam's posture as that of an angry little boy:

> You were in great *choller* against some women, and in the *ruffe* of
> your furie. . . . Alas (good Sir) wee may easily gather you were
> mightily transported with passion . . . Twere a pleasant sight to see
> you in your *great* standing *choller* and *furious ruffe* together. Your choller
> (no doubt) was too great for a Spanish *peccadillo,* and your shagge
> *ruffe* seemed so greesly to set forth your ill-looking visage, that none
> of your shee-aduersaries durst attempt to confront your follie. But
> now let vs talke with you in your cold bloud. Now the lees of your
> furie are settled to the bottome, and your turbulent minde is defæcated
> and clearer, lets haue a parle with you. (p. 7)

Munda, like Speght, calls Swetnam a dog. He had seen himself as
Cerberus, guard dog of Hades; satirists, on Diogenes's authority, had
often posed as snarling dogs. But Munda's Swetnam is neither fearsome
Hell-guardian nor the classical canine spirit of detraction. He is an ordinary English mutt—currish, mangy, vomiting in the streets. (She reminds him that Cerberus had three heads, not—as he claims—two.)

Munda turns some old antifeminist charges against Swetnam. He is "a
hare-brain'd scold" (p. 8), of "incredible impudence" (p. 15). She, in contrast, is a woman of erudition; she reveals this through Latinate neologisms, classical allusions, and (on page 25) syllogistic logic.

Although Munda chooses not to write a formal defense, she shows
awareness of the formal controversy. She follows convention in impugning Swetnam's motives: he has probably been unlucky with women. "You
hauing peraduenture had some curst wife that hath giuen you as good as
you brought . . . you run a madding vp and downe to make a scrole of
female frailties. . . . A priuate abuse of your owne familiar doxies should
not breake out into open slander of the religious matron together with
the prostitute strumpet" (pp. 8–9). Women who consort with the likes

of Swetnam might well be lewd, idle, froward, and unconstant; small wonder, being what he is, that he "happened (in some Stewes or Brothelhouses) to be acquainted with their cheats and euasions" (p. 11). Another familiar convention, the charge of filial ingratitude, Munda treats fully. She applies Swetnam's antifeminist insults to his mother, proving him "*Nero*-like in ripping vp the bowels of thine owne Mother" (p. 17). If woman sprang from the Devil, as Swetnam maintains, Swetnam is "the Deuils Grand-child" (p. 18). Munda, in contrast, dedicates her essay to her mother, who conventionally earns gratitude for so willingly undergoing childbirth pains and the difficulties of rearing and educating her child.[7]

Even Munda at times plays the literary critic. She is hampered by Speght's and Sowernam's thoroughness; but she adds objections to Swetnam's trite proverbs, mixed metaphors, and dismal doggerel. Like Sowernam, she complains that his work is derivative: "'Tis worthy laughter what paines you haue taken in turning ouer *Parismus,* what vse you make of the *Knight of the Sunne,* what collections out of *Euphues, Amadis a Gaule,* and the rest of *Don Quixotes* Library, sometimes exact tracing of Aesopicall Fables, and *Valerius Maximus,* with the like schooleboyes bookes" (p. 21). Like Speght and Sowernam, she taxes Swetnam with disorganization and self-contradiction: "these iarring and incongruous speeches, whose absurdities accrew to such a tedious and infinite summe" are but "vnsauorie non-sense" (p. 26). It is possible that Munda's interests too are primarily literary, that she was giving the old literary game a new twist. As Agrippa had adapted rhetorical paradox to the controversy's purposes, and Elyot had adapted the Platonic/Erasmian dialogue, so Munda is adapting the techniques of formal satire as developed by Marston, Hall, Guilpin, and others in the late 1590s and early 1600s. Again, it is difficult to say for certain that her interest in the woman question goes beyond its usefulness as a vehicle for wit and style.

She does, however, engage one important substantive issue—the war-and-peace view of sex roles (see part 2). Taking this issue by the throat, Munda provides one of the best Renaissance discussions of this centrally important matter. She sees clearly that women have no chance of equality as long as human dignity is defined in martial terms:

> You most graphically describe the difference and antipathie of man and woman, which being considered, you thinke it strange there should be any reciprocation of loue, for a man say you delights in armes, and hearing the ratling drum, but a woman loues to heare sweet musicke on the Lute, Cittern, or Bandora: I prethee who but the long-eard animall had rather heare the Cuckoe than the Nightingale? Whose eares are not more delighted with the melodious tunes of sweete musicke, then with the harsh sounding drum? Did not

Achilles delight himselfe with his harpe as well as with the trumpet? Nay, is there not more men that rather affect the laudable vse of the Citterne, and Bandore, and Lute for the recreation of their mindes, than the clamourous noyse of drums? Whether is it more agreeable to humane nature to march amongst murthered carkasses, which you say man reioyceth in, than to enioy the fruition of peace and plenty, euen to dance on silken Carpets, as you say, is our pleasure? What man soeuer maketh warres, is it not to this ende, that hee might enioy peace? Man loues to heare the threatning of his Princes enemies, but woman weepes when shee heares of warres, What man that is a true and loyall subiect loues to heare his Princes enemies threaten? . . . is it not more humane to bewaile the wars and losse of our countrimen, then to reioyce in the threats of an aduersary? but you goe forward in your paralelling a mans loue to lie on the cold grasse, but a woman must bee wrapped in warme mantles. I neuer heard of any that had rather lie in the could grasse then in a feather-bed, if he might haue his choyce; yet you make it a proper attribute to all your sexe. . . . This Antithesis you haue found in some Author betwixt a warrier and a louer, and you stretch it to shew the difference betwixt a man and a woman. (pp. 31–32)

Few writers affirm more stoutly that the basic human values are the values of peace: the man of peace, if more womanlike than his hawkish brother, is also more fully human.

It is Munda who articulates most clearly the Jacobean sense that it was time women stopped smiling off misogynist insult. She predicts that from now on, insulted women will refuse to keep silent: "Though feminine modesty hath confin'd our rarest and ripest wits to silence . . . opportunity of speaking slipt by silence, is as bad as importunity vpheld by babling. . . . Know therefore that wee will cancell your accusations, trauers your bils, and come vpon you for a false inditement" (p. 5).

A little over a year after the registration of Swetnam's *Arraignment* and about six months before the registration of Speght's rejoinder, Daniel Tuvil's *Asylum Veneris; or, A Sanctuary for Ladies. Iustly Protecting Them, their virtues and sufficiencies from the foule aspersions and forged imputations of traducing Spirits,* 1616, had been registered. This is not a direct reply to Swetnam; it never mentions him. Wright notes, "If his pamphlet was not an answer to Swetnam, its appearance was timely and its title seems to have been dictated with Swetnam's traducing work in mind" (p. 488), but this is only another example of the assumption that defenses of women are "answers": Tuvil's "traducing Spirits," like the "malicious detractors" in the title of Vaughan's dialogue, are most likely conventional and hypothetical. Tuvil says the finished work lay unpublished for some time; he summarizes antifeminist views before refuting them, suggesting that no recent attack was available when he wrote. His work is clearly in the pre-Swetnam tradition of defense as an independent genre rather than a response to an attack; as other defenses imitated defenses, so Tuvil's leans very heavily on the defenses of Castiglione and Agrippa.[8] But since the play *Swetnam the Woman-hater Arraigned by Women,* which crowned the Swetnam controversy, draws upon Tuvil's essay as well as on Speght's, Sowernam's, and Munda's (see chapter 12), I will discuss it in the context of the Swetnam war.

Each of Tuvil's ten chapters, one on "Womens worth in generall," nine on particular virtues (beauty, chastity, modesty, humility, silence, constancy, learning and knowledge, wisdom and discretion, and valor and courage), begins with a description of particular antifeminist charges, followed by refutations. Especially in the first seven chapters, Tuvil is overzealous in describing the charges: his examples of female misbehavior are so extreme, and the misogynistic comment so lively, as to overwhelm his colorless defense.[9]

Tuvil approaches beauty with a dangerous allusion to women whose beauty conquered great men—Samson, Solomon, David—as if daring hypothetical opponents to make snide jests about Delilah or Solomon's concubines. He courts rejoinder even more boldly by including Omphale, whose beauty emasculated Hercules. In his chapter on chastity he dwells on classical epigrams on the rarity of female chastity, including Martial's epigram suggesting that thousands of women are chaste only because no man would ask them. In his chapter on silence, Tuvil tells an anecdote wherein Socrates, asked how he could endure Xantippe's unceasing talk, replied "that for the children which she bare him he could as well abide hir prating, as he did the cackling of his Hennes for the Egges they laid him" (p. 63), and relates an old story of a man who petitioned to be executed, unable "to endure the disdainefull braues, and haughtie menaces, which his Wife like a triple-mouthed Cerberus did continually thunder out against him" (p. 64). The anecdote he relates in his chapter on modesty, concerning "a certaine Spanish Lasse" who thanked God for her gang rape by soldiers because "once in my daies I haue had my fill without sinning" (p. 40) is a hard act for virtue to follow. And Tuvil's examples of virtue in that chapter are bizarre—women who killed themselves and their female children to prevent rape, a woman who carried home in her lap the severed head of a rapist, a vestal virgin who tore out her eyeballs and presented them to the man who was tempted by her pretty eyes, a widow who sealed her vagina with fire to "cut off the importunacie" of her suitors, Queen Zenobia, who refused sex with her husband, a woman who swore her husband to a sexless marriage. To a modern reader, such modesty seems psychopathic, and I suspect that even Renaissance readers found the lusty Spanish lass wholesomer than the eye-gouging vestal.

That between the time he penned the table of contents and the time he penned chapters 5 and 6 Tuvil changed his mind and decided to write a formal attack rather than a formal defense is suggested by the fact that the table of contents shows chapter 5 as dealing with women's "Humility, and supposed Pride," while the chapter heading becomes "of their supposed Pride," and the chapter itself deals almost entirely with women's pride, while chapter 6, called in the table of contents "their Silence and falsly obiected Talkatiuenesse," becomes in the chapter heading "Of their Talkeatiuenesse." In this chapter Tuvil dwells on misogynists' complaints about women's talkativeness without saying anything to indicate that they are unjustified, except to adduce two women who could keep a secret and to assert that "want of Secrecie is as incident to Men and found as often in their bosomes, as in any of this Sex" (p. 79). The first seven chapters of the *Asylum* look like an attack masquerading as a defense, similar to Rich's *Excellency of Good Women*. But the last three chapters comprise an interesting (and sometimes nearly feminist) defense. It is possible that Tuvil was attempting a rhetorical paradox, with the *volta* at the beginning of chapter 8. His technique is inept, however; if he intended paradox, he achieved confusion.

At the turning point, Tuvil explains that he has been discussing passive virtues. He now turns to more active virtues: "I haue hitherto laboured . . . [to give] the liuely representation of Womens perfections in a louely *Venus* . . . I endeuour hereafter withall the art I can, to limme them foorth in an armed Pallas, . . . endued with such learning, wisdome, courage, and other the like abilities, which Men, ouerwhelmed with self-conceit presumptuously entitle Masculine" (p. 86). This distinction between virtues thought proper to women and virtues possessed by some women but thought proper only to men had occurred to almost no other writer. Tuvil may acquit himself better in the final section simply because the problems presented by antifeminist comment are here of a different order. Misogynists could allege that not many women possessed passive virtues. Of active virtues—learning, wisdom in government, courage— detractors might have said the same, but they had more frequently denied the appropriateness of active virtues to women. Tuvil is not a profound thinker, and he finds this argument easier to deal with: it is blatantly akin to the sin of pride. Men's arrogation of active virtue to themselves alone is "self-conceit," presumption.

The three chapters on active virtues are as long as the seven chapters on passive virtues. In chapter 8, on women's learning, Tuvil dismisses the proverbial notion that learning "doth not ballast their Iudgements, but onely addeth more saile to their ambition" (p. 87)[10] as "fond imagination," and is not tempted to linger on detraction. He protests against the common opinion that education, particularly literary education, is dangerous for women; he has a humanist's faith in education as the road to virtue: "To conuerse with Bookes, hath bin still [i.e., always] accounted the readiest way to moralise our harsher natures, and to weane them from all inbred Barbarisme to more humane and ciuill conuersation" (p. 89). He affirms the equality of the sexes: "I see no hinderance why [books] should not produce the same effect in [women], which they doe in vs, their bodies consisting of the same matter, and their mindes comming out of the same molde" (p. 90). He entertains the possibility that learning will allow a woman to dominate her husband: "But *Scientia inflat;* Knowledge puffeth vp, and there is nothing, say our opposites, more swelling and imperious, than a Woman, that seeth shee hath the superiority and start of her Husband" (p. 96), but his answer to this provides his most feminist moment: someone has to steer a household, and if the woman is better educated, perhaps it ought to be her. "He that is depriued of his bodily sight, is content to bee led, though by a childe: and shall hee, that is blinde in his vnderstanding disdaine to be directed by her, who by the ordinance of God, and the rules of sacred Wedlocke, is alotted him a fellow-helper in all his businesse? The Husband and the Wife are the eyes of a Familie; if the right one bee so bleared, that it cannot well discerne; the guiding of the Houshold must of necessity be left vnto the left, or on the sudden all will go to wracke. And surely I see no reason but the Henne may bee permitted to crowe, where the Cocke can doe nothing but cackle" (p. 97). (The right/left dichotomy appears again in Tuvil's epilogue.)

In chapter 9, concerning women in public life, Tuvil (following Agrippa) attacks the ideal of domesticity: "It hath bin our pollicie from the beginning to busie them in domestical affaires, thereby to diuert them from more serious imployments, in which if they had not surmounted vs, they would at least haue showne themselues our equals. . . . Spinning, knitting, sowing, preseruing, & the like, as we would make them beleeue, are their chiefest peices. But all ages haue affoorded some, whose Spirits being of a stronger temper, and harder edge, then to turne at such perswasions, haue trauailed beyond those Herculean Pillers" (p. 101; cf. Agrippa, Sig. [F8]ᵛ). He attacks Salic law as a French barbarity: "I . . . condemne the Salique law, and taxe it of iniustice, by which the worthinesse of Women is excluded, as a thing altogether eccentricall from the crown of France" (p. 110).

Chapter 10, on courage, is twenty-four pages long, by far the longest chapter—over twice as long as all but one of the first seven. Since courage, as Tuvil defines it, is the most aggressive of the active virtues, this special emphasis is one more example of the literary attention being paid during these years to assertive women. (See part 2).

Tuvil is at first uneasy about feminine aggression. As if remembering that it can tend toward undesirable extremes, he begins with revenge. Here again we find, as we would not if a firm *volta* existed at chapter 8, the self-defeating habit of placing negative examples first: the two examples here are the most lurid in the book. First, Parisatis, who in revenge for her son's maiming tortured the malefactor for ten days; his eyes were bored out, "and finally molten mettle [was] poured into his eares, till he breathed his last in this miserable torment" (p. 115). Parisatis subjected another enemy to seventeen days' "hellish torture" (p. 115) and had a third flayed alive, then completely dismembered (pp. 115–16). Second, the mother of Mahomet II, who in revenge for her son's death cut a hole in the culprit's side, "and by peece-meale cut out his Liuer, and cast it before his eyes to the Dogges" (p. 116). These overenthusiastic examples, perhaps revealing Tuvil's suppressed doubts about female assertiveness, soon give way to more positive remarks on female courage.

Women's apparent fearfulness, Tuvil argues, is actually only a reflex action, as any man would jump at a loud noise: after the initial shock, women usually pull themselves together and exhibit courage. He tells Courageous Women stories, mostly classical: some women killed themselves to prompt their husbands to the same noble act; some chose to die with husbands condemned to death; many excelled in battle. Tuvil's uneasiness over female aggression dictates that all his martial examples be women who defended themselves and their country in extremity and under siege: recalling Elyot's strategy with Zenobia in *The Defense of Good Women,* he speaks of no female military leaders who took the offensive. But although he emphasizes defense, he describes graphically the exploits of "generous and warlike Lasses": "Amongst other women was a tall Hungarian, who thrusting in amongst the souldiers . . . at one blow strucke off the heads of two Turkes, as they were climbing vppe the Rampier" (pp. 131, 130). Tuvil gradually overcomes his reluctance to portray women as strong, aggressive, courageous.

In his epilogue, Tuvil comes as close, probably, as he dared to affirming the equality of the sexes. He reiterates Plato's conclusions: "*Plato* yet maintaines, that if there be any distinction betwixt their sufficiencie: and ours, it is not essentiall, but accidentall, & such a one as is grounded meerely vpon vse. And therefore, saith hee, as both the Hands are by nature alike fit for all manner of actions, till application and imployment bring in a difference of Right and Left. So Women and Men haue in them the same aptitude and abilitie for the well managing of ciuill and militarie places, and it is exercise alone, which begets dexteritie" (pp. 138–39). Plato was wrong about right- and left-handedness; the dominance of one hand is now known to be more a matter of "Nature" than of "exercise." But never mind the metaphor; if the vehicle is weak, the tenor is strong: men are dominant only through custom; they seem better suited than women to be in control only because they have had more practice. Most differences between the sexes, Tuvil sees here, are cultural, not innate; in Plato's terms, accidental, not essential. The one further step necessary to feminism is to argue that equality of essence demands equality of opportunity. This step Plato took, and Tuvil followed him: "As those bodies are most perfect, and fitting for euery action, which can, if occasion require, as well apply their left-hand to the businesse, as their right: so is that Common-wealth the most absolute which for good gouernment can make vse of Women, as well as of Men" (p. 139) If the ideal individual is ambidextrous, then the ideal society is hermaphroditic. Tuvil, clearly indebted to Castiglione, uses this notion to refute Aristotle's contention that "nature intendeth alwaies to produce that, which is most perfect, and therefore willingly would still bring foorth the Male, counting Females . . . like those, that are borne blinde and lame, or any other way defectiue" (p. 138). If there is any state of imperfection in nature, Tuvil argues, "one Sex alone is an argument of imperfection; and therefore the Heathens did attribute both of them to God. *Orpheus* said of *Iupiter,* that he was Male and Female" (p. 141; cf. *The Courtier,* pp. 223–26).

A problem with the metaphor of ambidextrousness is that the Renaissance had inherited a long symbolic tradition associating right hand with good and left with evil. The word *dexterity,* which Tuvil employs to refer to the two hands' equal abilities, comes from the Latin *dexter,* "right hand." *Sinister,* which Tuvil uses to describe ill behavior (p. 148), originally meant "left hand." In the Bible, the saved sit on God's right hand. When Tuvil follows Plato in associating the right hand with men and the left with women, a value judgement creeps in. The ambidexter metaphor captures Tuvil's essential ambivalence. He argues that belief in male superiority is mere pride ("Self-conceitednesse hath like a canker eaten into the hearts of Men, and possessed them with such an admiration of their owne sufficiencie, that they looke but with a scornefull eye vpon the sufficiencie of others" [p. 142]). He endorses in theory equality between spouses (from the old proverb, "The woman was taken out of the side of man, to bee rankt in equall estimation with him; and not out of his foot, to become litier for his proud and insolent ambition to wallow on" [p. 149], he interestingly omits the usual "nor out of his head to be his superior"). But he assumes that the husband is head of the family. A husband can make his wife good if he takes the trouble. He must lead her gently, with private admonitions, rather than making her faults public. Marriage is here a tutor-pupil relationship—hardly a relationship of equality.

Tuvil's essay is a tribute to the power of custom. Here is an author who accepts major feminist tenets, which when pressed to their logical conclusions produce concepts like equal pay for equal work, equal responsibility for child care and housework. But Tuvil does not see the logical conclusions. Women had never been employed on an equal footing with men; men had never pulled their weight around the house. Tuvil, like virtually all his contemporaries of both sexes (and the majority of our own contemporaries), could not even imagine a world where such conditions prevailed. Equality was a beautiful theory, but custom militated against its being put into practice. I can admire Tuvil in the abstract, but if he were alive I would grasp him by the doublet and demand, "Talk is cheap, Daniel Tuvil. How many diapers have you washed today?" The maddening thing about the history of feminism is that while the theory has been there since Plato, the generality of womankind still awaits the man who wields a mop with a good will. For two thousand years, equality of the sexes has existed in the realm of Platonic Forms and literary games. Plato had his moments; but Plato is dead, and so, for all practical purposes, have been his theories on women.

Tuvil, like Sowernam, vacillates uncomfortably between a sincere desire to address the question of the nature and status of women, and pure literary gamesmanship. His ingenious argument that ribs aren't really crooked ("Art would haue termed it an Arch, which of all kindes of Architecture is both the firmest, and the fairest" [p. 8]) is the kind of tiny variation on an old theme that had delighted Tudor controversialists. His awkward overdose of misogynistic opinion perhaps reflects an unwillingness to forfeit the sheer literary effectiveness of the misogynists' half of the argument; for just as vice is nearly always more interesting in literature than is virtue, so the misogynists' ribald anecdotes were more successful as literature than the defenders' pious portraits of chaste matrons. Literary attacks on women always outsold literary defenses: not one of the three responses to Swetnam's smashingly successful essay ran to a second edition, and this was partly because, whatever else one can say apropos the relative merits of antifeminist attacks and pro-feminist defenses, the attacks were certainly more fun. Anyone primarily interested in his essay's popularity with readers would be tempted to do what Tuvil did—capitalize on the salacious and the sensational, as available in the works of his putative opponents.

Nevertheless, Tuvil's last chapters get a handle on substantive feminist issues in a way that was rare in the genre, however difficult it is to know where sport leaves off and a serious attempt to persuade begins. It would help if Tuvil had had a clearer sense of where he was going: he should have brushed up his Quintilian. Replete with hoary *exempla*, from Susanna, Lucrece, and Penelope to Minerva, Ceres, and Nicostrata, his essay is an overstuffed *refutatio* cum *confirmatio*, not lacking the odd *digressio*. He is badly in need of a firm *propositio*.

One final note on Tuvil. That ghastly title *A Sanctuary for Ladies*, which appears on his title page, was amended on all running page titles to *A Sanctuary for Women*. For this relief much thanks.

In the Jacobean period, the formal controversy was losing its generic consistency—it is difficult to find in this period a classic, pure example of a judicial oration or a Platonic/Erasmian dialogue—and was beginning to show signs of authorial uncertainty over the relationship between this charming parlor game and the realities of life for women.

During the Swetnam controversy, the debate lost an important element of artistic dishonesty; while earlier defenses only pretended to be answering a published attack on women, the defenses of Speght, Sowernam, and Munda actually did answer such an attack. When defense answered attack, the debate more nearly approached the kind of argument that occurs in real life than it had when attack was a generic subspecies of defense. The very fact that the entire Swetnam controversy was conducted in prose lent the later formal controversy an air of decreased artificiality as compared with the poetic orations of the Tudor controversy. And the increasing emphasis on aggressive women in the Jacobean controversy suggests a quite unprecedented brush with the real world, where contemporary women were donning breeches and challenging people to duels.

But the formal controversy was still recognizably a genre and still at heart a literary exercise. To engage in this sort of feminism, if feminism it was, one didn't need to discommode oneself by lobbying Parliament for the right of married women to own property, or by picketing the London trade guilds that were systematically excluding women, or by organizing shelters for battered wives, or by marshalling funds for the relief of starving women forced into prostitution by diminishing economic opportunities for women. All one needed was to sit in a study, searching through old books for historical and literary examples with which to rebut the latest witty slander upon womankind.

Looking back, we can see that through all its twists and permutations the formal controversy maintained throughout the Renaissance an underlying structure as fixed as liturgy. I use the word *liturgy* advisedly: there is a repetitiveness, an orthodoxy about the formal controversy that suggests ritual.

Francis MacDonald Cornford once threw out the provocative suggestion that *débat* as a literary form originated in ritual abuse that was part of the struggle between fertility and sterility, summer and winter, fullness and hunger, in the fertility rites that may also have given rise to both tragedy and comedy.[11] If this is true, the formal controversy about women, continuing the medieval *débat,* likely retains some of its ancient roots and possibly even preserves the antique purpose—promotion of fertility. I shall have more to say, in "The Stage Misogynist" (chapter 11), about the role of misogyny in the archetypal struggles surrounding human sexuality. For now, I will briefly touch on the structural implications of the formal controversy's possibly having roots in ancient ritual.

The forces of fertility are, in the formal controversy, on the side of the defense: the misogynist who attacks women is clearly a representative of winter, and women are defended against the assumed hostility of male readers because the world must be peopled. The *agon* of comedy, from the Greeks to *Much Ado,* is at bottom the struggle between the spirits of fertility and sterility; the rhetorical struggle in the formal defense is between Woman and the hypothetical misogynist. As in ancient comedy the wintry intruder Sterility is driven away with abuse, often personal invective, so in the formal defense's *exordium* and *refutatio* the frosty misogynist is discredited and driven away, often with the help of personal abuse—remarks about his manhood, his inadequacies as a son, and so forth. This structure has roots in the deepest subsoils of the human heart: the triumph of Woman in the formal defense is as natural as the seed bursting from the ground in spring, as archetypal as Easter. However ancient an impulse misogyny may be, the formal attack has no such ancient literary credentials as the formal defense has. The attack's *refutatio* is discordant with western tradition: no ritual, no festival, no comedy known to western man allows the spirit of sterility to triumph, driving out a fertility (the profemale argument) cast as intruding *alazon*. The triumph of sterility is rightly tragedy, but the formal attack is all comic buffoonery with no comedic regeneration.

The formal controversy's dialogues clearly reproduce the ancient comedic structure; as I have shown, in all Renaissance dialogues but one, defender triumphs over misogynist: summer's message, "Women are good; marry," prevails over winter's message, "Women are evil; remain single," as fertility triumphs over sterility in ritual. Whatever the case in noncontroversialist literature, in the formal controversy itself we never hear the argument "men are evil; remain single." The lopsidedness of the formal controversy, where fertility is salvaged by reconciling men to female company but not the other way around, may be given many explanations: we may adduce the myth of feminine evil; we may posit a Tudor assumption that the typical reader is male. Purely in terms of literary structure, though, the explanation that recommends itself is that in the formal controversy women are spotlighted because the principle of fertility is being associated exclusively with women.

This is in perfect accord with the regenerative comedy of Shakespeare, where women play so central a role. Feminist critics have occasionally been irritated, understandably enough, with Shakespeare's relegation of important female roles to the "fertility" world of comedy, sensing in it something of the baby machine attitude toward women's proper role. But the Renaissance association of women with the comedic world of fertility and the human life force was something relatively recent in western cultural history: comedy developed, Aristotle says, from phallic songs, and it was the phallus that had most often represented fertility; Aristophanes, who wrote three "women plays," still nearly always represented fertility through a protagonist who was an old man rejuvenated. Assigning Woman the role of fertility goddess was no step forward for feminism. But the structural position occupied by women in the formal controversy's literary architecture does foreshadow the very great prominence of female characters and the female principle in Renaissance literature as a whole.

NOTES

1. See Wright, *Middle-Class Culture,* p. 487n.

2. *Euphues* had been reprinted in 1613, two years before the publication of the *Arraignment;* fresh editions of *Euphues* appeared in 1617, 1623, 1631, and 1636, coinciding closely with the *Arraignment's* period of popularity (ten editions between 1615 and 1637). This suggests a revival of interest in Euphuistic style which may help account for Swetnam's popularity.

3. *Swetnam the Woman-Hater: The Controversy and the Play,* p. 7.

4. Ian Maclean notes that "hints about the historical nature of biblical texts (especially the Pauline epistles [precisely Speght's topic here]) may have suggested to some theologians that statements about women could be considered as relative to the society and *mores* of [the?] time and not as absolute religious prescriptions; but . . . there is no rigorous application of this exegetical method" (*The Renaissance Notion of Women,* p. 26).

5. Prefatory remarks to Margaret Tyler's translation of *The Mirror of Princely Deeds and Knighthood,* 1578.

6. See Erasmus's *Coniugium,* translated into English in 1557 as *A mery dialogue, declaringe the propertyes of shrowde shrewes, and honest wyues.*

7. It is charming to observe that Katharine Rogers, who with Freud views fear of a mother's power as the primary impetus to misogyny and who argues that attacks upon Mom are the most prominent feature of twentieth-century misogyny, reënacts Munda in dedicating *The Troublesome Helpmate* "To My Mother."

8. Tuvil and Agrippa both make an issue of Eve's name. Both take up beauty first and chastity second; in discussing feminine beauty, both cite Omphale, Sara, Hester, and Judith, in the same order. Both court rejoinder by alluding to three men captivated by women—Samson, David, and Solomon. In the space of two pages, Agrippa mentions Arthemisia, Julia, Portia, Alceste, and Hypsicratea (Sig. [D7]–[D7]ᵛ); Tuvil mentions the same group on pp. 82 and 84. Agrippa mentions Portia and Cornelia

consecutively on Sig. [D7]; Tuvil mentions Portia and Cornelia in the same sentence on p. 135. Castiglione had employed about thirty-five *exempla,* virtually all of which Tuvil appropriates; some are rare elsewhere in the controversy—Harmonia, Theodora, Anne of France, Lady Margaret, Queen Isabella, the women ruling Hungary and Naples. One cluster of four *exempla* occurring together is common to all three authors: Castiglione and Tuvil cite Aspasia/Diotima/Corinna/Sappho; Agrippa cites Aspasia/Diotima/Sappho/Corinna. Tuvil often plagiarizes directly; for example: "We have seene Ann Frenche Queen a verye great Ladye, no less in vertue then in State: and if in justice and mildenesse, liberalitye and holynesse of lief, ye lust to compare her to the Kinges Charles and Lewis (whyche had bine wyef to bothe of them) you shall not finde her a jott inferiour to them. Beehoulde the Ladye Margaret daughter to the Emperour Maximilian, whyche wyth great wysedome and justyce hitherto hath ruled and still doeth her State" (Castiglione, pp. 244–45); "What should I speake of Queene Anne of France, a Lady of no lesse worth, then wealth, wife to two Kings, *Charles* and *Lewis,* but to neither of them any way inferiour, either in iustice, clemency, liberality, or holinesse of life? What of Lady *Margaret,* Daughter to Maximilian the Emperour, who with no lesse wisedome, moderation and equity gouerned hir State a long time?" (Tuvil, p. 104).

Tuvil's is the longest defense in the controversy, and he draws his multitudinous *exempla* from a number of sources; that among these sources were the two founders of the Renaissance controversy (and the two who came closest to modern feminism) helps explain the occasional surfacing of radical thought in the work of so modest a thinker as Tuvil. Comparing Tuvil with his sources also reveals a marked increase in favorable attention to aggressive women which I believe was peculiarly Jacobean.

Examination of *exempla* and argument does not suggest that Tuvil knew the work of William Bercher (see chapter 3), who had previously combined Agrippa and Castiglione; whether Tuvil borrowed from Domenichi, Bercher's intermediary source, I have not been able to ascertain.

9. According to Ruth Kelso, this rhetorical problem was common in the continental controversy, where some, "like Domenico Bruni, who wrote to defend women, were severely reprimanded because they repeated the old charges before proceeding to the defense, as aid to refutation, they said, by revealing its strength in contrast. And there was no denying that the repetition served to perpetuate the charges and even to spread them among readers who would not have looked at the direct attacks because of their scurrility" (p. 7).

10. A proverb most recently available in Sir Thomas Overbury's *A wife now the widdow of Sir T. Overbury,* Sig. C.

11. Francis MacDonald Cornford, *The Origin of Attic Comedy,* p. 129.

CHAPTER FIVE

✠

The Influence of the Formal Controversy

THE FORMAL CONTROVERSY continued in later Stuart times. Authors adopted such pugnacious pseudonyms as Mary Tattle-well and Ioane Hit-him-home to prosecute the old arguments in essays like *The womens sharpe revenge*. The procession of Eves and Jezebels, Penelopes and Susannas marched on. But the controversy as it was carried on from 1540 to 1620 represents the genre fairly enough. What remains is to sketch briefly the formal controversy's influence on literature of other genres and to assess its influence on the Renaissance theory of women.

The impact of the formal controversy on other genres was probably not very great; but its tracks can be glimpsed wandering over ballads, stories, and plays from time to time. The influence is most prominent in prose fiction. This genre was strongly oriented towards women readers: in the numerous story collections of the 1560s, 1570s, and 1580s, dedications to women readers and interpolated remarks addressed to the feminine reader are the rule rather than the exception. George Pettie's collection of classical tales, *A petite pallace of Pettie his pleasure,* 1576, is dedicated "To the gentle Gentlewomen Readers"; R. B., who wrote the dedicatory epistle, speaks fawningly to "Gentle Readers, whom by my will I woulde haue onely Gentlewomen," avouching "the great desire I haue to procure your delight." He claims to be publishing the tales against Pettie's wishes and is perfectly willing to risk Pettie his displeasure: "I care not to displease twentie men, to please one woman." Displeased or not, Pettie's orientation was apparently the same: all the stories are about women, mostly women who gain sympathy for sufferings at the hands of men and fate. Authorial intrusions address women readers; for example, "This seemeth straunge vnto you (Gentlewomen) that a woman should die and then liue againe" (p. 117). At the end of "Cephalus and Procris," he lectures women on the evils of jealousy. "Appius and Virginia" he closes by warning women against *senes fornecatores,* or dirty old men. In preparing a book for women readers, Pettie seems to have turned naturally to the formal controversy. Not only is his last tale largely a formal defense (see above), but the controversy intrudes at other points as well. Pigmalion appears in the traditional character of a misogynist, indulging in a long rant against womankind (pp. 199–200); here Pettie himself plays defender, quickly seeking to make amends to his women readers: "Gentlewomen, you must vnderstande, this Gentleman was in a great heate, and therefore you must beare with his bolde blasphemy against your noble sexe: for my part, I am angry with my selfe to haue vttred it" (p. 200). Pettie employs *exampla* traditional to the controversy: Camma is "worthy to bee compared to *Lucrece, Penelope,* or what woman soeuer that euer had any preheminence of praise for her vertue" (p. 23). When he takes up (as had Gosynhyll) the story of Pasiphaë, he suggests that her lover may have been a man named Taurus, rather than a bull, in order to mollify the women who—according to the formal controversy's ancient convention—would otherwise rise in fury against him: "Gentlewomē, because you shal not enter into colorick conceites against me, for publishing . . . a hystorie whiche seemeth so mutch to sounde to the shame of your sexe . . . " And at any rate, he allows, again employing the formal controversy's *exempla,* the world is full of good women like Penelope, Lucrece, and Susanna, who compensate for the occasional Pasiphaë. (pp. 186–188).

Another collection of tales, George Whetstone's *An Heptameron of Ciuill Discourses,* 1582, also emphasizes the actions of virtuous women; like Pettie's work, it incorporates a small formal controversy. Whetstone includes a *Courtier*-like discussion on the relative merits of men and women in the Promos and Cassandra story: when one speaker catalogues illustrious women—Semiramis, the Amazons, Lucrece, the Sybils—the detractor Dondolo scoffs, "There be so few of these women, as an easy wit may remember them" (Sig. [O4]). Other male speakers are irritated by the defense: "The other Gentlemen although they were willinge to giue place vnto the Gentlewomē in small matters, yet this comparison of equal soueraignty, netteled them a lytil" (Sig. [O4]). One Soranso remarks, "Although there hath bene Women learned, and experienced in Mecanicall craftes, yet to heare a Woman plead at the Barre, preache in a Pulpit, or to see her build a House, is a wonder and no example in vse" (Sig. O4ᵛ). But the author pronounces sexual distinctions irrelevant: "*Orpheus* sayde, that *Iupiter* and Pluto, were both *Male* and *Female.* It is also read in Scripture: *That God fashioned bothe Man and Woman to his owne likenesse:* Moreover this worde, *Homo,* signifieth bothe kindes" (Sig. Piᵛ).

Occasionally a story collection would masquerade as a work of the formal controversy: an example is the anonymous *The deceyte of women, to the instruction and ensample of all men, younge and olde.*[1] Opening with the usual denial of general misogyny—only vicious women are intended—and then conventionally allowing his criticism to become universal (the serpent assailed Eve because "he knew the strength of the man and so he thoughte for to deceyue the woman for she is of much febler nature to w[ith]stand temptacion" [Sig. (A2)ᵛ]), the author casts his collection of tales as *exempla* supporting his argument: he has used the trappings of the controversy to mask his real purpose, which is to retail salacious stories. Traditional *exempla*—Lot's daughters, Jael, Judith, Jezebel, Delilah—mingle with modern malefactors whose sexual adventures with friars and clerks are related with gusto. In one of his concluding stories, the author cleverly weaves the literary tradition into his plot: a jealous husband has armed himself against cuckoldry by making a lifetime study of antifeminist literature; no shift of his wife's to escape from the household for an hour will catch him unawares, for literature has made him an expert on the deceits of women. When his wife finally makes time for a lover by having to send home for dry garments after arranging to have water spilled on her dress, the husband recognizes this immediately as a new device not found in any standard misogynist literature. Falling into despondency, he dies of melancholy at the thought of so much wasted study.

The single novella, too, might bear traces of formal controversy. In Robert Greene's *Mamillia. A Mirrour or looking-glasse for the Ladies of Englande,* 1583, appears the earnest lover Florion who, disappointed in love by a "kite of Cressids kind" (p. 2), has been tempted toward misogyny. He has, however, resisted: "Although hee had cause with *Euripides* to proclaime himselfe open enemie to womankinde . . . he knew . . . that there was as well a *Lucrece,* as a *Lais;* as well *Cornelia* as *Corinna,* as constant a *Penelope,* as a fleeting *Phania*" (p. 2). Greene, who obviously hoped to tap the enormous resources of the female reading public, devoted two pieces of prose fiction to two favorite *exempla* of the formal defense, Susanna in *The Myrrovr of Modestie,* 1584, and Penelope in *Penelopes Web . . . a Christall Mirror of feminine perfection,* 1587. Such echoes of the formal defense suggest that the author who wrote for the women's market might naturally trick out his pieces with ornaments garnered from the formal controversy.

The judicial oration's underlying image of a trial surfaces occasionally in "women's" fiction. In his *Palace of Pleasure,* Pettie calls upon women readers to be judges of who is more to blame in a case, the man or the woman. "Sinorix and Camma" ends, "Gentlewomen I leaue it to your iudgements to giue sentence, whether be more worthy reprehension, hee or she" (p. 24). "Tereus and Progne" concludes, "It were hard here gentlewoman for you to giue sentence, who more offended of the husband or the wife" (p. 38). Of Curiatius and Horatia, Pettie remarks, "Gentlewomen . . . I would heare your iudgementes to whom you thinke this lamentable end of these louers ought to be imputed" (p. 150). This use of the judicial metaphor anticipates the trial scene of *Swetnam the Woman-hater Arraigned by Women,* where the case involves the respective guilt of the sexes.

Elizabethan story collections often include tales about women who were familiar as *exempla* in the formal controversy. William Painter's *The Palace of Pleasure,* 1566, contains stories about Lucrece, Zenobia, Veturia, Sybilla, Virginia, and the Amazons. It is impossible to prove that these women were chosen with an eye to the formal controversy. Painter culled his stories from the works of Boccaccio, Bandello, Belleforest, Straparola, Masuccio, the Queen of Navarre, and other continental and classical sources. But it is conceivable that the gathering together of these women's names in the formal controversy influenced Painter's choice of their stories for his anthology. He does evince some familiarity with the formal controversy's conventions. In the introduction to "Faustina the Empresse," he discusses good and bad women in history; a servant in "Dom Diego and Gineura" recites classical misogynist verse. It is possibly because the Amazons were treated so positively by formal defenders that Painter was able to overcome his initial repugnance to this "monstrous Sexe," these "mankynde [i.e., masculine] women" (pp. 4–5); in the second tome's table of contents, he praises "the hardinesse and conquestes of diuers stoute and aduenturous Women called *Amazones.*" Painter was as eager as any Renaissance story compiler to gain female readers, and he designed his second tome specifically with this end in mind, as is clear from his stated reason for placing the Amazon story first: "The maners & qualities of which nation, bicause they were women of no common spirite and boldnesse, be thought good in the front of this second volume to be described: bicause of diuers womens liues plentiful varietie is offered in the sequele" (p. 5). Painter was one of the first Elizabethans to realize the great market potential of women readers and to cater to it: it is reasonable to assume that he was not entirely oblivious to the recent success of several books about women, the 1560–61 editions of *Mulierum Pean, The School House of Women,* More's *Defense,* and *The Courtier,* works of the formal controversy published just five years before *The Palace of Pleasure.*

Such links, however slender, between the formal controversy and Elizabethan prose fiction are interesting in light of the fact that prose fiction continued for some two centuries to be associated with women readers and to focus on female protagonists. Perhaps the formal controversy's shortcomings can be forgiven in view of the possibility that it contributed, in whatever modest a way, to the rise of the novel.

Ballads occasionally take up the formal controversy; I have not included them in my discussion of the Tudor and Jacobean controversies because of the difficulty of dating them. *The ballat of the prayis of Wemen*

in the Bannatyne Manuscript is a classic formal defense—except that it
places the *refutatio* after the *confirmatio*—with a large number of biblical
and classical *exempla*.[2] In view of the fact that Gosynhyll's *Mulierum Pean*
and *The School House of Women* were both apparently based on Agrippa's
defense, it is interesting that Alexander Arbuthnot's *Ane contrapoysoun to
the Ballat falslie intitulit the properteis of gud Wemen* in the Maitland Quarto
Manuscript is apparently a conflation of *Mulierum Pean* and *The School
House* to form a new defense.[3] Two ballads in Thomas Deloney's collection, *The garland of good will*, entered 1593, are entitled "A Song in praise
of Women" and "A Song in praise of a single life": these purport to be a
controversy between defender and misogynist, although both are quite
negative. Some lost ballads appear from their titles to have imitated the
formal controversy: *The Defence agaynste them that commonlye Defame
women*, 1560, *The prayse and Dysprayse of Women*, 1563–64. Ballads may
have been one channel through which the formal controversy was trans-
mitted to popular culture.

Epitaphs on women appear to draw *exempla* from the formal defense.
Joshua Sylvester, in *Monodia. An Elegie, in commemoration of the Vertuous
life, and Godlie Death of . . . Dame Helen Branch,* compares Dame Helen
with Ruth, Sara, and Judith; W. Har, in *Epicedivm, A Funerall Song, vpon
the vertuous life, and godly death, of . . . Lady Helen Branch,* compares her
with Lucrece, Helen of Troy, Judith, Virginia, and Cleopatra. Patrick
Hannay alludes to a common "defense" motif in his elegy on Queen
Anne: "The *Morallists* did all of *her* deuine, / When *they* made euery *vertue* foeminine" (Sig. Bᵛ).

The Theophrastan character, a Jacobean genre, would seem a likely
environment for the formal controversy, seeing that good and bad women
were often charactered as contrasting types in balanced prose characters:
the first two characters of the Overburian character collection, 1614, deal
respectively with a good woman and a bad; Richard Brathwait in *Essaies
upon the five senses,* 1619, creates the character of a shrew to balance his
character of a good wife. In fact, the Theophrastan character as a genre
does not lean very heavily on the formal controversy. One catches glimpses,
though. In the long piece about a good wife which opens the Overburian
collection, Overbury makes the traditional point that "*Eue* from *Liue-
flesh,* Man did from *Dust* proceed" (Sig. Bᵛ). Richard Brathwait conventionally accuses the misogynist of a sour-grapes attitude consequent on
maltreatment by one woman: "I conceiue how apt man is to iudge sin-
isterly of the weaker vessell, and I impute it either to a want of Braines,
in that they cannot diue into the excellencie of so pure and exquisite a
composition, or some hard hap they haue had in making choice of such
infirme creatures" (p. 123). He introduces a few *exempla*—Portia, Paulina, Octavia. Thomas Gainsford in *The Rich Cabinet Furnished with var-*

ietie of Excellent descriptions, exquisite Charracters, 1616, employs the balancing formula: "Woman . . . is a purgatory on earth . . . if she be honest, she will be imperious, if faire, she wil be venerious: if foule, she is loathsome; if a wanton, full of fraude or treason: if proud, costly aboue thy ability: if witty, impudent to shame thee or make thee weary . . . if familiar and affable, she will bee foolish and tell all" (p. 163). Gainsford makes succinctly the kind of point usually made with the help of exhaustive *exempla:* "Woman is endued with the same vertues as man: for there hath beene as valiant, wise, godly, magnanimous, pollitick, iudicious, great spirited, and learned women as men: yea, our histories are filled with the glorious actions and famous conquests of women" (p. 164). Such contradictory passages occur in close proximity to each other: Theophrastan characters shared the formal controversy's chameleon ability to bestow equal conviction on both sides of the question.

The formal controversy is occasionally visible in the "gossips' meeting" genre (see chapter 9). In *The Gossips Greeting,* 1620, Henry Parrot disclaims conventionally, "I speake not in my disdaine of the vertuous, for some there are of that sex, in vertue vnparalleled, but of the vicious," and predicts reprisals: "I doubt not but I shall be carped at by many whose calumnious accusations I respect not." After thus playing formal detractor in one dedication, Parrot plays formal defender in another, listing good women—Lucrece, Susanna.

Considering the fact that early in *The Faerie Queene* Spenser casts himself as the chivalric champion of women, referring to the "alleageance and fast fealtie, / Which I do owe vnto all woman kind" (I.iii.1.6–7), it is intriguing to note that that poem shares a large number of *exempla* with the formal controversy. Of course, such *exempla* were widely available in other sources, but Spenser does treat them in the same way the formal controversy treats them. Especially interesting is the small group of *exempla* which were regularly employed by both formal attackers and defenders—Cleopatra, Semiramis, Medea; Spenser employs them with the same kind of ambivalence. Cleopatra appears at V.vii.2.6–9 as an example of feminine beauty's power over men, and Semiramis is admired at II.x.56.1–3, where she is compared with Bunduca (Boudicca) as a famous female military leader. But in Book I, Cleopatra and Semiramis are condemned as "proud wemen, vaine, forgetfull of their yoke" (I.v.50.1). Medea was honored by defenders for her skill in sorcery and damned by misogynists for murdering her brother: in Book II Spenser refers to Medea's "mighty charmes" (II.xii.44.5) and in Book V to the fact that "her brothers bones she scattered all about" (V.viii.47.4).

Spenser's main discussion of womanhood comprises Book III;[4] it succeeds the synthesis of Christian and humanist thought on the nature of the ideal human being which occupies Books I and II. Spenser thus rep-

licates the shape of Books I through III of *The Courtier,* where the first
two books delineate the ideal courtier and the third the ideal female courtier: Castiglione's formal defense may well have influenced Spenser's
treatment of womankind. Another section on womankind occurs in Book
V, the book of Justice. One explanation for this allegorical incongruity
may lie in the formal controversy's use of the judicial oration: the controversy's rhetorical structure belonged to the courtroom and was intimately connected with justice. The rhetorical method shaped the argument:
theorists advanced simplified types of the Good Woman and the Bad
Woman in their efforts to judge womankind innocent or guilty. The central portion of Book V is a trial—albeit trial by combat. In the confrontation between Britomart and Radigund, Good Woman meets Bad Woman;
the triumph of Good Woman is one prerequisite to the establishment of
the just society.

In considering the multiple genre of *The Faerie Queene,* at once epic
and romance, allegory and courtesy book, one should not overlook the
fact that while epic was primarily a masculine genre, romance was by
Spenser's day primarily a feminine genre. The majority of contemporary
writers who purveyed romance, mostly as prose fiction, were making a
special pitch to women readers; like them, Spenser addresses a number
of authorial intrusions to women. It is not impossible that the poem's
whole Arthurian framework may have been chosen with an eye to women
readers. If that were true, it would be reasonable to suspect that Spenser,
like the collectors of prose fiction, had dabbled a bit in the formal controversy.

As for the drama, the formal controversy's most important contribution was a character type, the stage misogynist, modelled partly on the
misogynist as he presented himself as a *persona* in formal attacks, with
touches of the misogynist as he was satirically portrayed by formal defenders. This character type is the subject of my chapter 11. But there
are other traces of the formal controversy in Renaissance drama.

Some plays attacking or defending women are set up as matched pairs,
as if in imitation of the formal controversy's antithetical orations: the
clearest example is Nathan Field's duo, *A Woman Is a Weathercock,* acted
1609–10, and *Amends for Ladies,* acted ca. 1610–1611.[5]

A Woman Is a Weathercock is structured like a formal attack on women.
Its dedicatory epistle offers the standard disclaimer: only bad women are
meant; good ones should take no offense. Conventionally, it promises
amends in a future work (in this case, *Amends for Ladies*). Like formal
treatises, it takes up Eve early on: Scudmore says of Bellafront, "Hadst
thou bin the Beginning of thy sex, / I thinke the Deuill in the Serpents
skin, / Had wanted Cunning to orecome thy goodnesse, / And all had
liu'd and dy'de in Innocency / The white Originall Creation" (I.i.32–38).

This reminder that a woman initiated Original Sin is followed shortly by "proof" that Bellafront is no better than Eve; Scudmore later declares: "Oh woman, woman, woman, woman, woman, / The cause of future and Originall sinne, / How happy (had you not) should we haue beene" (III.i.193–195). Like Nashe in *The Anatomy of Absurdity,* Field saves opponents the trouble of impugning the misogynist's motives: he shows Scudmore turning misogynist as a result of disappointment with Bellafront: "None of your base sex / Shall know me from this time" (II.i.206–207). Like the *narratio* of a formal attack, the play enumerates women's faults. First is lust: "Women, women. / Hee's mad by Heauen, that thinkes you any thing / But sensuall Monsters . . . / Ye fillers of the world with Bastardy, / . . . Know I do hate you all, will write against you" (II.i.202–213). Next, vengefulness: Kate orders her husband to kill a man for insulting her. Then, deceit: a pregnant servant considers whom to accuse of paternity, not particularly bothered about whether she has slept with potential defendants. As the proverb-title suggests, inconstancy is a theme; Bellafront has allegedly been inconstant in throwing over Scudmore; when she repents this decision, Scudmore sees her change of heart as further evidence of inconstancy. He dismisses her weeping as "tears at command" and is not worried by her suicide threat because "tis a full houre since she spake the word, / And God forbid, that any womans minde / Should not be chang'd and chang'd in a long houre" (IV.i.51–53). Feminine social climbing is introduced through Wagtail, pursuing a knight through her paternity suit. Female drunkenness is introduced through Lady Ninnie, whose obesity gives further proof of habitual self-indulgence. Scudmore summarizes women's faults in III.ii. The author closes with the standard plea, "Women, forgiue me" (V.ii.233). The play does not list wicked women in history but is otherwise pure dramatized Gosyn-hyll.

Field adopts the tone of the formal misogynist; all is in good fun. Most of the charges against women prove unfounded. Bellafront marries Scudmore, and even Wagtail shows promise of being a good wife. Bellafront's tears were real; she really did intend to commit suicide. The criticism of women is so half-hearted that Field hardly needed to apologize; this is in line with the tone of the formal attack.

Amends for Ladies, which Field billed as a recantation, resembles a formal defense. Its account of the hardships of a woman's life uses the old device of the maid/wife/widow debate. The play demonstrates that there are in the world at least some virtuous (i.e., chaste) women: the maid proves herself chaste by turning down a lewd proposition, the wife by passing a chastity test with flying colors, the widow by fending off a seducer in her very bedchamber. In addition, a citizen's wife resists the importunings of a lady-killing aristocrat, Sir John Love-all. Again, lists of virtuous women are absent; but the two plays (the only known plays Field wrote on his own) seem designed as an attack/defense pair on the model of nondramatic pairs like Gosynhyll's or Pyrrye's. As is characteristic of the Jacobean controversy, attack preceded defense.

Two other plays might be considered an attack/defense pair. Middleton's *Women Beware Women* and *More Dissemblers Besides Women* were bound together in their earliest surviving edition, 1657: Middleton may possibly have considered them a matched pair. *More Dissemblers* was onstage about the time the Swetnam controversy was in its early stages, *Women Beware Women* rather later. Middleton may have hoped to capitalize on current interest in the formal controversy to keep the house full.

In Thomas Heywood's *The Rape of Lucrece,* a dispute over wifely chastity furnishes the context for a small formal controversy. Sextus, the detractor, uses the balancing formula: "What's *Lucrece* but a woman, and what are women / But tortures and disturbance vnto men? / If they be foule th'are odious, and if faire, / Th'are like rich vessels full of poisonous drugs." Brutus, the defender, takes up the challenge in chivalric terms: "*Sextus* sit fast for I proclaime my selfe a womans champion, and shall unhorse thee else." The list of women's good qualities is absent; the argument proceeds to examples of virtuous women—in this case, to suit dramatic context, the wives of the various disputants. Brutus advances a compromise view to undercut misogynist stereotype:

> I hold some holy, but some apt to sinne,
> Some tractable, but some that none can winne. . . .
> The purest oare contains both Gold and drosse,
> The one all gaine, the other nought but losse.
> The one disgrace, reproch, and scandall taints,
> The other angels and sweet featur'd Saints.
>
> (pp. 207–208)

Following this vision of women as an unpredictable lot, some good and some bad, the company races off to determine whose wife is which. Most wives fail the test, ratifying Sextus's view; but more emphasized is the fidelity of Lucrece, always a defender's favorite.

Another small controversy takes place in George Wilkins's *The Miseries of Enforced Marriage,* where Ilford declares, "A man is made a beast by being married . . . Married men, ye are cuckolds," and Scarborow primly rejoins, "I construe more divinely of their sex: / Being maids, methinks they are angels; and being wives, / They are sovereign cordials that preserve our lives." Ilford insists that "women are the purgatory of men's purses, the paradise of their bodies, and the hell of their minds; marry none of them. Women are in churches saints, abroad angels, at home devils." To this proverbial slander, Scarborow stiffly replies:

> Men that traduce by custom, show sharp wit
> Only in speaking ill; and practice it
> Against the best creatures, divine women,
> Who are God's agents here, and the heavenly eye,
> By which this orb hath her maturity:
> Beauty in women gets the world with child,
> Without whom she were barren, faint and wild.
>
> (Act I)

In a momentary fit of remorse over his jealousy, Sir Timothy Trouble-some in Edward Sharpham's *Cupid's Whirligig* spews out a good deal of lore familiar to the formal defense:

> O who would abuse your sex, which truely knowes ye? O women were we not borne of ye? should we not then honour you? nurs'd by ye, and not regard ye? begotten on ye, and not loue ye?. . . Mã was made when nature was but an apprentice, but woman when she was a skilfull Mistresse of her Arte . . . Are not all Vices masculine, and Vertues feminine? are not the Muses the loues of the learned? doe not all noble spirrits followe the Graces because they are women, there's but one Phoenix and shee's a female: Is not the Princes and foundres of good artes Minerua, borne of the braine of highest Ioue, a woman? (Sig. D3)

One Slack in the same play trots out a few defenders' chestnuts too, including "If strength of bodie make the noblest creature, / Why should not Lyons be the kings of nature?" and a commiseration with mothers, who "bring forth [men's] brats with your liues ieopardie" (Sig. F3).

Other familiar notions crop up from time to time in plays. The idea that men should be kind to women out of gratitude to their mothers appears in *Much Ado about Nothing* (I.i.240–242), *Troilus and Cressida* (V.ii.129–130), and Dekker and Middleton's *The Honest Whore, Part I* (IV.i.148–150). Woman's creation from a crooked rib is mentioned in Dekker's *The Honest Whore, Part II* (I.iii.111–112). In *Much Ado*, Beatrice inverts the balancing formula by which contrasting female character types were usually disqualified from consideration as wives: "He that hath a beard is more than a youth, and he that hath no beard is less than a man. And he that is more than a youth is not for me, and he that is less than a man, I am not for him" (II.i. 38–41). When Beatrice says she will not marry "till God make men of some other metal than earth" (*Much Ado*, II.i.62–63), she is likely playing on the defenders' argument that woman was created of finer stuff than man, since Eve was made of flesh, Adam of earth (her next line, "Adam's sons are my brethren," reinforces this interpretation). The formal controversy's treatment of Eve hovers in the background of other passages as well. Where the wife-abuser Arthur in Thomas Heywood's *How a Man May Choose a Good Wife from a Bad* betrays in his reference to Adam's cursing "vile Eve" a tendency to blame his own difficulties on women, his patient wife recalls Eden with nothing but sympathy for the woman she twice calls "poor Eve": "Tempt no more, devil! / . . . Thou gett'st an apple to betray poor Eve, / Whose outside bears a show of pleasant fruit; / But the vile branch, on which this apple grew, / Was that which drew poor Eve from paradise" (III.ii). Edward Sharpham's *The Fleire* makes the delightful misogynistic point that Eve was the only chaste woman Nature ever made: in her day, no other men existed with whom she could cuckold her husband (Sig. [E4]ᵛ); such ingenious convention-twisting is reminiscent of the early Tudor controversy. Occasionally a familiar item from defense literature is transmuted into a vehicle for attack, as when the expression "mother-wit," for defenders an example of the way language reflects women's contribution to culture, is introduced in Middleton's *Your Five Gallants* to mean the wit that teaches women to be good at illicit sex (I.i.238–241). Such stock notions were available from sources other than the formal controversy, but there is occasional evidence to suggest that dramatists were directly familiar with documents of the formal controversy; Dekker and Webster's *Westward Ho,* for example, makes two explicit references to Book III of *The Courtier* (I.i.13–14, 91–94), a new edition of which had come out the year before the play was first acted (1604).

When Jonson staged misogyny, it is difficult to know whether he turned to the formal controversy or directly to classical sources on which the formal controversy had drawn. In *Epicoene,* when Truewit is trying to dissuade Morose from marrying by "thundring into him the incommodities of a wife, and the miseries of marriage" (II.iv.14–15), he echoes Juvenal's Sixth Satire in telling Morose his friends are amazed that, with all the convenient modes of suicide open to him (throwing himself from London Bridge or the steeple of St. Paul's, hanging himself in a garret), Morose has chosen the more difficult course of suicide by matrimony (II.ii.20–32). But he continues with the balancing formula: "If shee be faire, yong, and vegetous, no sweet meats euer drew more flies; all the yellow doublets, and great roses i' the towne will bee there. If foule, and crooked, shee'll bee with them, and buy those doublets and roses, sir. If rich, and that you marry her dowry, not her; shee'll raigne in your house, as imperious as a widow. If noble, all her kindred will be your tyrannes. If fruitfull, as proud as *May,* and humorous as *April;* she must haue her doctors, her midwiues, her nurses, her longings euery houre: though it be for the dearest morsell of man" (II.ii.66–76). This too, of course, was ultimately classical; but his apparent echoes of *The Bachelor's Banquet,* both in the passage above and in *Epicoene* (II.ii.91–113) and *Eastward Ho* (II.iii.60–81) suggest that Jonson was not averse to gleaning misogynistic convention from more recent works.

Like the *narratio* of a formal attack, Renaissance plays continually adduce the faults of women. Women are credulous: "Alas, poor women!
Make us but believe, / Being compact of credit, that you love us" (*Comedy
of Errors*, III.ii.21–22). Women are easily tempted: "You are a woman;
you haue flesh and blood enough in you; therefore be not tempted; keepe
the doore shut vpon all cummers" (Jonson's *Every Man in His Humour*,
III.v.27–29). Women affect contrariety: "For women, when they may,
will not, / But, being kept back, straight grow outrageous" (the anonymous *Arden of Feversham*, i.51–52). Women lack reason: "The mettell of
our minds, / Hauing the temper of true reason in them, / Affoorde a
better edge of argument / . . . Then the soft leaden wit of women can"
(Henry Porter's *Two Angry Women of Abington*, Sig. [B4]ᵛ); for judgement, women substitute impulse and irrational obstinacy: "I have no
other but a woman's reason. / I think him so, because I think him so"
(*Two Gentleman of Verona*, I.ii.23–24). Women cry at will: "A woman's
gift / To rain a shower of commanded tears" (*Shrew*, Ind. I.124–125).
Women cannot keep a secret: "How hard it is for women to keep counsel!" (*Julius Caesar*, II.iv.8–9); "Constant you are, / But yet a woman.
And for secrecy, / No lady closer, for I well believe / Thou wilt not utter
what thou dost not know, / And so far will I trust thee" (*1 Henry IV*,
II.iii.111–115). Women are coy; for them, "no" means "yes": "Play the
maid's part—still answer nay, and take it" (*Richard III*, III.vii.51); "Maids,
in modesty, say 'no' to that / Which they would have the profferer construe 'aye'" (*Verona*, I.ii.55–56). Women are nosy: "Hath he no part of
mother in him, ha? / No licorish womanish inquisitiuenesse?" (Marston's *Antonio's Revenge*, Sig. D). Women run to extremes: "Their loue is
lightly wonne and lightly lost, / And then their hate is deadly and ex-
treame" (*Abington*, Sig. E2). Of course, such material is proverbial and
stereotypical, and cannot be traced directly to the formal controversy.
But the formal controversy's having dignified such stereotypes, by trick-
ing them out as formal treatises with the trappings of intellectualism,
may have facilitated their passage into the plays, where they are voiced
so glibly and examined so seldom.

The favorite *exempla* of the formal controversy recur extensively in the
drama. In the 1560s, a number of such exemplary women became the
subjects of whole plays—John Phillip's *Comedy of Patient and Meek Grissill*,
1558–61, Thomas Garter's *Most Virtuous and Godly Susanna*, 1563–69,
R. B.'s *Appius and Virginia*, 1559–67, Lewis Wager's *Life and Repentance
of Mary Magdalene*, ca. 1550–66, the anonymous *Godly Queen Hester*,
published 1561. Three of these female title figures—Hester, Susanna,
and Mary Magdalene—figured prominently in works of the formal controversy published in 1560–61; Grissill and Virginia were popular *exempla* later in the formal controversy, possibly because of their use in

these plays, but must already in the 1560s have been seen in the context of the debate about women; Chaucer had used Grissill (Griselda) in his debate on women in *The Canterbury Tales,* and Virginia appears in Boccaccio's omnipresent *De Claris Mulieribus.* All these plays use their title figures as the formal defense had used them—as exemplars of virtuous womanhood; four of the plays further the sense of controversy by staging characters who play the role of the detractor of women—Politic Persuasion in *Grissill,* Ill Report in *Susanna,* Haphazard in *Appius and Virginia,* Infidelity in *Mary Magdalene.* This is the point at which the formal controversy most clearly intersects with Tudor drama, converging with the secular morality play to produce a dramatized formal defense of women. In part 3, I will discuss further the role of these Vice / detractors as early essays in the type of the stage misogynist; for now I will point out that the direct influence of the formal controversy on these plays is fairly clear: the only one of the five which does *not* stage the detractor of women, *Godly Queen Hester,* was likely published in 1561 only to take advantage of the formal controversy's popularity, since it was onstage as early as 1525—too early to be influenced, like the others, by the *persona* of the Renaissance formal controversy.

Interest in the formal controversy during the 1560s may also account for the appearance of certain other plays devoted to favorite *exempla*— Thomas Nuce's *Octavia* and John Studley's *Medea,* both translations from Seneca published in 1566, and a lost *Samson* play acted in 1567, from which Delilah cannot have been absent.

A second flurry of plays centering on prominent *exempla* of the formal controversy appeared in the late 1580s and 1590s, with one or two more in the early 1600s—an anonymous *Octavia,* now lost, acted 1590–91; Mary Herbert's *Antonius,* a translation from Garnier published in 1592, in which Cleopatra was prominent; Samuel Daniel's *Cleopatra,* published in 1594; Kyd's *Cornelia,* published in 1594, and *Portia,* now lost, both translated about the same time from Garnier; Samuel Brandon's *Virtuous Octavia,* published in 1598; the lost *Zenobia,* acted before 1592; the lost *Hester and Ahasuerus,* acted ca. 1580–94; Chettle, Dekker, and Haughton's *Patient Grissil,* acted 1600; Heywood's *Rape of Lucrece,* acted ca. 1607. This was not a period of outstanding activity in the formal controversy: the controversy's influence on these plays is much less clear than that on the plays of the 1560s; but the plays do make considerable comment on the nature of women and often give the sense that their heroines are being considered as exemplars.

On the level of literary allusion, the drama is particularly rich in references to the stock *exempla* of the formal controversy, often using them in the same ways the formal controversy had. Lucrece, fabled for chastity, is alluded to in *The Taming of the Shrew* (II.i.298), *Titus Andronicus*

(IV.i.91), *Twelfth Night* (II.v.103, 116), *Cymbeline* (II.ii.12–14), the anonymous *Lust's Dominion* (III.ii.5–6), and *Westward Ho* (IV.ii.154). Grissill, model of patience, is honored as a paragon next to Lucrece: "For patience she will prove a second Grissel, / And Roman Lucrece for her chastity" (*Shrew,* II.i.297–298). The insistence with which formal defenders praised Portia may be reflected in Shakespeare's allusions: "Her name is Portia, nothing undervalued / To Cato's daughter, Brutus' Portia" (*Merchant of Venice,* I.i.165–166), and in the way Shakespeare stages Portia: "I grant I am a woman, but withal / A woman that Lord Brutus took to wife. / I grant I am a woman, but withal / A woman well reputed, Cato's daughter. / Think you I am no stronger than my sex, / Being so fathered and so husbanded?" (*Julius Caesar,* II.i.292–297). Portia is also a positive example of womanhood in Marston's *Malcontent* (V.iii.31) and Markham and Machin's *The Dumb Knight* (I.i). Jonson alludes to Susanna in *Every Man in His Humour,* Shakespeare to the Susanna story in *Twelfth Night* and *The Merchant of Venice;* a version of the story appears in the plot of Dekker and Webster's *Northward Ho,* where the slanderers are called "two wicked elders" (I.iii.44). As in the formal controversy, Susanna is always a positive exemplar. Allusions to other familiar *exempla* are predictably negative: Xantippe, a favorite *exemplum* of the formal misogynist, is mentioned (appropriately) in *The Taming of the Shrew*—"as curst and shrewd / As Socrates' Xanthippe" (I.ii.70–71); Job's wife is "wicked" in *The Merry Wives of Windsor* (V.v.164–165); Delilah is a negative example of womanhood in *Eastward Ho* (II.ii.33–34).

Some *exempla* which were ambidextrous in the formal controversy— used by attackers and defenders alike—are similarly ambivalent in the drama. Eve usually exemplifies pride, bequeathed to later generations of women ("She is proud. . . . It was Eve's legacy, and cannot be ta'en from her" [*Verona,* III.i.341–343]); her part in the Fall is not overlooked: "What Eve, what serpent, hath suggested thee / To make a second fall of cursèd man?" (*Richard II,* III.iv.75–76); but she is sometimes viewed more favorably, as in *How a Man May Choose* (see above). Medea, likewise ambiguous in the tradition, is seen as a famous sorceress in *The Merchant of Venice* (V.i.11–13), as a mixer of potions in *Epicoene* (IV.i.149), and as an exemplar of violent womanhood in *2 Henry VI* (V.ii.57–59). In *The Brazen Age,* where she is staged, Heywood emphasizes both sides of her character: she is at first a powerful magician, but later she butchers her brother and strews his mangled limbs behind her. Another ambiguous figure, Cressida, is sometimes the type of a famous lover (*Venice,* V.i.1– 6), sometimes the "lazar kite" of Henryson's imaginings (*Henry V,* II.i.80; *Troilus and Cressida*). Helen of Troy, one of the frequentest *exempla* of both formal defenders and attackers, is an exemplar of feminine beauty in Marlowe's *Dr. Faustus,* Middleton's *The Family of Love* (II.ii.7–8),

Middleton's(?) *Blurt, Master-Constable* (IV.ii.25–26), the anonymous *The Fair Maid of the Exchange* (Sig. C3ᵛ, [K4]ᵛ), Jonson's *Volpone* (II.ii.238), *All's Well that Ends Well* (I.iii.74–75), Elizabeth Cary's *Mariam* (Sig. G2), and even the Prologue to *Troilus and Cressida,* a play which otherwise presents her as a whore. Several plays defend Helen on the grounds that she was kidnapped. In the anonymous *London Prodigal* (I.v), *The Malcontent* (I.iii.52), and *Troilus and Cressida,* however, Helen is a paradigm of female fickleness ripening towards prostitution. Heywood, in *1 Iron Age,* explicitly repudiates the kidnapping theory: Helen lustfully elopes with Paris of her own volition. Helen is memorialized at once for beauty and for faithlessness in *3 Henry VI* (II.ii.146–149). Cleopatra, another frequent example shared by defense and attack, is regarded in *Mariam* as a faded beauty of immoral life (Sig. Bᵛ) and as wanton, alluring, and deceitful (Sig. [G4]), but *The Malcontent* (V.iii.31) and *The Dumb Knight* (I.i) recall only the courageous suicide which expressed her faithfulness to her dead lover. In the several plays in which Cleopatra appears as a character, she is always portrayed with the full ambiguity of the tradition.

For such characters, however, the drama had many other potential sources. And there are enough instances where the old *exempla* are treated differently from the way the formal controversy treated them to cast doubt on the controversy's influence. Semiramis was ambiguous in the formal controversy, employed as an *exemplum* by both sides; in the drama she is almost always connected either with damnable lust (*Titus Andronicus,* II.i.22, II.iii.118, *Taming of the Shrew,* Ind., ii.39–41) or with overbearing womanhood (*Epicoene,* III.iv.57). The Amazons were *exempla* most congenial to the formal defense; but in the drama they are sternly disapproved (*1 Henry VI,* I.ii.104; *3 Henry VI,* I.iv.113–114; *King John,* V.ii.154–158; *Epicoene,* V.iv.234). Penelope, darling of formal defenders, receives rather shabby treatment in the drama. In *Coriolanus,* Penelope's weaving is said to have accomplished nothing but to fill Ithaca with moths (I.iii.92–94); Chapman's *The Widow's Tears* suggests that Penelope deliberately led her suitors on: "It is . . . a certain itch in female blood: they love to be su'd to." Two plays voice the opinion that under modern conditions Penelope would not have been able to hold out (*Malcontent,* III.ii.24–50, *Epicoene,* IV.i.72–75). A character in *The Fleire* asserts that modern filthy minds can suspect even Penelope: "I haue heard some say *Penelope* was a Puncke [i.e., prostitute], hauing no reason to suspect her, but because she set vp late a nightes" (Sig. Eᵛ). *2 Honest Whore* stages a prostitute named Penelope Whore-hound.

While it would be a mistake, then, to take the drama's use of female *exempla* as evidence of the formal controversy's direct influence, the drama's habit of adducing historical/literary example when moralizing on women's nature may have been reinforced, even if it was not created, by the formal controversy's constant rhetorical practices.

The formal controversy's influence is clearest in genres obviously slanted toward female readers, like prose fiction from the 1560s onwards, or morality plays of the 1560s with female title figures. The implication is that authors hoping to attract women readers turned for materials and strategies to the formal controversy, apparently assuming that the genre was smiled upon by women. Such an assumption, if it existed, forms one of the only links between the controversy and flesh-and-blood women of the Renaissance. The formal controversy was not the kind of feminism which reaches beyond the covers of books to transform living women; we should consider, at least briefly, why the Renaissance defense of women never developed into anything resembling feminism as we know it.

The main reason is obvious: such was never its intention. The formal defense was a literary game; most authors who delicately and wittily defended the fair sex against hypothetical slanders would have been merely baffled by talk of job discrimination or women's property rights. Even the rare authors who did come to grips with issues more immediately compelling than whether Helen of Troy was abducted, or whether ribs are crooked, failed to pursue to its logical conclusions the doctrine of sexual equality. And few accepted the doctrine of equality at all.

A primary barrier to belief in sexual equality was Christian doctrine. The fabric of society was Christian, and the Renaissance typically (and not without reason) interpreted the Scriptures as endorsing male dominance. Defender after defender came up against this wall and retired without surmounting it. You could rebut Gosynhyll, but you couldn't rebut God. Some satiric works, like *The Virtuous Schoolhouse of Ungracious Women* (ca. 1550) or *The Proud Wife's Paternoster* (1560), portray shrews as ungodly: some shrews resent the church; others attend church in body only while their minds are elsewhere. Such portraits were a calculated slur on strong-minded women, but they offer a hint that women desiring liberty and equality were beginning to sense it was Christian doctrine which stood in their way. Occasionally, one glimpses the dissatisfaction of living women with the church's orthodox position on female subjection. After approving from the pulpit of the "law of Nations" which denied a married woman the right to own any property, even her own clothing, the Rev. William Gouge was astonished at the public outcry against his views. In his published marriage sermons, *Of Domesticall Duties,* he reminisced, "I remember that when these Domesticall Duties were first uttered out of the pulpit, much exception was taken against the application of a wives subiection to the restraining of her from disposing the common goods of the family without, or against her husband's consent" (pp. 3–4). But women opposed not only the law but also the fundamental biblical doctrine of wifely subjection! In a chapter entitled "A fond [i.e., foolish] conceit, that Husband and Wife are equall," Gouge marvels that "many wives . . . thinke themselves every way as good as their husbands, and no way inferiour to them" (p. 273). He records wonderingly that for showing wives their duty to be in subjection (a task every Protestant marriage preacher took on himself), he had been reviled as "an hater of women." Such evidence suggests that women were growing dissatisfied with the role the Bible had assigned them. But Christianity's precepts ran deep in everyone's character. Dissatisfaction with women's subjection was probably translated into irritation with the Rev. William Gouge. Perhaps a less abrasive preacher could be found; perhaps a change of congregation was in order. Few Renaissance women concluded that the problem lay with the Bible and consequently questioned their faith. Renaissance Englishwomen were often rebels, but refusing allegiance to a male chauvinist God was farther than they were prepared to go. The formal controversy, committed from the start to biblical arguments and *exempla,* and growing more pious than ever in Jacobean times, did nothing to encourage women either to question their religion or to protest against the male-centered way in which theologians and preachers interpreted Scripture.[6]

In secular terms, too, equality was foreign to the Renaissance mentality. Order was hierarchical. God was superior to angels, angels to man, man to animals, animals to plants. Within humanity, the monarch occupied a position parallel to God's in the universe; below monarch was aristocracy, below aristocracy the commonalty. All these were in subjection to the monarch and were called "subjects." The clergy had its hierarchy. According to Hooker, kinds of law had their hierarchy. And the sexes had their hierarchy too. Throughout the universe, some classes were in subjection to others, and women were in subjection to men. The husband's position in the family was parallel to God's in the universe: William Whately, noting in a marriage sermon, *A Bride-Bush,* that "in all good things the husband should excell more, because his place is higher and more excellent," called the husband "a little God in the family" (p. 113).

Even in this essentially feudal universe, the order of priority was sometimes reversed. While the wife expressed subservience in feudal diction when she called her husband "my lord," the roles were reversed in courtly/Petrarchan love: the man called the woman "my lady" or "my sovereign." ("My mistress" also suggested servant status; lovesick male suitors were often called "servants," which under the impetus of misogynistic writing eventually became a euphemism for "illicit lover.") What was not possible was a relationship of absolute equality. The great debate in Chaucer's *Canterbury Tales* concerns which sex should have "sovereignty" in marriage, not whether marital sovereignty should exist at all. Spouses in innumerable ballads fought for the breeches, assuming that *somebody* had to wear the breeches. The Renaissance household, like the medieval household, could not accommodate two pairs of breeches, knee to knee in equality. Just as the Renaissance could not conceive of democracy as other than mob rule, so the idea of marital equality was foreign, strange, hardly capable of entering the mind. And this extended to all relationships between the sexes, not only marriage.

But the system was disintegrating. Political theorists didn't know what to do with the middle class, just as theorists of men and women didn't know what to do with the various hermaphrodites of fashion and behavior: neither fit into the hierarchy. And democracy was stirring. Puritans, preaching each man's right to interpret Scripture by his own inner light, were seeking to abolish church hierarchy. The middle class was wresting power from king and aristocracy. All this would soon come to civil war, and Puritans and middle class would win. The hierarchical view of order would ultimately break down, and when it did, feminism could be born. But this did not happen in time to benefit Renaissance women.[7]

Another obstacle to feminism was the Renaissance habit of conducting all arguments in moral terms. Women's economic deprivation and political disenfranchisement were seldom discussed because formal argument got bogged down on whether women are good or bad. Because controversialists assumed that the only questions of real importance were moral questions, attacks and defenses concentrated on issues plainly moral, such as lechery and deceit, at the expense of questions more legal or social, such as women's right to own property, or shared responsibility for housework and child care. These latter issues were not ignored, but in comparison with "moral" issues were greatly deëmphasized.

The moral slant simply confused many issues. Take talkativeness. Sometimes a wife's loquacity was viewed as a mere irritant to her chagrined husband; in the drama, a number of comic scenes take this view. But the formal controversy saw morality even here. Misogynists saw women's talkativeness as morally reprehensible: it shaded off into scolding in one direction, deceit in the other; defenders argued that female loquacity was good, a sign of superior humanity: speech distinguishes mankind from the beasts. The very effort involved in deciding whether talkativeness is good or bad, as well as the rhetorical habit that reduced all questions to good versus bad, prevented analytic examination. Some questions could be asked about female talkativeness that would allow the argument to go somewhere. For example: are women really more talkative than men, or do their speeches loom larger because men assume that women have nothing worthwhile to say? If it is true that women talk more than men, why is it true? Does a woman inundate her husband with words when he comes home simply because she has had no adult company all day? Do women find outlet for their energies in talk because so few other outlets are permitted them? Is there physiological or neurological evidence that women have the more highly developed faculty of speech? Not all these questions could have been answered in the Renaissance, but all of them could have been asked. They were not asked: the restriction of debate to moral considerations prevented the asking.

The area of modern feminist concern most conspicuous by its absence from the formal controversy is the economic. Access to paid work outside the home, equal pay for equal work, legal protection from discrimination in employment, the right to own and dispose of property, maintenance for female single parents—none of these issues was seriously examined. The only one that received any attention, in or out of the formal controversy, was property ownership for women, which was opposed by preachers on moral grounds. The Renaissance was hardly oblivious to economic questions. Writers who lived during a crisis of economic change—the shift to a money-based economy, the growth of trade and manufacture, the centralization in cities of the primary means of production, the change from a social system based on heredity to a social system based on money; in short, the institutionalization of capitalism—did not fail to notice what was going on. But they never developed a vocabulary or a theory to deal with economic matters. They could not come to terms with women's economic position because, again, they reduced economic questions to moral questions. What we call capitalism, they called greed. The epithet is apt enough, but not useful. Capitalism's ills might be approached through legislation; the sin of greed called forth no more practical solutions than prayer.

Far from demanding legal protection for women from abuses of capitalism which were causing women to starve, moralists blamed economic ills on women. Almost nobody suggested that the extremely high incidence of prostitution had economic causes; it was a moral evil, attributable to prostitutes' lust and greed. Few writers saw that prostitution was the only employment available to a large number of women. Wives who did not work outside the home, because they were raising a family, because no jobs were open to them, or because their rich husbands were keeping an ornamental wife as a status symbol, were subjected to the moral charge of idleness. Wives who worked in their husbands' shops were caricatured as cuckolders. Women who as consumers helped to keep the vast clothing industry afloat were accused of extravagance. Women who wanted money of their own were derided in "gossip" poetry as tavern haunters. Almost nobody looked at the economic system's effect on women: some writers were engaged in blaming economic ills on women and others in defending women from this moral charge.

But while Renaissance literary treatment of such economic questions as prostitution, unemployment among women, female sartorial extravangance, and control of household monies was wholly without economic or sociological sophistication, at least these topics were aired, in the drama, in ballad, in sermon, in poems about gossips; in many genres, the topic of women and money was prosecuted with a good deal of heat and smoke. From all this full-blooded passion, the formal controversy remained sedately remote through the whole of its history, seldom coming closer to the problem of prostitution than to mention the classical courtesan Lais as an exemplar of vicious womanhood, or closer to female unemployment than to bandy abstractions about feminine idleness.

The formal controversy may in fact have actively prevented the development of true feminist debate. Formal defenders only obscured the issue by focussing on alleged slander, and their very rhetorical method was a barrier to constructive debate. The judicial oration was an unfortunate choice: it cast Woman as defendant, restricting the argument to clearing her of charges. The alternative (or simultaneous) posture of chivalric champion was also an unhappy device. The damsel in distress is not in a good position to demand legislation against discriminatory hiring practices. If the defender of women emerges through his imagery as an odd hybrid—part barrister and part knight in shining armor—the women so defended emerge as framed-up damsels in distress. Such images are not conducive to the argument for equality. The very existence of the formal controversy may have preëmpted more useful approaches. Despite the atmosphere of game, formal attacks and defenses were eruditely written; their classical form and their Christian-humanist opinions and *exempla* gave the impression of true intellectual theory; their rigid, closed structure imparted an air of the last word's having been said. The existence of so many treatises created the illusion that the topic was being discussed in a responsible way. The question of women, it must have seemed, was being taken care of.

To the cynical, formal attacks and formal defenses might seem two sides of the same coin. Attacks criticize bad women for gadding about, defenses praise good women for staying home; this is only negative versus positive reinforcement. Attacks and defenses disagree, or pretend to disagree, about whether there are more bad than good women in the world; but their definitions of female goodness and badness are identical. The formal defense ultimately accomplished little more than to proffer a stereotype of the good woman to complement the attack's stereotype of the bad. I rather prefer the bad. I would rather be Semiramis than Patient

Grissill any day of the week. Modern feminists who have called themselves shrews and bitches have recognized in those ancient opprobrious terms male attempts to discredit and stamp out qualities of assertiveness that women have always had and men have always feared.

If the formal controversy had any purpose at all beyond literary delight, then the purpose of attacks and defenses was likely the same—to enforce a certain mode of behavior. There is no inconsistency at all in an author's attacking women in one treatise and defending them in the next, as Gosynhyll and others did, if the whole formal controversy was behavior modification—a misogynistic slap in the face if you misbehave, a pat on the head by a barrister in shining armor if you behave. This is Spenser's avowed method in Book III of *The Faerie Queene,* where he encourages chastity in women by the positive example of Britomart, Florimell, Amoret, and Belphoebe, and discourages unchastity by the negative example of the Squire of Dames' fruitless quest for chaste women and of that second Helen of Troy, the promiscuous Hellenore. Tellingly, the two negative examples are comic: their broad sexual humor, so rare in Spenser, suggests the basically comic *modus operandi* of the formal attack on women. When Spenser apologizes to women readers for including Hellenore's sexual orgies with satyrs, he uses the formal misogynist's standard disclaimer that good women should not be offended, since he censures only the bad; but he explains more clearly than did formal misogynists the usefulness of misogynistic anecdotes:

> Redoubted knights, and honorable Dames,
>   To whom I leuell all my labours end,
>   Right sore I feare, least [i.e., lest] with vnworthy blames
> This odious argument my rimes should shend,
> Or ought your goodly patience offend,
> Whiles of a wanton Lady I do write,
> Which with her loose incontinence doth blend [i.e.,
> blemish]
> The shyning glory of your soueraigne light . . .
> But neuer let th'ensample of the bad
>   Offend the good: for good by paragone
> Of euill, may more notably be rad [i.e., read],
> As white seemes fairer, macht with blacke attone;
> Ne all are shamed by the fault of one.
>
>   (III.ix. 1–2)

It is largely true, I think, that the formal controversy prevented serious questioning by creating the illusion of real debate. Whatever its literary merits, as feminism the debate was a sham. Most of the time, it was worse than nothing: it blocked constructive thinking. But occasionally it was better than nothing: it kept the topic alive long enough for a real thinker to step in and engage real questions, for Agrippa to tackle the question of cultural influences on female behavior, for Castiglione to attack the seemingly innocuous habit of antifeminist jesting, for "Constantia Munda" to refuse to accept a military definition of men and women. For these isolated moments, women can thank the formal controversy; as far as feminism is concerned, only for these moments was the wilderness of Jezebels and Susannas worth creating.

The conservatism of both defenses and attacks may itself, however, bespeak the stirrings of more liberal thought in the outside world. Keith Thomas has postulated that Renaissance women's "actual independence . . . was always greater than theory allowed; and part of the evidence lies in the very frequency with which that independence was denounced."[8] Was literary misogyny itself a response to women's actual freedom? Renaissance attacks on women, by this view, were defensive, a paradox reflected in the fact that Renaissance formal attacks arose originally in response to defenses, rather than the other way around; misogyny was a method of fortifying the male's dominant position against the incursions of increasingly libertarian women. The same can probably be said of the defense: attacks and defenses were complementary efforts at keeping women housebound, nurturing, chaste, modest, and silent. But the nature and behavior of real Renaissance women can be deduced through the formal controversy only through a "no smoke without fire" interpretation of lectures on home keeping and chastity. It is to literature with a less tenuous relationship to real life that I now turn.

NOTES

1. STC 6451, dated ca. 1560. Utley (pp. 122–23) discusses the argument for an earlier date. He cites *Les Cent Nouvelles Nouvelles,* ca. 1435, as the source of the modern tales.

2. By one "Weddirburne," *The Bannatyne Manuscript,* III, pp. 327–34. The Bannatyne Manuscript is a four-volume compilation, made in 1568, of poems about women, both satiric and favorable. Although the manuscript is of great value to anyone interested in literature about women in this period, it is sparse in documents of the formal controversy.

3. *The Maitland Quarto Manuscript,* pp. 86–97. Almost all Arbuthnot's *exempla* can be found in Gosynhyll's two poems, and of these, Arbuthnot's Lucretia, Portia, and Penelope occur in the same order in which they occur in *Mulierum Pean,* while Arbuthnot's Jezebel, Herodias, and Delilah occur in the same order in which they occur in *The School House;* Herodias is an *exemplum* otherwise rare in the controversy. In addition, ll. 141–44 of Arbuthnot seem to echo stanza 5, Sig. [A]ᵛ of *The School House.* Arbuthnot's poem was composed ca. 1558–83.

4. Book III is not called the book of Womanhood, but the book of

Chastity. If this seems a narrowing of the ideal, it was a common Renaissance reduction: chastity was the one absolute demand made on virtuous womanhood. Sir Thomas Overbury was almost alone in protesting against the reduction of "virtue" in a woman to the niggling virtue of chastity: true virtue in women, as in men, he argued, comprises doing the good more than omitting the evil: "A *Wife* that's *Good*, doth *Chaste and more* containe, / For *Chaste* is but an *Abstinence* from ill: / And in a *Wife* that's *Bad*, although the *best* / of qualities; yet in a *Good* the *least*" (*A wife now the widdow of Sir T. Overbury*).

5. *The Plays of Nathan Field*, ed. William Peery. Throughout my discussions of drama, I accept the conclusions of the Harbage/Schoenbaum *Annals of English Drama* on dating and authorship.

6. The excellent opening chapter of Rogers's *Troublesome Helpmate* traces the way in which generations of medieval and Renaissance commentators distorted biblical texts to render them misogynistic. The deeply rooted biblical assumption of male superiority, however, required very little revision by Renaissance male supremacists. See the chapter on theology in Maclean's *The Renaissance Notion of Woman*, which demonstrates that "in theological terms woman is . . . the inferior of the male by nature" (p. 27).

7. Madelon Gohlke suggests that "the breakdown of hierarchical modes of thought, of vertical ways of imagining experience, finds its deepest resistance in our habits of imagining the relations between the sexes" (" 'I wooed thee with my sword': Shakespeare's Tragic Paradigms," in *The Woman's Part: Feminist Criticism of Shakespeare*, p. 163). This is borne out by the disappointing failure of seventeenth-century egalitarian thought to undermine middle-class dogmatism about women's proper role.

8. Keith Thomas, "The Changing Family," p. 1226.

Part Two

❧

Toward the Hermaphrodite

Swift *Hermes, Aphrodite!* him ô heare
Who was your sonne! who both your names doth beare!
May every man, that in this water swims,
Returne halfe-woman, with infeebled lims.

—Ovid, *Metamorphosis*
(Sandys translation)

Had ye them seene, ye would haue surely thought,
　That they had beene that faire *Hermaphrodite,*
　Which that rich *Romane* of white marble wrought,
　And in his costly Bath causd to bee site:
　So seemd those two, as growne together quite.

—Spenser, *The Faerie Queene*

The body of Nature is most truly described as biform . . . for
there is no nature which can be regarded as simple, every one
seeming to participate and be compounded of two. . . . All
things are in truth biformed.

—Bacon, "Pan, Or Nature"

CHAPTER SIX

Hic Mulier and Haec-Vir

In 1620, a controversy about women which had been simmering for nearly fifty years came to a boil in two essays, *Hic Mulier,* an attack on women who wear masculine clothing, and *Haec-Vir,* an answering defense which attacks male foppishness. In the unpromising context of fashion, the two essays really joined combat on the nature of the sexes. The perplexities of disentangling art from life, which dog the formal controversy at its every twist and turn, are diminished when we consider the *hic mulier/haec vir* controversy. The historical events surrounding the publication of these two essays are a matter of record;[1] they include public pronouncements by King James, comments in personal letters, remarks in sermons.

The transvestite controversy began, as nearly as we can tell, in about the 1570s, when some women began adopting masculine attire. In one of the earliest formal satires in English, *The Steele Glas,* 1576, George Gascoigne mentioned the new fashion in the course of denouncing other sorts of extravagant and ridiculous feminine attire: "Women? masking in mens weedes? / With dutchkin dublets, and with Ierkins iaggde? / With Spanish spangs, and ruffes set out of France, / With high copt hattes, and fethers flaunt a flaunt?" (Sig. Ii^v). But where Gascoigne dismissed this female transvestism as an outlandish fashion, Phillip Stubbes, writing seven years later, characterized the fashion as a deliberate challenge to the immutability of sexual distinctions:

> The Women . . . haue dublets & Jerkins as men haue . . . , but-toned vp the brest, and made with wings, welts and pinions on the shoulder points, as mans apparel is, for all the world, & though this be a kinde of attire appropriate onely to man, yet they blush not to wear it, and if they could as wel chaunge their sex, & put on the kinde of man, as they can weare apparel assigned onely to man, I think they would as verely become men indeed as now they degen-erat from godly sober women, in wearing this wanton lewd kinde of attire, proper onely to man.

It is writtē in the 22 of *Deuteronomie,* that what man so euer weareth womans apparel is accursed, and what woman weareth mans apparel is accursed also. . . . Our Apparell was giuen vs as a signe distinctiue to discern betwixt sex and sex, & therfore one to weare the Apparel of another sex, is to participate with the same, and to adulterate the veritie of his owne kinde. Wherefore these Women may not improperly be called *Hermaphrodita,* that is, Monsters of bothe kindes, half women, half men. (*Anatomy of Abuses,* Sig. [F5]–[F5]ᵛ)

Stubbes worried about male effeminacy as well: "We haue brought our selues into suche . . . effeminat condition, as we may seeme rather nice dames, and yonge gyrles, than puissante agents, or manlie men, as our forefathers haue bene" (Sig. Eᵛ–Eii). In 1588, William Averell wrote of the man-clothed woman, "though they be in sexe Women, yet in attire they appeare to be men, and are like Androgini, who counterfayting the shape of either kind, are in deede neither . . . they are neither men nor women, but plaine Monsters" (*A meruailous combat of contrarieties* [Sig. B1ᵛ]). Where Stubbes has spoken of hermaphrodites, Averell speaks of androgynes; both call such women "monsters."

The hermaphrodite was sometimes smiled upon in the Renaissance. The formal controversy, partly on the authority of Plato's myth of hermaphrodism in the *Symposium,* had called upon the hermaphrodite image to symbolize the essential oneness of the sexes, adducing the bisexuality of Greek divinities and occasionally even hinting at the early Christian notion that God is androgynous, as in Castiglione's "It is read in Scripture that God facioned male and female to his likeness" (*The Courtier,* p. 226); the old idea that Adam was hermaphroditic and that the separation into two sexes constituted the Fall, officially heretical since the thirteenth century, lingers in the background of the several defenses of women which view Adam as incomplete, a half-being, before the creation of Eve. Numerous literary works in the Renaissance use hermaphrodism for artistic and symbolic purposes, without denouncing it as monstrous: for example, Geoffrey Fenton's *Monophylo,* 1572, uses myths of androgyny as fables of love; Spenser in *The Faerie Queene* employs a vision of the *Venus biformis* as "the root of all that ioyous is, . . . welspring of blisse" (IV.x.41–47), and the original ending of Book III symbolizes the perfect union of true lovers by reference to a "faire *Hermaphrodite*"; Donne uses the hermaphrodite image in reference to the clerical calling.[2] Elyot in *The boke named The gouernour* implies that the Golden Mean which ideally governs human behavior is a hermaphroditic whole, wherein "masculine" fierceness, audacity, willful opinion, and desire for glory are moderated by "feminine" mildness, timorousness, tractability, and benignity to produce the ideal means between these extremes—severity, magnanimity, constancy, and honor (Book I). The central mystery of *Twelfth Night* is that Cesario is a being made up of both Viola and Sebastian—a hermaphroditic symbol of wholeness that calls forth love from Olivia and Orsino alike.

But the Renaissance was also heir to a tradition of fear of and contempt for physical androgyny and transvestism which went back to the Greeks; as Nancy Hayles points out, "Part of the ambivalence of androgyny comes . . . from a contrast between the symbolic and the concrete; what may be admired in the abstract becomes detestable when manifested in the flesh." Hayles traces the way Ovid's myth of Hermaphroditus became in Renaissance exegesis an emblem of bestial transformation, male effeminacy, and impotence, the way *hermaphrodite* became a term of contempt for either the effeminate male or the mannish woman.[3] Marie Delcourt, too, comments on the harsh light in which androgyny was usually viewed when it left the pages of philosophy and poetry and invaded real life: "Androgyny is at the two poles of sacred things. Pure concept, pure vision of the spirit, it appears adorned with the highest qualities. But once made real in a being of flesh and blood, it is a monstrosity."[4] There was certainly no shortage of preachers, satirists, and epigrammatists to stigmatize the man-clothed woman as a monstrosity; what is remarkable is that given the longevity and intensity of the tradition that bemonstered the nonsymbolic hermaphrodite, the real-life transvestites should have been defended as stoutly as they were, and viragos treated as favorably as literature often treated them. The ambivalence with which the hermaphrodite had always been greeted allowed Jacobean moralists to use the hermaphrodite image either to damn or to praise modern sex-role changes. It is surprising to see how many writers used it for praise.

Whether praising or damning, comment on women in masculine attire was almost always accompanied by remarks on male effeminacy, indicating that the issue went beyond fashion to embrace the compelling question, what really is the difference between men and women?

During the 1590s and early 1600s, the female transvestite movement was apparently quiescent: women in male attire received almost no literary attention, even from the formal satirists of the late 1590s, who—hungering and thirsting as they were after abuses to satirize—would hardly have let the man-clothed woman escape censure had she been a prominent feature of the London landscape. Literature again took notice of women wearing breeches and sporting weaponry beginning around 1606: Henry Parrot in *The Movs Trap* (epigram 24), 1606, and Richard Niccols in *The Cuckow* (Sig. C2ᵛ), 1607, both satirize women in male attire. From then on, the movement gained momentum, public and literary interest in it climaxing between 1615 and 1620.

In 1615, the year Swetnam published the *Arraignment of Lewd, Idle,*

Froward and Unconstant Women, Thomas Adams was having a good grumble about women in masculine attire: certain apparitions stalking the London streets seemed to be "both he and shee. For if they had no more euident distinction of sexe, then they have to shape, they would be all man, or rather all woman: for the *Amazons* beare away the Bell . . . *Hic mulier* will shortly bee good latine, if this transmigration hold: For whether on horsebacke, or on foot, there is no great difference."[5] By 1620, *hic mulier* was a by-word for the man-clothed woman, and the controversy about a fashion which had exercised moralists since the 1570s finally came to a full boil.

An odd alliance of satirists, epigrammatists, and preachers kept up a running commentary on man-clothed women all through these years. William Gamage included an epigram "On the feminine Supremacie" in *Linsi-Woolsie* in 1613: "I often hard [i.e., heard], but never read till now, / That Women-kinde the Codpeeces did weare; / But in those Iles, the men to women bow, / Which do their names of male, and female beare." Richard Niccols offered another in *The Furies,* 1614:

> T'is strange to see a Mermaide, you will say,
> Yet not so strange, as that I saw to day,
> One part of that which 'boue the waters rise,
> Is woman, th' other fish, or fishers lies.
> One part of this was man or I mistooke. . . .
> The head is mans, I iudge by hat and haire,
> And by the band and doublet it doth weare,
> The bodie should be mans, what doth it need?
> Had it a codpeice, 'twere a man indeed.
>
> (Sig. [A6]-[A6]ᵛ)

Henry Hutton's *Follie's Anatomie,* 1619, devotes one satire to "a woman creature most insatiate. / See the incarnate monster of her sex, / Play the virago, vnashamde, perplext. / See *Omphale* her effeminated king, / Basely captiue; make him doe any thing" (Sig. [B6]). The reference to an "effeminated king" strikes me as a little risky in the reign of James.

Preachers, too, took arms against the fashion. John Williams, in *A Sermon of Apparell,* 1619, declared that God "diuided male and female, but the deuill hath ioyn'd them, that *mulier formosa,* is now become *mulier monstrosa supernè,* halfe man halfe woman" (p. 7). Williams provides the fascinating information that women attended church in masculine attire, which took almost everyone's attention away from the sermon: "What flesh and blood hath his thoughts so staunch, but must be distracted in his Church-deuotions, at the *prodigious* apparition of our *women?* . . . For a woman therefore to come vnto a Church . . . halfe male, and halfe female . . . lifting vp towards his throne *two plaister'd eies* and a *polled* head . . . In *Sattin* (I warrant you) in stead of sackecloath . . . standing most manly vpon her *points,* by wagging a *Feather* to defie the *World,* and carrying a *dagger,* . . . to enter Gods house, as if it were a Play-house . . . what deuotion in the world but must start aside?" (pp. 20–22). Williams rages against extravagant male attire too; and this put him in a difficult position, since the sermon was preached at court. This embarrassment no doubt accounts for Williams's proving with weighty biblical arguments that for a king and courtiers to wear extravagant clothing is quite acceptable in the sight of God.

Entered in the Stationer's Register in December 1619, Thomas Gataker's sermon *Marriage Dvties Briefely Covched Togither* spends even more time than usual demonstrating wives' inferiority; this occupies fully a third of the sermon. Playing on the ancient symbolism of Adam's rib, Gataker uses "mankind" or masculine women as an example of modern marital insubordination: "As it were . . . a thing prodigious and monstrous in nature for the rib in the body to stand either equall with or aboue the head: so . . . that a mankinde woman or a masterly wife is euen a monster in nature" (pp. 9–10). Gataker's "prodigious" and "monstrous" ally him with Stubbes and Averell: all regard the absolute line between the sexes as a law of nature. (The sight of a man-clothed woman almost automatically prompted appeals to Nature: even the admirable Moll Cutpurse is at one point called "a creature . . . nature hath brought forth / To mock the sex of woman . . . a thing / One knows not how to name: her birth began / Ere she was all made: 'tis woman more than man, / Man more than woman" [Dekker and Middleton's *The Roaring Girl,* I.i.248–253].)

A month after Gataker's sermon was registered, King James himself entered the lists. On January 25, 1620, John Chamberlain wrote in a letter:

> Yesterday the bishop of London called together all his Clergie about this towne, and told them he had expresse commaundment from the King to will them to inveigh vehemently and bitterly in theyre sermons, against the insolencie of our women, and theyre wearing of brode brimd hats, pointed dublets, theyre haire cut short or shorne, and some of them stillettaes or poinards, and such other trinckets of like moment; adding withall that yf pulpit admonitions will not reforme them he wold proceed by another course; the truth is the world is very far out of order, but whether this will mend yt God knowes.

Chamberlain clarified the threat "he wold proceed by another course," and reported on the progress of the campaign, on February 12, 1620: "Our pulpits ring continually of the insolence and impudence of women:

and to helpe the matter forward the players have likewise taken them to taske, and so to the ballades and ballad-singers, so that they can come no where but theyre eares tingle; and yf all this will not serve the King threatens to fall upon theyre husbands, parents or frends that have or shold have powre over them and make them pay for yt."[6] This letter suggests that playwrights and balladeers, as well as preachers, felt obligated to fulfil the king's command. However, extant evidence does not suggest a sudden increase in literary barbs aimed at man-clothed women.[7] Literature had had plenty to say about women in masculine attire before King James burst upon the scene.

Women of any sort, let alone viragos, received short shrift from James, whose misogyny was legendary: "He piques himself on great contempt for women," reported the French ambassador.[8] His relationship with his favorites Carr and Buckingham was overtly homosexual. As I shall argue in the next chapter, James's pacifism helped create a climate where distinctions between the sexes broke down; but homosexuality allowed the nation's leading woman-hater to reëstablish barriers. Male homosexuality was peacetime's answer to the male-bonding of soldiers (which, of course, could also be homosexual): both excluded women. But homosexuality lent James and his courtiers, in the eyes of many observers, exactly the quality that James as woman-hater should have despised—effeminacy. Most courtiers in Jacobean literature are portrayed as effeminate in varying degrees. James's attack on man-clothed women was the real-life equivalent of a prominent literary motif—the confrontation between effeminate man and aggressive woman.

The anonymous *Hic Mulier; or, The Man-Woman: Being a Medicine to cure the Coltish Disease of the Staggers in the Masculine-Feminines of our Times* was registered on February 9, 1620. A woodcut on the title page shows one woman being fitted with a man's plumed hat, which she admires in a mirror; another woman awaits, in a barber's chair, the shearing of her locks. The essay plunges without preamble into why *hic mulier* is now good Latin: "For since the daies of *Adam* women were neuer so Masculine; Masculine in their genders and whole generations, from the Mother, to the youngest daughter, Masculine in Number, from one to multitudes; Masculine in Case, euen from the head to the foot; Masculine in Moode, from bold speech, to impudent action; and Masculine in Tense: for (without redresse) they were, are, and will be still most Masculine, most mankinde, and most monstrous" (Sig. A3).

The author firmly believes that women have a fixed nature: they are "crownes of natures worke, the complements of mens excellencies, and the Seminaries of propagation"; they "maintaine the world, support mankinde," are "modest," and "gentle" (Sigs. A3ᵛ, C2). The existence of masculine women does not invalidate this stereotype; such women are merely monsters of unnaturalness: in describing them, the author uses the words *deforme(d)* and *deformitie(s)* twenty-one times in the essay's eighteen pages. Such a woman is "most pernicious to the Commonwealth, for she hath power by example to doe it a world of iniury" (Sig. C2); but her aggressive behavior does not cast a moment's doubt on the weakness and tenderness of feminine nature: "Farre bee such cruelty from the softnesse of their gentle dispositions" (Sig. C2).

The author often connects transvestites' aggressiveness with moral laxity: they "haue laid by the bashfulnesse of [their] natures, to gather the impudence of Harlots" (Sig. [A4]). Dressing as men implies a mode of behavior, from swearing ("vile and horrible prophanations") to brawling ("ruffianly and vnciuill actions" [Sig. Bᵛ]). Bobbed hair is immodest: Nature designed hair to hide bosoms. Women who repudiate femininity will find all the romance gone out of their lives, "lose all the charmes of womens naturall perfections, haue no presence to winne respect, no beauty to inchaunt mens hearts" (Sig. B3ᵛ). The author quotes a stanza of *The Faerie Queene* (V.v.25) dealing with the horrendous implications of Radigund's transvestism (Sig. C2ᵛ), and labels man-clothed women "these new *Hermaphrodites*" (Sig. C2ᵛ). He gives the impression that vast numbers of women were involved. The fashion cut across social barriers; it was "as frequent in the demy-Palaces of Burgars and Citizens, as it is either at Maske, Tryumph, Tilt-yard, or Play-house" (Sig. C). It is "an infection that emulates the plague, and throwes it selfe amongst women of all degrees, all deserts, and all ages; from the Capitoll to the Cottage" (Sig. Bᵛ-B2). Significantly, the author blames city life for the disturbing sex-role changes (Sig. [B4]ᵛ-Cᵛ): I shall shortly discuss the effect of urbanization on literary images of women.

This author describes a costume consisting of a broad-brimmed hat with feather, a French doublet (unbuttoned to reveal naked breasts), bobbed hair, and a sword. At times he speaks of breeches, at other times of skirts. (The women in the title-page woodcut are in skirts.) Other descriptions of man-clothed women sometimes speak of skirts rather than breeches. I have seen woodcuts of armed women in doublets, ruffs, broad-brimmed feathered hats, and skirts. Williams, above, spoke of daggers and satin. I wonder whether a doublet and broad-brimmed hat would be enough to make a woman look masculine, if her breasts were exposed. To me the one unsatisfying feature of the otherwise stimulating transvestite movement is that it had to be transvestite: Renaissance women so far accepted the masculine rules of the game that they felt they had to look masculine to be "free." But as *Hic Mulier* shows, the costume was not strictly masculine. The bare-breasted woman with a sword is not a woman pretending to be a man. She is the great symbol of the age, often feared and hated but sometimes approved and welcomed—the hermaphrodite.

However flabbergasted he is by the clothing of these monstrous females, the author's main concern is their aggressive behavior. Why should women carry weapons? In more blessed times, "the weapon of a vertuous woman was her teares, which euery good man pitied" (Sig. B3). Women had exchanged "modest gestures" for "gyant-like behauiours" (Sig. [A4]ᵛ). (The essay's woodcut seems designed with this phrase in mind. The tailor fitting one woman with her broad-brimmed hat stands waist-high to his customer, and while it is true that the barber's head is slightly above the level of his female customer's, he is standing and she is sitting.) Perhaps the author, who had read his Spenser, remembered that giantesses could be lewd as well as aggressive. But aggression receives most emphasis: "They swimme in the excesse of these vanities, and will bee man-like not onely from the head to the waste, but to the very foot, & in euery condition: man in body by attyre, man in behauiour by rude complement, man in nature by aptnesse to anger, man in action by pursuing reuenge, man in wearing weapons, man in vsing weapons: And in briefe, so much man in all things, that they are neither men, nor women, but iust good for nothing" (Sig. B2).

Hic Mulier was answered one week later by another anonymous essay, *Haec-Vir; or, The Womanish Man: Being an Answere to the late Booke intituled Hic-Mulier. Exprest in a briefe Dialogue betweene Haec-Vir the Womanish Man, and Hic-Mulier the Man-Woman.* Here the characteristic Jacobean confrontation between aggressive woman and effeminate man is given its most articulate treatment. Again, the role reversal is not perfectly symmetrical. The man has simply lost his male attributes and become womanish; the woman has retained some female attributes. The dialogue's twice-repeated formula "Womanish-Man"/"Man-Woman" suggests effeminate man versus hermaphrodite rather than effeminate man versus mannish woman. The character Hic-Mulier appears in the title-page woodcut carrying a sword and wearing a skirt—a hermaphroditic image even though her breasts are not exposed. (In the dialogue itself, they *are* exposed.)

The dialogue is between Hic-Mulier, a female transvestite, and Haec-Vir, a young man who suspiciously resembles the foppish male courtier, King James version. It opens comically, with each speaker mistaking the other's gender. This cleared up, the man launches a verbal attack on the woman: as in the formal controversy, women are placed on the defensive. (The formal controversy's judicial image appears: Haec-Vir tells Hic-Mulier that "in that Booke [*Hic Mulier*] you are arraigned, and found guilty" [Sig. (A4)ᵛ].) The fop is piqued with the man-woman's shorn hair, "naked, lasciuious, bawdy Bosome," "*Leaden-Hall* Dagger" and "High-way Pistoll," and with the "mind and behauiour" he assumes must go with them (Sig. [A4]). He harangues her, repeating the charges of *Hic*

Mulier. Nothing daunted, the woman replies at length to his charge that she violates custom, ending cheerfully, "To conclude *Custome* is an Idiot" (Sig. B2ᵛ). She confesses to having sloughed off stereotypical feminine behavior: she refuses to stand in a modest pose, to move with womanly grace, to keep silent while courted by "wantons," to bear burdens "Asse-like," or to cry when she is hurt. Rejoicing in her freedom to cast off outmoded behavior, she proclaims, "We are as free-borne as Men, haue as free election, and as free spirits, we are compounded of like parts, and may with like liberty make benefit of our Creations" (Sig. B3).

The dialogue is not as revolutionary as isolated quotations make it sound. The author officially disapproves of the blurring of sexual distinctions "nowadays" that so many writers commented upon. S/he longs for the days when men were men and women women, and defends the man-clothed woman mainly by characterizing her behavior as a response to male effeminacy: *somebody* has to wear the breeches. Haec-Vir introduces a version of the old "if you get equal pay, men won't open doors for you" argument, which slips easily into the Renaissance plea for Order: "If you will walke without difference, you shall liue without reuerence: if you will conte[m]ne order, you must indure the shame of disorder" (Sig. B4ᵛ). Hic-Mulier claims that effeminate men originally blurred the line between the sexes: women have been forced to adopt "manly" behavior to preserve that all-important distinction: "Now since according to your own Inference, euen by the Lawes of Nature, by the rules of Religion, and the Customes of all ciuill Nations, it is necessary there be a distinct and speciall difference betweene Man and Woman, both in habit and behauiours: what could we poore weake women doe lesse . . . then to gather vp those garments you haue proudly cast away, and therewith to cloath both our bodies and our mindes; since no other meanes was left vs to continue our names, and to support a difference?" (Sig. C2ᵛ). With a little ingenuity, one might extricate the author from these unfeministi-cal straits. One could argue that the passage is tongue-in-cheek, that the reference to "poore weake women" by a woman sporting a Leaden-hall dagger is transparently ironic. One could argue that Hic-Mulier is show-ing off female rhetorical skill by cleverly turning her opponent's argu-ments against him. But I am very much afraid that the passage was meant literally. Transvestism is called a "deformity" from the outset (the author speaks of "deformitie[s]" six times). The praise of martial manliness and condemnation of peacetime effeminacy smack too much of Renaissance orthodoxy to be suspected of irony: "You [womanish men] haue demo-lish'd the noble schooles of Horsmanship . . . hung vp your Armes to rust, glued vp those swords in their scabberds that would shake all Christendome with the brandish, and entertained into your mindes such softnes, dulnesse and effeminate nicenesse, that it would euen make *Her-*

aclitus himselfe laugh against his nature to see how pulingly you languish in this weake entertained sinne of womanish softnesse" (Sig. C2). Hic-Mulier is disgusted that men have taken up women's sports. (In the title-page woodcut, the woman wears spurs and the man carries a racquet and battledores for shuttlecock.) If the author were not sincere in disapproving modern unisex tendencies, Hic-Mulier would not have expressed shame at wearing men's garments (Sig. C2ᵛ); nor would she have promised that women will again be subservient when men again are manly: "Be men in shape, men in shew, men in words, men in actions, men in counsell, men in example: then will we loue and serue you; then will wee heare and obey you; then will wee like rich Iewels hang at your eares to take our Instructions" (Sig. C3ᵛ). And the dialogue would not have ended with Haec-Vir's proposal, apparently accepted by Hic-Mulier, that they exchange clothes, behavior, and Latin pronominal prefixes and live happily ever after. Some contemporary writers, as I shall show, were willing to view diminished sexual distinctions as a step towards civilization; apparently the author of *Haec-Vir* was not among them. S/he officially endorses sexual apartheid on grounds of "the Lawes of Nature . . . the rules of Religion . . . the Customes of all ciuill Nations." But only, I think, officially.

Despite the eventual collapse of *Haec-Vir* into orthodoxy, the first half of the dialogue falls very little short of being a flaming manifesto of liberty for women. Hic-Mulier's speeches ring with the words *free* and *liberty*: "I was created free, born free, and liue free: what lets [i.e., prevents] me then so to spinne out my time, that I may dye free?" (Sig. Bᵛ– B2). She rejoices in city life and the freedom of action it can offer women (Sig. B3). And no writer since Agrippa—indeed, not even Agrippa himself—had so resoundingly repudiated custom. Whether or not she ultimately bows to the force of "the Customes of all ciuill Nations," her demolition of custom is thorough. She defends her male attire: "What we do weare is warme, thrifty and wholesome . . . where is then the error? onely in the Fashion, onely in the Custome" (Sig. B3ᵛ). And custom is illogical. It cannot reflect the laws of Nature because it differs from one culture to the next:[9] the English wash their hands before meals, while the ancient Romans anointed their bodies; the English mourn in black, but the Romans mourned in white: "I see not but we may mourne in *Greene, Blue, Red*" (Sig. B2ᵛ). Some customs are absurd, like the English custom of cross-examining fellow travellers about their itineraries. To expect women to dress and behave according to received custom is ridiculous: "O miserable seruitude chained onely to Basenesse and Folly! for then custome, nothing is more absurd, nothing more foolish" (Sig. B2). Hic-Mulier delights in doing things in new ways: "Nor do I in my delight of change otherwise then as the whole world doth, or as it becommeth a daughter of the world to doe. For what is the world, but a very shop or ware-house of change? Sometimes Winter, sometimes Summer; day and night: they hold sometimes Riches, sometimes Pouertie, sometimes Health, sometimes Sicknesse: now Pleasure; presētly Anguish; now Honour, then contempt: . . . there is nothing but change, which doth surround and mixe withall our Fortunes" (Sig. B).

Delight was not the usual response to change: mutability tormented generations of Renaissance writers. The malaise of the early seventeenth century was a response to change. A changing economic system, changing configurations of social class, new discoveries in astronomy—all these were feared; partly because they seemed un-Christian, immoral, antithetical to humanism and to Order. But partly just because they were new. The author of *Hic Mulier,* arguing against changing attire and behavior for women, had noted approvingly that "*Licurgus* the law-giuer made it death in one of his Statutes, to bring in any new custome into his Common-wealth" (Sig. C3). But Hic-Mulier in *Haec-Vir,* almost alone among her contemporaries, welcomed change. Because she did, this essay, for all of its disappointing passages, is a landmark for women. For custom indeed lies upon us with a weight heavy as frost. In the Renaissance, it was not the custom for women to work outside the family business, to go to grammar schools and universities, to enter the professions, to hold office, to write for the stage. It was not the custom for men to share housework and child care or to support themselves by spinning if unemployed. The overwhelming majority of Renaissance writers saw these sex roles as ordained by God or by Nature. The author of *Haec-Vir,* like Agrippa and one or two others, at least momentarily suspected that sex roles were sanctioned not by majestic Nature but by ordinary habit. When Hic-Mulier cried "Custom is an idiot," she flung open the door to reveal vistas of freedom and equality. And then her creator, growing alarmed, bustled in and shut it again. But at least the door had been found. Someday it would be opened again, and through it would march Mary Wollstonecraft and Emmeline Pankhurst, Susan B. Anthony and John Stuart Mill, Simone de Beauvoir and Betty Friedan, and all of us who can thank the dubious feminism of the English Renaissance for at least one indisputable battle-cry: *Haec-Vir's* "We are as freeborne as men."

Hic Mulier and *Haec-Vir* resemble works of the formal controversy about women in their formal rhetorical strategies and their controversialist methods of argument. They even reënact the formal controversy's two literary modes: *Hic-Mulier* is a kind of oration (the title page calls it a "briefe Declamation") and *Haec-Vir* a dialogue. But where the formal controversy had existed on a timeless literary plane, *Hic Mulier* and *Haec-*

Vir are contemporary, topical, anchored in the actions of living women. In the remaining chapters of part 2, while my main interest is in the ways literature portrayed women, I also want to suggest, with all seemly caution, what is nearly impossible to prove—that more canonical Renaissance literature dealing with women may have reflected contemporary reality too.

The problem is that the expression of reality is nearly always oblique: it must be extrapolated from recurring plot structures, unravelled from patterns of characterization, coaxed from odd twistings of stereotype, winkled out of costume and imagery and word. Sometimes, as with Shakespeare's giving up on the unmarried transvestite heroine after 1600 or the drama's dispensing with woman-as-food imagery after 1610, it must be inferred from what has disappeared. As in geometry one can increase the number of sides of a regular polygon infinitely and it will never be a circle, so one can pile up similarities between literature and life infinitely without being able to prove that literature is really reflecting life. But the Renaissance evidence, maddeningly oblique though it may be, seems to me to point so consistently in that direction that I must assure the reader that it is only my acceptance of epistemological absolutes, and not natural feminine timidity, that prevents me from trying to make my polygon a circle.

NOTES

1. Louis B. Wright was, I believe, the first to give a full account of the topical events surrounding this controversy (*Middle-Class Culture*, pp. 492–97).

2. "To Mr. Tilman After He had Taken Orders." See discussion by Julie Lepick, "'That Faire Hermaphrodite': The Transformation of a Figure in the Literature of the English Renaissance."

3. Nancy Hayles, "The Ambivalent Ideal: The Concept of Androgyny in English Renaissance Literature," pp. 11, 12–19.

4. Marie Delcourt, *Hermaphrodite: Myths and Rites of the Bisexual Figure in Classical Antiquity*, p. 45.

5. Thomas Adams, *Mystical Bedlam, or the world of mad-men*, p. 50.

6. John Chamberlain, *The Letters of John Chamberlain*, II, pp. 286–87, 289.

7. A piece suggestively entitled *Doublet, Breeches, and Shirt* was acted at Magdalen College, Oxford, in January of that year; it is unfortunately a lost play. Contemporary sermons on the topic, if they reached print, seem not to have survived, with the possible exception of Thomas Walkington's *Rabboni, Mary Magdalens tears*, entered in the Stationer's Register on January 25, 1620, the day after James's injunction to the clergy, and containing the following passage: "Are not the dayes farre worse, than those that were in *Isay* the Prophets time? . . . Are not the sexes altered?

Contrary to that in *Deut. 22.5 The woman shall not weare what pertaineth to man, nor man put on the attire of women*" (p. 158). The sermon was not wholly devoted to transvestism, however: this reference is buried in an avalanche of rhetoric on another topic and does not in itself seem enough to make women's ears "tingle." It is possible that the passage was a last-minute addition to the sermon, inspired by James's injunction.

8. D. Harrison Willson, *King James VI and I*, p. 196.

9. Montaigne's *Apology of Raymond Sebonde*, available in Florio's 1603 translation, was possibly an influence here.

CHAPTER SEVEN

❃

Civilian Impotence, Civic Impudence

THE CONFRONTATION between effeminate man and virago which *Haec-Vir* dramatizes as dialogue was a prominent literary device during the early seventeenth century. In the anonymous play *Every Woman in Her Humour,* a bevy of primping fops is counterbalanced by a domineering wife who, reversing sex roles, bullies her husband into home keeping and silence. In Middleton's comedy *More Dissemblers Besides Women,* a dandified gallant in a "smockified shirt" (I.iv.105) is pursued by a plucky young woman who assumes male disguise to infiltrate his household. In Shakespeare, Caesar declares that Antony "is not more manlike / Than Cleopatra, nor the Queen of Ptolemy / More womanly than he" (*Antony and Cleopatra,* I.iv.5–7); Cleopatra reminisces about the time she put her clothes on Antony, while she wore his sword (II.v.22–23). In *Troilus and Cressida,* Patroclus tells Achilles, "A woman impudent and mannish grown / Is not more loathed than an effeminate man / In time of action" (III.iii.217–219); Patroclus's views on confusion of sex roles are given added authority from the fact that he is Achilles's whore. Fops often appear in plays dominated by strong-minded women. The prissy Count Malateste, reluctant to enlist in the military service for fear gunpowder will spoil his perfume, is oddly enough considered, at one point, as a likely suitor for the strong-minded Duchess of Malfi. Valeria in Middleton's comedy *The Widow,* who disdains foppish men, takes to the law to outwit her own suitors. Contemporary epigrammatists and writers of formal satire often lampooned both fop and virago, as do Henry Fitzgeffrey in *Satyres: and Satyricall Epigrams* and Henry Hutton in *Follie's Anatomie.*

Effeminacy among men, mannishness among women, and related questions regarding behavior proper to each sex, which form the subject of the *hic mulier/haec vir* controversy, had a long career in noncontroversial literature. It is highly suggestive to find "canonical" literature voicing the same concerns and employing the same character configurations as the formal transvestite controversy. The influence of living women's behavior on the *hic mulier* controversy is indisputable; I will argue that a similar influence on canonical literature is probable. Unlike the formal controversy, the *hic mulier* controversy benefitted by an exhilarating contact with flesh and blood.

As I have shown, the real-life fashion of masculine attire for women was a recurrent phenomenon in Elizabethan times and a fairly permanent feature of the Jacobean landscape. All through these years, literature maintained a steady interest in female mannishness, male effeminacy, and the whole question of the "nature" of men and women, often suggesting that traditional sex roles were undergoing pronounced mutation in the modern world. The most obvious literary vehicle for exploring such issues was transvestite disguise in the drama.

During the 1590s, Shakespeare frequently used transvestite disguise in his plots; other dramatists used it occasionally. It is true that, as Juliet Dusinberre says, "disguise invites the dramatist to explore masculinity and femininity" (p. 241); it is probable, however, that the feminism resulting from such explorations has been overestimated. Writing that "Shakespeare's feminism is not optional, to be taken or left according to the critic's taste," Dusinberre notes that "disguise freed the dramatist to explore . . . the nature of women untrammelled by the custom of femininity" (p. 271). But most dramatists, lacking the rare insight of *Haec-Vir*'s author, regarded femininity as a matter of nature rather than custom; and as such it could never be sloughed off with clothes. Granted, masculine disguise gives heroines certain unwonted freedoms: sometimes a woman travelling alone adopts male clothing to discourage rape ("Beauty provoketh thieves sooner than gold," *As You Like It*, I.iii.112); sometimes, like Portia in *The Merchant of Venice*, she must adopt male dress to practice a profession barred to women; sometimes she dresses as a man to effect a daring escape or for the sheer love of adventure. The dramatists saw clearly enough that women *qua* women could not easily travel alone, plead a case at law, have adventures. It is at least possible, given the spirit and intelligence with which they endowed their heroines, that they saw something unfair about these restrictions. But the dramatists insistently remind us that such behavior, however necessitated by emergency circumstances, is unnatural. Julia, who dons a page's costume to "prevent / The loose encounters of lascivious men," worries about her reputation: "But tell me, wench, how will the world repute me / For undertaking so unstaid a journey? / I fear me, it will make me scandalized" (*Two Gentlemen of Verona*, II.vii.40–41, 59–61). She reproaches her lover for having forced her to such a shift: "O Proteus, let this habit make thee blush! / Be thou ashamed that I have took upon me / Such an immodest raiment" (V.iv.104–106). Jessica too sees her boy's disguise as shameful: "I am glad 'tis night, you do not look on me, / For I am much ashamed of my exchange. / . . . Cupid himself would blush / To see me thus transforméd to a boy. / . . . What, must I hold a candle to my shames?" (*Merchant of Venice,* II.vi.34–41). Viola's "masculine usurped attire" represents behavior, according to Orsino, "much against the mettle of your sex. / So far beneath your soft and tender breeding" (*Twelfth Night,* V.i.257, 330–331). The idea that wearing male clothing implies a change in her feminine nature shocks Rosalind: "Dost thou think though I am caparisoned like a man, I have a doublet and hose in my disposition?" (*As You Like It,* III.ii.204–206). Upon hearing that Orlando is near, she is as perturbed as Jessica before Lorenzo: "Orlando? . . . Alas the day! What shall I do with my doublet and hose?" (III.ii.229–231).

Dusinberre's most attractive theory about male disguise is that "the masculine woman and the woman in disguise are both disruptive socially because they go behind the scenes and find that manhood describes not the man inside the clothes, but the world's reaction to his breeches. . . . A woman in disguise smokes out the male world, perceiving masculinity as a form of acting" (pp. 244–45). This may well have been true for the "masculine woman," by which Dusinberre means the man-clothed woman of Jacobean times; but unfortunately it does not ring true for Shakespeare's transvestite heroines. When Rosalind dons curtle-axe and boar-spear to declare, "In my heart / Lie there what hidden woman's fear there will, / We'll have a swashing and a martial outside, / As many other mannish cowards have / That do outface it with their semblances" (*As You Like It,* I.iii.120–124), and when Portia takes up a dagger to disguise herself "like a fine bragging youth" (*Merchant of Venice,* III.iv.69), what they expose as "a form of acting" is not masculinity but the feigned masculinity of the braggadocio. This is to say nothing: the coward had hidden behind the braggadocio role in literature from classical antiquity to Falstaff. To advance from this convention to the perception that the "true" masculinity of an Orlando and the "true" femininity of a Rosalind are merely artificial roles is a large step—a step Shakespeare did not take. Nothing in Shakespeare suggests that but for a little artificial social conditioning, an Orlando would faint at the sight of blood, or a Rosalind challenge Charles the wrestler. Shakespeare's transvestite heroines do not approach any nearer to true manhood than do the fraudulent "mannish cowards." In the confrontation between Sir Andrew Aguecheek and Viola, we are invited to laugh with mild contempt at the male coward and with affectionate indulgence at the female coward: cowardice violates his nature but is a natural expression of hers. Transvestite disguise in Shakespeare does not blur the distinction between the sexes but heightens it: case after case demonstrates that not even masculine attire can hide a woman's natural squeamishness and timidity. King Lear must disrobe to find the essential nature of a human being; a woman's essential nature, Shakespeare insists, shines through any kind of clothes. When Shakespeare's romantic heroines play at being men, Shakespeare invites us to smile at their trepidations and their posturings, with the affection of a parent watching his child play at being grown-up. His obvious good will, and the central roles he assigns these heroines, keeps the condescension from being offensive. But neither is it feminist. As Paula S. Berggren notes, "While the wearing of pants allows expression of a talent otherwise dampened by convention, it does not, in Shakespeare, lead to a direct challenge of the masculine order." Shakespeare's transvestite heroines are "content to reassume their womanly duties."[1]

All but one of Shakespeare's transvestite heroines belong to the 1590s, when female transvestism was out of fashion on the London streets. After the fashion was revived in early Jacobean London, Shakespeare largely abandoned the device. His sole remaining female transvestite, Imogen in *Cymbeline*, is ill at ease in her masculine weeds: as Dusinberre points out, "Rosalind and Portia thrive on the masculine life where Imogen wilts beneath it" (p. 263). In *All's Well*, Shakespeare seems to avoid the device deliberately; Helena travels alone to the court and the wars without adopting male disguise. There are many possible explanations for Shakespeare's abandoning such a cherished plot device; among them is that he recoiled from the sight of real-life women in breeches.

Shakespeare's plays contemporary with the revival of masculine attire among London women (*Macbeth*, 1606, *Antony and Cleopatra*, 1607, *Coriolanus*, 1608) take a persistent interest in women who violate their "natural" sex roles. Shakespeare is not without sympathy, in these plays, for the frustrations of a woman who must live a vicarious life of action through a man who has more freedom to act than she does. But the yearnings of such women for masculinity must have disturbed him: none of his breeches-envying tragic heroines of this period is treated with unqualified approval.

Lady Macbeth's attempt to unsex herself, so as to put on the power and ruthlessness she attributes to men, is foreshadowed by the hermaphroditic witches—bearded women. Macbeth sees her driving ambition as masculine: "Bring forth men-children only, / For thy undaunted mettle should compose / Nothing but males" (I.vii.72–74). But she goads a man into action rather than acting herself. Volumnia's life of action is accomplished vicariously through her son, Coriolanus, whom she imagines fighting, bleeding; when he returns from battle she counts his fresh wounds to keep her tally up to date. "Thou art my warrior," she reminds him; "I holp to frame thee" (V. iii.63–64). When she is accused of being mannish, she considers it a compliment: "Aye, fool, is that a shame? . . . / Was not a man my father?" (IV.ii.17–18). Cleopatra, too, is frustrated by the narrow sphere of action allotted to her sex. She imagines Antony riding his horse, commanding his troops. She reports having tried on his sword. Her outburst to Antony, "I would I had thy inches" (I.iii.39), is telling; given her propensity for suggestive remarks, it is unlikely to refer solely to his height. Her one foray into battle is prefaced by a cool verbal sex change: she says she will "appear there for a man" (III.vii.19). The exercise is disastrous. But then Cleopatra has had little experience being a man.

Both the fact that in the 1590s Shakespeare took pains to assert through his transvestite heroines that despite appearances to the contrary, women have a fixed and immutable nature that will declare itself eventually, and the fact that during the early Jacobean years he interested himself in women who try to step out of that feminine nature, showing how such attempts invariably eventuate in failure, death, and/or authorial disapproval, suggest that Shakespeare had caught a whiff of the winds of sexual change blowing in his own culture. The idea that sex roles might alter was apparently an aroma which seared his nostrils.

Other dramatists continued to stage female transvestites in early Jacobean times, sometimes relating the device to the confusion of sex roles in modern times. Anabell in the anonymous *Fair Maid of Bristow*, ca. 1604, the second Luce in Heywood's *The Wise-Woman of Hogsdon*, ca. 1604, Susan and Nan in Sharpham's *The Fleire*, ca. 1608, Mary Fitzallard in *The Roaring Girl*, ca. 1608, all adopt masculine disguise. The somewhat darker tone of these plots may reflect authorial uneasiness over the implications of transvestism. The young men faithfully pursued by page/ mistresses in these plays are in general more unsavory than their counterparts in plays of the 1590s, and the device is used by prostitutes as well as virgins: Bellafront appears disguised as a page in *1 Honest Whore*; a group of prostitutes dress as shield boys in *Your Five Gallants*. But as the transvestite movement gained momentum once again on the London streets, the transvestite heroine, outside Shakespeare at least, came into her own again on the stage. No authorial qualms dampen the spirits of Bess Bridges, who in Heywood's *Fair Maid of the West*, ca. 1610,[2] dons male attire to challenge a bully to a duel, and later a sea-captain's disguise, apparently for the hell of it. Its function is not to protect her: she eventually tires of it and returns to female attire with no visible trepidation. Neither Bess nor the author frets about unnaturalness.

Most female transvestites appearing in plays at the height of the *hic mulier* controversy, ca. 1610 to 1620, are favorably regarded. As befits the age, they are more assertive than were the women disguised as pages in earlier plays: almost none of them explains her male disguise as necessitated by fear of rape or the danger of travelling alone. Aspatia in Beaumont and Fletcher's *The Maid's Tragedy*, ca. 1610, adopts masculine attire as a novel suicide method: dressed this way, she challenges an experienced swordsman to a duel and is killed. Kate in Middleton's *No Wit No Help Like a Woman's,* ca. 1613, adopts masculine disguise to regain her fortune, Alathe in Fletcher's *The Nightwalker,* ca. 1611, to win back her defecting fiancé, Martia in *The Widow,* ca. 1616, to escape enforced marriage. Several of the male-disguised women—for example, Kate and Martia—are courted boldly by women, as were Rosalind in *As You Like It* and Viola in *Twelfth Night:* a woman who takes a man's-eye view learns all sorts of things about her fellow women's assertiveness.

Veramour in Fletcher's *The Honest Man's Fortune,* 1613, whose feminine features lead more than one character to suspect he is a woman in disguise, comments on the frequency of masculine disguise as a plot device in this period. As a joke, he appears in feminine attire and claims to be female, explaining that he got the idea of dressing as a man from two or three recent plays. The convention, indeed, was so pervasive that the inevitable reaction set in; it began to be parodied. *More Dissemblers Besides Women,* ca. 1615, has great fun with a woman whose page's disguise subjects her to the torments of dancing lessons while in an advanced state of pregnancy. In the same play, convention breaks down entirely when Aurelia enters dressed as a man: unlike fathers in the old days of *As You Like It,* Aurelia's father recognizes her immediately and orders her to get rid of her disgraceful costume. This play comments on the sexual confusion of the day: "By this light, the boy's with child! / A miracle! some woman is the father. / The world's turn'd upside down: sure if men breed, / Women must get" (V.i.225–228). *Amends for Ladies,* ca. 1611, is a *tour de force* of transvestism; Lady Honor dresses as a foot-boy, Bould as a waiting gentlewoman, Ingen's brother and Lord Fee-simple as brides. (Moll Cut-purse appears in habitual male attire, not intended to disguise.) The convention reaches its zenith in II.iii, where a woman disguised as a man meets a man disguised as a woman. These plays are remarkably mild about female transvestism. Notes of criticism are sounded, but most dramatists seem to agree with a character in *No Wit No Help:* "Women are wiser than ever they were, since they wore doublets" (II.i.14–15).

Renaissance literature always regarded male transvestism as less attractive than female transvestism, just as in our day a man wearing a dress is in a different league from a woman in pant suit and tie. Men had a greater horror of effeminacy than women of mannishness: for a man to behave like a woman was shameful, but for a woman to behave like a man, while unnatural, was at least a step up—into the mannerisms of the higher-caste sex. Sometimes authors view male transvestism with open horror: when Hercules in Heywood's *The Brazen Age* "is so much with [Omphale's] inchantments blear'd, / That hee's turn'd woman . . . spinnes, / Cards, and doth chare-worke, whilst his mistres sits / And makes a cushion of his Lyons skin," Jason cries out, "This *Hercules?* / This is some base effeminate groome, not hee / That with his puissance frighted all the earth: / This is some woman, some *Hermaphrodite.*" Only when his former military companions recite his heroic deeds does Hercules begin to recover (pp. 240–243).

Usually, male transvestism is a comic device.[3] Only very rarely, as with Iustiniano in *Westward Ho,* does an author risk putting it to serious purposes. More often, male transvestites are involved in some semicomical seduction scheme which calls for infiltrating feminine society, as are Jupiter in Heywood's *The Golden Age,* Welford in Beaumont and Fletcher's *The Scornful Lady,* and Bould in *Amends for Ladies.* The absurdity of Antonio's disguise in Marston's *Antonio and Mellida* is increased by his revealing that he has rented the Amazon costume from a local Jewish merchant. Similarly comic female impersonators are the title figure of *Epicoene,* Falstaff and two young boys in *The Merry Wives of Windsor,* and Follywit in Middleton's *A Mad World, My Masters,* the last of whom sees his female garb as an emblem of modern sexual chaos: "'Tis an Amazonian time; you shall have women shortly tread their husbands" (III.iii.114–115).

The meaning of Pyrocles's Amazon disguise, maintained throughout the action of Sidney's *Arcadia,* remains ambiguous to this day. While it is true that all the sinister implications of the Hercules/Omphale story surface in Musidorus's argument against Pyrocles's transvestism, "This effeminate love of a Woman, dothe so womanish a man, that, yf yow yeelde to yt, yt will not onely make yow a famous Amazon but a Launder, a Distaff spinner," it is also true that in the *New Arcadia,* Pyrocles forthrightly adopts as his emblem "a *Hercules* made in little fourme, but a distaffe set within his hand as he once was by *Omphales* commaundement with a worde in Greeke, but thus to be interpreted, *Never more valiant.*"[4] Mark Rose argues that "Pyrocles's womanish dress . . . is the mark of that spiritual effeminacy which has resulted from his allowing his reason to be ruled by passion,"[5] while John F. Danby thinks that in Pyrocles Sidney "would seem to be insisting that man is capable of a synthesis of qualities that includes the womanly yet avoids the hermaphroditic,"[6] and Elizabeth Dipple believes that in the *New Arcadia* metamorphosis "becomes the natural instrument of love in any landscape, making transference of sex not a degrading but an ennobling thing."[7] Whether we regard *Never more valiant* as a triumphant proclamation of the irrelevance of artificial sexual boundaries or, with Rose, as "no more than Pyrocles's own foolish thought" (p. 362), we should not overlook Sidney's introduction into the *New Arcadia* of Zelmane, a woman in male disguise, in juxtaposition to the Pyrocles who assumes her name when he adopts female disguise. Once again, literature balances womanized

man against masculinized woman; the ambivalence with which Sidney
treats this duo reflects the ambivalence of his age toward the softened
men and toughened women it wavered between regarding as monsters
and regarding as symbols of human wholeness.

Literary concerns about the unisex tendencies of modern life, which
surface in the context of transvestite disguise and elsewhere, were intimately interwoven with literary attitudes toward war and peace. Closely
contemporary with Stubbes's attack on man-clothed women and effeminate men (see chapter 6) was Barnabe Rich's *Riche his farewell to Militarie
Profession: containyng very pleasant discourses fitte for a peaceable tyme: Gathered together for the onlie delight of the courteous Gentlewomen, both of Englande and Ireland for whose onlie pleasure they were collected together, And vnto
whom they are directed and dedicated*, 1581, a collection of stories whose
introductory remarks display intense hostility toward "feminine" peacetime culture.

Rich was a soldier: his previous books had dealt with the military
profession. Now, during the 1580s, he found himself a soldier in peacetime. Shelving a proposed book on warfare, he turned to writing prose
fiction for women. In his dedicatory epistle to English gentlewomen,
Rich explains: "Gentlewomen . . . will not a little wonder to see such
alteration in mee, that hauing spent my yoonger dayes in the Warres
amongst men, and vowed my selfe only vnto Mars: should now in my
riper yeeres, desire to liue in peace amongst women, and to consecrate
my selfe wholy vnto Venus. . . . I see now it is lesse painful to folowe a
Fiddle in a Gentlewomans chamber: then to march after a Drumme in
the field. And more sound sleeping vnder a silken Canopy close by a
friend, then vnder a Bush in the field, within a mile of our foe." Several
works of this period praise Elizabeth for the nation's long period of peace;[8]
but as Paul Jorgensen points out in *Shakespeare's Military World*, Elizabethans were never comfortable with peace, and military alarmists like Rich
himself made sure they were not, reminding the public in inflammatory
tracts of the dangers of peace. Peacetime society was considered a world
of women; the men who inhabited it were often stigmatized as effeminate. That Rich despised himself for becoming so effeminate as to earn
his bread by writing stories for women is clear from the *Farewell's* second
dedicatory epistle, addressed to the soldiers of England. Here he apologizes for having promised another work on warfare and delivered this
"women's" book instead: "But I trust I shall please Gentlewomen, and
that is all the gaine that I looke for. And herein I doe but folow the course
of the world. For many now adaies goe about, by as great deuise as may
be, how they might become women themselues. Howe many Gentlemen shall you see at this present day, that . . . in the wearing of their

apparrell, in the setting of their Ruffes, and the freesling of their haire, are more new fangled and foolish then any curtisan of Venice." The sight of a man carrying a feather fan moves Rich to excoriate violators of expected sex roles among both sexes: "It is as fond a sight to see a man with such a bable in his hand, as to see a woman ride through the streete with a launce in hers." Bitter about the slender estimation in which the military profession is presently held, Rich in a gesture of self-annihilation declares that one might as well give in and join the majority of effeminate civilians. Publishing this book was his way of doing so. The stories in Rich's collection sometimes reflect his introductory views on peacetime's unwholesomeness: in the story of Sappho, Duke of Mantona, for example, an honest soldier returns from the wars to find himself at severe social disadvantage in a polished court of elegant, effeminate courtiers.

Rich's bitterness with a society that could reduce a plainspoken soldier to the humiliating posture of woman-flatterer is matched by the cynicism that could not be kept out of the drama's scenes of warfare. There was a brief vogue, roughly coeval with the euphoria attending the Armada's defeat, for macho heroes. But the unalloyed manliness of a Talbot or a Tamburlaine gave way quickly to theatrical commentary on male cowardice and female mannishness. Marlowe's *Tamburlaine, Part 1* ends happily on a unisex note, as the great military conqueror allows his fury to be mitigated by the beauty and tenderness of a woman, Zenocrate. But in *Part 2*, Tamburlaine grows increasingly barbarized after resisting and finally losing through death the feminine influence of Zenocrate; he murders his effeminate son who had requested, "while my brothers follow arms, my lord, / Let me accompany my gracious mother" (I.iv.65–66). Scenes set in wartime in the drama of the 1590s are permeated with a sense of sexual chaos. Women become associated with war: in *King John*, "ladies and pale-visaged maids, / Like Amazons, come tripping after drums, / Their thimbles into arméd gauntlets change, / Their needles to lances, and their gentle hearts / To fierce and bloody inclination" (V.ii.154–158). The Amazons, beloved of formal defenders of women, Shakespeare found a disturbing race. Both of the female military leaders he compares with Amazons, Queen Margaret and Joan of Arc (*1 Henry VI*, I.ii.104, *3 Henry VI*, I.iv.113–115, IV.i.106), are unhappy examples of womanhood: one is an adulteress, the other is a witch, and both are French. Alongside the monstrous behavior of these masculinized women appears a running commentary on the effeminacy of men. York calls a truce "effeminate peace" (*1 Henry VI*, VI.iv.107). Warwick demands, "Why stand we like soft-hearted women here, / Wailing our losses, whiles the foe doth rage?" (*3 Henry VI*, II.iii.25–26). Bolingbroke brands his temporarily unwarlike son "effeminate boy" (*Richard II*, V.iii.10). Hotspur is incensed when a court messenger visits the battlefield "perfuméd like a milliner" and talking "like a waiting gentlewoman" (*1 Henry IV,* I.iii.36, 55). Sometimes a direct confrontation between masculine female and effeminate male appears, anticipating the pervasive Jacobean use of this motif, as for example when in Marlowe's *Edward II* Queen Isabella makes war on her husband, who through a debilitating homosexuality has lost his "masculine" decisiveness of action.

The malaise which attended literary treatments of war in the drama of the 1590s may have been a response to the protracted and demoralizing Spanish war which throughout these years was dragging its slow length along. But when fruitless war yielded to unpopular peace, literary unease about effeminacy in society only increased. James I was a pacifist; on his accession in 1603 he took immediate steps to end the Spanish war. Literature, I think, reflects the unease attending this action. Shakespeare's plays of this period are full of aborted battles and confused sex roles.

Apparently sensing a change in his culture, from "masculine" military values to peacetime values traditionally female, Shakespeare wrote three plays during this period which dramatize conflict between these two value systems. In *Troilus and Cressida,* Troilus loses his military courage because loving a woman has made him effeminate: "I am weaker than a woman's tear . . . Less valiant than the virgin in the night" (I.i.9, 11), a significant departure from the courtly love tradition, where love made a man a better warrior. (Barnabe Rich too voices the changed ethic: he has read of "conquerors whom Loue haue made effeminate, but I neuer heard of any whom Loue hath made truly valiant";[9] similarly, Spenser describes as "horrible enchantment" Verdant's amorous devotion to Acrasia, which has caused him to neglect armed combat [*Faerie Queene,* II.xii.80].) Achilles declines to fight, preferring to languish in the arms of a homosexual lover. In *Antony and Cleopatra,* military action climaxes with a great military leader's leaving the battle to follow a woman. The military action of *Coriolanus* culminates in a great military hero's calling off his greatest battle at a woman's behest. Even in contemporary Shakespearean plays which are not primarily military in focus, the theme keeps intruding. *All's Well* shows the soldier Parolles exposed for cowardice and lying; the hero himself spends more of his time at the wars wenching than fighting. The impending battle with the Turks which clouds the first act of *Othello* is disposed of in Act II with "News, friends. Our wars are done, the Turks are drowned," and the action shifts to the marital difficulties of a great general in peacetime. Alcibiades, who keeps two whores as travelling companions, calls off his invasion of Rome at the end of *Timon of Athens.* Cymbeline cancels his long-standing hostilities with Rome because a prophecy has foreseen a time of peace for Britain inaugurated by a piece of tender air, which a soothsayer interprets as *mollis aer,* or *mulier,* "woman."[10] Macduff is not considered "manly" until he pulls himself together and decides to fight (*Macbeth,* IV.iii.235), and he cannot do that until after his wife has been murdered.

Dissatisfaction with peacetime comes out in the large number of discontented soldiers, descendants of Barnabe Rich and his characters, on the Jacobean stage. These men return from the wars, having passed untold dangers and endured terrible hardship for their country, to find their worth neglected. Often they find themselves unemployed. In Field and Massinger's *The Fatal Dowry,* a faithful soldier has been allowed to rot in debtors' prison until he has committed suicide. Valentine in *The Honest Lawyer,* by S. S., out of work after returning from war, is forced to set up as a quack medic. Melantius in *The Maid's Tragedy* returns home from wholesome war to find his country sunk in a corrupt peace, whose only wars are the "naked wars" of women (II.i.2). Palamon laments the peacetime plight of the "unconsider'd soldier" (Shakespeare and Fletcher's *Two Noble Kinsmen,* I.ii).[11] Sebastian in Middleton's *The Witch* is rewarded for three years' military service with loss of his fiancée to a civilian. Flamineo says his way of thriving—by serving as pander to his sister—is rewarded better than a soldier's service (Webster's *White Devil,* III.i). When Francisco asks a returned soldier, "How have you thriv'd?" the soldier confesses, "Faith poorely." Francisco commiserates, "That's the miserie of peace . . . Some men i' th Court seeme *Colossuses* in a chamber, who if they came into the feild would appeare pittifull Pigmies" (*White Devil,* V.i.126–133). Montague vows to relieve "the poor neglected soldier" (*Honest Man's Fortune,* I.i). Bosola is a discontented soldier; he complains, "There are rewards for hawks, and dogs, when they have done us service; but for a soldier, that hazards his limbs in a battle, nothing . . . " (Webster's *Duchess of Malfi,* I.i.59–61). In *The Iron Age, Part 1,* military action is succeeded by civilian squabbling over the slain Achilles's armor; Ajax, viewing his defeat in this litigation as the final proof that his soldierly worth has been slighted, kills himself. In *Othello,* Iago responds to the supposed neglect of his worth as a soldier by contriving the ruin and death of a woman.

The conflict between "masculine" wartime values and "feminine" peacetime values was traditionally represented in literature by the Mars/Venus dichotomy which Barnabe Rich uses in the dedicatory epistle to *Farewell to Military Profession.* Marlowe uses imagery of Venus and Mars in his Tamburlaine plays, where Tamburlaine is torn between the claims of war, instinct in his driving ambition for world power, and the claims of love, personified in Zenocrate, his queen. Shakespeare uses Venus/Mars imagery to delineate conflicting claims on Antony in *Antony and Cleopatra.* Chaucer had used it in *The Knight's Tale,* and it appears again in the play based on that story, *The Two Noble Kinsmen;* Palamon is de-

voted to Venus, Arcite to Mars; the two worlds draw together as Palamon and Arcite join combat for the sake of love.

Love and war often conflict in Jacobean drama. In *The Two Noble Kinsmen,* when three queens request military aid on Theseus's and Hippolyta's wedding day, Theseus wants to marry first; the queens argue that
newly-wedded love will incapacitate him for war. Hippolyta, who has
been a soldier and should know, agrees; she defers consummation until
after the wars. In Fletcher's *Bonduca,* Junius mopes in his tent, unable to
fight because love for Bonduca's daughter has made him effeminate. He
tries to pull himself together, vowing, "I will be man agen" (II.ii.778).
Finally hating the young woman, he declares, "The warrs shall be my
mistress now" (IV.i.1759).

No compromise was possible. One was either a warrior or a lover; if
one attempted to be both, trouble followed. Aurelia in *More Dissemblers*
says of General Andrugio, "I like not him that has two mistresses, / War
and his sweetheart" (II.iii.97–98). In *1 Iron Age,* four separate stories of
love in the midst of war are all disastrous. Achilles mopes in his tent out
of love for Polixena; instead of fighting he plays upon an "effeminate
lute" (III.i). Troilus's love for Cressida, despite the play's softening of her
perfidy, doesn't do him any good. Helen and Paris are engaged in the
love affair which started the war; Helen says of Paris, "Hee was not made
for warre, but amorous play" (I.i). Hector is incensed by feminine pacifism: when his wife and child beg him not to fight on a certain day, he
cries, "Helpe to take off these burrs, they trouble mee" (IV.i). When
Hecuba and Helen join in, he lashes out, "Not all the diuells / Could
halfe torment mee like these women tongues" (IV.i). (It is somewhat
gratifying that for this callous disregard of feminine fears he is killed that
day.) In Rowley's *All's Lost by Lust,* where several amorous campaigns
coexist with a military campaign, two characters get into trouble because
of their conceptions of love and war. Roderigo sees love in terms of war,
while Iuliano sees war in terms of love. Roderigo lays siege to Iacinta,
employing the military metaphor for love which had been common in
Petrarchan poetry: "I would atchieve a victory from you." She insists,
"Sir, I am not your foe"; he informs her that "the war is love" (Sig.
[C4]). Because he cannot conceive of love in other than military terms,
his only course when she refuses him is to take the fort by force. Iuliano
gets sexual excitement out of war, calling it "a gallant Mistresse" and
"my second nuptials" (Sig. B3ᵛ). He ignores the fears of his daughter,
Iacinta, because he sees women as safely ensconced in the peacetime world.
"Methinkes thou shouldst be reading o're new fashions, / Conferring
with your Tire-woman for fair dressings, / Your Ieweller has new devices for yee" (Sig. [B4]). He cannot grasp that Roderigo has brought

war into her peacetime world, that she is under siege. She tries to make him understand by alluding to the soldier who took time out from war to rape Lucrece: "There has bin ravishers, remember *Tarquin*" (Sig. [B4]). But stereotypes about war and peace prevent him from hearing her; and anyway he would rather be off at the wars than at home listening to the problems of a woman.

Women soldiers fared as badly on the Jacobean as on the Elizabethan stage. Bonduca, who acts as general, is a military disaster. She has no understanding of the masculine military code. When she scoffs at the effeminacy of Roman soldiers, twice beaten by an army commanded by "a weake woman" (I.i.19), she is severely rebuked by Caratack, her soldier/advisor, who calls her attitude "Impudence" (I.i.93), informing her that the Romans are valiant soldiers, to be admired even though they are enemies. This bond between male soldiers is beyond Bonduca's comprehension; she tries to make sense of it in "female" terms: she will try to love them too; perhaps they should make peace. For this about-face, she is rewarded with stereotype: women are always changing their minds. Caratack instructs her patiently, as if she were a military idiot: although the Romans are worthy adversaries, they must be opposed. She is a mere fool throughout; the Romans fear Caratack, but they do not fear her. Her daughters, too, fail to understand the code. They treat captured soldiers cruelly; Caratack orders a good meal for captives. When the daughters capture some Roman soldiers by a cheap trick involving a promise of love, Caratack releases them and contemptuously dismisses the daughters: "Learne to spin" (III.v.1576). Caratack becomes a raging misogynist after Bonduca makes a stupid military decision: "O you have playd the foole. / the foole extreamely. the mad foole . . . the woeman ffoole . . . Home and spinne woeman spinne, goe spinne . . . O woeman, scuruy woeman beastly woman" (III.v.1632–1648). Possibly to avoid giving offense to women in the audience, Bonduca and her daughters are allowed to redeem themselves by committing suicide nobly, but the point has been made: women have no place in war.[12]

In 1 *Iron Age*, the Trojans welcome a battalion of female reinforcements: "*Penthisilea* Queene of *Amazons*, / With mighty troopes of Virgin warriers, / Gallant Veragoes, for the loue of *Hector*, / And to reuenge his death, are entred *Troy*" (IV.i); but at the opening of 2 *Iron Age*, the Greek warrior Pyrhus heaps scorn upon them. Observing "Penthesilea, and her traine of Viragoes," Pyrhus jeers; these women reflect discredit on Priam: "For want of men / Hee brings a troope of Women to the field" (I.i); he calls them harlots. Penthesilea is stout in her legion's defense: "Curbe thy irregular tong," she tells Pyrhus; "We are those women / That practise armes, by which we purchase fame" (I.i). She recites a list of their famous victories. When Penthesilea wounds Pyrhus in single combat, Pyrhus suffers such extremes of embarrassment at having been wounded by a woman that he claims it was somebody else's blood that happened to be spilled on him. For there on, it's all downhill for the Amazons. They get involved in a dubious cause—the defense of Cressida's good name—and Pyrhus finally defeats their whole army singlehandedly, beheading Penthesilea.

Women have no place in hunting either: this masculine pursuit is peacetime's nearest equivalent to war. Heywood treats Diana and her huntresses favorably in *The Golden Age*—although I am not sure he admired their man-hating—but *The Brazen Age* dramatizes all the outrage and contempt accruing to a mortal woman who, without Diana's divine immunity, dares to take up the hunt. Among the worthies who convene to hunt the Caledonian boar is Atalanta, "a virgin huntress," who boasts, "by a womans hand the beast shall dye" (II.ii). She is in illustrious company; the hunting party comprises Meleager, Theseus, Telamon, Castor, Pollux, Jason, Peleus, Nestor, Atreus, Toxeus, Plexippus, and Adonis; but Atalanta first wounds the boar. For this courageous deed, Meleager compliments Atalanta, but at her eagerness to be in on the kill, Meleager draws the line: "Thou hast purchast honour and renowne enough, / Oh staine not all the generall youth of *Greece*, / By thy too forward spirit" (II.ii). Meleager kills the boar; out of sportsmanship, and because he is half in love with Atalanta, he gives her the "spoil" and "the fame" of the kill. The reactions of other hunters are: "Ha, to a woman"; "And so many men, / Ingag'd in't, call backe thy gift againe"; "*Greece* is by this disparaged, and our fame / Fowly eclipst"; "Snatch't from that emulous Dame"; "We must not suffer this disgrace to *Greece*"; "Let women claime 'mongst women eminence, / Our Lofty spirits, that honour haue in chace, / Cannot disgest wrongs womanish and base" (II.ii). Meleager persists; a fight breaks out in which he kills his two uncles, a crime for which he ultimately dies. If Meleager had been a man of letters, he might have written in defense of women; he is one of many male characters in this period who admire women of strength and spirit. Heywood is noncommittal; the unfairness of barring a woman from such honors is apparent, but so is the trouble caused when a woman competes with men who hold women in contempt.

Although many dramatists regarded changing sex roles as a threat to society, some dramatists writing at the height of the Jacobean *hic mulier* controversy entertained the possibility that the unisex tendencies of peacetime could be a force for good. Most interesting in its skeptical attitude towards wartime masculinity is Heywood's Homeric cycle, where the macho hero returns in the persons of Hercules, Hector, Pyrhus, and others. The cycle's last two plays, the *Iron Age* plays, dramatize the Trojan War; these are replete with bombastic utterances and mighty threats reminiscent of Marlowe's *Tamburlaine* plays. All active participants get a kick out of war: boasting about their military prowess is a favorite pastime. In one scene, during a suspension of hostilities, opposing warriors dine together; like opposing soldiers in *Bonduca,* they admire each other in a male-to-male sort of way. The scene is like a visit to a rival football team's locker room, the camaraderie that of one good jock for another. Yet Heywood is not less cynical about the Trojan War than was Shakespeare in *Troilus and Cressida.* Hector is killed in an unsportsmanlike manner, Achilles by treachery and guile; the Greeks' victory is achieved through a cheap trick conceived by a perjured coward. Throughout, the action is governed more by cunning than by courage. Thersites, as in Shakespeare's play, keeps up a commentary on the baseness and futility of it all. Heywood drives home the fact that except for Aeneas and Ulysses, virtually the only survivors of the holocaust are the two characters who, never pretending to courage, refused to fight: Thersites and Synon. The cycle is not over when the war ends: in the second half of *Part 2,* a Vice figure, Cethus, schemes to undo the surviving Greeks. (Significantly, he several times echoes Iago.) The Vice triumphs: all the Greeks but Ulysses are destroyed. The end of this epic action, at best dubiously heroic, is wholesale slaughter and the denial of life. Masculine military values seem utterly repudiated.

In the *Iron Age* plays, male warriors become brutalized by unremitting spectacles of death. Synon, who like Cethus is a kind of Vice figure in his mirthful enjoyment of evil and destruction, articulates the Greeks' joy in Troy's ruin: "Hauing spitt young children on our speares, / We'le rost them at the scorching flames of *Troy*" (*Part 2,* II.i). When these bloodthirsty warriors return to a civilian world, they can no longer feel normal emotions or behave in a manner appropriate to civilization. Pyrhus, told that his general Agamemnon has been murdered on his first night home, is undismayed and turns immediately to wooing Agamemnon's niece. Shocked, she tells him this is not the appropriate time for amorous pursuits. He sees women's values as negated by men's experience: "Tush faire *Hermione,* / These sights that seeme to Ladies terrible, / Are common to vs souldiers; when from field returning / All smear'd in blood, where Dukes and Kings lie slaine, / Yet in our Tents at mid-night it frights not vs / From courting a sweete Mistresse" (V.i). War's brutalizing effects have inured Pyrhus to civil murder, which he is no longer capable of distinguishing from death in battle. Kinship ties are so meaningless to him that the fact that he is conversing with the murdered man's niece does not seem to register. He is so far out of touch with civilized behavior that the unseemliness of alluding to frolics with camp followers while proposing marriage to a princess does not occur to him. The masculine code he is so proud of has deprived him of the stature of a civilized being. Men have lost their humanity; civilization has come into the sole possession of women. That Heywood did not share Pyrhus's views is evidenced by the fact that they are seconded by the scurvy Thersites and Synon. The dramatist is clearly saying that if these perverted values are masculine, men would do better, even at the cost of effeminacy, to adopt the values of women.

Jacomo, title figure of *The Captain,* is another returning soldier unfit for civilian life, especially female society. He cannot approach a woman unless roaring drunk or angry enough to rush into battle. Before he can meet a woman on common ground and grow to love her, he must become more feminine and she more masculine. When a woman finally ties him in a chair, harangues him, and proposes to him, he responds, "I'le have my head curl'd, and powder'd tomorrow / By break of day" (V.iv).

This motif, important in Jacobean drama, had surfaced occasionally in earlier plays. Richard returns from the wars a monster in *Richard III* (here, war accentuates monstrous tendencies present from birth). Where Achilles displays effeminacy by playing a lute, Richard does not attempt to "caper nimbly in a lady's chamber / To the lascivious pleasing of a lute" (I.i.12–13): he believes he is too ugly to bring it off. He remains a monster, like Pyrhus immune to kinship's claims, like Pyrhus unperturbed by the bloodiest of murders. In *Much Ado about Nothing,* it is only after Beatrice grows more masculine (in one scene she wishes she were male) and the returned soldier Benedick grows more feminine (he shaves off his beard and begins wearing makeup) that they become lovers in a civilized, civilian world.

War and love are symbolically reconciled in *The Brazen Age* with the copulation of Venus and Mars. Civilian and military are reconciled in Middleton and Rowley's *The World Tossed at Tennis:* "Scholar and soldier must both shut in one, / That makes the absolute and complete man" (ll. 868–869). While Jacobean drama still excluded women from the military world, it often called the military world into question as a repository of human values, sometimes advancing a rival, almost hermaphroditic ideal— a world in which, brawn not constituting the basis of human worth, the sexes could work on an equal footing to forge the values of civilization.

That the Renaissance, whether it knew it or not, was gradually growing accustomed to a less military concept of civilization is suggested by the age's very prosody. From the time of Chaucer through the early years of the sixteenth century, pentameter had struggled to oust tetrameter as the standard national meter. After major gains under Chaucer, pentameter suffered serious setbacks during the fifteenth century, only to triumph in the second half of the sixteenth. In the High Renaissance, for the first time in the history of the language, it was possible to make the general statement that the basic line of English poetry has five feet. This marked the first time in English literary history that the basic line of poetry had an odd number of feet, and the military implications are clear: pentameter is one of the few meters in poetry to which it is virtually impossible to march.

Because of the traditional association of masculinity with martial pursuits, feminism cannot flourish while society defines human value by military standards; as soon as peacetime values prevail, women's status rises. It was no accident that the feminist movement of our own time made its greatest gains after pacifism ended the Viet Nam War: if men who refused to fight could still be considered "real men," military prowess was no longer the cornerstone of virtue, and traditionally female values became respectable. Peacetime diminishes the distinction between the sexes. King James's pacifism focussed public attention on the question which Renaissance humanism made inevitable: if humanity is defined by qualities of mind and spirit, why should we grant preëminence to the physically stronger sex? The military side of the woman question which came to such prominence in Jacobean literature had been latent in the Renaissance debate about womankind from the very beginning. The pronouncements on education for women of the early Renaissance humanists Erasmus, More, and Vives were far from feminist in our sense of the term; but that the Erasmus/More circle turned to the question of women as a logical consequence of its concerted pacifist campaign against the literary glorification of war (and, incidentally, of hunting), as Robert P. Adams has persuasively argued that it did, is strong evidence that the war-and-peace issue was a potent force shaping the Renaissance view of womankind.[13] In Castiglione's *The Courtier,* the first virtue discussed is distinction in feats of arms; but this criterion for distinguishing the ideal courtier is gradually abandoned as speakers begin defining virtue in terms of the values of civilization—just governing, the exercise of the arts, love. (The thin end of the wedge is Bembo's sturdy defense, in Book I, of literature as worthier than arms.)[14] Only when man ceases to be defined as a warrior can discussion proceed to the ideal female courtier, who, despite the protestations of conservatives like Gaspar Pallavicino, turns out to be virtually identical to the ideal male courtier. In a civilized, civilian society, the immutable difference between the roles of the sexes cannot be maintained by logic.

If England was becoming more and more oriented toward the peaceable, mercantile values of a nonchivalric age, its view of the roles of men and women in society was also strongly influenced by the fact that it was becoming an urban society. The astronomical growth of London, the literary center of the country, is reflected in a literature with urban heroes.[15] Macho heroes thundering at the pampered jades of Asia would have been theatrical dinosaurs among the sophisticated legacy hunters of Jacobean city comedy, a drama whose satiric exposures of London wickedness so closely resemble celebrations of London urbanity. In the new urban civilization, men were valued more for qualities of mind than for physical strength, and women who had tasted new city freedoms were beginning to insist on an equal partnership in civilized life. In any culture where wit replaces brawn as the primary earner of wealth and status, the distinction between the sexes becomes diminished. Many writers viewed as effeminate the new city men who lived by wit and as outrageously aggressive the new city women who showed any signs of assertiveness; others proved readier to accept the changes. Literature of the High Renaissance in England offers a fair amount of comment on male effeminacy and an enormous amount of comment on female aggressiveness; although literary convention is still operating, it is not unreasonable to suspect that this intense interest in unorthodox male/female behavior reflects changing conditions in the real world.

Male effeminacy is a recurrent theme in the formal satires of the 1590s: the satires of Marston, Hall, and Guilpin are full of commentary on foppishness; and such other specialized perversions of true manliness as female impersonation, male prostitution, and buggery in academe receive mention as well. These are "city" satires, concerned with urbanization and rural depopulation, rueing the decline of hospitality and of the virtuous life of the rural gentry and yeomanry. In *Virgidemiarum*, Hall posits a pastoral Golden Age: "Then men were men, but now the greater part / Bestes are in life, and women are in heart" (Book III, Satire 1). Coming on the heels of the craze for sonnet sequences, these satires view Petrarchan lovers as effeminate. In *The Scourge of Villanie*, among those Marston considers unqualified to judge his work is the effeminate, perfumed lover who "nere in his life did other language vse, / But *Sweete Lady, faire Mistres*" (Sig. B^v); *Satyre VIII, Inamorato Curio* attacks writers of "puling sonnets," whom he characterizes as both sensual and effeminate.

Jacobean satire, seething with fops, is no less harsh than Elizabethan satire on the male denizens of London's peaceable urban society. George Wyther complains in *Abuses stript and whipt*, 1613, that men nowadays "vaunt and bragge of their lasciuious facts [i.e., deeds], / No less then of some braue *Heroick* acts" (p. 28). Richard Niccols, who in his satiric epigrams *The Fvries*, 1614, scoffs at women in male attire, also wrote the poem *Londons artillery*, 1616, a tribute to England's past military glories, nostalgic for the days of sturdy yeomen and long bows. Niccols laments the present softness of "this our peacefull cittie," populated by "eldest sonnes of idle ease, / Whom nothing but the Taylors cut can please" (pp. 100–101).

Especially after the turn of the century, the drama abounded in Osric-style fops. A group of them enter an inn in *Every Woman in Her Humour* and sit preening themselves before looking glasses; they are attacked by Accutus, a fop baiter. When the smoke clears, one fop is piqued that the fray has "put my hat quite out of fashion" (Sig. B3ᵛ). Later, in an echo of *1 Henry IV,* an inventory is made of the contents of a sleeping fop's pockets, which contain a brush, comb, looking glass, tobacco pipes, half an ounce of tobacco, and very little money.

Shakespeare is reasonably tolerant of "feminine" qualities in men. Compared with his Jacobean contemporaries, he created remarkably few fops. Contempt for male effeminacy he mainly limits to the battlefield, and even there, allegations of effeminacy are often only manipulative tools.[16] Shakespeare agrees that weeping is a feminine trait but does not necessarily despise male characters who weep. The clerical misogyny latent in Friar Laurence's rebuke to Romeo, "Thy tears are womanish, thy wild acts denote / The unreasonable fury of a beast. / Unseemly woman in a seeming man!" (*Romeo and Juliet,* III.iii.110–112) is quite exceptional. Rosalind believes that "to cry like a woman" would "disgrace my man's apparel," and Celia believes "that tears do not become a man" (*As You Like It,* II.iv.4–5, III.iv.3), but Shakespeare may not have agreed. Certainly he presents for our approval the tears of Sebastian and Exeter, although both men feel ashamed of the tears, as an inheritance from their mothers: Sebastian's admission "I am yet so near the manners of my mother that upon the least occasion more mine eyes will tell tales of me" (*Twelfth Night,* II.i.41–43) does not sully him in the audience's eyes any more than his twin sister's masculine disguise sullies her; and to Exeter's apologetic "All my mother came into mine eyes / And gave me up to tears," the manly King Henry V responds, "I blame you not, / For hearing this, I must perforce compound / With mistful eyes, or they will issue too" (*Henry V,* IV.vi.31–34).

Often in Shakespeare, context invalidates remarks about effeminacy. When Clarence calls on his murderers to "relent, and save your souls," one replies, "Relent! 'Tis cowardly and womanish" (*Richard III,* I.iv.263–265). Clarence's counterargument, "Not to relent is beastly" anticipates Macbeth's "I dare do all that may become a man. Who dares do more is none": both see pity and compassion as human rather than feminine attributes; pitilessness is not masculine but subhuman. The dramatic irony of Romeo's "O sweet Juliet, / Thy beauty hath made me effeminate, / And in my temper softened valor's steel" (III.i.118–120) is apparent; to refrain from killing Tybalt might be effeminate, but had Romeo chosen this course, tragedy might have been averted.[17] Hubert, another would-be murderer, tries to quell his pity for Arthur: "I must be brief, lest resolution drop / Out at mine eyes in tender womanish tears" (*King John,*

IV.i.35–36); again, to be womanish is preferable to murdering a child. In most civilian situations (even feuds), Shakespeare valued tender-heartedness in either sex, looking askance at those who would confuse compassion with effeminacy. It is true, though, as Madelon Gohlke maintains, that "while Shakespeare may be said to affirm the values of feeling and vulnerability associated with femininity, . . . he does not in dramatic terms dispel the anxiety surrounding the figure of the feminized male."[18] This anxiety reflects, I think, society's ambivalence toward the modern civilian/urban male.

Comment on male effeminacy in Renaissance literature was complemented, if immensely overshadowed, by comment on aggressiveness in women. Since aggressiveness was always considered a trait properly masculine, any sign of it in women was viewed as a violation of Nature, at least as serious as male effeminacy, and probably more serious.

Literature voices the common belief that English women had much more freedom than their European counterparts: "What confirmes the liberty of our women more in *England*, then the Italian Prouerbe, which saies if there were a bridge ouer the narrow Seas, all the women in *Italy* would shew their husbands a Million of light paire of heeles, and flie ouer into *England*?" (*Westward Ho*, III.iii.85–88). In *Volpone* the difference between Italian and English wives is made plain: Celia, the Italian, is never permitted to leave the house, while Lady Politic Would-be, the English tourist, astonishes the locals by going boldly about the streets of Venice and even paying calls on Volpone in his chamber, accompanied only by her maids. The pestered Volpone grumbles, "I wonder at the desperate valure / Of the bold *English,* that they dare let loose / Their wiues, to all encounters" (I.v.100–102). Lady Politic's morals are called into question by the fact that she fraternizes with Italian courtesans, seeking their advice on fashion: dramatists often besmirched feminine liberty by connecting it with libertinism. Envy for Mistress Page's freedom— "Never a wife in Windsor leads a better life than she does. Do what she will, say what she will, take all, pay all, go to bed when she list, rise when she list, all is as she will"—is put into the mouth of that dame of dubious virtue, Mistress Quickly (*Merry Wives of Windsor,* II.ii.121–125). It is the bawd Maquerelle who sees the ideal of chastity as a male plot to deprive women of liberty: "Pray ye, what's honesty, what's constancy, but fables feigned, odd old fools' chat, devised by jealous fools to wrong our liberty" (*Malcontent,* V.iii.11–13).

There is much to suggest that the Renaissance literary obsession with aggressive women reflected the realities of London life. Foreign visitors to England marvelled at Englishwomen's liberty, particularly their visiting playhouses and taverns unescorted: Thomas Platter, a Swiss traveller, went so far as to maintain that women frequented taverns and alehouses more than men did.[19] Frederick, Duke of Württemberg, who visited England in 1602, wrote that "the women have much more liberty than perhaps in any other place."[20] Fynes Moryson voiced a common proverb in 1617: "England in generall is said to be the Hell of Horses, the Purgatory of Servants and the Paradice of Weomen."[21]

The ideal of feminine home keeping was trumpeted from city pulpits. The Rev. William Gouge preached that "affaires abroad do most appertaine to the man, and are especially to be ordered by him. That which the wife is especially to care for, is the businesse of the house" (p. 257). Robert Cleaver pontificated, "the dutie of the husband is, to trauell abroad to seeke liuing: and the wiues dutie is to keep the house" (p. 170). William Whately hammered it home: "He without doores, she within: he abroad, she at home" (p. 84). Englishmen were very attracted by Antonio de Guevara's *Golden Book of Marcus Aurelius,* which went through seventeen editions in two separate English translations; its second antifeminist diatribe is touched off by Aurelius's daughter, who disgraces herself by talking and laughing with her uncles and cousins, and later by gadding about the streets of Rome with her mother. This depth of depravity provokes a lengthy harangue, some of it put in Aurelius's mouth and some proceeding directly from the author, against liberty for women. Women should never talk to any man but their husbands, not even to male relatives (incest is always a possibility). To talk to a man is to be a fallen woman; an example is adduced of a woman who so far abjured male company during her husband's absence at the wars that she sent her little sons away lest they introduce male playmates into the household; this is proffered as the only sure method of avoiding both temptation and slander. The fearful danger of windows is constantly emphasized: through windows women may glimpse men; a woman gazing through a window is to be presumed a whore.

But English Renaissance literature is full of women who gad about visiting each other, shopping, attending plays, drinking in taverns, and (especially in Jacobean city comedy) making merry with gallants. Coaches, symbols of idle extravagance to satirists and moralists, were in the drama a favored mode of transportation on gadding sprees, although one citizen's wife demurs: "O fie vpont: a Coach? I cannot abide to be iolted." The sexual double entendre of the rejoinder is inevitable: "Yet most of your Cittizens wiues loue iolting" (*Westward Ho,* II.iii.69–70). Boating down the Thames to a secluded spot, in company with her lover, her gossips, and her gossips' lovers, is a preferred gadding mode for many a wife. The waterman's cry furnished titles for three plays, *Westward Ho, Northward Ho,* and *Eastward Ho,* all involving journeys by river for immoral purposes. (In *Eastward Ho,* gadding lovers and pursuing husband are shipwrecked; the latter is humiliated to be washed up at that bend in the river known as Cuckold's Haven.) Purge, standing outside the meeting house of the orgiastic Family of Love, to which he has followed his wife, counsels, "Look too't, you that have such gadders to your wives! self-willed they are as children, and, i'faith, capable of not much more than they, peevish by custom, naturally fools" (*Family of Love*, III.iii.113–116). (Purge is embittered: his wife is revelling within, and he has forgotten the password.) In *Coriolanus*, Volumnia is nonplussed by her daughter-in-law's refusal to join the gossip Valeria in a gadding expedition:

> *Virgilia.* No, good madam, I will not out of doors.
> *Valeria.* Not out of doors!
> *Volumnia.* She shall, she shall.
> *Virgilia.* Indeed, no, by your patience. I'll not over the threshold till my lord return from the wars.
> *Valeria.* Fie, you confine yourself most unreasonably. Come, you must go visit the good lady that lies in.
> *Virgilia.* I will wish her speedy strength, and visit her with my prayers, but I cannot go thither. . . .
> *Valeria.* You would be another Penelope. Yet they say all the yarn she spun in Ulysses' absence did but fill Ithaca full of moths.
>   (I.iii.77–94)

It is partly as a reaction against the liberty of city women that I would explain the large number of promiscuous citizens' wives onstage in the early Jacobean private theatre. When these women practice deceptions in order to gain liberty, the object is nearly always adultery. They are quick to seize opportunity when their husbands leave the house ("Wheres the Gentleman your Maister?—Wher many women desire to haue their husbands, abroad" [*Westward Ho*, I.i.44–45]), and they have plenty of excuses to get out of the house themselves: "You must to the pawne to buy Lawne: to Saint Martins for Lace; to the Garden: to the Glasse-house; to your Gossips: to the powlters: else take out an old ruffe, and go to your Sempsters: excuses? Why, they are more ripe then medlers at Christmas" (*Westward Ho*, II.i.214–218). Beaumont and Fletcher's *The Woman-Hater* lists, as common shifts, pretended visits to distant churches and pretended calls on mourning widows, adding that some women, in order to enjoy adultery in the comfort of their own homes, have their husbands arrested. The reformed courtesan in Middleton's *A Trick to Catch the Old One* promises never to practice any of the usual tricks of wives:

> Henceforth for ever I defy
> The glances of a sinful eye . . .
> Wringing of fingers, biting the lip,
> The wanton gait, th' alluring trip;
> All secret friends and private meetings,

Close-borne letters and bawds' greetings;
Feigning excuse to women's labours
When we are sent for to th' next neighbour's . . .
Removing chambers, shifting beds,
To welcome friends in husbands' steads.

(V.ii.169–182)

That this courtesan knows so much about the ways of wives is believable in a dramatic world where the activities of wives and whores are so similar as to make possible a transition from whore to wife with little or no retraining. Some city wives in these plays employ bawds; several bawds run private consulting services for married women as a sideline to their normal professional activities. The bawd in *The Widow's Tears* makes arrangements "for the pleasure of two or three poor ladies that have prodigal knights to their husbands" (II.ii.58–60). The bawd in *1 Honest Whore* subcontracts the trade in citizens' wives to her pander at "sixpence a lane" (III.ii.78–80). Professional prostitutes are understandably resentful of this amateur intrusion, just as Shylock resents Antonio's interest-free loans. Mistress Newcut is charged with unfair business practices by a gang of irate prostitutes in *Your Five Gallants;* her merchant husband being at sea, she has paid a bawd for the privilege of viewing through a spy hole the gallants who enter the brothel; choosing one Tailby, a "smockster," she has arranged to keep him.

Such unflattering portraits of middle-class wives arose in the private theater, patronized as it was by the upper class, partly as literary revenge on the affluent London citizenry which was gaining so much power at the expense of the aristocracy; these two classes would meet head-on in civil war within a generation, and class tensions are evident in Jacobean literature from the very beginning. It is unlikely that young aristocrats cuckolded prosperous merchants with such regularity in real life: gallants would have had little motive for patronizing a drama based on such wish-fulfilment fantasies if they were getting their own social revenge by cuckolding real citizens.

There is one way, though, in which the satire on citizens' wives may have been more directly provoked by reality—one suspicious element of the citizen's wife's behavior that would almost certainly have called her morals into question: she worked outside the home. The drama is full of women who mind the store—shopkeepers' wives who serve customers, often in their husbands' absence. Outside the servant class, the only other city women who worked and brought in money were whores. The inference is obvious.

The type of work, too, invited comparisons with prostitution. Gallants called in at all hours at the mercer's shop, as at the brothel; and the mercer's wife met them with a smile, as the prostitute did. Like a harlot, the shopkeeper's wife did not stay home with the children but dealt at first hand with the public. During slack times in the shop, she often stood in the doorway or sat just outside on a bench, watching the world go by. This forward behavior was easily construed as solicitation; even prostitutes were more discreet, sending forth their panders to bring in business rather than displaying themselves at brothel door. Sitting in a doorway seems innocuous to the modern reader, but Renaissance observers often found it shocking.

The private theater consistently satirized the middle-class working wife. In Marston's *The Dutch Courtesan,* a speech approving the practice of using a wife as a sexual lure for customers is put into the mouth of a vintner's wife, who, since she goes with a friendly neighborhood bawd to the orgiastic "services" of the sect called the Family of Love, is hardly a spokesman for the author's values: "He [a goldsmith] comes forward in the world well, I warrant him; and his wife is a proper woman, that she is. Well, she has been as proper a woman as any in Cheap; she paints now, and yet she keeps her husband's old customers to him still. In troth, a fine-fac'd wife in a wainscot carved seat is a worthy ornament to a tradesman's shop, and an attractive, I warrant; her husband shall find it in the custom of his ware, I'll assure him" (III.iii.6–13).

Plays of the public theater occasionally display genuine enthusiasm for the shop-minding wife, as in the apotheosis of the Royal Exchange in Heywood's sanguine piece of bourgeois propaganda, *If You Know Not Me, You Know Nobody, Part 2,* where the Exchange's founder, Sir Thomas Gresham, rhapsodizes: "It shall be in the pleasure of my life / To come and meet our merchants at their houre / . . . Twill do me good to see shops, with faire wiues / Sit to attend the profit of their husbands." But more often, plays of the public theater are defensive about the practice; several passages hasten to assure the audience that a wife who attends customers is not necessarily fair game. *The Miseries of Enforced Marriage* displays some uneasiness over the accessiblity of shopkeepers' wives: the dishonorable gallant Bartley walks up and down Goldsmith's Row, spending "some conference with the shopkeeper's wives; they have seats built a purpose for such familiar entertainment" (Act IV). In *The Wise-Woman of Hogsdon,* a sempster's shop is minded by Luce, this time the tradesman's daughter. When Luce's father instructs her to mind the shop by herself for a while, Luce asks the apprentice to stay with her:

> I doe not love to sit thus publikely:
> And yet upon the traffique of our Wares,
> Our provident Eyes and presence must still wayte.
> Do you attend the shop, Ile ply my worke [i.e., needlework].
> I see my father is not jelous of me,

That trusts mee to the open view of all.
The reason is, hee knowes my thoughts are chast,
And my care such, as that it needes the awe
Of no strict Overseer.

                                                        (I.ii)

Grissil, before her marriage, declines her father's invitation to join him
in working outside on a warm day: "Me thinkes it doth not fit a maide, /
By sitting thus in view, to draw mens eyes / To stare vpon her . . . I
could be more content to worke within" (Chettle, Dekker, and Haughton's *Patient Grissil*, I.ii.25–28).[22]

Another persistent motif, one which recalls *The Golden Book of Marcus
Aurelius,* is the woman at the window. Mistress Taffeta hails gentlemen
in the street from her window in Barry's *Ram-Alley.* A prostitute is
glimpsed sitting at her window in *How a Man May Choose.* Mall Berry
applies her makeup before a window, for all passers to behold, in *The
Fair Maid of the Exchange.* Often lascivious gallants must approach a woman
by calling at her window because she has been locked up by a husband
or relative. This is why Volpone masquerades as a mountebank under
Celia's window, and why Maria in *The Family of Love* must make arrangements through her window to have her lover smuggled up to her
chamber in a trunk. Sitting in a window, like sitting in a doorway, often
allied a woman with prostitution in the popular imagination. Italian
prostitutes were popularly believed to solicit mainly from their windows; Lady Politic Would-be is not the only Englishwoman in the drama
to learn something from Italian courtesans.

If even windows were suspect, the only place a woman was really safe
from seducers was deep in the bowels of her house, preferably surrounded by six children and no gossips. In an age when a woman's going
outside was an aggressive and probably immoral act, it is easy to see
how the assertive, businesslike citizen's wife was transformed by the drama
into a model of loose morals. Economic changes were producing new
lifestyles for city women, which brought down on them the antifeminist
wrath of those whose conservatism could not accommodate such changes.

Nothing short of an encyclopedia could do justice to Renaissance
treatments of female sexual transgressions, from John Dickenson's Fair
Valeria, who belongs to a club that keeps a stable of male whores, to the
legion of deceitful wives (from *The Deceit of Women* in 1560 to Jacobean
city comedy) who smuggle lovers into their chambers disguised as music
masters or hidden in luggage, concealing lovers under their farthingales
when a husband unexpectedly appears. The plot lines are as ancient as
the sentiments: the cynical stories go back to the Middle Ages or even

classical antiquity; the belief that most women are incontinently lustful is a logical extension of the doctrine that the virtuous woman has hardly any sexual desires at all.

Many literary passages show chastity nearly extinct in the modern female. A man who wishes for an "honest" woman is in for a long search. "Marry a harlot, why not? . . . If none should be married but those that are honest, where should a man seek a wife after Christmas?" (Middleton's *Michaelmas Term*, V.iii.125–129). "Those women which haue it, / Keepe their honesty so close, that not one / Amongst a hundred is perceiued to haue it"; "Women and honesty are as neere alyde, / As parsons liues are to their doctrines" (*Ram-Alley*, II.i.941–942, IV.i.1666–1667). "Say thou are not a Whore, and that's more then fifteene women (amongst fiue hundred) dare sweare without lying" (*2 Honest Whore*, V.ii.179–180). "It is so rare a thing to bee honest amongst you, that some one man in an age, may perhaps suspect some two women to be honest, but neuer beleeue it verily" (*The Woman-Hater*, Sig. [C4]ᵛ). "Honest Countrey Wenches! in what hundred shall a man find two of that simple vertue?" (*Westward Ho*, I.i.21–22). Vindice has a fine passage on global female immorality:

> Now 'tis full sea a-bed over the world,
> There's juggling of all sides; some that were maids
> E'en at sunset are now perhaps i'th'toll-book.
> This woman in immodest thin apparel
> Lets in her friend by water; here a dame
> Cunning nails leather hinges to a door
> To avoid proclamation.
> Now cuckolds are a-coining, apace, apace, apace, apace!
> And careful sisters spin that thread i'th'night
> That does maintain them and their bawds i'th'day.
> (Tourneur's *Revenger's Tragedy*, II.ii.136–146)

What is striking about Renaissance sexual cynicism is the frequency with which the charge of sexual immorality is levelled at female characters who have attained some measure of freedom of action. One of the major charges in the Renaissance misogynist's catalogue, lust, may have been no more than a backlash against feminine freedom and assertiveness in the real world.

This seems particularly apparent in the Renaissance stereotype of the widow as unregenerately lecherous, which Roger MacDonald has argued was a reaction against the uniquely independent status of widows.[23] The widow stereotype, as it appears full-blown in Valeria in Dickenson's *Fair Valeria*, Eudora and Cynthia in *The Widow's Tears*, Mistress Taffeta in *Ram-Alley*, Lady Plus in the anonymous *Puritan: or, The Widow of Watling Street*, Gertrude in *Hamlet*, Regan in *Lear*, the heroine of Marston's

The Insatiate Countess, and many others, consists of a widow's turning a lascivious eye, with indecent haste, upon another man. Gertrude remarries so quickly that "the funeral baked meats / Did coldly furnish forth the marriage tables" (*Hamlet,* I.ii.180); Cynthia in *The Widow's Tears* takes a lover in the tomb of her lately-deceased husband. The raison d'être of this stereotype is complex. The idea that lust is the only conceivable reason for remarriage is related to the Patristic reverence for celibacy—the notion goes back to Tertullian. Probably the lustful widow stereotype contains a generous portion of male wishful thinking: the old belief that widows are an easy sexual mark has passed intact to the twentieth century, now merely transferred to the divorcee. More important, the stereotype suggests nagging worry on the part of husbands about what was to become of their wealth and their name if they predeceased their wives. In many Renaissance epigrams, a woman wastes her late husband's wealth on a young man who has married her for her money. The issue united the high concern of the Renaissance with posterity and earthly immortality with the lower Renaissance concern with cash. A man left behind him his children, his good name, and his fortune; his fears about what would become of all three after he died are reflected in stereotypes about widows. Renaissance literature is full of Fair Valerias: many an incontinent widow marries away her late husband's fortune, neglects his children, and by her lewd behavior brings his name posthumously into ridicule. The remarriage of widows was, in fact, often considered posthumous cuckoldry. "Widows' marriages" are "a kind of lawful adultery, like usury, permitted by the law, not approv'd . . . To wed a second [is] no better than to cuckold the first" (*Widow's Tears,* II.iv.26–28).[24] Like cuckoldry, the widow's remarriage endangers legitimate heirs: "My sister [in law] hath so possess'd my brother's heart with vows and disavowings, seal'd with oaths of [i.e., against] second nuptials, as in that confidence he hath invested her in all his state, the ancient inheritance of our family, and left my nephew and the rest to hang upon her pure devotion; so as he dead, and she matching (as I am resolv'd she will) with some young prodigal, what must ensue but her post-issue beggar'd, and our house, already sinking, buried quick in ruin?" (*Widow's Tears,* II.iii.72–81).

But allowing for the complexity of Renaissance attitudes toward widows, the conjunction of charges of lust with widowhood's inherent freedom of action combines with other literary evidence to suggest that the charge of lechery was a smear tactic against assertiveness and liberty.

Writers were clearly envisioning lewdness as an expression of women's struggle for power when they created women who practice cuckoldry as revenge upon their husbands, usually for shrew-taming attempts. When Glister threatens, "I say you are a scold, and beware the cucking-stool," his wife rejoins, "I say you are ninnihammer, and beware the cuckoo; for as sure as I have ware, I'll traffic with the next merchant venturer" (*Family of Love*, V.i.25–29). When Gerillo, a young bachelor in the anonymous *Wit of a Woman*, wonders what a husband should do with a brawling, scolding wife, another bachelor repeats his father's advice: "Either say nothing to her, that will fret her: or out-scolde her, and that will mad her: or cudgell her, and that will tame her: or keepe her bare, and that will kill her." But a third bachelor is dubious: "Peace man, then she will either poyson thee, or cut thy throate, or do some other mischiefe vnto thee, or make thy head like Cuckoldes hauen" (Sig. G). In Egypt, too, wives practice cuckoldry as revenge: Iras believes "it is a deadly sorrow to behold a foul knave uncuckolded" (*Antony and Cleopatra*, I.ii.76–77).

The man-clothed woman herself was branded lecherous on account of her aggressiveness. Henry Parrot, in *The Gossips Greeting; or, A new Discovery of such Females meeting*, 1620, impugns the morals of such female swaggerers as "in the suburbs domineere and roare; / Each being a swagering swearer, and a whore" (Sig. [C4]). The suburbs, where the brothels were located, are the proper venue for these assertive dames: a woman whose behavior is in any way "masculine" is as good as a whore in Parrot's view. And this view was widely shared.

Some writers, though, were alive to the possibility that the outgoing personality of the modern woman was open to misinterpretation—that men frequently misconstrue female friendliness as an invitation to immorality: "Kindnesse, is tearmed Lightnesse, in our sex" (John Cooke's *Greene's Tu Quoque*, Sig. [H4]). Falstaff misconstrues Mistress Ford's friendliness in *The Merry Wives of Windsor:* "I do mean to make love to Ford's wife. I spy entertainment in her. . . . She gives the leer of invitation" (I.iii.47–49). He also means to make love to Mistress Page, "who even now gave me good eyes too, . . . did so course o'er my exteriors with such a greedy intention that the appetite of her eye did seem to scorch me up like a burning glass!" (I.iii.65–74). On receipt of Falstaff's love letter, Mistress Page ransacks her memory: "What an unweighed behavior hath this Flemish drunkard picked . . . out of my conversation, that he dares in this manner assay me? Why, he hath not been thrice in my company! . . . I was then frugal of my mirth" (II.i.24–29). She concludes that such lascivious misconstructions are typical of the male sex: "Why, I'll exhibit a bill in the Parliament for the putting down of men" (II.i.29–31). Later, Mistress Page insists, "Wives may be merry, and yet honest [i.e., chaste] too. / We do not act that often jest and laugh" (IV.ii.107–108). Moll Cutpurse, in *The Roaring Girl*, challenges her would-be seducer to a duel,

> To teach thy base thoughts manners: thou'rt one of those
> That thinks each woman thy fond flexible whore:
> If she but cast a liberal eye upon thee,

Turn back her head, she's thine. . . .
How many of our sex, by such as thou,
Have their good thoughts paid with a blasted name
That never deserv'd loosely.

(III.i.72–84)

Iago's insinuations about Desdemona—"What an eye she has! Methinks
it sounds a parley to provocation"—are rebuffed by Cassio: "An inviting
eye, and yet methinks right modest" (*Othello*, II.iii.22–25). Othello, too,
at first resists interpreting Desdemona's friendliness as wantonness: " 'Tis
not to make me jealous / To say my wife is fair, feeds well, loves company, / Is free of speech, sings, plays, and dances well. / Where virtue is,
these are more virtuous" (III.iii.183–186).

Several plays demonstrate that the safest response to misconstrued
friendliness is more assertiveness: Mistresses Ford and Page salvage their
reputations by seeing Falstaff pitched into the river; Moll Cutpurse thrashes
her importuner in a duel. Desdemona, who adopts the approved mode
of wifely submissiveness, is promptly throttled.

Whether or not the world had grown significantly lewder, the charge
of feminine lewdness, levelled at citizens' wives, widows, shrews, and
man-clothed women, maintained a suspicious connection with dislike
for feminine liberty, especially the new liberties of the city. If, in the
popular imagination, to step outside the door of one's home was to court
defloration, what maidenhead could possibly survive attendance at bawdy
plays and other city entertainments? As True-wit says to Morose: "Alas,
sir, doe you euer thinke to find a chaste wife, in these times? now? when
there are so many masques, plaies, puritane preachings, mad-folkes, and
other strange sights to be seene daily, priuate and publique? if you had
liu'd in king Ethelred's time, sir, or Edward the Confessors, you might,
perhaps, haue found in some cold countrey-hamlet, then, a dull frostie
wench, would haue been contented with one man: now, they will as
soone be pleas'd with one leg, or one eye" (*Epicoene*, II.ii.32–41).

When John Chamberlain reported in 1620 that the clergy were carrying out King James's orders to discourage female transvestism on the
London streets, "Our pulpits ring continually of the insolence and impudence of women" (see chapter 6), and when the author of *Hic Mulier*
accused man-clothed women of possessing the "impudence of harlots,"
their diction was typical of the times: "impudence" was a charge frequently levelled at Jacobean womankind. Meaning literally "shameless-
ness" or "lack of modesty," "impudence" derives from the Latin *pudēre*,
"to be ashamed," as does "pudendum," an organ which it is a breach of
modesty to expose. As the Renaissance used the word, an impudent
woman was without sexual shame, a concupiscent woman; but she was
also bold of speech and action, an insolent, aggressive woman. The term

draws together the concupiscible and irascible faults of womankind, uniting aggression with lust. It is little wonder that a term with this dual meaning should have evolved, given the persistent connection in the Renaissance imagination between assertiveness and lewdness.

Jonson's Epicoene, whose name means "androgynous," stands accused of "Amazonian impudence" (III.v.41). Jonson was one among many male writers in the Renaissance who recoiled in indignation from the sort of women who would leave home and meet together, to "crie downe, or vp, what they like, or dislike . . . with most masculine, or rather *hermaphroditicall* authoritie" (*Epicoene,* I.i.78–80).

Literature of the English High Renaissance abounds in dialogue, epithet, incident, and costume which suggest changing sex roles—the constant juxtaposition of fop and virago, each of whom partakes of the other's sexual "nature"; the high incidence of transvestism in the drama; the imputing of effeminacy to civilian men; the literary attention being paid to assertive city women; the charge of lewdness which can so often be read obliquely as a protest against liberty. What we know about the real-life female transvestite movement, about the dandified gallants of King James's court, about the traumas of transition to a peacetime society, about the new way of life women were encountering and creating in a London which was suddenly a large city, suggests that literature was here reflecting life—that sex roles were changing and the distinction between the sexes diminishing, just as literature showed.

Ovid's tale of Hermaphroditus and Salmacis, extant in at least four Renaissance translations and adaptations in English, can stand as an emblem of the unisex tendencies of Renaissance life, so often feared and contemned, but occasionally welcomed. In Ovid, the hermaphrodite is created when the sexually aroused Salmacis wraps herself around the shy, retiring Hermaphroditus and refuses to let go: the essential ingredients of the story are male timidity and female lasciviousness, the latter expressing itself in aggression. Not much imagination is required to see why this story appealed to Renaissance England.

NOTES

1. Paula S. Berggren, "The Woman's Part: Female Sexuality as Power in Shakespeare's Plays," in *The Woman's Part*, p. 19.

2. A number of scholars believe that *The Fair Maid of the West* was written before the death of Elizabeth, although the Harbage/Schoenbaum *Annals of English Drama* assigns it to 1610. Judging by its treatment of female transvestism, the play could belong either to the 1590s or to the second decade of the seventeenth century, but not, I think, to the years 1600 to ca. 1608.

3. As Berggren notes, "For Anglo-Saxon audiences, . . . a man in travesty, as the term suggests, remains an instrument of farce. In a society where men are ashamed to weep, to appear womanly can only be a humiliation" (*The Woman's Part*, p. 21). Given such attitudes, the occasional serious use of male transvestism as a plot device is the more remarkable—and its seriousness the more open to dispute.

4. *The Prose Works of Sir Philip Sidney*, ed. Albert Feuillerat, IV, p. 17; I, pp. 75–76.

5. Mark Rose, "Sidney's Womanish Man," p. 357.

6. John F. Danby, *Poets on Fortune's Hill*, p. 56.

7. Elizabeth Dipple, "Metamorphosis in Sidney's *Arcadias*," p. 62.

8. Edward Hake's *A Commemoration of the most prosperous and peaceable Raigne of our gratious and deere Soueraigne Lady Elizabeth*, 1575, for example, celebrates seventeen years' peace and prosperity under Elizabeth.

9. Barnabe Rich, *Favltes favlts, and nothing else but favltes*, Sig. [F4]ᵛ.

10. This wholly favorable treatment of the motif of war stopped by the intervention of the female principle is a rarity in Shakespeare. It is complemented, in pre-Jacobean Shakespeare, by the fact that Falstaff is not a woman: it is the antagonist Hotspur in *1 Henry IV* who scorns the soft world of women and music in favor of war, while the peacetime world which the hero puts aside in favor of battle is not associated with femininity, as it might so easily have been. As a result, the peaceable influence of women emerges as a positive (if minor) force in the play.

11. Dyce's edition of Beaumont and Fletcher.

12. Celeste Turner Wright connects the drama's dislike of women soldiers with the *hic mulier* issue: "One reason for such vehemence against fighting-women was doubtless the roughness and immodesty of such Roaring Girls as London actually knew" ("The Amazons in Elizabethan Literature," p. 448).

13. Robert P. Adams, *The Better Part of Valor: More, Erasmus, Colet, and Vives on Humanism, War, and Peace, 1496–1535*, chapter 13.

14. Adams, documenting the decay of chivalric war during the fifteenth century, cites the late fifteenth-century *Boke of Noblesse*'s lament that the sons of aristocratic houses were deserting chivalry for civilian professions like law; he concludes that "the old chivalry was already clearly decaying though still cherished by old-fashioned courtiers" (*The Better Part of Valor*, p. 15).

15. Louis B. Wright notes that "in Chaucer's prime, London had a population of probably fewer than 50,000 inhabitants. The population in 1563 has been estimated at 93,276; in 1580, 123,034; in 1593–95, 152,478; in 1605, 224,275; in 1622, 272,207; in 1634, 339,824" (*Middle-Class Culture*, p. 10).

16. A frequent rhetorical device in wartime contexts is the attempt to shame men into action by claiming that women would dare more than they have dared: "Had I been there, which am a silly woman, / The soldiers should have tossed me on their pikes, / Before I would have granted to that act"; "Women and children of so high a courage, / And

warriors faint! Why, 'twere perpetual shame" (*3 Henry VI*, I. i.243–245, V.iv.50–51). Some characters seek to impress a sense of emergency upon political leaders by proclaiming the situation so desperate that even women have been moved to action. Scroop reports to King Richard that "boys with women's voices / Strive to speak big and clap their female joints / In stiff unwieldy arms against thy crown. / . . . Yea, distaff women manage rusty bills / Against thy seat" (*Richard II*, III.ii.113–119).

17. Coppélia Kahn, in "Coming of Age in Verona," shows how the feud in *Romeo and Juliet* fosters "fear and scorn of women, associating women with effeminacy and emasculation," arguing that "Romeo's death in the tomb of the Capulets rather than in that of his own fathers reverses the traditional passage of the female over to the male house in marriage and betokens his refusal to follow the code of his fathers" (*The Woman's Part*, pp. 173, 190).

18. Madelon Gohlke, *The Woman's Part*, p. 163.

19. Thomas Platter, *Thomas Platter's Travels in England*, p. 170.

20. "A True and Faithful Narrative of the Bathing Excursion," in William Brenchley Rye, *England as seen by Foreigners in the Days of Elizabeth and James the First* (New York: Benjamin Blom, 1967; first published 1865), p. 7.

21. Quoted by Louis B. Wright, p. 466. Cf. also Carroll Camden, *The Elizabethan Woman*, p. 17.

22. Bowers's edition of Dekker.

23. Roger MacDonald, "The Widow: A Recurring Figure in Jacobean and Caroline Comedy."

24. For this reason among others, we need not take the Ghost's "adulterate beast" (*Hamlet*, I.v.42) as evidence that Gertrude and Claudius were lovers before the death of Hamlet Senior.

CHAPTER EIGHT

Saints of Sonnet and the Fight for the Breeches

LITERARY EXPRESSIONS of what might be called sexual chiasma (the crossing-over of qualities between the sexes), widespread and intense during the *hic mulier* years of the Jacobean period, are visible throughout the Renaissance in literature dealing with love and marriage, where women are so often powerful and dominant, men passive and downtrodden. With regard to love and marriage, the Renaissance inherited from the late Middle Ages two literary traditions in which the conventional sexual hierarchy is reversed to give dominance to the woman—the aristocratic tradition of courtly love and the bourgeois tradition of the wife wearing the breeches. Both are important to the question of the nature of the sexes which came to the fore in the *hic mulier* controversy.

Medieval courtly love was inimical to marriage: the knight humbled himself in chivalrous devotion to the lady who was goods and chattels to her husband, and it was only by maintaining a strict separation between the two institutions that the male-dominated, property-oriented institution of marriage could be prevented from destroying the fragile female dominion that existed in courtly love. When Shakespeare and Spenser finished what Chaucer had begun and united romantic love once and for all with marriage, the whole notion of courtly love grew increasingly illogical. Chaucer had proposed a compromise between woman as worshipped mistress and woman as submissive wife: a man might be a woman's "servant in love, and lord in mariage";[1] and the Renaissance followed his lead. But linking courtly love to marriage showed up courtly love in an odd light: why should a man grovel before a woman he is shortly to dominate in marriage?

Grovelling came to be viewed with a jaundiced eye for another reason, too: where courtly love, always romantically adulterous, had provided no scope at all for matrimonial intentions, the Protestant Renaissance, by positing courtly love as a stage of courtship, shackled itself with the problem of dishonorable intentions; more and more, the male courtly/Petrarchan lover came under suspicion as a seducer. And the seducer, in

Renaissance England, did not have a manly image: no true, stout Englishman, the seducer insinuated himself with words, especially with poetry; he had a smooth, deceitful tongue—like a woman's. Conscious of their image, some of Shakespeare's most articulate male characters present themselves as bluff manly soldiers when they woo: "I wooed thee with my sword," Theseus reminds Hippolyta (*Midsummer Night's Dream,* I.i.16); "Rude am I in my speech, / And little blest with the soft phrase of peace," the soldier-turned-lover Othello mendaciously maintains (*Othello,* I.iii.81–82); but it is an Englishman, the consummate actor Henry V, who is eagerest to avoid the smooth-talker image: "I speak to thee plain soldier. If thou canst love me for this, take me"; he has nothing but disdain for "these fellows of infinite tongue that can rhyme themselves into ladies' favors" (*Henry V,* V.ii.155–164). The medieval courtly lover, while an excellent ladies' man, went on beheading Saracens with unimpeachable virility; by the end of the sixteenth century, however, the specter of seduction conspired with doubts about the virility of civilian men to create a new image of the male courtly/Petrarchan lover as an effeminate fop. The natural identification of courtiers with courtly love in the popular imagination doubtless contributed to the Jacobean image of the male courtier as an effeminate, emasculated dandy—a central image of the essay *Haec-Vir.*

Love poetry of the courtly and Petrarchan tradition, like the formal controversy about women, was chiefly a literary game. Not until the nineteenth century did men light upon the inspired strategy of installing living women upon pedestals, where, once stranded, they were effectually barred from meddling in this world's affairs; in the Renaissance, only fictional women were placed for veneration above eye level. (Whatever the case with Stella, Penelope Devereux was hardly a woman to remain marooned on anybody's pedestal.) Courtly love was, by the time of the Renaissance, no longer peculiar to the court—there are enough languishing lovers and pearly teeth blazons in popular ballads to indicate that courtly love had joined other traditions in descending the social scale—but it was still chiefly literary: its conventions remained too static over the last two-thirds of the sixteenth century to admit of very much contact with real human lovers. Sidney sensed the literary artificiality of contemporary love poetry: "Many of such writings as come under the banner of unresistable love, if I were a mistress, would never persuade me they were in love; so coldly they apply fiery speeches, as men that had rather read lovers' writings."[2]

Its remoteness from the world of action may be reflected in the fact that courtly love, in the Renaissance at least, did not travel well among genres; short lyric, from sonnet to ballad, seemed its natural soil; it did not fare very well when transplanted to fiction or drama, where devel-

opment of plot and character was fuller. Petrarchan passions are subjected to gentle parody, and ultimately dismissed as irrelevant, when they
appear in Shakespeare's plays, from *The Two Gentlemen of Verona* to *Romeo and Juliet* and *As You Like It.* One scornful lady, whose story was
told and retold in prose fiction by Bandello, Belleforest, Painter, Fenton,
and John God, and finally dramatized by Gervase Markham and Lewis
Machin as *The Dumb Knight,* disdains her lover a little too long: when
her life is in his power, he has his way with her for fifteen consecutive
days, in God's version, in revenge for her cruelty. Here the brisk, cynical
brutality of the fabliau is turned directly on courtly love's burning devotion, with the ardor-dampening force of a fire hose; but what is interesting is that the dumb knight eventually marries his humiliated lady.
Faced with the courtly situation, this author has provided the bourgeois
solution: nothing takes the wind out of an uppity lady's sails like a good
shrew taming. Bridging the gap between courtly love and marriage in
no-nonsense fashion, this popular story turns an Astrophel's Stella into a
Petruchio's Kate.

To be taken seriously during the Renaissance, the courtly elevation of
Woman had to be safely circumscribed in lyric. The sonnet sequence did
not tell a story; it rang changes on a confined group of related emotions—the repeated push of the masochistic tongue against the exquis-
itely aching tooth of unrequited love. Once propelled into the literature
of plot and action, courtly love is so lated in the world as to lose its way
forever. Romeo must simply get over his hopeless love for Rosaline,
with all its literary affectations, before he can find a true love, in Juliet,
that will eventuate in marriage. The heroine of the dumb knight story
finds herself catapulted out of her complacent role as sonnet mistress into
the role of embattled shrew. Outside lyric poetry, the bourgeois model
of the fight for the breeches had far greater influence on literature than
had the courtly model of goddess and adorer.

A tantalizing question is whether the backlash against Petrarchan poetry suggests that for all its literary artificiality the tradition was taken
seriously as a symbol of women's enhanced stature in the real world. A
certain amount of resentment of the male lover's abject grovellings is
conventional to Petrarchan poetry. The poem "A carelesse man, scorning
and describing, the subtle vsage of women towarde their louers" in *Tottel's Miscellany* suggests that the spectacle of male suffering gratifies a
mistress's power hunger: "She, that fedes him so, I fele, and finde it
plain: / Is but to glory in her power, that ouer such can reign." Now and
then a recalcitrant Petrarchan lover refuses to die of unrequited love:
"The louer waxeth wiser, and will not die for affection" (a title in *Tottel's*). Some lovers go so far as to contemplate revenge:

There's nothing grieves me but that age should haste
That in my days I may not see thee old . . .
Thy pearly teeth out of thy head so clean
That when thou feed'st, thy nose shall touch thy chin.
These lines that now [thou] scorn'st, which should
     delight thee,
Then would I make thee read but to despight thee.[3]

In the "rebellious lover" tradition, a number of Petrarchan lovers give up love altogether, resolving to shun the company of women henceforth.[4] But all this is conventional. In fact, the rebellious lover convention comes so close to the convention of the misogynist as a man disappointed in love, prominent in the formal controversy about women (see part 1), as to suggest a direct influence in one direction or the other;[5] and any link with the formal controversy only heightens the sense of literary artificiality in the Petrarchan tradition.

But courtly love poetry was attacked by writers in other genres, and those who turned viciously upon the Petrarchan tradition repeatedly referred the argument to living women: where the sonnet mistress is beautiful in literature, basking in adoration, her real-life counterparts (according to opponents of Petrarchanism) are physically repulsive, leading a life of drudgery and degradation. Joseph Hall, who declares in *Virgidemiarum* that he chooses to write formal satires rather than to "sonnet of my Mistresse face / To plaint some Blowesse with a borrowed grace" (Book I, Satire I), satirizes the Petrarchan sonneteer:

Then can he terme his durtie ill-fac'd bride,
Lady and Queene, and virgin deifide:
Be shee all sootie-blacke, or bery-browne,
Shees white as morrows milk, or flaks new
     blowne.
And tho she be some dunghill drudge at home,
Yet can he her resigne some refuse roome
Amids the well-knowne stars: or if not there,
Sure will he Saint her in his Calendere.
(Book I, Satire VII)

The misogynist Gondarino in *The Woman-Hater* is nauseated by the courtly/ Petrarchan tradition: "How familiar a thing is it with the Poets of our age, to extoll their whores, which they call mistresses, with heauenly praises? . . . How many that would faine seeme serious, haue dedicated graue works to ladies tooth-lesse, hollow ei'd, their haire shedding, purplefac'd, their nayles apparantly comming off; and the bridges of their noses broken downe; and haue called thē the choyse handy workes of nature, the patterns of perfection, and the wondermēt of women" (Sig. [F4].) *Cupid's Whirligig* provides another such antiblazon: "Teeth like two rowes of orient pearle . . . But the string is broken & many of them are fallen out" (Sig. I3). It is true that some such comments are meant to reflect discredit upon their speakers, who are stock misogynists, but their disgust with the female body is delineated a little more enthusiastically than is really necessary for such a purpose. *How a Man May Choose a Good Wife from a Bad,* a putative defense of good women, seems to exult in the contrast between the adored sonnet mistress and the downtrodden Patient Grissill figure, as a Petrarchan blazon is startlingly employed to describe the heroine's brutal beating at the hands of her husband:

> Nay, did he not
> With his rude fingers dash you on the face,
> And double-dye your coral lips with blood?
> Hath he not torn those gold wires from your head . . .
> Hath he not beat you, and with his rude fists
> Upon that crimson temperature of your cheeks
> Laid a lead colour with his boist'rous blows?
>
> (IV.iii)

As well as working to re-degrade the women so unnaturally elevated by Petrarchan poetry, many authors heaped contempt upon the men who so abdicated manly dominance as to abase themselves before a woman. Contemplating the sonneteer, John Marston declares, "I doe sadly grieue, and inly vexe / To view the base dishonors of our sexe" (*Scourge of Villanie,* Satyre VIII, "Inamorato Curio"). Hall accuses those who are "o'er-ruld with loue, and tyrannous disdaine" of displaying the "folly of a feeble braine" (*Virgidemiarum,* Satire VII). The male courtly lover staged in the drama was often a fool. The Petrarchan lover in *A Woman Is a Weathercock,* whose sonnets are studded with such gems as "I sigh thou precious stonie Iewell, / Wearing of silke, why art thou still so cruell" (III.iii.25–26), is aptly named Abraham Ninnie; when the tobacco fiend Petoune in *The Fleire,* absurdly directing Petrarchan attentions to a bawd, simpers "I protest I cannot but commend the whitenes of your skin," the bawd comments sardonically, "I thinke a be a Tanner, and meanes to buy me for my skin" (Sig. [F4]ᵛ). Other Petrarchan suitors in the drama are downright wicked: the unspeakable Syphax argues that Sophonisba deserves rape "for all thy scornful eyes, thy proud disdain, / And late contempt of us" (Marston's *Sophonisba,* III.i.7–8), and he is not the only male character whose renewed sense of masculine dominance, once he is cured of the follies of Petrarchan respect for women, expresses itself in violence toward women: Vallenger in *The Fair Maid of Bristow,* who employs Petrarchan religious diction to repent his former misogyny ("False tongue that spoke such blasphemy before, / That I dispraised, now doth my soule adore" [I.i.33–34]), soon recovers and plots the lady's murder.

Sometimes Petrarchan idolatry was rejected on Christian grounds—not surprising since the religious diction typical of courtly love since its medieval inception sets it up as a rival of Christian devotion: Edward Guilpin objects to the blasphemy of the love poets, inveighing against "committing idolatry" with a "painted saint" (prefatory epigrams to *Skialetheia); The Fair Maid of the Exchange* expresses shock that a man could "wrong the adoration of his Maker, / By worshipping a wanton female skirt, / And making Loue his Idoll" (Sig. C2ᵛ). But the most frequent charge levelled at the male Petrarchan was effeminacy, indicating that it was the inversion of sex roles that authors found most disturbing. When Anselm, a Petrarchan lover in *How a Man May Choose,* speaks in conceits of drowning and burning, affects the lover's melancholic dishabille, keeps tokens of his lady's, and fears death by frowning, his friend Fuller upbraids him for effeminate behavior, "female fooleries"; he advises different amatory strategies:

> First, be not bashful, bar all blushing tricks:
> Be not too apish-female; do not come
> With foolish sonnets to present her with,
> With legs, with curtsies, congees, and such like:
> Nor with penn'd speeches, or too far-fetch'd sighs.

When Anselm interrupts, "O, but I cannot snatch occasion: / She dashes every proffer with a frown," Fuller cannot conceal his disgust: "A frown, a fool! art thou afraid of frowns?" The proper manly way to woo, Fuller counsels, is by force. He describes how he once jettisoned Petrarchan techniques in favor of the cave-man approach, with very satisfactory results: the wench was in bed with him before he could finish bullying her (I.iii).

Even so refined, so conventional, so pronouncedly literary a genre as courtly/Petrarchan love poetry, then, was capable of being propelled into the arena where the changing nature of masculinity and femininity was being debated. As well it might be: for all her artificiality and for all her gentility, the sonnet mistress at her best is as potent a symbol of feminine dominance and power as the Renaissance ever provided. And the Renaissance regarded her with exactly the attitude we should by now have come to expect—extreme ambivalence.

The bourgeois reversal of sexual hierarchy gave literature the juxtaposition of domineering shrew and milksop husband which was a common end result of Renaissance fights for the breeches. The spirit of the Wife of Bath broods over bourgeois marriages in Renaissance literature:

although male authors created in great numbers wish-fulfillment fantasies on the Patient Grissill model, it is hard to think of a Renaissance literary wife who really sets her heart on dominating her husband who does not succeed in the project.[6] So many shrews appear in Renaissance literature that a shrew can even be found among the Petrarchan sonnet mistresses in *Tottel's Miscellany:* in "An epitaphe written by w. G. to be set vpon his owne graue," we hear that the subject's shrewish wife "was the shortnyng of his life / By many daies and yeres." (This poem is accompanied by a rejoinder: if what the poet says is true, he should be glad to be dead; but if he is given to unjustly blaming his wife, she should be glad he is dead.)

John Lydgate set the stage for the Renaissance preoccupation with the domineering wife in his delightfully hyperbolic early-fifteenth-century *Mumming at Hertford,*[7] wherein a group of rustics—a reeve, a cobbler, some farmers, a butcher, a tinker, and a tiler—present a petition to the king begging relief from the tyranny of their "fierce wyves" (l. 12), several of whom drink, gad, and scold, and all of whom beat their husbands. Even the butcher, a giant of a man who regularly kills bulls and boars, quakes before his wife: "Thoughe his bely were rounded lyche an ooke / She wolde not fayle to gyf the first[e] strooke" (ll. 99–100); her fist "ful offt made his cheekis bleed" (l. 108). One wife, by trade a wafermaker, pelts her husband's face with cakes hot from the oven, until his hairs glow red. The husbands, described as holy martyrs, as patient as Chaucer's Griselda (ll. 135, 170–176), acknowledge that the sovereignty of wives has long been established in England but plead that this "Olde Testament" matriarchy be modified so as to allow for New Testament values like mercy. The wives then bustle in before the king, waving the example of the "worthy Wyff of Bathe" (l. 168) before them like a banner, to demand that "the statuyt of olde antiquytee" granting wives the "maystrye" (ll. 213, 203) be reconfirmed. The king feels sorry for the downtrodden husbands but is impressed by the argument that wives' right to govern their husbands is confirmed by "custome, nature, and eeke prescripcyoun, / Statuyt vsed by confirmacyoun, / Processe and daate of tyme out of mynde, / Recorde of cronycles . . ." (ll. 235–38); he promises to ponder the matter, meanwhile granting sovereignty to the wives for another year, seeing that for husbands to have sovereignty over their wives would be "a thing vnkouthe, which was neuer founde" (l. 245).

Even the thoroughgoing delineation of meek husbands' miseries at the hands of tyrannical wives furnished by *Le Quinze Joyes de Mariage* did not go far enough for English tastes: the English translator who refurbished it as *The Batchelars Banquet*[8] added whole new stretches of dialogue, wherein women instruct each other in husband management: "I got the bridle into my owne handes, so that I may now say, I do what I list: for be it right or wrong, if I say it, hee will not gainsay it, for by this Golde on my finger, let him doo what he can, I will be sure to haue the last word: so that in very deed, if that women be made vnderlings by their husbands, the fault is their owne: for there is not any man aliue, be he neuer so churlish, but his wife may make him quiet and gentle enough if shee haue any wit" (Sig. C^v–C2).

The milksop husband was the domestic, bourgeois equivalent of the male courtly lover: both, by abdicating masculine dominance, perverted what Renaissance orthodoxy took to be the natural order of things. The milksop is a very common figure in Renaissance literature. When the husband in Thomas Ingelend's *The Disobedient Child* is loaded with firewood like a donkey by the wife who has beaten him into submission, all he can say is, "I will do your commandments whatsoever" (p. 305). When Mistress Purge in *The Family of Love,* in a fit of hypochondria, commands her husband to send for the doctor, he responds, "Thy will is known; and this for answer say, / 'Tis fit that wise men should their wives obey" (I.iii.62–63). The widow in *The Puritan* praises her late husband: "O, out of a million of millions, I should ne'er find such a husband; he was unmatchable, unmatchable. Nothing was too hot, nor too dear for me. I could not speak of that one thing that I had not. Beside, I had keys of all, kept all, receiv'd all, had money in my purse, spent what I would, went abroad when I would, came home when I would, and did all what I would. O, my sweet husband! I shall never have the like" (I.i).

Mistress Otter in *Epicoene* threatens her husband with humiliation ("I'll ha' you chain'd vp, with your bul-dogs, and beare-dogges, if you be not ciuill the sooner. I'll send you to kennell" [III.i.2–4]) and then reminds him of their marriage contract, an outrageous document which embodies fears expressed in *The Bachelor's Banquet*—that a man may find himself dominated by his wife, dependent on her money, and constantly twitted with his inferior social station:

> Is this according to the instrument, when I married you? That I would bee Princesse, and raigne in mine owne house: and you would be my subiect, and obay me? What did you bring me, should make you thus peremptory? Do I allow you your halfe-crowne a day, to spend, where you will? . . . Who giues you your maintenance, I pray you? who allowes you your horse-meat, and mans-meat? your three sutes of apparell a yeere? your foure paire of stockings, one silke, three worsted? your cleane linnen, your bands, and cuffes when I can get you to weare 'hem? . . . Who graces you with courtiers, or great personages, to speake to you out of their coaches, and come home to your house? Were you euer so much as look'd vpon by a lord, or a lady, before I married you? (III.i.32–47)

In the same play, Mavis's advice to a bride, "Looke how you manage him at first, you shall haue him euer after," parodies the marriage theorists' usual advice to husbands.

When Cornutus in *Every Woman in Her Humour* encounters his wife in a tavern, she (in a delightful reversal of the homekeeping-wife convention) upbraids him for being there: "twere more seemely you were at your owne house" (Sig. F4ᵛ). He obeys her and goes home. One Graccus marvels, "I thought it had bene but a fable all this while, that Iole shold make great Hercules spit on his thombes, & spin, but now I see, if a man were as great as Caesar . . . a woman may take him downe" (Sig. F4ᵛ).[9] The host of the tavern believes Cornutus has given "her tongue to much string" (Sig. F4). Later, when the host is having trouble with his own wife and rages, "I am her top, i'me her head," Cornutus cringingly counsels, "Not so my sweet Host, mum, mum, no words against your wife, he that meanes to liue quiet, to sleep in cleane sheetes, a Pillow vnder his head, his dyet drest cleanly, mum, mum, no words against his wife" (Sig. G4ᵛ). (This glimpse of the domestic guerrilla warfare a wife will wage to maintain her sovereignty recalls scenes in *The Bachelor's Banquet.*) The host calls Cornutus a fool and advises him to tame his own wife: "Kicke thy heele at her huckle bone" (Sig. G4ᵛ). But Cornutus will not attempt it; and the host's wife, too, makes a fool of her husband and retains her wilful liberty.

The shrew-ridden husband was always a figure of ridicule and contempt in literature; his abdication of authority was resented by other men, who feared the consequences of letting women acquire the habit of command. The milksop husband is frequently lectured by male friends on the importance of getting his wife under control: the host lectures Cornutus in *Every Woman in Her Humour;* Gwalter lectures Sir Owen in the 1600 *Patient Grissil*, offering, "Ile teach you how to win the soueraigntie" (IV.iii.271); a male friend counsels Candido in *2 Honest Whore*, "May not you I pray bridle her with a sharpe bit?" (II.ii.33). The taming of the individual shrew is thought to be in everyone's best interests; Renaissance literature affords numerous examples of accomplished shrews who matriculate from their marital apprenticeship and go on to scold or dominate other people. In *The Two Angry Women of Abington*, Mistresses Goursey and Barnes scold not only their husbands but each other and anyone else unfortunate enough to come within scolding distance. Mistress Barnes tells Mistress Goursey, "Tis not time of night to hold out chat, / With such a scold as thou art, therefore now, / Thinke that I hate thee as I do the diuell" (Sig. Hᵛ), which is itself an instance of scolding. Goneril and Regan, having practiced on their husbands, behave shrewishly toward their father, subjecting him to ranting lectures. Regan addresses him with the formula, "Be ruled" (*Lear*, II.iv.150); wherever this phrase is put in a woman's mouth, it is an ironic transference of a husband's proper injunction to his wife.

Husband domination in Renaissance literature is almost always connected with shrewishness. It is not a necessary connection: domination by icy stare is theoretically possible. But this is not the style of Renaissance wives, whose aggressiveness ranges from shrill scolding to physical violence. The drama in particular had a long history of violent wives. Among the literary descendants of Mrs. Noah in the mystery plays, the most dynamic is Strife, the shrew in the anonymous *Tom Tyler and His Wife,* ca. 1560. Strife's boasting to her female drinking companions about her marital dominance is interrupted when her husband, thirsty from a hard day's work, comes into the tavern; for his presumption, Strife administers one of her regular beatings, after which she must have another drink, the labor has tired her so. A close second is the termagant wife in *The Disobedient Child,* who makes good such threats as "By Cock's bones, I will make thy skin to rattle, / And the brains in thy skull more deeply to settle" (p. 305): her violence, specified in stage directions like *"Here the Wife must strike her Husband handsomely about the shoulders with something"* (p. 303), is punctuated by laments from her weeping husband: "Alas, alas! I am almost quite dead! / My wife so pitifully hath broken my head!" (p. 306). The husband in John Heywood's (?) *Johan Johan, the Husbande, Tyb, His Wife, and Syr Johan, The Preest* defends himself with a shovel full of hot coals against a wife who threatens to "make the blood ronne about his erys" with her distaff or shears (p. 395). In Greene and Lodge's *A Looking-Glass for London and England,* a poor man describes his wife: "She is too eloquēt for a poore man, and hath her words of Art, for she will call me Rascall, Rogue, Runnagate, Varlet, Vagabond, Slaue, Knaue. Why alasse sir, and these be but holi-day tearmes, but if you heard her working-day words, in faith sir they be ratlers like thunder sir, for after the dewe followes a storme, for then am I sure either to be well buffetted, my face scratcht, or my head broken" (Sig. [C4]). Shakespeare never staged a husband beating; but Adriana beats Dromio in *The Comedy of Errors,* while the premarital shrew Kate strikes both tutor and suitor in *The Taming of the Shrew.* Cleopatra's messenger beating is a variant of such comic scenes.

The drama likely exaggerated women's violence for comic effect. Still, there is historical evidence of contemporary uxorial violence. William Whately warned in a marriage sermon that if a husband used violence with his wife, she might "rebel against him." An unmastered wife, Whately told his parishioners, was "wilfull in cursing, swearing, drunkennesse," and would "raile vpon [her husband] with most violent and intollerable terms, . . . out-face him with bold maintaining, that she will doe as she doth, in despight of him," or even strike him (pp. 123–24). When one

Katherine Francis murdered her husband, Martin Parker commemorated the marriage breakdown in a ballad: "She oftentimes would beat him sore, / and many a wound she gave him, / . . . Till she with one inhumane wound, / Threw him (her husband) dead to th' ground."[10] Thomas Platter, a Swiss visitor to England, observed that English wives "often beat their men."[11]

Scolding, though, is much more frequent in literature than is husband beating. A henpecked husband in Chettle, Dekker, and Haughton's *Patient Grissil* complains, "A shrewes sharpe tongue is terrible as hell" (III.ii.279); a henpecked husband in *The Roaring Girl* sighs, "I cannot endure the house when she scolds: sh'as a tongue will be heard further in a still morning than Saint Antling's bell" (II.i.314–316). Filenio in *The Wit of a Woman* describes a wife who "would scolde till she slauerd, and looked blacke in the face, sweare like a ruffin, and curse like a hel-hounde, frowne and leere like a Bearewhelpe, and sling that was next her at her husband, sweare shee loued him not, reuile him out of order" (Sig. Gᵛ). A character in *Cupid's Whirligig* laments, "There is no pece in marriage, vnlesse it bee with a dumbe woman" (Sig. G3). Candido's wife in *1 Honest Whore* describes the frustrations of being married to the world's most patient man: "He . . . is so free from anger, that many times I am ready to bite off my tongue, because it wants [i.e., lacks] that vertue which all womens tongues haue (to anger their husbands)" (I.ii.74–77). "Husband" in the anonymous *A Yorkshire Tragedy* lays down a principle that dozens of male characters would ruefully have accepted: "The surest way to charm a woman's tongue, / Is—break her neck" (Scene V).

Some shrews are simply ill tempered, but for most of them, scolding is an instrument for gaining power. Renaissance literature is full of references to women who actively dominate their husbands, sometimes achieving political power at the same time. In the anonymous *King Leir,* Ragan as queen of Cambria boasts, "I rule the King of Cambria as I please" (Sig. D2). Gloucester in *1 Henry VI* is told, "Thy wife is proud. She holdeth thee in awe / More than God or religious churchmen may" (I.i.39–40); later, Suffolk anticipates similar behavior from Margaret: "Margaret shall now be Queen, and rule the King" (V.v.107). The Duchess of Gloucester in *2 Henry VI* is perturbed by the king's subjection to his wife but acknowledges it a common case: "In this place most master wear no breeches" (I.iii.149). Gloucester in *3 Henry VI* wishes that Queen Margaret "might still have worn the petticoat, / And ne'er have have stol'n the breech" (V.v.23–24). Boyet in *Love's Labor's Lost* refers to shrewish wives who "strive to be / Lords o'er their lords" (IV.i.37–38). A wife's political influence is often wielded, in the drama, with criminal intent: Tullia in Heywood's *The Rape of Lucrece,* who persuades her husband to murder her royal father that the two of them may reign in his place, is a shrew: her husband rules the kingdom "in publike" but is "over-rul'd by a curst wife in private"; Lady Macbeth, who talks her husband into regicide, has a chastising tongue that would be a credit to any shrew.[12]

The wife who dominates a military officer may influence military decisions or affect the morale of the troops. Captain Otter's wife "commands all at home . . . She is Captaine *Otter*" (*Epicoene*, I.iv.27–30). Iago seeks to create the same impression of Desdemona: "Our General's wife is now the General" (*Othello*, II.iii.319–320). Cassio voices the same opinion, with less insidious intent: "The divine Desdemona . . . our great Captain's captain" (II.i.73–74). Although Desdemona is no domineering shrew, her behavior at one point comes dangerously close to stereotype: "My lord shall never rest. / I'll watch him tame and talk him out of patience, / His bed shall seem a school, his board a shrift. / I'll intermingle every thing he does / With Cassio's suit" (III.iii.22–25). The line between allowable influence and domineering behavior was exceedingly fine. The distinction had been drawn by dramatists and biblical commentators with regard to the biblical Queen Hester (Esther): Hester was perfectly within her conjugal rights in seeking to influence a public policy decision by private cajolery and manipulating her husband's affections, as long as she did not openly command.[13] Desdemona does not command Othello to receive Cassio back into favor, but the tactics she outlines in the passage above would have been regarded with deep suspicion by a marriage theorist like Erasmus, who hated to see a husband pestered, especially in the sanctity of the bedroom. The "bolster-lecture"— a wife's haranguing her husband in bed—was a stock feature of the shrew stereotype: in vowing that her husband's "bed shall seem a school," Desdemona, by adopting the shrew's attributes, is making Iago's task easier. The Renaissance regarded sin as a seamless whole: as literature repeatedly demonstrates, the woman who dabbles her feet in a little gadding or facial painting will soon find herself drowning in seas of sensuality.[14] The least hint of shrewishness, even without the suspicion that it was employed on a lover's behalf, would lend credence to charges that Desdemona was prone to adultery as well, especially since the charge of lust was so frequently connected with feminine liberty and aggression.

Antony is another military leader at whom the charge of undue influence by women is levelled. Shakespeare plays down Plutarch's remarks on the way Antony was dominated by his first wife, Fulvia, to the point where Cleopatra had an easy job when it came her turn; but the notion surfaces at one point. When Fulvia makes war on Caesar, Antony apologizes by claiming she was always an uncontrollable shrew: "So much uncurbable, her garboils, Caesar, / Made out of her impatience, which not wanted / Shrewdness of policy too, I grieving grant / Did you too

much disquiet. For that you must / But say I could not help it" (II.ii.67–
71). As Shakespeare presents the Antony/Cleopatra relationship, Antony
is not dominated by Cleopatra. She exercises her manipulative powers
to their height to prevent his going to Rome in Act I, but he goes anyway. When he returns, it is of his own volition. It is partly Antony's
history of being henpecked by Fulvia and partly adherence to stereotype
that persuades one of Antony's followers that Cleopatra dictated the decision to fight at sea: "Our leader's led / And we are women's men"
(III.vii.70–71).[15] Antony's following her from the battle of Actium is
shown more as an impetuous act of lust than as an unduly influenced
military decision. But the military influence of a strong-minded woman
is an issue in the play, however ambiguously it is treated.

Occasionally a play will make the point that shrewish wives secretly
long to be dominated. When the hag-ridden Candido in *2 Honest Whore*
is finally provoked beyond the limits of his preternatural patience by the
behavior of his second shrewish wife, he takes after her with a yardstick;
whereupon she, adoring his manliness, kneels before him in gratitude:

> Downe I will be throwne
> With the least blow you giue me, I disdaine
> The wife that is her husbands Soueraigne.
> She that vpon your pillow first did rest,
> They say, the breeches wore, which I detest:
> The taxe which she imposed vpon you, I abate you,
> If me you make your Master, I shall hate you.
>
> (II.ii.107–113)

Mistress Gallipot in *The Roaring Girl* feels the same way; she upbraids
her indulgent husband, "Your love is all words; give me deeds: I cannot
abide a man that's too fond over me. . . . Thou dost not know how to
handle a woman in her kind." He responds with an early version of "you're
so cute when you're angry": "Ha, ha, 'tis such a wasp! it does me good
now to have her sting me." This refusal to accede to her demand that he
dominate her irritates Mistress Gallipot even further: "Now, fie, how
you vex me! I cannot abide these apron husbands; such cotqueans!"
(III.ii.24–33). (A "cotquean" is a man who meddles with "women's work.")

Such scenes are one part homily and three parts male wishful thinking;
this stereotype is a cousin of the belief that all women adore the caveman
approach and secretly crave rape. Most Renaissance shrews, however,
betray no occulted longing to be dominated: Renaissance literature brims
over with women eager to bear the whip hand in a relationship with a
man. When Lazarillo in *Blurt, Master-Constable* advises a group of female
auditors, "Since, then, a woman's only desire is to have the reins in her
own white hand, your chief practice, the very same day that you are

wived, must be to get hold of these reins," his listeners are not offended: they are taking notes. And they are delighted with his conclusion: "If you can get these reins into your lily hand, you shall need no coaches, but may drive your husbands" (III.iii.70–72, 151–53). Fletcher's *Women Pleased,* a play adapted from *The Wife of Bath's Tale,* culminates in three husbands' giving their wives sovereignty in marriage; the play's closing lines point the moral: "You, young men, that know not / How to preserve a wife, and keep her fair, / Give 'em their sovereign wills, and pleas'd they are."

Many literary hints create the impression that what the Renaissance really feared about shrews was that, armed with governing skills acquired in their own households, they might advance into the political arena. As John Knox had troubled to point out in *The First Blast of the Trumpet Against the Monstrous Regiment of Women,* Europe was already pestered with an alarming number of female rulers; so convinced was Knox of the connection between the epidemic of female monarchs and the widespread failure to heed biblical injunctions toward wifely subjection that his political treatise reads like a marriage sermon. Richard Brathwait, who theorized about marriage in pieces like "The good wife," created in *Essaies upon the five senses* a Theophrastan character of a very politically minded shrew: "shee approues of no ancient soueraigntie, but that of *Amazon,* where the gouernment was feminine: and for the *Salique* law [which disqualified women from hereditary succession] she hath already repeald it, as expresly preiudiciall to their sex" (p. 139). Such a passage reveals what was so frightening about shrewishness: Brathwait's shrew is a feminist.

Marital insubordination, it was felt, was contagious. A clear biblical example lay in the story of Queen Vashti, who refused to come at her husband's command and display her beauty before princes assembled at a state dinner. Vashti was punished for this public act of disobedience with divorce, for fear her behavior would set a dangerous precedent: "Vashti the queen hath not done wrong to the king only, but also to all the princes, and to all the people that are in all the provinces of the king Ahasuerus. For this deed of the queen shall come abroad unto all women, so that they shall despise their husbands" (Esther 1:9–17, *KJV*). The final scene of *The Taming of the Shrew* may owe something to the Vashti story: the two wives who refuse to come to the table at their husbands' command fill Vashti's role, and Kate fills the role of Vashti's successor Esther or Hester, the exemplary submissive wife.

A remarkable example of one wife's marital disobedience touching off a veritable women's movement is Fletcher's *The Woman's Prize; or, The Tamer Tamed,* ca. 1611, a sequel to *The Taming of the Shrew* in which

Petruchio's second wife adopts *Lysistrata* tactics to break her husband of wife taming. Vowing to sleep alone on her wedding night, she is joined in her garrisoned chamber first by her feisty cousin Bianca and then by her conservative sister Livia; eventually, as news of Maria's bold stand for marital freedom spreads throughout the land, the house is surrounded by an army of cheering women from both city and country. A country wife shouts at Petruchio, "To the comfort of distressèd damsels, / Women out-worn in wedlock, and such vessels, / This woman has defied you." And the women sing a rousing song:

> A health, for all this day,
> To the woman that bears the sway,
> And wears the breeches;
> Let it come, let it come!
> Let this health be a seal,
> For the good of the common-weal
>   The woman shall wear the breeches!
>   (II. vi)

*   *   *   *   *

Female insubordination is sometimes defended in Renaissance literature. Three dramatic characters in particular, all outspoken servant-confidantes of downtrodden mistresses victimized by their husbands, were created by authors willing to excuse insubordination on grounds of justifiable shrewishness—the nurse in Phillip's *Patient Grissill,* Paulina in *The Winter's Tale,* and Emilia in *Othello.* In *The Winter's Tale,* Leontes, pestered by Paulina's insistent truth telling, cries "A gross hag!" and tells her husband he is "worthy to be hanged, / That wilt not stay her tongue." Even in these grim circumstances, Paulina's husband cannot refrain from the predictable jest: "Hang all the husbands / That cannot do that feat, you'll leave yourself / Hardly one subject" (II.iii.108–112). In *Othello,* Iago paints his wife Emilia as a shrewish bolster-lecturer: "Too much [speech], / I find it still when I have list to sleep. / Marry, before your ladyship, I grant, / She puts her tongue a little in her heart / And chides with thinking." Emilia objects, "You have little cause to say so" (II.i.103–109), and a prudent reader is reluctant to take Iago's word for anything; but later we see Emilia in full cry. Standing fearlessly alone with a murderer, Emilia gives him (and Iago, when he comes in) a tongue-lashing that lasts from line 130, with interruptions, until she is stabbed at line 235 (V.ii). Iago treats her like a disobedient wife. "Go to, charm your tongue," he charges her; she answers, "I will not charm my tongue, I am bound to speak" (ll.183–84). "Be wise, and get you home," he orders; she answers, "I will not" (ll.223–224). Surrounded by men, Emilia knows her boldness may be construed as shrewishness, but she persists: "I will speak as liberal as the north. / Let Heaven and men and devils, let them all, / All, all, cry shame against me, yet I'll speak" (ll. 220–222). Iago's stabbing Emilia to silence her is an admission of defeat. He can ruin the careers and lives of Cassio, Roderigo, Othello, Desdemona; he can plume up his will in double knavery; he can undermine the army and the state; but he cannot (except by murdering her) stop his own wife talking. It is a joke on Iago, a kind of black comedy turned by the playwright into a criticism of arguments for the silence of women. It is a woman, and a shrew at that, who is the play's spokesman for truth and justice.

In Phillip's *Patient Grissill,* both the compliance of Grissill and the nurse's spirited defense of her mistress against male tyranny and injustice attest to the indebtedness of the Desdemona-Emilia-Othello scenes to the Griselda story and the theory of marriage it exemplified. Phillip's nurse is the literary ancestor of Emilia and Paulina: all three speak up when the situation calls for a statement of moral condemnation on a husband's behavior. That such statements are consistently given to female characters, when a male character could as easily have spoken them, suggests an externalization of feelings which the virtuous wife has had to suppress. It is as if the respective authors had split one female personality into two, giving to her companion the wife's chafing sense of injustice, of moral indignation: a virtuous wife could not herself accuse her husband of injustice.

As a rule, writers sanctioned female insubordination only in cases of pronounced male wrongdoing, and even then they most often granted the privilege to someone other than the offender's wife. However extreme the misery resulting from the heroines' wordless submission to their husbands' misdirected will, the good wife was expected to suffer in silence.[16] In the rare cases where a good wife takes steps to get control of the matrimonial reins, she usually gives them back again in the end, as Maria does in *The Woman's Prize.*

A number of women in the drama wish they were men—a kind of breeches envy. *King Leir*'s domineering Ragan cries:

> O God, that I had bin but made a man;
> Or that my strength were equall with my will!
> These foolish men are nothing but meere pity,
> And melt as butter doth against the Sun.
> Why should they haue preeminence ouer vs,
> Since we are creatures of more braue resolue?
>
> (Sig. I)

Since Ragan's inversion of conventional sex roles involves perverting values so that pity becomes a liability, her sexual egalitarianism would have been suspect, as such egalitarianism nearly always was. Such statements seldom go unchallenged: women who make them are usually vicious and are frequently punished, in accordance with Luciana's principle "Headstrong liberty is lashed with woe." The Duchess of Gloucester wishes she were a man: "Were I a man . . . / I would remove these tedious stumbling blocks / And smooth my way upon their headless necks; / And, being a woman, I will not be slack / To play my part" (2 Henry VI, I.ii.63–67). Her presumption is lashed with woe: after three days' public penance, she is sent to prison.

When Shakespeare's female characters express a wish to be men, it is almost always to shame some man into taking action; and they usually pervert the meaning of manhood to exclude pity and compassion, on the illogical principle that if women are compassionate, men cannot be. Suppression of women's natural pity usually figures; the speaker hints that if a tenderhearted woman such as herself can divest herself of pity, the situation must be so desperate that the least a man can do is to sacrifice his own compassion—a smaller sacrifice since his is less developed than hers. This is Lady Macbeth's line; its context in Macbeth establishes it as a villain's argument. Shakespeare usually sees something monstrous about a woman who wishes she were a man.

The only exception is Beatrice, who incites Benedick to kill Claudio by an argument similar to Lady Macbeth's: "Oh, God, that I were a man! I would eat his heart in the market place. . . . Oh, that I were a man for his sake! Or that I had any friend would be a man for my sake! But manhood is melted into courtesies, valor into compliment, and men are only turned into tongue" (Much Ado, IV.i.308–323). There are differences between Beatrice's case and Lady Macbeth's: Beatrice's cause is just; a challenge is involved rather than murder; and Claudio is never killed after all. But Shakespeare does seem willing to concede that a woman's position is frustrating in times of crisis, that there are moments when a woman's wishing to be a man does not indicate outlandish perversion. Beatrice's speech is clearly indebted to Ragan's speech in King Leir, quoted above: compare Ragan's "O God, that I had bin but made a man" with Beatrice's "Oh, God, that I were a man!," Ragan's "These foolish men are nothing but meere pity, / And melt as butter doth against the Sun" with Beatrice's "Manhood is melted into courtesies"; both speakers begin a sentence with "Or." The changes Shakespeare made when he assigned this villain's speech to a virtuous woman, however, are telling: Beatrice never denigrates pity; and although she wishes as an individual woman that she were a man, she does not, like Ragan, claim equality or superiority on behalf of the female sex.

Then, too, Beatrice is not yet a wife. When Renaissance authors betray admiration for an aggressive virago, she is usually a single woman—

Long Meg of Westminster, Moll Cutpurse, Bess Bridges, Rosalind; if such a character eventually marries, she is expected to hand over the sovereignty to her husband forthwith, if she hopes to retain that admiration. It was thought rather charming when an assertive virgin took command of the situation, but the sky changed when she was a wife: the charm of a domineering wife was a topic the Renaissance entirely neglected. Although, as I have noted, the drama occasionally exonerated (or partially exonerated) a scold on grounds of justifiable shrewishness, most authors were pretty obviously put off by the overbearing wife, and they employ several literary strategies against her: they subject her to shrew tamings, they satirize her for the use of her tongue, they attempt to overbalance her with a heavyweight of submissiveness—the Patient Grissill figure, and they declare her (along with aggressive women in general) an abnormality. The remainder of this chapter will focus on these strategies, the frequency of which in literature is itself a testimony to the ubiquity of feminine aggression.

Shrew-taming tales haunt Renaissance literature of many genres, ranging from exemplary anecdote to narrative (in verse or prose) to scenes in the drama and occasionally a whole play. The most brutal of the taming stories, *A merry Ieste of a Shrewde and curste Wyfe lapped in Morrelles skin* makes explicit the sadism latent or covert in most of the others.

The anonymous author of the Morel's skin tale has a distinctive style, the hallmark of which is formulaic expression: his poem is heavily padded with rhyme tags and other formulae, most of them indigenous to medieval metrical romance—"with reason and right," "sorrow and mickle shame," "ye shall vnderstande," "I tell thee playne," "I make God avow," "withouten miss," "so mote I thee," "by sweete saynt John." Though most of the popular literature of the fifteenth and early sixteenth centuries employs a certain number of narrative formulae, rhyme tags, and expletives, *Morel* uses the same tags and expletives so frequently as to become a tour de force of limited vocabulary. Even if one deleted the tags and formulae, which would deflate the poem by perhaps a third, the remaining vocabulary would be marked by extremes of repetition. The author develops enthusiasms for certain words and phrases, and will use them over and over within the space of a few pages: *diligent* appears four times; *depart, good will, peer,* and *trow* eight times each; *in fay* thirteen times; *withouten* eighteen times, in a poem of about 1000 lines; appropriately for a work of sadism, *payne* appears eleven times and *smart* ten. Rhymes, too, repeat themselves hypnotically: the poet rhymes *heart* with *smart* six times; *have* five times with *save,* once with *crave,* and three times with *knave; also* with *go* eight times, *mother* with *other* six times. It is as if the author had wagered on his ability to write a poem with a fixed number of words; *The Wife Lapped in Morel's Skin* at times sounds like Books for Beginning Readers.

The hypnotic quality of verbal repetitions in the Morel's skin story produces an incantatory tone oddly appropriate to this brutal tale. The author uses the word *charm* five times in reference to the shrew taming, and the air of primitive ritual that clings to the taming in this poem makes one wonder what anthropological secrets may be embalmed in the habitual Renaissance use of the word *charm* in reference to shrew taming. The shrew in *Morel* is tamed when her husband drags her into a deep cellar, tears off her clothes, beats her bloody from head to toe with birch rods, and wraps her senseless body in the salted hide of Morel, a horse he has had killed for the purpose. When the salt in her wounds revives her and her husband threatens to keep her in Morel's skin for the rest of her life, the wife vows eternal submission. Francis Utley has suggested some connection with primitive magical curing rituals (p. 176). At times, the poem's rhythmic repetitions take on the aura of magic spells, and the isolated couplet "Now good Morels skin, / Receiue my curst wife in" (Sig. [E4]), appearing suddenly among eight-line stanzas, has a quality almost liturgical. It is singularly appropriate that for this poem the author chooses the pseudonym "Mayster Charme her" (Sig. [F4]).

The author achieves extraordinary effects by juxtaposing a style appropriate to romance, even to fairy tale, first with bourgeois social realism and then with sadistic fantasy. The juxtaposition with social realism is charmingly comic. The author employs the stock phrase "gold and silver"—an expression that in metrical romance had conjured visions of treasure hordes, kings' ransoms, aristocratic largesse—three times in the context of the young man's haggling with his future mother-in-law over the dowry and once in reference to wedding gifts. The incongruity reminds the reader that even in romance "gold and silver" was often a euphemism for cash. All through the poem's first section, scenes of domestic realism—a henpecked husband telling a prospective son-in-law the truth about his daughter's shrewishness, negotiations over the dowry, details of the wedding feast, including seating arrangements, the guests' attire, remarks by the mother of the bride, bestowal of wedding gifts, dancing—are developed in diction conventional to the literature of dragons and giants: the effect is subtly and quietly amusing. But the juxtaposition of the language of romance with sadistic fantasy is another matter.

Despite Furnivall's genial description of *Morel* as "an interesting and amusing old poem . . . capitally told,"[17] it is clear that beginning with the wedding-night scene, the poem becomes a rather timeless sort of pornography. The initiation of the bride is brutal: the groom keeps her awake all night, hitting her, tearing her clothes to shreds, and forcing her to adopt various positions—an obvious appeal to the reader's prurience. The author insists on having witnesses present to view the wife's various humiliations: the mother comes in during an intermission of the wedding-night athletics to check on the progress of the defloration and passes on the masochistic information, "so was I dealt with the fyrst night. / . . . Me thought neuer night to me so good, / As that same was, when I tooke such payne" (Sig. [C4]); wedding guests greet with "mirth" the deeply ashamed and disturbed bride who is forced to appear among them immediately following her husband's brutal sexual advances; the wife's family and friends are invited to dinner after the Morel's skin episode to watch the wife parade her new-found subjection; the mother is taken to the cellar to view Morel's skin and the birch rods and hear from the wife's lips the whole grisly story. All of this suggests voyeurism. And the wrapping in Morel's skin, whatever its magical antecedents, is also a form of the sexual perversion known as bondage. The effect of relating such stuff in the language of romance and fairy tale is startling, a grim and cynical commentary on a loveless, deromanticized world where a man has no dragons to conquer but his wife.[18] In a metrical romance like *Sir Cleges,* it is the courteous knight who is described as being "so gentyll and fre"; in the Morel's skin poem, the hero described as being "so gentle and so free" (Sig. A4) is quite another sort of fellow. There are ways in which this poem does not belong among Books for Beginning Readers.

In this tale, the wife's shrewishness is only an excuse for her husband to indulge sadistic inclinations which have been in evidence earlier: he brutally breaks her in sexually on her wedding night, before she begins behaving shrewishly; considerably shaken the next morning, the wife describes to her mother her pain and shame, wishing she could have lain alone. In a work of more psychological subtlety, her subsequent shrewish and domineering behavior might have been traced to the unhappiness of her first sexual experiences with her husband, but here the wife's wedding-night diffidence is simply out of character; the author explains that she was brought up a shrew by her shrewish mother. Nor can the author be praised for careful preparation, in the wedding-night scene, for the brutality that emerges in the husband's character in the Morel's skin scene; his insistence throughout that the wife simply gets what she deserves makes clear that he imputes no perversity to the husband. It is simply that the author likes writing this sort of scene and knows that a certain sort of reader will like reading it. Sexual titillation is the poem's main object. The attempt to persuade the reader that the wife requires taming since her sharp tongue is causing unrest among the hired hands is perfunctory; more to the point, the taming is explicitly connected with the husband's sexual desires: he wants to "make her shrinke / And bow at my pleasure, when I her bed" (Sig. Eiii).

The Wife Lapped in Morel's Skin calls itself a "merry jest," and shrew-taming tales are often to be found in Renaissance jest books: authors seem to have assumed that the physical torment and psychological humiliation of a woman would strike readers as side-splittingly funny, filling them with mirth and good spirits. The formal controversy about women, too, had its affinities with jest and jest books; but where Gosynhyll had intended his misogynistic work to provide men with "somewhat to jest with the femynye," the most optimistic of poets could hardly have expected women to laugh along or find anything "merry" in a sadistic fantasy like the Morel's skin story. Shrew-taming tales are jests of quite a different order.

As time passed, the physical brutality of the shrew-taming jest was played down, but the element of humiliation and psychological torment loomed as large as ever, perhaps larger. The transmutation can be seen in a popular story as it appears in *Scoggin's Jests* (STC 21851; earlier editions not extant), a work of the early sixteenth century, and later in the anonymous play *The Wit of a Woman,* published in 1604. In the earlier work, Scoggin's wife begs forgiveness for her shrewishness and promises eternal submissiveness after she has been bound to a "forme" by Scoggin and a servant and had a good deal of blood let by a surgeon who has been persuaded by Scoggin that bloodletting is necessary to cure her madness. This wife is not even shrewish; a little mild teasing of her husband is enough to call forth an extreme of physical retaliation; as usual, all is in fun. In the later work, although the bondage motif remains (the wife in this anecdote is tied to a chair), the bloodletting is replaced by psychological torments: the wife, who cannot move, must be fed "like a childe" and is lectured with much good counsel by the church clerk and his wife ("whom she hated"), for "a fewe monthes" (Sig. G2).

The wife taming related anecdotally in *The Wit of a Woman* is stunningly successful; it makes the wife "an other woman: the winde of her tongue was so calme, that it would scarce haue mooued an aspin leafe" (Sig. G2), a reference which recalls the old story of the Devil, the aspen leaf, and the wife's tongue. But this optimistic view of the relative ease with which a shrew may be tamed is proffered by a young bachelor who has never had reason to put it to the test. Shrew-taming attempts in Renaissance literature fail at least as often as they succeed.

The host in *Every Woman in Her Humour* fails in his planned shrew taming, and in the same play the milksop Cornutus flinches at the mere mention of shrew taming; in the 1600 *Patient Grissil*, Sir Owen's sporadic attempts to get his shrewish wife under control are utterly ineffectual. The play *Tom Tyler and His Wife* centers on the miscarriage of a shrew-taming project. When the milksop Tom Tyler is afraid to act on the advice of his friend Tom Tayler, to return his wife's blows, Tom Tayler impersonates Tom Tyler, beards Tyler's wife in her tavern, and beats her nearly unconscious. One beating is enough to vanquish this shrew: upon Tom Tyler's reappearance, Strife (the wife) vows eternal obedience. Moved with pity for her bloody and bruised state, however, Tom Tyler foolishly confesses it was not he who gave her the beating. This news so revives Strife that she recovers health instantly and resumes beating him. An Italian jest anthologized in Humfrey Gifford's *A Posie of Gilloflowers* features two sworn brothers who marry two sisters. The first spoils his wife, and she becomes wilful, contrary, and shrewish. The second takes a tough line with his wife from the start. Taking her to the stable to view his horses, he illustrates his methods by beating a horse which is headstrong and unmanageable. The horse still kicks, however, and so the husband takes his sword and kills it. The wife gets the message and becomes completely subservient. The other husband, informed of this foolproof method of wife control, tries it on his own wife. She laughs him to scorn for his unreasonableness in killing a perfectly good horse and says she'd like to see him try such tactics on her. The husband retires defeated, and the moral of the story is, "A woman that is by nature obstinate, had rather suffer a thousand deaths, then alter her setled determination" (p. 25). Chapter IX of *The Bachelor's Banquet* describes a fight for the breeches that lasts at least twenty years, until the husband finally loses by default, out of sheer exhaustion; the wife is still fresh, partly because the life of women is so easy: as earlier chapters make clear, it is the husband who is the prime sufferer through a woman's many pregnancies.

Some shrew tamings last the lifetime of a marriage; among the least pleasant of Renaissance stories are those wherein a shrew suffers protracted torment at the hands of a cynical adventurer, to the eventual ruin of both spouses. In John Heywood's *Two Maner of Maryages*,[19] a man marries a rich and ugly widow, considerably his senior, for her money. At first the couple is happy, but later the husband loathes his wife, and she responds by growing shrewish. The scenes wherein the husband, suffering sexual nausea in the presence of his wife, avoids sex by staying up late and getting up early, or wherein he excuses his wenching and profligacy on grounds of his home life's having been made so intolerable by his wife's shrewishness that he has no choice but to eat out, make painful reading. With considerable insight into the timeless elements of domestic misery, Heywood brings to life the couple's mutual recriminations, the neighbors' hopeless efforts to reconcile them, the poignant occasional moments of truce and loving words followed by relapses into prodigality on the husband's part, into embittered shrewishness on the wife's, the inevitable final separation and eventual lonely and impoverished death of husband and wife. The heroine of John Dickenson's *Fair Valeria* is both shrewish and lewd; her second husband, the adventurer

Arthemio who has been promoted from his former position as Valeria's
chief whore, does not trust his new bride—understandably—and "to
reforme her lewdnesse, he restraind her libertie" (p. 47). Over a period
of years, Arthemio tames Valeria by cursing and beating her, causing the
servants to be rude to her, bringing his harlots home and making her
prepare and serve dinner to them. When Arthemio forces Valeria to watch
him copulating with his whores and she is unable to speak for fear of
beating, Dickenson comments approvingly, "Loe here an instance proouing
it not wholly impossible to ouer-master for the time the miraculous vol-
ubilitie of a womans tongue" (p. 52). Like the husband in Heywood's
story, Arthemio eventually spends all his wife's money, and the tale ends
in marital estrangement, poverty, and death. As in the Morel skin story,
moralizing is here no more than a thin mask covering the brutal face of
sadism. Dickenson has no genuine interest in shrewishness: Valeria's faults
must be made glaring enough to serve as an excuse for her torments and
humiliations, the main appeal of the story being to the reader's prurience
and delight in the degradation of women.

It is true that *The Taming of the Shrew* is less offensive than earlier
shrew-taming tales; the extreme physical brutality of the earlier shrew-
taming tradition had, after all, been muted into mere psychological sadism by the 1590s, when Shakespeare wrote the play. Shakespeare does
retain, in the taming metaphor, the implication that a wife should be
treated like an animal; but he softens this, by creating the metaphor of a
falcon, an animal which although subhuman is a primate among birds
and is allowed a certain amount of autonomy and aggressiveness, rather
than comparing a wife to a recalcitrant horse, as did Humfrey Gifford's
jest. (Though in another context, Petruchio's amending the tenth com-
mandment's comparison of a wife with "ox . . . ass . . . any thing" [Ex-
odus 20:17, *KJV*] to "she is . . . My horse, my ox, my ass, my anything"
[III.ii.232–234] would seem almost to suggest a deliberate recalling of
Gifford's jest.) Granted, the Petruchio who comes "to wive it wealthily
in Padua" (I.ii.75) is clearly a literary descendant of the sort of adventurer
who torments his wealthy wife in Heywood's *Two Manner of Marriages*
and Dickenson's *Fair Valeria;* but then he does not spend all his wife's
money on whores, as they did—at least he hasn't yet, by the end of Act
V. It must be confessed that Kate is obliged, as in the voyeuristic closing
scene of *The Wife Lapped in Morel's Skin,* to parade her total subjection
before family and friends; but at least the playwright demonstrated his
approval of women of spirit by leaving us to conclude that a woman of
spirit, once thoroughly broken in, will prove more tractable than an ultrafeminine, obedient daughter like Bianca.

When all is said and done, however, I find it hard to regard this play
as much of an improvement over the earlier shrew-taming tradition. Pe-

truchio starves Kate, deprives her of sleep, publicly humiliates her; for this he is celebrated as having done the state some service. I cannot overcome my impression that Shakespeare—like the authors of the Morel's skin story and *Fair Valeria*—relished his heroine's humiliation, in the same not altogether wholesome way he seems to have enjoyed the degradation and public humiliation of other of his early female characters, like the Duchess of Gloucester and Joan of Arc. *The Wife Lapped in Morel's Skin* may actually have been one source of *The Taming of the Shrew*,[20] and it is customary to praise Shakespeare's superior humanity in the handling of this unsavory old story. But physical brutality in shrew tamings was already out of style when he wrote anyway, and other authors had always made at least perfunctory attempts to mask the sadism that is so undeniably at the center of the tale: Shakespeare's softening of the story is in line with his usual policy of expurgating whatever might prove offensive to the middle-class element of his audience[21] and does not prove that he was quintessentially humane or even that he was free from prurience and sexual perversity, much less that he was a proto-feminist, as some of *Taming*'s critics have suggested.[22] There is no denying that *The Taming of the Shrew* is less disgusting than *The Wife Lapped in Morel's Skin;* but to my mind, it does not speak well of a hero that the best thing to be said in his favor is that he neither beats his wife senseless nor wraps her in a salted horsehide.

The shrew-taming story was one authorial strategy for mitigating the threat posed by strong-minded wives in literature. That they dramatize the advisability of knocking a wife into shape indicates that a good number of Renaissance writers were male supremacists; that they emphasize the difficulty of knocking a wife into shape indicates that a good number of Renaissance writers were realists. Taming a wife in literature is a tough proposition as it is; if living wives had been any more easily tamable, it is hard to see why male readers and audiences would have needed to take refuge in this sort of fantasy.

Feminine aggressiveness being more frequently verbal than physical, women's speech was the object of volleys of satiric abuse, expressed in characteristic clichés. Men may find glory in battle; women's weapons are their tongues: "T'is but a womans iarre, / Their tongues are weapons, words there blowes of war" (*Abington*, Sig. [B4]); " 'Tis not the trial of a woman's war, / The bitter clamor of two eager tongues, / Can arbitrate this cause" (*Richard II*, I.i.48–50); "Keepe close your womanish weapon, hold your tongue" (*Ram-Alley*, V.i.2189); "Wife . . . the two-edged sword of thy tongue hath drawn blood o' me" (*Family of Love*, V.i.5–8); "She has prevail'd; a woman's tongue and eye / Are weapons stronger than artillery" (*Lust's Dominion*, IV.iii). This central metaphor harks back to the war and peace issue: women's use of weapons, even such cowardly weapons as the tongue, is seen as an intrusion on male turf; battle is for men.

Male characters in Renaissance literature scold fairly frequently, but characteristic diction excuses male scolding (which is dignified by titles like "exhortation" and "oratory") and condemns female scolding. George Webbe's use of adjectives in *The Araignment of an Vnruly Tongue*, 1619, is revealing: "There are . . . Husbands tongues which are too bitter against their wiues; Wiues tongues too sharp against their Husbands" (p. 43). Women's tongues are very often, in Renaissance literature, said to be sharp; the submerged metaphor suggests a weapon. (A particularly graphic image of sharpness occurs in *Bussy d'Ambois:* "Here's one, I think, has swallowed a porcupine, she casts pricks from her tongue so" [III.ii.243–244].) The tongues of men, especially of husbands rebuking their wives, are often called "bitter," suggesting unpalatable but necessary medicine. Women's tongues are instruments of aggression or self-defense; men's are the tools of authority. In either case, speech is an expression of power; but male speech represents legitimate authority, while female speech attempts to usurp authority or rebel against it.

Many literary barbs aimed at female speech concern mere volubility rather than verbal aggression. Most of these are jests, intended—like most Renaissance antifeminist humor—to be greeted good-naturedly by women and to effect subtle changes in women's behavior. Ero in *The Widow's Tears* cites as Aristotle's opinion "that when a man dies, the last thing that moves is his heart; in a woman, her tongue" (IV.ii.152–153). When Speed counts among his wench's vices that "she is slow in words," Launce sets him straight: "O villain, that set this down among her vices! To be slow in words is a woman's only virtue" (*Two Gentlemen of Verona*, III.i.336–339). The main intention is comic: that is the sort of thing that clowns said. It was also, however, the sort of thing that marriage preachers said. Henry Smith preached that "the ornamēt of a woman is silence," and "as it becommeth her to keepe home, so it becommeth her to keep silence,"[23] Robert Cleaver that "the dutie of the man is, to bee skilfull in talke: and of the wife, to boast of silence."[24] The loquacity that preachers discouraged by dogma, authors discouraged by witticism; in an age when literary theory favored the didactic, the goals of sermon and comedy were not always dissimilar.

Ben Jonson enjoyed creating scenes of female talkativeness. Lady Politic Would-be in *Volpone* floods the hero with a torrent of words until he cries, "Oh, / Rid me of this my torture, quickly, there; / My Madam, with the euerlasting voyce: / The bells, in time of pestilence, ne're made / Like noise, or were in that perpetuall motion" (III.v.2–6). The whole plot of *Epicoene; or, The Silent Woman* turns on female talkativeness. Morose, whose sensitive ears cannot endure noise of any kind, is searching for a dumb or very quiet woman for a wife. A man in his employ has searched England for six months without finding such a woman. Morose's nephew, who for reasons of inheritance does not want his uncle to marry, presents him with a silent woman, Epicoene. Morose tests her at some length. (To his question, "Can you . . . not taking pleasure in your tongue, which is a womans chiefest pleasure . . . answer me by silent gestures?" Epicoene merely curtsies.) Delighted, Morose marries Epicoene; she bursts into unremitting speech the moment the ceremony is concluded. To be rid of her, Morose is forced to settle his estate on his nephew and resolves never to marry. The fact that Epicoene turns out to be a man in disguise does not negate the satire on female logorrhea; Epicoene's part had to be taken by a man partly to facilitate annulment of the marriage, but more significantly because no real woman would be able to keep silent long enough to play the premarital scenes in which Epicoene says nothing at all.

Shakespeare, too, often plays upon the stereotype of loquacity. Cleopatra is a great talker. She almost preëmpts the weakened Antony's deathbed speech, interrupting his opening, "I am dying, Egypt, dying. / Give me some wine, and let me speak a little" with "No, let me speak, and let me rail so high / That the false housewife Fortune break her wheel, / Provoked by my offense"; Antony must weakly reinsist, "One word, sweet Queen" (*Antony and Cleopatra,* IV.xv.41–45). The stereotype lingers behind her "I dreamed there was an Emperor Antony" speech, into which Dolabella repeatedly tries to break with "If it might please ye—," "Most sovereign creature—," "Cleopatra—," "Gentle madam, no," "Hear me, good madam" (V.ii.76–100). Shakespeare here asserts the stereotype with a gentle humor but leaves no doubt that this is a very great speech, which deserves to be uninterrupted.

Women's intense fear of losing the faculty of speech was the subject of popular jest. In *Love's Labor's Lost,* women are forbidden to come within a mile of the court on pain of losing their tongues, "to fright them hence with that dread penalty" (I.i.128). When a bogus fortune-teller in *The Puritan* predicts that a widow and her elder daughter shall go mad and "with most impudent prostitution, show your naked bodies to the view of all beholders," while the younger daughter shall be struck dumb, the younger is by far the most perturbed: "Dumb? out, alas! 'tis the worst pain of all for a woman. I'd rather be mad, or run naked, or any thing. Dumb!" (II.i).

Mere loquacity, like aggressive female speech, often provoked remarks on the relative nature of the sexes. Talkative men were often styled effeminate: Northumberland upbraids Hotspur, "Why, what a wasp-stung and impatient fool / Art thou to break into this woman's mood, / Tying thine ear to no tongue but thine own!" (*1 Henry IV,* I.iii.236–238). Shakespeare's most articulate tragic hero heaps contempt on his own verbal excesses by characterizing them as feminine: "I, the son of a dear father murdered, / Prompted to my revenge by Heaven and Hell, / Must, like a whore, unpack my heart with words / And fall a-cursing like a very drab" (*Hamlet,* II.ii.612–615). The formal satirists of the 1590s, while condemning vices in women, were not blind to the paradox that their own satiric railing resembled stereotypical feminine scolding: this they neatly rationalized by blaming their satiric posture and tone on a woman—their muse. The satirist's muse is often presented as a whore; as such she can take the blame for the author's prurience as well as his shrewish tone. Marston twice calls his muse a scold (*Scourge of Villainy,* Satire II); Guilpin instructs his muse to "play the scold brauely, feare no cucking-stoole," later giving her other "female" attributes: "How now my *Muse,* this is right womans fashion, / To fall from brawling to a blubbering passion" (*Skialetheia,* Satire I).

That the stereotype of female talkativeness in literature is false is statistically demonstrable: a line count of dialogue in Renaissance drama would reveal that men overwhelmingly out-talk women. It does depend, though, on one's definition of talkativeness: the Renaissance never actually said that women talk more than men; it maintained that women talk too much. In the view of many male characters and authors, almost anything was too much. Queen Margaret is derided as a "wrangling woman" after speaking only twenty-three of the 177 lines of Act II, Scene ii in *3 Henry VI:* her longest single speech in that scene is five lines long. No one condemns the volubility of any of the men who speak the scene's remaining 154 lines; indeed, King Henry responds to Clifford's thirty-four-line speech, "Full well hath Clifford played the orator" (II.ii.43). Men were not ordinarily considered talkative, because they had a right to speak. In *Sophonisba,* although Carthalon, a male character, has just delivered a thirty-six-line speech with no apologies for wordiness, Sophonisba is made to end her twenty-nine-line speech with the apology, "My tongue / Swears I am a woman still, I talk too long" (I.ii.183–184).

According to literary pronouncements, female speech is less rational than male speech in general; authors' diction often characterizes female speech as meaningless sound, babbling, prating, chattering: "a prating wrangling toung, / A womans ceaselesse and incessant babling" (Haughton's *English-men for My Money; or, A Pleasant Comedy Called A Woman Will Have Her Will,* Sig. Cᵛ); "women will be prating" (*Arden of Feversham,* xiv.201); "a long-tongued babbling gossip" (*Titus Andronicus,* IV.ii.150); "tame a shrew and charm her chattering tongue" (*Taming of the Shrew,* IV.ii.58). Such literary tactics are clearly designed to help neutralize a woman's most effective tool of aggression—her tongue.

Where the formal controversy took Eve and the Virgin Mary as its main paradigms of womankind, the mainstream of late medieval and Renaissance literature neglected the old temptress/saint dichotomy in favor of a more secular model: after the confrontation between Patient Griselda and the Wife of Bath in *The Canterbury Tales,* the central confrontation between opposing female character types in literature was that between the Patient Grissill figure and the aggressive, liberty-minded woman, either a shrew or a whore. Chaucer's Clerk had put Griselda to exemplary and homiletic purposes; so did the Renaissance. In the 1600 *Patient Grissil,* Grissil is juxtaposed with the shrew Gwenthian. Grissil's husband, observing Gwenthian's antics, makes the contrast explicit: "Oh my deare *Grissill,* how much different / Art thou to this curst [i.e., shrewish] spirit, heere, I see / My *Grissils* vertues shine" (IV.iii.156–158). Later he interprets the whole course of his wife tormenting as a preventative measure against shrewishness (V.ii.240–243). In *How a Man May Choose a Good Wife from a Bad,* Mistress Arthur, who interprets her husband's behavior in Grissillian terms ("Only to try my patience he puts on / An ugly shape of black intemperance"), is juxtaposed with Mistress Mary, both a shrew and a whore. Anabell in *The Fair Maid of Bristow,* believing that her husband's abuse is "to try my patience" (V.i.847), is balanced against a false Grissill (in the manner of Spenser's technique with False Florimell), the harlot Florence, who tells Sentloe: "I will become as mild and duetyfull, / As ever Grissel was unto hir Lord, / And for my constancie, as Lucrece was, / And if that Sentloe will but live with me" (I.ii.109–112). In contrast to Anabell, she forgets her vow on the least provocation; eventually, she plots to murder Sentloe.

Part of the strain we experience in trying to interpret Queen Isabella's character in *Edward II* results from Marlowe's having attempted to combine the Patient Grissill figure with the aggressive/lewd wife in a single character. We are not sure whether she undergoes a radical character change or whether her earlier Grissillian behavior is simple hypocrisy; there was little in English literature up to the time *Edward II* was acted to prepare audiences for a Grissill figure who behaves in either of these ways.[25]

Plays of the early seventeenth century were especially rich in Grissill figures: *Patient Grissil,* acted in 1600, *How a Man May Choose,* acted ca. 1602, *All's Well that Ends Well,* acted ca. 1602, *The London Prodigal,* acted ca. 1604, *The Fair Maid of Bristow,* acted ca. 1604, *Othello,* acted ca. 1604, *The Miseries of Enforced Marriage,* acted ca. 1606, all have heroines who remain patient and submissive through scenes of gruesome abuse by their husbands. Significantly, this dismal literary fad was contemporary with the rejuvenation of the female transvestite movement:[26] the Patient Grissill figure in literature was, I believe, a male wish-fulfillment fantasy appropriate to historical periods when few living wives behaved like Patient Grissill. When women began swaggering the streets in male attire and weaponry, male authors provided male readers and playgoers with a comforting fantasy into which they could retreat. The Grissill story and its analogues are cunningly constructed for use during periods of female aggressiveness: by masquerading as a defense of women, they avoid incurring the ire of dangerously aggressive females, they serve a hortatory purpose for wives and daughters, and they allow men to luxuriate in the spectacle of a woman humiliated and punished while she is being praised.

Matthew Flowerdale in *The London Prodigal,* abandoning his wife Luce, charges her, "Look you do not follow me; look you do not: / If you do, beggar, I shall slit your nose." To her "Alas, what shall I do?" he replies helpfully, "Why turn whore: that's a good trade; / And so perhaps I'll see thee now and then" (III.iii). Young Arthur's wife in *How a Man May Choose* out-Grissills Grissill:

> If you delight to see me drudge and toil,
> I'll be your drudge, because 'tis your delight.
> Or if you think me unworthy of the name
> Of your chaste wife, I will become your maid,
> Your slave, your servant—anything you will,
> If for that name of servant and of slave
> You will but smile upon me now and then.
>
> (I.ii)

He answers that there is, in fact, some practical service she can do him: "Die suddenly, / And I'll become a lusty widower: / The longer thy life lasts, the more my hate / And loathing still increaseth towards thee. / When I come home and find thee cold as earth, / Then will I love thee." Arthur persists in his shameless behavior even before relatives; his father-in-law issues a mild rebuke: "You might have us'd my daughter better, / Than to have beat her, spurn'd her, rail'd at her / Before our faces." This boldness upsets the wife:

> O father, be more patient; if you wrong
> My honest husband, all the blame be mine,
> Because you do it only for my sake.
> I am his handmaid; since it is his pleasure
> To use me thus, I am content therewith,
> And bear his checks and crosses patiently.
>
> (I.iii)

Anabell in *The Fair Maid of Bristow* follows faithfully the husband who taunts her with his whore and tries to murder her; refusing to prefer charges against him, she offers to be executed in his place.

These prodigal husbands see the error of their ways: all are reformed through their wives' fidelity. In the closing lines of *How a Man May*

Choose, Young Arthur, enlightened by bitter experience with a shrew, propounds the value of a Grissill: "A good wife will be still [i.e., always] / Industrious, apt to do her husband's will; / But a bad wife, cross, spiteful and madding. Never keep home, but always be a-gadding." Another prodigal husband, Scarborow in *The Miseries of Enforced Marriage,* sets forth with admirable clarity the great ideal of the submissive, home-keeping wife which every prodigal was thought to deserve:

> To be a wife, is to be dedicate,
> Not to a youthful course, wild and unsteady,
> But to the soul of virtue, obedience,
> Studying to please, and never to offend.
> Wives have two eyes created, not like birds
> To roam about at pleasure, but for sentinels,
> To watch their husbands' safety as their own.
> Two hands; one's to feed him, the other herself:
> Two feet, and one of them is their husbands'.
> They have two of everything, only of one,
> Their chastity, that should be his alone.
> Their very thoughts they cannot term their own.
> Maids, being once made wives, can nothing call
> Rightly their own; they are their husbands' all.
>
> (Act I)

The Patient Grissill plot has the air of an over-correction: probably few Renaissance husbands would have liked to see their wives quite such self-effacing, grovelling martyrs as were the literary Grissill figures; but they may have hoped that if wives aimed at the Grissill mark, even a shortfall would be preferable to husband beating. Chaucer had balanced the exaggerated obedience of Griselda against the wife of Bath's uxorial power hunger which was itself an exaggeration in the other direction; in Jacobean times, the liberty and libertinism of citizens' wives was likely as exaggerated as the patience of a Grissill. But when women are sauntering the streets of London in breeches, armed with pistols and daggers, literature will be hard put to exaggerate the aggressiveness of women. I think the Patient Grissill figure was fantasy; the aggressive female character more accurately reflected reality, transmuted only by the often-felt necessity to portray women of any degree of assertiveness as either shrews or whores.

Shakespeare's plays bristle with strong-minded female characters—Joan of Arc, Queen Margaret, Constance, the Duchess of Gloucester, Portia, Rosalind, Beatrice, Adriana, Kate, Viola, Mistresses Page and Ford, Helena, Isabella, Marina, Imogen, Juliet, Volumnia, Cordelia, Goneril, Regan, Lady Macbeth, Cleopatra, Paulina, Emilia, Katharine of Aragon.

The roll call is impressive: for good or for ill, these women's muscular personalities demand audience response. The same can be said for dozens of other women in Renaissance literature, from the heroine of *Appius and Virginia* to the heroine cf *The Duchess of Malfi*. Yet despite the truly spectacular number of assertive women in Renaissance literature, female assertiveness continued to be widely regarded as abnormal. Assertiveness was supposedly a male trait, and assertive women were often stigmatized as "mankind," or masculine. Of the strong-willed scold Mistress Barnes in *The Two Angry Women of Abington* we hear, "She is mankind, therefore thou mayest strike her" (Sig. F3). When in *Coriolanus* the submissive Virgilia is at last galvanized into assertiveness, she astonishes herself by speaking two lines to a tribune in a public place and is rewarded for this piece of courage by being labelled mannish: "Are you mankind?" (IV.ii.16). When the shrew Xantippe contemplates husband beating in Robert Snawsel's *A looking glasse for maried folkes,* her fellow shrew Margery commends her "manly courage," while the virtuous Eulalie cries, "O terrible mannish woman!" (Sig. Cᵛ, C2). Hall satirized domineering women as "mannish housewives" (*Virgidemiarum,* Book III, Satire III). Female shrewishness is described in *Epicoene* as "masculine, and lowd commanding" (IV.i.9).

Renaissance orthodoxy viewed women as *by nature* timid, passive, and tender of heart: the courageous, aggressive, and tough minded it typically regarded as unnatural. No amount of contrary evidence could shake the faith of the average Renaissance man in the existence of behavior dictated by nature: if a vast majority of women had failed to conform to expectations about timidity, passivity, and tenderness of heart, that would have proved only that a good many women were unnatural nowadays.

This Renaissance mental habit—the trick of maintaining a generalization about women by dismissing contrary evidence as aberrant behavior—helps account for the fact that sweeping generalizations about women's weak nature appear in literature abounding in women of formidable strength. After all the tongue-lashings delivered by female characters in the drama, nobody bats an eyelid when Luce in *The London Prodigal* sighs, "My voice grows weak, for women's words are faint" (III.iii). Several plays notable for strong-minded female characters describe Woman by the biblical formulation "the weaker vessel" (cf. *As You Like It,* II.iv.6, *Cupid's Whirligig,* Sig. [L3]), *The Fleire,* Sig. H3ᵛ). Unembarrassed by the staging of Joan of Arc, Moll Cutpurse, Cordelia, or the Duchess of Malfi, authors went on declaring women fearful by nature. Credulity was apparently not strained when Constance, that militant champion of her son's claim to the English throne, described herself as "a woman, naturally born to fears" (*King John,* III.i.15), or when a character in *The Fleire,* a play whose main characters are murderous prostitutes and sturdy female transvestites, says "Let foolish feare goe dwell with women" (Sig. Gᵛ). Hamlet, whose own mother remains unruffled by her husband's death, a murder she witnesses in her bedchamber, her son's banishment for criminal insanity, and the suicide of her prospective daughter-in-law, can still describe his fears as the sort of thing that "would perhaps trouble a woman" (V.ii.225–226). Despite the guzzling gossips of Skelton's *The Tunning of Elinor Rumming*, Dunbar's *The Twa Marrit Wemen and the Wedo*, the play *Tom Tyler and His Wife*, and Rowland's *'Tis Merry when Gossips Meet* (see chapter 9), authors could still maintain that women cannot hold their liquor and must be given weak drinks: "Women are weak, and we must bear with them: / Your frolic healths are only fit for men," opines Sir John Harcop in *Enforced Marriage* (Act II), while Lucrece drinks "a womans draught" in Heywood's *The Rape of Lucrece*, explaining, "Your grace must pardon / The tender weaknesse of a womans braine" (p. 218).

Certain stock devices enabled authors to reassert the weak nature of Woman in the face of steel-backboned female behavior. The sturdiest of women faint when circumstances become too trying: Rosalind faints in *As You Like It*, Luce in *The Wise-Woman of Hogsdon*, Phillis in *The Fair Maid of the Exchange*, Celia in *Volpone*, Thaïsa in *Pericles*, Cleopatra in *Antony and Cleopatra*. Lady Macbeth faints too, although she may be shamming, like Tamyra in Chapman's *Bussy d'Ambois*. At other times women—Constance in *King John*, Ophelia, Lady Macbeth—retreat from unpleasant reality into madness and sometimes suicide.

Madelon Gohlke's formulation, "It is not the female herself who is perceived as weak, but rather the feminized male" (*The Woman's Part*, p. 162), while expressing the paradox that a man could be made to feel "effeminate," or weak, by the presence of a strong woman, is not really accurate. The true paradox is that the female sex *was* perceived as weak, although an infinite number of individual women might be perceived to be strong.

Lady Macbeth's behavior does not really raise questions about women's tender-heartedness: she has to be unsexed before she can divest herself of tenderness, and even so she can hardly be said, judging by her later words and actions, to have succeeded. *Lear's* imagery consistently makes monsters of Goneril and Regan: they cannot be women, for women aren't like that. Albany sees Goneril as a fiend disguised as a woman: "Howe'er thou art a fiend, / A woman's shape doth shield thee" (IV.ii.66–67). A servant feels that Regan's behavior calls forth a whole new stereotype encompassing all women: "If she live long, / And in the end meet the old course of death, / Women will all turn monsters" (III.vii.100–104); the inadequacy of stereotypes to deal with individuals, he never considers. The Duke of York in *3 Henry VI*, defeated by an army under the generalship of Queen Margaret, declares (in a somewhat unsports-manlike manner) that Margaret is an ugly, unvirtuous, mannerless trull and proceeds to reëxamine stereotype: "Women are soft, mild, pitiful, and flexible— / Thou stern, obdúrate, flinty, rough, remorseless" (I.iv.141–142). If the minor premise of this fledgling syllogism is not to invalidate the major premise, the only possible conclusion is, "Therefore, you are not a woman." This, indeed, is York's implied conclusion: Margaret is "inhuman" (I.iv.154); specifically, a tiger disguised as a woman ("O ti-ger's heart wrapped in a woman's hide" [I.iv.137]). Shakespearean women who depart from the stereotype of weak, tender, pitying vulnerability are usually seen either as temporarily behaving unnaturally in an emergency situation (as are the romantic heroines), or as being permanently dehumanized, warped, monstrous, "fiend-like" (as are the villainesses of tragedies and history plays). The validity of the stereotype is seldom challenged.

Partly because real Renaissance women were decidedly un-Grissillian, and partly for artistic reasons (the submissive wife is among the most boring literary characters yet conceived by the mind of man), aggressive women enormously outnumber timid and passive women in Renaissance literature. Yet the authority of stereotype was such that authors were continually shaking their fingers at their own characters, continually evincing the helpless conviction that these vigorous, aggressive hordes of women forcing themselves so ebulliently into the plots of plays and the warp and woof of epigram were, however arresting, however delightful, not quite feminine. While the behavior of their own female characters insistently battered at the bulwark of faith in immutable sexual distinctions, the women taking on more and more "masculine" attributes and remaining as attractive as ever, authors in their generalized pronouncements about women clung tenaciously to ancient beliefs in the unchangeable nature of womankind.

Germaine Greer's perception that "where the choice lies between the ultrafeminine and the virago, Shakespeare's sympathy lies with the virago"[27] holds true for other Renaissance writers as well: much in their writings suggests that if unencumbered by the dead weight of social orthodoxy, Renaissance males might have blossomed into a race of viragophiles. But encumbered they were. Clara Claiborne Park has shown how Shakespeare neutralizes his viragos by tempering their behavior in various ways to render it acceptable to society. Park attributes the continued popularity of Shakespeare's transvestite heroines partly to the persistence of orthodox, stereotyped notions of submissive femininity: "That he could create women who were spunky enough to be fun to be with, and still find ways to mediate their assertiveness so as to render them as nonthreatening as their softer sisters, is one of the secrets of his perennial appeal."[28]

Other writers, having created female characters every bit as "spunky" as Shakespeare's, were also doing all they could to vitiate the threat such characters posed: by taming shrews, praising Grissills, satirizing scolds, and declaring female aggressiveness abnormal, authors strove desperately to shield themselves from the specter of feminine strength.

When women wore breeches on the streets of London, they brought to life the old cliché about domineering wives wearing the breeches. London's female transvestites cannot have been unaware of this: their gesture was deliberately symbolic. So automatically did the Renaissance mind equate feminine breeches with domineering wives that the issue is raised even with regard to transvestite virgins in the comedies: Mellida's page's livery is twice seen in relationship to modern women's figurative breeches wearing: "*Mellida* . . . Turnd man, turnd man: women weare the breeches" (*Antonio and Mellida,* Sig. G4ᵛ; see also Sig. [A4]). Lyly treats the matter symbolically in *The Maid's Metamorphosis,* where a maid is changed by Apollo into a man, which saves her life but is a fairly severe disappointment to her boyfriend; one character relates the metamorphosis to the question of sovereignty in marriage: "In sooth, me-thinks the breech becomes her well: / And might it not make their husbands feare then, / Wold all the wiues in our town might wear them" (Sig. G). So inextricably were breeches and shrewishness intertwined that sometimes it is difficult to tell whether a given passage refers to literal or figurative breeches wearing, or to both. When Bos in *Every Woman in Her Humour* inquires in a tavern, "Which of you fiue is the Hostis of the house?" a boy answers, "Thats easily discernd, for foure weare breeches." Bos replies, "Women now adaies weare breeches as well as men, mary the difference lies in the bawble" (Sig. B3ᵛ). ("Bawble," at least, needs no gloss.) Living Jacobean transvestites must have known they would be characterized as domineering wives; and they must not have cared.

When fop confronted virago, as he did in *Haec-Vir* and in many contemporary texts, he was in some ways representing the courtly tradition against a champion of the bourgeois tradition—the woman who wears the breeches. Both traditions were founded upon female dominance: the fop was the courtly lover, sadly run to seed through generations of composing "puling sonnets" to disdainful mistresses; the virago confronted him after mastering a milksop husband or father at home, with the venerable bourgeois strategies of the shrew. If we did not know that Jacobean courtiers *were* foppish, and that Jacobean women *did* stalk the streets in male attire, we would be tempted to read *Haec-Vir* and related documents as allegories of class antagonism, appropriate to an age darkened by the gathering clouds of impending civil war.

But living women did don the breeches, to the horror of royalty, aristocracy, and bourgeoisie alike. The issue went considerably beyond the class war, to involve the deeply ingrained Renaissance reverence for order. Feminine aggression, whose icon was the man-clothed virago of the Jacobean London streets but which left its tracks all across Renaissance literature, was more than just one more symptom of the wickedness of the age; it was, for many, the herald of impending chaos: "Is change strange?" asks Candido. "Tis not the fashion vnlesse it alter: Monarkes turne to beggers; beggers creepe into the nests of Princes, Maisters serue their prentises: Ladies their Seruingmen, men turne to women . . . And women turne to men" (*1 Honest Whore*, IV.iii.130–135). Constabarus in *Mariam* spins a vision of chaos out of Salome's masculine demand for a divorce:

> Are . . . women now trāsform'd to men?
> Why do you not as well our battels fight,
> And weare our armour? suffer this, and then
> Let all the world be topsie turued quite.
> Let fishes graze, beastes, swine, and birds descend,
> Let fire burne downewards whilst the earth aspires:
> Let Winters heat and Summers cold offend,
> Let Thistels growe on Vines, and Grapes on Briers,
> Set vs to Spinne or Sowe.
>
> (Sig. [B4]ᵛ-C)

This is reminiscent of passages in Hooker and Elyot, of Ulysses's speech on degree in *Troilus and Cressida*—visions of the cosmic chaos that will certainly result if due degree, due hierarchical distinction between superiors and inferiors, is not preserved. The laws of God and of Nature declared beasts inferior to humans, serfs inferior to lords, women inferior to men. "Nowadays" serfs were purchasing knighthoods, and women usurping male attire. Could the distinction between man and beast be preserved under such circumstances? Would not the moon leave its course and the stars fall? Breeches were a serious matter.

Two prominent literary traditions dealing with love and marriage, the courtly love tradition and the woman wearing the breeches, portray men as weaklings helplessly languishing under the tyrannous rule of formidably powerful women. Both traditions regard their dominant women ambivalently: the courtly mistress is basically a revered figure, although she is sometimes complained of by a suffering lover within the tradition and sometimes reviled and debunked from outside the tradition; the domineering wife is basically a detested figure, although scolding in a just cause is occasionally excused, and sympathy sometimes extended to a woman who turns shrewish in response to her husband's abuse. But whether these two female character types are satirized or praised, the pattern is still female dominance and male subjection.

Literature celebrating women's power, a literature envisioning men in subjection to women, is what one would expect to find in a tradition which developed under feminine auspices: Joan Kelly-Gadol remarks astutely upon the fact that courtly love poetry was created largely under female sponsorship.[29] But this does not account for the fact that the complementary tradition, the wife wearing the breeches—a satiric tradition clearly not under the patronage of women—exhibits the same pattern of female dominance. It seems not unreasonable to argue, again, that the similarity was mediated by real life—that late medieval and Renaissance males felt their dominant position in society threatened.

NOTES

1. Geoffrey Chaucer, *The Franklin's Tale*, l. 793, in *The Works of Geoffrey Chaucer.*

2. Sir Philip Sidney, *The Defense of Poesy*, in *The Renaissance in England*, p. 622.

3. Michael Drayton, *Idea*, in *The Renaissance in England*, p. 427.

4. See Louis Salomon's *The Devil Take Her! A Study of the Rebellious Lover in English Poetry.*

5. Shakespeare hints several times at an anti-Petrarchan component in Hamlet's misogyny. Hamlet's love letter to Ophelia is Petrarchan in its religious diction ("to the celestial, and my soul's idol") and its reference to lover's groans; Hamlet's reported appearance in Ophelia's chamber has the earmarks of Petrarchan dishabille, as Ophelia's father (considerably quicker than Romeo's father in spotting Petrarchan symptoms) immediately recognizes—the only complication being the possibility that seeing a ghost might produce the same symptoms. Although this Petrarchan motif is not, I think, successfully integrated into the play, the replacement of Petrarchan sentiments by bitter misogyny in Hamlet's character does complete a well-established literary pattern, however much distorted by Gertrude's behavior. For more on Hamlet's misogyny, see chapter 11.

6. Rare exceptions like the anonymous *A merry Ieste of a Shrewde and curste Wyfe lapped in Morrelles skin,* where a wife determined to dominate her husband is successfully tamed, demonstrate the extreme measures that must be adopted to bring a recalcitrant wife to heel. Also, *A merry Ieste* (as I argue in my essay "New Light on *The Wife Lapped in Morel's Skin* and *The Proud Wife's Paternoster*") is a work of the very early English Renaissance.

7. In *Minor Poems of Lydgate,* pp. 675–82.

8. STC 6476, 1603. The translation is no longer commonly attributed to Dekker.

9. The host refers to the Hercules/Omphale story. A number of Renaissance texts confuse Omphale with Iole.

10. Martin Parker, *A warning for wives, by the example of one Katherine Francis.*

11. *Thomas Platter's Travels in England, 1599,* p. 182.

12. Domineering wives could also make pushy mothers, sometimes a public nuisance. Constance, disputing the royal succession on behalf of her son, is dismissed as an "unadviséd scold" (*King John,* II.i.191)—a risk run by any politically assertive woman in the period. Volumnia dominates her son and always has: Coriolanus confesses he learned his contempt for plebeians from her (*Coriolanus,* III.ii.7–13), and his other major trait, his warlike nature, she clearly instilled as well. Coriolanus admires his mother's strength: "Mother, / Resume that spirit when you were wont to say / If you had been the wife of Hercules, / Six of his labors you'd have done, and saved / Your husband so much sweat" (IV.i.15–19)—ambiguous praise, since Hercules was dominated and made effeminate by a woman, just as Coriolanus is ultimately dismissed as "thou boy of tears" for giving way to his mother's wishes. Volumnia meditates (in a passage dripping with Freud), "If my son were my husband, I should freelier rejoice in that absence wherein he won honor than in the embracements of his bed" (I.iii.2–5). Manipulating him to do her will in the stereotypical manner of wives, she lectures him at great length and at two moments of crisis produces her trump card, the threat that if he does not do as she wills, she will die (III.ii.125–28, V.iii.172–73). She also addresses him with that telling phrase, "Be ruled" (III.ii.89).

13. *Godly Queen Hester,* ca. 1527, enunciates the principle: "Sometyme more for loue than for awe / The king is content to be counselled by the queene." Carefully avoiding "awe"—domination through shrewishness, Hester adopts Erasmian tactics (as set forth in the closely contemporary *Coniugium*) to sweeten up her husband by providing him an "exquisite" repast and treating him with great deference before advancing her political petition. A German commentary translated into English in 1584, *A Right Godly and learned discourse vpon the booke of Esther* (STC 3602), argues: "Howe did the Queene *Ester* wring this from so mightie a king: Doubtlesse, not by foule wordes, not by contempt, not by disdayne, not by brawling, not by chyding, not by lewde demeanour. For by these maners women are wont rather to carry away blowes and stripes then rule and maistrie. But by godlines towardes God, reuerence towardes their husbandes, chastitie, patience, and other commendable vertues. For thus women by seruing and obeiing do rule, by which waye onely the rule bearing of women is lawfull" (Sig. [I6]ᵛ-[I7]).

14. John Dickenson, whose Fair Valeria proceeds from one sin (playing the lute to the neglect of her needlework) to a repertoire of others— gossiping, demanding a dainty diet, excessive drinking, singing lewd

songs, wearing sumptuous attire, using cosmetics and perfume, indulging in group sex, keeping male whores, and scolding her husband, enunciates the principle of sin's seamlessness: "Most vices are linked together in such an union of affinity, & cleaue so sister-like in one knot . . . that neuer any is imployed alone" (p. 23). Similarly, Thomas Tuke in *A Discovrse Against Painting and Tincturing of Women. Wherein the abominable sinnes of Murther and Poysoning, Pride and Ambition, Adultery and Witchcraft are set foorth and discouered* demonstrates that the use of rouge and mascara leads directly to such "neighbour sins" as poisoning, adultery, and witchcraft. This principle helps account for the extreme leaps of the imagination so typical of Renaissance literature: a finely dressed woman is bound to be a whore; women who use makeup would think nothing of murdering their husbands.

15. See my essay "Egyptian Queens and Male Reviewers: Sexist Attitudes in *Antony and Cleopatra* Criticism," pp. 311–312.

16. In "The Victim's Side: Chaucer's *Clerk's Tale* and Webster's *Duchess of Malfi*," Harriett Hawkins argues cogently that Chaucer's version of the Griselda story, *The Clerk's Tale,* should be read as a criticism of unquestioning obedience to authority, even divine authority. In Renaissance versions of the Grissill story, though, the husband is excoriated for cruelty, but the wife seldom encouraged to stand up for herself; abuse of authority is condemned, but obedience to authority continues to be recommended.

17. Frederick J. Furnivall, ed., *Captain Cox, his Ballads and Books; or, Robert Laneham's Letter,* pp. lxiv–lxv.

18. The juxtaposition of romance and sadism in *The Wife Lapped In Morel's Skin* seems to justify the belief of the Erasmus/More circle that chivalric romance itself has a brutalizing effect on readers. See Robert P. Adams's *The Better Part of Valor,* chapter 13.

19. *A dialogue conteynyng the number of the effectuall prouerbes in the Englishe tounge, compact in a matter concernynge two maner of maryages,* in *John Heywoodes woorkes.* Heywood ingeniously constructed this dialogue by stringing together a large number of proverbs: that a compendium of English proverbs works out to be the story of an unhappy marriage says a good deal about the nature of English proverbs.

20. See Richard Hosley, "Sources and Analogues of *The Taming of the Shrew,*" pp. 295–99.

21. See Alfred Harbage's essay "Shakespeare as Expurgator," appended to *Shakespeare and the Rival Traditions.*

22. Feminist criticism of *The Taming of the Shrew* has become a small industry, or perhaps a sport resembling the Renaissance formal controversy in its competitive spirit: which critic can most ingeniously exonerate Shakespeare? Germaine Greer writes that "the submission of a woman like Kate is genuine and exciting because she has something to lay down, her virgin pride and individuality" (*The Female Eunuch,* p. 221); Coppélia Kahn argues that "unlike other misogynistic shrew literature, this play satirizes not woman herself in the person of the shrew, but *male attitudes*

toward women" ("*The Taming of the Shrew:* Shakespeare's Mirror of Marriage," in *The Authority of Experience: Essays in Feminist Criticism,* p. 86); John C. Bean insists that "Shakespeare's play does *not* preach the subjection of women" ("Comic Structure and the Humanizing of Kate in *The Taming of the Shrew,*" in *The Woman's Part,* p. 67); Juliet Dusinberre judges *Taming* a feminist play because Shakespeare's Kate justifies the subjection of women on political grounds rather than (as does Kate in the anonymous *Taming of A Shrew*) on religious grounds (*Shakespeare and the Nature of Women,* pp. 78–79). Robert Heilman discusses several critics' "revisionist" attempts to show that Kate is not really tamed at all ("The *Taming* Untamed, or, The Return of the Shrew," pp. 147–61). One can certainly sympathize with the "can this play be saved?" response of those feminists who cannot bring themselves to believe that their favorite author, on whom they have lavished so much scholarly effort, could be quite such a male chauvinist as he appears in *Taming;* but as I have shown in the course of this book, there are plenty of indications that Shakespeare was no proto–Mary Wollstonecraft with a knack for blank verse.

The rescuing of Shakespeare by feminists, who view him as a feminist ahead of his time, might well be seen as a species of that idolatry that Alfred Harbage has labelled "the myth of perfection": we feministical Shakespeareans often fall into a class with Harbage's "various musicians, sailors, soldiers, doctors, and others, especially lawyers," who have "fostered the idea that Shakespeare not only knew and loved music, as he truly did, but could take down and reassemble a spinet (if he did not invent the instrument) as well as navigate a ship, command an army, and perform a frontal lobotomy, while his exhaustive knowledge of the law might have ruptured even the capacious brain of the Lord Chief Justice" (*Conceptions of Shakespeare,* p. 24). We are tempted to assume that not only did Shakespeare know and love women, as he truly did, and not only does he occasionally allow them to speak movingly in their own defense (a privilege he grants even to villains, so why not to women?), but he was also conversant with all modern notions about sex-role stereotyping, socialization, the economics of sexism, and so on.

But feminism as we know it did not exist in Shakespeare's time, and I see little evidence that he was ahead of his time in his attitudes toward women. If critics feel they cannot enjoy any of Shakespeare's works without first cleaning up *The Taming of the Shrew,* I wish them luck; but I suspect that not even the love of a good woman will ultimately salvage that play. And it is, perhaps, both presumptuous and fruitless to try to reform the opinions of an author so immeasurably great and so irretrievably dead: it would be more respectful and less exhausting to forgive him.

23. Henry Smith, *A Preparatiue to Marriage,* pp. 38, "61" (i.e., 81).

24. Robert Cleaver, *A Godlie Forme of Household Government,* p. 170.

25. See Sara Munson Deats's perceptive essay "*Edward II:* A Study in Androgyny," pp. 30–41.

26. Regular references to female transvestites resume in 1606–7. I am

assuming that the fashion was revived a couple of years before that, allowing for references to it in works now lost, or in works that I have simply missed.

27. Greer, *The Female Eunuch,* p. 220. Celeste Turner Wright (p. 442) traces the literary tradition wherein the tall, muscular Amazonian type "inspires men with the hope of superior offspring": remarks on the puissant children to be hoped from such women appear in *The Life of Long Meg of Westminster,* Sidney's *Arcadia, The Roaring Girl,* and *Swetnam the Woman-hater.* That such admiration for big women went beyond literary convention is evidenced by the fact that such a matrimonial sermonizer as Alexander Niccholes could advise against marrying a short woman, lest one produce "pigmy children" (*A Discourse of Marriage and Wiving,* published in 1615, at the height of the *hic mulier* movement).

28. Clara Claiborne Park, "As We Like It: How a Girl Can Be Smart and Still Popular," in *The Woman's Part,* p. 103.

29. Joan Kelly-Gadol, "Did Women Have a Renaissance?" *Becoming Visible: Women in European History,* pp. 146–148.

✂

CHAPTER NINE

The Gossips' Meeting

IF THE LITERATURE of love and marriage suggests that men felt threatened by individual women, the way in which feminine friendships were satirized suggests masculine suspicion of women meeting together. Such satire is particularly prominent during the early Jacobean years: again, suggestively contemporary with the reawakening female transvestite movement. Samuel Rowlands produced during the early *hic mulier* years two satiric portraits of domineering and libertarian women, *Tis Merrie when Gossips meete,* 1602, and *A whole crew of kind Gossips, all met to be merry,* 1609, both representative of a genre which can be called the gossips' meeting.

"Gossip," from Old English *godsib* or spiritual relative, originally meant "godparent." Its transferred meaning, "familiar acquaintance," was probably acquired through women's frequently-satirized habit of congregating at christenings. The *Oxford English Dictionary* dates the meaning "a person, mostly a woman, who delights in idle talk; a tattler" to the 1560s, a period rich in literary cynicism about women. The term had both favorable and unfavorable connotations throughout the Renaissance—favorable for women, who apply the term affectionately to close friends, and unfavorable for men, who apply the term satirically to their wives' close friends.

Tis Merry When Gossips Meet is a dialogue which fails to accomplish its satiric objectives and bumbles instead into being a work of art. Rowland's characters got out of control, as literary characters sometimes do, and took over the piece for themselves.

The original object, it would seem, was to satirize female gadding, gossiping, swearing, and drinking. A widow, a wife, and a maid meet fortuitously near a tavern and stop in for just one pint: drunkenness ensues. The widow, by definition the most emancipated, is the ringleader. She swears valiantly (preferring blasphemies like "Christ" and "Jesu-Christ"), keeps ordering rounds while the others timidly consider going home, and initiates much of the offending conversation. But the other two warm to the drinking and swearing as time goes on. The wife has been tempted away from duty: with her husband away, she is supposed to be tending the shop. The maid is initially shy: "You are to blame, in trueth we drinke like men, / Now by my truely I am e'ne ashamed" (Sig. C3ᵛ). But as the second pint of claret is succeeded by a quart of white wine and later by sack and sugar, all three grow relaxed and expansive.

They discuss the relative merits of the three estates of womankind—maidenhood, marriage, and widowhood. The widow enjoys her freedom: when she goes home there will be no husband to sniff her breath and call her to account. She has seen all three estates and can judge: next to widowhood, she prefers maidenhood, for all the suitors with their sighs of Petrarchan subjection and their gifts. The wife defends marriage; it is better, she proverbializes, than leading apes in hell. The maid is not so sure; she has witnessed marital brawls.

Another topic of discussion is men. The widow complains about her late husband, a wencher. The maid, advised to marry a youth who is courting her, exclaims that she could never marry such a dwarf; she is holding out for a really handsome man. The wife praises her own husband; no worry about breath sniffing from him: he is the soul of indulgence, addressing all sorts of endearments to her and becoming terribly alarmed if she shows any hint of illness. The widow says she has a suitor like that; when she tested his love by feigning illness, he wept. For this good quality, plus his attractive lands, she is inclined to marry him. Considerable energy goes into discussing men's physical appearance—hair color, complexion, beards. Their habits, too, are scrutinized; tobacco smokers are odious: the wife says her husband would never dream of smoking if she asked him not to. It is delightful to observe that what these women look for in a "good" man is precisely what, judging from the Patient Grissill plays or Erasmus's *Coniugium,*[1] Renaissance men looked for in a woman—a physically attractive doormat. The reciprocation may seem fair enough; but these women, remember, are being satirized.

As they get deeper in drink, the two older women begin schooling the maid in feminine manipulations. The wife explains how she manages to drink as much as she likes at home:

He [i.e., her husband] knowes (efaith) to please me in my diet,
Or for a month I shall be out of quiet.
Then if he sees me out of patience once,
Oh Christ, how [he] will seeke to [make] amends,
Then do I sigh to grieue him for the nonce,
Wherewith, hee'le kisse and say, Sweet loue be frends:
I let him kisse, and speake me faire a while,
And when the sullen humor's past, I smile.

(Sig. E3–E3ᵛ)

The widow congratulates her: "I cannot chuse but praise thy pretty wit, / It is the very course that I would take." The naïve maid is incredulous: "Why, I thought men had lou'd for kindnesse sake?" The wife scoffs: "Alas plaine wench, God knowes thou art not in it, / She that will settle loue, must this way win it." The maid cannot believe her ears: "I neuer heard that tricke before, / I thought mens loue must still be fed with kindnesse." The wife disabuses her: "God helpe thee *Besse,* not one among a score, / That poore opinion is but Maidens blindnesse" (Sig. E3ᵛ), adding that if a wife feigns disinclination to consort with gossips, her husband will insist that she get out of the house a bit. This advice is seen as schooling: "This for instruction *Besse,* I haue disclosed" (Sig. E4).

Much of this is pure stereotype, pure commonplace, part of the cultural cargo of misogynist jest and satire inherited from the Wife of Bath's Prologue and *Le Quinze Joyes de Mariage,* from *The School House of Women,* from *The Golden Book of Marcus Aurelius,* from jest book and ballad. But the piece bursts from its satiric confines, as characters and situation become too real for stereotype.

For one thing, the tavern and the mechanics of drinking are too thoroughly imagined for satire. The women have little debates on whether to drink upstairs or down, which wine to choose, whether the sack should be burnt or sugared, whether they should order sausages, whether the sausages are too salty, whether they should go home or order another round. The psychological effects of drinking are finely rendered. One loses track of time while drinking: although they order drinks every two or three stanzas on average, they still complain about slow service. The more one drinks, the better cheap wine tastes: *Wife:* "Beshrew my heart this wine is not the worst." *Widow:* "Good-faith me-thinkes t'is better then the first" (Sig. C4ᵛ). And an alcohol-befuzzed conscience can be assuaged by declaring that each round will be absolutely the last.

The characters, too, come alive. The maid, at first a little prissy, experiences a childish thrill at drinking like a grown-up: "In trueth (forsooth) a full cup doth excell, / Good Lord, I am become a mightie drinker" (Sig. Cᵛ); her oaths progress from the ladylike "forsooth" to the more daring "Good Lord" in the space of two lines. She says nothing when the widow confesses she would not drink so freely before men, but once in her cups the maid owns that when she drinks with men she feigns maidenly inability to drink much:

> An odde conceite *I* thinke on makes me smile:
> When I am forth in company, or so,
> How by the dram I take in Wine that while,
> Kissing the Cup, vpon the Wine I frowne,
> And so with smelling it, I set it downe.

Some simple fooles (all manners for his wit)
Comes on me with the French salute most quaintly,
And sayes, Sweet, mend your draft, you drink no whit,
Introth you shew your selfe too mayden-dainty:
Drinke better Lady at my kind request,
I say sweet Sir, *I* can no wine digest.

(Sig. E4^v)

The maid (who is almost sixteen) wants very much to appear an accomplished swizzler in the eyes of her two adult companions; this tavern visit is for her the apogee of worldly sophistication. But the widow points out that the maid has a way to go before she can hold her liquor: "Ile take my oath . . . The last full cup hath made you mightie ill / . . . See how pale she lookes" (Sig. F). (The widow's remedy is to order "another pynt of that she tasted last.") But nauseous or no, the tipsy maid has found a whole new side to her personality; she makes a slightly coarse remark in too loud a voice, at which the vintner's boy cannot help laughing.

The wife is well realized. Intensely proud of (and quite fond of) her husband, she seems hardly to realize, before she gets drunk, the way she manipulates him. Describing his compliance, she adds that the desire to please is mutual: she never serves him goose, which he detests. The transition to satiric comment is graceful: the mention of goose leads into a discussion of kinds of food the women like; this melts naturally into the wife's description of dainties she craves during pregnancy, which her indulgent husband readily provides. No reader could miss the satiric implications of this time-honored theme,[2] but the wife misses them; the twisting of the husband around the proverbial little finger is in her almost entirely unconscious. Only when she is pretty heavily into the wine does she begin schooling the maid in manipulations, and this appears similar in kind to the maid's self-congratulation on her drinking. Both are attempts to appear worldly, perhaps to gain the approval of the trio's dominant member, the widow. The wife's essay into worldliness gives her a queasy stomach, too; as the party gets noisier and she considers how they look to others, she retreats into respectability: "Talke not so loude, what will folke thinke that heares? / The very Vintners Boy laugh'd when you spake" (Sig. F). In anguish, she tries to hush the loud, thick-tongued widow and to escape from the tavern; her fear of rebuke from her husband when she comes home late and inebriated reveals her earlier remarks as mere bravado: "Cousen you do forget your selfe, me-thinke, / When *Besse* and I come home, we shall be chid" (Sig. [F3]).

The widow also transcends stereotype. Widows' proverbial lechery is not made part of her character. For all her posture of worldly experience, there is something wistful in her recollection of her youth—the romantic

days when suitors flocked about her. She does not harp very much on
the joys of liberty, as was conventional in maid/widow/wife dialogues.
While she claims that having seen all three estates she can best judge their
relative merits, she does not really fulfil this promise, and indeed is nearly
cut out of the conversation while maid and wife discuss matrimony versus the single life. As if it becomes painfully apparent during this part of
the conversation that she lacks both romantic youth and marital compan-
ionship, she interjects that she is thinking of marrying a wealthy and
indulgent man. Although she dominates the dialogue, at this one point
she seems insecure; she tries to impress the other two as they at times try
to impress her. There is at least a hint that her brash self-confidence conceals essential loneliness. The other two women arrived together, and
people are waiting for them at home: it is the widow who insists on
having company at the tavern and who is most reluctant to go home.
Rowlands does not paint her an evil temptress, seducing virtuous women
away from hearth and home. She is not satirized nearly as harshly as she
might have been; I wonder whether Rowlands didn't find unexpected
sympathy for this woman to whom a tavern is infinitely more congenial
than an empty house.

Near the end, satire dissolves utterly into realism. The vintner's boy
laughs; the wife is embarrassed, but the widow is indignant. Priding
herself on familiarity with various taverns, she is that perennial social
type for whom savoir faire consists of knowing the names of waiters.
She calls the vintner over and demands his name; thereafter, she calls him
William. To the wife's vast embarrassment she interrogates the inoffen-
sive William: "Brother, I pra'y, is it your Maisters minde, / Your fellow
Boy should flout guests when they drinke? . . . What is thy name? . . .
William, say the case were but your owne / And that you were as we are
at this season / With friends a drinking where you are not knowne /
Would you be flouted? . . . *William,* when cam'st thou in this house to
dwell?" (Sig. Fᵛ– F2ᵛ). The vintner humors and mollifies her; the wife
tries to shut her up. The widow is at that stage of drunkenness where it
suddenly seems terribly important to prove that one is sober; she asserts
her staunch respectability: "And therefore *William,* this abuse we scorne, /
For we are *London Gentle-women* borne" (Sig. F2). This is succeeded by
another familiar phase of inebriation: maudlin intimacy with the barten-
der. Inviting William to drink with her, the widow asks him personal
questions. Apprised that his master's wife is pregnant and hopes for a
boy, the widow boozily confides, "So would not I, *William,* for Boyes
be wilde, / Though Girles cry, *William,* till they be bepist, / *William,* giue
me a Girle, take boyes who list" (Sig. [F3]). The wife, telling the widow
she is forgetting herself, hastily pours the rest of the wine into the vintner's cup and pulls the widow away. The widow makes one last magnan-

imous gesture: sweeping away the small change proffered by wife and maid, she pays the bill herself.

This final scene could be staged today and ring true to life. It has the timelessness of real literary art, growing out of accurate observation of how real people behave in a timeless human situation. It is at the same moment satiric and affectionate, like much great comic art; and like all great comic art, it is sad around the edges. The three women of *Tis Merry When Gossips Meet* are in the company of other literary figures who outgrew their function as satiric butts, tempters, and villains to become flesh and blood—the Wife of Bath, Falstaff, Shylock. It is distinguished company.

Tis Merry is Rowlands's best poem: the light of genius illuminated his pedestrian poetry but this once. His second gossip poem, *A Whole Crew of Kind Gossips, All Met to Be Merry,* published seven years later, is by contrast a lifeless, mean-spirited piece of work. But it is at least thorough; it combines with *Tis Merry* to make Rowlands England's laureate of gossip verse. The nominal dramatic situation—gossips again sit drinking in a tavern—is here only a frame for six declamations. All these gossips are aggrieved wives. The first complains that her husband's "mind's of Money bags" (Sig. A2ᵛ). He keeps her short of drinking money. He allows her to wear fine clothing, "But that's his credit, full as much as mine" (Sig. A3). (This is one of several Renaissance comments suggesting that complaints about wives' extravagance were unfair, that husbands wanted smartly-dressed wives to parade their own prosperity.) This wife resents being in her husband's financial power: "I scorne to take allowance like a child" (Sig. A3), admiring her sister's success in obtaining her own money by louring, pouting, weeping, and complaining; she intends to try a "sick and sullen" routine herself. "A Shroe [i.e., shrew]," she believes, "is ten times better then a sheepe" (Sig. [A4]).

The second wife wishes she were a maid again, recalling the halcyon days when she chalked up forty-five suitors, received their gifts, and in return did them favors which shall be nameless. Her husband crosses her humors. When he hits her, she hits him back, as her mother taught her. He is still a braggart, but she has nearly broken him of wife beating:

> [I] valiantly tooke vp a Faggot-sticke.
> (For he had giuen me a blow or twaine)
> But as he likes it, let him strike againe,
> The blood ran down about his eares apace,
> I brake his head, and all bescratch't his face:
> Then got him downe, and with my very fist
> I did bepommell him vntill he pist.
>
> (Sig. B)

The third wife admires the second's physical prowess. Since her own husband is too strong for her to beat, she contents herself with endless scolding and occasional guerilla warfare: once she put a stool in front of him when he came in drunk, feigning surprise and grief when he went flying. The fourth is married to a gamester; his cards and dice keep her dressed poorly. When she told him of envying another woman's hat at church, he upbraided her for undevout thoughts during the service—a clear case of pot calling kettle black.[3] The fifth wife's husband is a drunkard and smoker. The sixth's is a wencher: he wastes money on whores; she goes ill dressed. She abhors the bawdy songs he brings home from the bordello.

These complaints are the equivalent of complaints about wives in works like *The Bachelor's Banquet;* Rowlands even notes that hearing such complaints will dissuade young people from marriage: "What will our Batchelers and Maidens say, / That are preparing for their wedding day?" (Sig. A2). But unlike the *Banquet's* author, who professed determination to dissuade young men from marrying, Rowlands is highly critical of women who thus sully matrimony's good name: "Thinke whether ther's not much discretion lackes, / When men are wronged thus behind their backes." In the legions of literary works proclaiming wives' faults, nobody ever complained that husbands lacked discretion for saying such things behind their wives' backs. This double standard so little troubles Rowlands that he gives the gossips' husbands what nobody gave wives— the right of rejoinder. He brings on the six husbands to call their wives liars.

The first husband says he keeps his wife short of money because she is a shrewish spendthrift, inclined to idleness. (Her gossiping in the tavern itself dramatizes her idleness.) The second checks his wife's humors because she is domineering. He denies taking pleasure in her extravagant attire: she badgers him into providing it. The third regrets having married a widow; she is a scold, "impudent" and "bold," always comparing him unfavorably with her first husband, who was agreeably tractable and indulgent, like the husband described in *Tis Merry*. She once got a gossip to fetch her to a sick friend's bedside; he had them followed to a bawdy-house. He said nothing: he plans to give her enough rope to hang herself and then divorce her. The fourth husband says his wife was a kitchen drudge before he married her; now she is completely idle, sleeping late, amusing herself with a lap dog, beating her maid, and gadding with her gossips. She is a notorious scold. He denies being a gamester: she made all that up because women are ceaseless talkers, and she had to have something to say. Suspecting that he is a cuckold, he plans to put her out to pasture at his earliest convenience. The fifth husband confesses that he drinks a lot but says he is seldom too drunk to stand up. He does not deny his wife's charges but is furious that she made them public: wives have a duty to put up with anything in silence. The sixth husband denies wenching. It was unreasonable of his wife to jump to conclusions when she found him coming out of a bordello; as it happened, he avers with a perfectly straight face, he had just dropped by there for a smoke.

The fifth husband's remarks reflect the orthodox attitude toward women complaining about their husbands: a wife's duty is to suffer in silence, while her husband drinks, smokes, wenches, bankrupts the family by gambling, begrudges her spending money, and beats her. This, of course, was the burden of many a contemporary play: every prodigal deserves a Patient Grissill.

Almost all the elements of Rowlands's poems find parallels in other Renaissance literature of gossips' meetings. In most of these meetings, gossips complain about their husbands, in the process revealing what the authors consider their own unreasonable demands. A wife in William Dunbar's *The Twa Cummeris*[4] (The Two Gossips) complains of her husband's sexual inadequacy: "In bed he is nocht wirth a bene." In Dunbar's *Tretis Of The Twa Marrit Wemen and the Wedo* (The Two Married Women and the Widow), ca. 1508, a wife complains of her husband's loutishness, impotence, and jealousy. She prides herself on never consenting to intercourse without a great fee—a common motif. Another wife in this poem hates her husband: he is a whoremaster, impotent through too much wenching. Blaming her kinfolk for getting her into this marriage, she is sure she could have done better. Gossips in the anonymous *A Talk of Ten Wives on Their Husbands' Ware* grumble about the inadequacies of their husbands' erotic equipment. Gossips on their way to an upsitting[5] in Henry Parrot's *The Gossips Greeting,* 1620, plan to discuss their "husbands powers" (Sig. [B3]ᵛ). Gosynhyll incorporated a gossips' meeting in *The School House of Women,* wherein wives complain of being beaten and of their husbands' verbal abuse and sexual impotence. With Gosynhyll's usual fine sense of domestic detail, one wife complains that her husband pulls all the covers off her while he sleeps. One says she could have married better. In Chapter III of *The Bachelor's Banquet* a crew of gossips amuse themselves by running down the husband of a woman they are visiting. In *Every Woman in her Humour,* acted ca. 1607, a wife tells her gossips that her husband gives her no money for clothes. She receives rather suggestive advice: "Does he not sleepe some times? has hee no pockets about him? cannot you search his breeches? anye thing you finde in his breeches is your owne" (Sig. G2ᵛ). Shortness of money is a common complaint, reminding the reader that wives in Renaissance England had no legal right to own property or possess money; authors characterize such complaints as evidence of greed and extravagance.

Advice is central to the tradition: what literary husbands feared most from gossips was the wicked tricks women might learn from each other.

The "instruction" the wife gives the maid in *Tis Merry* has a long tradition behind it. The belief that women "school" other women in untoward behavior gave Gosynhyll's *School House of Women* its title: "Thus lerne the yonger, of the elders guiding / Day by day, kepynge suche scoles / The symple men, [they] make as foles" (Sig. [A4]). Tom Tyler's wife is "to well schooled with too many shrowes / To receive any blowes." The widow in Dunbar's *Two Married Women and the Widow* instructs the wives with what reads like a Machiavellian parody of Erasmus's advice to wives: although she hated her first husband, she treated him with supreme sweetness; this not only made him tractable (as Erasmus promises) but also allowed her to cuckold him without suspicion.[6] All wives, she says, could profit from her "sovereign teaching." In *The Proud Wife's Paternoster,* one gossip counsels another on methods of sweet-talking her husband into providing her with fine clothes; if he refuses, the gossip advises, she should confiscate his money and goods. A gossip schools John Dickenson's Fair Valeria by introducing her to a ladies' club that keeps male whores; here she learns a good deal about contemporary manners. Often a wife takes instruction merely by example: a wife in Ercole Tasso's *Of Marriage and Wiuing* envies another wife's gown, jewels, girdle, purse, furs, and freedom: the friend can "goe abroade here and there as best liketh her, without needing either to giue account where she hath bin, or asking any leaue to take her pleasure" (Sig. [D4]ᵛ–E). This wife goes home to agitate for similar benefits; feigning weeping, she tells her husband she might have married better. True to the age's fear that marital insubordination was contagious, the gossip's most energetic educational effort is to teach younger gossips how to get the marital bridle into their own hands: the usual advice is relentless scolding varied by histrionic scenes of feigned illness and artificially induced weeping.

The scene in *Epicoene* where the "collegiates" advise the newly wedded Epicoene on husband management draws on the long tradition of women schooling each other:

> *Daw.* Learne to chastise. Mistris *Otter* corrects her husband so, hee dares not speake, but vnder correction. . . .
> *Mavis.* Looke how you manage him at first, you shall haue him euer after.
> *Centaure.* Let him allow you your coach, and foure horses, your woman, your chamber-maid, your page, your gentleman-vsher, your *french* cooke, and foure groomes.
> *Haughty.* And goe with vs, to *Bed'lem,* to the *China* houses, and to the *Exchange*.
> *Centaure.* It will open the gate to your fame.
> *Haughty.* Here's *Centavre* has immortaliz'd her selfe, with taming of her wilde male. (IV.iii.8–28)

Tis Merry's discussion of the relative merits of marriage and the single life has precedent in Dunbar's *Two Married Women and the Widow,* where the widow demands to know what mirth can be in marriage, and neither wife can think of much mirth. One wife longs for freedom: could she break out of these "chains" she would wear silk, go to plays, preachings, and pilgrimages, keep much company, change lovers often. The other hates marriage too: if she had half a chance, "then chastite, adew!" The widow relishes her freedom: she has a lover, and flirts with everyone, even at church.

The maid/widow/wife formula appears in a poem by John Davies in Francis Davison's anthology *A Poetical Rapsody;* that this poem appears in the 1608 but not the 1602 edition suggests the influence of *Tis Merry.* Davies's "A contention betwixt a Wife, a Widdow and a Maide" consists entirely of a debate on the relative merits of the three estates. The major issue is freedom. The widow believes "Most maides are Wards, and euery wife a slaue, . . . / I am free" (p. 8). All three claim some power: the wife is mistress of her family, the widow runs her own household without male intrusion, and the maid controls her own desires. But power is not freedom. Not even the wife, who defends marriage throughout, denies that marriage is a cage; luckily, she enjoys being a canary:

Maid: Wiues are as birds in golden cages kept,
Wife: Yet in those cages chearefuly they sing:
Widow: Widdowes are birds out of those cages lept,
 Whose ioyfull notes makes all the forrest ring. (p. 10)

Each estate has its own prized possessions: the wife has her husband's reflected prestige, the widow her husband's fortune, and the maid her maidenhead: "Maids loose their value, whẽ they match with mẽ," she notes. The wife, perhaps more attracted by widowhood than she cares to admit, is put off mainly by widowhood's sexlessness: "If I were widdow, my merry dayes were past" (p. 13). The widow puts her mind at rest on this score.

Amends for Ladies, acted ca. 1611, opens with a small maid/wife/widow debate; the play examines problems peculiar to each of the three estates of womankind and closes with the wife exulting as the maid and widow both choose to marry. It will be recalled that the maid/wife/widow formula comes up in Swetnam's *Arraignment* and is regarded with a jaundiced eye in "Sowernam's" *Ester Hath Hanged Haman.* Any of these works might well have been influenced by Rowlands's *Tis Merry.*

Most gossips' meetings feature fairly heavy drinking. All of Rowlands's gossips are enthusiastic tipplers. The gossips in "The Twa Cummeris" sit drinking wine while rueing the deprivations of Lent. Dunbar's married women and widow quaff wine in a garden as they rake their husbands over the coals. In the anonymous carol "Hoow, gossip myne,"[7] a convivial group of gossips complain mildly about their husbands while drinking "wyne of the best" (Version A, stanza 22). *Fair Valeria's* gossips use drink as an aphrodisiac. In *Tom Tyler and His Wife*, Strife guzzles ale in a tavern with her gossips, Sturdie and Tipple. One group of gossips in *The Bachelor's Banquet* drink all day with a friend recuperating from childbirth. In a section considerably expanded by the *Banquet's* English translator, one gossip tipples while moralizing upon the high living that has bankrupted an absent gossip: she "loued euer to goe fine and fare daintily, and by my faith gossip, this is not a world for those matters, and thervpon I drinke to you" (Sig. C). In the last chapter of the *Banquet*, another group of gossips fortify themselves with wine, the better to advise a friend on how her daughter should deal with a domestic crisis: the daughter's husband has just surprised her lover in her bedchamber and chased him down the street. In Parrot's *The Gossip's Greeting*, a group of gossips sit in a tavern complaining of their husbands' jealousy, profligacy, and drinking; they punctuate their conversation with demands: "What is the wine quite out? drawer another quart" (Sig. C2[v]). Parrot provides a fanciful etymology for "gossip": it derives from the frequency with which such women "go sipping." The drunken gossips tradition goes back at least as far as the pageant of Noah's Flood in the Chester Mystery Cycle,[8] where Mrs. Noah sits drinking malmsey wine with her gossips while the waters rise; these gossips sing a song: "And lett us drinke or [i.e., before] wee departe, / for oftetymes wee have done soe. / For at one draught thou drinke a quarte, / and so will I doe or I goe" (ll. 229–32).

The apex of feminine drunkenness in Renaissance literature is undoubtedly reached in John Skelton's *The tunning of Elynor Rumming*, reprinted in 1609 perhaps as a result of *Tis Merry's* popularity. Elinor Rumming is an alewife who adulterates her ale with hens' dung. Her customers are gossips in huge numbers. They pay for their ale in kind: one with her wedding ring, one with her needle and thimble, others with spinning wheels, kitchen utensils, and babies' cradles. They keep coming and coming; alehouse turns warehouse as their pawned possessions mount to nightmare proportions. This is all in a day's work for serious drinkers. The women get horribly drunk: one falls down, revealing her "token" to all the world; another pisses where she stands.

Drunkenness was the image of idleness. The charge of wifely idleness, so frequent in Renaissance literature, comes to life in the gossips' meeting. Authors could count on most readers' agreeing that wives should be home spinning and looking after children, not rising at noon to prepare for a drinking bout. Underlying all these pieces is an unspoken indictment: not only are the gossips drinking and complaining about their husbands, they are drinking on their husbands' money and complaining on their husbands' time.

The famous "proviso" scene in Congreve's *The Way of the World*, 1700, has behind it the gossips' meeting. Millamont views marriage as had maids, wives, and widows before her: "My dear liberty, shall I leave thee?" But she insists on preserving idleness: "I'll lie abed in a morning as long as I please." Like Renaissance wives, she craves liberty to pay and receive visits without interrogation by her husband. This proviso touches off fear of gossips in her intended, Mirabell: he insists that she "admit no sworn confidante or intimate of your own sex." Mirabell's longest proviso is against the gossips' meeting. He bans alcoholic beverages from her meetings with female friends and opposes "masculine" drinking behavior, stipulating "that on no account you encroach upon the men's prerogative, and presume to drink healths, or toast fellows."

In one Renaissance play, *The Wit of A Woman*, the satiric conventions of the gossips' meeting give way to a momentary glimpse of a woman's despair at the despised condition of the female sex. Taking literally the charge that women school each other, the play opens in a schoolroom: an old schoolmistress is teaching needlework to her young female charges. This was the approved course of study for young women, according to such educational writers as Thomas Salter, who deplored the practice of teaching girls to dance, play the lute, read, and write.[9] Something sinister, however, is afoot: one of the girls feigns illness to discontinue her needlework and is allowed to recuperate by dancing and playing the lute. The expected happens: all the girls lay down their needlework, vow sisterhood, and begin to talk about men. One has apparently been reading Petrarchan poetry; she believes that all men can be brought to adore and serve women. But here is the moment of truth. Gianetta, the only girl who has been studying writing rather than needlework, has this to say about male attitudes toward women: "If we be wittie, they will play with vs like Apes: If foolish, they will skorne vs like Asses: if fayre, like pictures make vs gaye to looke vpon; if foule, keepe vs like Owles to laugh at: And the house must be kept as a prison, or else called gazers, or gossips: cookes of their dyet, Launders for their linnen, seruants for charge, and companions but for idlenes" (Sig. [A4]ᵛ).

But such moments of devastating perception are rare in the tradition. Most gossip literature is an unsubtle attempt to stigmatize as alcoholic louts women who do not stay strictly at home, who prefer female company on occasion, and who dare to criticize men. Authors may really have believed that such literature could shame women into home keeping and silence; more likely, they simply meant to entertain men by wit-

tily airing their grievances, and to entertain women too, for this is the
sort of antifeminist literature that women themselves might have enjoyed. The gossips' meeting is at heart a comic genre of considerable
charm. But it does suggest widespread male defensiveness, a general unwillingness to brook criticism from an inferior species, as well as fear of
women acting in concert: the authors consistently assume that wherever
two or three women are gathered together, some plot against men is
afoot. At the very least, these writings imply widespread male curiosity
about what women talk about when they are alone together. Several
contain an eavesdropping motif. Dunbar portrays himself as an eavesdropper on women's conversation in *The Two Married Women and the
Widow.* An eavesdropper on the conversation of two gossips in J. Wallys's
ballad "Good awdience, harken to me in this cace"[10] discovers that widows' worst grief is the problem of where to find another husband. Diogenes, disguised as a woman, infiltrates a gossips' meeting in William
Goddard's *A Satirycall Dialogve . . . betweene Allexander the great, and that
truelye woman-hater Diogynes,* 1616. The gossips in *Tis Merry* drink in a
private room, declaring that they would never carry on like this before
men; but they are overheard by male waiters, which alarms them. *Tis
Merry* is prefaced by a conversation between a bookseller's apprentice and
a customer; the apprentice finally makes his sale of *Tis Merry* by adver-
tising it as a chance to eavesdrop on women's conversation. Beatrice in
The Dutch Courtesan reminds the bawdy-speaking Crispinella that although "we are private," the "world would censure you" (III.i.45–46).
Mistress Taffeta in *Ram-Alley,* negotiating with a suitor, introduces as a
marital proviso, "Shall I haue / A Carotch of the last edition, / The
Coatchmans seate a good way from the Coatch, / That if some other
Ladies and my selfe / Chance to talke bawdy, he may not ouer-heare vs?"
(III.i.1221–1225).

What men hear when they eavesdrop on female conversation (as imagined by male authors) is just what they feared: what women talk about
when they are alone together is men. A character in *The Widow's Tears*
expresses men's nervous fears: "Pray sister, tell me—you are a woman—
do not you wives nod your heads and smile one upon another when ye
meet abroad? . . . As who should say, "Are not we mad wenches, that
can lead our blind husbands thus by the noses?" Do you not brag amongst
yourselves how grossly you abuse their honest credulities? How they
adore you for saints, and you believe it, while you adhorn their temples,
and they believe it not?" (I.i.95–104). The anonymous ballad *Cuckolds
haven* voices similar fears: "When these good Gossips meet / In Alley,
Lane, or Street, / Poore men, we doe not see't! / with Wine and Sugar
sweet, / They arme themselues, and then, beside, / their husbands must
be hornify'd" (Part 11, ll. 73–78). *A Whole Crew of Kind Gossips* suggests

that men were outraged not only by complaints against husbands or vaunted cuckoldry but even by women's talking about the men they knew:

> Their mouths cannot containe their tongues within,
> For when they're maids, ere wedlocke they begin,
> At euery meeting, then they do discouer
> The disposition of each kind of louer.
> *Ione* hath a propper handsome man in truth,
> But *Iudiths* is not halfe so kinde a youth:
> *Nan* knowes not what a Iewell she hath got,
> But *Dorothies* sweet-hart, I like him not.
> Thus being Maides, they do their Louers vse,
> And being Wiues their Husbands they abuse.
>
> (Sig. E2-E2^v)

Many Shakespearean women talk about men and sex when they are alone together: witness Rosalind and Celia, Beatrice and Hero, Desdemona and Emilia. Outside Shakespeare it is common too: Mistress Taffeta in *Ram-Alley* discusses with her maid Adriana men's beards, stockings, and codpieces; Crispinella in *The Dutch Courtesan* regales Beatrice and a nurse with a lively comparison of various men's kissing abilities; a lady in *Cupid's Whirligig* discusses men and sex with her maids, while they are dressing her; Dulcimel in Marston's *The Parasitaster; or, The Fawn* descants upon the irksomeness of virginity with her lady-in-waiting. Whether male authors' imaginings were accurate, men had no way of knowing. They were perhaps flattering themselves; but we have no way of knowing either. For all we know, Renaissance women might have used the tavern as a forum for discussing the war with Spain, or predestination versus free will, or the double time scheme in *Othello*.

Men of the Renaissance resented gossips for a number of rather obvious reasons: they disapproved of feminine intrusions upon male preserves like the tavern;[11] they were inconvenienced by their wives' being occupied with women friends when they needed clean shirts; they feared domestic disturbances if their wives got ideas, from other married women, about liberty, better clothes, spending money, control of the household budget. But there is a less obvious reason for men's resentment of married women's friendships: they envied them.

There was simple jealousy, of course; what husband would wish to divide his wife's affection and attention with a friend, if he might have it all for himself? But it was more than that. Women could consort with their friends after marriage in ways men felt they could not. A man did not disrupt a woman's life in the way a woman could disrupt a man's. Or if he did, it was an expected disruption: marrying a man was in the game plan of every woman's life; she had so few other choices. She could marry and keep her female friends; men were expected to shed their former companions when they settled down in marriage, as Bertram sheds Parolles at the close of *All's Well*. With the growing cult of bourgeois respectability and the official adulation of domesticity, men as well as women were being urged toward home keeping; the early seventeenth-century glut of prodigal plays was propaganda in that direction, operating under the influence of Puritanism, and marriage theorists like Erasmus had been singing this tune in pieces like *Coniugium* since the early sixteenth century. Such preachments were eroding the double standard by which society had long sanctioned a man's night out with the boys while insisting that mother stay home with the kids. Although many middle-class wives worked in shops, the growing practice of maintaining an idle wife as a symbol of affluence meant that women who stayed home had time to cultivate friendships with kinswomen and neighbors, as their working husbands, under pressure to give up the night out with the boys, did not.

On a more literary level, the same went for falling in love. In the Renaissance, in literature at least, love was thought to alter a man in alarming ways. Male characters under the influence of Petrarchanism wept, sighed, complained, exchanged their manly freedom for abject slavery to feminine whim. Such a male lover became effeminate and gave up his former friendships partly because he was no longer fit for masculine society. But neither marriage nor love worked a corresponding alteration in women; their close same-sex friendships could continue as if nothing had happened. Shakespeare has gentle fun with this situation in *Much Ado About Nothing,* where Benedick shaves off his beard and begins wearing makeup after falling in love, much to the amusement of his male friends. But the transformation holds when the play darkens; as the women band together during Hero's crisis, Benedick finds himself cut off from his former male companions: he sides with the women.

Satiric sketches of gossips are complemented in Jacobean drama by a characteristic plot structure—male friendship threatened by female intrusion. In Beaumont and Fletcher's *The Captain,* the friendship of Julio and Angelo is endangered when both are attracted to the fatal Lelia; but male friendship reasserts itself against woman's bewitching wiles. In the anonymous *The Costly Whore,* Otho's friendship with Constantine is broken up when Otho falls in love with Constantine's intended. In *The Maid's Tragedy,* the friendship of Amintor and Melantius is threatened when Amintor tells Melantius his sister is an adulteress. In *The Two Noble*

Kinsmen, the intense friendship of Palamon and Arcite is ruined through their rivalry to the death over a woman. Leontes and Polixenes in *The Winter's Tale* have been close friends since childhood; then Leontes suspects Polixenes of sleeping with his wife. In *The Fatal Dowry,* Romont's friendship with Charolais is disrupted when Romont informs Charolais that he is a cuckold. After Charolais has put his wife to death, the two are reconciled; Charolais cries, "Who would love a woman / That might injoy in such a man, a friend?" (V.ii.134–135). The age was much moved by scenes of *amicitia* but prone to conclude that such male bonding was endangered by close contact with women. The gossips' meeting genre expresses male chagrin at finding that female friendships, by nature so much less noble, less lofty than male friendships, can absorb such a formidable male intrusion as marriage with scarcely a ripple. Female friendships were portrayed as coarse and crude by such writers as Skelton, Dunbar, and Rowlands, one suspects, because men, rather in awe of the resilience of female friendships, assumed that anything so tough must lack all delicacy.

Possibly the most enviable facet of female friendship was the warmth and spontaneity of the emotional support women seemed able to give each other in times of crisis. By contrast, many male friendships in Renaissance literature merely crumble during a crisis, and even such scenes of *amicitia* as remain are marked by a Roman formality and restraint that is stark and frosty compared with a scene like that in which Rosalind and Celia's mutual love stands up against Duke Frederick's insinuations and death threats (*As You Like It,* I.iii). Men in Renaissance literature are nearly always ashamed of weeping, while women are less uncomfortable about displaying emotion, a state of affairs that has not changed very much. It is a commonplace of modern grief therapy that women often cope with bereavement better than men can, because women have friends who will rally round and weep with them, while a man's male associates feel almost too awkward, in the face of emotional trauma, to mention the bereavement to him. The Renaissance understood this well: even Lady Macbeth is not such a monster that her death fails to elicit a "cry of women," but Macduff's male friends—chiefly interested in recruiting his military aid anyway—are as incapable of comforting him for the loss of his wife and children as he is incapable of "giving sorrow words."

*   *   *   *   *

Against the satiric gossips' meeting must be set the favorable portraits of female friendship abounding in Renaissance literature. In *The Two Noble Kinsmen,* an idealized female friendship is counterpoised with the play's disrupted male friendship: Emilia is moved by Hippolyta's paean to male friendship to describe her own intense childhood friendship with Flavina:

> You talk of Pirithous' and Theseus' love:
> Theirs has more ground, is more maturely season'd,
> More buckled with strong judgment, and their needs
> The one of th' other may be said to water
> Their intertangled roots of love; but I,
> And she I sigh and spoke of, were things innocent,
> Lov'd for [i.e., because] we did, and like the elements
> That know not what nor why, yet do effect
> Rare issues by their operance, our souls
> Did so to one another; what she lik'd
> Was then of me approv'd; what not, condemn'd,
> No more arraignment.
>
> (I.iii)

Emilia concludes "that the true love 'tween maid and maid may be / More than in sex dividual," apparently meaning "more than in hetero-sexual love." Emilia is consistently more interested in women than in men: of her suitor Arcite she remarks, "Believe, / His mother was a wondrous handsome woman; / His face methinks goes that way"; to her sister's rejoinder "But his body / And fiery mind illustrate a brave father" (II.iv), she makes no reply. When her suitors are on the verge of fighting to the death over her, Emilia thinks of the pain their death would cause their mothers (IV.ii). But even this interesting portrait of a latent lesbian takes pains (in the passage quoted above) to characterize female friend-ship as immature, irrational, remote from the world of action where mature and rational male friendships are forged in the heat of the battle-field.

Renaissance literature has several strategies for diluting the strength of female friendships. Where male friendships of the highest order are en-tered into by the free, mature, rational choice of both parties, many of the female friends—Rosalind and Celia in *As You Like It,* Beatrice and Hero in *Much Ado,* Hippolyta and Emilia in *The Two Noble Kinsmen,* Maria, Bianca, and Livia in *The Woman's Prize*—are kinswomen: their friendships thus date to childhood rather than maturity and lose, by their connection with love as a family responsibility, at least part of the ele-ment of free and rational choice. Where female friends are not kins-women, they tend to be mistress/waiting woman, as is the case with Desdemona and Emilia in *Othello,* Hermione and Paulina in *The Winter's Tale,* Leonora and Winifred in Webster's *The Devil's Law-Case,* Mistress Taffeta and Adriana in *Ram-Alley,* Crispinella and the nurse in *The Dutch*

Courtesan, and many others: such a relationship is a hybrid between true friendship and a mistress/servant relationship. Where idealized male friendships are usually between social equals, the female friendships often have a note of social dependency that is inimical to the highest forms of friendship. Male friendships in Renaissance literature often have a Platonic/Ciceronian flavor, while female friendships exist more on the level of "let's have a chat about men while you stiffen my ruff." Male friendships have been forged in a world of war and statesmanship, female friendships in a world of courtship and social trivia: the "separate spheres" approach to male and female endeavor inevitably cheapened female friendship. The Christ-like gesture of two characters in *The Costly Whore* is tellingly bifurcated according to social class: Julia, offering to lay down her life for Euphrata, says, "I ask to dye for my deare Ladies sake"; Otho, offering to die for Constantine, "I for my friend" (V.i).

In the literature of love and marriage, adulatory and satiric portraits of women display a comparable pattern of female dominance; similarly, in the literature of female friendship, satiric portraits of gossips who band together to outwit and manipulate men display a comparable pattern to more favorable portraits. Both, whether by satirizing or by trivializing female friendship, betray a need to diminish its power. And both characterize female friendships as crystallizing in opposition to men: the gossips' meeting is a closed society plotting to gain the upper hand over men, while a number of more favorable portraits of female friendship are structured as defensive maneuvers against male abuse: Desdemona and Emilia, Hermione and Paulina, Beatrice and Hero, Maria, Bianca, and Livia draw together like a circle of covered wagons against the Indian savagery of the male sex.

The kind of sexual antagonism such structures suggest is ancient and primitive. The anthropologist Ernest Crawley, after describing a number of primitive male strategies (from devil dances to sorcery) for keeping women in subjection, described a female counterattack that sounds for all the world like the Renaissance gossips' meeting: "Women . . . form such organisations amongst themselves, in which, for instance, they discuss their wrongs and form plans of revenge. Mpongwe women have an institution of this kind which is really feared by the men. Similarly amongst the Bakalais and other African tribes."[12]

That atavistic male fears of female secret societies should emerge as so prominent an element of the literature of women during the late Middle Ages and the Renaissance, a literature so constantly expressive of women's power, and that the gossips' meeting should enjoy a particular vogue during the *hic mulier* years of the early seventeenth century, a period of aggressiveness among living women, suggests male apprehensiveness that women, intractable enough as individuals, might begin making a habit of banding together to improve their lot.

NOTES

1. Erasmus's colloquy "Marriage," translated into English in 1557 as *A mery dialogue, declaringe the propertyes of shrowde shrows, and honest wyues,* found numerous adapters and imitators. Its recommended wifely policy of calculated submissiveness proved influential.

2. The thesis that the husband, pestered for dainty foods, is the prime sufferer in pregnancy, memorably developed in *Le Quinze Joyes de Mariage,* crops up in a number of English works. Even an admirable figure like the Duchess of Malfi can develop a "vulturous" appetite for apricots while she is breeding, but such longings are more frequently seen as a species of that "feminine" tactic, feigned illness—a device for manipulating husbands. Pregnancy's cravings figure not only in literary stereotype but even in "scientific" works: Jacques Guillemeau's medical/obstetrical treatise *Child-birth; or, The Happy Delivery of Women,* translated into English in 1612, discusses pregnancy's "depraved appetite," which can extend to longings for "Mans flesh, Ashes, Coles, old Shoes, Chalke, Waxe, Nutshels, Morter, and Lime"; Guillemeau speaks of one woman who died from eating "the plastering of wals" (pp. 34–35).

3. This episode recalls the anonymous *Proud Wife's Paternoster,* an early sixteenth-century sketch wherein a wife indulges in reveries about fine clothing while repeating the Lord's Prayer in church.

4. William Dunbar, *The Poems of William Dunbar,* p. 84.

5. *Upsitting:* the occasion of a woman's first sitting up to receive company after childbirth. Most gossip literature shows the ceremony as superfluous, since gossips swarm around a newly delivered mother almost from the moment of parturition.

6. Actually Dunbar's poem significantly predates Erasmus's *Coniugium,* which was first printed in 1523. I see Erasmus's *Coniugium,* along with imitations like *The vertuous scholehous of vngracious women* or Robert Snawsel's *A looking glasse for maried folkes,* as an adaptation of the gossips' meeting; a wife complains about her husband's drinking, beating her, and keeping her short of clothing money, but the "schooling" is by a virtuous woman, to break her of the habit of complaining.

7. *The Early English Carols,* ed. R. L. Greene, rev. ed. (Oxford: Oxford University Press, 1977), pp. 249–53.

8. *The Chester Mystery Cycle,* ed. R. M. Lumiansky and David Mills, pp. 42–56.

9. See Salter's *A mirrhor mete for all mothers, matrones and maidens.*

10. *Songs and Ballads, With Other Short Poems, Chiefly of the Reign of Philip and Mary,* ed. Thomas Wright (New York: Burt Franklin, 1970; first published 1860), pp. 129–32.

11. That the literary portraits of women carousing in taverns, though

obviously exaggerated, were not entirely satiric fabrications is suggested by the observation of a Swiss traveller to England, who reported in 1599, "What is particularly curious is that the women as well as the men, in fact more often than they, will frequent the taverns or alehouses for enjoyment" (*Thomas Platter's Travels in England, 1599*, p. 170).

12. Ernest Crawley, *The Mystic Rose: A Study of Primitive Marriage and of Primitive Thought in its Bearing on Marriage*, I, p. 55.

❊

CHAPTER TEN

Pistolas in the Playhouse

THE LITERATURE exactly contemporary with the height of the controversy over women in male attire, that is, from about 1610 to about 1620,
rejoices in assertive women. When Martia, whose name suggests com-
bativeness, is held up by a highwayman in *The Widow*, ca. 1616, she pulls
a pistol and demands her purse back. When Subtle and Face quarrel in
the opening scene of Jonson's *The Alchemist* (1610), Doll Common draws
a sword and orders them to desist. (They desist.) The title figure of
Fletcher's *Bonduca*, ca. 1613, acts as general in the wars against the Romans. Women crowd to see the infant Elizabeth christened in *Henry VIII*,
1613; the porters wish for heavier cudgels to beat them back but are
overwhelmed. The porter's man reports, "There was a haberdasher's wife
of small wit . . . that railed upon me till her pinked porringer fell off her
head for kindling such a combustion in the state" (V.iv.49–52). Renaissance literature in general, as I have shown, abounds in assertive women.
But in the literature of the *hic mulier* years, especially the drama, women
are more assertive than ever before, and their aggressive actions are likelier than before to lead to successful conclusions and happy endings. Assertive women are in general more favorably regarded than ever before.

Throughout this period, women speak their minds. They are likelier
to rail than to weep. In *The Devil's Law-Case*, ca. 1617, a waiting-woman
says to her suffering mistress, "I could weepe with you, but tis no matter,
I can doe that at any time—I have now / A greater mind to rayle" (I.ii.224–
226). Public opinion disapproves the Duke of Orleans' turning his wife
out of doors: "The men do a little murmur at it, and say, 'Tis an ill
precedent in so great a man. / Marry, the women, they rail outright"
(*Honest Man's Fortune*, 1613, II.i). Iacinta, raped by the king and impris-
oned under the custody of a keeper who plans to have a taste of the same
dish as soon as it cools off, doesn't waste time weeping; she vigorously
curses her keeper before resourcefully escaping (*All's Lost By Lust*, ca.
1619). The Duchess of Malfi, for all her courage to face adversity, is no
patient Grissill: at one point she cries, "I could curse the stars" (IV.i.96).

Many men are tongue-lashed by women during this period; most of them thoroughly deserve it. Paulina harangues Leontes in *The Winter's Tale*, ca. 1610–11. In *The Nightwalker*, ca. 1611, Wildbrain's aunt denounces him for his part in the breakup of Maria's marriage to Algripe. Evicting this mooching nephew from her house, she joins with several other women in haranguing Algripe and threatening to burn his house down.

Outspoken as these women are, they are hardly as domineering as men, and at least one of them rues that fact: Gartred in *Greene's Tu Quoque*, 1611, says, "Could women learne but that imperiousnesse, / By which men vse to stint our happinesse, / When they haue purchast vs for to be theirs / . . . how happy were we then" (Sig. C3). Female characters who had expressed such sentiments before had been satiric butts; Gartred is well regarded throughout the play.

A number of female dramatic characters court their men, rather than the other way around. Sometimes this is seen as brazen impudence: Lelia in *The Captain*, ca. 1612, proposes marriage to Julio, who is shocked, despite her fatal attractiveness; she later courts an elderly gentleman who turns out to be her father. Beaumont and Fletcher do not view this kind of assertiveness with approval. Yet in the same play, the lady Frank courts Jacomo with the dramatists' full approbation: he is intensely shy with women, and this is the only way the two can be brought together. Like the soldier he is, Jacomo can gather courage to approach a woman only when drunk or angry; when drunkenness fails, Frank resolves to enrage him: she and her women hurl piss pots down on him from a window. Jacomo breaks all the windows on the street and departs. Finally Frank and her friends tie Jacomo to a chair, and she boldly declares herself, inserting a small disclaimer to obviate charges of impudence: "Let not this boldness make me be believ'd / To be immodest" (V.iv). Their happy marriage ends the play: wooing by women is in some cases a practical and blameless course of action. In *More Dissemblers Besides Women*, ca. 1615, the duchess maneuvers for marriage with Andrugio; at one point she offers herself to him and has him locked up before he can say no. In *The Tempest*, ca. 1611, Miranda proposes to Ferdinand: "Hence, bashful cunning!/ . . . / I am your wife, if you will marry me" (III.i.81–83). In *Greene's Tu Quoque*, Joyce proposes marriage to Staines. In *All's Lost By Lust*, Dionysia writes to Antonio, suggesting that the two of them would "be well matcht" (Sig. E). Venus woos Adonis in *The Brazen Age*, ca. 1611. Abigail in *The Scornful Lady*, ca. 1613, throws herself at Welford, one of her lady's suitors. Amazed, Welford inquires, "What a skin full of lust is this? I thought I had come awoeing, and I am the courted party" (I.i.255–256). Abigail is a foil to the lady: she is a kind of Scornful Lady grown old, a reminder that she who scorns her suitors for too long will sue herself when youth and beauty are gone. But Abigail is treated fairly sympathetically and allowed a happy marriage at the end. Montague in *The Honest Man's Fortune* is courted by a waiting-gentlewoman, Charlotte, described as "a ravening woman" (IV.i). When Charlotte at last confesses that her wooing was only a test, the situation seems to be saved from the specter of female wooing; but Charlotte was testing Montague on behalf of her lady, who now proposes herself. The honest man's fortune is to have a beautiful lady propose to him; the playwright sees nothing improper in her behavior.

A few female characters distinguish themselves as leaders of government. There are a fair number of widowed duchesses in contemporary plays, all strong-minded women. The Duchess of Malfi keeps tight control over her realm's purse strings, partly by marrying her treasurer. The opening speech of *Women Pleased,* ca. 1620, praises the Duchess of Florence as a just and able governor.

Women commit noble suicide in the literature of the day, just as men do—in fact, rather more frequently than men. Bonduca and her two daughters earn the undying admiration of their Roman adversaries by taking the Roman way after their final military defeat: they kill themselves on the battlements, in full view of the assembled armies. Dionysia and Margaretta stab themselves in *All's Lost By Lust.* Althea falls on her son's sword in *The Brazen Age.*

The women of this period are litigious; a number go to law for redress of grievances. When the usurer Algripe repudiates his bride and refuses to refund her dowry, the bride's mother is soon "up to th' ears in law" to have him hanged (*The Nightwalker,* IV.i). The title figure of *The Widow* goes to law for release from a marriage contract obtained by trickery. Leonora in *The Devil's Law-Case* becomes so fed up with her no-good son that she sues to have him disinherited in favor of her daughter; because she claims that she cuckolded her husband, and hence that her son is illegitimate, the play's subtitle is *When Women goe to Law, the Deuill is full of Businesse.*

Women in court against their will acquit themselves with courage and intelligence. Katharine of Aragon in *Henry VIII,* quickly grasping the kangaroo-court nature of the proceedings against her, seizes upon the one course which will hamstring the opposition: she refuses to remain in the courtroom. Hermione in *The Winter's Tale* faces a false accusation with courage and dignity. Vittoria Corombona in *The White Devil,* ca. 1612, puts up a good fight in her trial for murder. She refuses to testify if the lawyers speak Latin; although she understands Latin, "amongst this auditory / Which come to heare my cause, the halfe or more / May bee ignorant int'" (III.ii.19–21). Vittoria is caught in a double bind: meek acquiescence will be interpreted as guilt, while boldness in her own defense will be considered shrewish or impudent. She opts for the latter course, with the expected result. "What is my just defence / By him that is my Judge cal'd impudence?" she demands. "My modesty / And womanhood I tender; but withall / So intangled in a cursed accusation / That my defence . . . / Must personate masculine vertue to the point" (III.ii.155–156, 163–167). The English ambassador (accustomed to female assertiveness at home?) admires her pluck: "Shee hath a brave spirit" (III.ii.171).

The women-in-court scenes may reflect interest in the sexual inequities of judicial proceedings. Agrippa had complained of laws prohibiting women from pleading a case. Shakespeare's Portia had proved that a woman could do it, but only if male disguise co-opted charges of impudence. In *The Devil's Law-Case*, Leonora suffers through the bumbling ineptitude of her male lawyer. Most of the women are allowed no counsel at all, or only lawyers in the pockets of their accusers. The scene of one woman in a courtroom full of accusing men was a common one during the period. Whether such scenes were intended to provoke thought or simply to appeal to the women in the audience, they were good theater and provided an opportunity for the embattled women's strength of character to shine forth.

There are a number of contemporary references to fights for the breeches. In *Women Beware Women*, Leantio pleads with his mother, "I pray do not you teach her to rebel / When she's in a good way to obedience; / To rise with other women in commotion / Against their husbands, for six gowns a year" (I.i.74–77); and while Bianca pities Isabella for her marriage to the witless Ward, she admits that "she has the better hope o' th' upper hand indeed, / Which women strive for most" (III.iii.210–211). *Women Pleased,* that dramatic refashioning of the *Wife of Bath's Tale,* leaves the impression that there is nothing wrong with a wife's having her will, as long as she uses her liberty responsibly. When a character advises, "Come, Lopez, let us give our wives the breeches too, / For they will have 'em," Lopez cheerfully agrees: "Whilst they rule with virtue, / I'll give 'em, skin and all" (V. iii). This reference to husband beating is good-natured: the former wife beater recognizes that beating is no more than he deserves. Here, as elsewhere, female assertiveness is acceptable; women can possess dominant personalities without being denigrated as shrews.

In a number of plays, women direct the action: like Shakespeare's Rosalind two decades earlier, they stage-manage events to achieve a happy ending. The title figure of *The Nightwalker; or, The Little Thief* is Alathe, a "virgin spurned" figure not content with the traditional role of patiently following her man about in page's disguise until such time as he repents. Her disguise indicates more active intentions; she dresses as a young underworld type and apprentices herself to a burglar. She and the burglar, Lurcher, gain access to the house of her faithless fiancé, bind and gag him, and purloin her marriage contract. Alathe prevents Maria from being buried alive, works to reunite Maria with Frank Heartlove, restores Lurcher's mortgage from a usurer's hands, induces Algripe and Wildbrain to repent, and finally, yes, gets her man. The play's closing lines give credit where credit is due: "The cure of all our grief / Is owing to this pretty little thief." A similar stage manager is Kate Low-water in *No Wit No Help Like a Woman's,* ca. 1613. Financially distressed because of the machinations of Sir Avarice Goldenfleece, and lewdly importuned by Gilbert Lambstone, a fortune-hunting suitor to Goldenfleece's widow, Kate pursues a bold course. Disguised as a swashing gallant, with her husband posing as her servant, she crashes a party to present Widow Goldenfleece with a lewd letter she has received from Lambstone, in the very presence of that dastard. This definitely queers Lambstone's pitch with the widow; she falls in love with the "gallant," Kate. (Many elements of this play make it a kind of depastoralized *As You Like It.*) Kate regains her fortune, reforms Lady Goldenfleece and marries her off to Kate's brother, and engineers a denouement in which lost children are restored and weddings abound.

Paulina in *The Winter's Tale* is a stage manager too. Her spirits undampened by the loss of her husband, eaten by a bear in Act III, she hides the maligned queen and lectures the king on his sins for sixteen years. The spectacular statue scene is her play-within-a-play; the denouement with its weddings, restored children, restored spouses, and restored friendships owes much to her benign direction. In her old age, she even gets a new husband.

The oddest stage manager is Valentia, title figure of *The Costly Whore,* ca. 1620, who after a very shaky start pulls herself together and saves the dukedom. Initially a figure of overweening pride, she is ambitious and unscrupulous once married to the duke. She clings to power throughout a civil war brought about by the duke's having married a whore, turns with vicious ingratitude on the duke's son (who spared her while she was in his power) and gets him condemned to death for treason, abets the duke in his plan to execute his daughter (ironically enough) for marrying beneath herself, tries to seduce the duke's son, and generally carries on in a manner unbecoming a duchess. The playwright redeems her at the latest possible moment. The poison she gave the duke's son turns out to be a sleeping draught administered in the hope of reconciling him with the duke; the seduction attempt is explained as a test of the son's loyalty. Repenting her lustful life, Valentia suggests to the duke that they retire to a hermitage to spend their declining years in contemplation of the Divine. Her former enemies, entranced, beg her to stay on as duchess, but she is adamant, only pausing before her journey to the hermitage to reconcile the duke to his daughter, purge the court of flatterers, and cure the country's economic ills by banishing oppressors of the poor. This wholly unbelievable conclusion says a good deal about the temper of the age: the playwright was willing to titillate the audience with visions of costly courtesans and to provoke cynical laughter by allusions to women's perfidy, ambition, and ruthlessness; but there was a line he would not cross. He could not leave a cynical last impression of a woman; instead he chose, at the expense of artistic integrity, to convert villainess into savior. It is as if a seventeenth-century Hayes Office were operating: titillating antifeminism could be allowed free rein through nine-tenths of the play, as long as the ending showed women virtuous, strong, loyal, and true. The Hayes Office, I believe, consisted of the women in the audience.

The first decade of the seventeenth century had witnessed unprecedented misogyny in the drama; the basically satiric temper of the early Jacobean theater, in part a literary fashion and in part a response to a genuine malaise prompted by change and instability in the nation's political, social, economic, and even scientific life, produced a body of plays which delineated with savage cynicism the lewdness, infidelity, aggression, shallowness, cupidity, and deceit of a legion of faithless citizens' wives, insatiable widows, and homicidal whores. Women had joined other character types as scapegoats for the ills of society. Toward the end of the century's first decade, however, the image of women in the drama changed startlingly for the better.

The decline of bitter antifeminist satire during these years was partly a function of the decline of the satiric mode in general; if satire on women was going out of fashion in the theater, so was satire on prodigals, gamesters, usurers, panders, intelligencers, social climbers, smokers, and lawyers, and on the corrupt society of which such types were symptomatic. The increasingly Puritanical inclinations of society were a contributing factor: some kinds of antifeminist satire faded away less because audiences took a warm view of women than because audiences took a dim view of adultery, prostitution, and lechery as subject matter for plays.

Some of the changes can be put down to the eclipse of the private theater, the former venue of facetious cuckold plots. Most plays featuring cuckolds, especially citizen cuckolds, had been the property of two companies which played private theaters exclusively—Paul's and the Chapel Royal; the latter became the Queen's Revels after 1603. Paul's disbanded in 1606, and the Queen's Revels was dormant after 1610: of 242 plays known to have been acted between 1610 and 1620, only two were certainly acted by the Queen's Revels; three others may have been. The Queen's Revels disappeared altogether about 1615, probably merging with Lady Elizabeth's Men, who played to both private and public theaters. The majority of plays acted between 1610 and 1620, then, were the property of companies that played either exclusively to the public theater or to both theaters; to be acceptable, a play had to pass muster at the public theater, bastion of the citizenry. Under the circumstances, the disappearance of citizen cuckoldry from plots is understandable. And the public theater now occasionally took its own literary revenge: in Fletcher's *The Honest Man's Fortune,* the citizen Mallicorn prosecutes a prodigal aristocrat for debt, as revenge on behalf of his class for all the citizens cuckolded by the aristocracy: "An honest citizen / Cannot wholly enjoy his own wife for you / . . . which is a lamentable thing, and truly / Much hardens the hearts of us citizens / Against you" (II.i).

But if the view of woman as born adulteress had belonged to the private theater, the view of woman as born shrew had belonged to the public theater: the overwhelming majority of theatrical shrews had appeared in plays designed for the public theater. Yet with the triumph of the public theater after 1610, shrews disappeared as completely from the stage as did adulteresses. Play succeeded play without a single old-fashioned scold. No shrew tamings were staged; to the contrary, *The Woman's Prize,* ca. 1611, showed the shrew tamer tamed by his wife: significantly, Maria tames her tamer without ever becoming shrewish herself. Clearly, the decline of the private theater is insufficient to explain the drama's changed stance toward women.

The new image of women in the Jacobean drama is suggestively contemporary with the revived female transvestite movement. References to women in male attire begin to appear around 1606–7, which (given the number of literary works which have not survived) probably represents a time lag of several years after the reappearance of the fashion. By 1608 the first stirrings of the new attitude can be discerned in *The Roaring Girl,* which gives favorable treatment to a man-clothed virago. After 1610 the drama was regularly presenting Woman in her new untarnished character. Modern feminists, who have struggled so long to improve the image of women in our most popular medium of drama, television, and have witnessed progress at such glacial speeds, may find it difficult to believe, but some evidence suggests that the radical change in the drama's image of women that occurred around 1610 is directly attributable to pressure applied by female playgoers.

Prologues and epilogues, which allow dramatists and their companies to address the audience directly and speak of its reactions to the play, display in these years an increased nervousness, a fear of hissing, an apologetic pleading for applause that is unlike earlier witty requests for applause. *The Two Noble Kinsmen's* prologue, ca. 1613 (the opening line of which, incidentally, is the provocative "New plays and maidenheads are near a-kin"), begs the audience not to hiss: the plot came from that most famous of English poets, Chaucer, who will turn over in his grave if they do hiss. The epilogue begins, "I would now ask ye how ye like the play; / But, as it is with schoolboys, cannot say, / I am cruel fearful. Pray, yet stay a while, / And let me look upon ye. No man smile? / Then it goes hard, I see." The audience is begged not to "hiss, and kill / Our market!" *Henry VIII*'s prologue assures the audience its money's worth: "I'll undertake [they] may see away their shilling / Richly in two short hours." The epilogue grumbles, "'Tis ten to one this play can never please / All that are here." Many other prologues and epilogues display similar insecurity. Whatever the audience wanted—and the timorous prologues and epilogues suggest that the companies were not sure what that was—it had obviously become very vocal about its likes and dislikes. Women in the audience were apparently among the most vocal.

The Captain, one of the few contemporary plays to offer an unrelievedly cynical portrait of a woman, displays fear of hissing in both prologue and epilogue; the prologue fears the play may offend women: "Damsels, if they mark the matter through, / May stumble on a foolish toy, or two / Will make 'em shew their teeth": the graphic image of snarling damsels provides an insight into contemporary female playgoers. The quasi-epilogue of *A Woman Is A Weathercock,* 1609–10, a play whose antifeminism is exceeding mild, begs "Women forgiue me." Plays designed to please women do not stick to say so. The epilogue of *The Woman's Prize* offers an exhortation to marital equality. *Henry VIII*'s epilogue states openly that the company is counting on women to make the play a success, for they will surely like its favorable view of Katharine of Aragon; woe betide the man who dares not to clap when female Londoners decide he should:

> All the expected good we're like to hear
> For this play at this time is only in
> The merciful construction of good women;
> For such a one we showed 'em. If they smile
> And say 'twill do, I know within a while
> All the best men are ours; for 'tis ill hap
> If they hold when their ladies bid 'em clap.

Playwrights and companies had finally recognized the economic importance of female playgoers. It took them nearly half a century after the founding of the public theaters to do so,[1] but then it took printers and authors nearly a century after the introduction of the printing press in England to recognize the potential of the women's market in printed books. But something else was operating too. Women had always flocked to the theater,[2] even when the plays abused women. They were expected to laugh at themselves and probably did. In the years 1610 to 1620, women

stopped laughing. Women who stalked the streets with pistols and daggers were not likely to put up with constant literary abuse in the theater.
They would hiss, they would walk out. They would stop attending. The
assertive female characters who populate the plays had counterparts in
real life, and these women were using their economic and vocal power
to influence the way women were presented onstage.

Contemporary literature affords some glimpses of female playgoers.
Amends for Ladies, ca. 1610–11, posits group excursions by female co-
workers: the play's swaggerers sit forlornly in a tavern with no whores
to console them, for as the drawer reports, "All the Gentlewomen went
to see a Play at the Fortune, and are not come in yet . . . they sup with
the Players" (III.iv.25–27). In the same play, a virtuous widow talks bawdy
to her lady-in-waiting (who, being a man in disguise, is unaccustomed
to such talk from a woman). When the lady-in-waiting expresses shock
at this filth, the widow counters, "Dost not thou goe to *Black-fryers?*"
She defends bawdy jokes as wholesome: "An ill tale vnutter'd, is like a
maggot in a nut, it spoiles the whitest kernell" (III.iii.43–44). This widow
later defends herself with a sword. One imagines that neither the prostitutes nor the respectable but assertive widow would be reticent about
expressing displeasure with drama that demeaned women. The man-
clothed woman herself appears as a playgoer in Henry Fitzgeffrey's "humours" sketch *Notes from Black-Fryers,*[3] 1617, where two men sit watching people arrive at the Blackfriars theater. A Cheapside dame and later
another woman arrive unescorted; but the observers are most struck by
a woman dressed like a man: "Now *Mars* defend vs! seest thou who
comes yonder? / Monstrous! A *Woman* of the *masculine Gender*" (Sig. F2).
The speaker begs his friend not to point at this monstrosity lest she come
over and beat them up. She seats herself in the gallants' row, and the next
arrival, true to the period's constant juxtaposition of these two types, is
an effeminate fop.

Dramatists' determined efforts to present women in a flattering light
are sometimes amusing. Reminiscent of Thomas Deloney's *The garland
of good will,* a ballad collection which took great pains to create sympathy
for both wronged wife and usurping mistress, *Henry VIII* manages to
present Katharine of Aragon as "the Queen of earthly queens" (II.iv.141)
and her rival Anne Boleyn as an angelic being: "Heaven bless thee! /
Thou hast the sweetest face I ever looked on. / Sir, as I have a soul, she
is an angel" (IV.i.42–44). *All's Lost By Lust* presents sympathetically both
Margaretta and the woman who usurps her conjugal rights. Both wives
and mistresses attended the theater; both had paid their shilling, and the
playwright made sure that all were "women pleased."

But while pistol-packing London dames were making it necessary for
the drama to flatter women, they were not making it easy. Theaters also

had to keep the patronage of male playgoers, who might well be out-raged by contemporary female assertiveness and hence resent theatrical praise of women. Would the drama go so far as to praise "mannish" women?

A masque like *The World Tossed at Tennis,* ca. 1620, committed with the masque's elegant distance from gritty reality to the ideal of Rural Simplicity, could still take pleasure in ritually purging society of the man-clothed woman: "How civilly those fair ladies go yonder! by this hand, they are neither trimmed, nor trussed, nor poniarded" (ll. 832–834). This was the sort of thing that pleased the king. But viragos more often earn admiration in plays of the period.

All's Lost By Lust adapts Bandello's story of the violent Violenta—a tale suited to the temper of the times. The audience is temporarily lulled into believing that Margaretta, the Violenta figure, plans to play Patient Grissill to her faithless husband: testing her maid's opinions on violence, Margaretta asks whether she would second her if she challenged some-one to a duel but hastily assures the maid, "I do intend no such viragoes part" (Sig. F2). Once confident of the maid's tolerance of bloodshed, however, Margaretta reveals that she intends a different "virago's part": she will murder her husband in his bed. The sex-role reversal in this inside-out *Othello* is underlined by the husband's employing a friend in a rare masculine use of the conventional bed trick: the friend is murdered in the husband's stead. When Margaretta flies into a rage at discovering her mistake, Mulymuman, the lustful Moorish king, happens to be standing by; he is quite taken with her: "A noble girle," he cries, "a lusty stout Virago" (Sig. Iᵛ). Whether Mulymuman is an accurate spokesman for the play's values is a matter of some doubt. His innocent enjoyment in blinding Iuliano and plucking out Iacinta's tongue, and his childlike pleasure in engineering Iacinta's death, make him seem a reincarnation of Aaron the Moor; but when he succeeds to the Spanish throne at play's end, the implication is that everyone will live happily ever after (al-though it is also true that almost everyone else is dead by that time). The play's moral values are simply confused, but it is at least clear that in his way Mulymuman is a connoisseur of women: that he finds a virago par-ticularly attractive sexually reflects the changing tastes of the age.

In *The Golden Age,* ca. 1610, Jupiter (who outdoes even Mulymuman in amorousness) finds much to attract him in Diana's bold huntresses. Infiltrating this group while pursuing Calisto, a new recruit, Jupiter en-ters "like a Nimph, or a Virago." He allays his fears of discovery by assuring himself he can easily pass for "a *Virago,* or a good manly Lasse." He is right; Diana is really impressed with this new nymph's size and musculature: "A manly Lasse, a stout Virago, / Were all our traine pro-portion'd to thy size, / We need not feare mens subtill trecheries." The

remark might provoke comparison with modern women combatting the
danger of rape with courses in karate. But "subtill trecheries" does not
suggest rape: it suggests seduction. Diana implies that a woman's best
course against a seducer is to thump him. According to Diana, the historical frequency of seduction demands that all women turn virago in
self-defense. The oath of allegiance to Diana makes reference to "hated
men" (II.i). The portrait here is of a certain kind of feminist, familiar in
our own time, whose achieved liberty and self-respect involves hatred of
men, withdrawal into the society of mannish women pursuing sports
traditionally masculine (here, hunting), and limitation of sexual activity
to other women (the play portrays Diana and her followers as lesbians).
Again, the viragos are viewed with favor. Calisto *is* raped the minute she
is separated from her sisters' support: what Diana says about men is justified.

Rare satire on a virago occurs in *Amends for Ladies,* where Moll Cutpurse, hero of *The Roaring Girl,* makes a cameo appearance in vicious
caricature. Her masculine attire is identified with that of real-life London
women of the *hic mulier* movement: in one of the earliest uses of the *hic/
haec* formula (ca. 1610–1611), Moll is called "Mistris *hic & haec*" (II.i.19).
Where the Moll of *The Roaring Girl* had been militantly chaste, this Moll
is a kind of bawd, bearing a gallant's love letter to a citizen's wife. The
wife denounces her: "Hence lewd impudent / I know not what to tearme
thee man or woman, / For nature shaming to acknowledge thee / For
either, hath produc'd thee to the World / Without a sexe, some say thou
art a woman, / Others a man; and many thou art both / Woman and
man, but I thinke rather neither" (II.i.32–38). She compares Moll (herself
based on the historical Mary Frith) with two other real-life viragos in
masculine attire, Mary Umbree or Ambree and Long Meg of Westminster. The tenor of this topical scene has a simple explanation: the play
was acted at court, and King James was outraged at women dressing as
men. This play is in fact a defense of women, but the playwright was
obligated to include a scene wherein James's least favorite type of woman
was exempted from the general defense.

But Moll Cutpurse as she appears in *The Roaring Girl* is an astonishing
creation. If the playwrights excuse her from cutting purses, that is the
only touch of whitewash: Moll is shown ordering breeches from a tailor,
sending for drink and tobacco, conversing on terms of easy familiarity
with various underworld characters, bestriding the streets of London in
her transvestite costume. Laxton, however dishonorable his intentions,
finds her mannish aggressiveness as sexually attractive as Mulymuman
finds Margaretta's: "Heart, I would give but too much money to be nib-
bling with that wench! life, sh'as the spirit of four great parishes, and a
voice that will drown all the city" (II.i.191–193). Moll's response to this

rake provides one of the period's only clear-sighted comments on the economic pressures being exerted on contemporary women: having accepted gold in return for a promised rendezvous with Laxton, she shows up at the meeting dressed as a man and armed with a sword. To avenge poverty-stricken women who have sold themselves to scrape a living, Moll challenges the randy gallant to a duel and beats him soundly. He exits, humiliated and bleeding, with her stirring speech still ringing in his ears:

> In thee I defy all men, their worst hates
> And their best flatteries, all their golden witchcrafts,
> With which they entangle the poor spirits of fools,
> Distressed needle-women and trade-fallen wives;
> Fish that must needs bite, or themselves be bitten;
> Such hungry things as these may soon be took
> With a worm fasten'd on a golden hook:
> Those are the lecher's food, his prey; he watches
> For quarrelling wedlocks and poor shifting sisters;
> 'Tis the best fish he takes.
>
> (III.i.93–102)

Moll, almost alone among dramatic characters of her day, recognizes that prostitution, professional or improvised, is less often a result of greed and lust than of need and hunger.

Viragos and shrews were not the only female character types whose image was cleaned up during the height of the transvestite movement. Most striking among the transformations of the period is the rehabilitation of the widow.

The stereotype of the lustful widow, forged partly as a response to widows' independence, was not entirely taboo onstage during the *hic mulier* years. The heroine of *The Insatiate Countess*, 1610, is a widow who burns with lust and goes through a record number of men in five acts. *Bonduca*, whose title figure is a widow, refers to widows' lust—to hungry soldiers whose "stomack[s] are like a widdows lust nere satisfied" (II.ii.821–822). The widow Lelia in *The Captain* lusts after her father, whom she does not recognize because he has been given a decent suit; entertained at a lascivious banquet by his own daughter, the elderly gentleman is startled by her idea of a good time: they will feast "till both our bloods / Shoot up and down to find a passage out, / Then mouth to mouth will we walk up to bed, / And undress one another as we go; / Where both my treasure, body, and my soul / Are your's to be dispos'd of" (IV.iv). In a delightful reversal of the patient Grissill theme, he wonders whether she is doing this to test his patience. Yet even Lelia is not past reformation. Her father locks her up in a vacant house until she repents; after exactly one day, he declares her penitent and marries her off. Her marriage forms part of the play's happy ending.

But most of the many widows onstage during this period are not lustful, nor does their behavior ratify stereotypes about widows' hasty remarriage. The duchess in *More Dissemblers* has been true for seven years to her vow not to remarry. Paulina in *The Winter's Tale* remarries after sixteen years of widowhood. Most of the widows of these years are more interested in governing their states or seeing to their children's welfare than in chasing after young men.

Many widows resent the widow stereotypes; several actively combat them. Dionysia in *All's Lost* refuses to weep at her husband's death: "Who does beleeve a widows teares to be her hearts sorrow? / Are they not then better spar'd then derided?" (Sig. I2). (She kills herself instead.) When Spendall courts a widow violently in *Greene's Tu Quoque,* she ironically acquiesces in stereotype: "Thou art worthy / Of the best widdow liuing . . . / Those that will win widdowes must doe thus" (Sig. L). Then she binds him to a post.

Amends for Ladies exonerates widows as part of its campaign to defend all three estates of womankind—maids, wives, and widows. Widow Bright, she who defends bawdy jokes as wholesome, perhaps works out her sexual frustrations in bawdy talk, for she displays no signs of lust. No man hater, she still enjoys her freedom: sensitive to matrimony's miseries, she holds at arm's length her main suitor (appropriately, for a widow's suitor, named Bould) until he infiltrates her household disguised as a waiting-gentlewoman. To Bould's delight, the widow asks "her" to share her bed. Early in the night, Bould makes bold; on discovering his true gender, the widow pitches him out of bed and draws a sword. He threatens to turn slanderer, to tell the world he has slept with her, unless she yields. She calmly calls his bluff and disabuses him of his complacent belief in the caveman stereotype:

> You haue trusted to that fond [i.e., foolish] opinion,
> This is the way to haue a widdow-hood,
> By getting to her bed: Ahlas young man,
> Should'st thou thy selfe tell thy companions
> Thou hast dishonour'd mee (as you men haue tongues
> Forked and venom'd gainst our subiect sexe)
> It should not moue me, that know 'tis not so:
> Therefore depart.

> (IV.i.32–39)

Bould rejoins, "Few widdowes would doe thus" (IV.i.40). He remains wedded to stereotype, certain that "no" means "yes":

To be in bed and in possession
Euen of the marke I aim'd at, and goe off
Foild and disgrac't, come, come, you'll laugh at me
Behind my back, publish I wanted [i.e., lacked] spirit,
And mock me to the Ladies, call me childe,
Say you denide me but to trie the heate
And zeale of my affection toward you,
Then clap't vp with a rime, as for example.
> *Hee coldly loues, retires, for one vaine triall,*
> *For wee are yeelding, when we make deniall.*
>   (IV.i.42–51)

The widow assures him that "no" means "no," adding dryly that "there are amongst vs good" (IV.i.55). When he argues that sex is natural, adducing the birds and the bees, she replies in humanist terms: control of sensual urges by reason is what sets humankind above the animals. Bould wonders aloud if the widow likes to be forced; she warns him she would cry rape, and if he persisted would kill herself with her sword. As a last resort, Bould proposes marriage. The widow declines and turns him out into the street.

Not only does the title of Middleton's *The Widow* promise a racy play, but Middleton's widow is named Valeria—likely an allusion to the man-eating widow of Dickenson's *Fair Valeria;* yet the play sets up these expectations only to explode them. Valeria holds three suitors at bay. She ridicules one for wearing makeup; she has never thus offended her Maker: "I'm a woman; / Yet, I praise heaven, I never had th' ambition / To go about to mend a better workman" (II.i.11–12). She goes to law to break a marriage contract obtained by trickery, making over her estate to her brother to keep it out of her husband's hands should she be forced to marry; when she wins her case after all, she tests her suitors by telling them her estate is forfeit. Only one of them agrees to marry her now that she is penniless. Another, recalling horror stories of matrimonial poverty, predicts with malicious glee, "He'll give her a black eye within these three days, / Beat half her teeth out by All-hallowtide, / And break the little household stuff they have / With throwing at one another: O sweet sport!" (V.i). But Valeria is too resourceful and assertive to allow that: to her brother's chagrin, she tears up the deed granting him her estate. With her fortune restored and her suitors tested, she marries on her own terms.

The widow in *More Dissemblers,* the Duchess of Milan, is renowned for faithfulness to her vow never to remarry. Lactantio, who makes an old gibe, "She has kept the fort most valiantly, / To th' wonder of her sex, this seven year's day, / And that's no sorry trial. A month's constancy / Is held a virtue in a city-widow" (I.i.11–14), is soon discredited as an utter cad. The cardinal lectures a group of lords, apparently assembled for this very purpose, on the duchess' admirable chastity: "O my fair lords, / When we find grace confirm'd, especially / In a creature that's so doubtful as a woman, / We're spirit-ravish'd" (I.ii.15–18); the lords share in the cardinal's public raptures over the duchess' sexlessness. This odd scene has certain qualities of soap opera. It is the Renaissance equivalent of the soap-operatic scene where handsome young doctors pause between quadruple bypasses to discuss whether a spinster aunt is feeling lonely and resolve to call on her during their lunch break. Now, no physician in the entire world ever called on his maiden aunt during his lunch break, any more than any real cardinal ever invited real peers to reflect upon a duchess' chastity. Such scenes are dramatized in modern times because maiden aunts watch soap opera and may be moved, by the touching spectacle of important men worrying about unimportant women, to buy the sponsor's detergent. Such scenes were dramatized in the Renaissance because the substantial number of unimportant women attending the play wanted to believe that high-ranking public figures would take time out from political duties to praise a woman. The lords do not consider the cardinal mentally unbalanced for introducing such a topic in a public gathering; they take the duchess' chastity very seriously. One suggests that she may be chaste only because reclusive; all agree that her chastity should be tested: the cardinal should induce her to terminate her seclusion. This scene is at such a fantastic remove from the behavior of real males as to leave only one motive for its existence—to keep women coming to the playhouse. Middleton had earlier specialized in vicious satire on women. Now, something had dawned on him. If he were alive today, Middleton would be selling a lot of Tide.

Induced to end her seclusion, *More Dissemblers'* duchess looks out a window, apparently for the first time in seven years. The first object that meets her liberated eyes is the dashing general Andrugio, returning home from a military victory. The duchess is a goner. She has the grace to feel upset about falling in love at first sight, despite her vow. She is not seriously criticized for doing so: it has been seven years, after all; and she is still under thirty. But the Cardinal, coming to call, quotes her husband's dying exhortation: "Once to marry / Is honourable in woman, and her ignorance / Stands for a virtue, coming new and fresh; / But second marriage shows desire in flesh; / Thence lust, and heat, and common custom grows" (III.i.76–80). The late duke's sexual views were a little peculiar, even by Renaissance standards: being willing to have sex is acceptable, but wanting to have sex is damnable. His drawing his breath in pain to tell this story reflected the fear of many a husband—that his estate might be ruined and his good name sullied by his wife's behavior after his death. Undaunted by this timely reminder, the duchess reveals that she is in love. This spoils the cardinal's day.

The duchess pursues Andrugio with all the assertiveness of the day; but Andrugio prefers Aurelia, a spoiled young thing who is using him to further her own pursuit of Lactantio. When Andrugio finally recognizes that she has used him, he forgives her: in this "drama for women" even a cheap charmer must have adorers. The duchess proves extremely reasonable, acknowledging that it is only natural for Andrugio to prefer a woman "younger, fairer" than herself (V.ii.128). She has had her little fling; graciously bowing out of the sexual world, she returns to her vow. The validity of the widow stereotype is once again denied.

The great vindication of the widow, though, belongs to the finest non-Shakespearean tragedy of the Jacobean age, Webster's *The Duchess of Malfi*, ca. 1614. Closely contemporary with *More Dissemblers,* this play has its duchess and its chastity-minded cardinal too, but is subtler and more daring than the other play in its treatment of widowhood—subtler in that the motives of those opposing the widow's remarriage, the Cardinal and Ferdinand, are complex and ambiguous, ranging from family honor to self-interest to psychopathology; more daring in that the duchess' behavior comes perilously close to stereotype. When the duchess announces, "I'll never marry," the cardinal is cynical: "So most widows say: / But commonly that motion lasts no longer / Than the turning of an hour-glass—the funeral sermon / And it, end both together" (I.i.302–305). He is right: she already intends to remarry. Moreover, the Duchess fulfills stereotype in marrying a man of greatly inferior social class—the fear of all wealthy husbands and male relatives. But Antonio is no fortune hunter; significantly, he is her treasurer—the guardian rather than the squanderer of her wealth.

The legality of the duchess' marriage is a tantalizing point. Assertiveness is here carried to an extreme: not only does she propose marriage to her man, but when he accepts she herself performs the ceremony on the spot, and doesn't bother with reciting "particular duties" either. The need for secrecy is apparent, given her brothers' views, but isn't there a single discreet clergyman in the duchy? The duchess trusts no one but her woman Cariola, who acts as a witness; it is possible that Webster is introducing a wry irony: only a woman can be relied upon to keep a secret. But since the marriage is without benefit of clergy, the relationship is very close to "living in sin"; any children would almost certainly have difficulty maintaining their legitimacy in a court of law. The marriage's questionable legality lays the duchess open to conventional charges of illicit lust.

The question of female sexuality is precisely what Webster seems interested in exploring. The whole tenor of the play is that sexual desire is wholesome and natural, that distaste for sexuality is the mark of a twisted, pathological personality like Ferdinand's. The play comes very close to asking "what's wrong with a little good old-fashioned lust?" The duchess challenges the idea of chastity vows for widows, incidentally arguing that they are the exception rather than the rule: "Why might not I marry? / I have not gone about, in this, to create / Any new world, or custom . . . / Why should only I, / Of all the other princes of the world, / Be cas'd up, like a holy relic? / I have youth, / And a little beauty" (III.ii.109–11, 137–140).

There is nothing in all Jacobean drama to match, in its sane naturalness, the duchess' and Antonio's easy banter and mutual teasing about sex in III.ii. Whether they are really married or not, they are the happiest and most faithful couple in Jacobean drama. I have the impression that, this being true, Webster didn't think it mattered whether they were really married.

Any defender of women could show a widow remaining chaste. But to turn a widow who does not remain chaste into a tragic hero was revolutionary. Ferdinand sneeringly calls the duchess a "lusty widow." A lesser dramatist would have absolved her of this charge; Webster makes clear that she really is a lusty widow and implies that there is nothing in the world the matter with that. The duchess has much in common with Cleopatra: both Webster and Shakespeare offer the audience a woman with all the antifeminist stereotypes on her head, who becomes a tragic hero. Defenders of women almost never got beyond contending that the old ugly charges were not true, or not universally true. The duchess and Cleopatra are virtually the only women whose creators dared to maintain that the old ugly charges weren't really ugly. Other authors were still piously arguing that not all women are strong willed, lustful, vain about their looks, possessive of their men. Shakespeare and Webster gave literature two women who were strong willed, lustful, vain about their looks, and possessive of their men—and told the world they were fine women, and heroes. Shakespeare's vindication of Cleopatra is the more impressive because, as *Antony and Cleopatra* was acted ca. 1607, it predates the drama's general shift to a more favorable view of women and is contemporary with such cynical portraits as *The Widow's Tears*. With the words "Husband, I come. / Now to that name my courage prove my title" (V.ii.290–291), Cleopatra turns herself into wife and widow at the same moment; paradoxically, it is the courtesan of genius who becomes one of the only widows of early Jacobean literature to remain true to her vow of constancy. The Webster who created the Duchess of Malfi a few years later must, I think, have appreciated that irony; his duchess, whose marriage like Cleopatra's is self-declared and needs no paltry clerical ceremonies, stands with Cleopatra as the virtuous and lustful widow triumphant.

In both of the other surviving plays known to be exclusively his work (he was largely a collaborator), Webster displays the same willingness to grapple with antifeminist stereotypes in unusual ways. *The White Devil*'s Vittoria Corombona is in some ways a first draft of the Duchess of Malfi. She is not so clearly the protagonist (the play does not really have one), and she is morally culpable as the duchess is not. Nevertheless, she defends herself valiantly in her trial scene and dies courageously. The moral ambiguity readers experience in the play stems partly from Webster's attempt to achieve sympathy for a fallen woman, to turn a whore into a hero. The attempt is unsuccessful, but one can see in it the seeds of his daring "so what?" attitude toward female sexual indiscretions in *The Duchess of Malfi.* In *The Devil's Law-Case,* he tackles the charge of idleness. The usual defense was the claim that not all women are idle; Webster stages a woman who, like so many high-caste women, lives in enforced idleness. All that has been expected of Leonora is that she dress finely. In her advancing years she looks back with regret over a lifetime frittered away at her toilette, sadly addressing her woman,

> Thou hast lived with me
> These fortie yeares, we have growne old together,
> As many Ladies and their women doe,
> With talking nothing, and with doing lesse:
> We have spent our life in that which least concernes life,
> Only in putting on our clothes.
>
> (III.iii.418–423)

Webster wasted no time debating whether women were idle; he addressed himself to *why* they were idle and to the psychological effects of idleness.

Even the image of prostitutes underwent a face-lifting in the drama during the *hic mulier* years. In the satirically inclined early Jacobean years, hardly a comedy was acted which did not have a full complement of whores, bawds, and panders; during the second decade of the century, such characters virtually disappeared from the *dramatis personae.* The few remaining "whores," like Valentia in *The Costly Whore* and Lelia in *The Captain,* repent and become wives and useful citizens; and, unlike their immediate dramatic forebears, they are hardly "six-penny mutton": figures of fatal attractiveness and great power, they are at times Circes.

Lelia is more a merry widow than a whore: she is called a whore and considered a whore, but there is no evidence that she accepts money for her enthusiastic promiscuity. (The failure—or refusal—to draw a distinction between prostitution and amateur promiscuity was common in Renaissance literature and persisted at least as late as *Moll Flanders*.) Her effect on men is devastating. In one scene a young man, resembling the speaker of Shakespeare's sonnets in his agonized revulsion from a lust he cannot control, takes a friend along on his mission to sever relations with Lelia: he does not trust himself alone with her. The friend, too, falls under Lelia's power. Desperately (and rather comically) they prop each other up in an attempt to tear themselves away. One has the feeling that each longs for a mast to tie himself to.

Valentia is a professional, but more properly a courtesan than a whore. She is extremely popular with the men (not surprising, since she is the only prostitute in the realm) but restricts her clientele to the nobility. She is like a Petrarchan sonnet mistress: her "servants" adore her and are sometimes satisfied with the sight of her face; her high-class male bawd serves her for no salary but the joy of being near her. Her attraction has magical elements: the duke falls in love with her without having seen or heard of her, merely from picking up her lost glove. This is more the stuff of fairy tale than of satiric comedy. The rare remaining prostitutes of this period were a far cry from the cheap tarts who had gone before.

Gone too were the worldly bawds who had provided so much anti-feminist comment in the earlier Jacobean drama. One lonely bawd in *All's Lost By Lust* carries valiantly on: enlisted in a campaign to seduce the virgin Iacinta, she merrily remarks, "Men follow / The traditions of their forefathers, so should / Women follow the trades of their foremothers" (Sig. B2ᵛ). But this jest is negated by Iacinta's stubborn virtue, and the bawd drops out of the play.

The very imagery of the drama reflects the changed attitude toward women. Favorite satiric images of women drop completely out of sight between 1610 and 1620 in the drama: women are no longer connected in the imagery with gold and money;[4] they are no longer seen as food,[5] or as animals,[6] or as marketable commodities.[7] They are no longer said to be the source of man's damnation.[8] Almost nothing is said of their rich attire,[9] or any other kind of extravagance.[10] Barbed remarks about facial paint have disappeared.[11] Women are very seldom portrayed as ambitious,[12] lecherous,[13] or deceitful.[14]

The prologue to *The Roaring Girl* paints an intriguing portrait of modern assertive women:

> I see Attention sets wide ope her gates
> Of hearing, and with covetous listening waits,
> To know what girl this roaring girl should be,
> For of that tribe are many. One is she
> That roars at midnight in deep tavern-bowls,
> That beats the watch, and constables controls;

Another roars i' th' daytime, swears, stabs, gives
    braves,
Yet sells her soul to the lust of fools and slaves:
Both these are suburb-roarers [i.e., whores]. Then
    there's beside
A civil city-roaring girl, whose pride,
Feasting, and riding, shakes her husband's state,
And leaves him roaring through an iron grate [i.e.,
    debtors' prison].
None of these roaring girls is ours; she flies
With wings more lofty.

                                              (ll. 13–26)

The idea that London women, both prostitutes and wives, tended to be
rampant viragos owes quite a bit to the antifeminist tradition; as I have
shown, the mere act of sitting in an open doorway was construed as
libertine aggression. Still, London did have its Moll Friths and its Long
Megs, and references to women in male attire were increasing steadily.
City women were apparently demanding and getting more freedom. In
giving favorable treatment to women of all sorts during the *hic mulier*
years, the drama, I submit, was bowing to necessity. In creating a gallery
of assertive female characters, the drama, one cannot help suspecting,
was holding the mirror up to nature.

                          *   *   *   *   *

    Nondramatic literature, by nature less immediately responsive than
the drama to the likes and dislikes of its patrons, was more critical than
the drama of the doings of viragos and of unisex tendencies in general,
and more likely to lampoon women. Although "Ester Sowernam" seemed
to be calling for a boycott of Joseph Swetnam's pamphlet in 1617, and
although Henry Parrot worried in 1620 that some book buyers might
"refuse the patronizing" of his piece *The Gossip's Greeting* "because it is
against women" (Sig. A3ᵛ), the most ostentatious refusal to buy a book
will hardly be as noticeable as will jeering women in the theater—or
empty seats.
    Formal satirists, and writers of Theophrastan character, took a dim-
mer view of aggressive women than had the dramatists. John Heath, in
Two Centuries of Epigrams, 1610, obliquely connects wilfulness with unisex tendencies:

Philip, and *Franck,* and such like names there bee
That alike to both sexes doe agree:
Will is a name to men alonely due,
Women so call'd as yet I neuer knew.
Yet mought they well, being for the most part still,

So awkward, and so giuen to their will.
Or else, that the confusion may be lesse,
Will, be a mans name: womans, wilfulnesse.

                              (Sig. [E5])

In another of Heath's epigrams, an allusion to unisex apparel (cunningly connected with the Fall of man) leads into a remark on modern domineering women: "Ovr common parents straight vpon their fall / Made breeches for to hide their shame withall / And as we read, both alike wore them then / Now females weare the breeches more than men" (Sig. E3ᵛ). William Gamage, in *Linsi-Woolsie; or, Two Centvries of Epigrammes,* 1613, mentions the "poys'ned stings" of women's tongues (Sig. C4), notes that even Socrates was not wise enough to avoid marrying a scold (two epigrams treat Xantippa [Sig. (D7), E3]), and includes a dialogue wherein a man, outraged when a woman proposes marriage, declares, "Fie 'tis not fit for females, for to sue," and is answered, "It is the fashion new" (Sig. [D8]). He makes a snide remark about the famous virago, Long Meg of Westminster (Sig. [C6]ᵛ). In one epigram, he speculates on woman's grammatical mood: it cannot be indicative, for that requires reason, nor subjunctive, for she is not subject to her husband; it must be imperative: that is her usual marital mood. Henry Fitzgeffrey has an epigram on "A manly woman the best wife" in his *Satyres: and Satyricall Epigrams,* 1617: "Giue me the *Woman halfe a Man:* / So I shall (happy) haue but *halfe a Woman*" (Epigram 26).

   Two assertive women are charactered in John Stephens's *Satyrical essayes, characters and others,* 1615. The widow is masculine in forwardness: "She is indeed a mungrell woman, or the worst part of both sexes, bound vp in one volume" (p. 309). "An Hostesse" is a working woman who does not mind her husband's being unemployed: "Her husbands sloth make[s] her imployed proudly; being heartily ambitious of labour, if shee can boast well, that her paines alone keepe her husband and his family" (p. 268). Richard Brathwait appended to his *Essaies upon the five senses,* 1619, the character of a shrew who is a menace even in the gossip circle: "Shee goes weekly a catter-wauling, where shee spoiles their spice-cup'd gossiping with her tart-tongued calletting" (p. 135). Even her assets are liabilities: "She hath an excellent gift for memorie, and can run diuision vpon relation of iniuries" (p. 135); and "Silence shee hates as her sexes scandall" (p. 137). She seeks to wear the breeches in her household. And "shee approues of no ancient soueraigntie, but that of *Amazon*" (p. 139). In one of the satiric sketches in Roger Sharpe's *More Fooles yet,* 1610, a wittol tolerates his wife's gadding to plays, drinking with other men, and staying out late, because "she keepes the house, keepes him, & paies the rent" (Sig. B). "A woman hater" is counselled, "O peace *Misoginos,* why do'st thou wrong them? / Thou wilt cõmend them whẽ thou art among thẽ: / But will you know how this his hate was bred, / A wench in Turnbull street did breake his head" (Sig. B3). The claim that misogynists lack courage to maintain their antifeminist posture when women are present goes back to Elyot's *Defense of Good Women;* the habit of impugning the misogynist's motives is also of ancient pedigree. The more modern note is Sharpe's substituting for the conventional charge that the misogynist has been unlucky in love the alternate explanation that the misogynist has been beaten up by a whore. Sharpe's version is a specialized case of unluckiness in love, particularly appropriate to an age of assertive women.

When Robert Snawsel translated and recast Erasmus's *Coniugium* in 1610, it is significant that he doubled the number of shrews in the piece. Beset by Xantippe's new ally Margery, who approves of husband beating, Snawsel's Eulalie shudders, "Will you haue all the world to exclaime on our sexe, and cry out vpon women kinde?" Like the living women of this time, Margery disdains the idea of adjusting her behavior to obviate misogyny; misogynists should be outfaced: "Why, none but men will speake against vs; and if they do, we can giue them two words for one in the hottest manner" (Sig. C2ᵛ).

* * * * *

That both dramatic and nondramatic literature of the *hic mulier* years portray women as strong and aggressive, during a period when living women were behaving aggressively, is highly suggestive, but does it necessarily imply that sex roles were changing and women growing more assertive? An alternate explanation might be that the defenders of patriarchy were growing more repressive than before, that literature exaggerated women's aggressiveness because men (for whatever reasons) were feeling more threatened by it than ever before. Coppélia Kahn rightly points out the "disparity between the extent and nature of Kate's 'shrewish' behavior [in *The Taming of the Shrew*] and the male characters' perceptions of it";[15] is it possible that the aggressiveness of female characters in Renaissance literature is entirely a product of the oversensitivity of male authors committed to a patriarchal society and does not reflect living women's behavior at all?

Indeed, we must allow for exaggeration and distortion if we adopt the mirror theory of literature: as I have persistently argued, the connection between literature and life in the Renaissance was oblique rather than direct, as in good literature it nearly always is. But the theory of patriarchal repressiveness, while it might account for the satiric attack upon assertive women in nondramatic literature of the *hic mulier* years, cannot account for the drama's shift, during the same years, to a decidedly more favorable view of women. As far as the drama is concerned, patriarchy was definitely not exercising a more despotic power during the *hic mulier* years: King James's attempt, as reported by Chamberlain, to enlist the support of literature in his campaign against aggressive women was, as far as can be judged from extant plays, a signal failure. We can account for the drama's new image of women, forged during the *hic mulier* years, by positing increased pressure by female playgoers, which is itself an index of living women's actual power, and/or by positing increased tolerance of women, increased sophistication about the nature of masculinity and femininity, on the part of male dramatists. The fact that such tolerance and sophistication did not extend to nondramatic literature of the same period would seem to rule out the latter hypothesis, but it is true that the best writers of the day who took up this topic were writing for the theater: lightweight nondramatic writers like Parrot, Heath, Fitzgeffrey, or Sharpe cannot be expected to exhibit the sophistication of such dramatic heavyweights as a Webster or a Shakespeare.

Just how strong and assertive were living women of the Renaissance we shall never be able to gauge with certainty. But we do know that for a few years they were strong enough and assertive enough to influence the drama's image of womankind; considering the power of literature to create images which can govern human behavior, that power (had women kept it) possessed tremendous potential.

The Renaissance, committed in the titles of dozens of books (from *The Mirror for Magistrates* to *The Steel Glass*) to the mirror theory of literature, sometimes employed—to follow M. H. Abrams's formulation—the lamp theory instead. Sidney sometimes believed that art mirrored nature ("an art of imitation . . . a speaking picture") and sometimes that art created a new nature: "The poet . . . lifted up with the vigor of his own invention, doth grow in effect into another nature, in making things either better than nature bringeth forth, or, quite anew, forms such as never were in Nature. . . . Nature never set forth the earth in so rich tapistry as divers poets have done."[16] Sidney's belief that literature might mend character was dear to the hearts of Renaissance literary critics: the mirror metaphor itself, as the Renaissance used it, was active rather than passive: in aiming at amending behavior in the real world, it sought to affect as well as to reflect. Surely the female playgoers who "showed their teeth" when dramatists staged a monstrous stereotyped figure like *The Captain*'s Lelia recognized the power of literary stereotype to affect living women: they recognized that literary images might influence both the way women behaved and the way men treated them. For generations, literature had sought to modify women's behavior by praising Grissills and damning shrews; during the heady *hic mulier* years, women forced the drama, at least, to provide models more to their taste—Katharine of

Aragon, the spurned wife who stands up for herself; Maria, the rebellious wife whose insubordination is celebrated; the Duchess of Malfi, the widow allowed a sex life with no authorial condemnation. Whether any insubordinate wife was ever celebrated by any living creature in the real world is finally a secondary question: a real world whose literature admits to her celebration as an imaginative possibility is capable of celebrating her in the flesh eventually.

Renaissance literature both followed human behavior, in being "an art of imitation," and sought to lead it, to "grow another nature" into which our imperfect natures might strive to enter. In the drama of the *hic mulier* years we can glimpse where the behavior of the two sexes might have been led had women kept hold of the reins.

* * * * *

The two essays which crowned the transvestite controversy in 1620, *Hic Mulier* and *Haec-Vir*, did not spring unheralded onto the literary scene. This ground had long been tilled, not only by satirists, moralists, and preachers who commented directly on a provocative fashion over a period of some fifty years, but also by writers in many genres who were moved—partly by the behavior of flesh-and-blood Englishwomen—to explore the nature of women and of men.

From the housewife in *Cambyses* who confronts evil by thrashing the Vice, first with her broom and then with her bare hands, until like the milksop husband he cries "Even now I yield, and give you the mast'ry," to Spenser's "mighty Giauntesse," who "bore before her lap a dolefull Squire, / Lying athwart her horse in great distresse, / Fast bounden hand and foote with cords of wire, / Whom she did meane to make the thrall of her desire" (*Faerie Queene*, III.vii.37), to Fletcher's Maria, turning the tables on the shrew tamer, Renaissance literature shows a propensity to choose women of spirit as its subjects. The literature, especially the drama, of the *hic mulier* years adopts attitudes toward women which demonstrate the power of real-life women of spirit to mold literature after their own image.

What is telling is that both laudatory and satiric portraits of Renaissance women, from sonnet mistress to shrew to gossip to breeches-clad virago, endow them with formidable power over men; even the Patient Grissill figure has the power to chasten and subdue, and ultimately triumphs over her husband's ill behavior. I am not arguing against the persistence of convention. All of these female character types remain literary conventions: I suspect that Renaissance writers almost never drew characters directly from the life. I am arguing that conditions in contemporary life influenced the choice of these conventions rather than others and that the strong-mindedness of contemporary women was one of those conditions.

Katharine Rogers notes that "neither secular nor religious writers in this period felt any need to moderate their criticism of women by consideration for the supposed fragility of the female sex" (*Troublesome Helpmate*, p. 134), and this is most certainly true: the quality of Renaissance misogyny was itself a tribute to the sturdiness of Renaissance women. With one important manifestation of that misogyny I conclude this study.

NOTES

1. The plays with female heroes that were published in the 1560s or slightly later—*Godly Queen Hester, Patient Grissill, Susanna, Mary Magdalene*—may have been designed for female readers; there is no evidence that any of these plays was acted before a live audience.

2. For evidence on women's playgoing, see Alfred Harbage, *Shakespeare's Audience*, pp. 75–78.

3. A section of *Satyres: and Satyricall Epigrams*.

4. Women were frequently hoardable property in the imagery of plays acted before 1610: Shylock in *The Merchant of Venice*, Barabas in Marlowe's *Jew of Malta*, Pisaro in *Englishmen for My Money*, Jaques de Prie in Jonson's *The Case Is Altered*, Pietro in *The Malcontent*, Security in *Eastward Ho*, and Mosca and Volpone in *Volpone*, along with a few nondramatic characters like Malbecco in *The Faerie Queene*, are misers of both gold and women. A woman in *The Wise-Woman of Hogsdon* is called a "little property" (I.ii), a courtesan in *Blurt, Master Constable* a "rich argosy of all golden pleasure" (III.iii.193). The connection between women and property was so deeply engrained in Renaissance thought that such diction was often used as an innocent compliment: Octavia is "a gem of women" (*Antony and Cleopatra*, III.xiii.108), Anne Frankford "a chain of gold to adorn [her husband's] neck" (Heywood's *A Woman Killed with Kindness*, i.64), Bess Bridges "A Girl Worth Gold" (subtitle of *The Fair Maid of the West*). Given its pervasiveness in Renaissance thought, the sharp decline of such imagery during the *hic mulier* years is the more striking.

5. In plays acted before 1610: Mistress Taffeta in *Ram-Alley* fears that Boutcher will not want to marry her because she is a widow: "Belike you thinke it base and seruant-like, / To feed vpon reuersion, you hold vs widdowes, / But as a pie thrust to the lower end / That hath had many fingers int before, / And is reseru'd for grose and hungry stomackes. / . . . Though a capons wings and legges be caru'd, / The flesh left with the rumpe I hope is sweet" (I.i.346–356); a bawd in *Pericles* orders up a "dish of chastity with rosemary and bays" (IV.vi.160); Emilia remarks memorably, "They [men] are all but stomachs and we all but food. / They eat us hungerly, and when they are full / They belch us" (*Othello*, III.iv.104–106). "Mutton" was a slang term for "whore" (see

Roaring Girl, III.ii.181, *Blurt*, I.ii.1–6, *2 Honest Whore*, V.ii.148–149), as was "mackerel" (see *The Widow's Tears*, II.i.34); the bawd in *The Malcontent* is named Maquerelle. Traditional imagery linking women with food gives rise to many double entendres in *The Woman-Hater*, where the gourmet Lazarello reverses tradition by calling a choice fish head a "chast virgin," "pure and vndeflowred" (Sig. C); in pursuit of the fish head, he comes to rest in a brothel, amongst other kinds of mackerel. In *Antony and Cleopatra*, Cleopatra's affair with Caesar is said to have taken place during Cleopatra's "salad days" (I.v.73); thereafter, she proceeded from being a Caesar salad to being Antony's favorite repast: as Enobarbus puts it, "Other women cloy / The appetites they feed, but she makes hungry / Where most she satisfies" (II.ii.241–243); she is "Egyptian cookery" (II.vi.64), an "Egyptian dish" (II.vi.134), a "morsel for a monarch" (I.v.31), and spends one of her dying moments wondering of the asp, "Will it eat me?" To Cleopatra's clown, a woman is "a dish for the gods, if the Devil dress her not" (V.ii.272–276).

6. "Wiues are nasty sluttish *animalls*" (*Epicoene*, 1609, IV.ii.56); "Why should women only aboue all other creatures that were created for the benefit of mã, haue the vse of speech?" (*The Woman-Hater*, 1606, Sig. G); "Women are like fish, / Which must be strooke when they are prone to byte" (*Ram-Alley*, ca. 1608, II.i.841–842); "Their beasts?—Their wenches, I mean, sir; for your worship knows that those that are under men are beasts" (Middleton's *The Phoenix*, ca. 1604, I.iv.9–11); "Well, I'll pray for women while I live; / They're the profitablest fools, I'll say that for 'em, / A man can keep 'bout his house; the prettiest kind fowl; / So tame, so gentle, e'en to strangers' hand / So soon familiar; suffer to be touch'd, / Of those they ne'er saw twice" (*Your Five Gallants*, ca. 1605, I.i.136–141).

7. In earlier plays, we hear that women "sell their maiden-heads, / As men sell cloth, by yard and handfull" (*Ram-Alley*, III.i.1045–1046), that a maidenhead is "a commodity will lose the gloss with lying. The longer kept, the less worth. Off with 't while 'tis vendible" (*All's Well*, I.i.166–168), that "if you buy ladies' flesh at a million a dram, you cannot preserve it from tainting" (*Cymbeline*, I.iv.146–148), that "a bawd, first for her profession or vocation, it is most worshipful of all the twelve companies; for as that trade is most honorable that sells the best commodities—as the draper is more worshipful than the pointmaker, the silkman more worshipful than the draper, and the goldsmith more honorable than both . . . so the bawd above all. Her shop has the best ware; for where these sell but cloth, satins, and jewels, she sells divine virtues as virginity, modesty, and such rare gems, and those not like a petty chapman, by retail, but like a great merchant, by wholesale" (*Dutch Courtesan*, I.ii.29–39).

8. The connection was persistent in early Jacobean drama: "One woman serues for mans damnation" (*1 Honest Whore*, IV.i.139); "If there be a hell / Greater then whore, and woman; a good catholique / May make the doubt" (*Volpone*, IV.v.129–131); "When woman's in the heart, in the

soul hell" (*Dutch Courtesan,* IV.ii.30); "Oh women / You were created Angels, . . . / But since the first fell, tempting Deuils you are. . . . / Were there no Women, men might liue like gods" (*2 Honest Whore,* III.i.161–165); "Were't not for gold and women, there would be no damnation" (*Revenger's Tragedy,* II.i.257). "Damnation" was a slang term for "whore": Maquerelle calls prostitutes "sixpenny damnations" (*Malcontent,* V.vi.99).

9. In pre-1610 plays, the Lord Protector's wife in *2 Henry VI* "bears a duke's revénues on her back" (I.iii.83); Jaques complains that "the city woman bears / The cost of princes on unworthy shoulders" (*As You Like It,* II.vii.74–75); Vindice speaks of women who "walk with a hundred acres on their backs" (*Revenger's Tragedy,* II.i.216).

10. In pre-1610 plays, Mistress Newcut must have milk-baths, rose-leaves, and bean-flower bags to make her "soft, smooth, and delicate, for lascivious entertainment" (*Your Five Gallants,* V.i.13–20); Maquerelle dispenses a fabulous posset compounded of Barbary hens' eggs, cock-sparrow bones, Ethiopian dates, candied Indian eryngoes, pearl of America, amber of Cataia, and lamb-stones of Muscovia (*Malcontent,* II.iv.8–21).

11. A courtesan in *Blurt, Master Constable,* ca. 1601, barks at her maid, "Away; fie, how thou blowest upon me! thy breath . . . takes off all the painting and colour from my cheek" (II.ii.9–12); Mall Berry in *The Fair Maid of the Exchange,* ca. 1602, has been observed "curling [her] haire, then practising smiles, / Sometimes rubbing [her] filthy butter-teeth, / Then pull[ing] the haires from off [her] beetle-browes. / Painting the veins vpon [her] breasts with blew" (Sig. I2ᵛ); in a grotesque echo of *Romeo and Juliet,* Glister in *The Family of Love,* ca. 1602, lyricizes, "The jocund morn looks more lively and fresh than an old gentlewoman's glazed face in a new periwig" (II.ii.1–3); Hamlet, ca. 1601, complains of women, "God hath given you one face and you make yourselves another" (III.i.148–150).

12. Lady Macbeth and Tullia in Heywood's *Rape of Lucrece* are only the most extreme examples of female ambition in early Jacobean literature; women's "mindes mount aboue their estates" (*Bachelor's Banquet,* Sig. A2ᵛ), and many a husband would be content with his modest social position were his wife not constantly pushing. Marriage itself, in early Jacobean literature, was frequently no more than a method of social climbing: "Though my father be a low-capped tradesman, yet I must be a lady" (Gertrude in *Eastward Ho,* I.ii.3–4).

13. In early Jacobean plays, women were valiant in lust: a knight being dragged off to a bedroom by a jeweler's wife in *The Phoenix* marvels, "A man so resolute in valour as a woman in desire, were an absolute leader" (I.v.37–38); Montsurry in *Bussy d'Ambois* exclaims, " 'Tis miraculous to think with what monsters women's imaginations engross them when they are once enamoured, and what wonders they will work for their satisfaction" (III.ii.294–297). Female characters in early Jacobean drama make extreme demands on the sexual energies of gentleman-ushers, pages, obliging blackamoors, each other's husbands, and any other male who

can be found, including the males of other species: "Oh who would trust your corcke-heeld sex? I thinke / To sate your lust, you would loue a Horse, a Beare, / A croaking Toade, so your hot itching veines / Might have their bound" (2 *Honest Whore,* III.i.175–78). No wonder, for "down from the waist they are Centaurs, / Though women all above" (*Lear,* IV.vi.126–127).

14. "There's more deceit in women, then in hel" (1 *Honest Whore,* 1604, III.iii.86); "She is a woman—that is, she can lie" (*Dutch Courtesan,* ca. 1604, V.iii.133); "In anything a woman does alone, / If she dissemble, she thinks 'tis not done" (*Bussy d'Ambois,* ca. 1604, II.ii.179–180).

15. Coppélia Kahn, "*The Taming of the Shrew:* Shakespeare's Mirror of Marriage," in *The Authority of Experience: Essays in Feminist Criticism,* p. 90.

16. Sir Philip Sidney, *The Defense of Poesy, The Renaissance in England,* pp. 607–8.

Part Three

❧

THE WOMAN-HATER

Fie upon women!—this shall be my song.

—*Arden of Feversham*

I little weigh the *Woman-haters* of our Age,
whose subiect is euer in dispraise of woman,
they shew the vnworthinesse of their Nature
in Satyrizing vpon the weaker.

—Richard Brathwait, 1620

We'll . . . go hear our husbands' lamentations.
They say mine has compiled an ungodly vol-
ume of satires against women, and calls his book
The Snarl.

—Marston, *The Insatiate Countess*

CHAPTER ELEVEN

The Stage Misogynist

T HE MISOGYNISTIC PRONOUNCEMENTS which so frequently punctuate Renaissance drama have not been accorded very helpful interpretation. When the clown tells Cleopatra, "I know the devil himself will not eat a woman" (*Antony and Cleopatra*, V.ii.273–274), critics and audiences laugh and forget it: so much misogyny seems designed for no higher purpose than comic relief. When Enobarbus declares, "under a compelling occasion, let women die. It were pity to cast them away for nothing, though between them and a great cause they should be esteemed nothing" (*Antony and Cleopatra*, I.ii.141–144), critics are likely to agree with him: E. C. Wilson calls these lines an "incisive judgment."[1] The problem is not only that so many critics are themselves misogynists, but also that we have not thoroughly enough explored the conventions governing misogynistic comment in plays. As a small start in the direction of understanding the context of dramatic misogyny, I will here draw attention to the fact that a large number of the drama's antifeminist jibes are made by representatives of a recognizable character type, as much a dramatic convention as the stage Machiavel: I will call him the stage misogynist.

In his pure form, he is a kind of humours character, whose governing trait is a testy disregard for the female sex. Pure representatives of the type are Joseph Swetnam in *Swetnam the Woman-hater Arraigned by Women*,[2] Gondarino in *The Woman-Hater*, Benedick in *Much Ado about Nothing*, Algripe in *The Nightwalker*, Accutus in *Every Woman in Her Humour*. Dozens of characters adopt the stage misogynists's attributes for part of a play, donning or shedding the role as character and circumstance dictate. Their behavior is drawn from several literary sources, and they perform several functions within their respective plays.

Literary sources for the character include certain stock figures from nondramatic literature, the *persona* of the misogynist as developed in the formal controversy, certain Vice figures from the popular drama, and the returning-soldier figure from the debate over the unisex tendencies of peacetime. The formal controversy united with the hermaphrodite controversy to produce a character who embodied, almost allegorically, the Renaissance controversy about women.

Among the nondramatic sources for the character is the Renaissance version of the Cynic Diogenes, who sometimes made satirical pronouncements on such topics as prodigality, whoring, dicing, drinking, usury, lawyers, and social climbing, as in Samuel Rowlands's *Diogines Lanthorne*, 1607, but was more often the quintessential misogynist. When Euphues turns against women, he advises, "Learne of . . . Diogenes to detest women bee they neuer so comely."[3] The Diogenes Lodge created in *Catharos, Diogenes in his Singularitie*, 1591, counsels, "Multiply not too many wordes with a woman, for the auncient sages haue taught vs, that as often as a man talketh long time with a woman, hee procureth his ruine and withdraweth himselfe from the contemplation of celestiall things" (p. 24ᵛ). Diogenes indulges in mild misogyny in Lyly's *Campaspe*. He takes on the role of the formal detractor of women in one work of the formal controversy, William Goddard's *A Satirycall Dialogve Or a Sharplye invectiue conference, betweene Allexander the great, and that truelye womanhater Diogynes* (see above). The misogynist was also a stock figure, especially in Jacobean times, in epigram and Theophrastan character. Misogunes in R. West's *Wits ABC*, 1608, "being wrong'd by some, saith constantly, / That all women want shame and honesty. / In briefe heele falsely sweare, in his mad mood, / That neuer any of that sexe prou'd good" (Sig. C). Misoginos is satirized in the Theophrastan character "A woman hater" in Roger Sharpe's *More Fooles yet*, 1610; the misogynist Vindex is lampooned in one of Richard Niccols's epigrams in *The Fvries*, 1614; "All women monsters euery where proclaimes: / Which to affirme the *Stagirite* he names, / Who sayes they are imperfect Creatures all. / Then what doth *Vindex* his owne mother call? / A monster? yes; then this must current passe, / A monster woman bore a monstrous Asse" (Sig. C3). Richard Brathwait writes in a character in *Essaies upon the five senses*, 1620, "I finde Mysogenes opinion grosse and erroneous . . . I little weigh the *Woman-haters* of our Age" (pp. 121, 129).

Most prominent among the woman haters of Brathwait's age was Joseph Swetnam; the most important nondramatic source of the stage misogynist's character was the *persona* elaborated by writers in the formal controversy, going back to Gosynhyll's *persona* and Elyot's Caninius. The formal attack on women, from the *School House of Women* to Swetnam's *Arraignment*, bestowed upon the misogynist certain stock character traits: he was often genial, witty, good-natured about his insults, often professed to fear attack by outraged females;[4] he sometimes affected remorse and promised to make amends at some future date. From the formal defense of women, stretching from *Mulierum Pean* to Speght and Sowernam, the misogynist picked up a few more traits: he was ungrateful toward his mother (or at least, like Benedick, felt obliged to defend himself against this charge); his misogyny grew out of a sour-grapes attitude—he had turned on all women after an unhappy experience with one; he had a cowardly streak and would not always maintain before a woman's face what he would say noisily enough behind her back.

Several Jacobean stage misogynists engage in debate about women which closely resembles the formal controversy. Sextus in *The Rape of Lucrece* and Ilford in *The Miseries of Enforced Marriage* I discussed in chapter 5. *The Iron Age, Part 2* stages a confrontation between misogynist and defender, in which some *exempla* from the formal controversy, Cressida and the Amazons, are involved. Synon opens, "I hate all women, painted beauty / And I am opposites: I loue thee lesse / Because thou doat'st on Troian *Cressida*" (I.i). "Leaue this detraction," Diomed commands. Synon predicts Cressida's inconstancy: "Neuer was woman constant to one man"; as proof, he tests Cressida's constancy by wooing her while Diomed eavesdrops. She fails the test. Diomed is converted: "Now *Synon* Ile beleeue / There is no truth in women." Cressida lashes out at Synon: "Thou art a Traytor to all woman kinde"; he answers conventionally, "I am, and nought more grieues me then to thinke, / A woman was my mother." Craving revenge, Cressida calls upon Penthesilea and her Amazons. Suppressing her own faithlessness, Cressida explains only that Synon is a notorious misogynist. Penthesilea charges Synon: "You betray Ladies, enuy all our sexe, / And that you now shall pay for." The Amazons surround Synon, who stands firm: "I recant nothing." The stage picture of angry women besieging a misogynist anticipates Swetnam's arraignment in *Swetnam the Woman-hater*.

The stage misogynist also owed some character traits to Vice figures in earlier Tudor drama. Ill Report, the Vice in Garter's *Comedy of the Most Virtuous and Godly Susanna*, ca. 1569, comments on women's natural envy, sloth, and lechery. Politic Persuasion, the Vice in Phillip's *Comedy of Patient and Meek Grissill*, 1558–61, accuses women of extravagance, loquacity, fractiousness, craftiness, and impatience, and wives of domestic power hunger: "Moast wyues are so knappish and cutted now, / That they will be knowen to beare rule . . . / Oft times they conquer ther husbands in battell" (Sig. Cii^v). The Vice Haphazard in R. B.'s *Appius and Virginia*, ca. 1564, also snipes at domineering wives, whom he connects with the chaos of modern sex-role inversions;

> Hap may so hazard, the moon may so change,
> That men may be masters, and wives will not range:
> But in hazard it is, in many a grange,
> Lest wives wear the codpiece, and maidens coy strange . . .
> Maids would be masters by the guise of this country.
>
> (Sig. C)

Infidelity, the Vice in Wager's *The Life and Repentance of Mary Magdalene* (1560's), pontificates, "This is a true prouerbe, and no fained fable, / Few womens words, be honest, constant, and stable" (Sig. Di^v); he is seconded by a chorus of sub-Vices, who are also misogynists: Cupidity comments on women's viciousness, ambition, and pride, Pride on women's vanity and mercilessness; Carnall Concupiscence remarks, "Both damsels and wiues vse many such feates, / I know them that will lay out their faire teates, / Purposely men to allure" (Sig. [C4]^v).

As Dusinberre points out, "satire on women was the property of the Vice in the morality play";[5] but before concluding that audiences would have recognized antifeminism as a tool of the Devil, we should note that misogynistic Vices belong to a particular type of morality play—the later, secular sort—and to plays of other genres into which the vice was eventually imported. Ill Report, Politic Persuasion, Haphazard, and Infidelity belong to plays with female protagonists. Their function is to tempt and test these protagonists; their misogyny, appropriate to dramatic context, has little bearing on larger questions of good and evil. *Susanna, Patient Grissill, Appius and Virginia,* and *Mary Magdalene* were all contemporary with intense activity in the formal controversy, the 1560s; they are dramatic equivalents of the formal defense, as indeed their heroines' names are familiar to the formal defense's lists of good women. The presence of the formal detractor, in the person of the Vice, is a structural and generic necessity: the defense of women had always adopted a posture of rebuttal; if a contemporary detractor did not exist, the formal defense had always found it necessary to invent one. This use of the Vice figure owes a great deal to the formal controversy: a character like Politic Persuasion is part allegorical figure, part embodiment of the spirit of Edward Gosynhyll. This type of play saw the first transmutation of the formal controversy's detracting *persona* into the stage misogynist. L. W. Cushman, who analyzes the speeches of Vice figures, cites only isolated instances of misogynistic comments by Vices prior to the 1560s.[6] Beginning in the 1560s, however, a spate of antifeminist comment occurs in such speeches: the Vices in *Cambyses* (ca. 1561), *Horestes* (1567), *The Trial of Treasure* (1569), and *The Tide Tarrieth No Man* (1576), along with the four already named, all make misogynistic remarks. The prominence of the formal controversy during the period when this character type was developing suggests a direct influence from that controversy, with its heavy freight of conventionalism, upon the stage misogynist, who so often has about him an aura of bookish artificiality, close in spirit to the formal controversy's *personae*.

Equally important as a source, however, was a figure from the debate about changing sex roles in peacetime—the soldier who returns to find his martial masculinity inappropriate in a civilian world where women's tastes and values prevail. All the most prominent stage misogynists are or have been soldiers: Sextus in *The Rape of Lucrece*, Benedick in *Much Ado*, Gondarino in *The Woman-Hater*, Troilus in *Troilus and Cressida*, Caratack in *Bonduca*, Accutus in *Every Woman in Her Humour*, Posthumus in *Cymbeline*, Jacomo in *The Captain*, Enobarbus in *Antony and Cleopatra*, Bosola in *The Duchess of Malfi*, Iago, Hamlet; Swetnam affects a militant posture. By making their stage misogynists soldiers, dramatists imported into the character type the potential for comment on unisex themes arising from the war and peace issue. Since the "hermaphrodite" debate was always livelier, more radical, and more firmly rooted in reality than was the formal controversy's debate about Eve and the Virgin, militarizing the stage misogynist made him a considerably more promising figure than he might otherwise have been.

The diminished sexual distinctions accompanying the end of a war form a major theme in *Much Ado*. Claudio transforms himself resolutely from soldier to lover; when he left for the wars,

> I looked upon her with a soldier's eye,
> That liked but had a rougher task in hand
> Than to drive liking to the name of love.
> But now I am returned and that war thoughts
> Have left their places vacant, in their rooms
> Come thronging soft and delicate desires,
> All prompting me how fair young Hero is,
> Saying I liked her ere I went to wars.
>
> (I.i.300–307)

Claudio, as "Constantia Munda" said of Joseph Swetnam, has found in some author an antithesis betwixt a warrior and a lover; but whether war thoughts have truly left their places vacant, whether Claudio is ready for civilian life and female society, is a question to be asked. He volunteers to forego his honeymoon in order to escort his commanding officer to Aragon and needs to be reminded that this would be "as great a soil in the new gloss of your marriage as to show a child his new coat and forbid him to wear it" (III.ii.1–7). His readiness to believe slanders against his fiancée is, after this, not surprising: Claudio values his reputation among fellow officers more highly than any relationship with a woman. Janice Hays, noting that "his association with the male world, his silence in the presence of women, and his hesitation about affirming his tentative feelings for Hero imply that he is more at home with the actions of war than the emotions of love," suggests that he "has embraced the duties of a soldier because he is disinclined, or afraid, to embrace a woman."[7]

Benedick, returning from the wars a misogynist, is full of a genial contempt for Claudio's transformation: "I have known when there was no music with him but the drum and the fife; and now had he rather hear the tabor and the pipe. I have known when he would have walked ten mile afoot to see a good armor; and now will he lie ten nights awake carving the fashion of a new doublet. He was wont to speak plain and to the purpose, like an honest man and a soldier, and now . . . his words are a very fantastical banquet" (II.iii.12–18). Like a proper misogynist, Benedick is aware that he may be charged with ingratitude toward his mother: he begins one antifeminist speech with the disclaimer, "That a woman conceived me, I thank her; that she brought me up, I likewise give her most humble thanks; but . . ." (I.i.240–242). Benedick's misogyny is a good-natured pose, a self-conscious humour, and everyone knows it: "Do you question me, as an honest man should do, for my simple true judgment?" he asks Claudio, "or would you have me speak after my custom, as being a professed tyrant to their sex?" (I.i.167–170)— certainly a more self-aware pose than Claudio's pose as a lover. But before Benedick can enjoy successful integration into the civilian world, he must shed not only his highly artificial pose as a misogynist, but the very trappings of masculinity which belong to the soldier's world. Benedick's shaving off his beard (not to mention wearing cosmetics), as a prerequisite to becoming the lover of a Beatrice who wishes she were a man that she might eat Claudio's heart in the marketplace, is an unmistakable surrender to the hermaphrodism of civilian life. Beatrice, reversing sex roles in a rare feminine use of the balancing formula, had ruled out both bearded and unbearded men as candidates for husband; in the process, she had put the effeminacy of the beardless man beyond question:

> *Beatrice:* I could not endure a husband with a beard . . .
> *Leonato:* You may light on a husband that hath no beard.
> *Beatrice:* What should I do with him? dress him in my apparel and
>   make him my waiting gentlewoman? . . . He that hath no beard
>   is less than a man. (II.i.31–39)[8]

Ensuing scenes make clear, however, that a shaven Benedick is both a more desirable lover and a more honorable soldier than the Claudio who continues to make camp jokes with his fellow soldier Don Pedro, in the face of Hero's tragedy. Leonato early approves of "feminine" qualities in a man, praising a weeping uncle: "A kind overflow of kindness. There are no faces truer than those that are so washed" (I.i.26–27), and the play continues to smile upon cross-sex behavior to the end. The reform of a misogynist in such a context combines with the debearding of a soldier to endorse the hermaphrodism of a civilized world.

Jacomo, identified as a "Woman-hater" in the *dramatis personae* of *The Captain,* is less comfortable with his misogynistic pose than is Benedick: his is an expression of insecurity, a cover for his soldier's shyness with women. "Pox o' peace," he cries like a veritable Barnabe Rich, "that makes the toughness, and the strength of Nations / Melt into Women" (II.i); he so lacks confidence, in civilian surroundings, that when women compliment him he thinks they are mocking him and lashes out against womankind with a macho fury. The cowardice at the heart of the misogynist's aggressive posture had been part of the character type since Caninius's embarrassed retreat from misogyny when a warlike queen enters the room, in Elyot's *Defense of Good Women*. Jacomo's successful reëntry into the civilian world, symbolized by his promise "I'le have my head curl'd and powder'd tomorrow / By break of day" (V.iv), is accomplished when a woman exposes the hollowness of his aggressive stance by being more aggressive than he is. It is with a kind of relief that Jacomo abandons his macho posture to embrace a sane hermaphrodism that welcomes the razor.

The misogynist sometimes opens his antifeminist remarks by affecting to hate himself because born of woman. Gondarino "doeth seeme to loath all woman kind, / To hate himselfe, because he hath some part / Of woman in him" (*Woman-Hater*, Sig. C3). Posthumus agonizes:

> Could I find out
> The woman's part in me! For there's no motion
> That tends to vice in man but I affirm
> It is the woman's part. Be it lying, note it
> The woman's; flattering, hers; deceiving, hers;
> Lust and rank thoughts, hers, hers; revenges, hers;
> Ambitions, covetings, change of prides, disdain,
> Nice longing, slanders, mutability,
> All faults that may be named, nay, that Hell knows,
> Why, hers, in part or all, but rather all.
> For even to vice
> They are not constant, but are changing still
> One vice, but of a minute old, for one
> Not half so old as that. I'll write against them,
> Detest them, curse them.
>   (*Cymbeline*, II.v.19–33)

This diatribe, like formal attacks on women, lists feminine faults, a practice followed by most stage misogynists. Constabarus delivers a forty-four line diatribe against female inconstancy, bloodthirstiness, pride, troublemaking, emotional extremism, lawlessness, foolishness, frowardness, wantonness, vanity, murderousness, wilfulness, and adultery (*Mariam*, Sig. [F4]ᵛ-G, lines 1575–1619). To the defender's argument that women replenish the human race he responds, "T'were better that the humane race should faile, / Then be by such a mischiefe multiplide." He does not neglect Eve. Accutus in *Every Woman In* lists feminine faults too—outrageous fashions, extravagance, moodiness, husband bankrupting, pouting, scowling, railing, mincing demureness, and spleenfulness. Mendoza, rejected by Aurelia, delivers a formula antifeminist diatribe:

> Women! Nay, furies; nay, worse; for they torment only the bad, but women good and bad. Damnation of mankind! . . . O, that I could rail against these monsters in nature, models of hell, curse of the earth, women that dare attempt anything, and what they attempt they care not how they accomplish; without all premeditation or prevention; rash in asking, desperate in working, impatient in suffering, extreme in desiring, slaves unto appetite, mistresses in dissembling, only constant in unconstancy, only perfect in counterfeiting; their words are feigned, their eyes forged, their sights dissembled, their looks counterfeit, their hair false, their given hopes deceitful, their very breath artificial. Their blood [i.e., lust] is their only god; bad clothes and old age are only the devils they tremble at. That I could rail now! (*Malcontent*, I.vi.78–93)

The stage misogynist is often thinly motivated, betraying roots in allegorical traditions like the Vice. Influenced by the formal defense, the misogynist's low opinion of womankind often results from a snub by one woman. The incidents which touch off misogyny vary greatly in their degree of seriousness, but all involve hasty generalization from one woman to all womankind. Constabarus in *Mariam* turns against women when his wife seeks a divorce, Posthumus in *Cymbeline* and Zuccone in *The Fawn* when they believe their wives unfaithful, the heroes of Beaumont and Fletcher's *Philaster* and of Greene's *Orlando Furioso* when they believe their lady loves unfaithful; Scudmore and Neville in *A Woman Is a Weathercock* conclude that "women all are false" (I.i.170) when Scudmore's fiancée throws him over; Rowland in *The Woman's Prize* misogynizes upon Eve's faults when his fiancée breaks their engagement; Algripe in *The Nightwalker* turns misogynist when he believes he has been cuckolded on his wedding night, Troilus in *Troilus and Cressida* and Lysander in *The Widow's Tears* when their women actually are unfaithful, Mendoza in *The Malcontent* when a woman resists his advances; Gondarino in *The Woman-Hater* hates the memory of his dead wife, and "for her sake all women" (Sig. C^v).[9] Although Accutus in *Every Women In* attributes his misogyny to his close observation of "the muliebritie / of female scandal" (Sig. A3^v), a woman interprets it as sour grapes: "I warrant he ranne mad for loue, because no good face could endure the sight of him, and euer since he railes against women like a whot shot" (Sig. [H4]). William the Conqueror in the anonymous *Fair Em* turns misogynist after being rejected: "Conseit hath wrought such generall dislike / Through the false dealing of *Mariana*, / That vtterly I doe abhore their sex. / They

are all disloyall, vnconstant, all vniust" (Sig. Fᵛ). After hearing of Em's
constancy, he reconsiders: "I see that women are not generall euils" (Sig.
F2ᵛ). Manuile, too, threatens to turn misogynist; this is specifically identified as a sour grapes attitude: "The Foxe will eat no grapes, and why?"
(*Fair Em,* Sig. F3).

Hamlet turns misogynist through disappointment with one woman;
his mother's "o'erhasty marriage" leads him to generalize, "Frailty, thy
name is woman" (II.ii.57, I.ii.146). Unhappy Ophelia is snared in the
wide net of Hamlet's misogyny: one can hardly believe that the Polonius
who frowns "Beautified is a vile phrase" (II.ii.111–112) would permit his
docile daughter to wear makeup, but it is to Ophelia that Hamlet gen-
eralizes about women, "I have heard of your paintings. . . . God hath
given you one face and you make yourselves another" (III.i.148–150).

The misogynist's credibility is continually undercut by his subjectivity
and his habit of jumping to conclusions. Several are mistaken even in
their suspicions of one woman: the wives of Posthumus, Zuccone, and
Algripe, for example, are innocent of the suspected infidelity. Some
(Scudmore, Mendoza, Rowland) unfairly level accusations against all
womankind because one woman does not happen to fancy them. Other
women are guilty as charged. When Lysander in *The Widow's Tears* rants
"What is a woman? What are the worst when the best are so past naming? As men like this, let them try their wives again. Put women to the
test; discover them; paint them . . . ten parts more than they do themselves, rather than look on them as they are" (V.i.220–225), he has some
reason: his wife has just failed her chastity test in a spectacular way. But
even where the woman is guilty, the invalidity of the misogynist's hasty
generalization disqualifies him from consideration as the author's mouthpiece.

The misogynist is portrayed as a man who slanders a whole sex out of
personal disappointment or inadequacy frequently enough to establish
the character type as discreditable by nature—no less suspect as a com-
mentator than the braggadocio. The formal controversy had always suspected his motives and morals; evidence that ulterior motive was regularly
suspected in cases of misogyny exists in a witty parody, *A lyttle treatyse
called the Image of Idlenesse, conteynynge certeyne matters moued betwene Walter Wedlocke and Bawdin Bacheler. Translated out of the Troyane or Cornyshe
tounge into Englyshe, by Olyuer Oldwanton, and dedicated to the Lady Lust,*
entered in the Stationer's Register in 1558–59. Its subtle parodic quality
has proved elusive: the ironic deference to women in the dedication to
Lady Lust points towards its being what Louis B. Wright suggests—"a
burlesque of the books in praise of women."[10] The work itself, however,
is a wry commentary on misogynists, or on the way misogynists were
being viewed by defenders of women.

The form is epistolary: Bawdin Bachelor addresses two long letters to
Walter Wedlocke; in the first he encloses correspondence dealing with his
unsuccessful career as a suitor, on the flimsy excuse of defending himself
from Walter's charge that he is opposed to matrimony. To show that he
has done his best to enter into that blessed state, Bawdin documents the
history of his wooing, revealing in the process his inept and insensitive
amatory methods. The first enclosure, a letter to the kinsman of a woman
he hopes to wed, makes his primarily fiscal interest in the marriage only
too clear, compounding that faux pas by a blatant attempt to bribe the
kinsman into furthering his suit; although he puts this in the form of a
wager (betting the kinsman a large sum that the suit will not be successful), the kinsman could hardly be deceived or fail to be offended. This
suit is a decided failure. The next letter addresses the recent widow of a
close friend. Upon being informed that she already has somebody else
in mind, Bawdin cheerfully responds that if she finds herself widowed
again soon he will still be interested (and will gladly break off any engagement he may have contracted in the interim). He also provides a few
stanzas of execrable verse which he commands the widow to have carved
on her husband's tombstone. The answers to Bawdin's letters are not
usually included; part of the piece's humor arises from our imagining the
amazement of those who receive these very odd epistles.

Undaunted, Bawdin presses on to a third eligible; this one responds
that she has vowed never to marry. Bawdin returns a long, fatherly letter
advising her on how to get rid of suitors in her future career as a virgin.
He outlines his own theory of the three male motives for wooing—true
love, desire for money, and enjoyment of wooing for its own sake—
wooing as recreation. Bawdin's own amorous pursuits reveal all three
motives: money is the primary motive of his first suit, true love (or so
he alleges) of his fourth suit, recreation of his fifth.

The next letter from Bawdin's amorous archives is to a woman who
refuses to see suitors. (Is this only her excuse for refusing to see Bawdin?)
Declaring desperate love, Bawdin accuses her of narcissism, delivering
himself of a windy lecture on various historical narcissists. Apparently
the lady remains unmoved; Bawdin lays siege to a fifth. The letter ex-
emplifying this ill-starred romance has been written after the lady has
stood him up. To his recriminations she has returned a bitter answer, of
which he ruefully complains, "Women are or shulde be of a myld and
gentle nature" (Sig. [C5]ᵛ). To save face, he tells her he wooed her only
for "recreation" (Sig. [C6]), never intending marriage: he considers the
"pastyme of wooynge . . . muche better then the penaunce of weddynge" (Sig. [C6]). This is the second time Bawdin has taken refuge in
a sour grapes attitude; after an earlier refusal he persuaded himself that

taking the woman away from family and friends would have been too great a hardship. This personality trait will prove important.

Bawdin has made a "kalender" of all maidens and widows in his neighborhood, including in this list of eleven eligibles the wife of an old man not expected to live out March. Confiding to his correspondent his decision not to be too particular (he will overlook some faults, as long as they are minimally gross and the marriage is "for myne owne advauncement" [Sig. (C8)ᵛ]), Bawdin outlines his plan of attack: to lessen the sorrow of a repulse to his "tender simple hart" and to save time, he will woo several simultaneously, allowing himself two or three meetings with one woman before launching another campaign. At this writing he has exhausted seven of the eleven possibilities but not lost heart.

After an ellipsis during which the remaining four have obviously refused him, Bawdin writes to an old army friend with gentlewomen "to spare":[11] Bawdin asks for a spare gentlewoman. Here he does include the responding letter: the army friend reminds Bawdin that he cannot merely send him a woman; such matters are at the woman's discretion. He has, however, put Bawdin's case before the women he knows, and none is interested: a man who has been refused so often must have something wrong with him.

Bawdin, despairing at last, writes that he is giving up wooing forever and plans to live alone in the wilderness. In the meantime, he is taking comfort in antifeminist literature; a number of misogynistic couplets (e.g., "Lybertie they couet, to do what they wyl, yet what they take in hand commenly they spyll") are now providing solace. It is here, when Bawdin's sour-grapes habit leads him to damn all women because some refuse to marry him, that the purport of the work suddenly becomes clear. Like Elyot, Gosynhyll, and Vaughan before him, the pseudonymous Oliver Oldwanton is impugning misogynists' motives: "detractors" have cursed women after disappointments in love. This allegation, which had a long career in the formal controversy, is here brought to life, with comic intent; the amorous struggles of Bawdin Bachelor have a mock-heroic tone which trivializes the misogynist's bluster.

Bawdin Bachelor, though appearing in a nondramatic context, can serve as a paradigm for the type: a survey of the field reveals that most stage misogynists lash out at women out of a personal grudge. While their bitterness is usually understandable in context, their misogyny can almost never be taken as authorial comment on the nature of women.

Like Bawdin, many stage misogynists are basically comic figures. This again betrays their origins: from the time of Gosynhyll's "somme what to ieste with the femynye," misogynists were jesters in formal attacks

and the butts of jest in formal defenses; and all the Vice/misogynists—
Infidelity, Haphazard, Ill Report, Politic Persuasion, Ambidexter—are
jokers: vices and devils had always been comic figures in the drama. Two
stage misogynists are outright clowns—Cleopatra's clown and *All's Well's*
clown, who both traffic in percentages. The former offers, "These same
whoreson devils do the gods great harm in their women; for in every ten
that they make, the devils mar five" (*Antony and Cleopatra,* V.ii.274–276);
the latter makes it nine out of ten: "One good woman in ten, madam,
which is a purifying o' the song. . . . An we might have a good woman
born but one every blazing star, or at an earthquake, 'twould mend the
lottery well" (I.iii.86–92). Others, less literally clowns, expend considerable energy on antifeminist quips. Benedick makes one too many jests
for Beatrice's taste: she describes him as "the Prince's jester, a very dull
fool" (*Much Ado,* II.i.142). Swetnam in *Swetnam the Woman-hater* persists
in antifeminist jests while arraigned before a tribunal of angry women.
Gondarino's jests sometimes have the quasi-theological trappings of the
formal controversy: "Deuils were once good, there they excel'd you
women" (Sig. [D4]); and he lampoons the formal controversy's cherished *exempla:*

> The much praysed *Amazones,*
> Knowing their owne infirmities so well,
> Made of themselues a people, and what men
> They take amongst them, they condemne to die,
> Perceiuing that their follie made them fit
> To liue no longer, that would willingly
> Come in the worthlesse presence of a woman.
> (*Woman-Hater,* Sig. D^v)

Enobarbus rejoices in the obscene jests of the soldier: when Cleopatra
proposes to attend the war, he remarks, "If we should serve with horse
and mares together, / . . . the mares would bear / A soldier and his horse"
(III.vii.8–10), a remark that allies him with characters like *Mary Magdalene's* Vices:

> *Infidelity:* It skilleth not though in the buttocks you [i.e., Mary] be
>   great.
> *Carnall Concupiscence:* No for there she is like many tymes to be
>   beate.
>   (Sig. Di)

Several stage misogynists become the object of laughter by falling in
love. Valentine in *The Two Gentlemen of Verona* falls in love after disdain-
ing "to be in love, where scorn is bought with groans, / Coy looks with
heart-sore sighs" (I.i.28–29), following the pattern of Chaucer's Troilus,

who laughs at love before succumbing to it. In *Love's Labor's Lost,* very little time elapses between the lords' forswearing women's company and their falling in love. Jacomo in *The Captain* is a woman-hater who falls in love, as is Vallenger in *The Fair Maid of Bristow,* who in the opening scene is a formal misogynist, "an enemy to women still," but soon falls in love with Anabell, marries her, and passes from woman-hater to wife-baiter with the shortest stint as a lover on record. Tiberio in *The Fawn,* who has "ever loathed / A thought of woman," resolves "to sigh, read poets, look pale, go neatly, and be most apparently in love" after being courted by Dulcimel (III.i.471–2; IV.i.689–90). Benedick obligingly ties his own noose: "I do much wonder that one man, seeing how much another man is a fool when he dedicates his behaviors to love, will, after he hath laughed at such shallow follies in others, become the argument of his own scorn by falling in love—and such a man is Claudio" (II.iii.7–12). Two hundred lines later, Benedick is "horribly in love" with Beatrice (II.iii.243). Swetnam in *Swetnam the Woman-hater* attempts to seduce a woman by cynically posing as the misogynist-fallen-in-love; when his plan is foiled, he becomes an object of laughter for the ludicrousness of the attempt.

In *The Nightwalker,* comic poetic justice is meted out to the misogynist Algripe, who has declared of women that he hates

> Their noise, and do abhor the whole sex heartily!
> They are all walking devils, harpies, I will study
> A week together how to rail sufficiently
> Upon 'em all: and, that I may be furnish'd,
> Thou shalt buy all the railing books and ballads
> That malice hath invented against women:
> I will read nothing else, and practise 'em,
> Till I grow fat with curses.
>
> (II.iv)

Algripe will rue the day he thus charged a servant with antifeminist book buying: it undoes him. To gain access to Algripe's papers, Alathe poses with her confederate as an itinerant bookseller, whose stock includes "a new book of women . . . a book of wicked women . . . of rude, malicious women, of proud women, / Of scolding women," and other antifeminist books, along with "a little, very little book, / Of good and godly women, a very little one, / So little you may put it in a nutshell" (III.iii). The device works: admitted to Algripe's house, they distract the servants by distributing books and ballads, bind and gag Algripe, and purloin his papers. The misogynist has been hoist with his own petard.

Dramatists may have made the misogynist a figure of fun—either a jester or a laughing-stock or both—to avoid offending female playgoers:

this would have been especially important during the *hic mulier* era. But while the plays superficially suggest that the woman-hater is not to be taken seriously, events in these plays often suggest the opposite.

The misogynist is frequently found in conjunction with a related type, the slanderer.[12] Misogynists libel womankind; slanderers blacken one woman's reputation. The slanderer, unlike the misogynist, is nearly always treated with deadly seriousness: his machinations lead to the slandered woman's ruin or near ruin, and sometimes death. The slanderer was remarkably appealing to Shakespeare, who created Don Juan, Iago, Leontes, and Iachimo. But other authors were enthusiastic too, creating a number of characters who impugn an innocent woman's chastity,[13] up to the *hic mulier* days when so many sex roles were reversed and the slanderer began to be female: Francisca in *The Witch,* acted ca. 1615, and Megra in *Philaster,* acted ca. 1608–10, slander women; Aurea in Heywood's *The Silver Age,* acted ca. 1611, slanders a man; Leonora in *The Devil's Law-Case,* acted ca. 1617, slanders herself.

The prototype is the biblical Susanna story, where the virtuous heroine is slandered by two unjust elders. (In light of Shakespeare's interest in the slanderer, it is appropriate that one of his daughters was named Susanna.)[14] In Garter's dramatization, *The Comedy of the Most Virtuous and Godly Susanna,* the Vice, Ill Report, is both a slanderer and a misogynist (he comments on women's proneness to all seven deadly sins). The very spirit of slander, he inspires the elders, here allegorized into lieutenant Vices (Voluptas and Sensualitas), to impugn Susanna's chastity: "If you meane to haue my helpe, to fortefy your forte, / All that I can doe is, to giue her an ill Reporte" (Sig. Cii). Iago in *Othello* is a slanderer who is occasionally a misogynist; a number of later plays divide Ill Report's functions between misogynist and slanderer.

The misogynist Benedick coexists in *Much Ado* with the slanderer Don John, whose lies nearly cost Hero her marriage, and endanger her life. The misogynist Posthumus coexists in *Cymbeline* with the slanderer Iachimo, whose lies result in Imogen's banishment and endanger her marriage and her life. The misogynist Scudmore in *A Woman Is a Weathercock* shares the stage with the slanderer Captain Pouts, whose lies disrupt a wedding ceremony as had Don John's. Philaster's misogyny is prompted by the slanders of Megra and Dion (*Philaster,* II.iv.ff.), Orlando's by the slanders of Sacripant (*Orlando Furioso,* II.i.ff.). Sextus in *The Rape of Lucrece* is a misogynist who threatens a woman with a form of slander,[15] which helps drive her to suicide; but the two character types reunite most firmly in Gondarino of *The Woman-Hater,* a misogynist who slanders a woman for two good misogynistic reasons—to save the duke from women and to make all women hate Gondarino, and hence leave him alone; his slanders nearly cause the death of Oriana. The conjunction of misogynist with slanderer may suggest that misogyny, however genial, is far from harmless: it can create a climate in which slander against one woman is likelier to be believed.[16]

Even in plays featuring a misogynist but not a slanderer, women regularly suffer cruel mistreatment, near ruin, or death. The heroine of *Appius and Virginia* is beheaded, partly by the help of the Vice/misogynist Haphazard; Phillip's Patient Grissill is tormented for some sixteen years at the instigation of the Vice/misogynist Politic Persuasion; misogynists appear in all the tormented-wife plays of the early seventeenth century, modelled on the Grissill story—Ilford in *Enforced Marriage*, Fuller in *How a Man May Choose*, Vallenger in *The Fair Maid of Bristow*, the clown in *All's Well*. In *Mariam*, with its misogynist Constabarus, and *Swetnam the Woman-hater*, with its misogynist Swetnam, the heroines are condemned to death; in *The Honest Lawyer*, with its misogynist Vaster, an honest wife is sold to a brothel by her husband; in *The Nightwalker*, with its misogynist Algripe, a young wife narrowly averts being buried alive. In plays where women as a group are libelled in jest, individual women come to grief in earnest. The implication seems to be that misogyny is by no means as harmless as it appears. These plays dramatize an insight of Castiglione's: antifeminist jest is dangerous because, however light-hearted its tone when practiced by conversationalists of superior intellect, it creates in the less sophisticated the habit of contempt.

Almost all the stage misogynists are indigenous to plays mainly about a woman or women. A majority appear in plays where a woman is the title figure—Infidelity in *Mary Magdalene*, Haphazard in *Appius and Virginia*, Ill Report in *Susanna*, Politic Persuasion in *Patient Grissill*, Sextus in *The Rape of Lucrece*, Vallenger in *The Fair Maid of Bristow*, the clown and Enobarbus in *Antony and Cleopatra*, Constabarus in *Mariam*, Laxton (who feigns misogyny for immoral purposes) in *The Roaring Girl*, Algripe in *The Nightwalker*, Troilus in *Troilus and Cressida*, Bosola in *The Duchess of Malfi*. Misogynists also regularly appear in plays with the word *woman* or *women* in the title—Accutus in *Every Woman in Her Humour*, Gondarino in *The Woman-Hater*, Scudmore in *A Woman Is a Weathercock*, Rowland in *The Woman's Prize*, Swetnam in *Swetnam the Woman-hater*, the Cardinal (who, out of venerable Patristic misogyny, "not endures the sight of womankind / About his lodgings" [I.i.50–51]) in *More Dissemblers besides Women*. Other misogynists appear in plays primarily devoted to courtship—Benedick in *Much Ado*, Jacomo in *The Captain*—or marriage—Ilford in *Enforced Marriage*, Fuller in *How a Man May Choose*, the clown in *All's Well*, Posthumus in *Cymbeline*. Most of these plays seem designed to appeal mainly to the women in the audience.

Why are misogynists native to plays about and for women? Misogynistic comment could be a sop to the men in the audience, attending the theatre in tow and applauding at the insistence of some strong-willed Renaissance wife. If that were the case, however, why should misogynists be discredited so frequently? To see a misogynist made a laughing-stock would hardly buck up a henpecked husband. The misogynist is more likely present to initiate comment, pro and con, on the nature of women; the Renaissance found it virtually impossible to focus literary attention on one woman without embarking on discussions about womankind in general.

A number of these plays are almost ritual vindications of Woman, wherein the misogynist performs an antimasque function, embodying the discordant and disruptive elements of reality which must be banished before a woman can achieve wholeness, happiness, human respect. The misogynist objectifies all the doubts, fears, and antagonisms likely to be aroused in any play focussing primarily on women: when he is converted, discredited, or simply drops out of the play, he is intended (not unlike the classical *pharmakos* or scapegoat) to carry the doubts, fears, and antagonisms out of the play with him, leaving the heroine the closing scenes in which to bask in our newly unskeptical approval.

The play with a female protagonist faces special problems of skepticism and hostility which do not trouble the play with a male protagonist: it must overcome a prejudice against women that runs deep in society. The stage misogynist is a tool for overcoming that prejudice through forcing it into the open. At the deepest structural level of such plays, Woman is on trial, as she was on trial in the writings of the formal controversy; the misogynist is her accuser.

A number of plays are structured around a test of character. The misogynist, who sometimes proposes the test himself, predicts that the female hero will fail. Politic Persuasion in *Patient Grissill* proposes the grueling and inhuman test of the hero's patience; Grissill's husband plays defender, comparing Grissill's virtues to those of the formal defender's *exempla*—Dido, Penelope, Thisbe, Cassandra—while Politic predicts failure: "Try hir that waye and by myne honestie I sweare, / You shall see hir decline from Vertues so rife, / And alter topsie turuie hir saintish lyfe: / Hir pacyence quicklye shall chaunged bee" (Sig. Eiiᵛ). Because he argues that Grissill will fail on account of her feminine nature, her test becomes a test of womankind, a sex Politic claims is "stoberne and vnkynde / . . . Ether brauling, iaulynge, sknappinge, or snarringe" (Sig. Ciii). Politic even manages to convince Grissill's husband that wife torment is a sign of virility: "I sweare by mine honor ye shalbe deempt a man" (Sig. Giiᵛ). When Grissill passes her test, Politic tries valiantly to make her out as the one earthly exception to womankind's general vile-ness; lest we take him at his word, the dramatist peoples the play with other good women, from the nurse to the Countess of Pango.

Mary Magdalene undergoes two trials: she fails the first, succumbing to the temptations of the flesh, but passes the second—fidelity to the Christ who has rescued her from a life of sin. The misogynist sub-Vice Malicious Judgment predicts that Mary will prove unfaithful to Christ, women's nature being what it is: "Womens heartes turne oft as doth the wynde" (Sig. [G3]ᵛ). He is proved wrong and disappears from the play; immediately after his exit, Mary reënters accompanied by the allegorical figure Justification. Ill Report in *Susanna* expects an easy victory over the hero, on grounds of a precedent central to the formal controversy: the Devil has conferred on him "the blessing giuen to the Serpent which tempted *Eue*" (Sig. Aiii). Susanna is accused in a courtroom trial; when she is acquitted, vilification of women is stamped out with unusual thoroughness: not only the two unjust elders, but even the Vice Ill Report, are executed. The misogynist Sextus in *The Rape of Lucrece* suggests the test of wives; if womankind is not so completely vindicated by Lucrece's steadfast chastity, since most wives in this play fail the test, her vindication shines all the more brightly for their failure; the misogynist's predictions once again prove false.

On the public level, the misogyny in the plays may represent distrust of civic and civilian society, a fear that a demilitarized, urban society will be an emasculated society. The banishment of misogyny in some plays represents the absorption of more primitive, battle-oriented elements into the hermaphroditic fabric of civilized life, through the recognition that gentleness and nonviolence are attributes not of the ideal woman but of the ideal human.

On the personal level, the misogyny that must be overcome in the plays may represent adolescent fears—fear of sex, fear of women and their mysterious ways, fear of the murky unknown that is the adult world: the banishment of misogyny in some plays marks a rite of passage to adulthood. Here the frequent remarks about mothers are intriguing: Gondarino in *The Woman-Hater* and Posthumus in *Cymbeline* hate themselves because born of woman; Synon in *2 Iron Age* hates "all woman kinde," declaring "nought more grieues me then to thinke, / A woman was my mother" (I.i). Defenders of women conventionally charged the misogynist with having turned upon his own mother. Considering that almost all misogynists accuse women of sexual wrongdoing (those who do not do so appear alongside slanderers who do), the pattern is suggestive: while dwelling upon women's sexual appetites, a man turns against his mother and against women in general.

Renaissance writers needed no acquaintanceship with Freud to observe that there comes a time in the life of a maturing child when he learns about sex and sees his parents in a whole new light. Whether or not one has harbored Oedipal longings, the transformation of a mother from nurturer to sexual being in a child's eyes is bound to come as a shock. The recoil from a mother's sexuality is nowhere clearer than in *Hamlet,* but it is sublimated in many other Renaissance texts.

Misogyny, as I read Renaissance treatments of it, is an expected phase of a young man's life. Under normal circumstances, he will grow out of it, fall in love, and marry into normal heterosexual society. Young men in these plays who turn misogynist after a repulse by a young woman reveal the bumpiness of the road that leads to such normality. Abnormal circumstances can cause a delayed adolescent misogyny like Hamlet's; and if a character does not grow out of his misogynistic phase, psychopathology may be suspected: this is the case with Ferdinand in *The Duchess of Malfi,* who, dwelling with lascivious horror on his sister's sex life, retreats neurotically from all sexuality.

Jacomo is not the only stage misogynist who fears women: Algripe and Swetnam suspect themselves of impotence; the aggressive stance of the stage misogynist often masked fear of normal sexuality, as the braggadocio's militant posture masked cowardice. It is appropriate that the opening scene of *The Captain,* whose title figure Jacomo hides his fear of women behind a mask of soldierly woman hatred, should set the stage with an antifeminist conversation between Lodovico and Piso, identified in the *dramatis personae* as "two cowardly gulls."

Surprising though it may be, the character type closest to the stage misogynist is the transvestite heroine. Rosalind and Portia, as I have shown, take on the false valor of the braggadocio, as does the title figure of *Swetnam the Woman-hater.* Where the stage misogynist's aggressive posture conceals fear of women, the female transvestite adopts "a swashing and a martial outside" (I.iii.122) for fear of men—overtly, for fear of rape; covertly, I suggest, for fear of sexuality itself. It is not a neurotic fear, like Ferdinand's, but plain, normal adolescent panic at the thought of the undiscovered country of sex—a fear that makes them want to buy a little time by hiding behind a mask. Why else does Rosalind retain her male apparel once in the Forest of Arden? Surely she does not conceive of Silvius, Corin, or Jaques as potential rapists. She wants time to relax with Orlando, to get to know him, before sex is an issue. She wants, for a little time, to postpone growing up.[17]

The closeness of these two character types is apparent when Rosalind, as female transvestite, adopts the role of the stage misogynist (*As You Like It,* II.ii.361–377, IV.i.116–179). Celia is irate: "You have simply misused our sex" (IV.i.205), but the disguised Rosalind abuses men too, most particularly the man she loves. That, in the germinal stages of sexuality, abuse of the opposite sex is itself an expression of sexual interest is known to every girl whose pigtails have ever been pulled by the handsomest boy in the class—or at least that's what she hopes. As if the question of women and misogyny is not pestered enough by paradox already, I will bring up the fact that ritual slanging matches between choruses of men and women were a feature of ancient fertility rites.[18] What was ultimately driven away by such abuse was not the opposite sex but sterility—an interpretation suggested by the fact that most ritual abuse, in the rites that gave rise to both tragedy and comedy, was directed at the forces that oppose fertility. The persistence of such patterns, from the rites of preclassical Greece through the comedies of the High Renaissance through the pigtail pulling of modern life, suggests that something in the psychological makeup of humankind renders hostility to the opposite sex a logical first step toward sexual consummation and fertility.[19]

The ways in which society pressures girls to grow out of their tomboy phase with its intense female friendships, a phase which Shakespeare's transvestite heroines clearly exemplify, and into the adult world of femininity and heterosexuality, are well understood.[20] But literature reflects society's tactics for propelling men into heterosexual adulthood too. Since "the world must be peopled," misogynists are pried loose from a soldier's world and transvestite heroines are called from the bosom of an intimate female friendship. Both pass through the latent homosexuality of adolescence, where the girl guards the chrysalis of her sexual self by dressing like a boy and the boy by cracking jokes against girls, to emerge into that domestic hermaphrodism that is marriage.

For the women, much is lost when femininity strikes: as Dusinberre says, "Viola is Viola in her breeches" (p. 266). Some modern feminists would argue that such heroines might better hunt forever with Diana's virgin band, and the refusal to grow up and marry *is* an option considered by those heroines who can afford to consider it: Julia revises in an instant our whole view of the action in the 1600 *Patient Grissil* by refusing to marry in a world where wives are treated like Grissil: "Why this it is to be married, thus you see those that goe to wooe, goe to woe . . . Sir *Owen* is maistred by his Mistris, that makes you [men] mad, poore *Grissil* is martred by her Lord, that makes you merrie, for I alwaies wish that a woman may neuer meete better bargaines, when sheele thrust her sweet libertie into the hands of a man: fye vpon you" (IV.iii.176–214). The female misogamist was expected, like Beatrice, to mellow into marriage; but Julia ends the play a confirmed bachelor, calling upon fellow "mayden batchelers . . . those that liue in that freedome and loue it, those that know the war of mariage and hate it," to "set their hands to my bill, which is rather to dye a mayde and leade Apes in hell, then to liue a wife

and be continually in hell" (V.ii.275–283). At the end of *The London Prod-*
igal, Delia refuses a marriage proposal after observing the matrimonial
torments of the play's Grissill figure: "My vow's in heaven, on earth to
live alone; / Husbands, howsoever good, I will have none" (V.i).

But of the several models of marriage the Renaissance evolved, the
marriage of reformed misogynist to benevolent virago, as we see it in
Benedick and Beatrice, Jacomo and Frank, Algripe and Martia (this last
a case of misogynist marrying female transvestite) is the most admirable:
these couples meet each other half way—the men growing more "feminine" through their abdication of the misogynist's macho pose, the women
growing more "masculine" through their assertiveness. Granted, this
combining of stereotypical qualities is not as admirable as abandoning
sexual stereotypes altogether would be; but the hermaphroditic marriage
of misogynist and virago is a step in the right direction. Other models,
from the eternal fight for the breeches to the settling of the wild prodigal
into adult sobriety through the cathartic effect of letting him abuse his
Patient Grissill wife for the first few years of marriage, simply can't
compare.

An important stage misogynist is Enobarbus in *Antony and Cleopatra:*
understanding how Shakespeare intended his misogyny is essential to
understanding how Shakespeare meant us to interpret Cleopatra's relationship with Antony, and this lies at the heart of the play. Unless we
know whether Shakespeare agreed with Enobarbus that in the face of
military or political duty women "should be esteemed nothing" (I.ii.141–
144), we cannot know whether the play is high tragedy, a political fable
that happens to end with some deaths, or a cynical farce.

Enobarbus has a soldier's contempt for women, and the woman he
dislikes most is Cleopatra; not despite his recognizing her extreme attractiveness (the greatest accolades to Cleopatra's beauty and charm are
his), but because he recognizes her extreme attractiveness. He dislikes
her because he fears her: he sees her relationship with Antony as destructive—to Antony, to the army, to Rome, to all whose fortunes are dependent on Antony's, including himself. He is right, as far as he goes; but
while others have seen that relationship as both dangerous and beautiful,
Enobarbus sees only the danger. He is a spokesman for Roman military
values. Since Shakespeare invented Enobarbus, though, many critics assume that he is Shakespeare's mouthpiece, that his view of the action,
one-sided as it is, is the correct one. Misogyny accepted at face value,
Antony and Cleopatra joins the ranks of *The Widow's Tears* and *The Dutch*
Courtesan as one more antifeminist tract adapted for the theater.

Enobarbus's behavior, however, shows him anything but a mouthpiece for Shakespeare: Shakespeare undermines Enobarbus's credibility

as authors so often discredited stage misogynists. In I.ii, Antony's ambivalent response to his wife's death is dramatized seriously: "There's a great spirit gone! Thus did I desire it. / What our contempts do often hurl from us, / We wish it ours again. . . . / She's good, being gone, / The hand could pluck her back that shoved her on" (ll. 126–131). At this point Enobarbus, in the comic tradition of the stage misogynist, bustles in with a cheery packet of slanders on Cleopatra and women in general. He cannot know at first that his tone is inappropriate to Antony's present mood, but even after he is apprised of Fulvia's death he is not astute enough to sense Antony's new seriousness; he continues in a frivolous tone which proves offensive: "When it pleaseth their deities to take the wife of a man from him, it shows to man the tailors of the earth, comforting therein, that when old robes are worn out there are members to make new. If there were no more women but Fulvia, then had you indeed a cut, and the case to be lamented. This grief is crowned with consolation. Your old smock brings forth a new petticoat. And indeed the tears live in an onion that should water this sorrow" (I.ii.167–177). Antony says tersely, "No more light answers." He has just called Fulvia "a great spirit"; Enobarbus's reducing her to an "old smock" shows insensitivity to Antony's moods. Cleopatra immediately senses and responds to Antony's new seriousness: she understands him better than Enobarbus does.

In II.ii, Enobarbus ham-fistedly intrudes on delicate negotiations between Antony and Caesar. Antony is embarrassed, as Hal is embarrassed when Falstaff presumes on their friendship by jesting before the king. Both Hal and Antony are trying to live down a reputation for riotousness, gained partly by their treating social inferiors as drinking buddies; neither wants the process of reinstatement into respectability undermined by the intrusion of those with whom he has been unduly familiar. Antony rebukes Enobarbus by reminding him of his inferior rank: "Thou art a soldier only. Speak no more." Enobarbus, stung, tries to cast himself as a choric figure: "That truth should be silent I had almost forgot"; like Iago, he represents himself as the blunt soldier who must tell the truth in whatever rude terms. Antony insists that such bluntness is inappropriate in exalted company: "You wrong this presence, therefore speak no more." Caesar agrees, allowing the truth of Enobarbus's words but protesting his "manner" (II.ii.108–114). Enobarbus has shown himself a boor. Would Shakespeare create a boor to be his mouthpiece?

Finally, in III.xiii, the "Thyreus" scene, Caesar sends a messenger to try to wean Cleopatra from Antony; Enobarbus, whose ability to judge people's moods has never been acute, assumes that Cleopatra will leave Antony and takes this as a precedent for himself: "Sir, sir, thou art so leaky / That we must leave thee to thy sinking, for / Thy dearest quit

thee" (ll. 63–65). Despite the unflattering image of a rat deserting a sinking ship, the usual interpretation is that as a choric figure Enobarbus
embodies audience feelings; at this low point, where Antony has dis-
graced himself by fleeing the battle of Actium, the departure of audience
sympathy from Antony is said to be objectified in Enobarbus's decamp-
ing. Audience sympathy returns when Enobarbus returns. (Enobarbus
in fact never does return, but his dying of remorse is supposed to accomplish the aim). If this is the correct interpretation, if Enobarbus is pure
choric figure, then like a chorus he is right in everything he says, right
at least in reflecting the author's views. But there is another possible
interpretation of the Thyreus scene. Both Enobarbus and Cleopatra spend
the scene deciding whether to desert Antony. By scene's end, Enobarbus
has decided to leave, and Cleopatra has decided to stay. Her decision is
foolish in practical terms; his is dishonorable in military terms and dis-
loyal in human terms. Shakespeare always treated sympathetically the
character who ignored his own welfare to stay with a master whose fortunes had declined, from Adam in *As You Like It* to Kent and the Fool in
King Lear. It doesn't matter that Enobarbus is wiser or more circumspect
in this scene than Cleopatra; it doesn't matter that her loyalty expresses
itself in a desire for one last orgy. What matters is that he leaves, and she
stays. If audience sympathy departs with Enobarbus, then audience sympathy will have to learn, as Enobarbus learns, that that was a mistake.

Enobarbus does perform limited choric functions insofar as he, along
with Scarus, Philo, Octavius, and others, articulates the Roman view of
the action; in a play which seems deliberately to hold in suspension opposing perspectives on the same characters and actions, the Roman view
cannot be discounted as wholly "wrong"; but to see Enobarbus as Shakespeare's mouthpiece is to grant the Roman view an unqualified approval
which the play's action and tone do not warrant. In a play whose very
meaning seems to lie in its ambivalence, the idea of a mouthpiece character is incongruous. But why, then, did Shakespeare invent Enobarbus?

As stage misogynist Enobarbus performs two important functions which
critics have neglected. First, he is a foil to Cleopatra. Enobarbus and
Cleopatra are Antony's closest friends; one deserts him and the other
remains faithful. Practicality, military astuteness, and correct political
opinions cannot stand up to a crisis the way love can. Second, Enobarbus
is introduced because the surest way to control a revolutionary is to give
him a seat in Parliament. Cleopatra's actions are bound to provoke antifeminist thoughts in the audience; Shakespeare knew, as he had known
when he introduced Mercutio and Touchstone into romantic plays to
make wisecracks about romantic love, that it is best to objectify these
thoughts, to articulate them forthrightly so that they can be measured
against characters' actual behavior.

From the time of Politick Persuasion in *Patient Grissill* to the time of Sextus in *The Rape of Lucrece,* misogynists had been stock figures in plays with female heroes. They grumble along through the play making anti-feminist remarks and predicting that the heroine will prove unfaithful if tested, right up to the point where the test comes and the heroines prove them wrong. Enobarbus, who is wrong in his prediction that Cleopatra will "quit" Antony, and who is written out of the play before Cleopatra's triumphal death scene, is one of their number.

*   *   *   *   *

Critics discuss the stage Machiavel as an important conventional char-acter type on the basis of a very few existing examples. Far more stage misogynists exist; but as a type, they have been sadly neglected and, I think, largely misunderstood. Critics have been wrong to assume that dramatists agreed with the misogynists they created: it is difficult to find, among the more than three dozen stage misogynists I have discussed, a single one whose misogynistic pronouncements are not undercut by context or deflated by humor. Genuine contempt for women may emerge as an authorial attitude in a number of Renaissance literary contexts, but the character of the stage misogynist is not one of them. Paradoxically, the stage misogynist is a figure belonging to the defense of women.

NOTES

1. E. C. Wilson, "Shakespeare's Enobarbus," in *Joseph Quincy Adams: Memorial Studies,* p. 392. The two most reasonable discussions of drama-tized misogyny I have come across are both by female critics—Katharine Rogers (*Troublesome Helpmate,* pp. 118–23) and Juliet Dusinberre (*Shake-speare and the Nature of Women,* pp. 185–93).

2. *Swetnam the Woman-hater: The Controversy and the Play,* ed. Coryl Crandall.

3. Lyly, *Euphues: The Anatomy of Wyt,* p. 41.

4. Asked "Dost thou rail upon the ladies as thou wert wont?" a former misogynist in *The Malcontent* replies, "I were better roast a live cat, and might do it with more safety" (V.i.20–23). Given the assertiveness of Renaissance women, such pronouncements may have been more than mere convention.

5. *Shakespeare and the Nature of Women,* p. 185.

6. L. W. Cushman, *The Devil and the Vice in English Dramatic Literature Before Shakespeare.*

7. Janice Hays, "Those 'soft and delicate desires': *Much Ado* and the Distrust of Women," in *The Woman's Part,* pp. 81–82.

8. *Haec-Vir* comments, "For you [men] to cut the hayre of your vpper lips, familiar heere in England, euery where else almost [is] thought

vnmanly" (Sig. B2ᵛ). Is Shakespeare possibly attributing Beatrice's remarks on the effeminacy of the beardless to Messina prejudice? Would Shakespeare's audience, at least those who saw the play during the *hic mulier* years, have viewed Benedick's shaving and Beatrice's loving the shaven Benedick as behavior proper to an English couple?

9. Gondarino's misogyny also represents the backlash against Petrarchan excess, as I have shown in chapter 8, above. Such a backlash also helps explain the otherwise poorly motivated misogyny of Hercules in *The Fawn,* who creates anti-blazons: "Oh, this is the fair lady with the foul teeth. Nature's hand shook when she was in making, for the red that should have spread her cheeks, nature let fall upon her nose, the white of her skin slipped into her eyes, and the gray of her eyes leapt before his time into her hair, and the yellowness of her hair fell without providence into her teeth" (III.i.79–85).

10. *Middle-Class Culture,* p. 469.

11. As befits a misogynist, Bawdin himself has been a soldier, and "serued in Garryson" (Sig. Diᵛ). He notes that women and war don't mix, except that some married men make valiant soldiers, fighting "by waye of desperation, chosynge rather to dye . . . then longer to liue vnder such yoke of seruytude" [i.e., marriage] (Sig. Diiᵛ).

12. Joyce H. Sexton in *The Slandered Woman in Shakespeare* discusses the slanderer but, disappointingly, not the slandered woman: that is, she attempts no explanation of the fact that in Shakespeare's four main plots turning upon slander the victim is always a woman. Sexton makes some good points about the slanderer, but her discussion of the "proofs" brought against Hero in *Much Ado* is most unsatisfactory, and her identification of slander with envy proves very inadequate to cope with *The Winter's Tale.* The important topic of the slanderer needs further exploration; many critics actually confuse the slanderer with the misogynist.

13. For example, the slanderers Greenshield and Featherstone, connected with the Susanna story in being called "two wicked elders" (*Northward Ho,* I.iii.44).

14. Shakespeare never names Susanna in his plays, but the first line of the ballad *The Constancy of Susanna,* dating to the early 1560s, is quoted by Sir Toby Belch in *Twelfth Night;* and Shakespeare alludes to the Susanna story in references to Daniel in *The Merchant of Venice.*

15. "Ile broach thee on my steele, that done, straight murder / One of thy basest Groomes, and lay you both / Graspt arme in arme, on thy adulterate bed, / Then call in witnesse . . . / So shalt thou die, thy death be scandalous, / Thy name be odious" (Vol. 5, p. 224).

16. Castiglione had connected the misogynist with the slanderer; although one speaker in *The Courtier* views misogynistic jests as harmless unless they drift into slander (impugning a woman's chastity), Lord Julian regards both as dangerous. See chapter 2.

17. Shakespeare does not often write pure "humours" comedy, but he sometimes uses humours characters as what Northrop Frye calls "blocking characters"—characters who stand in the way of the comic resolu-

tion. (See *Anatomy of Criticism* and *A Natural Perspective: The Development of Shakespearean Comedy and Romance*.) Since comic resolution for Shakespeare almost always includes marriage and/or the reunion of estranged spouses, the humours with which he endows these blocking characters are those which work against marriage—the ascetic scholarship of the lords in *Love's Labor's Lost,* the jealousy of Leontes in *The Winter's Tale* and Posthumus in *Cymbeline,* the misogyny of Posthumus and of Benedick in *Much Ado,* the withdrawal from courtship into transvestite disguise of Rosalind in *As You Like It* and Viola in *Twelfth Night.* To these we must add the shrewishness of Kate in *The Taming of the Shrew:* since she must be cured of this antimarital humour before comic resolution can be reached, her shrewishness brings her into structural parallel with the female transvestite and the misogynist, and her humour may, in psychological terms, be as much a self-protective device as theirs. However, her cure is much more protracted and painful than theirs: Rosalind changes clothes offstage and comes forth to wed; Benedick's "Happy are they that hear their detractions and can put them to mending" (*Much Ado,* II.iii.237–38) is an easy conversion. Comparing Kate with characters who perform the same structural function in other plays only heightens my sense of the unnecessary viciousness with which Shakespeare treats her.

18. See Cornford, *The Origin of Attic Comedy,* pp. 110–111.

19. Documenting extensively the primitive dread of the dangers of contact with the opposite sex, Ernest Crawley persuades me that for the human animal, sex has never been comfortably regarded as "doing what comes naturally" (*The Mystic Rose*).

20. See, for example, Germaine Greer's discussion in *The Female Eunuch,* pp. 77–83.

CHAPTER TWELVE

Swetnam the Woman-hater Arraigned by Women

After the publication of all the essays in the Swetnam controversy, probably around 1618, a play was acted which grew out of that controversy—the anonymous *Swetnam the Woman-hater Arraigned by Women.* Besides crowning the Swetnam war, that flower of the formal controversy, the play makes sophisticated comments on the nature of femininity and masculinity, taking up issues raised during the transvestite controversy; and this dramatized defense of women makes use of that character type which evolved out of both controversies, the stage misogynist. Joseph Swetnam, author of *The Arraignment of Lewd, Idle, Froward and Unconstant Women,* is staged as a character: this is the clearest extant case of a stage misogynist developing directly from a *persona* of the formal controversy, and the fact that he is so similar to other stage misogynists says a good deal about the origin and nature of the type.

Besides the fact that the play incorporates a formal controversy dramatized as judicial oration and feeds our nostalgia (such as it may be) for the formal controversy with a few morsels of historical and literary example, a large cast of issues common in both Renaissance controversies about women step forth in this play as if making a curtain call—the relative culpability of the sexes, feminine seductiveness and coyness versus masculine Petrarchan wiles, masculine justice versus feminine mercy, alleged feminine cruelty, sinfulness, frailty, deceit, scolding, gullibility, patience, timidity, aggression, vengefulness, talkativeness, inability to keep secrets. The returning-soldier figure appears, as does transvestite disguise; imagery of chivalric mistress is set against imagery of citizen's wife, while images of hermaphrodism pervade the play.

But the author of *Swetnam the Woman-hater* accomplishes much more than simply to bring out all the old motifs for one last bow: s/he actively challenges stereotype, exposes prejudice, probes the affinities of misogyny and jest, explores fresh ways of viewing the sexes. With extraordinary deftness, the unknown author of this now obscure comedy has woven a delightful and really interesting literary fabric from a large number of threads gathered together from the very controversies I have been examining, and the play makes a satisfying finale to this study.

Swetnam is the subplot's major figure. Fleeing England for Sicily after the uproar created by *The Arraignment,* he sets up as a fencing instructor named Misogynos, with the grudging help of his servant, the clown Swash. Swetnam's role is limited to quoting *The Arraignment* to prospective students, until he is caught up in the main plot.

In the main plot, Atticus king of Sicily mourns the loss of his sons, one killed in battle, the other long missing in action. He locks up his daughter Leonida, since many promising youths are dying of love for her. The missing son Lorenzo, returning to Sicily in disguise to observe the kingdom's health, witnesses a sinister situation—the increasing power of the ambitious, treacherous Lord Nicanor—and a more immediate crisis: Leonida is discovered in compromising circumstances with her young man, Lisandro, whom she has been unable to marry because their fathers are enemies. Atticus invokes a law requiring death for the prime offender in a sexual transgression, banishment for the lesser offender. The story, from a tale by Juan de Flores,[1] was well-chosen for purposes of the debate about women: because Leonida and Lisandro each admit guilt to save the other, more general issues must be raised; the trial becomes a debate over the relative culpability of the sexes. Lorenzo disguised as an Amazon defends women; Swetnam, alias Misogynos, acts as advocate for men. When a judgement in favor of men is brought in by an all-male tribunal, Leonida is condemned to die, Lisandro banished. After Leonida's execution and Lisandro's attempted suicide are reported, the queen and Lorenzo (still supposed an Amazon) plot revenge on Misogynos, who makes their task easier by claiming to have fallen desperately in love with "Atlanta," the Amazon. Using "her" as a lure, the women trap Misogynos, arraign him at their own tribunal, gag him, and torment him. With the speed and improbability which characterize the fifth act in so many Jacobean plays, Leonida and Lisandro return alive, Atticus and Nicanor repent, the lovers are reunited, Lorenzo unmasks and is welcomed home. In the epilogue, Swetnam recants and is pardoned.

The trial scene uses the judicial oration as rhetoricians had originally intended: it was an oral form, designed for courtroom use. The basic format is accusation and defense. While each advocate is in theory to argue the innocence of one sex and the guilt of the other, women are on the defensive from the beginning. The trial scene is introduced with chivalric rather than judicial imagery: advocates for each sex are recruited by heralds with royal proclamations in the medieval fashion; once found, they are proclaimed "champions." This chivalric/judicial blend, combining Speght's controlling metaphor with Sowernam's, had a long tradition in the formal controversy, where defenders of women had often seen themselves as "champions"; though their oratorical methods were judicial, their motives were chivalrous: they wanted to defend damsels in distress. This confusion between justice and chivalry has long been an obstacle to feminism. A cherished argument against women's rights has always been that the demand for rights is unladylike: true ladies can get anything they want from true gentlemen without resort to such demands. Women's pursuit of justice has been blocked by men's appeal to chivalry. Men argue that women will be the ultimate losers in the struggle for equal rights; when women receive equal pay for equal work, men will not open doors for them or give them a seat in the bus. Chivalry is itself a subtle method of maintaining distinctions between sexes, posited as it is on the assumption that women are weak and defenseless. This is one of many problems limiting the usefulness of the formal defense of women. And this is exactly where Lorenzo, disguised as Atlanta, begins his defense:

> It is an honour farre beyond my weaknesse,
> (Most equall Iudges) that I am accepted,
> I but a woman, before men to plead,
> Dumbe feare and bashfulnesse to speake before
> Bold Orators of State, men graue and wise,
> That can at euery breathing pause, correct
> The slipp'ry passages of a womans speech:
> But yet withall my hopes are doubly arm'd . . .
> First, that my bashfull weaknesse claymes excuse,
> And is to speake before such temp'rate Iudges,
> Who in their wisdome will, no doubt, conniue
> At small defects in me a silly woman.
>
> (III.iii.45–57)

One lawyer comments, "Smoothly put on"; another remarks, "A quaint insinuation" (III.iii.58). They rightly see this stance as a clever rhetorical pose, which disarms the opposition by suggesting that misogynists are unchivalrous, that only cowards bring charges against such weak and defenseless creatures. Female helplessness is also vital to Atlanta's case: "she" will shortly argue that women are putty in the hands of seducers and not to be blamed for sexual transgressions. But Lorenzo is chivalrous even out of the courtroom: witness his incensed reaction to Swetnam's antifeminist jibes in III.ii. The chivalric flavor of the formal defense, imported into this play, is essentially medieval, intimately related to courtly love and Mariolatry. A world where women's defender is a Redcrosse Knight, the misogynist the dragon, will not be given to debating the sex-role stereotyping of Una.

Atlanta's opening remarks are described by one lawyer, a connoisseur of the judicial oration, as "a promising *Exordium*" (III.iii.65). In the *narratio,* Atlanta outlines the facts of the case, which she casts plainly as a defense of women against a charge: she outlines not the Leonida/Lisandro case, but Misogynos's allegations against women:

> I need not tell you what I come to prooue:
> That rayling Woman-hater hath alreadie
> With his foule breath belcht forth into the Ayre,
> The shamelesse cause in question, and doth charge
> The supple wax, the courteous-natur'd woman,
> As blamefull for receiuing the impression
> Of Iron-hearted man . . .
>
> (III.iii.66–72)

Atlanta follows the advice of classical rhetoricians in flattering the judges by intimating that they are already familiar with the case; but this is not the case that was to be tried: casting Misogynos as plaintiff, women as defendant, puts women at a considerable disadvantage. The argument should have been put as a disjunctive syllogism: Either A or B is guilty; if not A, then B. (Or, better, if B, then not A.) Reducing the case to whether A is guilty as charged is a serious tactical error. It was an error which defenders had been making all along.

Misogynos interrupts, objecting to Atlanta's claim that women are feeble and passive: "In all their passions, women are impetuous, / And beyond men, ten times more violent" (III.iii.92–93). Surprisingly, since the admission damages "her" position, Atlanta yields this point but shrugs it off as begging the question: "I grant you that. But who begins the motion, / And is first agent? . . . / That's the cause in question" (III.iii.94–96). Atlanta is right about the question here: the trial is not a full-blown controversy about women; it is limited to one facet of the controversy— which sex is to blame for sexual offenses. But although limited, this question had often been addressed in the formal controversy and is still an important issue: similar arguments are heard in modern rape trials. Atlanta argues that men, accomplished seducers, are more to blame; Misogynos blames women, who use their charms to allure. Historical/ literary examples are used as proof: Atlanta argues that Helen of Troy was raped, a prey to Paris's lust, Misogynos that Helen tempted Paris with her "inticing beautie" (III.iii.98). Atlanta's major argument is that women, both helpless and compassionate, fall easy prey to masculine wiles—the Petrarchan lover's pose of abject misery used with the calculated intent to seduce:

> Lust tempteth Beautie:
> Witnesse the vowes, the oaths, the protestations,
> And Crocadile teares of base dissembling men,

To winne their shamelesse purpose: Whereof missing,
Then but obserue their Gifts, their Messages,
Their wanton Letters, and their amorous Sonnets,
Whereby they vent the smoke of their affections,
Readie to blind poore women, and put out
The Eye of Reason. . . .
. . . They at hand with fained languishment,
Make shew as if they meant to dye for loue,
When they but swelter in the reeke of Lust.
But heere's not all: for if this all preuaile not,
Then they are vp againe, and with pale cheekes,
Like some poore Starueling, or some Mimick Ghost,
They stalke into the presence of their Mistris,
Fold vp their armes, hang downe their wanton heads,
Cast loue-sicke glances, and as wofull Commas,
In this dumbe Oratorie, now and then they breathe
A passionate sigh, whereat the gentle nature
Of milde compassionate woman once relenting,
Straight they fall out into such sweet complaints
Of their sad suffrings, tuning words of Art,
Able to melt a gentle Eye in teares.
                                        (III.iii.101–127)

   If the image of courtly lady permeates Atlanta's remarks, the private
theater's old stereotype of citizen's wife as amateur prostitute permeates
Misogynos's; the one speaks the language of courtly and Petrarchan love,
the other the language of commerce. "What a foolish reason, / Is it to
say, Lust tempteth garish Beautie," Misogynos counters.

                    There's not
A Citie Tradesman throughout all the Streets,
From the East Chappell, to the Westerne Palace,
But knowes full well the garish setting out
Of Beautie in their shops will call in Customers
To cheapen ware: Beautie set forth to sale,
Wantons the bloud, and is mans tempting Stale . . .
And this is woman, who well knowes her strength,
And trimmes her Beautie forth in blushing Pride.
                                        (III.iii.151–162)

Damning "Painting, Curling, Powdring / . . . Periwigs, pin knots,
Bordrings" (III.iii.176–177), he adduces coyness and feminine wiles:

They are instructed by like Art,
How to giue entertainment, and keepe distance
With all their Sutors, Friends, and Fauourites,
When to deny, and when to feed their hopes,

Now to draw on, and then againe put off,
To frowne and smile, to weepe and laugh out-right,
All in a breath, and all to trayne poore man
Into his ruin.

(III.iii.181–188)

The two advocates conclude with a few thrusts and parries of historical/
literary example: Misogynos adduces Helen, Cleopatra, and Messalina
as paragons of lust and deceit; Atlanta cites insatiate men.

When the verdict is handed down ("that women are the first and worst
temptations / To loue and lustfull folly" [III.iii.259–260]), Atlanta announces intention to appeal: "You are impartiall [i.e., prejudiced], and
we doe appeale / From you to Iudges more indifferent: / You are all men,
and in this weightie businesse, / Graue Women should haue sate as Iudges
with you" (III.iii.262–265). It was a motif frequent in contemporary
drama—a woman fruitlessly seeking justice in a male-dominated court.

The trial scene dramatizes the formal controversy's confrontation between detractor and defender by means of the formal controversy's favored literary form, the judicial oration. (Misogynos is called an "orator,"
IV.iii.6.) The rest of the play takes up the woman question as the hermaphrodite controversy typically did—as part of action and dialogue.

The action suggests a different verdict on the case. As to who is to
blame for the sexual indiscretion, there is some ambiguity. Although
Lisandro steals into Leonida's chamber, against her express command-
ment that he see her no more, he rationalizes this by interpreting her
command as an oblique invitation. This is difficult to judge. Once he
appears, though, she lets him remain; the action here ratifies the faithful
Iago's opinion: "To say the truth, / Both Sexes equally should beare the
blame; / For both offend alike" (IV.i.11–13). But in two other instances,
men employ the masculine wiles on which Atlanta had based "her" case.
Nicanor feigns love for Leonida: he hopes to improve his chances of
succeeding Atticus by marrying his daughter. His Petrarchan religious
diction ("my owne harts blisse . . . the dew of her coelestiall breath"
[I.i.182–191]) is undercut by his revealing to his servant Scanfardo his
true intentions: "Nothing then / Is wanting but her loue; that once ob-
tain'd / Sicill is ours. *Scanfardoe!* if we win, / Thou shalt be Lord *Nicanor*,
I the King" (I.i.196–199). Misogynos's Petrarchan passion for Atlanta
amounts to just what Atlanta had argued, in the trial, such passions usually amount to—disguised lust. The audience is left for some time believing that Misogynos's love is genuine—one more misogynist comically
falling in love, like Benedick in *Much Ado*. Misogynos deceives even his
servant, in whom he usually confides, by posing as the stereotyped Petrarchan: "Looke I not pale? / Are not my armes infolded? my eyes fixt, /
My head deiected, my words passionate? / . . . I tell thee, *Swash,* I am

in loue (IV.iii.8–19)—surely a deliberate echo of Atlanta's court-room portrait of Petrarchan seducers ("with *pale* cheekes, / [They] *fold vp their armes, hang downe their wanton heads,* / . . . they breathe / A *passionate sigh*" [III.iii.117–123, italics mine]). After Atlanta pretends to yield, Misogynos comes forward in his true colors: when Swash asks him, "Doe you loue / This Lasse sincerely?" he replies, "Ha, ha, ha. Loue? that were a iest indeed, / To passe away the time for sport, or so; / Th'are made for nothing else: / And he that loues vm longer, is a foole" (V.ii.82–85). There follows another deliberate echo, this time of Misogynos's diction in the trial scene, where he had blamed all sexual offense on "deluding woman" (III.iii.97): to Swash's " 'Tis pittie to delude her, Sir," Misogynos replies, "Away, you Asse. / Delude? what are they good for else?" (V.ii.89). Misogynos thus ratifies his opponent's main thesis: sexual offenses are initiated by "flattring and periur'd man" (III.iii.97).

Coyness, another of Misogynos's allegations in the trial, is an issue in the play. Misogynos had claimed, "They are instructed . . . how to giue entertainment, and keepe distance / With all their Sutors . . . Now to draw on, and then againe put off / . . . and all to trayne poore man / Into his ruine" (III.iii.181–188). Leonida's coyness has supposedly ruined many men. Her father locks her up as a public service: "She must not haue her libertie to match, / The Girle is wanton, coy, and fickle too: / How many Princes hath the froward Elfe / Set at debate, desiring but her loue?" (I.i.161–164). Atticus's charges here echo the title of Swetnam's *Arraignment:* he calls Leonida wanton (cf. Swetnam's "lewd"), fickle (cf. Swetnam's "vnconstant"), and, like Swetnam, "froward." Coyness, inconstancy, and frowardness are interrelated: a woman coyly draws on a number of suitors, not intending constancy to any, out of frowardness (perverse wilfulness). Also related are cruelty and disdain: although Leonida has been loved by "the chiefe Italian Princes . . . their Loues / Were quitted with contempt and crueltie: / And many of our braue Sicilian Youths / Haue sacrific'd their liues to her disdaine" (I.iii.47–50). The play challenges this cluster of Petrarchan charges. Far from glorying in the number of men perishing for love of her, Leonida does not believe these stories. Accused of "too much crueltie / To one that dearely loues you," Leonida is unable to imagine any such suitor: "Whom in the name of wonder?" she inquires (II.ii.67–69). Leonida is absolutely constant to Lisandro; her receiving him into her chamber is hardly coyness. Traditionally, the lady's constancy to one suitor was called inconstancy by other suitors; the play belittles this. Iago quashes the charge of lethal disdain. When another argues, "Her disdaine . . . hath bin the cause / Of many hopefull Youths vntimely end," Iago says that the youths' love for Leonida did not obligate her to love them: "Why, what of that? / It is not fit affection should be forc'd" (IV.i.83–87). As the last word on coyness, this is important: however difficult it is to accept the word of a character named Iago, this Iago is a choric figure, the main spokesman for the play's moral values.

And the play reverses stereotype. Atticus's severe sentence on the lovers, one his own child, is called "cruelty" by other characters, a charge usually levelled at women. His persistence in this course, against the advice of his most trusted counsellors, is clearly masculine wilfulness.

One after the other, ancient stereotypes about women are introduced and then demolished. Sometimes a stereotype is shown to be untrue, or not consistently true. Sometimes it is robbed of all value by proof that it applies equally to men. And occasionally a stereotype about women holds true *only* for male characters.

The frailty stereotype is twice introduced and twice shown untrue. First, Nicanor is undiscouraged by Leonida's refusals:

> 'Tis the generall fault
> Of women all, to make shew of dislike
> To those they most affect: and in that hope
> Thou shalt to her againe: No Citie
> Euer yeelded at first skirmish. Before,
> You came but to a parley, thou shalt now
> Giue an assault: There's nothing batters more
> A womans resolution, then rich gifts.
> (II.i. 102–109)

Leonida, though, stoutly affirms, "My faith is past alreadie, and my heart / Ingag'd vnto a farre more worthy man" (II.ii.84–85). Second, Misogynos preens himself on his conquest: "I told thee she would yeeld, / No woman in the world can hold out long" (V.ii.76–77). But Atlanta is leading him into a trap. Atlanta is not really a woman, of course; but the playwright still undermines male complacency about feminine frailty.

Leonida's maid Loretta, the play's only frail woman, yields to Nicanor's servant Scanfardo with such rapidity as to render her perfunctory resistance a travesty of the institution of coyness:

Scanfardo. Shall we to bed?
Loretta. Fye, seruant, how you talke?
　Troth you are to blame, to offer to assault
　The chastitie of any Gentlewoman,
　Vpon aduantage.
Scanfardo. Pox, leaue this forc'd modesty: for by this hand, I must
　enioy you now before we part.
Loretta. I haue so farre ingag'd my selfe, you know, 'Tis now vaine
　to resist. (II.ii.142–149)

One case, however, does not establish feminine frailty. Anyway, servants' peccadilloes were always treated leniently; the high standard of

chastity expected of ladies did not necessarily apply to their maids. Loretta, fulfilling the stereotype of women's insatiable lust, goes into a minor sexual frenzy while fantasizing about Leonida and Lisandro:

> Heigho! now could I wish my Sweet-heart
> Heere too, I feele such a tickling, somewhere
> About me: if he were here now, I would
> Neuer cast such an vnwilling deniall vpon him
> As I haue done, hauing so good a president
> [i.e., precedent] as I haue.
>
> (II.ii.105–109)

But her fantasies about Leonida are apparently inaccurate: Lisandro insists that, despite appearances, she remains chaste. And if some women
are lustful, so are some men: Scanfardo and Misogynos prove lechers.

The deceit stereotype, introduced by Misogynos ("dissemblers, the
very curse of man" [I.ii.117]), is similarly undercut. Loretta deceives
Nicanor in pretending to further his suit, but no other woman is a de-
ceiver. Leonida tells one lie—that she sent the costume to Lisandro to
smuggle him into her chamber; but this is a white lie, told to save his
life, at the cost of her own. The play's real dissemblers are men. Nicanor
pretends to love Leonida, Misogynos to love Atlanta. Nicanor feigns
loyalty to Atticus, revealing his treachery in asides; Swash feigns loyalty
to Misogynos, wishing him ill in asides. Male aptness for deception is
suggested by the disguises which even good male characters adopt: Lisandro adopts two disguises, Lorenzo three—two of them simultaneously. Swetnam adopts a false identity as Misogynos, and eventually even
his "real" identity as a fencer is shown to be a fraud. Atticus pretends to
be just but is eventually unmasked as a tyrant: his "Crueltie" has mas-
queraded "vnder the forme of Iustice" (IV.v.38–39).

Another stereotype is treated as Daniel Tuvil had treated it: if women
cannot keep secrets, neither can men. Loretta tells Scanfardo that the
"friar" in Leonida's chamber is Lisandro in disguise; although she swears
him to secrecy, he immediately tells Nicanor. In the act of deciding to
reveal this secret for his personal gain, Scanfardo rationalizes with
stereotype: "What will not women blab to those they loue?" The irony
is transparent.

During the trial, Atlanta gets carried away and directs *ad hominem* remarks at Misogynos. This leaves women wide open to the usual charge,
and Misogynos is quick to make it: "O doe not scold, good woman!"
(III.iii.215). One of the judges reprimands her as well: Atlanta is forced
to confess, "I forgot my selfe" (III.iii.216). But this scolding woman is a
man in disguise. Several other stereotypes undergo a sex change: skeptical about Misogynos's fencing prowess, Iago takes a jaundiced view of

the woman hater's prattling: "He fights not with his hands, but with his tongue" (IV.i.76). Nicanor has "tears at command" (IV.ii.37). Atticus is gullible, consistently susceptible to flattery. Misogynos is twice said to be a shame to his sex (III.ii.49, V.ii.344).

The play's two scolding women, "Scold" in the arraignment scene and Queen Aurelia, engage in justifiable shrewishness. The scold attacks Misogynos and Aurelia scolds her husband; both men deserve it. Aurelia, like Emilia in *Othello* and Paulina in *The Winter's Tale,* is unjustly called a scold when she tells truths that ought to be told.

The playwright is very uneasy about generalizations on men's and women's "nature." He rightly objects to positive stereotypes of women as well as to negative. Patience, a virtue recommended to female characters since the early days of the Patient Grissill story, he regards skeptically. It is a male character, Iago, who consistently counsels patience—first to Atticus and later to Aurelia. Aurelia is in a position very similar to Grissill's: her child has apparently been killed through her husband's cruelty. Yet she staunchly refuses to play Patient Grissill:

> How, *Iago,* patience?
> 'Tis such a sinne, that were I guiltie of,
> I should despayre of mercie. Can a Mother
> Haue all the blessings both of Heauen and Earth,
> The hopefull issue of a thousand soules
> Extinct in one, and yet haue patience?
> I wonder patient Heauen beares so long,
> And not send thunder to destroy the Land.
> The Earth, me thinkes, should vomit sulph'rous Damps,
> To stifle and annoy both man and beast,
> Seditious Hell should send blacke Furies forth,
> To terrifie the hearts of tyrant Kings.
>
> (IV.v.74–86)

That stereotypes can be dangerously unreliable guides to action is emphasized in Atlanta's entrapment of Misogynos. Counting on his familiarity with stereotypes available in *Fair Valeria* or *The Captain,* Atlanta orders a fine banquet. Swash reminds Misogynos that insatiate women arrange banquets as aphrodisiacs: "This is but onely a prouocatiue, / To make you strong and lustie for the incounter" (V.ii.29–30). Lulled into complacency, Misogynos is easy prey for the ambush.

One of *Swetnam the Woman-hater*'s major themes is justice and mercy. The playwright challenges the commonplace attribution of justice to men, mercy to women, staging men who are not particularly just, women not especially merciful.

One important literary treatment of orthodox Renaissance ideas on "masculine" justice and "feminine" mercy, Book V of Spenser's *Faerie Queene,* allegorizes the unjust society by a variant of the Hercules-Omphale story: a stable of emasculated men are kept spinning by a crew of Amazonian dames—again, effeminate man juxtaposed with mannish women. Spenser views this as a perversion: in the just society men must be manly and women must stay in their place. That place is honorable: every society needs softness and gentleness, and women's stereotypical tenderheartedness makes them ideal representatives of mercy in Book V. Mercilla, a female character, stands for mercy; Britomart often feels pity and the need for mercy; Radigund induces Justice itself, Artegall, to show mercy. But mercy must subserve justice. The unwise mercy Artegall shows Radigund puts Justice in jeopardy; Britomart, accepting the fact that mercy is sometimes inappropriate, beheads Radigund. The stereotypical association of men with justice and women with mercy works perfectly in the allegory: in the just society, men respect but dominate women, and justice, although tempered with mercy, is ultimately superior to mercy. Justice can dominate mercy with no strain upon Christian ideals, for justice is itself a kind of mercy: one can best show mercy to society by providing it with even-handed justice. This is a man's kind of mercy, better (Book V insists) than women's mercy, which consists of indiscriminate sympathy and forgiveness. In a dream, Britomart sees the female god Isis, as clemency, restraining the male god Osiris, identified as Artegall, Justice: "Clemence oft in things amis, / Restraines those sterne behests, and cruell doomes [i.e., judgments] of his" (V.vii.22.8–9). In the just society, women or the female part of every individual can occasionally persuade men or the masculine part of every individual not to be too harsh. But masculinity and justice still dominate.

Although Shakespeare's sympathies, unlike Spenser's, lie with unconditional mercy, Shakespeare too associates justice with men, mercy with women. In two plays about justice and mercy, male characters—Shylock, Angelo—demand letter-of-the-law justice, while female characters—Portia, Isabella—argue that "earthly power doth . . . show likest God's / When mercy seasons justice" (*Merchant of Venice,* IV.i.196–97) and that "the marshal's truncheon, nor the judge's robe, / Become them with one half so good a grace / As mercy does" (*Measure for Measure,* II.ii.61–63).

In *Swetnam,* although Iago initially describes Atticus as a ruler whose throne is "borne vpon two Columnes, / Iustice and Clemencie" (I.iii.19–20), clemency soon shows itself a shaky column. Of his daughter's crime, Atticus declares, "This offence / . . . cals for Iustice from vs, as a King" (III.i.13–15); after coolly sentencing Leonida to death, he rebuffs his wife's anguish, echoing the words Shakespeare's Julius Caesar uttered before his assassination: "A King is like a Starre, / By which each Subiect, as a

Mariner, / Must steere his course. Iustice in Vs is ample" (III.iii.276–278). Atticus views mercy as effeminate: he casts off his wisest counsellor for his excess of womanly pity:

> Old *Iago* is a froward Lord,
> Honest, but lenatiue, ore-swaid too much
> With pittie against Iustice, that's not good:
> Indeed it is not in a Counsellor.
> And he has too much of woman, otherwise
> He might be Ruler of a Monarchie,
> For policie and wisdome.
>
> (V.iii.40–46)

Iago *is* a pitying character: of the death sentence he cries out, "This cruel-tie afflicts my very soule" (IV.i.78). But Atticus's dichotomy is false. Mercy is not necessarily feminine, as is evident when women get their hands on Misogynos. What they want is justice: they arraign him in their own court. And Atticus, representing male justice, is himself unjust. His regime has repressed freedom of speech: characters repeatedly warn each other against criticizing Atticus, for "the time is full of danger euery-where" (IV.iv.10). Justice, for Atticus, amounts to brutal retaliation for trifling offenses and imagined slights. When three counsellors hesitate to answer him, he threatens, "If once agen / We doe but aske the question, Death tyes vp / Your soules for euer. Call a Heads-man there" (V.i.14–16). He threatens Aurelia and Iago with death for criticizing him: "If agen / They dare but vtter the least syllable, / . . . / They shall not breathe a minute" (V.iii.9–12). During the last act, Atticus comes out of the closet as a tyrant. His false definition of mercy as feminine has diminished his humanity to the point where he can be neither merciful nor just: belief in stereotypes about the sexes is not merely inadequate, not merely silly, but dangerous.

Appropriately for the *hic mulier* years, the play examines stereotypes of masculine courage and feminine timidity. One male character, Miso-gynos, is exposed as a contemptible coward, and two women are very courageous: Aurelia criticizes Atticus in the face of death threats; Leonida faces death bravely. Leonida and Lisandro prove equally courageous in facing death: each claims guilt in order to save the other's life. But Leo-nida's courage is the more persistently stressed. Tuvil had written at length of female "magnanimity"—courage to face death; his anecdotes about women whose courage strengthened the flagging courage of their men are recalled when the lovers are surprised in Leonida's chamber. Lisandro is completely at a loss: "What shall we doe?" he helplessly asks Leonida. She takes the initiative: "*Lisandro,* stand: the worst, / We can but dye"

(II.iii.30–32). She has enough composure to aim a heroic insult at Nicanor, the disappointed suitor who has led the raid on her chamber: "Hence, doting Foole, more welcome far is death, / Then to bee linkt to Ages Leprosie" (II.iii.38–39). Lisandro is led off meekly without another word. Tuvil is recalled again in Iago's speech relating Leonida's death. Tuvil had seen women's initial fearfulness in any frightful situation as a reflex action; after recovering, women would prove brave. The playwright takes the same tack:

> She began to quake and shrinke away . . .
> . . . When she saw her Executioner
> Stand readie to strike out that fatall blow,
> Nature, her frailtie, and the alluring world,
> Did then begin to oppose her constancie:
> But she, whose mind was of a nobler frame,
> Vanquish'd all oppositions, and imbrac'd
> The stroke with courage beyond Womans strength.
>   (V.i.41–50)

This is a fabrication; Leonida has not really been executed. It looks as if the author wanted Leonida to live, but wanted to include a statement on feminine courage, and took this method of having it both ways.

If Tuvil had problems deciding where courage left off and aggression and vengefulness began, so does the play: the one stereotype allowed to stand is that of women's penchant for revenge. The play shows women extremely aggressive. Swash's remarks on the meekness of English women must have raised hoots of audience laughter: "Would we had kept / In our owne Countrey," laments the English emigrant; "there w'are safe enough: / You might haue writ and raild your bellifull, / And few, or none would contradict you, Sir" (I.ii.39–42). Since all the rejoinders to the historical Swetnam had seen print before the play was acted, the statement is resoundingly absurd; in any case, the play's Swetnam has been forced by women's rage to flee England. (He says he was hit especially hard by "one that writ against me" [I.ii.43]. Which of the rejoinders was considered the most devastating?) Swetnam and Swash find Sicilian women as aggressive as English; Swetnam's reputation must have preceded him to Sicily, for on our first sight of the pair, Swash is licking his wounds:

> Puffe, giue me some ayre,
> I am almost stifled, puffe, Oh, my sides! . . .
> I thinke all the Deuils in Hell,
> Haue had a pinch at my hanches;
> I haue beene among the Furies, the Furies:

A Pox on your Booke: I haue been paid ifaith;
You haue set all the women in the Towne in an vprore. . . .
Ne'r was poore *Swash,* so lasht, and pasht,
And crasht and dasht, as I haue beene;
Looke to your selfe, they're vp in armes for you. . . .
Weapons, Sir, I, Ile be sworne they haue.
And cutting ones, I felt the smart of 'em,
From the loines to the legs, from the head to th' hams,
From the Front to the foot, I haue not one free spot.

(I.ii.10–29)

This is why Swetnam adopts a new identity as Misogynos. At the trial, he finds women as aggressive as ever: after one of his speeches, the Queen cries, "Stop the Detractors mouth: Away with him"; other women shout, "Teare him in pieces" (III.iii.248–49). When the women capture him, they take revenge by binding and gagging him, scratching him with their nails, and stabbing him with pins. Some have even more picturesque plans, but Aurelia believes him unworthy of proper assassination:

Aurelia. Now, thou inhumane wretch, what punishment
    Shall we inuent sufficient to inflict,
    According to the height of our reuenge?
Omnes. Let's teare his limmes in pieces, ioynt from ioynt.
Misogynos. Oh, oh.
Scold. Three or foure paire of Pincers, now red hot,
    Were excellent.
Loretta. Will not our Bodkings serue?
Aurelia. Hang him, Slaue, shall he dye as noble a death
    As *Caesar* did? No, no: pinch him, pricke him. (V.ii.156–164)

Perhaps the playwright allowed himself this one stereotype because it wasn't really a stereotype—not adopted from stale literary models but drawn from the life. All the evidence suggests that contemporary women *were* aggressive. But the author did soften the revenge: in the source, the women had tortured the woman-hater to death. And in the epilogue, Leonida pardons Swetnam, explicitly to counter any notions about women's vengeful cruelty: "The greatest wrong was mine; he sought my life: / Which fact [i.e., deed] I freely pardon to approue [i.e., prove] / Women are neither tyrannous, nor cruell, / Though you report vs so."

One of the best things in the play is its subtle treatment of masculinity; here it takes up issues central to the transvestite controversy. The macho soldier versus delicate woman stereotype had come up in Swetnam's *Arraignment* and was queried by Constantia Munda. The play queries it again. Swetnam is the macho hero; the playwright was in luck that the historical Swetnam was a fencing master. Swetnam/Misogynos adopts a posture of the virile man of weapons, "a Master, Sir, of the most magnanimous Method of Cudgell-cracking" (I.ii.67–68). Scanfardo calls him "my noble Gladiator" (I.ii.66). Swash compares Misogynos's amatory methods to combat—love as sexual conquest. To Misogynos's "Beware when a man of Art courts a woman," Swash adds, "Or a Fencer, Sir: We lay vm flat before vs" (V.ii.78–79).

The play ruthlessly exposes Misogynos's militant masculinity as fraudulent. His virility is questioned: doubting his ability to perform sexually, he gets drunk before facing Atlanta; only when inebriated does he declare, "I would she would come . . . Now, methinks, / I could performe" (V.ii.38–39). (This recalls Jacomo, the soldier in *The Captain* who cannot approach a woman unless drunk or angry.) The implication is clear: it is sexual impotence that has made him a woman-hater. Misogynos's prowess with weapons is also annihilated: Atlanta defeats him in a fencing duel. Here it is too bad that Atlanta is not really a woman: her defeating a braggart/seducer in a duel is no more than what women like Moll Cutpurse had done in other plays. (For other reasons, though, not least his failure to win his court case, it was important that "Atlanta" be a man.)

Misogynos shows himself cowardly in the arraignment scene:

Aurelia. Darest thou denie a truth so manifest?
  Didst thou not lately both by word, and deed,
  Publish a Pamphlet in disgrace of vs,
  And of all women-kind?
Misogynos. No, no, no, not I. (V.ii.266–270)

But the ultimate exposure comes from Swash:

He is no Fencer, that's but for a shew,
For feare of being beaten: the best Clarke,
For cowardise that can be in the World,
To terrifie the Female Champions,
He was in England a poore Scholer first,
And came to Medley, to eate Cakes and Creame,
At my old Mothers house . . .
And then he tooke the habit of a Fencer:
And set vp Schoole at Bristow: there he liu'd
A yeere or two, till he had writ this Booke:
And then the women beat him out of the Towne.
                              (V.ii.300–317)

The inefficacy of his fearsome posture—the Bristow women beat him despite his fencer's guise—should not obscure the fact that Swetnam adopts his aggressive stance out of fear, specifically fear of women, which confirms the impression that his misogyny grew out of sexual inadequacy.

Misogynos owes much to the braggadocio, the braggart soldier who is actually a coward. The play suggests that this is what ostentatious masculinity finally amounts to—a cover for cowardice and other insecurities. The macho hero is a man uncertain of his own masculinity,[2] who takes refuge from self-doubt in attacks on women, as if seeking assurance that there is some difference between women and himself. As in the formal controversy, aggressive misogyny is paradoxically defensive.

After Misogynos's exposure, the characteristic structure of the *hic mulier* period emerges—the confrontation between effeminate man and aggressive women. The sexes have exchanged roles, as they have been throughout the play, in the repeated insistence that sexual stereotypes break down under scrutiny and can be applied to either sex or to both.

Misogynos's fraudulent masculinity is balanced by Lorenzo's healthy masculinity. Lorenzo's military prowess is heavily emphasized in the opening scenes. An eye witness testifies to his epic valor in battle:

> He did demeane himselfe so manfully,
> That he perform'd wonders aboue beliefe;
> For when the Nauies ioyn'd, the Cannons plaid,
> And thundring clamors rang the dying knels
> Of many thousand soules; He, void of feare,
> Dalli'd with danger, and pursu'd the Foe
> Thorow a bloudy Sea of Victorie.
>
> (I.i.126–132)

Lorenzo's homecoming is that common motif, a soldier returning from war to a corrupt peace, sunk in tyranny and flattery. There is a reference to the neglected soldier (I.i.151–152). But most returning-soldier figures, from whose ranks the stage misogynist was regularly recruited, had difficulty adapting; they had troubles with women and saw peace as effeminate. Not so Lorenzo. This heroic soldier's first act upon returning is to become a female impersonator: the play connects Lorenzo's disguise to the transvestite controversy with Swash's reference to this "Amazon" as a "Masculine Feminine" (IV.iii.65). He has no trouble stepping into a woman's world: he simply becomes a woman. Lorenzo's Amazon disguise is important, not only because the Amazons were favorite defenders' examples of female courage, but also because it symbolizes Lorenzo's accommodation to peacetime. Lorenzo believes in civilization; if civilized peacetime values are feminine, he will allow his "feminine" side to emerge. Unlike Misogynos, he has no doubts about his masculinity; he is so comfortable with it that wearing women's clothes does not threaten him at all. Lorenzo is an intellectual hermaphrodite. He makes no false distinctions between "masculine" valor and justice and "feminine" amiability and mercy. A complete human being, he seems to assume, will have all these qualities. Iago's vision of the ideal ruler as a model of justice and clemency is a hermaphroditic image; the heroic soldier dressed as a woman repeats that image. Lorenzo in female clothing is a figure neither of fun nor of disgrace. He is the all-sided human being, the union of male and female, which should be the goal of civilized humankind.

The image is enhanced by Lorenzo's final disguise: "an old Shepherd." He uses this "Siluan disguise" primarily to introduce the slanderer figure so often juxtaposed with the stage misogynist:

> Know, that all the Happinesse
> I did in this World possesse,
> Was my onely Daughter . . .
> But it chanced so, God wot,
> That an old decrepit man
> Most prepostrously began,
> With flatt'ring words to woo my Daughter,
> But being still deny'd, he after
> Turn'd his loue to mortall hate
> *Claribell* to ruinate,
> Striuing to o'rpresse her fame,
> With Lust, Contempt, Reproch, and Shame.
>   (V.iii.126–143)

The Susanna story hovers; and the audience is aware that the unjust elder Lorenzo has in mind is the aged Nicanor, who brought all this trouble on Leonida because of his own frustrated intentions. This places Nicanor and Misogynos in the same camp: both malign women out of deprivation. Further, the Renaissance saw heroic and pastoral as two extremes: Sidney called the heroic the highest literary genre, pastoral the humblest; these extremes might represent the active and contemplative modes. Tamburlaine is a shepherd turned conqueror; Lorenzo, for the moment, the military hero turned shepherd. The sylvan disguise is one more emblem of the complete man: Lorenzo unites heroic and pastoral as he unites masculine and feminine. The last scene's complicated unmasking may be only a light-hearted send-up of disguise conventions: Lorenzo's throwing off shepherd's disguise to reveal Amazon disguise, and within fifteen lines throwing off his Amazon disguise to reveal himself, could hardly help provoking audience laughter. But I think that despite the comic effect, the wholeness image is meant seriously. First we see a man who combines military heroism with rural simplicity; next, a man who combines masculine valor and justice with feminine love and compassion. Beneath all this is one man, certain of his identity.

This scene also provides the play's only disguised woman: Leonida appears as "a Siluan Nymph." The ideal of rural simplicity which was part of the Golden Age myth had always included the ideal of feminine purity. Leonida, like her brother, combines aggressiveness/magnanimity with rural simplicity: the wholeness the play endorses is available to women too, and feminine purity can coexist with valor.

In contrast to Lorenzo's and Leonida's wholeness, the two detractors, Misogynos and Nicanor, are truncated beings. Both are obsessive: Nicanor is obsessed with ambition, Misogynos with antifeminism. Both have a diminished capacity for human feeling: Nicanor disguises ambition as love, Misogynos disguises lust as love; neither feels a dram of compassion for the lovers condemned to death. Atticus makes a third in an unholy trinity; amputating his sense of mercy, he forfeits all human values, even justice. All these narrowed beings are guilty of contempt for women. This comedy makes a serious point: when the sexes are sundered (and the attempts of Nicanor, Misogynos, and Atticus to separate the lovers symbolize this sundering), humanity is the loser. In the play's terms, the complete human being is both male and female.

The play is a comedy, while its source ended tragically, with lovers and misogynist dead; but we should not conclude that it has no serious intent. Coryl Crandall concludes, from the sparing of Misogynos, that England did not take misogyny as seriously as did Spain, where the story originated (pp. 25–26). But surely tragic evidence that misogyny leads to chaos and destruction, and comedic insistence that life demands integration of male and female, are two sides of the same coin. After an orgy of satiric bitterness in the century's opening years, the drama had moved away from satiric comment toward positive example; that is the direction in which this story was adapted. Nonsatiric comedy was at its best an exploration of human happiness. *Swetnam the Woman-hater's* hermaphroditic vision of happiness is a subtle and important contribution to that serious enterprise.

*   *   *   *   *

Swetnam is himself a comic figure. He is a comic butt in some scenes; in others he must have drawn laughs with his witticisms (or with *The Arraignment's* plagiarized witticisms). In making Swetnam a comic figure, the author denies him the stature of great figures of evil. Several characters believe him unworthy of notice: when even the judicious Iago is moved to draw upon Misogynos, Sforza counsels, "He is not worth our indignation" (IV.i.40); Atlanta advises the Queen, "He is not worth your wrath" (IV.v.121). But Swetnam, however contemptible, cannot be ignored; with the help of his low jests, a woman is condemned to death. The playwright saw that jest is misogyny's medium and showed where jesting could lead.

There is much of the Vice figure in Swetnam. Like the old Vice, he is often laughing. When Lorenzo demands, "Dar'st thou behold that too much wronged Sex, / Whose Vertues thou hast basely slander'd?" Misogynos replies, "Ha, ha, ha" (III.ii.65–67). Asked whether he loves Atlanta, he answers, "Ha, ha, ha. Loue? that were a iest indeed, / To passe away the time for sport" (V.ii.82–83). The word *sport* is a trademark of latter-day Shakespearean Vice figures like Aaron the Moor and Iago, characters for whom wickedness is recreation; descended from allegorical figures of evil, they need no further motivation. We have seen that the Vice evolved into a misogynist in plays vindicating Woman against detraction. This was a natural, even an inevitable, development. The Vice, always a figure of comic evil, was the logical character type to play the misogynist, since misogyny so often works through jest. Casting Swetnam as a Vice makes clear his connection with evil; and the comic elements do not alleviate the evil. The horror of comic evil is apparent in *King Lear*'s world, where the very gods are Vice figures: "As flies to wanton boys are we to the gods, / They kill us for their sport" (IV.i.38–39). Laughter implies distance; the Vice is remote from human sympathy. That a character could cause pain is one thing; that he could laugh at that pain quite another. This play's comic elements do not rob it of seriousness; laughing evil is if anything more shocking than sober evil. Nicanor's selfish ambition causes pain but has a recognizably human motivation. Swetnam's enjoyment of the pain he causes women exists in a vacuum of human feeling. He can gain nothing by it, as Nicanor hopes to gain a crown. The evil of misogyny is gratuitous evil; behind the misogynist's laughing mask is blank indifference to suffering.

Swetnam is the best of a long line of stage misogynists. Like the others, he is enjoyable, at times almost lovable. In the arraignment scene, surrounded by furious females, Swetnam keeps blurting out old antifeminist jokes—not because he is brave, but because (out of lifetime habit) he simply can't help himself. To the command, "Silence in the Court," he responds "Silence? and none but women? That were strange!" (V.ii.248–249). Threatened with being "bayted by all the honest women in the Parish," he cries "Is that the worst? there will not one be found / In all the Citie" (V.ii.333–335). It is hard to dislike these sprightly fellows; one is tempted to admire them, if only for their persistence and their good-natured cussedness. Most are granted enough human touches to make us want to forgive them. (Would the love of a good woman cure what ails them?) But this dramatist knew what he was doing in making Swetnam a Vice. For behind the smiling faces of all literary misogynists, from

Gaspar Pallavicino to Politic Persuasion to Joseph Swetnam, is a kind of evil, a deprivation of feeling, an antihuman principle. Women in the play go to court seeking justice and find a laughing opponent. It is an image of the frustration of women's movements throughout history. Seeking human justice, we confront the inhuman face of the Jester.

The author researched thoroughly; there is evidence that he read Swetnam, Speght, Sowernam, Munda, and Tuvil. Swetnam/Misogynos quotes numerous passages from *The Arraignment*. References to Speght's essay occur in the indictment, "*Ioseph Swetnam, alias Misogynos, / Alias Molastomus*" (V.ii.255–56) and the sentence, "He shall weare this Mouzell, to expresse / His barking humour against women-kind" (V.ii.328–329). The arraignment scene stems from a scene in Sowernam's essay; Swetnam pleads "not guilty" in both. Iago's speech at III.ii.31–47 is cast in the satirists' diction Munda had used and contains two of Munda's ideas about Swetnam—that "His acquaintance / Has bin altogether amongst Whores and Bawds, / And therefore speakes but in's owne element" (ll. 37–39), and that "he is the Viper, that . . . gnawes / Vpon his Mothers fame" (ll. 45–46). The play's repeated charge that Swetnam is ungrateful to his mother may reflect Munda's vehemence in prosecuting this time-honored theme. The play often uses the word *impious* to characterize Swetnam, as had Speght, Sowernam, and Munda. Like these three women, the play constantly applies the epithet *dog* to Swetnam. It is Tuvil, though, who is most frequently echoed. (One feels with sadness that there must be some special reason for his work being given the most careful consideration.) The play emphasizes that the "female Sexe cannot inherit here" (I.i.90), recalling Tuvil's disapproval of the Salic law. Loretta uses the marigold image Tuvil had used twice (II.ii.17–18; this was a cleaned-up version of a bawdy antifeminist jest to be found in *Ram-Alley*). The play makes much of female magnanimity, as Tuvil had, and Atlanta echoes Tuvil in alluding to women committing suicide to preserve their honor (III.iii.200–223).

The play is topical to some degree. Some of the humor would be lost on an audience unfamiliar with its immediate literary context; the playwright assumed that the audience of the Red Bull, a public theater, were up on the controversy. He alludes several times to the great stir it created. Swetnam/Misogynos glories in his infamy in England:

> Oh, but for one that writ against me, *Swash*,
> Ide had a glorious Conquest in that Ile.
> How my Bookes tooke effect! how greedily
> The credulous people swallowed downe my hookes!
> How rife debate sprang betwixt man and wife!

The little Infant that could hardly speake,
Would call his Mother Whore. O, it was rare!
                                                    (I.ii.43–49)

Swash says the book "made a thousand men and wiues fall out" (V.ii.320)
and alludes to the counterattack: "Two or three good wenches, in meere
spight, / Laid their heads together, and rail'd him out of th' Land" (V.ii.321–
322). The play hints at the reception *The Arraignment* got from men:
although judicious men like Iago, Lorenzo, and Sforza hold Misogynos in
contempt, the man in the street may congratulate him:

First Gentleman: Worthie *Misogynos*.
Second Gentleman: Noble Champion,
    We doe applaud your merit, in the report
    Of your late conquest.
Misogynos.   Thanke you, Gentlemen;
    Truth will preuaile, you see. I speake not for my selfe,
    In my owne quarrel; but the generall good
    Of all men in the world.
First Gentleman: We know it, Sir. (IV.i.51–56)

But the play is intelligible without knowledge of the Swetnam war.
The stereotypes on which the play depends were so widespread as to be
recognizable by the totally illiterate. And, sadly, they are so today. A
modern audience would have little difficulty following this play.

A note on authorship. This playwright was *au courant* with the theatrical scene as well as the controversialist landscape. The play echoes *The
Duchess of Malfi* (II.i.121–122), acted three or four years earlier, *Dr. Faustus* (II.i.155–157), out in a revised edition in 1616, and *King Lear* (III.ii.83),
published in quarto in 1608 and perhaps recently onstage. As Crandall
indicates, the main candidates for the play's authorship are Dekker and
Heywood (p. 28). Heywood is a logical choice; his plays evince considerable familiarity with the formal controversy, and he later produced two
defenses, *Gunaikeion: or, Nine Bookes of Various History Concerninge Women*,
1624, and *The Exemplary Lives and memorable Acts of nine the most worthy
Women of the World*, 1640. Louis B. Wright goes so far as to call Heywood
"perhaps woman's staunchest literary advocate in the first half of the
seventeenth century (p. 117). Nevertheless, *Swetnam the Woman-hater* seems
rather too thoughtful and too carefully worked out to have been solely
the work of an author capable of the scattershot approach to women that
characterizes Heywood's Homeric cycle. I wonder if Webster shouldn't
be added to the list of possibles. He was very active at this time, and the
habit of literary borrowing, which shows up in the echoes of plays above,
is characteristic of Webster.[3] His fondness for "women in court" scenes
is evident from *The White Devil* and *The Devil's Law-Case*, and the motif

of one family member seeking the death or ruin of another, which appears in Atticus, is one of Webster's most persistent themes, occurring in *The Duchess of Malfi, The White Devil,* and *The Devil's Law-Case.* The latter two plays, like *Swetnam the Woman-hater* with which they are closely contemporary, were acted by Queen Anne's Men at the Red Bull. Among contemporary dramatists, Webster most consistently saw through stereotypes of women. It is not at all farfetched to suggest that he may have had a hand in this play.

Comedy depends, more than other genres, on shared cultural experience. The author of *Swetnam the Woman-hater Arraigned by Women* counted on his audience's having read or heard about Speght's essay and thus catching the allusion to Melastomus; more important, he counted on audience familiarity with stereotypes about masculine and feminine behavior, without which the play's role reversals would lose power to provoke either laughter or thought. The existence of this play, in this form, is evidence that the Renaissance public was conversant both with formal debate about women and with a repertoire of popular stereotypes which have come down to us very little altered. Literary controversy about women, which had always drawn upon popular lore, merged in the popular imagination with ancient stereotype, proverb, hoary anecdote, and jest to create a coherent body of woman lore upon which the comic dramatist could play with confidence.

But few authors dealing in this material have so consistently resisted the temptation to cheap shots and easy laughter at women's expense as has the author of *Swetnam the Woman-hater.* It is a very good play—a play that achieves the twin Renaissance literary goals "to teach and to delight"; the sort of play (a rarity in any age) that manages to address important intellectual notions without resort to fifth-act sermons engorged with abstractions; its ideas are perfectly dissolved in a solution of plot and character, and hence perfectly dramatic. The fact that the play succeeds as literature is the more gratifying in view of its being, finally, one of the few literary documents of the English high Renaissance about which one can *almost* say, "this is a feminist piece of work."

NOTES

1. Chapter 2 of Crandall's *Swetnam the Woman-hater: The Controversy and the Play* provides an account of the play's continental sources.

2. Madelon Gohlke puts this same idea in Freudian terms: the "macho mystique" she characterizes as "a demonstration of phallic power in the face of a threatened castration" (*The Woman's Part,* p. 162). In Jacobean times, the sexual braggadocio was beginning to develop as a character

type; although seeds of sexual boasting exist in Swetnam's character, a pure specimen of the type is Herod Frappatore in Marston's *The Fawn,* whose vaunted sexual conquests are exposed as fictitious when one character produces a letter Herod has sent to a bawd, confessing his desperation for feminine attention—just as the martial braggadocio is always exposed as a coward.

3. See Robert W. Dent, *John Webster's Borrowing.*

Peroratio: Hot Ice and Wondrous Strange Snow

How shall we find the concord of this discord?
—*A Midsummer Night's Dream*

Perish the man whose mind is backward now!
—*Henry V*

To READ ABOUT WOMEN in Renaissance literature is to be met with the paradoxical at every turn. Like Hamlet's crab, the reader must "go backward" to cope with the fact that it was defenses of women that sparked attacks on women, rather than the other way around; that it was the formal attack on women, rather than the formal defense, that provided satisfactory role models for modern feminists; that attacks and defenses, apparently so inimical to each other, may have had very similar goals. No less paradoxical are the age's blithe grafting of female-dominated courtly love upon male-dominated marriage, its use of the acerbic stage misogynist as a tool in the defense of women, its portrayal of stage misogynists as comic figures whose actions have serious consequences, its insistence on describing women in general as weak and vulnerable while portraying individual women as strong and aggressive, its pretense that the brutal humiliations of women in the Patient Grissill story and its analogues were essays in the praise of womankind. It was an age when masculine weakness expressed itself in macho aggressiveness and when a purported humanist like Erasmus could recommend slyly-feigned submissiveness as a more useful program than shrewishness for the power-minded wife; an age that elaborated, in Madelon Gohlke's words, "structures of dominance and submission in which dominance becomes the mask of weakness and submission a subversive strategy in the mutual struggle for power" (p. 166). A period capable of remaining unconfused through such inversions, dilemmas, and masquerades would find the restoration of male-dominated society by Spenser's female knight Britomart as natural as breathing, and might unblinkingly accept such mind-boggling pronouncements as Erasmus's "the natural ouerthwartnesse of the womanishe minde, doth now and then burst out as of the frayler and weaker vessell" (STC 10499, Sig. Aiiii). It is no more than to be expected that one of the leading feminist theorists of the day, Henry Cornelius Agrippa, should cast his defense of women as a rhetorical paradox.

Paradox is central to Renaissance literature, as it was habitual in Renaissance thought. Paradox is the very essence of Shakespeare's work. *Hamlet,* as Bradley says, impresses us at once with a sense of the limitless potential of man and his powerlessness in his own "petty sphere of action."[1] In *Macbeth,* Pity is personified as "a naked new-born babe, / Striding the blast" (I.vii.21–22); Paul Jorgensen shows how the paradoxical power of innocence, as exemplified by this "paradoxical view of the babe as both helpless pity and as an agent of retribution," is central to the play.[2] In *King Lear,* the protagonist learns more in one night of madness than he had learned in eighty years of sanity; in a long tradition of wise fools in Shakespeare, the Fool speaks wisdom; and Gloucester embraces the same paradox Milton would explore in Book III of *Paradise Lost*—that growth in spiritual sight can accompany physical blindness: "I stumbled when I saw" (IV.i.21). Shakespeare's generic hybrids are of tension and paradox all compact: in *Antony and Cleopatra*'s world, where the public and political orientation of the history play confronts the private orientation of the tragedy, behavior that is right in the public figure is wrong in the private person, and vice versa. And Shakespeare ended his career experimenting in the paradoxical realm of tragicomedy.

Norman Rabkin's fruitful thesis that Shakespeare tends to structure his plays "in terms of a pair of polar opposites" and that "always the dramatic structure sets up the opposed elements as equally valid, equally desirable, and equally destructive" applies to a certain extent, as Rabkin argues, to "all great writers."[3] But in the Renaissance the spirit of paradox imbued the works of pigmies as of giants. Not only does *King Lear* stand as a magnificent embodiment of the paradox that self-knowledge grows as the soul is afflicted, but we have the modest John Davies's word for it too: "If ought can teach us ought, Affliction's looks / (Making us look into ourselves so near) / Teach us to know ourselves beyond all books / Or all the learned schools that ever were." Shakespeare was not alone in the grand paradoxical conception of tragicomedy; the humble Thomas Preston conceived in *Cambyses* "A Lamentable Tragedy, Mixed Full of Pleasant Mirth."

Paradox expresses the essence of the age. The highest literary achievement of the Renaissance, tragedy, affirms by the very intensity of its grieving the value of what is lost, the individual human life: it is this genre, wherein human beings are crushed, which is most firmly humanistic. The most ethereal and other-worldly philosophy of the Renaissance, Neoplatonism, paradoxically came to serve as a rationale for sensuality and worldliness: as Herschel Baker puts it, "Neoplatonism . . . enabled man to take a legitimate delight in the world and the flesh by rationalizing such delight as the first necessary step toward that condition of virtue which spiritual wisdom makes possible."[4] The Christianity so fundamental to Renaissance thought was a religion informed by paradox: "If any man desire to be first, the same shall be last of all" (Mark 9:35, KJV), "The wisdom of this world is foolishness with God" (I Cor. 3:19), "He that findeth his life shall lose it: and he that loseth his life for my sake shall find it" (Matthew 10:39) were basic tenets of a faith whose king was cradled in a manger. And the central philosophy of the age, Christian humanism, where Christian humility and belief in human sinfulness were yoked by violence together with the humanist belief that man was "confined by no bounds" and could recreate himself "at the higher levels which are divine,"[5] is so quintessentially paradoxical that the very term "Christian humanism" is something very like an oxymoron. It was indeed an age of "living deaths, dear wounds, fair storms, and freezing fires."

The yoked incompatibilities of Renaissance thought produced, by a kind of fission, a literature of great energy: drama thrives on conflict, as all literature thrives on tensions and ambiguities. But such incompatibilities reflected a world view disturbed to the point of schizophrenia. The hermaphrodite figure, which so appealed to the Renaissance passion for paradox, was always an uneasy symbol: Nancy Hayles believes that the frequent iconographic representation of the hermaphrodite as a grotesque with two heads indicates that "the disunity of the figure, its composite and discontinuous nature, is being deliberately stressed."[6] An appropriate emblem of the age: if the orthodox Renaissance view of mankind, expressed in Christian humanism, betrayed a radical discontinuity between Christian theory and human inclination, the orthodox Renaissance view of womankind, expressed in the formal controversy, in marriage sermons, in plays of the Patient Grissill formula, betrayed a radical discontinuity between theory and reality—the reality of the aggressive, liberty-minded Englishwoman whose portrait emerges from the *hic mulier* controversy and from the preponderance of aggressive female characters in the literature of the day.

The marriage of Christianity and humanism was a precarious and fragile thing from the start, and it ended in divorce. Douglas Bush notices symptoms of marriage breakdown occurring very early: from immediately post-Thomist times, "the divorce between reason and faith opened the way for those two extreme positions of the Renaissance, anti-Christian rationalism and anti-rational fideism."[7] The Renaissance view of women, too, was an unstable compound. Even the Renaissance mind, shot through with paradox from infancy, could not indefinitely hold in colloidal suspension the theory that women were weak and the fact that the women one knew were strong, the theory that virtuous women never left the house and the fact that seemingly virtuous women one knew worked in shops and attended the Globe. Either the Renaissance theory of women or the behavior of Renaissance women would have to be revised.

It was, in the main, the behavior that was revised. Alice Clark demonstrates that "able business women might be found in every class of English society throughout the seventeenth century, but their contact with affairs became less habitual as the century wore away."[8] What was true of business was true of many other spheres of life: as the Renaissance ebbed, woman after woman shrank back to the cloister of the hearth.

The evaporation of aggression from the blood of Renaissance Englishwomen testifies to the crucial role theory plays in the success of a feminist movement: as I have shown in chapter 5, the Renaissance did not generate a workable body of feminist theory, especially theory that could cope with changing economic conditions. The spirit did not depart easily from women who had stalked London streets in breeches and weaponry, but the habit of liberty and even the habit of self-employment could not sustain individual women against the pressure of public opinion and against massive discrimination. The London Weavers' Ordinance of 1596, for example, decreed that "no woman or mayd shall use or exercise the Arts of weaving . . . except she be the widow of one of the same Guild"; as a corollary, if such a widow remarried, she could be forced to give up the trade. In 1667, one Widow Goodale "gave bad words" to the London Weavers' Company when she was forced to give up weaving.[9] But bad words were not enough. What was needed was group action, feminist pressure on the trade union model, even if it came to the exercise of women's last source of power in hard times—the *Lysistrata* tactics Maria turns to advantage in *The Woman's Prize*.

But Renaissance women could not take group feminist action, partly for reasons I have mentioned—the force of Christian doctrine, the Renaissance reverence for hierarchical authority and horror of civil disobedience—and partly because they must have believed what literature said about them. Women may not have dreamed of seeking power through uniting with other women because whenever women were considered as a group, as a sex, they were seen to be feeble. Literature repeatedly took refuge in an unexamined paradox: while one bad woman "shamed her sex" and served as an impetus to general misogyny, one good, strong, self-sufficient woman was dismissed as an exception to the general rule. Such mental habits proved divisive to women: a single strong woman could not extrapolate the strength of the female sex from her own sufficiency, because literature had taught her to shrug off her own strength as a rare exception: she could say with Portia "I am . . . stronger than my sex" (*Julius Caesar,* II.i.296), or believe that like Leonida she possessed "courage beyond Womans strength" (*Swetnam the Woman-hater,* V.i.50). Such habits of thought do not impel a woman to seek out other women: the final barrier to feminism was the habit of paradox itself.

But—paradoxically—what was to living women's disadvantage was to literature's advantage. What if Renaissance literature had consistently created women who lived up to its own stated ideal? One has only to imagine a literature that is all Grissills and no Gwenthians, all Octavias and no Cleopatras, all Lady Macduffs and no Lady Macbeths, to be thankful that Renaissance writers were able to salve their consciences by reminding us that assertive women are wicked and to diminish the threat such women pose by declaring them to be rare. Otherwise, they might not have created them at all.

Renaissance literature was always better than Renaissance literary theory: Sidney might have shackled literature with a theory of strict poetic justice as outlined in *The Defense of Poesy;* but when he wrote the *Arcadia* he paid no attention to poetic justice, and neither, during most of the Renaissance, did anybody else. We are relieved that Shakespeare never bothered much about the unities, and we should rejoice that Renaissance authors allowed their stultifying theory of womankind to interfere as little as it did with the women they created in their literature. Their stuffy pronouncements on women show that their minds accepted the orthodox theory, but the lively women they created show that their hearts were very impressed with (and often quite fond of) exuberant English Woman exactly as they found her. Though they write of Grissills for their peace, in the Rosalinds their pleasure lies.

NOTES

1. A. C. Bradley, *Shakespearean Tragedy,* p. 109.

2. Paul A. Jorgensen, *Our Naked Frailties: Sensational Art and Meaning in "Macbeth",* pp. 94–109. The paradoxical power of weakness was sometimes adduced in defense of women, who were always presumed weak. Agrippa, for example, writes, "Those thynges that be folysshe before the worlde, god hathe chosen, that he myghte confounde wise menne: and those thynges that be feble and weake in this worlde, he hathe chosen to confounde the mighty": women, foolish and feeble in this world's terms, achieve power as tools of the Almighty (*The Nobility and Excellency of Womankind,* Sig. [C8]–[C8]ᵛ). Ian Maclean, tracing in theological texts the idea that "if woman is generally considered to be weaker than man, her virtuous acts become as a consequence much more admirable" and that "God delights in confounding the mighty by the agency of the weak," rightly points out that such a use of paradox

"strengthens the presumption of female weakness" (*The Renaissance Notion of Women*, pp. 21, 26)—again, the paradoxical fact that the defense of women was as damaging as the attack.

3. Norman Rabkin, *Shakespeare and the Common Understanding*, pp. 12, 17; Rabkin's essay "Rabbits, Ducks, and Henry V" extends this thesis.

4. Herschel Baker, *The Image of Man: A Study of the Idea of Human Dignity in Classical Antiquity, the Middle Ages, and the Renaissance*, pp. 248–49; see also my essay "Humanism Questioned: A Study of Four Renaissance Characters."

5. Pico della Mirandola, *Oration on the Dignity of Man*, 1487, my translation.

6. Nancy Hayles, "The Ambivalent Ideal: The Concept of Androgyny in English Renaissance Literature," p. 40.

7. Douglas Bush, *The Renaissance and English Humanism*, p. 85.

8. Alice Clark, *Working Life of Women in the Seventeenth Century*, p. 35. Although bourgeois values triumphed in the long run, the relative freedom of women in the Restoration—most highly visible among the emerging class of professional actresses—strengthens my impression that a solid royalist regime had more to offer feminism than had the hegemony of the middle class.

9. Ross Davies, *Women and Work*, pp. 30–32.

Bibliography

I. Reference Works

Harbage, Alfred, ed. *Annals of English Drama, 975–1700.* Rev. by Samuel Schoenbaum. Philadelphia: University of Pennsylvania Press, 1964.

Pollard, A. W., and G. R. Redgrave. *A Short-Title Catalogue of Books Printed in England, Scotland, and Ireland, and of English Books Printed Abroad, 1475–1640.* London: Bibliographical Society, 1926. Revised edition, vol. 2, ed. W. A. Jackson *et al.* London: Bibliographical Society, 1976. References to the revised edition, only the second volume of which was in print when I wrote, are cited "Revised STC."

Rollins, Hyder E. *An Analytical Index to the Ballad-Entries(1557–1700) in the Register of the Company of Stationers of London.* Chapel Hill: University of North Carolina Press, 1924.

Utley, Francis. *The Crooked Rib: An Analytical Index to the Argument about Women in English and Scots Literature to the End of the Year 1568.* New York: Octagon, 1970 (first published 1944).

Wing, Donald. *Short-Title Catalogue of Books Printed in England, Scotland, Ireland, Wales, and British America and of English Books Printed in Other Countries, 1641–1700.* 2nd ed. New York: Modern Language Association, 1972.

II. Primary Sources

Adams, Thomas. *Mystical Bedlam; or, The world of mad-men.* 1615. STC 124.

Agrippa, Henry Cornelius. *Female Pre-eminence; or, The Dignity and Excellency of that Sex, above the Male.* 1670. Trans. Henry Care. Wing STC 784.

———. *Opera.* Lyons, 1531.

———. *A Treatise of the Nobilitie and excellencye of woman kynde.* Trans. David Clapham. 1542. STC 203.

Anger, Jane. *Iane Anger her Protection for Women. To defend them against the scandalovs reportes of a late Surfeiting Louer, and all other Venerians that complaine so to bee ouer cloyed with womens kindnesse.* 1589. STC 644.

Arbuthnot, Alexander. *Ane contrapoysoun to the Ballat falslie intitulit the properteis of gud Wemen*. In *Maitland Quarto Manuscript*, ed. W. A. Craigie. Edinburgh and London: Blackwood for Scottish Text Society, 1920.

Arden of Feversham. In *Elizabethan Plays*, ed. Arthur H. Nethercot, Charles R. Baskervill, and Virgil B. Heltzel. New York: Holt, Rinehart, and Winston, 1971.

Averell, William. *A meruailous combat of contrarieties*. 1588. STC 981.

B., R. *Appius and Virginia*. In *Five Anonymous Plays*, ed. John S. Farmer. London: Early English Drama Society, 1908.

Barry, Lording. *Ram-Alley*. Ed. Claude E. Jones. Louvain: Uystpruyst, 1952.

The Batchelars Banquet. 1603. STC 6476.

Beaumont, Francis, and John Fletcher. *The Captain*. In *The Works of Francis Beaumont and John Fletcher*, ed. A. Glover and A. R. Waller. Cambridge: Cambridge University Press, 1905–12.

———. *The Maid's Tragedy* and *Philaster*. In *English Drama 1580–1642*, ed. C. F. Tucker Brooke and Nathaniel Burton Paradise. Boston: Heath, 1933.

———. *The Scornful Lady*. In *The Dramatic Works in the Beaumont and Fletcher Canon*, ed. Fredson Bowers. Cambridge: Cambridge University Press, 1966–.

———. *The Woman-Hater*. STC 1692.

Bercher, William. *The Nobility of Women*. Ed. Warwick Bond. Roxburghe Club, 1904.

Boccaccio, Giovanni. *Concerning Famous Women [De Claris Mulieribus]*. Trans. Guido A. Guarino. New Brunswick, N.J.: Rutgers University Press, 1963.

Brathwait, Richard. *Essaies upon the five senses*. 1619. STC 3566.

———. "The Good Wife." See Patrick Hannay.

Brentius, Joannes. *A Right Godly and learned discourse vpon the booke of Esther*. Trans. John Stockwood. 1584. STC 3602.

Breton, Nicholas. *The Praise of vertuous Ladies. An inuectiue against the discourteous discourses, of certain Malicious persons, written against Women*. In *The Will of Wit*. 1597. STC 3705.

A C. Mery Talys [A Hundred Merry Tales]. ca. 1525. STC 23663.

Captain Cox, his Ballads and Books; or, Robert Laneham's Letter. Ed. F. J. Furnivall. Hertford: Stephen Austin, 1890.

Cary, Elizabeth. *Mariam, Fair Queen of Jewry*. Malone Society Reprint.

Castiglione, Baldassare. *The Courtier*. Ed. W. E. Henley. London: David Nutt, 1900. (Hoby translation.)

Chamberlain, John. *The Letters of John Chamberlain*. Ed. Norman Egbert McClure. Philadelphia: American Philosophical Society, 1939.

Chapman, George. *Bussy d'Ambois*. In *Five Stuart Tragedies*, ed. A. K. McIlwraith. London: Oxford University Press, 1953.

———. *The Widow's Tears*. Ed. Ethel M. Smeak. Lincoln, Nebr.: University of Nebraska Press, 1966.

Chaucer, Geoffrey. *The Works of Geoffrey Chaucer*. Ed. F. N. Robinson. Boston: Houghton Mifflin, 1957.

The Chester Mystery Cycle. Ed. by R. M. Lumiansky and David Mills. London, New York, and Toronto: Oxford University Press for EETS, 1974.

Chettle, Henry, Thomas Dekker, and William Haughton. *Patient Grissil*. In *The Dramatic Works of Thomas Dekker*, ed. Fredson Bowers. Cambridge: Cambridge University Press, 1953–.

Cicero, Marcus Tullius (ascribed to). *Rhetorica ad Herennium*. Trans. Harry Caplan. London: Heinemann; Cambridge: Harvard University Press, 1954.

Cleaver, Robert. *A Godlie Forme of Household Government*. 1598. STC 5383.

Cooke, John. *Greene's Tu Quoque*. Tudor Facsimile Text.

The Costly Whore. In *A Collection of Old English Plays*, ed. A. H. Bullen. New York: B. Blom, 1882–1889.

Cuckolds haven; or, The marry'd mans miserie. STC 6101.

Davison, Francis. *A Poetical Rapsody*. STC 6375.

The deceyte of women, to the instruction and ensample of all men, younge and olde. ca. 1560. STC 6451.

Dekker, Thomas. *The Honest Whore, Part 2*. In *The Dramatic Works of Thomas Dekker*, ed. Fredson Bowers. Cambridge: Cambridge University Press, 1953–.

Dekker, Thomas, and John Webster. *Westward Ho* and *Northward Ho*. In *The Dramatic Works of Thomas Dekker*, ed. Fredson Bowers. Cambridge: Cambridge University Press, 1953–.

Dekker, Thomas, and Thomas Middleton. *The Honest Whore, Part 1*. In *The Dramatic Works of Thomas Dekker*, ed. Fredson Bowers. Cambridge: Cambridge University Press, 1953–.

———. *The Roaring Girl*. In *The Works of Thomas Middleton*, ed. A. H. Bullen. New York: AMS Press, 1964 (first published 1885).

Deloney, Thomas. *The garland of good will*. 1593. STC 6554.

Dickenson, John. *Greene in conceipt: new raised from his graue to write the tragique historie of Faire Valeria of London*. 1598. STC 6819.

Drayton, Michael. *Idea*. In *The Renaissance in England*, ed. Hyder Rollins and Herschel Baker. Boston: Heath, 1954.

Dunbar, William. *The Twa Cummeris*. In *The Poems of William Dunbar*, ed. W. Mackay Mackenzie. Edinburgh: Porpoise, 1932.

———. *The Twa marrit wemen and the wedo*. ca. 1508. STC 7350.

Elyot, Sir Thomas. *The boke named The gouernour*. 1531. STC 7635.

———. *The Defence of Good Women*. 1545 (first published 1540). STC 7658.

Erasmus, Desiderius. *Coniugium*. ca. 1523. Trans. into English as *A mery dialogue, declaringe the propertyes of shrowde shrewes, and honest wyues*. 1557. STC 10455.

Every Woman In Her Humour. 1609. STC 25948.

An excellent ballad intituled, The constancy of Susanna. STC 23436.

Fair Em. Malone Society Reprint.

The Fair Maid of Bristow. Ed. Arthur Hobson Quinn. Philadelphia: University of Pennsylvania Press, 1902.

Fenton, Geoffrey. *Monophylo.* 1572. STC 10797.

Feylde, Thomas. *A contrauersye bytwene a louer and a Jaye.* ca. 1509–35. STC 10839.

Field, Nathan. *A Woman Is A Weathercock* and *Amends for Ladies.* In *The Plays of Nathan Field,* ed. William Peery. Austin: University of Texas Press, 1950.

Field, Nathan, and Philip Massinger. *The Fatal Dowry.* Ed. T. A. Dunn. Berkeley: University of California Press, 1969.

Fitzgeffrey, Henry. *Satyres: and Satyricall Epigrams.* 1617. STC 10945. Includes *Notes from Black-fryers.*

Fletcher, John. *Bonduca.* Malone Society Reprint.

———. *The Honest Man's Fortune.* In *The Works of Francis Beaumont and John Fletcher,* ed. A. Glover and A. R. Waller. Cambridge: Cambridge University Press, 1905–12.

———. *The Nightwalker, The Woman's Prize,* and *Women Pleased.* In *The Works of Beaumont and Fletcher,* ed. Alexander Dyce. New York: Appleton, 1890.

Fletcher, John, and William Shakespeare. *The Two Noble Kinsmen.* In *The Works of Beaumont and Fletcher,* ed. Alexander Dyce. New York: Appleton, 1890.

The fyftene joyes of maryage. 1509. STC 15258.

G., I. *An Apologie For Women-Kinde.* 1605. STC 11497.

Gainsford, Thomas. *The Rich Cabinet Furnished with varietie of Excellent discriptions, exquisite Charracters.* 1616. STC 11522.

Gamage, William. *Linsi-Woolsie; or, Two Centvries of Epigrammes.* 1613. STC 11544.

Garter, Thomas. *The Most Virtuous and Godly Susanna.* Malone Society Reprint.

Gascoigne, George. *The Steele Glas.* 1576. STC 11645.

Gataker, Thomas. *Marriage Dvties Briefely Covched Togither.* 1620. STC 11667.

Gibson, Anthony. *A Womans Woorth, defended against all the men in the world. Prouing them to be more perfect, excellent and absolute in all vertuous actions, then any man of what qualitie soeuer.* 1599. STC 11831.

Gifford, Humfrey. *A Posie of Gilloflowers.* 1580. STC 11872.

Goddard, William. *A Satyricall Dialogue Or a Sharplye invectiue conference, betweene Allexander the great, and that truelye woman-hater Diogynes.* 1616. STC 11930.

Godly Queen Hester. Ed. W. W. Greg. Louvain: Uystpruyst, 1904.

Gosynhyll, Edward. *The prayse of all women, called Mulierū pean.* ca. 1542. STC 12102.

———. *The Scole house of women.* ca. 1542. I use the edition of 1560, STC 12105.

Gouge, William. *Of Domesticall Duties.* 1634 (first published 1622). STC 12121.

Greene, Robert. *Mamillia. A Mirrour or looking-glasse for the Ladies of Englande.* 1583. STC 12269.

————. *The Myrrovr of Modestie.* 1584. STC 12278.

————. *Orlando Furioso.* In *The Plays and Poems of Robert Greene,* vol. 1, ed. J. Churton Collins. Oxford: Clarendon, 1905.

————. *Penelopes Web . . . a Christall Mirror of feminine perfection.* 1601 (first published 1587). STC 12294.

Greene, Robert, and Thomas Lodge. *A looking-Glass for London and England.* Malone Society Reprint.

Guevara, Antonio de. *The golden boke of Marcus Aurelius.* Trans. J. Bourchier, Lord Barners, 1535. STC 12436–12447. Trans. Thomas North, 1557. STC 12427–12430.

Guillemeau, Jacques. *Child-birth; or, The Happy Delivery of Women.* 1612. STC 12496.

Guilpin, Edward. *Skialetheia.* 1598. STC 12504.

Haec-Vir; or, The Womanish Man: Being an Answere to the late Booke intituled Hic-Mulier. Exprest in a briefe Dialogue betweene Haec-Vir the Womanish Man, and Hic-Mulier the Man-Woman. 1620. STC 12599.

Hake, Edward. *A Commemoration of the most prosperous and peaceable Raigne of our gratious and deere Soueraigne Lady Elizabeth.* 1575. STC 12605.

Hall, Joseph. *Virgidemiarum.* 1598. STC 12717 (first published 1597).

Hannay, Patrick. *A happy husband. To which is adjoyned the Good Wife,* by R. Brathwaite. 1618. STC 12747.

————. *Two Elegies on the late death of our Souereigne Queen Anne.* 1619. STC 12749.

Har, W. *Epicedivm, A Funerall Song, vpon the vertuous life, and godly death, of . . . Lady Helen Branch.* 1594. STC 12751.

Haughton, William. *English-men for My Money; or, A Pleasant Comedy called A Woman Will Have Her Will.* Malone Society Reprint.

Heale, William. *An Apologie for Women.* 1609. STC 13014.

Heath, John. *Two Centuries of Epigrams.* 1610. STC 13018.

Heywood, John. *Johan Johan, the Husband, Tyb, His Wife, and syr Johan, The Preest.* In *Chief Pre-Shakespearean Dramas,* ed. Joseph Quincy Adams. Cambridge, Mass.: Houghton-Mifflin, 1924.

————. *John Heywoodes Woorkes.* 1562. STC 13285.

Heywood, Thomas. *The Exemplary Lives and memorable Acts of nine the most worthy Women of the World.* 1640. STC 13316.

———— (?). *The Fair Maid of the Exchange.* Malone Society Reprint.

————. *The Fair Maid of the West.* Ed. Robert K. Turner. Lincoln, Nebr.: University of Nebraska Press, 1967.

————. *Gunaikeion; or, Nine Bookes of Various History Concerninge Women.* 1624. STC 13326.

———— (?). *How A Man May Choose A Good Wife From A Bad.* In *A Select Collection of Old English Plays Originally Published by Robert Dodsley,* ed. W. Carew Hazlitt. London: Reeves and Turner, 1875.

———. *The Rape of Lucrece, The Iron Age, Parts 1 and 2, The Golden Age, The Silver Age, The Brazen Age, The Wise-Woman of Hogsdon,* and *If You Know Not Me, You Know Nobody, Part 2.* In *The Dramatic Works of Thomas Heywood,* ed. R. H. Shepherd. London: John Pearson, 1874.

———. *A Woman Killed with Kindness.* In *Elizabethan Plays,* ed. Arthur H. Nethercot, Charles R. Baskervill, and Virgil B. Heltzel. New York: Holt, Rinehart, and Winston, 1971.

Hic Mulier; or, The Man-Woman: Being a Medicine to cure the Coltish Disease of the Staggers in the Masculine-Feminines of our Times. 1620. STC 13374.

"Hoow, gossip myne." In *The Early English Carols,* ed. R. L. Greene. Oxford: Oxford University Press, 1977.

Hutton, Henry. *Follie's Anatomie.* 1619. STC 14028.

Ingelend, Thomas. *The Disobedient Child.* In *A Select Collection of Old English Plays Originally Published by Robert Dodsley,* ed. W. Carew Hazlitt, London: Reeves and Turner, 1874.

Interlocucyon with an argument betwyxt man and woman whiche of them could prouve to be most excellēt, ca. 1525. *STC 14100.*

Jonson, Ben. *The Alchemist, The Case Is Altered, Epicoene, Every Man in His Humour,* and *Volpone.* In *Ben Jonson,* ed. C. H. Herford and Percy Simpson. Oxford: Clarendon, 1925–52. (1601 version of *Every Man*).

Jonson, Ben, George Chapman, and John Marston. *Eastward Ho.* Ed. C. G. Petter. London: E. Benn, 1973.

King Leir and His Three Daughters. Tudor Facsimile Text.

Knox, John. *The First Blast of the Trumpet Against the Monstrous Regiment of Women.* 1558. STC 15070.

The life and pranks of long Meg of Westminster. 1582. STC 17782.

Lloyd, Lodowick. *The Choyce of Iewels.* 1607. STC 16618.

Lodge, Thomas. *Catharos, Diogenes in his Singularitie.* 1591. STC 16654.

The London Prodigal. In *Disputed Plays of William Shakespeare,* ed. William Kozlenko. New York: Hawthorn, 1974. (Reprint of *The Doubtful Plays of Shakspere,* ed. Henry Tyrrell. London and New York: John Tallis, 1860.)

Lust's Dominion. In *A Select Collection of Old English Plays Originally Published by Robert Dodsley,* ed. W. Carew Hazlitt. London: Reeves and Turner, 1875.

Lydgate, John. *A Mumming at Hertford.* In *Minor Poems of Lydgate,* ed. Henry N. MacCracken and Merriam Sherwood. London: EETSES, 1911.

Lyly, John. *Campaspe.* 1584. STC 17048.

———. *Euphues. The Anatomy of Wyt.* 1578. STC 17051.

———. *The Maid's Metamorphosis.* Tudor Facsimile Text.

A lyttle treatyse called the Image of Idlenesse, conteynynge certeyne matters moued betwen Walter Wedlocke and Bawdin Bacheler. Translated out of the Troyane or Cornyshe tounge into Englyshe, by Olyuer Oldwanton, and dedicated to the Lady Lust. ca. 1558. STC 25196.

Markham, Gervase, and Lewis Machin. *The Dumb Knight.* In *A Select Collection of Old English Plays Originally Published by Robert Dodsley,* ed. W. Carew Hazlitt. London: Reeves and Turner, 1875.

Marlowe, Christopher. *Dr. Faustus*. In *The Complete Works of Christopher Marlowe*, ed. Fredson Bowers. Cambridge: Cambridge University Press, 1973.

———. *Tamburlaine, Parts 1 and 2, Edward II*, and *The Jew of Malta*. In *The Works and Life of Christopher Marlowe*, ed. R. H. Case. London: Methuen, 1930–33.

Marston, John. *Antonio and Mellida, Parts 1 and 2 (Part 2* also known as *Antonio's Revenge)*. Malone Society Reprint.

———. *The Dutch Courtesan*. Ed. M. L. Wine. Lincoln, Neb.: University of Nebraska Press, 1965.

———. *The Malcontent*. Ed. M. L. Wine. Lincoln, Nebr.: University of Nebraska Press, 1964.

———. *The Parasitaster; or, The Fawn*. Ed. David A. Blostein. Manchester: Manchester University Press; Baltimore: Johns Hopkins University Press, 1978.

———. *The Scourge of Villanie*. 1598. STC 17485.

———. *Sophonisba*. In *John Marston: The Works*, ed. A. H. Bullen. Hildesheim: G. Olms, 1970 (first published 1887).

Marston, John, and William Barkstead. *The Insatiate Countess*. In *The Plays of John Marston*, ed. H. Harvey Wood. Edinburgh: Oliver and Boyd, 1935–39.

A merry Ieste of a Shrewde and curste Wyfe lapped in Morrelles skin. STC 14521.

Middleton, Thomas. *More Dissemblers Besides Women; Your Five Gallants; The Family of Love; Blurt, Master-Constable(?); The Widow; No Wit No Help Like a Woman's; A Mad World, My Masters; The Witch; A Trick to Catch the Old One; Michaelmas Term; The Phoenix*. In *The Works of Thomas Middleton*, ed. A. H. Bullen. New York: AMS Press, 1964 (first published 1885).

———. *Women Beware Women*. Ed. J. R. Mulryne. London: Methuen, 1975.

Middleton, Thomas, and William Rowley. *The World Tossed At Tennis*. In *The Works of Thomas Middleton*, ed. A. H. Bullen. New York: AMS Press, 1964 (first published 1885).

More, Edward. *A Lytle and Bryefe tretyse, called the defence of women, and especially of Englyshe women, made agaynst the Schole howse of women*. 1560. STC 18067.

Munda, Constantia [pseud.]. *The Worming of a mad Dogge; or, A Soppe for Cerbervs the Iaylor of Hell*. 1617. STC 18257.

Nashe, Thomas. *The Anatomie of Absurditie, Contayning a breefe confutation of the slender imputed prayses to feminine perfection*. 1589. STC 18364.

Newman, Arthur. *Pleasvres Vision: With Deserts Complaint, And A Short Dialogve of a Womans Properties, betweene an old Man and a Young*. 1619. STC 18496.

Newstead, Christopher. *An Apology for Women; or, Womens Defence*. 1620. STC 18508.

Niccholes, Alexander. *A Discourse of Marriage and Wiving*. 1615. STC 18514.

Niccols, Richard. *The Cuckow.* 1607. STC 18517.

———. *The Fvries.* 1614. STC 18521.

———. *Londons artillery.* 1616. STC 18522.

Overbury, Sir Thomas. *A Wife now the widdow of Sir T. Overbury.* 1614. STC 18904.

Ovidius Naso, Publius. *The pleasant fable of Hermaphroditus and Salmacis.* Trans. T. Peend. 1565. STC 18971.

———. *Salmacis and Hermaphroditus.* Translation and expansion attributed to Francis Beaumont. 1602. STC 18972.

Painter, William. *The Palace of Pleasure.* Vol. II. 1567. STC 19124.

Parker, Martin. *A warning for wives, by the example of one Katherine Francis.* STC 19280.

Parrot, Henry. *The Gossips Greeting; or, A new Discovery of such Females meeting.* 1620. STC 19331.

———. *The Movs-Trap.* 1606. STC 19334.

Pettie, George. *A petite pallace of Pettie his pleasure.* 1576. STC 19819.

Phillip, John. *The Commodye of Pacient and Meeke Grissill.* Malone Society Reprint.

Pickering, John. *The Interlude of Vice [Horestes].* 1567. Malone Society Reprint.

Pico della Mirandola. *Oration on the Dignity of Man.* 1487. My translation.

Platter, Thomas. *Thomas Platter's Travels in England.* 1599. Trans. Clare Williams. London: Jonathan Cape, 1937.

Porter, Henry. *The Two Angry Women of Abington.* Malone Society Reprint.

Preston, Thomas. *Cambyses.* In *Elizabethan Plays,* ed. Arthur H. Nethercot, Charles R. Baskervill, and Virgil B. Heltzel. New York: Holt, Rinehart, and Winston, 1971.

The proude wyues Pater noster that wolde go gaye, and vndyd her husbonde and went her waye. STC 25938.

The Puritan; or, The Widow of Watling Street. In *Disputed Plays of William Shakespeare,* ed. William Kozlenko. New York: Hawthorn, 1974. (Reprint of *The Doubtful Plays of Shakspere,* ed. Henry Tyrrell. London and New York: John Tallis, 1860.)

Pyrrye, C. *The praise and Dispraise of Women, very fruitfull to the well disposed minde, and delectable to the readers thereof.* ca. 1569. STC 20523.

Quintilianus, Marcus Fabius. *Quintilian's Institutes of Oratory.* Trans. John Selby Watson. 2 vols. London: George Bell, 1891.

Rich, Barnabe. *The Aduentures of Brusanus Prince of Hungaria.* 1592. STC 20977.

———. *The Excellency of good women.* 1613. STC 20982.

———. *Favltes favlts, and nothing else but favltes.* 1606. STC 20983.

———. *Riche his Farewell to Military Profession: containing very pleasant discourses fitte for a peaceable tyme: Gathered together for the onlie delight of the courteous Gentlewomen, both of Englande and Ireland for whose onlie pleasure they were collected together, And vnto whom they are directed and dedicated.* 1594 (first published 1581). Revised STC 20996.7.

Rowlands, Samuel. *Diogines Lanthorne.* 1607. STC 21368.

―――. *Tis Merrie When Gossips Meete.* 1602. STC 21409.

―――. *A Whole Crew of Kind Gossips, All Met To Be Merry.* 1609. STC 21413.

Rowley, William. *All's Lost By Lust.* 1633. STC 21425.

Rye, William Brenchley. *England as seen by Foreigners in the Days of Elizabeth and James the First.* New York: Benjamin Blom, 1967. (First published 1865.)

S., S. *The Honest Lawyer.* Tudor Facsimile Text.

Salter, Thomas. *A Mirrhor mete for all mothers, matrones, and maidens.* 1579. STC 21634.

Scoggin, John. *Scoggin, his jestes.* 1613. STC 21851; first published in the reign of Henry VIII (?).

Seneca, Lucius Annaeus. *Medea.* Trans. John Studley. 1566. STC 22224.

―――. *Octavia.* Trans. Thomas Nuce. 1566. STC 22229.

Shakespeare, William. *The Complete Works.* Ed. G. B. Harrison. New York: Harcourt, Brace, and World, 1948.

Sharpe, Roger. *More Fooles yet.* 1610. STC 22379.

Sharpham, Edward. *Cupids Whirligig.* 1607. STC 22380.

―――. *The Fleire.* 1607. STC 22384.

Sidney, Sir Philip. *The Defense of Poesy.* In *The Renaissance in England,* ed. Hyder Rollins and Herschel Baker. Boston: Heath, 1954.

Skelton, John. *The tunning of Elinor Rumming.* 1609. STC 22612. (First published in the reign of Henry VIII.)

Smith, Henry. *A Preparatiue to Marriage.* 1591. STC 22685.

Snawsel, Robert. *A looking glasse for maried folkes.* 1610. STC 22886.

Songes and sonettes [Tottel's Miscellany]. 1557. STC 13861.

Sowernam, Ester [pseud.]. *Ester hath hang'd Haman; or, An Answere To a lewd Pamphlet, entituled, The Arraignment of Women. With the arraignment of lewd, idle, froward, and vnconstant men, and Hvsbands.* 1617. STC 22974.

Speght, Rachel. *A Movzell for Melastomvs, The cynicall Bayter of, and foule mouthed Barker against Evahs Sex; or, An Apologeticall Answere to that Irreligious and Illiterate Pamphlet made by Io. Sw. and by him Intituled "The Arraignment of Women."* 1617. STC 23058.

Spenser, Edmund. *The Poems of Spenser.* Ed. J. C. Smith and F. De-Selincourt. London: Oxford University Press, 1912.

Stephens, John. *Satyrical essayes, characters and others.* 1615. STC 23249.

Stubbes, Phillip. *The Anatomy of Abuses.* 1583. STC 23376.

Swetnam, Joseph. *The Araignment of Lewde, idle, froward, and vnconstant women: Or the vanitie of them, choose you whether.* 1615. STC 23533.

Swetnam the Woman-hater Arraigned by Women. In *Swetnam the Woman-hater: The Controversy and the Play,* ed. Coryl Crandall. Lafayette, Ind.: Purdue University Studies, 1969.

Sylvester, Joshua. *Monodia. An Elegie, in commemoration of the Vertuous life, and Godlie Death of . . . Dame Helen Branch.* 1594. STC 23579.

A Talk of Ten Wives on Their Husbands' Ware. In *Jyl of Breyntford's Testament,* ed. F. J. Furnivall. London: privately printed, 1871.

Tales, and quicke answeres, very mery, and pleasant to read. ca. 1535. STC 23665.

Tasso, Ercole, and Torquato Tasso. *Of Mariage and VViuing. An Excellent, pleasant, and Philosophicall Controuersie, betweene the two famous Tassi now liuing, the one Hercules the Philosopher, the other, Torquato the Poet.* Trans. R. T. 1599. STC 23690.

Tilney, Edmund. *A brief and pleasant discourse of duties in Mariage, called the Flower of Friendship.* 1568. STC 24076.

Tom Tyler and His Wife. Malone Society Reprint.

Tottel's Miscellany. See *Songes and sonettes.*

Tourneur, Cyril. *The Revenger's Tragedy.* In *Three Jacobean Tragedies,* ed. Gāmini Salgādo. Harmondsworth: Penguin, 1965.

Tuke, Thomas. *A Discovrse Against Painting and Tincturing of Women. Wherein the abominable sinnes of Murther and Poysoning, Pride and Ambition, Adultery and Witchcraft are set foorth and discouered.* 1616. STC 24316ᵃ.

Turberville, George. *Epitaphes, Epigrams, Songs and Sonets.* 1567. STC 24326.

Tuvil, Daniel. *Asylum Veneris; or, A Sanctuary for Ladies. Iustly Protecting Them, their virtues and sufficiencies from the foule aspersions and forged imputations of traducing Spirits.* 1616. STC 24393.

Tyler, Margaret, trans. *Mirror of Princely Deeds and Knighthood.* 1578. STC 18859.

Vaughan, Robert (?). *A Dyalogue defensyue for women, agaynst malycyous detractours.* 1542. STC 24601.

The vertuous scholehous of vngracious women. ca. 1550. STC 12104.

Wager, Lewis. *The Life and Repentance of Mary Magdalene.* Tudor Facsimile Reprint.

Wager, W. *The Trial of Treasure.* 1567. STC 24271.

Walkington, Thomas. *Rabboni, or Mary Magdalen's tears.* 1620. STC 24970.

Wallys, J. "Good awdience, harken to me in this cace." In *Songs and Ballads, Chiefly of the Reign of Philip and Mary,* ed. Thomas Wright. New York: Burt Franklin, 1970 (first published 1860).

Wapull, George. *The Tide Tarrieth No Man.* 1576. STC 25018.

Webbe, George. *The Araignment of an Vnruly Tongue.* 1619. STC 25156.

Webster, John. *The Devil's Law-Case.* In *The Complete Works of John Webster,* ed. F. L. Lucas. New York: Gordian Press, 1966 (first published 1927).

——. *The Duchess of Malfi.* Ed. John Russell Brown. London: Methuen, 1964.

——. *The White Devil.* Ed. Clive Hart. Edinburgh: Oliver and Boyd, 1970.

Weddirburne. *The ballat of the prayis of wemen.* In *The Bannatyne Manuscript,* ed. W. Tod Ritchie. Edinburgh and London: Blackwood for Scottish Text Society, 1928.

West, R. *Wits ABC.* 1608. STC 25262.

Whately, William. *A Bride-Bvsh; or, A Direction For Married Persons. Plainly Describing The Duties common to both, and peculiar to each of them. By Performing Of Which, Marriage shall prooue a great helpe to such, as now for want of performing them doe find it a little hell.* 1623 (first published 1616). STC 25298.

Whetstone, George. *An Heptameron of Ciuill Discourses.* 1582. STC 25337.

Wilkins, George. *The Miseries of Enforced Marriage.* In *A Select Collection of Old English Plays Originally Published by Robert Dodsley,* ed. W. Carew Hazlitt. London: Reeves and Turner, 1875.

Williams, John. *A Sermon of Apparell.* 1619. STC 25728.

The Wit of a Woman. Malone Society Reprint.

Wyther, George. *Abuses stript and whipt.* 1613. STC 25891.

A Yorkshire Tragedy. In *Disputed Plays of William Shakespeare,* ed. William Kozlenko. New York: Hawthorn, 1974. (Reprint of *The Doubtful Plays of Shakspere,* ed. Henry Tyrrell. London and New York: John Tallis, 1860.)

III. Secondary Sources

Adams, Robert P. *The Better Part of Valor: More, Erasmus, Colet, and Vives, On Humanism, War, and Peace, 1496–1535.* Seattle: University of Washington Press, 1962.

Baker, Herschel. *The Image of Man: A Study of the Idea of Human Dignity in Classical Antiquity, the Middle Ages, and the Renaissance.* New York, Evanston, and London: Harper, 1961 (first published 1947).

Bean, John C. "Comic Structure and the Humanizing of Kate in *The Taming of the Shrew.*" In *The Woman's Part: Feminist Criticism of Shakespeare,* ed. Carolyn Ruth Swift Lenz et al., 65–78. Urbana, Chicago, and London: University of Illinois Press, 1980.

Berggren, Paula. "The Woman's Part: Female Sexuality as Power in Shakespeare's Plays." In *The Woman's Part: Feminist Criticism of Shakespeare,* ed. Carolyn Ruth Swift Lenz et al., 17–34. Urbana, Chicago, and London: University of Illinois Press, 1980.

Bergson, Henri. *Laughter* (first published 1900). Trans. Fred Rothwell. In *Comedy: Meaning and Form,* ed. Robert W. Corrigan. San Francisco: Chandler, 1965.

Boas, George. *The Happy Beast in French Thought of the Seventeenth Century.* Baltimore: Johns Hopkins University Press, 1933.

Bradford, Gamaliel. *Elizabethan Women.* Ed. Harold Ogden White. Boston: Houghton Mifflin, 1936.

Bradley, A. C. *Shakespearean Tragedy.* Greenwich, Conn.: Fawcett, 1965 (first published 1904).

Bridenthal, Renate, and Claudia Koonz. *Becoming Visible: Women in European History.* Boston: Houghton Mifflin, 1977.

Bush, Douglas. *The Renaissance and English Humanism.* London: Oxford University Press, 1941.

Camden, Carroll. *The Elizabethan Woman*. Houston, New York, and London: Elsevier, 1952.

Cartwright, Julia. *Baldassare Castiglione, the Perfect Courtier: His Life and Letters, 1478–1529*. 2 vols. London: John Murray, 1908.

Clark, Alice. *Working Life of Women in the Seventeenth Century*. London: Frank Cass, 1968 (first published 1919).

Colie, Rosalie. *Paradoxia Epidemica: The Renaissance Tradition of Paradox*. Princeton, N.J.: Princeton University Press, 1966.

Cornford, Francis MacDonald. *The Origin of Attic Comedy*. Cambridge: Cambridge University Press, 1914.

Crandall, Coryl. "The Cultural Implications of the Swetnam Anti-Feminist Controversy in the 17th Century," *Journal of Popular Culture* 2 (1968): 136–148.

———. Introduction to *Swetnam the Woman-hater: The Controversy and the Play*. Lafayette, Ind.: Purdue University Studies, 1969.

Crawley, Ernest. *The Mystic Rose: A Study of Primitive Marriage and of Primitive Thought in its Bearing on Marriage*, vol. 1. Rev. by Theodore Besterman. London: Methuen, 1927.

Cushman, L. W. *The Devil and the Vice in English Dramatic Literature before Shakespeare*. London: Frank Cass, 1970 (first published 1900).

Danby, John F. *Poets on Fortune's Hill*. London: Faber and Faber, 1952.

Davies, Ross. *Women and Work*. London: Hutchinson, 1975.

Deats, Sara Munson. "*Edward II:* A Study in Androgyny," *Ball State University Forum*, 22 (1981): 30–41.

Delcourt, Marie. *Hermaphrodite: Myths and Rites of the Bisexual Figure in Classical Antiquity*. Trans. Jennifer Nicholson. London: Studio Books, 1961 (first published in French in 1956).

Dent, Robert W. *John Webster's Borrowing*. Berkeley: University of California Press, 1960.

Diamond, Arlyn, and Lee R. Edwards, eds. *The Authority of Experience: Essays in Feminist Criticism*. Amherst: University of Massachusetts Press, 1977.

Dipple, Elizabeth. "Metamorphosis in Sidney's *Arcadias*," *Philological Quarterly* 50 (1971): 47–62.

Dunn, Catherine M. "The Changing Image of Woman in Renaissance Society and Literature." In *What Manner of Woman: Essays in English and American Life and Literature*, ed. Marlene Springer, 15–38. New York: New York University Press, 1977.

Dusinberre, Juliet. *Shakespeare and the Nature of Women*. London: Macmillan, 1975.

Fitz, L. T. (See also Woodbridge, Linda.) "Egyptian Queens and Male Reviewers: Sexist Attitudes in *Antony and Cleopatra* Criticism," *Shakespeare Quarterly*, 28 (1977): 297–316.

———. "Humanism Questioned: A Study of Four Renaissance Characters," *English Studies in Canada* 5 (1979): 388–405.

———. "'What Says the Married Woman?': Marriage Theory and Feminism in the English Renaissance," *Mosaic* 13 (1980): 1–22.

Freud, Sigmund. *Jokes and their Relation to the Unconscious.* Trans. James Strachey. New York: Norton, 1960 (first published 1905).

Frye, Northrop. *Anatomy of Criticism.* Princeton, N.J.: Princeton University Press, 1957.

———. *A Natural Perspective: The Development of Shakespearean Comedy and Romance.* New York: Columbia University Press, 1965.

Furnivall, F. J., ed. *Captain Cox, his Ballads and Books; or, Robert Laneham's Letter.* Hertford: Stephen Austin, 1890.

Gohlke, Madelon. " 'I wooed thee with my sword': Shakespeare's Tragic Paradigms." In *The Woman's Part: Feminist Criticism of Shakespeare,* ed. Carolyn Ruth Swift Lenz et al., 150–70. Urbana, Chicago, and London: University of Illinois Press, 1980.

Greer, Germaine. *The Female Eunuch.* New York: Bantam, 1972 (first published 1970).

Grosart, A. B., ed. Introduction to *Swetnam the Woman-hater, Arraigned by Women.* Manchester: C. E. Simms, 1880.

Harbage, Alfred. *Conceptions of Shakespeare.* New York: Schocken, 1968 (first published 1966).

———. *Shakespeare's Audience.* New York and London: Columbia University Press, 1961 (first published 1941).

———. *Shakespeare and the Rival Traditions.* New York: Macmillan, 1952.

Hawkins, Harriett. "The Victim's Side: Chaucer's *Clerk's Tale* and Webster's *Duchess of Malfi,*" *Signs* 1 (1975): 339–61.

Hayles, Nancy. "The Ambivalent Ideal: The Concept of Androgyny in English Renaissance Literature." Ph.D. diss., University of Rochester. 1976.

Hays, Janice. "Those 'soft and delicate desires': *Much Ado* and the Distrust of Women." In *The Woman's Part: Feminist Criticism of Shakespeare,* ed. Carolyn Ruth Swift Lenz, et al., 77–99. Urbana, Chicago, and London: University of Illinois Press, 1980.

Heilman, Robert. "The *Taming* Untamed; or, The Return of the Shrew," *Modern Language Quarterly* 27 (1966): 147–61.

Henze, Catherine. "Author and Source for *A Dyalogue Defensyue for Women,*" *Notes and Queries* 221 (1977): 537–39.

Hobbes, Thomas. *Leviathan, Parts I and II.* Ed. Herbert W. Schneider. New York: Bobbs-Merrill, 1958 (first published 1651).

Hosley, Richard. "Sources and Analogues of *The Taming of the Shrew,*" *Huntington Library Quarterly* 27 (1963–4): 289–308.

Jorgensen, Paul A. *Our Naked Frailties: Sensational Art and Meaning in "Macbeth."* Berkeley, Los Angeles, and London: University of California Press, 1971.

———. *Shakespeare's Military World.* Berkeley and Los Angeles: University of California Press, 1956.

Kahin, Helen Andrews. "Jane Anger and John Lyly," *Modern Language Quarterly* 8 (1947): 31–35.

Kahn, Coppélia. "Coming of Age in Verona," *Modern Language Studies* 8 (1977–8): 5–22. Reprinted in *The Woman's Part: Feminist Criticism of*

Shakespeare, ed. Carolyn Ruth Swift Lenz, et al., 171–210. Urbana, Chicago, and London, 1980.

———. "The *Taming of the Shrew:* Shakespeare's Mirror of Marriage," *Modern Language Studies* 5 (1975): 88–102. Reprinted in *The Authority of Experience,* ed. Arlyn Diamond and Lee R. Edwards, 84–100. Amherst: University of Massachusetts Press, 1977.

Kelly-Gadol, Joan. "Did Women Have a Renaissance?" In *Becoming Visible: Women in European History,* ed. Renate Bridenthal and Claudia Koonz, 137–64. Boston: Houghton Mifflin, 1977.

Kelso, Ruth. *Doctrine for the Lady of the Renaissance.* Urbana: University of Illinois Press, 1978 (first published 1956).

Lenz, Carolyn Ruth Swift, Gayle Greene, and Carol Thomas Neely, eds. *The Woman's Part: Feminist Criticism of Shakespeare.* Urbana, Chicago, and London: University of Illinois Press, 1980.

Lepick, Julie. "'That Faire Hermaphrodite': The Transformation of a Figure in the Literature of the English Renaissance." Ph.D. diss., University of Buffalo, 1976.

MacDonald, Roger. "The Widow: A Recurring Figure in Jacobean and Caroline Comedy." Ph.D. diss., University of New Brunswick, 1978.

Maclean, Ian. *The Renaissance Notion of Woman: A Study in the Fortunes of Scholasticism and Medical Science in European Intellectual Life.* Cambridge: Cambridge University Press, 1980.

Moncada, Ernest J. "The Spanish Source of Edmund Tilney's *Flower of Friendshippe,*" MLR 65 (1970): 241–47.

Morley, Henry. *The Life of Henry Cornelius Agrippa von Nettesheim.* 2 vols. London: Chapman and Hall, 1856.

Park, Clara Claiborne. "As We Like It: How a Girl Can Be Smart and Still Popular," *The American Scholar* 42 (1973): 262–278. Reprinted in *The Woman's Part: Feminist Criticism of Shakespeare,* ed. Carolyn Ruth Swift Lenz, et al., 100–116. Urbana, Chicago, and London: University of Illinois Press, 1980.

Rabkin, Norman. *Shakespeare and the Common Understanding.* London: Collier-Macmillan, 1967.

———. "Rabbits, Ducks, and Henry V," *Shakespeare Quarterly* 28 (1977): 279–296.

Rogers, Katharine. *The Troublesome Helpmate: A History of Misogyny in Literature.* Seattle and London: University of Washington Press, 1966.

Rose, Mark. "Sidney's Womanish Man," *Review of English Studies* n.s., 15 (1964): 353–365.

Saloman, Louis. *The Devil Take Her! A Study of the Rebellious Lover in English Poetry.* New York: Barnes, 1961 (first published 1931).

Scott, David. "William Patten and the Authorship of 'Robert Laneham's Letter' (1575)," *English Literary Renaissance* 7 (1977): 297–306.

Sexton, Joyce H. *The Slandered Woman in Shakespeare.* Victoria: University of Victoria Monographs, 1978.

Springer, Marlene, ed. *What Manner of Woman: Essays in English and American Life and Literature.* New York: New York University Press, 1977.

Stempel, Daniel. "The Transmigration of the Crocodile," *Shakespeare Quarterly* 7 (1956): 59–72.

Thistleton-Dyer, T. F. *Folk-lore of Women*. Chicago: A. C. McClurg, 1906.

Thomas, Keith. "The Changing Family," *Times Literary Supplement,* 21 October 1977, 1227.

Thorp, Willard. "The Position of Women in Elizabethan Drama." In *The Triumph of Realism in Elizabethan Drama, 1558–1612*. New York: Haskell, 1965 (first published 1916).

Watson, Foster. *Vives and the Renascence Education of Women*. New York: Longmans, 1912.

Wiley, Autrey Nell. "Female Prologues and Epilogues in English Plays." *PMLA* 48 (1933): 1060–1079.

Willson, D. Harrison. *King James VI and I*. Oxford: Alden, 1956.

Wilson, E. C. "Shakespeare's Enobarbus." In *Joseph Quincy Adams: Memorial Studies,* ed. James G. McManaway et al.. Washington: Folger Shakespeare Library, 1948.

Wilson, Violet. *Society Women of Shakespeare's Time*. London: Lane, 1924.

Woodbridge, Linda. (See also Fitz, L. T.) "New Light on *The Wife Lapped in Morel's Skin* and *The Proud Wife's Paternoster,*" *English Literary Renaissance* 13 (1983): 3–35.

Wright, Celeste Turner. "The Amazons in Elizabethan Literature," *Studies in Philology* 37 (1940): 433–456.

Wright, Louis B. "The Popular Controversy over Women." In *Middle-Class Culture in Elizabethan England*. Chapel Hill: University of North Carolina Press, 1935.

Index

Items are indexed by short title, in modern spelling.
For full title and old spelling, see the Bibliography.

Abrams, M. H., 266
Abuses Stripped and Whipped (Wyther),
169
Adam: as hermaphrodite, 140; mentioned, 28, 33, 34–36, 39–40, 51,
69, 70, 75, 84, 123, 144
Adams, Robert P., 168, 182n14,
221n18
Adams, Thomas: *Mystical Bedlam*, 142
Adventures of Brusanus. See Rich, Bar-
nabe: *Brusanus, Prince of Hungaria*
Aggressiveness of women. *See*
Women
Agrippa, Heinrich Cornelius, von
Nettesheim, 7, 38–44, 45, 47–
48n19, 48n25, 54, 61, 71–72n5, 90,
98, 102, 104, 112–13n8, 118, 135,
148, 149, 247, 324; *De Nobilitate et
Praecellentia Foemenei Sexus*, 16, 38,
58–59, 72n5; *Female Pre-eminence*,
41, 47; *Nobility and Excellency of
Womankind*, 4, 38–44, 47n17, 57,
327n2; *Vanity of the Arts and Sci-
ences*, 41
Alchemist, The. See Jonson, Ben
All's Lost by Lust. See Rowley, Wil-
liam
All's Well That Ends Well. See Shake-
speare, William
Alphonsus of Aragon, 67
Amazons. *See Exempla* of the formal
controversy
Ambree, Mary, 254
Amends for Ladies. See Field, Nathan
Anatomy of Absurdity, The (Nashe),
62–63, 67, 70, 121

Anatomy of Abuses (Stubbes), 139–40
Androgynes, androgyny. *See* Her-
maphrodites, hermaphrodism
Anger, Jane, 4, 88; *Protection for
Women*, 4, 63–66, 70
Annals of English Drama (Harbage/
Schoenbaum), 136n5
Antiblazons. *See* Blazons and antibla-
zons
Antisthenes, 67
Antonio and Mellida. See Marston,
John
Antonio's Revenge. See Marston, John
Antonius (Mary Herbert), 126
Antony and Cleopatra. See Shake-
speare, William
Apology for Women, An (Heale), 81
Apology for Women, An (Newstead), 79
Apology for Womenkind, An (I. G.),
74–76
Apology of Raymond Sebonde, An
(Montaigne), 41, 42, 151n9
Appius and Virginia (R. B.), 125–26,
214, 277, 278, 289
Aquinas, Thomas: *Summa Theologica*,
47–48n19
Arbuthnot, Alexander: *Contrapoison
to the Ballad Falsely Entitled the Prop-
erties of Good Women*, 118, 135n3
Arcadia. See Sidney, Philip
Archilochus, 100
Arden of Feversham (anonymous), 125,
210
Aristocracy, Renaissance, 54–55, 58
Aristophanes, 67, 112
Aristotle: on comedy and phallic

songs, 112; on physiology of
women, 68, 73n9; *Rhetoric,* 25; on
women's aptness for certain tasks,
19; on women's innate imperfection, 15, 19, 56, 61, 108; on wom-
en's wish to be male, 61, 68;
mentioned, 62, 66, 84, 208, 276
Arraignment of an Unruly Tongue, The
(Webbe), 208
*Arraignment of Lewd, Idle, Froward,
and Unconstant Women. See* Swetnam, Joseph
Assertiveness of women. *See* women:
aggressiveness of
Asylum Veneris. See Tuvil, Daniel
As You Like It. See Shakespeare, William
Augustine, Saint: *De Civitate Dei,* 15
Aurelius, Marcus, 63, 66
Averell, William: *Marvelous Combat of
Contrarieties,* 140

B., R.: *Appius and Virginia,* 125–26,
214, 277, 278, 289
Bachelor's Banquet, The (anonymous),
14, 124, 190, 191, 192, 205, 230,
231, 234, 270n12. *See also Quinze
Joyes de Mariage, Le*
Baker, Herschel, 325
Balancing formula, 67, 84, 85, 89,
122, 124, 199
Ballad of the Praise of Women, The
(Weddirburne), 117–18
Ballads, 117–18, 185, 236
Bannatyne Manuscript, 118, 135n2
Bansley, Charles: *Pride and Abuse of
Women Nowadays,* 14
Barry, Lording: *Ram-Alley,* 176, 177,
207–8, 236, 237, 240, 268n5,
269n6,n7, 319
Bath, Wife of. *See* Chaucer, Geoffrey:
Canterbury Tales (Wife of Bath's
Prologue and Tale)
Bawds, 174
Bean, John C., 222n22
Beaumont, Francis, and John
Fletcher: *The Captain,* 167, 238,
245, 251, 255, 261–62, 266, 279,
280–81, 287, 289, 292, 309, 314;
Maid's Tragedy, 156–57, 162, 238;
Philaster, 282, 288; *Scornful Lady,*

158, 246–46; *Woman-Hater,* 173,
177, 187, 269n5,n6, 275, 279, 281,
282, 286, 288, 289, 291. *See also*
Fletcher, John.
Beauty. *See* Virtues of women
Bercher, William: *Nobility of Women,*
4, 58–59, 113n8
Bergamo, Foresti of, 16
Berggren, Paula S., 155, 182n3
Bergson, Henri, 32
Bias, 67
Bion of Boristhenes, 67
Blackwood, G., 67
Blazons and antiblazons, 187–88,
298n9
Blurt, Master-Constable. See Middle-
ton, Thomas
Boas, George, 41
Boccaccio, Giovanni, 30, 33, 45, 53;
De Claris Mulieribus, 15, 16, 21, 33,
72n5, 126
Boke his Surfeit in Love (anonymous,
lost), 63
Bond, R. Warwick, 5, 48n25, 59
Bonduca. See Fletcher, John
Book Named the Governor, The. See
Elyot, Thomas: *The Governor*
Bradford, Gamaliel, 1, 8
Bradley, A. C., 324
Braggadocio, 154, 283, 292, 315,
321–22n2
Branch, Helen, 118
Brandon, Samuel: *Virtuous Octavia,*
126
Brathwait, Richard: *Essays upon the
Five Senses,* 118, 197, 264, 276;
"The Good Wife," 197
Brazen Age, The. See Heywood,
Thomas
Brentius, Joannes: *Right Godly Dis-
course upon the Book of Esther,* 220–
21n13
Breton, Nicholas: *Praise of Virtuous
Ladies,* 69
Bride-Bush, A (Whately), 130, 172,
193–94
*Brief and Pleasant Discourse of Duties in
Marriage, A. See Flower of Friend-
ship, The*
Brusanus, Prince of Hungaria. See Rich,
Barnabe

Bush, Douglas, 325
Bussy d'Ambois. See Chapman,
    George

Cambyses (Preston), 267, 278, 324
Camden, Carroll, 2–4, 183n21
Campaspe. See Lyly, John
Canterbury Tales. See Chaucer, Geof-
    frey
Capella, Galeazzo Flavio, 59
Captain, The. See Beaumont, Francis,
    and John Fletcher
Care, Henry, 41, 42, 48n20
Carmenta. See Exempla of the formal
    controversy
Cartwright, Julia, 72n5
Cary, Elizabeth: Mariam, 128, 218,
    281, 282, 289
Case Is Altered, The. See Jonson, Ben
Castiglione, Baldassare, 64, 71–72n5,
    98, 103, 108, 113n8, 135; Il Cortegi-
    ano, 16, 72n5; The Courtier, 4, 5,
    14, 47n16, 52–58, 94, 115, 117,
    120, 124, 168, 298n16
Catharos (Lodge), 276
Cato, 30, 67
Cerberus, 82, 101, 104
Ceres. See Exempla of the formal con-
    troversy
Chamberlain, John, 143–44, 180, 266
Chapman, George: Bussy d'Ambois,
    208, 215, 270n13, 271n14; Widow's
    Tears, 14, 128, 174, 177, 178, 208,
    236, 260, 269n5, 282, 283, 294. See
    also Jonson, Ben, George Chap-
    man, and John Marston
Characters. See Theophrastan charac-
    ters
Chastity, 136n5. See also Virtues of
    women
Chaucer, Geoffrey, 167; Canterbury
    Tales: 131 (Clerk's Tale, 126,
    221n16; Franklin's Tale, 184;
    Knight's Tale, 162; Nun's Priest's
    Tale, 31; Wife of Bath's Prologue
    and Tale, 30, 67, 190, 197, 211,
    213, 226, 247); Legend of Good
    Women, 16; Troilus and Criseyde, 286
Chester Mystery Cycle, 234
Chettle, Henry, Thomas Dekker, and

William Haughton: Patient Grissil,
    126, 176, 192, 194, 204, 211, 293
Child-birth (Guillemeau), 243n2
Chivalry: of defenders of women, 50,
    52, 87, 100, 119, 122, 133, 301–2;
    feminism hampered by, 302; lack
    of, among misogynists, 39
Choice of Jewels, The (Lloyd), 74
Christianity: and feminism, 65, 90–
    92, 129–30, 326; paradoxical nature
    of, 325; and the medieval/Renais-
    sance view of women, 15, 136n6
Christine de Pisan: City of Ladies, 16,
    47n16
Cicero, Marcus Tullius: as misogy-
    nist, 63, 67; Rhetorica ad Herennium,
    25; as rhetorician, 33, 91
Citizens' wives, 173–76, 304
City comedy, Jacobean, 169, 172, 176
City life, impact on women. See Ur-
    banization
City of Ladies. See Christine de Pisan
Clapham, David, 59
Clark, Alice, 326
Cleaver, Robert: Godly Form of House-
    hold Government, 172, 208
Cleopatra. See Daniel, Samuel: Cleo-
    patra; Exempla of the formal con-
    troversy; Herbert, Mary: Antonius;
    Shakespeare, William: Antony and
    Cleopatra
Clerk's Tale, The. See Chaucer, Geof-
    frey: Canterbury Tales
Colet, John, 16, 72n5
Colie, Rosalie L., 48n23
Comedy of Errors, The. See Shake-
    speare, William
Comedy of Patient and Meek Grissill,
    The. See Patient Grissill
Commemoration of the Peaceable Reign
    of Elizabeth (Hake), 182n8
"Concerning Famous Women." See
    Boccaccio, Giovanni: De Claris
    Mulieribus
Congreve, William: The Way of the
    World, 235
Coniugium. See Erasmus, Desiderius
Constancy of Susanna, The (anony-
    mous), 298n14
Constancy of women. See Virtues of
    women

Contrapoison to the Ballad Falsely Entitled the Properties of Good Women, A (Arbuthnot), 118, 135n3
Controversy. See Formal controversy about women
Controversy between a Lover and a Jay (Feylde), 46n4
Cooke, John: Greene's Tu Quoque, 179, 245, 256
Cooling Card for Euphues and All Fond Lovers, A. See Lyly, John
Coriolanus. See Shakespeare, William
Cornelia (Kyd), 126
Cornford, Francis MacDonald, 110–11, 299n18
Cortegiano, Il. See Castiglione, Baldassare
Costly Whore, The (anonymous), 238, 241, 248–49, 262
Courage of women. See Virtues of women
Courtier, The. See Castiglione, Baldassare
Courtly love, 15, 130, 184–89, 302
Cox, Captain, 49
Crandall, Coryl, 4, 88, 317, 320
Crawley, Ernest, 241, 299n19
Cressida. See Exempla of the formal controversy; Heywood, Thomas: Iron Age; Shakespeare, William: Troilus and Cressida
Cruelty of women. See Faults of women
Cuckolding of husbands. See Faults of women
Cuckold's Haven (anonymous), 236
Cuckow, The. See Niccols, Richard
Cupid's Whirligig. See Sharpham, Edward
Cushman, L. W., 278
Cymbeline. See Shakespeare, William

Danby, John F., 158
Daniel, Samuel: Cleopatra, 126
Davies, John, 324
Davison, Francis: Poetical Rhapsody, 233
Deats, Sara Munson, 222n25
Debate about women. See Formal controversy about women

Deceit, dissembling of women. See Faults of women
Deceit of Women, The (anonymous), 115, 135n1, 176
De Civitate Dei (Augustine), 15
De Claris Mulieribus. See Boccaccio, Giovanni
De Factis Dictisque Memorabilibus (Valerius Maximus), 15, 72n5
Defense against Them that Commonly Defame Women, The (anonymous, lost), 118
Defense of Good Women, The. See Elyot, Thomas
Defense of Poesy, The. See Sidney, Philip
Defense of Women, The. See More, Edward
De Flores, Juan, 301
Dekker, Thomas: 2 Honest Whore, 128, 177, 192, 196, 269n5, 270n8, 271n13; mentioned, 320. See also Chettle, Henry, Thomas Dekker, and William Haughton: Patient Grissil; Dekker, Thomas, and John Webster; Dekker, Thomas, and Thomas Middleton
Dekker, Thomas, and John Webster: Northward Ho, 127, 172, 298n13; Westward Ho, 124, 127, 158, 171, 172, 173, 177
Dekker, Thomas, and Thomas Middleton: 1 Honest Whore, 123, 156, 174, 194, 218, 269n8, 271n14; Roaring Girl, 143, 156, 179–80, 194, 196, 223n27, 250, 254–55, 262–63, 269n5, 289
Delcourt, Marie, 141
Delilah. See Exempla of the formal controversy
Deloney, Thomas: Garland of Good Will, 118, 252
Democritus, 63
Demosthenes, 63, 67, 84
De Nobilitate et Praecellentia Foemenei Sexus. See Agrippa, Heinrich Cornelius
Dent, Robert W., 322n3
De Nuptiis (Theophrastus), 67
Detraction, 50–51, 53

Devereux, Penelope, 185
Devil's Law-Case, The. See Webster, John
Dialogue between the Common Secretary and Jealousy (anonymous), 14, 49
Dialogue Defensive for Women. See Vaughan, Robert
Dialogues, 14, 18, 21, 22, 58, 59–60, 77–79, 102, 110, 150
Dickenson, John: *Fair Valeria*, 14, 106, 176, 177, 178, 205–6, 207, 220–21n14, 232, 234, 257, 309
Diogenes, 62, 66, 67, 77, 83, 101, 276
Diogenes' Lanthorne. See Rowlands, Samuel
Dipple, Elizabeth, 158
Discourse against Painting and Tincturing of Women, A (Tuke), 221
Discourse of Marriage and Wiving (Niccholes), 223n27
Disobedient Child, The (Ingelend), 191, 193
Dr. Faustus. See Marlowe, Christopher
Domenichi, Lodovico, 59, 113n8
Domestical Duties, Of (Gouge), 129–30, 172
Domineering wives. *See* Shrews
Doublet, Breeches, and Shirt (anonymous, lost), 150n7
Drayton, Michael: *Idea*, 187
Drunkenness of women. *See* Faults of women
Duchess of Malfi, The. See Webster, John
Dumb Knight, The. See Markham, Gervase, and Lewis Machin
Dunbar, William, 239; *Twa Cummeris* (The Two Gossips), 231, 234; *Two Married Women and the Widow*, 215, 231, 232, 233–34, 236, 242n6
Dunn, Catherine M., 4
Dusinberre, Juliet, 2, 3, 63, 153, 154, 155, 222n22, 278, 293, 297n1
Dutch Courtesan, The. See Marston, John

Eastward Ho. See Jonson, Ben, George Chapman, and John Marston

Eating imagery. *See* Women: as food
Economic problems of women, 132–33
Edward II. See Marlowe, Christopher
Effeminate men: city men, 169–71; confrontation with aggressive women, 144, 146, 150, 152, 153, 158–59, 161, 181, 189, 191, 217–19, 252, 315. *See also* War and peace
Elizabeth, Queen, 71n1, 159
Elyot, Thomas, 7, 16, 37, 38, 102, 218, 285; *Defense of Good Women*, 18–22, 36, 58, 265, 276, 281; *The Governor*, 140
Englishmen for My Money. See Haughton, William
Epicedium (Har), 118
Epicoene. See Jonson, Ben
Epitaphs, Epigrams, Songs and Sonnets (Turberville), 61, 67
Epitoma Historiarum Philippicarum Pompei Trogi (Justinus), 72n5
Equality of the sexes, 3, 39, 42, 76, 91, 94, 106, 107, 109, 129, 130, 131. *See also* Feminism
Erasmus, Desiderius, 14, 16, 21, 41, 59, 60, 66, 85, 98, 102, 168, 195, 221n18, 232, 323, 324; *Coniugium*, 60, 225, 238, 242n6, 265; *Merry Dialogue of Shrews and Honest Wives*, 14, 242n1; *Praise of Folly*, 41, 42
Essays upon the Five Senses. See Brathwait, Richard
Estates of womankind. *See* Maid/wife/widow classification
Ester Hath Hanged Haman. See Sowernam, Ester
Esther, Ester, or Hester. *See* Brentius, Joannes; *Exempla* of the formal controversy; *Godly Queen Hester*; Sowernam, Ester
Euphues. See Lyly, John
Euphues his Censure to Philautus. See Greene, Robert
Euphuistic prose style, 81–82
Euripides, 67, 95, 116
Eve. *See Exempla* of the formal controversy; Rib, crooked
Every Man in His Humour. See Jonson, Ben

Every Woman in Her Humour (anonymous), 152, 170, 192, 204, 217, 231, 275, 279, 282, 289
Excellency of Good Women, The. See Rich, Barnabe
Exempla of the formal controversy: *Alceste*, 112n8; *Amalasunta*, 72n5; *Amazons*, 15, 39, 69, 80, 117, 128, 142, 158, 160, 164–65, 181, 197, 264, 277, 301, 310, 315; *Anna*, 36, 97; *Anne of France*, 57, 113n8; *Artemisia, Artimesia, or Arthemisia*, 71–72n5, 80, 112n8; *Aspasia*, 71n5, 113n8; *Athaliah*, 30, 45; *Athena*, 69 (*see also* Minerva, Pallas, Pallas Athena); *Boudicca*, 80, 119; *Byblis*, 30; *Canaan*, woman of, 36, 44–45; *Carmenta (or Carmentes)*, 15, 19, 22, 34, 47n16, 57, 61, 76, 97 (*see also* Nicostrata); *Cassandra*, 20, 22, 290; *Ceres*, 15, 34, 47n16, 57, 61, 97, 109; *Cicero's wife*, 30; *Circe*, 39, 61; *Claudia*, 62; *Cleopatra*, 15, 57, 61, 71, 118, 119, 126, 128, 305; *Clodia*, 62; *Clytemnestra*, 15; *Corinna*, 71n5, 113n8, 116; *Cornelia*, 112n8, 116, 126; *Cressida*, 61, 127, 277; *Deborah*, 36, 61, 72; *Deianira*, 15; *Delilah*, 15, 30, 41, 45, 69, 77, 104, 116, 126, 127, 135n3; *Diana*, 97; *Dido*, 15, 39, 290; *Diotima*, 20, 22, 39, 57, 71n5, 113n8; *Elizabeth* (biblical), 97; *Esther*, 93, 197 (*see also* Hester); *Eve*, 15, 22, 28–29, 30, 33, 34, 35–36, 39–40, 51, 57, 59, 64–65, 70, 75, 79, 80, 82–83, 89–90, 94, 97, 112n8, 116, 120, 123, 127, 140, 211, 279, 282; *Faustina*, 66, 117; *Graces*, 97; *Grissill or Griselde*, 61, 125, 127, 133–34 (*see also* Patient Grissill figure); *Harmonia*, 113n8; *Helen of Troy*, 15, 23, 30, 61, 62, 64, 74, 80, 118, 127–28, 129, 134, 303, 305; *Herodias*, 30, 135n3; *Hester*, 15, 36, 47n18, 112n8, 125–26, 195 (*see also* Esther); *Hypsicratea*, 112n8; *Isabella, Queen*, 57, 113n8; *Jael (or Jahel)*, 36, 45, 116; *Jezebel*, 30, 62, 77, 116, 135n3; *Joan of Arc*, 80; *Job's wife*, 30, 41, 45; *Judith*, 15,

36, 51, 112n8, 116, 118; *Julia*, 112n8; *Katherine of France*, 80; *Lais*, 62, 69, 116, 133; *Leontium*, 22; *Lot's daughters*, 41, 45, 116; *Lot's wife*, 30; *Lucrece*, 15, 36, 51, 61, 62, 71, 85, 109, 115, 116, 117, 118, 119, 122, 126, 135n3, 164, 211; *Margaret of Austria*, 54, 57, 72n5, 113n8; *Martha*, 36; *Mary, Virgin*, 15, 22, 35, 36, 39, 57, 85, 90, 97, 211, 279; *Mary Magdalene*, 15, 36, 97, 125; *Medea*, 15, 39, 61, 119, 126, 127; *Medullina*, 62; *Medusa*, 74; *Messalina*, 30, 45, 305; *Minerva*, 15, 19, 22, 33, 34, 109 (*see also* Athena, Pallas, Pallas Athena); *Muses*, 20, 22, 74–75, 97; *Myrrha*, 30; *Nicostrata*, 109 (*see also* Carmenta); *Octavia*, 57, 118, 126; *Omphale*, 104, 112n8, 142, 157–58, 220n9, 310; *Pallas or Pallas Athena*, 33, 47n16, 57, 105 (*see also* Athena, Minerva); *Parisatis*, 107; *Pasiphaë*, 30, 115; *Paulina*, 118; *Penelope*, 15, 19, 36, 61, 62, 69, 71, 79, 109, 115, 116, 128, 135n3, 290; *Phania*, 116; *Pharaoh's wife*, 30; *Pilate's wife*, 45; *Portia*, 15, 19, 36, 57, 112n8, 118, 126, 127, 135n3; *Pyrrha*, 30; *Queen of Sheba (or Saba)*, 45; *Rebecca*, 36; *Ruth*, 36, 118; *Samaria*, woman of, 97; *Sappho*, 15, 34, 39, 57, 71n5, 76, 113n8; *Sara (or Sarah)*, 15, 36, 85, 112n8, 118; *Scylla*, 62; *Semiramis*, 15, 39, 57, 61, 71n5, 80, 115, 119, 128, 133; *Sulpitia*, 62; *Susanna*, 37, 51, 85, 109, 115, 116, 119, 125, 127, 316; *Sybilla*, 117; *Sybils*, 15, 20, 22, 34, 39, 57, 69, 115; *Tarpeya*, 62; *Theodelinda*, 72n5; *Theodora*, 113n8; *Thisbe*, 290; *Thomiris*, 71–72n5; *Timoclea*, 62; *Venus*, 32, 33, 80, 105, 140, 159, 162–63; *Veturia (or Volumnia)*, 15, 45, 117; *Virginia*, 117, 118, 125; *Xantippe*, 69, 74, 104, 127; *Zenobia*, 15, 20–21, 61, 76, 104, 117
Exemplary Lives of Nine the Most Worthy Women of the World. See Heywood, Thomas

Extravagance of women. *See* Faults
 of women

*Factis Dictisque. See De Factis Dictisque
 Memorabilibus*
Faerie Queene, The. See Spenser, Ed-
 mund
Fair Em (anonymous), 282–83
Fair Maid of Bristow, The (anony-
 mous), 156, 188–89, 211, 212, 287,
 289
Fair Maid of the Exchange, The. See
 Heywood, Thomas
Fair Maid of the West, The. See Hey-
 wood, Thomas
Fair Valeria (Dickenson), 14, 106,
 176, 177, 178, 206, 207, 221n14,
 232, 234, 259, 309
Family of Love, The. See Middleton,
 Thomas
Farewell to Military Profession. See
 Rich, Barnabe
Fasti. See Ovid
Fatal Dowry, The. See Field, Nathan,
 and Philip Massinger
*Faults, Faults and Nothing Else but
 Faults. See* Rich, Barnabe
Faults of women: Renaissance lists of
 faults, 14, 26–27, 60, 68, 281–82;
 ambition, 27–28, 270n12; *changing
 minds,* 60, 164; *contrariety,* 64, 125;
 covetousness, 60, 68; *coyness,* 125,
 306–7; *credulity,* 60, 125; *cruelty,* 23,
 60, 71, 83, 306–7; *cuckolding of husbands,* 27, 78, 79, 132, 178–79; 230;
 deceit, dissembling, 26, 27, 60, 61,
 68, 71, 78, 79, 83, 116, 121, 131,
 176, 271n14, 308; *drunkenness,* 60,
 121, 224–29, 234–35, 243n11; *extravagance,* 23, 60, 77, 83, 132, 229,
 230, 270n9; *gadding,* 77, 224, 230;
 gossiping, 68, 78, 224–43; *greed,* 132;
 husband-beating, 190–94; *inability to
 keep secrets,* 79, 86, 125, 259, 308;
 idleness, 77, 83, 92, 132, 230, 234–
 35; *ill temper,* 26; *impiety,* 60, 129;
 impatience, 60; *impudence,* 68, 77; *inconstancy, fickleness,* 19, 23, 26, 29,
 60, 79, 80, 121, 306; *ingratitude,* 60,
 83; *jealousy,* 83; *lack of reason, judgment, logic,* 19, 22, 26, 68, 88, 125;
 laziness, 23; *lust, sensuality,* 23, 26,
 57, 60, 62, 68, 78, 121, 132, 176–
 80, 227, 260, 270–71n13, 305, 308;
 malice, 26; *moodiness,* 60, 79, 83;
 nosiness, 125; *pride,* 60, 68, 83, 105;
 shrewishness, scolding, 19, 23, 27–28,
 31, 51, 60, 64, 68–69, 78, 94, 100,
 131, 230, 308–9; *superstition,* 60;
 sexual frailty, 79, 125, 307–8; *talkativeness,* 26, 29, 31, 41, 60, 86, 105,
 131–32, 207–11; *timidity,* 19, 68, 77,
 107, 311; *vanity,* 23, 60, 68; *vengefulness,* 60, 83, 99, 107, 121, 312–
 13; *weakness,* 19, 22, 31, 214–15;
 wilfulness, 26, 28, 64, 79, 83, 306
Fawn. The. See Marston, John: *Parasitaster*
Female Pre-eminence. See Agrippa,
 Heinrich Cornelius
Feminism: and *Agrippa,* 58, 113n8;
 and *belief in women's "nature,"* 86;
 and *Castiglione,* 58, 113n8; and
 Christianity, 65, 90–92, 99, 129–30,
 326; *defined,* 3, 8n5; *failure of, in
 Renaissance,* 129–35, 326–27; *hampered by chivalry,* 302; *hampered by
 custom,* 42, 109, 149; and *justice,*
 302; and *ladylike behavior,* 58; and
 lesbianism, 254; and *man-hating,* 254;
 and *marital equality,* 106; and the
 media, 250; and *pacifism,* 168; and
 Plato, 108–9; and the *Renaissance aristocracy,* 54–55; and the *Renaissance
 association of women with fertility,*
 112; and *Renaissance defenses of
 women,* 2–3, 92, 98, 110, 129–35;
 and the *Renaissance middle class,* 54–
 55; and *Shakespeare,* 153, 155, 221–
 22n22; and *sisterhood,* 99; and *Tuvil,
 Daniel,* 108–9. *See also* Equality of
 the sexes; Order, Renaissance concept of; Women
Fenton, Geoffrey: *Monophylo,* 140
Feudalism, 130
Feylde, Thomas: *Controversy between a
 Lover and a Jay,* 46n4
Fiction, prose, 114–17, 120, 129, 159
Field, Nathan: *Amends for Ladies,*
 120–22, 157, 158, 233, 252, 254,

256–57; *Woman Is a Weathercock*, 120–21, 188, 251, 282, 288, 289. *See also* Field, Nathan, and Philip Massinger

Field, Nathan, and Philip Massinger: *Fatal Dowry*, 162, 239

First Blast of the Trumpet against the Monstrous Regiment of Women, The (Knox), 197

Fitzgeffrey, Henry, 152, 266; *Notes from Blackfriars*, 252; *Satires and Satirical Epigrams*, 264

Fleire, The. See Sharpham, Edward

Fletcher, John: *Bonduca*, 163, 164, 166, 244, 246, 255, 279; *Honest Man's Fortune*, 157, 162, 244, 246, 250; *Nightwalker*, 157, 245, 246, 247–48, 275, 282, 287, 289; *Woman's Prize*, 197–98, 199, 240, 250, 251, 282, 289, 326; *Women Pleased*, 197, 246, 247. *See also* Beaumont, Francis, and John Fletcher: *The Captain, Maid's Tragedy, Philaster, Scornful Lady, Woman-Hater;* Fletcher, John, and William Shakespeare: *Two Noble Kinsmen*

Fletcher, John, and William Shakespeare: *Two Noble Kinsmen*, 162–63, 238–39, 239–40, 250–51

Florio, John, 151n9

Flower of Friendship, The (Tilney), 4, 59–60

Folly's Anatomy (Hutton), 142, 152

Food imagery. *See* Women: as food

Formal controversy about women, 4–5, 6–7, 11–137, 149–50, 275, 278, 300, 305, 315. *See also* Exempla of the formal controversy; Ritual and the formal controversy

Franklin's Tale, The. *See* Chaucer, Geoffrey: *Canterbury Tales*

Frederick, Duke of Württemberg, 172

Freedom of English women. *See* Women

Freud, Sigmund, 32, 112n7, 292, 321n2

Friendship, female, 237–41

Frith, Mary (or Moll), 254, 263

Frye, Northrop, 298–99n17

Furies, The. See Niccols, Richard

Furnivall, Frederick J., 202, 221n17

G., I.: *Apology for Womenkind*, 74–76

Gainsford, Thomas: *Rich Cabinet*, 118–19

Galen, 73n9

Gamage, William: *Linsey-Woolsy*, 142, 264

Garland of Good Will, The (Deloney), 118, 252

Garnier, Robert, 126

Garter, Thomas: *Susanna*, 125–26, 268n1, 277, 278, 288, 289

Gascoigne, George: *Steel Glass*, 139

Gataker, Thomas: *Marriage Duties Briefly Couched Together*, 143

Gibson, Anthony: *Woman's Worth*, 4, 69, 73n10

Gifford, Humfrey: *Posy of Gillyflowers*, 205

God, John, 186

Goddard, William: *Satirical Dialogue*, 77–79, 236, 276

Godly Form of Household Government, A (Cleaver), 172, 208

Godly Queen Hester (anonymous), 125–26, 220n13, 268n1

Gohlke, Madelon, 136n7, 171, 215, 321n2, 323

Golden Age, The. See Heywood, Thomas

Golden Book of Marcus Aurelius, The (Guevara), 81, 83, 172, 176, 226

"Good audience, harken to me" (Wallys), 236

"Good wife, The." *See* Brathwait, Richard

Gossiping. *See* Faults of women

Gossips, 27, 119, 224–43

Gossip's Greeting, The. See Parrot, Henry

Gosynhyll, Edward: *Mulierum Pean*, 24, 32–37, 44, 47n10, 49, 60–61, 117, 118, 135n3, 276; *School House of Women*, 24–31, 44, 46n5, 47n10, 49, 117, 118, 135n3, 226, 231, 232, 276; mentioned, 5, 7, 38, 85, 94, 121, 122, 129, 134, 204, 278, 285

Gouge, William: *Of Domestical Duties*, 129–30, 172

Governor, The. See Elyot, Thomas

Great Chain of Being, 76

Greene, Robert: *Euphues his Censure to Philautus*, 63; *Mamillia*, 14, 116; *Mirror of Modesty*, 116; *Orlando Furioso*, 282, 288; *Penelope's Web*, 14, 116. *See also* Greene, Robert, and Thomas Lodge

Greene, Robert, and Thomas Lodge: *Looking-Glass for London and England*, 193

Greene in Conceit. See Fair Valeria

Greene's Tu Quoque (Cooke), 179, 245, 256

Greer, Germaine, 216, 221n22, 299n20

Grissill, Griselde. *See* Patient Grissill figure

Grosart, A. B., 2

Guevara, Antonio de: *Golden Book of Marcus Aurelius*, 81, 83, 172, 176, 226

Guillemeau, Jacques: *Child-birth*, 242n2

Guilpin, Edward: *Skialetheia*, 189, 210; mentioned, 102, 169

Gunaikeion. See Heywood, Thomas

Haec-Vir (anonymous), 23, 139, 146–49, 152, 185, 217, 267, 297n8

Hake, Edward: *Commemoration of the Peaceable Reign of Elizabeth*, 182n8

Hall, Joseph, 102; *Virgidemiarum*, 169, 187, 188, 214

Hamlet. See Shakespeare, William

Hannay, Patrick: *Two Elegies on the Death of Queen Anne*, 118

Hannibal, 84

Har, W.: *Epicedium*, 118

Harbage, Alfred, 221n21, 222n22, 268n2

Haughton, William: *Englishmen for My Money*, 210, 268n4. *See also* Chettle, Henry, Thomas Dekker, and William Haughton: *Patient Grissil*

Hawkins, Harriett, 221n16

Hayles, Nancy, 141, 325

Hays, Janice, 279

Heale, William: *Apology for Women*, 81

Heath, John, 266; *Two Centuries of Epigrams*, 263–64

Heilman, Robert, 222n22

Helen of Troy. *See Exempla* of the formal controversy

Henderson, Katherine Usher, 46n1

Henry IV, Part 1. See Shakespeare, William

Henry V. See Shakespeare, William

Henry VI. Parts 1, 2, and 3. See Shakespeare, William

Henry VIII. See Shakespeare, William

Henryson, Robert, 127

Henze, Catherine, 46n3

Heptameron of Civil Discourses, An (Whetstone), 115

Herbert, Mary: *Antonius*, 126

Hermaphrodite controversy. *See Hic mulier* movement, *hic mulier* controversy; Transvestite controversy

Hermaphrodites, hermaphrodism, 140–41, 146, 293, 316, 317, 325

Hermaphroditus, 141, 181

Heroides. See Ovid

Hesiod, 67

Hester. *See Exempla* of the formal controversy; *Godly Queen Hester*

Hester and Ahasuerus (anonymous, lost), 126

Heywood, John: *Johan Johan, the Husband*, 193; *Two Manner of Marriages*, 205–6, 221n19

Heywood, Thomas: *Brazen Age*, 127, 157–58, 165, 167, 245, 246; *Exemplary Lives of Nine the Most Worthy Women in the World*, 320; *Fair Maid of the Exchange*, 128, 176, 189, 215, 270n11; *Fair Maid of the West*, 156, 181–82n2, 268n4; *Golden Age*, 158, 165, 253–54; *Gunaikeion*, 320; *How a Man May Choose a Good Wife from a Bad*, 14, 123, 127, 176, 188, 189, 211, 212–13, 289; *If You Know Not Me, You Know Nobody, Part 2*, 175; *1 Iron Age*, 128, 163, 164–66; *2 Iron Age*, 164–65, 166–67, 277, 291; *Rape of Lucrece*, 122, 126, 194–95,

215, 270n12, 277, 279, 288, 289, 297, 298n15; *Silver Age*, 288; *Wise-Woman of Hogsdon*, 156, 175–76, 215, 268n4; *Woman Killed with Kindness*, 268n4

Hic Mulier (anonymous), 7, 139, 144–46, 180, 267

Hic mulier movement, *hic mulier* controversy, 156, 165, 184, 223n27, 241, 244, 254, 287, 288, 298n8, 311, 315. *See also* Haec-Vir; Hic Mulier; Transvestism

Hierarchy. *See* Order, Renaissance concept of

Historiarum ab Urbe Condita (Livy), 15

Hobbes, Thomas, 32

Hoby, Thomas, 52–54

Homer, 63, 67, 75

Homosexuality, 144, 254

Honest Lawyer, The (S. S.), 78, 162, 289

Honest Man's Fortune, The. See Fletcher, John

Honest Whore, The, Part 1. See Dekker, Thomas, and Thomas Middleton

Honest Whore, The, Part 2. See Dekker, Thomas

Hooker, Richard, 130, 218

Horestes (Pickering), 278

Hosley, Richard, 221n20

How a Man May Choose a Good Wife from a Bad. See Heywood, Thomas

"How, gossip mine" (anonymous), 234

Humanism, 15, 16, 18, 23, 41, 42, 46n4, 56, 72n5, 106, 119, 324–25

Hundred Merry Tales, A (anonymous), 30

Hutton, Henry: *Folly's Anatomy*, 142, 152

Iane Anger her Protection for Women. See Protection for Women

Idea (Drayton), 187

Idleness of women. *See* Faults of women

If You Know Not Me, You Know Nobody, Part 2. See Heywood, Thomas

Image of Idleness, The (Oldwanton), 283–85, 298n11

Impudence, 144, 180–81, 247. *See also* Faults of women

Inconstancy, fickleness of women. *See* Faults of women

Ingelend, Thomas: *Disobedient Child*, 191, 193

Insatiate Countess, The. See Marston, John, and William Barkstead

Institutio Oratoria (Quintilian), 24, 29, 32, 33, 36, 38, 91, 92, 109

Interlocution betwixt Man and Woman (anonymous), 15, 21

Interlude of Vice, The. See Horestes.

Iron Age, The, Parts 1 and 2. See Heywood, Thomas

James I, King, 139, 143–44, 146, 151n7, 161, 168, 180, 181, 266

Jerome, Saint, 30

Jest, 6, 30–32, 37, 41, 43, 44, 52–53, 66, 68, 79–81, 88, 89, 92, 93–94, 95–96, 97, 99, 135, 203–4, 318–19

Jest books, 30–31

Jew of Malta, The. See Marlowe, Christopher

Johan Johan, the Husband. See Heywood, John

Jokes. *See* Jest

Jonson, Ben: *Alchemist*, 244; *Case is Altered*, 268n4; *Epicoene*, 124, 127, 128, 158, 180, 181, 191–92, 195, 208–9, 214, 232, 269n6; *Every Man in His Humour*, 125, 127; *Volpone*, 128, 171, 176, 208, 215, 268, 269n8. *See also* Jonson, Ben, George Chapman, and John Marston

Jonson, Ben, George Chapman, and John Marston: *Eastward Ho*, 124–25, 127, 268, 270n12

Jorgensen, Paul, 159, 324

Judicial imagery, 37–38, 96, 100, 116–17, 120, 146

Judicial oration. *See* Orations

Julius Caesar. See Shakespeare, William

Justice: and chivalry, 302 (*see also* Chivalry); need for both justice and mercy, 311, 316; traditionally associated with males, 99, 309–11, 316;

and women, in Spenser, 120, 310.
See also Judicial imagery; Mercy
Justinus, Marcus Junianus: Epitoma
Historiarum Philippicarum Pompei
Trogi, 72n5
Juvenal (Decimus Junius Juvenalis),
95, 124

Kahin, Helen Andrews, 5, 63, 65
Kahn, Coppélia, 183n17, 221–22n22,
265
Kelly-Gadol, Joan, 219
Kelso, Ruth, 4, 5, 13, 113n9
King John. See Shakespeare, William
King Lear. See Shakespeare, William
King Leir (anonymous), 194, 199–200
Knox, John: First Blast of the Trumpet
against the Monstrous Regiment of
Women, 197
Kyd, Thomas: Cornelia, 126; Portia,
126
Kynge, John, 49, 52

Legend of Good Women, The. See
Chaucer, Geoffrey
Lepick, Julie, 150n2
Life and Pranks of Long Meg. See Long
Meg of Westminster
Life and Repentance of Mary Magdalene.
See Mary Magdalene
Linsey-Woolsy (Gamage), 142, 264
Little and Brief Treatise. See Defense of
Women, The
Little Treatise. See Image of Idleness,
The
Livy (Titus Livius), 45; Historiarum ab
Urbe Condita, 15
Lloyd, Lodowick: Choice of Jewels, 74
Lodge, Thomas: Catharos, 276. See
also Greene, Robert, and Thomas
Lodge: A Looking-Glass for London
and England
Logic and women. See Women: and
logic
London Prodigal, The (anonymous),
128, 211, 212, 214, 294
London's Artillery. See Niccols, Rich-
ard
London Weavers' Ordinance, 326
Long Meg of Westminster, 254, 263,
264; Long Meg of Westminster,
223n27
Looking-Glass for London and England,
A. See Greene, Robert, and
Thomas Lodge
Looking Glass for Married Folks, A
(Snawsel), 214, 243n6, 265
Love. See Courtly love; Petrarchan
love
Love's Labor's Lost. See Shakespeare,
William
Luciana (in Comedy of Errors), 200
Lucrece. See Exempla of the formal
controversy; Heywood, Thomas:
Rape of Lucrece
Lucretia. See Lucrece
Lust, sensuality of women. See Faults
of women
Lust's Dominion (anonymous), 127,
207
Lycurgus, 43, 149
Lydgate, John: Mumming at Hertford,
190
Lyly, John, 65; Campaspe, 276; Cool-
ing Card for Euphues and All Fond
Lovers, 14, 61; Euphues, 14, 61, 63,
81, 95, 102, 112n2, 276; Maid's
Metamorphosis, 217

Macbeth. See Shakespeare, William
MacDonald, Roger, 177
Maclean, Ian, 73n9, 112n4, 136n6,
327–28n2
Mad World, My Masters, A. See Mid-
dleton, Thomas
Magdalene, Mary. See Exempla of the
formal controversy: Mary Magda-
lene; Mary Magdalene
Maid's Metamorphosis, The. See Lyly,
John
Maid's Tragedy, The. See Beaumont,
Francis, and John Fletcher
Maid/wife/widow classification, 84,
93, 121, 224, 228, 233
Maitland Quarto Manuscript, 118
Malcontent, The. See Marston, John
Mamillia. See Greene, Robert
Mariam (Cary), 128, 218, 281, 282,
289
Mariolatry, 15, 302. See also Exempla

of the formal controversy: Mary,
Virgin
Markham, Gervase, and Lewis Machin: *The Dumb Knight*, 127, 128,
186
Marlowe, Christopher: *Dr. Faustus*, 5,
127, 320; *Edward II*, 161, 211; *Jew
of Malta*, 268n4; *Tamburlaine, Parts 1
and 2*, 160, 162, 166
Marquess of Northampton, 52, 54
Marriage, 26–27, 77–78, 84–85, 293–
94. *See also* Feminism: and marital
equality; Maid/wife/widow classification; Milksop husbands; Shrews
*Marriage and Wiving. See Of Marriage
and Wiving*
*Marriage Duties Briefly Couched To-
gether* (Gataker), 143
Marston, John, 102, 169; *Antonio and
Mellida*, 158, 217; *Antonio's Revenge*, 125; *Dutch Courtesan*, 175,
236, 237, 241–41, 269n7, 269–
70n8, 271n14, 294; *Malcontent*, 127,
128, 171, 268n4, n5, 269n8,
270n10, 282, 297n4; *Parasitaster
(The Fawn)*, 237, 282, 287, 298n9,
322n2; *Scourge of Villainy*, 169, 188,
210; *Sophonisba*, 188, 210. *See also*
Jonson, Ben, George Chapman,
and John Marston; Marston, John,
and William Barkstead
Marston, John, and William Barkstead: *Insatiate Countess*, 14, 177–78,
255
Martial (Marcus Valerius Martialis),
104
Marvellous Combat of Contrarieties, A
(Averell), 140
Mary, Virgin. *See Exempla* of the formal controversy; Mariolatry
Mary Magdalene. *See Exempla* of the
formal controversy; *Mary Magdalene*
Mary Magdalene (L. Wager), 125–26,
268n1, 278, 286, 289
Mary Tudor, Queen, 57, 71n1
Massinger, Philip. *See* Field, Nathan,
and Philip Massinger
Maximilian, 72n5, 113n8
McManus, Barbara F., 46n1

Measure for Measure. See Shakespeare,
William
Medea (Studley), 126
Menander, 67, 95
Merchant of Venice, The. See Shake-
speare, William
Mercy: need for both justice and,
311, 316; traditionally associated
with women, 309–10; and women,
in Spenser and Shakespeare, 310.
See also Justice; Virtues of women:
mercy
*Merry Dialogue of Shrews and Honest
Wives. See* Erasmus, Desiderius
*Merry Jest of a Shrewd and Curst Wife.
See Wife Lapped in Morel's Skin*
Merry Wives of Windsor. See Shake-
speare, William
Metamorphoses. See Ovid
Metellus, 67
Michaelmas Term. See Middleton,
Thomas
Middle class, Renaissance, 54–55, 58
Middleton, Thomas: *Blurt, Master-
Constable*, 128, 196–97, 268n4,
269n5, 270n11; *Family of Love*, 127,
173, 175, 176, 178–79, 191, 207,
270n11; *Mad World, My Masters*,
158; *Michaelmas Term*, 177; *More
Dissemblers besides Women*, 152, 157,
163, 245, 256, 257–59, 289; *No Wit
No Help Like A Woman's*, 157, 248;
Phoenix, 269n6, 270n13; *Trick to
Catch the Old One*, 173–74; *Widow*,
152, 157, 244, 246, 257; *Witch*, 162,
288; *Women Beware Women*, 122,
247; *Your Five Gallants*, 124, 156,
174, 269n6, 270n10. *See also* Dek-
ker, Thomas, and Thomas Middle-
ton; Middleton, Thomas, and
William Rowley
Middleton, Thomas, and William
Rowley: *World Tossed at Tennis*,
167, 253
Midsummer Night's Dream, A. See
Shakespeare, William
Military values. *See* War and peace
Milksop husbands, 189–201
Millett, Kate, 56
Milton, John: *Paradise Lost*, 324

Minerva. *See Exempla* of the formal controversy

Mirandola, Pico della, 325, 328n5

Mirror of Modesty, The. See Greene, Robert

Mirthus, 67

Miseries of Enforced Marriage, The. See Wilkins, George

Misogamy, 293–94

Misogynist as a literary character: in dialogues of the formal controversy, 115 (as coward, 20; as dog, 18, 64; as jester, 22, 59; sour grapes attitude of, 19, 22, 54, 62, 66, 79); as *persona* in formal literary attacks on women (Gosynhyll, 25–32; Pyrrye, 60; Lyly, 61–62; Nashe, 62–63; E. Tasso, 67–69; Swetnam, 81–87 [*see also* 88–103]); as a character in other nondramatic literature, 276, 283–85; stage misogynist, 120, 126, 275–99. *See also* Misogyny

Misogyny: and anti-Petrarchan backlash, 219n5; distinguished from male supremacy, 2, 43; and filial gratitude/ingratitude, 34, 50, 70–71, 102; jest as vehicle of, 31, 318–19 (*see also* Jest); of King James, 144; neglect of, by modern scholars, 1–2; Patristic, 15, 289; Renaissance treatments of, 291–93. *See also* Misogynist as a literary character

Moncada, Ernest J., 72n6

Monodia (Sylvester), 118

Monophylo (Fenton), 140

Montaigne, Michel de, 41, 42, 151n9

Morality plays, 126, 129. *See also* Vice figures

More, Edward, 16, 60; *Defense of Women,* 49–52, 117

More, Thomas, 16, 168, 221n18

More Dissemblers besides Women. See Middleton, Thomas

More Fools Yet (Sharpe), 264–65, 276

Morley, Henry, 72n5

Moryson, Fynes, 172

Most Virtuous and Godly Susanna, The. See Susanna

Motherhood, 34, 80, 85, 220n12, 291–92

Mouse Trap, The. See Parrot, Henry

Mouzell for Melastomus. See Speght, Rachel

Much Ado About Nothing. See Shakespeare, William

Mulierum Pean. See Gosynhyll, Edward

Mulierum Virtutis (Plutarch), 15

Mumming at Hertford, A (Lydgate), 190

Munda, Constantia [pseudonym]: *Worming of a Mad Dog,* 99–103; mentioned, 104, 110, 135, 279, 313, 319

Munday, Anthony, 73n10

Muzzle for Mealstomus, A. See Speght, Rachel

Mystical Bedlam (T. Adams), 142

Nashe, Thomas: *Anatomy of Absurdity,* 62–63, 67, 70, 121

Neoplatonism, 69, 325

Newman, Arthur: *Pleasure's Vision,* 79

Newstead, Christopher: *Apology for Women,* 79

Niccholes, Alexander: *Discourse of Marriage and Wiving,* 223n27

Niccols, Richard: *Cuckow,* 141; *Furies,* 142, 169, 276; *London's Artillery,* 169

Nice Wanton (anonymous), 49

Nightwalker, The. See Fletcher, John

Nobilitate et Praecellentia. See Agrippa, Heinrich Cornelius

Nobility and Excellency of Womankind, The. See Agrippa, Heinrich Cornelius

Nobility of Women, The (Bercher), 4, 58–59, 113n8

Northward Ho. See Dekker, Thomas, and John Webster

Notes from Blackfriars (Fitzgeffrey), 252

Novel, rise of, 117

No Wit No Help Like A Woman's. See Middleton, Thomas

Nuce, Thomas: *Octavia,* 126

Nun's Priest's Tale, The. *See* Chaucer,
  Geoffrey: *Canterbury Tales*
Nuptiis, De (Theophrastus), 67
Nurturing of mankind, women's. *See*
  Virtues of women

Octavia (anonymous, lost), 126
Octavia (Nuce), 126
Of Domestical Duties (Gouge), 129–30,
  172
Of Marriage and Wiving (Tasso), 67–
  69, 75, 232
Oldwanton, Oliver [pseudonym]:
  Image of Idleness, 283–85, 298n11
Orations, 14, 25–26, 38, 41–42, 51–
  52, 75, 91, 110, 120, 133, 150, 300,
  301–2, 303, 305
Order, Renaissance concept of, 75–
  76, 84, 130–31, 147, 218–19
Orlando Furioso. See Greene, Robert
Orpheus, 54, 56, 108, 115
Othello. See Shakespeare, William
Overbury, Thomas, 4; *A Wife Now
  the Widow of Sir T. Overbury*,
  113n10, 118, 136n4
Ovid (Publius Ovidius Naso), 30,
  141, 181; *Fasti*, 15; *Heroides*, 15;
  Metamorphoses, 15

Pacifism, 144, 161, 168
Painter, William: *Palace of Pleasure*,
  117
Palace of Pleasure, The (Painter), 117
Pamphlet as a literary term, 7
Pankhurst, Christabel, 58
Paradise Lost (Milton), 324
Paradox, 324–26, 327–28n2; *rhetorical
  paradox*, 41–42, 44, 69, 102, 105,
  324
Park, Clara Claiborne, 216–17
Parker, Martin, 194
Parrot, Henry, 266; *Gossip's Greeting*,
  119, 179, 231, 234, 263; *Mouse
  Trap*, 141
Patient Grissil. See Chettle, Henry,
  Thomas Dekker, and William
  Haughton
Patient Grissill. See Phillip, John
Patient Grissill figure, 3, 61, 125–26,
  127, 133–34, 188, 190, 198–99,
  201, 211, 212–17, 225, 231, 244,
  253, 255, 266, 267, 296, 309. *See
  also Exempla* of the formal contro-
  versy: Grissill; Chaucer, Geoffrey:
  Canterbury Tales (Clerk's Tale);
  Chettle, Henry, Thomas Dekker,
  and William Haughton: *Patient
  Grissil;* Phillip, John: *Patient Grissill*
Paul, Saint, 90
Peacetime, effeminacy of. *See* War
  and peace: effeminacy of peacetime
Penelope. *See Exempla* of the formal
  controversy
Penelope's Web. See Greene, Robert
Pericles. See Shakespeare, William
*Petite Palace of Pettie his Pleasure, A.
  See* Pettie, George
Petrarch (Francesco Petrarca), 57, 67,
  75
Petrarchan convention, 75, 76, 80,
  82, 97, 163, 219n5, 235, 262,
  298n9, 303–4
Petrarchan love, 19, 57–58, 64, 130,
  169, 184–89, 238, 305–6
Pettie, George: *Petite Palace of Pettie
  his Pleasure*, 61, 95, 114–15, 116
Philaster. See Beaumont, Francis, and
  John Fletcher
Philemon, 67
Phillip, John: *Patient Grissill*, 14, 125–
  26, 198–99, 268n1, 277, 278, 289,
  290–91, 296
Phoenix, The. See Middleton,
  Thomas
Pickering, John: *Horestes*, 278
Pisan, Christine de. *See* Christine de
  Pisan
Pitacus Mitalenus, 67, 69
Plato, 15, 18, 19, 21, 43, 56, 58, 63,
  67, 80, 84, 102, 107–8, 109, 140
Platter, Thomas, 171–72, 194, 243n11
Plautus, Titus Maccius, 63, 67, 95
Playgoers, female, 250–52, 258
Pleasure's Vision (Newman), 79
Plutarch, 45, 63; *Mulierum Virtutis*, 15
Poetical Rhapsody, A (Davison), 233
Politics, women and, 197–98
Pont-aymeri, Alexandre de, 69
Porter, Henry: *Two Angry Women of
  Abington*, 125, 192–93, 207, 214
Portia (Kyd, lost), 126
Posy of Gillyflowers, A (Gifford), 205

Praise and Dispraise of Women. See Pyr-
rye, C.
Praise and Dispraise of Women, The
(Serle, lost), 118
Praise of All Women, The. See Gosyn-
hyll, Edward: *Mulierum Pean*
Praise of Folly, The. See Erasmus, De-
siderius
Praise of Virtuous Ladies, The (Breton),
69
Preparative to Marriage, A (Smith), 208
Preston, Thomas: *Cambyses,* 267,
278, 324
Pride and Abuse of Women Nowadays
(Bansley), 14
Pride of women. *See* Faults of
women
Prieneus, 67
Private theater, 249–50
Property ownership for women, 129,
231
Prose fiction, 114–17, 120, 129, 159
Prostitutes, prostitution, 132, 174–75,
176, 261–62
Protagoras, 5, 67
Protection for Women (Anger), 4, 63–
66, 70
Proud Wife's Paternoster, The (anony-
mous), 49, 129, 232, 242n3
Puritan, The (anonymous), 177, 191,
209
Puritanism, 131, 238, 249
Pyrrye, C., 5, 122; *Praise and Dis-
praise of Women,* 60–61, 72–73n7
Pythagoras, 62, 66

Quintilian (Marcus Fabius Quintilianus): *Institutio Oratoria,* 25, 30, 32,
34, 36, 38, 91, 92, 109
Quinze Joyes de Mariage, Le (anonymous), 14, 27, 190, 226, 242n2. *See
also Bachelor's Banquet, The*

Rabboni (Walkington), 150–51n7
Rabkin, Norman, 324
Ram-Alley. See Barry, Lording
Ramus, Peter, 5, 37
Rape of Lucrece, The. See Heywood,
Thomas
Ravisius, Joannes (Ravisius Textor),
16

Readers, female, 114–17, 120, 129
Revenger's Tragedy, The (Tourneur),
177, 270n8, 270n9
Rhetoric. *See* Aristotle
Rhetorica ad Herennium (ascribed to
Cicero), 25
Rhetorical paradox. *See* Paradox
Rib, crooked, 29, 82, 109, 123, 129
Rich, Barnabe, 162, 281; *Brusanus,
Prince of Hungaria,* 14, 66–67; *Ex-
cellency of Good Women,* 76–77, 105;
Farewell to Military Profession, 159–
60, 162; *Faults, Faults, and Nothing
Else But Faults,* 77, 161
Richard II. See Shakespeare, William
Richard III. See Shakespeare, William
Rich Cabinet, The (Gainsford), 118–19
Rich his Farewell. See Rich, Barnabe:
Farewell to Military Profession
*Right Godly Discourse upon the Book of
Esther* (Brentius), 220–21n13
Ritual and the formal controversy,
110–12. *See also* Formal contro-
versy about women
Roaring Girl, The. See Dekker,
Thomas, and Thomas Middleton
Rogers, Katharine, 1, 9n10, 47n11,
48n24, 112n7, 136n6, 268, 297n1
Romance as a "women's" genre, 120
Romeo and Juliet. See Shakespeare,
William
Ronsard, 75
Rose, Mark, 158
Rowlands, Samuel, 239; *Diogenes'
Lanthorne,* 276; *Tis Merry When
Gossips Meet,* 215, 224–29, 230,
232, 233, 236; *Whole Crew of Kind
Gossips,* 224, 229–31, 236–37
Rowley, William: *All's Lost By Lust,*
163–64, 244, 245, 246, 252, 253,
256, 262. *See also* Middleton,
Thomas, and William Rowley

S., S.: *Honest Lawyer,* 78, 162, 289
Salomon, Louis, 219n4
Salter, Thomas, 235
Samson (anonymous, lost), 126
Sanctuary for Ladies, A. See Tuvil,
Daniel: *Asylum Veneris*
Sappho. *See Exempla* of the formal
controversy

Satire, formal, 100, 102, 249, 263–65
Satires: and Satirical Epigrams. See
  Fitzgeffrey, Henry
Satirical Dialogue, A (Goddard), 77–
  79, 236, 276
Satirical Essays, Characters, and Others
  (Stephens), 264
Scapegoats, 290
School House of Women, The. See Go-
  synhyll, Edward
School of the Noble Science of Defense
  (Swetnam), 92
Scoggin's Jests (anonymous), 204
Scornful Lady, The. See Beaumont,
  Francis, and John Fletcher
Scourge of Villainy, The. See Marston,
  John
Secrets, women's inability to keep.
  See Faults of women
Seducers, 58, 184–85, 254, 303–4,
  304–6
Semiramis. See Exempla of the formal
  controversy
Seneca, Lucius Annaeus, 63, 66, 126
Seres, William, 52
Serle, Richard: Praise and Dispraise of
  Women (lost), 118,
Sermon of Apparel, A (Williams), 142–
  43, 145
Sexton, Joyce, 298n12
Sforza, Lodovico, 72n5
Shakespeare, William, 184, 213–14,
  216, 221–22n22, 266; All's Well
  That Ends Well, 128, 155, 161, 211,
  238, 269n7, 286, 289; Antony and
  Cleopatra, 30, 152, 155, 156, 161,
  162, 179, 193, 195–96, 209, 215,
  260, 268n4, 269n5, 275, 279, 286,
  289, 294–97, 324; As You Like It,
  153, 154, 157, 170, 186, 214, 239,
  240, 248, 270n9, 292, 296, 299n17;
  Comedy of Errors, 125, 193, 200;
  Coriolanus, 76, 128, 155, 161, 173,
  214, 220n12; Cymbeline, 127, 155,
  161, 269n7, 279, 281, 282, 288,
  289, 291, 299n17; Hamlet, 177, 178,
  183n24, 210, 215, 219n5, 270n11,
  283, 292, 324; 1 Henry IV, 50–51,
  125, 160–61, 170, 182n10, 209–10;
  Henry V, 127, 170, 185; 1 Henry VI,
  128, 160, 194; 2 Henry VI, 127,
  194, 200, 270n9; 3 Henry VI, 128,
  160, 182–83n16, 194, 210, 215–16;
  Henry VIII, 244, 246, 251, 252; Julius Caesar, 125, 127, 310, 327; King
  John, 128, 160, 170–71, 214,
  220n12; King Lear, 154–55, 177,
  192, 215, 271n13, 296, 318, 320,
  324; Love's Labor's Lost, 194, 209,
  286–87, 299n17; Macbeth, 155, 161–
  62, 170, 195, 200, 215, 239,
  270n12, 324; Measure for Measure,
  310; Merchant of Venice, 127, 153–
  54, 247, 268n4, 298, 310; Merry
  Wives of Windsor, 127, 158, 171,
  179, 180; Midsummer Night's Dream,
  185; Much Ado about Nothing, 123,
  167, 200, 238, 240, 275, 279–80,
  286, 287, 288, 289, 297–98n8,
  298n12, 299n17, 305; Othello, 161,
  162, 180, 185, 195, 198–99, 211,
  240, 268n5, 279, 288, 309; Pericles,
  215, 268n5; Richard II, 127, 160,
  183n16, 207; Richard III, 125, 167,
  170; Romeo and Juliet, 170, 183n17,
  186, 270n11; Taming of the Shrew,
  125, 126, 128, 193, 197, 206–7,
  210, 221–22n22, 265, 299n17; Tempest, 245; Timon of Athens, 161; Titus Andronicus, 126–27, 128, 210;
  Troilus and Cressida, 50, 123, 127,
  152, 161, 166, 218, 279, 282, 289;
  Twelfth Night, 127, 141, 154, 157,
  170, 298, 299n17; Two Gentlemen of
  Verona, 125, 127, 153, 186, 208,
  286; Winter's Tale, 198, 239, 240,
  245, 246, 248, 256, 298, 299n17,
  309. See also Fletcher, John, and
  William Shakespeare: Two Noble
  Kinsmen
Sharpe, Roger: More Fools Yet, 264,
  265, 276
Sharpham, Edward: Cupid's Whirligig,
  123, 188, 194, 214, 237; Fleire, 124,
  128, 156, 188, 214–15
Shrews, 129, 189–201; shrewishness,
  justifiable, 51, 86–87, 98; shrew
  taming, 201–7. See also Faults of
  women: shrewishness, scolding
Sidney, Philip, 75, 316; Arcadia, 158–
  59, 223n27, 327; Defense of Poesy,
  25, 185, 266, 327

Silence of women. *See* Virtues of women

Silver Age, The. See Heywood, Thomas

Simonides, 95

Skelton, John, 14, 239; *Tunning of Elinor Rumming*, 14, 215, 234

Skialetheia. See Guilpin, Edward

Slanderers, 288–89, 298n12

Smith, Henry: *Preparative to Marriage*, 208

Snawsel, Robert: *Looking-Glass for Married Folks*, 214, 242n6, 265

Socrates, 27, 31, 58, 63, 66, 67, 69, 74, 83, 84, 104

Soldiers: female, *see* War and peace; returning discontented from war, 162, 275, 278–81, 315–17

Solomon, 30, 83, 90, 104, 112n8

Songs and Sonnets. See Tottel's Miscellany

Sonnets, 42, 185. *See also* Petrarchan love, Petrarchan convention

Sop for Cerberus, A. See Munda, Constantia: *Worming of a Mad Dog*

Sophocles, 95

Sophonisba. See Marston, John

Sowernam, Ester [pseudonym]: *Esther Hath Hanged Haman*, 92–99, 233; mentioned, 100, 102, 104, 109, 110, 263, 276, 301, 319

Speght, Rachel: *Muzzle for Melastomus*, 4, 87–92; mentioned, 93, 94, 95, 100, 102, 103, 104, 110, 112n4, 276, 301, 319, 321

Spenser, Edmund: *Faerie Queene*, 26, 72n5, 119–20, 134, 135n4, 140, 145, 161, 267, 268n4, 310, 323–24; mentioned, 26, 75, 146, 184, 211

Stage misogynist. *See* Misogynist as a literary character

Steel Glass, The (Gascoigne), 139

Stempel, Daniel, 4

Stephens, John: *Satirical Essays, Characters, and Others*, 264

Stubbes, Phillip: *Anatomy of Abuses*, 139–40

Studley, John: *Medea*, 126

Summa Theologica. See Aquinas, Thomas

Susanna. *See Exempla* of the formal controversy; Garter, Thomas: *Susanna*

Swetnam, Joseph: *Arraignment of Lewd, Idle, Froward, and Unconstant Women*, 25, 28, 67, 81–103, 141–42, 233, 263, 276, 300, 301, 313–14, 317, 319–20; *School of the Noble Science of Defense*, 92; mentioned, 7, 279, 300, 312

Swetnam the Woman-hater Arraigned by Women (anonymous), 23, 38, 54, 57, 96, 104, 117, 223n27, 275, 279, 286, 287, 289, 292, 300–322, 327

Sylvester, Joshua: *Monodia*, 118

Tales and Quick Answers (anonymous), 31

Talkativeness of women. *See* Faults of women; *see also* Virtues of women: silence

Talk of Ten Wives on Their Husbands' Ware (anonymous), 231

Tamburlaine, Parts 1 and 2. See Marlowe, Christopher

Taming of a Shrew, The (anonymous), 222n22

Taming of the Shrew, The. See Shakespeare, William

Tasso, Ercole and Torquato: *Of Marriage and Wiving*, 67–69, 75, 232

Tel-troth, Thomas [pseudonym]. *See* Swetnam, Joseph

Tempest, The. See Shakespeare, William

Tender-heartedness. *See* Virtues of women

Terence (Publius Terentius Afer), 67

Tertullian (Quintus Septimius Florens Tertullianus), 66, 178

Thales Miletius, 67

Theophrastan characters, 118–19, 197, 263–65, 276

Theophrastus, 63; *De Nuptiis*, 67

Thomas, Keith, 135

Tide Tarrieth No Man, The (Wapull), 278

Tilney, Edmund: *Flower of Friendship*, 4, 59–60

Timidity of women. *See* Faults of women

Timon of Athens. *See* Shakespeare, William

Tis Merry When Gossips Meet. *See* Rowlands, Samuel

Titus Andronicus. *See* Shakespeare, William

Tom Tyler and His Wife (anonymous), 193, 204–5, 215, 232, 234

Tongues, women's, 207–8

Tottel's Miscellany, 61, 67, 186, 190

Tourneur, Cyril: *Revenger's Tragedy*, 177, 270n8,n9

Tragedy, 324–25

Tragicomedy, 324

Transvestism: transvestite disguise in drama, 153–59, 182n2, 182n3; transvestite heroine, 153–55, 156–57, 217, 292–93; transvestite movement, transvestite controversy, 139–51, 153, 180, 212, 216–17, 222–23n26, 224, 250, 254, 255, 267, 300, 313, 315. *See also Hic mulier* movement, *hic mulier* controversy

Treatise of the Nobility and Excellency of Womankind. *See* Agrippa, Heinrich Cornelius

Treatise of the Two Married Women and the Widow. *See* Dunbar, William

Treatise Showing the Pride of Women. *See Pride and Abuse of Women Nowadays*

Trial of Treasure, The (W. Wager), 278

Trick to Catch the Old One, A. *See* Middleton, Thomas

Troilus and Cressida. *See* Shakespeare, William

Troilus and Criseyde. *See* Chaucer, Geoffrey

Tuke, Thomas: *Discourse against Painting and Tincturing of Women*, 221

Tunning of Elinor Rumming, The (Skelton), 14, 215, 234

Turberville, George: *Epitaphs, Epigrams, Songs and Sonnets*, 61, 67

Tuvil, Daniel: *Asylum Veneris*, 103–10, 112n8; mentioned, 308, 311–12, 319

Twa Cummeris, The. *See* Dunbar, William

Twa Marrit Wemen. *See* Dunbar, William: *The Two Married Women and the Widow*

Twelfth Night. *See* Shakespeare, William

Two Angry Women of Abington (Porter), 125, 192–93, 207, 214

Two Centuries of Epigrams (Heath), 263–64

Two Gentlemen of Verona, The. *See* Shakespeare, William

Two Manner of Marriages. *See* Heywood, John

Two Married Women and the Widow, The. *See* Dunbar, William

Two Noble Kinsmen, The. *See* Fletcher, John, and William Shakespeare

Tyler, Margaret, 91

Umbree, Mary. *See* Ambree, Mary

Upsitting, 243n5

Urbanization, 145, 148, 168–76, 182n15

Utley, Francis, 1, 5, 6, 13, 15, 17n1, 18, 24, 46n3,n4,n6, 47n7,n8,n10, 59, 81, 82, 135n1, 202

Valeria. *See Fair Valeria*

Valerius Maximus: *De Factis Dictisque Memorabilibus*, 15, 63, 72n5, 102

Vanity of the Arts and Sciences, The. *See* Agrippa, Heinrich Cornelius

Varro, Marcus Terentius, 67

Vashti, Queen, 197

Vaughan, Robert: *Dialogue Defensive for Women*, 22–24, 46n3–6, 103; mentioned, 7, 38, 53, 285

Venus. *See Exempla* of the formal controversy; War and peace: Venus/Mars imagery

Vice figures, 166, 275, 277–78, 282, 286, 288, 289, 318. *See also* Morality plays

Vincent, N., 67

Viragos. *See Hic mulier* movement, *hic mulier* controversy; Transvestism

Virgidemiarum. *See* Hall, Joseph

Virgil, 67, 75

Virgin Mary. *See Exempla* of the for-

mal controversy: Mary, Virgin;
Mariolatry
Virtues of women: Renaissance lists
of virtues, 14; *beauty,* 69, 79, 104;
chastity, 20, 60, 64, 104, 121, 136n5;
cleanliness, 40; *constancy,* 55, 64, 71;
courage, 55, 106–7, 311–12; *eloquence,* 40, 80; *fortitude,* 80; *helpfulness,* 64, 79; *homekeeping,* 77;
humility, 69, 105; *learning,* 105; *liber-
ality/charity,* 69; *magnanimity,* 80;
mercy, 39, 309–11 (*see also* Justice;
Mercy); *modesty,* 60, 78, 104, 147;
nurturing of mankind, 33, 34, 39, 80,
90; *obedience,* 20, 60, 99; *patience,*
309; *piety,* 20, 23, 80; *reason,* 19, 22;
silence, 77, 104, 105, 147; *temperance,* 69; *tender-heartedness,* 23, 69,
310; *thriftiness,* 23; *wisdom,* 55
Virtuous Octavia (Brandon), 126
*Virtuous Schoolhouse of Ungracious
Women, The* (anonymous), 129,
242n6
Vives, Juan Luis, 16, 18, 59, 168
Volpone. See Jonson, Ben

Wager, Lewis: *Mary Magdalene,* 125–
26, 268n1, 278, 286, 289
Wager, W.: *Trial of Treasure,* 278
Walkington, Thomas: *Rabboni,* 150–
51n7
Wallys, J.: "Good audience, harken to
me," 236
Wapull, George: *Tide Tarrieth No
Man,* 278
War and peace: drama's treatment of
war and women in 1590s, 160–62;
effeminacy of peacetime, 75, 147,
159–60, 162, 182n10, 291; female
soldiers, 20–21, 75, 80, 107, 164–
65; love/war conflict, 163–64; love/
war reconciled, 167; men's military
values versus women's civilian values, 85, 102–3, 135, 162–63, 208,
315–16; military values as barrier to
feminism, 167–68; Shakespeare on
war, peace, women, effeminacy,
160–62, 182n10, 279–80; soldiers
unfit for civilian life, 162, 165–67;
278–81; soldiers as misogynists,
278–81; unwarlike men more fully

human, 103, 315–16; unwarlike nature makes women more fully human, 75; Venus/Mars imagery,
162–63; war as brutalizing to men,
165–67. *See also* Pacifism; Soldiers
Watson, Foster, 18, 21
Way of the World, The (Congreve), 235
Weakness of women, 214–15. *See also*
Faults of women
Webbe, George: *Arraignment of an Un-
ruly Tongue,* 208
Webster, John: *Devil's Law-Case,* 240,
244, 246, 247, 261, 288, 320–21;
Duchess of Malfi, 152, 162, 214,
242, 244, 246, 259–61, 279, 289,
292, 320, 321; *Swetnam the Woman-
hater,* 320–21; *White Devil,* 162,
246–47, 261, 320–21; mentioned,
266. *See also* Dekker, Thomas, and
John Webster
Weddirburne: *Ballad of the Praise of
Women,* 117–18
West, R.: *Wit's ABC,* 276
Westward Ho. See Dekker, Thomas,
and John Webster
Whately, William: *Bride-Bush,* 130,
172, 193
Whetstone, George: *Heptameron of
Civil Discourses,* 115
White Devil, The. See Webster, John
Whole Crew of Kind Gossips, A. See
Rowlands, Samuel
Widow, The. See Middleton, Thomas
Widows, 20, 177–78, 224, 255–61.
See also Maid/wife/widow classifi-
cation
Widow's Tears, The. See Chapman,
George
Wife Lapped in Morel's Skin (anony-
mous), 201–4, 206, 207, 219n6,
221n18
*Wife Now the Widow of Sir T. Over-
bury, A. See* Overbury, Thomas
Wife of Bath. *See* Chaucer, Geoffrey:
Canterbury Tales (Wife of Bath's
Prologue and Tale)
Wilkins, George: *Miseries of Enforced
Marriage,* 122–23, 175, 211, 213,
215, 277, 289
Williams, John: *Sermon of Apparel,*
142–43, 145

Will of Wit, The. See Praise of Virtuous Ladies

Willson, D. Harrison, 151n8

Wilson, E. C., 275

Wilson, Violet, 2

Winter's Tale, The. See Shakespeare, William

Wise-Woman of Hogsdon, The. See Heywood, Thomas

Witch, The. See Middleton, Thomas

Wit of a Woman, The (anonymous), 179, 194, 204, 235

Wit's ABC (West), 276

Wives. *See* Marriage; Maid/wife/widow classification

Woman-Hater, The. See Beaumont, Francis, and John Fletcher

Woman-hating. *See* Misogyny

Woman Is a Weathercock, A. See Field, Nathan

Woman Killed with Kindess, A. See Heywood, Thomas

Woman's Prize, The. See Fletcher, John

Woman's Worth, A (Gibson), 4, 69, 73n10

Woman Will Have Her Will, A. See Haughton, William: *Englishmen for My Money*

Women: *aggressiveness of,* 107, 146, 169, 171, 176, 193–98, 211–17, 218, 242, 244–71, 312–13 (*see also* Effeminate men: confrontation with aggressive women); *as animals,* 268n6; *and damnation,* 269–70n8; *economic problems of,* 132–33; *and fertility,* 111–12; *as food,* 65, 268–69n5; *freedom of, in England,* 171–73, 177–81; *friendship with other women,* 237–41; *and hunting,* 165, 168, 254; *literature as a reflection of attitudes toward,* 3, 45; *and logic,* 88–89, 95–96, 98, 101 (*see also* Faults of women: lack of reason, judgment, logic; Virtues of women: reason); *as playgoers,* 250–52, 258; *and politics,* 197–98; *as property,* 268n4; *property ownership for,* 42–43, 129, 231; *as readers,* 114–17, 120, 129; *and romance as a genre,* 120; *as marketable commodities,* 269n7; *tongues of,* 207–8; *weakness of,* 214–15 (*see also* Faults of women: weakness). *See also* Chivalry; Courtly love; Detraction; *Exempla* of the formal controversy; Faults of women; Feminism; Formal controversy about women; Gossips; *Hic mulier* movement, *hic mulier* controversy; Justice; Marriage; Mercy; Misogamy; Misogyny; Motherhood; Patient Grissill figure; Petrarchan love; Shrews; Transvestism; Urbanization; Virtues of women; War and peace

Women Beware Women. See Middleton, Thomas

Women Pleased. See Fletcher, John

World Tossed at Tennis, The. See Middleton, Thomas, and William Rowley

Worming of a Mad Dog, The. See Munda, Constantia

Wright, Celeste Turner, 182n12, 223n27

Wright, Louis B., 1, 2, 4, 16, 46n5, 103, 150n1, 182n15, 283, 320

Wyther, George: *Abuses Stripped and Whipped,* 169

Xantippe. *See Exempla* of the formal controversy

Yorkshire Tragedy, A (anonymous), 194

Your Five Gallants. See Middleton, Thomas

Zenobia. *See Exempla* of the formal controversy

Zenobia (anonymous, lost), 126

A Note on the Author

Linda Woodbridge received her Ph.D. from UCLA and is now professor of English and associate chairman of the English Department at the University of Alberta. She has published articles on subjects ranging from the Renaissance to twentieth-century literature. *Women and the English Renaissance* is her first book.